America's Housing:
Prospects and Problems

America's Housing

Prospects and Problems

George Sternlieb
James W. Hughes
and
Robert W. Burchell
Stephen C. Casey
Robert W. Lake
David Listokin

Rutgers University
Center for Urban Policy Research
New Brunswich, New Jersey

Published by the Center for Urban Policy Research
Building 4051, Livingston Campus
New Brunswick, New Jersey 08903

Grateful acknowledgement is accorded to the following publishers who granted
permission to include articles that originally appeared in whole or in part, in
their respective journals:

Areuea Journal - *Multifamily Housing Demand:
                      1980-2000 and Condominium
                      Conversion Profiles: govern-
                      mental Policy*
Annals of the American Academy of Political and Social
Science - *Racial Transition and Black Homeownership*
Traffic Quarterly - *Back to Central City: Myths and
                         Realities*
Public Interest - *The Post-Shelter Society*
Appraisal Journal - *Rent Control's Impact on the
                         Community Tax Base*
Policy Studies Journal - *The Uncertain Future of
                              Rental Housing*

Library of Congress Cataloging in Publication Data
Main entry under title:

America's housing.

  Includes index.
  1. Housing—United States—Addresses, essays, lectures.
  I. Sternlieb, George. II. Hughes, James W.
  HD7293.A688   373.5'0973   80-10700
  ISBN   0-88285-063-6

Contents

v

vi

Introduction and Organization

Introduction

There is no industry of comparable significance to housing whose literature is as diffuse and as difficult to secure. Certainly, important strides have been made by the federal Department of Housing and Urban Development in terms of promulgating research results. And its colloboration with the U.S. Bureau of the Census, which has yielded the Annual Housing Survey, is of prime importance. Nevertheless, the housing industry, whose output is the focal point of most Americans' aspirations, still lacks a journal of record. Instead both the student and the professional in the field must search out a host of media. Often, some of the more significant works are buried in consultant's reports, in fugitive and transient publication forms that surface, at best only briefly, and then disappear. Their existence may be unnoted—or is subject to the good luck and serendipity of the researcher of a particular topic.

In part this difficulty stems from the sheer number of topics which must be encompassed in order to grasp housing's reality. The specialized sub-fields of land use, of housing finance, of legal constraints and strictures and so many others, which define the field, each have a unique literature. Unfortunately in the very press of partitioning and concentration within the subsets, there is the danger of a loss of perspective on the ultimate product. When to these are added various aspects of demand, such as demographics, spatial shifts and the like, the scale of the problem becomes evident.

This dilemma, however, is not merely one that is built into the very nature and complexity of the topic, but rather indicates some of the shortcomings of perspective within the field. A surprising amount of effort, particularly in governmental sectors, for example, concentrates on estimating and forecasting housing starts within a very brief time set. A deputy assistant secretary in charge of economic research at HUD once commented that three-quarters of his time, and that of his staff, was spent on predicting housing starts for the following month. I do not wish to belittle the virtues and the necessities that give rise to this, but it has often precluded a longer term focus. Efforts at the latter have been given a relatively low order of priority because of the axiomatic belief in an eternal housing shortage. Thus demand was always seen as a given; study focal points were on the immediate barriers to its fulfillment whether in terms of financing mechanisms or spot prices of lumber. Two generations of this circumscribed horizon have severely limited the field. But this is a surety which is now a luxury. The end of the baby boom generation, in terms of new household generation, is in sight within a very few years. And housing is a good whose economics and required longevity calls out for lengthier demand analysis.

There is a strong tendency for the targets of learned literature to lag reality. This is strikingly the case when the focus is turned to the areal shifts which are dominating and will continue to dominate America's growth. The issues of future demand for housing in central cities, for example, is a monumental one, all too frequently met with reflections of philosophy rather than of data. It is the subject more of wishful thinking and fearful myth than of a solid research base. There has been a comparatively rigorous—and perhaps a most harmful —segmentation in the literature. Analysis of the total system requires a level of integration which is just beginning to secure sponsorship.

The essays which follow were written at the very least with an awareness of these limitations, if not a competence adequate to completely cope with their strictures. With one exception they represent some of the work done in the last two years at the Rutgers University, Center for Urban Policy Research. The one deviant is an earlier effort—on condominium conversion— which has been incorporated because of the interest, and lack of data in the field.

Wherever possible all the pertinent data appropriate to the subject at hand is included in the presentations. While this may leave much to be desired from a literary point of view, it is reflecting a continuing attempt by the Center to avoid the "black box" approach—to provide the analyst with the appropriate building blocks of information with which to criticize our own analyses—and, we hope, to generate meaningful alternatives. We welcome any comments and criticisms of the materials as presented, and will, within our limitations, provide elaborations and suggestions on additional materials to the interested reader.

Organization

The choice of organizational partitions in a work such as this can be based on any of a number of alternative logics. These can range from the spatial—central city, suburb and regional, for example—to the purely functional, such as demand, supply and market parameters. The contributions to this volume, however, tend to crosscut most conventional schemes of organization. Thus, rather than establishing rigid sectional partitions and attempting to classify essays via criteria and constraints they would inevitably violate, the materials are presented simply in broad sequences. The ordering is based upon general clusters of commonality, of materials grouped according to some common focus. Within the latter, however, a number of overlapping policy issues are discerned.

The first two papers of this collection establish general baselines and perspectives, setting the stage for the more specialized areas that follow. They isolate the broad national parameters of America's housing markets as they have evolved into the decade of the 1980s. *Housing in the United States: An Overview* provides the statistical foundation delineating the basic supply and demand profiles over

time and their changing interrelationships. This empirical quantification of general trendlines is complemented by *The Post-Shelter
Society*, a qualitative evaluation of the shifting housing environment
and the evolving rationales of America's housing consumers. Some
of the detailed topics encompassed within these two papers include:

1. The Dynamics of the Housing Inventory

2. The Boom-Bust-Cycle of Housing Starts

3. Tenure Shifts, Homeownership and Race

4. Regional, SMSA and Central City Supply Variations

5. The Changing Matrix of Housing Costs: Inflation,
   Prices and Values

6. America's Demographics and Demand Profiles

7. Household and Income Variations: Rental versus
   Owner Occupancy

8. Supply-Demand Interrelationships, Market Constraints
   and Shelter Dilemmas

9. The Political-Economic Environment: Housing as
   Investment versus Housing as Shelter

10. Fragmentation and Consensus in the Housing Market Arena

The sequence which immediately follows comprises a confederation
of essays whose major linkage is a focus on the central city. *Housing
and Shelter Costs: The Schizoid Problem of the Central City* approaches three major questions. What are the realities of central city
housing costs? What are the dynamics of the inventory? And how do
they impact the consumer? Again, a quantitative baseline is forged,
setting the stage for subsequent papers of this cluster. *Some Economic
Effects of Recent Migration Patterns on Central Cities* then profiles
the demand attributes of central city households via analyses of
shifting demographic patterns. Migration trends, racial changes,
household alterations and income and poverty levels are subjected
to extensive statistical detailing. *Back to the Central City: Myths
and Realities* builds upon the quantitative bases of the two preceding
papers in an exploration of the question of whether or not there is a

long-term swing toward a return to the cities and a revitalized housing market there. *The "Two-Cities" Phenomenon* subsequently speculates on the most likely urban future in the decade ahead and the political environment likely to envelop the housing market. *Physical Revitalization Strategies: Adaptive Reuse*, the final central city contribution, describes the redevelopment strategies possible for the use of surplus properties in various types of declining neighborhoods. Overall, the prominent concerns of this set of contributions include:

1. Central City Supply Parameters

2. Inventory Additions and Deletions

3. House Values: Central City versus Suburbia

4. Central City Demographic Trendlines: Population, Households and Migration

5. Race, Household Configurations and Income

6. Market Imperfections, Poverty and Lagging Demand Functions

7. Employment Change and Market Segmentation

8. Gentrification and Return to the City

9. The Bifurcation of the Housing Market: The Elite City versus the Poverty City

10. Housing Abandonment, Neighborhood Preservation, and Adaptive Reuse

Rental housing is the thread which binds together the next sequence of papers. *Multifamily Housing Demand: 1975-2000* establishes a quantitative projection of future demand for multifamily rental housing and poses a series of policy concerns and recommendations. Then, *The Uncertain Future of Rental Housing* isolates five major phenomena that promises to shape the future viability of the private rental housing market. Rent control and condominium conversion, two of these forces, are subsequently examined in *Rent Control's Impact on the Community Tax Base* and *Condominium Conversion Profiles: Governmental Policy*. Within this section, the detailed analyses center on the following considerations:

1. Market Profiles of Renters.

2. Household Formation and the Future Demand for Multifamily Housing

3. The Baby Bust and Demographic Strictures

4. Construction Requirements, Inventory Attrition and Supply Barriers

5. The Post-Shelter Society and Rental Housing

6. The "Cream Skimming" of the Rental Inventory

7. Operating Cost Structures and Income Lags

8. Rent Control: Rationales and Impacts

9. The Condominium Conversion Phenomenon: Impacts and Policy Alternatives

10. Rental Housing Governmental Policy Recommendations

The dilemma of housing costs as influenced by government regulation is the theme of the next two papers. *The Impact of Local Government Regulations on Housing Costs and Potential Avenues for State Ameliorative Measures* details the different housing costs associated with various forms of governmental regulation and defines the state's role in mitigating these costs, while *Design Standards in Developing Areas: Allowing Reduced Cost Housing While Maintaining Adequate Community Development Standards* analyzes zoning/subdivision/environmental design requirements and explores government policy ensuring adequate community design and minimum shelter costs. Specific foci include:

1. Relationship of Housing Costs and Resident Income Changes Over Time

2. The Costs of Excess Government Regulation

3. Land Development Strictures: Zoning Ordinances, Subdivision Regulations and Building Codes

4. Design Standards in Developing Areas

5. Environmental Controls

6. Meliorative Strategies for State Level Government Intervention

7. Policy Changes: State, Regional and Local

8. Fair Share Housing

9. Fiscal Change

10. The Minimization of Shelter Costs

The final cluster centers about issues of race and housing. *Racial Transition and Black Homeownership in American Suburbs* examines rates of black suburbanization and homeownership in relation to equity accumulation. This macro-analysis is followed by *Housing Search Experiences of Black and White Suburban Homebuyers*, a micro-level investigation of the differences between the search process experiences of black versus white suburban homebuyers. The last paper of this section, *The Effect of Race on Opinions of Housing and Neighborhood Quality*, explores the impact of race on both owner- and renter-specified opinions on housing and neighborhood condition. Within these three contributions, major emphasis is placed on the following subjects:

1. Black Suburbanization Trendlines

2. Race and Tenure Change in the Suburban Housing Stock

3. Black Homeownership, Wealth Generation and Equity Accumulation

4. Market Realities and Racial Transition

5. Models of Racial Differences in the Search Experience

6. Mobility Behavior

7. Component Factors of the Search Process

8. Empirical Analysis of Racial Differences in Search Behavior

9. Modeling Racial Differences in Specifying Housing and Neighborhood Quality

10. Empirical Analysis of Racial Differences and Opinions
on Housing and Neighborhood Quality

The final paper, *Epilogue: A Note on Federal Housing Policy*,
examines the barriers, constraints and dilemmas of present federal
housing policies.

Housing in the Unites States: An Overview

George Sternlieb
James W. Hughes

Introduction

A subject as vast as housing in the United States defies casual generalization or simple detailing. The sources of information vary in currency, coverage, comprehensiveness, availability and, all too frequently, in consistency as well. Indeed, in many instances the key phenomena are not integral to the standardized data accounts, necessitating the use of surrogates from which inferences must be drawn.

In the material which follows we have attempted to aggregate sufficient data to define the basic parameters of housing markets, the supply inventories of which are now in excess of 80 million units with a replacement cost easily in excess of $2.5 trillion. The supply runs the gamut from near-abandoned, pre-Civil War share-croppers' shacks to virtual palaces. In between stands a vast heartland which has made middle America by all standards the most substantially housed citizenry in the world.

1

The limitations not only of data availability—but of space—(and the authors' competence—not least of all) mean that only the highlights and outlines of the phenomena can be presented here. Nevertheless, it is essential that the broad parameters of the inventory—of the extant stock, the patterns of additions and deletions, and of changes in tenurial (ownership versus rental) character—be reviewed in detail.

Paralleling the latter in importance is the evolution of the demand sector. Researchers and policymakers are increasingly aware of the importance of long-term demographic shifts in reshaping shelter markets. While housing availability clearly has a significant impact on the formation and configuration of households, the latter is, to say the least, a semi-independent variable feeding back in turn upon demand functions for shelter—and the physical arrangements and tenurial partitions of the housing supply. The last section of this essay will be devoted to the market intersections and bridges which bring the supply and demand functions together.

In the shaping and design of housing policy in the United States, it is essential that the basic building blocks of data be kept in mind. Without a grasp of these realities, there is a temptation to formulate policy in a vacuum. The sheer leverage involved in the value of extant housing, coupled with the impact that the housing industry as a whole has on the national economy, makes this an increasingly important injunction. As housing investment has increasingly become the preferred vehicle in the flight from the dollar, as levels of implicit and explicit leverage are expanded not merely through formal mortgage instruments, but also through consumer overextension in terms of share of income resources devoted to housing investment, the dynamics of this situation become more precarious; the care and feeding of the housing stock a much more delicate and potent matter.

Indeed there is another dimension to this concern: the issue of overinvestment in housing serving as a crucial factor in undermining the savings and investment rates in the United States. The decade-ago speculator in high-technology stocks, the buyer of mutual funds, the providers of the wherewithal that made industrial investment costs relatively cheap in the United States, is increasingly devoting his or her assets to housing. Thus the issue of preemption of growth productive dollars by housing investment arenas becomes increasingly important. Are these really matters of choice? Are the two forms of investment antithetical? As the reshaping of the housing mortgage market and financing sources takes place over the next several years, these are issues which will increasingly come front and center. But they represent merely one among a score of other shelter dilemmas the resolution of which is crucial to the future of the United States and to the amenity level which its inhabitants will enjoy.

The data and analysis presented in this overview is projected to form a base for future policymaking. It also provides a foundation for the subsequent sections of this book, each of which details a particular substantive area of importance. The latter, typically written with housing specialists as the potential audience, depend upon a broader evolutionary context in order to secure an appropriate perspective. Thus this introductory essay is not distinct from the latter material but rather complementary. It, and they, are to be read in conjunction.

ORGANIZATION

The organization of this overview is empirically based, i.e., the format is ordered via published data accounts available to describe the major elements of the nation's housing markets. The descriptive parameters are subdivided into sections evaluating the *supply* (or inventory) of housing, the *demand* for shelter, and their interaction—the market—or the adequacy of the match of supply and demand.

The sequence of this overview—initially evaluating the parameters of supply before the demand sector—is based on the availability of a supply side quantitative base the descriptive detail of which more readily facilitates direct isolation of major trendlines. The demand equation, on the other hand, must be extrapolated from the extant data accounts, as it is less definitively measured. The inferential process of filling in the gaps is aided by the previous documentation of the actual trends and shifts in supply.

The geographic partitions used in the supply side analysis are derived from the examination of the shifting spatial distribution of the nation's population within the demand section. Hence a brief preview of their structure is useful at this stage.

The conventional wisdom of the last several decades, whose major perspective had centered about urban- suburban tensions (the decline of the central city and the resynthesis of many dimensions of American life in suburbia) gradually came into question as the initial population accounts of the post-1970 period were tabulated. The broader reference framework encompassing this phenomenon—the metropolitan area—had long been the dominant population growth arena in the United States. But as fragmentary accounts pyramided into a critical mass of evidence, limited reservations about past assumptions were transformed into a new reality. Metropolitan areas no longer were the unquestionable growth poles of the nation; the resurgence of nonmetropolitan areas in the decade of the 1970s has provided a new contender as the leading locus of population growth. A metropolitan-nonmetropolitan perspective has emerged, not yet supplanting its urban-suburban predecessor, but rapidly approaching parity. Consequently one set of geographic benchmarks employed throughout this work comprises the following formal and informal terminology.

Formal		Informal
Inside SMSAs	—	Metropolitan Areas
(In) Central Cities	—	Urban Centers or Cores
Not in Central Cities	—	Balance of SMSA or Suburban
Outside SMSAs	—	Nonmetropolitan Areas or Exurbia

Within the nonmetropolitan context, a definitional problem is unavoidable. Since the designations of metropolitan areas have changed over time—the classic extension or redesignation of boundaries required to capture spillover growth, as well as the formal registration of new metropolitan concentrations within hitherto rural territories—there may be some inconsistencies between data sets; these are noted where appropriate.

A second major spatial transformation of the nation's demographic and economic contours has engendered an additional analytical paradigm, one which stresses interregional comparisions. While the evolution of marked changes in the regional dimension can be seen now to extend back almost two decades, awareness of its significance only began—and then, with tentative interpretations of ambiguous indicators—in the early 1970s. Slowly but with gathering momentum came the realization that the aging industrial heartland of America—stretching from Boston to St. Louis—was experiencing the residual strains of sustained industrial relocation and population migration. By mid-decade, the invocation of the regional framework for analyzing an array of critical issues become commonplace. The "Decline of the Northeast" and "Rise of the Sunbelt" have become so embedded in day-to-day language that it is difficult to recall a time without them. Yet they are relatively recent newcomers to our conceptual armory. The phenomena they represent however, are not transient but rather aspects of a long-term structural readjustment the ramifications of which, for housing markets, will pervade the final quarter of the twentieth century. Hence the data which follows also will be subject to regional partitioning where appropriate.

Housing Supply

INTRODUCTION

The decade of the 1970s has been characterized by a number of challenges to the historic assumptions underpinning American society. Relatively inexpensive, ubiquitous supplies of energy and natural resources, a secular philosophy of growth and sustained economic development, and high expectations of future living standards are but a few of the nation's traditions which have been harshly questioned by the events of the recent past.

But as the morale of America's citizenry sags in the context of the broader sweep of events, the evolution of the nation's housing markets—while beset by rising cost thresholds frustrating to shelter seekers—also has become a unique source of solace for many. Despite somber perceptions, the realities of housing production and the changes in the overall supply parameters appear much more sanguine upon detailed scrutiny. While serious reservations are voiced on the future, a number of basic trendlines have been substantially positive in nature.

1. *Net additions (11.6 million units) to the all-year-round housing supply over the 1970-to-1976 period have already exceeded the net additions secured during the entire 1960-to-1970 decade (11.1 million units).*

2. *Additionally, 2.0 million private housing starts per year occurred in 1977 and 1978, rates of production comparable to that of the 1970-to-1976 period. Consequently, the present decade promises to dwarf the housing inventory expansion of any previous ten-year period.*

3. *Homeownership, despite popular media allusions to the contrary, is experiencing large absolute and relative gains. Indeed, the 1970-to-1976 period appears to represent an acceleration of long-term trendlines.*

   a) *In 1940, 43.6 percent of all occupied dwelling units were owner occupied. By 1976, the proportion soared to 64.7 percent.*

   b) *This is a basic phenomenon encompassing all sectors of America's populace. In 1940, for example, 23.6 percent of the occupied units sheltering blacks and other races were owner occupied. By 1976, their rate of owner occupancy had increased to 43.6 percent.*

    c) *During 1977 and 1978, the production (housing starts) of single-family units was at virtual record levels (over 1.4 million units per year). This assures that the 1970-to-1980 period will represent the greatest absolute expansion in homeownership in the nation's history.*

4. *The fractured landscapes of abandoned housing in the nation's core cities obscure another basic long-term trendline—improvement in the quality of the overall housing inventory—one which has strongly persisted throughout the post-World War II period. While the standardized measures of housing inadequacy are limited in scope and reliability, the extant indicators are still sufficient to document the sweep of this change.*

    a) *As recently as 1940, 45.2 percent of the housing units of the United States lacked some or all plumbing facilities. By 1976, the proportion declined to 3.4 percent.*

    b) *In 1940, 17.8 percent of all units were dilapidated or needed major repairs. By 1970, this conditional measure was reduced to 4.6 percent.*

    c) *The size of housing units (rooms per unit) is steadily increasing, the result of deletions from the inventory of smaller, obsolete configurations, and the addition of larger facilities, particularly in the owner-occupied sector.*

5. *The characteristics of new one-family homes completed from 1970 to 1976 amplify the effect of new additions to the inventory. More than half the units built in 1977 had the following attributes (with the percentages increasing annually):*

    a) *A floor area greater than 1,600 square feet,*

    b) *Two or more bathrooms, and*

    c) *Central air conditioning.*

6. *The significance of the data is accentuated when the proportional share of all extant housing accounted for by units constructed from 1970 to 1976 is isolated:*

    a) *Almost 16 percent of the total United States occupied inventory in 1976 was constructed post-1970. However, substantial regional variations are present.*

    b) *In the South and West, the nation's high growth regions, one out of every five units (20 percent) was constructed from 1970 to 1976.*

    c) *In the Northeast and North Central Regions, the proportion is one out of ten (slightly below and above 10 percent, respectively).*

7. *All the measures of improvement in the housing supply are reflected across all geographical partitions—inter-regional, inside central city-outside central city, and inside SMSA-outside SMSA demarcations. The sole major variation is absolute new building rates.*

8. *But the shifts outlined above have been accompanied by a more troubling element—sharply escalating cost and price thresholds.*

    a) *Over the 1970-to-1976 period, when the consumer price index increased by 46.6 percent, the rents associated with the rental inventory increased by between 50 and 65 percent across the nation's various geographic sectors.*

b) *Rental units, built between 1970 and 1976, have rents approximately 20 to 35 percent higher than the total inventory of such units.*

c) *During the same time period, the median house value (owner-occupied) within the United States increased by 89 percent. The 1976 median house value of units constructed from 1970 to 1976 was between 20 and 45 percent higher than that of the overall 1976 supply.*

d) *The median sales prices of new one-family homes sold over the 1970-to-1978 period soared by 138 percent; similarly the median sales prices of existing single-family homes sold jumped by 112 percent. The consumer price index for the same time frame increased by only 68 percent.*

The ramifications occasioned by the evolution of these supply parameters can best be observed within the broader market context—the intersection of supply and demand elements. This task is reserved for the second and third sections of this introduction.

CHANGES IN THE HOUSING INVENTORY: 1960 To 1976

In the post-1970 period, America's housing inventory has been expanding at an accelerated pace. In the 1960-to-1970 decade there was a net addition of 10.3 million housing units of all kinds to the inventory—or an increase over ten years of 17.7 percent (Exhibit 1). In the brief six-year period from 1970 to 1976, the total increment of the 1960s was exceeded by nearly 2.1 million housing units as the housing stock grew by 12.2 million units. Indeed the percentage gain in the six-year period (17.8 percent) was more than equal to that of the entire previous decade. By 1976, the nation contained 80.9 million units, 79.3 million of which were classified as all-year-round facilities.

The dominant form of housing tenure was increasingly owner occupancy. From 1960 to 1970 the inventory of such units increased by 21.6 percent—and this growth was nearly matched in the later six years (20.1 percent). In renter-occupied units, on the other hand, the growth was much more modest. From 1960 to 1970, the net additions to the owner-occupied supply increased at 2.1 times that of the renter equivalent (7.1 million versus 3.3 million units). In the period from 1970 to 1976, the ratio increased to 3.2, i.e., 8.0 million owner-occupied units were added to the inventory while the rental sector gained 2.5 million units. But even in the latter category the absolute increase in the number of units was substantial; 5.9 million renter-occupied facilities were added during the sixteen year period from 1960 to 1976.

EXHIBIT 1

CHANGES IN THE HOUSING INVENTORY, UNITED STATES AND REGIONS, 1960 TO 1976

(Numbers in thousands)

	1960	1970	1976	Change: 1960 to 1970 Number	Change: 1960 to 1970 Percent	Change: 1970 to 1976 Number	Change: 1970 to 1976 Percent
United States Total							
All Housing Units	58,326	68,672	80,881	10,346	17.7	12,209	17.8
All-Year-Round Units	56,584	67,699	79,316	11,115	19.6	11,617	17.2
Occupied Units	53,024	63,445	74,005	10,421	19.7	10,560	16.6
Owner Occupied	32,797	39,886	47,904	7,904	21.6	8,018	20.1
Percent of Total	61.9	62.9	64.7	–	–	–	–
Renter Occupied	20,227	23,560	26,101	3,333	16.5	2,541	10.8
All Housing Units by Region							
Northeast	14,798	16,642	18,283	1,844	12.5	1,641	9.9
North Central	16,798	18,971	21,381	2,173	12.9	2,410	12.7
South	17,173	21,030	26,115	3,857	22.5	5,085	24.2
West	9,558	12,029	15,102	2,471	25.9	3,073	25.5

Note: Numbers and/or persons may not add due to rounding.

Source: U.S. Department of Commerce, U.S. Bureau of the Census, *Current Housing Reports*, Series H-150-76, *General Housing Characteristics for the United States and Regions: 1976*, Annual Housing Survey: 1976, Part A, U.S. Government Printing Office, Washington, D.C., 1978.

Regional Variations. There were marked regional variations in the growth of the housing stock. While the rapid rise of the Sunbelt and the comparative stagnancy of the Northeast and North Central states only recently has received significant attention, the gap between the regions—at least in terms of total housing inventory growth—was clearly marked in the decade of the 1960s. The two slow-growth regions, for example, secured percentage gains of 12.5 and 12.9 percent; the South and West experienced increases of 22.5 and 25.9 percent, respectively. In anything, this differential widened over the 1970-to-1976 period. The Northeast was the only region in this six-year time span which did not have an absolute level of increase higher than that of the previous decade (1.6 million units as against 1.8 million). In contrast, from 1970 to 1976 the South experienced 1.2 million net additions to its housing stock over and above the absolute growth of the previous decade (5.1 million units versus 3.9 million units). The patterns of inventory gains of the West paralleled that of the South, with the 1970-to-1976 additions (3.1 million units) exceeding by 600,000 units the gains of the 1960-to-1970 period (2.5 million units). The North Central States, on the other hand, had an inter-period differential of 240,000 units.

The sharp regional variation is thus apparent: in the last six years under consideration (1970 to 1976), the South and West had growth increments to their total housing stocks of nearly one in four; in the North Central states, it was one in eight, with the Northeast lagging at the one in ten level.

THE SMSA/CENTRAL CITY PATTERN

In 1960, central cities had a plurality of the nation's housing stock—they contained fully 35 percent of the total national inventory (Exhibit 2). Over the following sixteen years the central city share progressively declined to 32.9 percent (1970) and to 30.4 percent (1976). The proportion of the housing stock outside SMSAs declined from 1960 (when its share, 33.8 percent, ranked second) to 1970, but its earlier status was regained by 1976, when fully a third (33.3 percent) of the nation's housing stock was in areas exclusive of SMSAs. This clearly defines the newly burgeoning exurbanization of America. Nonetheless, it is suburban America which has ascended to geographic dominance, encompassing 31.2, 32.6 and 36.3 percent of the nation's supply for the three benchmark years under consideration.

The central cities of the Northeast and North Central states had only minimal net changes in their total housing stocks over the sixteen-year period. The former gained less than 300,000 units, the latter, slightly more than 400,000 units. The situation was markedly different in the South and West; the former secured a net addition of 1.9 million units, the latter gained 1.5 million units.

Despite these absolute shifts, by the terminal year shown, the Northeast still had the largest proportion of its housing located within central cities, 34.5 percent, although the latter represents a diminution from the 1960 incidence of 40.6 percent. By 1976, the South had the smallest share of its housing in central cities—27.3 percent versus 30.3 percent in 1960. It is striking to note, however, that the West as late as 1976 still had a third (33.1 percent) of its total housing stock within central cities. Its profile comes closer to matching that of the Northeast rather than that of the South in terms of areal distribution.

EXHIBIT 2

ALL HOUSING UNITS BY REGION AND SMSA STATUS: 1960 TO 1976

(Numbers in thousands)

Year and Location	TOTAL					PERCENT DISTRIBUTION				
	U.S.	North-east	North Central	South	West	U.S.	North-east	North Central	South	West
1960, total	58,326	14,798	16,798	17,173	9,558	100.0	100.0	100.0	100.0	100.0
Inside SMSAs	38,633	11,834	10,514	9,052	7,233	66.2	80.0	62.6	52.7	75.7
Central cities	20,440	6,005	5,695	5,208	3,531	35.0	40.6	33.9	30.3	36.9
Not in central cities	18,193	5,829	4,818	3,844	3,701	31.2	39.4	28.7	22.4	38.7
Outside SMSAs	19,693	2,964	6,284	8,121	2,325	33.8	20.0	37.4	47.3	24.3
1970, total	68,672	16,642	18,971	21,030	12,029	100.0	100.0	100.0	100.0	100.0
Inside SMSA	46,289	13,036	12,206	11,651	9,395	67.4	78.3	64.3	55.4	78.1
Central cities	22,608	6,212	5,978	6,166	4,252	32.9	37.3	31.5	29.3	35.3
Not in central cities	23,681	6,824	6,228	5,486	5,143	34.5	41.0	32.8	26.1	42.8
Outside SMSAs	22,383	3,606	6,765	9,379	2,634	32.6	21.7	35.7	44.6	21.9
1976, total	80,881	18,283	21,381	26,115	15,102	100.0	100.0	100.0	100.0	100.0
Inside SMSAs	53,934	13,972	13,673	14,553	11,736	66.7	76.4	63.9	55.7	77.7
Central cities	24,576	6,300	6,153	7,122	5,001	30.4	34.5	28.8	27.3	33.1
Not in central cities	29,359	7,672	7,521	7,432	6,734	36.3	42.0	35.2	28.5	44.6
Outside SMSAs	26,947	4,311	7,708	11,562	3,366	33.3	23.6	36.1	44.3	22.3

Note: Data refers to 243 SMSAs as defined in 1970 Census.

Source: U.S. Bureau of the Census, *Census of Housing, 1960,* Vol. I; and *Current Housing Reports,* Series H-150, *Annual Housing Survey: 1976,* part A, *General Housing Characteristics for the United States and Regions.*

The South has by far the greatest proportion of its housing situated outside of SMSAs, with fully 44.3 percent of its total units in non-metropolitan locations as of 1976. This represents a small but significant shrinkage from the 1960 pattern when nearly half (47.3 percent) of the South's housing was located outside SMSAs. The nonmetropolitan focus of southern housing may have diminished in proportion but it is still the single most significant spatial construct in the region, with a proportion nearly double that of the Northeast and West.

Tenure and Location. Rental housing, particularly in political debate, often has been viewed as essentially the domain of the central city, with measures to aid it seen as equally limited in appeal. Whatever the historical merits of this statement, its validity has long since eroded with the growth of such accommodations in non-central city locations. The data in Exhibit 3, which partitions the nation's occupied housing units by tenure and geographic location for 1970 and 1976, amplifies the reality. For both years, approximately three-fourths of the total rental housing stock was located inside SMSAs with the proportion showing a small but perceptible decline over the period. Moreover, the central city share was reduced from 47.1 percent in 1970 to 44.4 percent in 1976. *By the latter year, over 55 percent of the total national rental housing stock was located outside of central cities, with approximately 8.0 million suburban units comprising 30.6 percent of the total, and an additional 6.5 million nonmetropolitan units accounting for 25.1 percent of the stock.*

The absolute change in the inventory from 1970 to 1976 is particularly striking. Occupied rental units within central cities increased by under 500,000. In contrast, the suburban increase was 1.3 million units; even nonmetropolitan areas (outside SMSAs) gained more units (750,000) than central cities.

While rental housing in the United States as a whole is increasing much more slowly than tenant-owned dwelling units, it is doing so in a much more dispersed fashion than historically has been the case. *Thus programs having application to rental housing are not central city programs alone.*

The pattern in owner-occupied housing from an areal perspective is even more accentuated than that of the rental sector. In central cities, for example, the number of owner-occupied units from 1970 to 1976 increased by slightly over 1.0 million. Concurrently, the net gain in suburbia was nearly four times that amount (3.8 million), with more than a 3.2 million increase experienced outside of SMSAs.

EXHIBIT 3

OCCUPIED HOUSING UNITS, TENURE BY SMSA STATUS: 1970 AND 1976

(Numbers in thousands)

	Total	Total	INSIDE SMSAs In Central Cities	INSIDE SMSAs Not in Central Cities	Outside SMSAs
Occupied Units					
1970: Number	63,445	43,859	21,395	22,464	19,586
Percent	100.0	69.1	33.7	35.4	30.9
1976: Number	74,005	50,452	22,930	27,522	23,553
Percent	100.0	68.2	31.0	37.2	31.8
Owner Occupied					
1970: Number	39,886	26,090	10,300	15,790	13,796
Percent	100.0	65.4	25.8	39.6	34.6
1976: Number	47,904	30,895	11,349	19,546	17,009
Percent	100.0	64.5	23.7	40.8	35.5
Renter Occupied					
1970: Number	23,560	17,769	11,095	6,674	5,790
Percent	100.0	75.4	47.1	28.3	24.6
1976: Number	26,101	19,557	11,581	7,976	6,544
Percent	100.0	74.9	44.4	30.6	25.1

Note: Numbers and/or percents may not add due to rounding.

Source: U.S. Department of Commerce, U.S. Bureau of the Census, *Current Housing Reports*, Series H-150-76; *General Housing Characteristics for the United States and Regions: 1976*, Annual Housing Survey: 1976, Part A, U.S. Government Printing Office, Washington, D.C., 1978.

The sum of these two processes, i.e., the total number of occupied units regardless of tenure, is shown in the top of Exhibit 3. To summarize the case, the number of occupied housing units in central cities in the six years under consideration increased by barely 1.5 million; in contrast, the growth in suburbia was 5.1 million units, while the gains outside of SMSA's approached 4.0 million units.

By 1976, less than a third of the nation's occupied housing stock was in central cities. Indeed by the terminal year shown in the exhibit, the number of housing units outside SMSAs exceeded the number within central cities.

To the degree that housing programs, therefore, are specifically geared for central cities, they may have difficulty securing as broad a constituency and support level as was once the case. Transportation, infrastructure (water and sewer grants) and similar policy-oriented funding devices which apply to exurban areas, based upon the number of households in such regions, may have accelerated political potency. This becomes an increasingly significant element as the stringencies of energy assert themselves, with renewed calls for a recompaction of America's population into less diffuse patterns.

Housing Tenure Trends and Race. In reviewing the changes in housing tenure over time, it is worthwhile to secure a longer perspective. The data in Exhibit 4, therefore, indicates housing tenure in the decades from 1920 to 1970 and for 1976. The United States was long a nation predominately of renters. In the base year for example—1920—some 54.4 percent of all occupied housing units were of rental status; 45.6 percent were owner occupied. The proportion of homeownership accelerated in the relative prosperity of the 1920s so that by 1930 the proportion of homeowners had moved up to 47.8 percent. The disasterous impact of the Great Depression was reflected in a retreat to the 43.6 percent level at the end of the decade (1940). It was the enormous expansion of homeownership through increased sophistication of mortgage mechanisms as well as the forced savings accumulated during war-induced prosperity that moved American housing ownership past the halfway mark. By 1950, the 55.0 percent level was achieved, with continued increments experienced through 1976 to 64.7 percent. Current estimates, as of mid-1979, indicate that two-thirds of United States households now own their residences.

In the lower part of Exhibit 4, the data are partitioned by race. In 1920 less than a quarter—23.9 percent—of nonwhites resided in owner-occupied units, a proportion less than half that of whites (48.2 percent). While nonwhites still lag, their pattern of acceleration in homeownership is indicated by the statistics for the terminal year, when the ratio of homeownership of whites to nonwhites was approximately three to two—with the latter standing at 43.6 percent and the former at 64.7 percent.

While the pattern of change is pervasive, there are substantial regional variations in homeownership by race. These are indicated in Exhibit 5. Fully half of all black households in the North Central Region as of 1976 owned their own homes. The Northeast, in contrast, was characterized by a 30 percent incidence, far lower than the South's 48.6 percent or the West's 41.9 percent. And this is a result of more than historic differentiation; the growth rate for

EXHIBIT 4

OCCUPIED HOUSING UNITS–TENURE
BY RACE OF HOUSEHOLD HEAD: 1920 TO 1976

(PRIOR TO 1960, EXCLUDES ALASKA AND HAWAII.
TENURE ALLOCATED FOR HOUSING UNITS WHICH DID NOT REPORT)

OCCUPIED UNITS[1]
(Numbers in thousands)

Year, Race, and Residence	Total	Owner-Occupied Number	Owner-Occupied Percent	Renter-Occupied Number	Renter-Occupied Percent	Average Annual Percent Change[2] Total Occupied Units
TOTAL						
1920	24,352	11,114	45.6	13,238	54.4	1.9
1930	29,905	14,280	47.8	15,624	52.2	2.1
1940	34,855	15,196	43.6	19,659	56.4	1.5
1950	42,826	23,560	55.0	19,266	45.0	2.1
1960	53,024	32,797	61.9	20,227	38.1	2.2
1970	63,445	39,886	62.9	23,560	37.1	1.8
1976	74,005	47,904	64.7	26,101	35.3	2.0
RACE						
White:						
1920	21,826	10,511	48.2	11,315	51.8	(NA)
1930	26,983	13,544	50.2	13,439	49.8	2.1
1940	31,561	14,418	45.7	17,143	54.3	1.6
1950	39,044	22,241	57.0	16,803	43.0	2.2
1960	47,880	30,823	64.4	17,057	35.6	2.1
1970	56,529	36,979	65.4	19,551	34.6	1.7
1976	65,114	44,024	67.6	21,090	32.4	2.0
Black and Other:						
1920	2,526	603	23.9	1,923	76.1	(NA)
1930	2,922	737	25.2	2,185	74.8	1.5
1940	3,293	778	23.6	2,516	76.4	1.2
1950	3,783	1,319	34.9	2,464	65.1	1.4
1960	5,144	1,974	38.4	3,171	61.6	3.1
1970	6,920	2,907	42.0	4,014	58.0	3.0
1976	8,891	3,880	43.6	5,011	56.4	2.6

Notes: 1. Statistics on the number of occupied units are essentially comparable although identified by various terms—the term "family" applies to fugures for 1910 and 1930; "occupied dwelling unit," 1940 and 1950; and "occupied housing unit," 1960, 1970, 1975 and 1976. For 1920, includes the small number of quasi-families; for 1930, represents private families only.
2. For 1920, change from 1910.

Source: U.S. Bureau of the Census, *Census of Population and Housing: 1960 and 1970*; and *Current Housing Reports*, Series H-150-76, Annual Housing Survey: 1976, Part A, *General Characteristics for the United States and Regions.*

EXHIBIT 5

OCCUPIED HOUSING UNITS—PERCENT OF HOME OWNERSHIP, BY RACE OF HOUSEHOLD HEAD, INSIDE AND OUTSIDE SMSAS, BY REGION: 1960 TO 1976

(Refers to 243 standard metropolitan statistical areas [SMSAs] as defined in 1970 census publication.)

| | Total | | INSIDE SMSAs | | | | | | OUTSIDE SMSAs | |
| | | | Total | | In Central Cities | | SMSA Remainder | | | |
Year and region	White	Black[1]	White	Black[1]	White	Black[1]	White	Black[1]	White	Black[1]
1960: United States	64.4	38.4	62.1	35.7	51.1	31.7	73.4	51.6	69.0	44.8
Northeast	58.1	27.0	55.5	26.4	37.5	22.3	72.6	46.7	70.0	42.0
North Central	69.1	35.8	67.3	34.2	56.0	31.4	79.2	56.5	72.0	54.3
South	66.4	41.6	65.9	39.7	60.5	35.9	72.3	51.3	67.1	43.6
West	62.5	44.6	61.6	42.5	55.0	38.4	67.7	54.0	65.5	54.6
1970: United States	65.4	41.6	62.3	38.5	51.3	34.8	71.1	54.1	72.1	51.7
Northeast	60.4	28.6	57.4	28.1	38.8	24.2	71.7	47.3	72.1	42.6
North Central	70.2	42.0	67.8	41.3	56.5	38.9	76.5	58.8	74.4	56.3
South	68.2	46.9	65.3	43.4	59.5	39.1	70.7	57.3	71.9	52.0
West	60.2	40.1	58.6	40.0	52.0	36.6	63.6	49.6	66.1	42.1
1976: United States	67.6	43.7	64.6	40.4	53.3	37.5	72.3	50.3	73.7	55.3
Northeast	63.1	30.0	60.3	29.6	41.5	26.5	72.7	43.1	72.5	37.2
North Central	71.6	50.0	69.6	44.0	58.6	42.0	76.8	55.0	75.0	60.6
South	70.2	48.6	65.9	43.8	57.9	40.0	72.2	54.4	75.4	56.3
West	63.3	41.9	62.2	42.0	55.5	42.1	66.6	41.7	66.9	42.1

Note: 1. For 1960, represents Black and other races.

Source: U.S. Bureau of the Census, Census of Population and Housing: 1970, PHC (2), *General Demographic Trends for Metropolitan Areas, 1960 to 1970*; and *Current Housing Reports*, Series H-150-76, Part A.

black homeownership in the North Central states since 1960 far exceeded that which took place in the other regions.

The incidence of homeownership for blacks, regardless of whether central cities, suburban areas, or areas outside SMSAs are considered, is consistently lower than holds true for whites. The ratios are relatively constant as of 1976 at the three-to-two level. On the whole, however, the data indicate an increased proportion of minority homeownership and certainly one which is not confined to any region or areal subset within the country.

Summary. The nation's housing inventory is marked by several key parameters:

1. *The sheer pace of expansion of the overall supply throughout the 1970s marks a phase of growth with few parallels in recent history.*

2. *But the visibility and impact is not universal; the major beneficiaries have been the new economic growth regions—the South' and West—on the macro scale, and the suburbs and nonmetropolitan areas on the micro level.*

3. *Within the inventory, the major tenure dynamic is the long-term swing toward owner occupancy. This shift has gained momentum through the present decade and involves all racial sectors of American society.*

4. *The rental supply has expanded mainly in the suburbs and non-metropolitan areas—this is a much more dispersed pattern than historically has been the case.*

These trendlines are given added clarity as the new additions to the inventory are isolated. It is to this subset of the supply sector that attention must be directed.

ADDITIONS TO THE INVENTORY

Housing can be viewed as essentially a reservoir, into and out of which new and old units flow continuously. The outflow occurs through demolition, abandonment, or conversion of units to non-residential purposes. The purpose of the inflow of new housing is to replace this attenuation, as well as to provide accommodations for increased demand.

Studies conducted at the Center for Urban Policy Research indicate that, all other elements being equal, the real maintenance costs of housing are largely a function of age. The geriatric diseases of roof decay, plumbing interruptions and the like are clearly age linked. In turn, much of the wealth of a region is a function of its housing stock and the level of replenishment, both in terms of rehabilitation and new construction, which flows into it. In this latter context, the data in Exhibit 6 is particularly pertinent. It indicates by region, the total 1976 housing inventory (both owner- and renter-occupied), the number of units constructed from 1970 to 1976, plus "new" construction as a percentage of the 1976 total. For the United States as a whole, 15.6 percent of the owner-occupied units meet this "new" (constructed from 1970 to 1976) criterion. The equivalent share for the rental supply is 14.7 percent, i.e., one out of seven units has been constructed post-1970.

Most striking, however, is the variation between regions. Only one in twelve of the Northeast's units, both owner-(8.7 percent) and renter-(8.6 percent) occupied, is "new." The equivalent proportion for the North Central Region is slightly more than one in eight (approximately 13.0 percent). This contrasts very markedly with the South and West; in those regions, more than one in five (between 21 and 22 percent, respectively) of the owner-occupied units were constructed after 1970. The proportion of "new" rental units is somewhat lower (18.9 percent) in the South, and a much more modest 15.3 percent in the West. In both cases, however, post-1970 rental construction is far in excess of that of the slow-growth regions.

To the degree that the appeal of an area is a function of modernity of housing, the South and West are advantageously positioned relative to the other two regions of the country. The contingent liability built into an aging stock—the requirement for replenishment of mechanical systems and the like—based on these data should be a greater concern in the older regions of the country than in those which have benefited from higher rates of new construction.

When we view the proportion of pre-1939 units—not shown here— this is even more strikingly the case. They account for 52.2 percent of the inventory of the Northeast, 42.8 percent of the inventory in the North Central Region, 22.4 percent in the South and 21.6 percent in the West. The housing capital of the older regions is of considerable vintage.

THE BOOM-BUST CYCLE IN NEW HOUSING STARTS

The roller coaster ride of privately-owned housing starts in the United States—the extreme variations in annual construction rates— has been the subject of much discussion. The inefficiencies attributed

EXHIBIT 6

UNITS CONSTRUCTED 1970 TO 1976, PERCENT OF 1976 TOTAL, BY TENURE AND REGION
(Numbers in thousands)

	Total 1976	New Construction 1970 to 1976	New Construction Percent of 1976 Total
U.S. Total			
Occupied (Total)	74,005	11,520	15.6%
Owner Occupied	47,904	7,786	16.3
Renter Occupied	26,101	3,734	14.3
Northeast			
Occupied (Total)	16,544	1,435	8.7
Owner Occupied	9,882	861	8.7
Renter Occupied	6,662	574	8.6
North Central			
Occupied (Total)	19,723	2,527	12.8
Owner Occupied	13,672	1,719	12.6
Renter Occupied	6,051	808	13.4
South			
Occupied (Total)	23,741	4,831	20.3
Owner Occupied	15,766	3,333	21.1
Renter Occupied	7,975	1,498	18.8
West			
Occupied (Total)	13,997	2,728	19.5
Owner Occupied	8,584	1,873	21.8
Renter Occupied	5,414	855	15.8

Note: Numbers and/or percents may not add due to rounding.

Source: U.S. Department of Commerce, U.S. Bureau of the Census, *Current Housing Reports*, Series H-150-76; *General Housing Characteristics for the United States and Regions: 1976*, Annual Housing Survey: 1976, Part A, U.S. Government Printing Office, Washington, D.C., 1978.

to it are discussed at great length in such seminal reports as those of the Kaiser and Douglas Commissions. The turbulence of the building cycles is shown in Exhibit 7. As is evident, the fluctuations are extreme. From 1970 to 1971, for example, there was an increase of nearly half in the number of housing starts, from 1.4 to 2.1 million units. Conversely, between 1973 and 1974, starts plummeted from 2.0 million units to 1.3 million, a decline of over a third. The gap between 2.4 million housing starts in 1972 and the less than 1.2 million of 1975 epitomizes the boom and bust nature of housing construction in America. This, in turn, has structured the supply

EXHIBIT 7

NEW PRIVATELY OWNED HOUSING UNITS STARTED,
BY STRUCTURE, SIZE, UNITED STATES TOTAL:
1964 TO 1978

(Numbers in thousands)

	Total		1 Unit		IN STRUCTURES WITH— 2 to 4 units		5 Units or More	
Year	*Number*	*Percent*	*Number*	*Percent*	*Number*	*Percent*	*Number*	*Percent*
1964	1,529	100.0	971	63.5	· 108	7.1	450	29.4
1965	1,473	100.0	964	65.4	87	5.9	422	28.6
1966	1,165	100.0	779	66.9	61	5.2	325	27.9
1967	1,292	100.0	844	65.3	72	5.6	376	29.1
1968	1,508	100.0	899	59.6	82	5.4	527	34.9
1969	1,467	100.0	811	55.3	85	5.8	571	38.9
1970	1,434	100.0	813	56.7	85	5.9	536	37.4
1971	2,052	100.0	1,151	56.1	120	5.8	781	38.1
1972	2,356	100.0	1,309	55.6	141	6.0	906	38.5
1973	2,045	100.0	1,132	55.4	118	5.8	795	38.9
1974	1,338	100.0	888	66.4	68	5.1	382	28.6
1975	1,160	100.0	892	76.9	64	5.5	204	17.6
1976	1,538	100.0	1,162	75.5	87	5.7	289	18.8
1977	1,987	100.0	1,451	73.0	122	6.1	414	20.8
1978	2,020	100.0	1,433	70.9	125	6.2	462	22.9
Total 1964 to 1978	24,364	100.0	15,499	63.6	1,425	5.8	7,440	30.5

Note: Percents may not add due to rounding.

Source: U.S. Bureau of Census, Department of Commerce *Construction Reports*, Housing Starts," C20-78-10, (Washington, D.C.: U.S. Government Printing Office, December 1978); also C20-79-2, February 1979.

system. It has severely inhibited the capacity and willingness of the building trades to invest in capital-intensive forms of production. It also has occasioned vast accompanying swings in the scale of the labor force—forcing an adaptation to relatively unskilled labor on the one hand—with relatively high wages, at least in times of employment, for skilled individuals on the other.

The Trend Toward Single-Family Units. Within the overall context of housing starts, there are long-term trends in the types of units which have been constructed. Single-family units, for example, have gone from a mid-1960s peak of 66.9 percent of total construction down to a low of 55.4 percent in 1973, before ascending over the 70 percent plateau during the last four years, 1975 through 1978. Indeed, the last two years for which data is provided—1977 and

1978—have seen the absolute number of single-family starts at a virtual all-time high.

The greatest level of variation, however, is found in the multi-family sector—structures with five units or more. The peak in the fifteen years under consideration was the 906,000 starts achieved in 1972. By 1975, this had declined to 204,000, a reduction of 77.5 percent. The earlier multifamily relative prosperity of the late 1960s and early 1970s was a tribute to unity in time of substantial program inputs in the aided housing sector, plus demands spurred on by the early wave of baby boom-related household formations. In a later section of this introduction, the issue of whether or not future demographic trends portend an equivalent level of activity will be examined.

(On a more mundane level, market analysts have suggested that the seeds of the recent decline in multifamily housing starts was underlaid by the drastic overbuilding in the 1969-to-1973 period, which generated about 3.6 million such units.)

The two-to-four family sector has had a relatively modest role in the provision of new, privately owned housing, with peak starts in 1972 of 141,000 units. Even at this level, they represented only 6.0 percent of the total national construction. There is some issue as to the proportion of nominal one-family homes, however, which actually are housing two or more households (if sometimes illegally). This pattern of conversion, though not shown in housing start statistics, is undoubtedly significant.

Privately Owned Housing Starts by Region. In order to secure a grasp of the realities of housing starts by region, without the aberrants of individual year fluctuations, the data in Exhibit 8 have been grouped into average annual rates for three-year intervals. The variance earlier indicated is much muted, but still is a dominant element. For example, the annual average of 1.3 million starts for the 1966-to-1968 period stands in contrast to the 1.9 million annual average for the 1972-to-1974 years. The latter, in turn, declined by over 20 percent to 1.6 million during the 1975-to-1977 period. The level of housing starts of 1978 clearly would be uniquely high by past standards, if continued. However, preliminary 1979 data presently in hand are far below that level.

Within this overall context, the regional variations is marked. The Northeast, which secured 17.1 percent of the total national private housing starts in the 1963-to-1965 period, has experienced continual erosion in more recent years. By 1978, it captured only 9.9 percent of the total starts. In the earlier period, the South's absolute increment was more than twice that of the Northeast. By the latter date

EXHIBIT 8

NEW PRIVATELY OWNED HOUSING UNITS STARTED BY REGION: 1963 TO 1978 ANNUAL AVERAGES

(Numbers in Thousands)

		REGION			
Period	*U.S. Total*	*Northeast*	*North Central*	*South*	*West*
1963 to 1965	1,535	262	344	580	350
1966 to 1968	1,322	216	331	537	237
1969 to 1971	1,651	229	359	690	374
1972 to 1974	1,913	263	400	836	414
1975 to 1977	1,562	173	386	598	404
1978	2,020	200	451	824	545

Percent Distribution

1963 to 1965	100.0	17.1	22.4	37.8	22.8
1966 to 1968	100.0	16.4	25.1	40.7	17.9
1969 to 1971	100.0	13.9	21.7	41.8	22.6
1972 to 1974	100.0	13.7	20.9	43.7	21.6
1975 to 1977	100.0	11.1	24.7	38.3	25.9
1978	100.0	9.9	22.3	40.8	27.0

Notes: 1. Where numbers do not add because of rounding, percentages are based on regional summations. Percentages may not add due to rounding.

Source: U.S. Bureau of the Census, Department of Commerce, *Construction Reports*, "Housing Starts" C20-78-10, (Washington, D.C.: U.S. Government Printing Office, December 1978); also C20-79-2, February 1979.

it expanded to four times that of the Northeast. Clearly, the capital replenishment of the latter's supply system is lagging.

Government Subsidized Production. The increasing significance of government subsidized multifamily housing in the United States is underscored by the data in Exhibit 9, prepared by our colleague David Listokin, which indicates total production partitioned by program and building type. While a direct comparison to the preceding data on housing starts (Exhibit 7) is limited by accounting variations (i.e., fiscal versus calendar years) the increased presence of government subsidy within the privately owned production sector is clear. (It should be noted that the public housing totals of Exhibit 9 include leased privately owned units, and are not directly comparable to subsequent public housing data, which are limited to the publically owned sector.) The recent stagnation in multifamily construction would be even more accentuated were government supported elements removed from the production equation.

EXHIBIT 9

FEDERALLY SUBSIDIZED HOUSING PRODUCTION FISCAL YEARS 1969-1979 TOTAL PRODUCTION
(NEW CONSTRUCTION STARTS AND REHABILITATED UNITS)

Housing Production/Programs	1969	1970	1971	1972	FISCAL YEAR 1973	1974	1975	1976	Transition Quarter	1977	(6) 1978	(6) 1979
I. Total Subsidized Production	202,700	328,010	482,970	429,790	331,830	171,660	128,840	137,240	59,400	217,440	274,330	406,920
HUD	166,950	276,790	397,400	338,190	234,170	90,520	46,540	51,130	26,110	130,030	181,440	298,950
FMMA	35,750	51,220	85,570	91,600	97,660	81,140	82,300	86,110	33,290	87,410	92,890	107,970
A. 1-4 Family, Total	48,120	128,280	233,110	211,990	154,110	86,480	70,110	82,020	23,660	74,740	87,190	103,520
1. HUD	15,050	80,320	150,180	124,940	65,920	15,110	5,080	7,960	4,290	4,610	20,440	29,750
Sec. 235	7,980	70,180	137,590	113,300	57,640	8,420	1,800	3,200	2,030	3,080	19,000	29,750
Sec. 115/312	5,760	8,670	12,250	11,600	8,260	6,680	3,200	4,740	2,260	1,630	1,440	2,250
Sec. 221 (h)	1,320	1,470	340	40	20	10	80	20	—	—	—	—
2. FMMA	33,070	47,960	83,930	87,050	88,190	71,370	65,030	74,060	19,370	70,180	66,750	73,770
Low Income	(2)	(2)	(2)	61,730	56,680	38,070	46,400	49,680	12,280	46,120	48,750	60,579
Moderate Income	(2)	(2)	(2)	25,310	31,520	33,300	18,630	24,380	6,550	24,010	18,000	13,200
B. Multifamily, Total	154,580	199,730	249,860	217,800	177,720	85,180	58,730	55,220	35,740	142,700	187,140	303,400
1. HUD	151,900	196,470	247,220	213,250	168,250	75,410	41,480	43,170	21,820	125,420	161,000	269,200
Public Housing	80,290	87,880	99,700	53,930	36,700	26,150	17,100	11,110	2,100	12,020	30,000	65,000
Sec. 8	—	—	—	—	—	—	—	11,750	15,140	106,310	125,000	200,000
Sec. 236	1,000	91,390	106,980	113,060	95,070	37,090	17,240	16,570	4,380	6,640	4,700	4,200
Rent Supplement	16,640	22,530	16,800	12,480	11,740	4,520	2,510	1,380	—	390	1,300	—
State Asst. Projects	3,410	1,800	9,860	28,690	23,530	7,360	4,410	2,360	200	(3)	(3)	(3)
Sec. 221(d)/(3) BMIR	43,590	26,870	11,640	3,880	520	120	—	—	—	(3,410)(4)	(27,900)(4)	(35,800)(5)
Sec. 202	6,590	5,830	1,430	200	220	—	—	—	—	—	—	—
Sec. 312	(5)	170	810	1,010	470	170	200	(5)	(5)	(5)	(5)	(5)
2. FMMA	2,680	3,260	2,640	4,550	9,470	9,770	17,270	12,050	13,920	17,280	26,140	34,200
Without Sec. 8 Asst.	2,680	3,260	2,640	4,550	9,470	9,770	17,270	12,050	13,920	17,280	26,140	34,200
With Sec. 8 Asst.	—	—	—	—	—	—	—	(1,090)(4)	(2,030)(4)	(11,630)(4)	(10,000)(4)	(10,00)(4)

Notes:
1. Projected starts under Sec. 235 in FY 1977 and FY 1978 are under the revised Sec. 235 program.
2. Breakdown between low and moderate income FMHA starts was not available prior to 1972.
3. Included in Sec. 236.
4. Included as a nonaddition since it is expected that each unit will receive Section 8 assistance and is already counted under the Section 8 program.
5. Included in Sec. 115/312 under 1-4 family totals.
6. Estimate.

Source: *Annual Report on the National Housing Goals* for indicated years.

EXHIBIT 10

NEW PUBLICLY OWNED HOUSING UNITS STARTED BY REGION: 1963 TO 1978 ANNUAL AVERAGES

(Numbers in Thousands)

U.S. TOTALS

Year	Total	Year	Total
1963	31.8	1971	32.3
1964	32.1	1972	21.9
1965	36.9	1973	12.2
1966	30.9	1974	14.8
1967	30.3	1975	10.9
1968	37.8	1976	10.1
1969	32.8	1977	2.7
1970	35.4	1978	3.0

Source: U.S. Bureau of Census, Department of Commerce, *Construction Reports*, "Housing Starts" C20-78-6, Issued July 1978, U.S. Government Printing Office, Washington, D.C. also C20-79-2, issued February 1979.

The Role of Public Housing. Public housing has played a relatively minute role in terms of the units added to the inventory since 1963. As shown in Exhibit 10, for example, the number of new units started under this program was constrained to a relatively narrow production band from 1963 through 1971—slightly in excess of 30,000 units annually. Its level since that time has diminished very sharply and indeed, by 1977 and 1978, was at or under the 3,000-unit mark.

It is striking to see in the overall totals the change in regional location within which public housing was provided, as shown in Exhibit 11. The South, at the very beginning of the first time period capsulized, secured 35.4 percent of the public housing starts; but, from 1972 on, this increased to more than 50 percent. The Northeast's share, on the other hand, diminished from 29.5 percent in the early 1960s to less than 4 percent by 1978.

This spatial variation is particularly provocative, given the overall view of public housing as essentially being confined to the large, aging industrial cities of the Northeast. Regardless of the validity of that perspective in the early days of the program's inception, it certainly does not hold for the last two decades.

EXHIBIT 11

NEW PUBLICLY OWNED HOUSING UNITS STARTED BY REGION
1963 TO 1978 ANNUAL AVERAGES
(Numbers in Thousands)

		REGION			
Period	*U.S. Total*	*Northeast*	*North Central*	*South*	*West*
1963 to 1965	33.6	9.9	6.8	11.9	5.0
1966 to 1968	33.0	9.1	8.0	12.6	3.3
1969 to 1971	33.5	6.8	7.2	15.5	4.0
1972 to 1974	16.3	2.0	2.5	8.3	3.5
1975 to 1977	7.9	0.3	0.8	4.7	2.1
1978	3.0	——————discontinued————————			

Percent Distribution

Period	*U.S. Total*	*Northeast*	*North Central*	*South*	*West*
1963 to 1965	100.0	29.5	20.2	35.4	14.9
1966 to 1968	100.0	27.6	24.2	38.2	10.0
1969 to 1971	100.0	20.2	21.5	46.3	11.9
1972 to 1974	100.0	12.3	15.3	50.9	21.5
1975 to 1977	100.0	3.8	10.1	59.5	26.6
1978	100.0	——————discontinued————————			

Source: U.S. Bureau of Census, Department of Commerce, *Construction Reports*, "Housing Starts" C20-78-6, issued July 1978, U.S. Government Printing Office, Washington, D.C. also: C20-79-2, issued February 1979.

SUMMARY

At this point, it is again useful to consolidate the basic trends in force. Despite the boom-bust nature of the residential construction industry, its output throughout the 1970s has been substantial.

1. *One out of every seven (15.6 percent) units in the total 1976 inventory was constructed after 1970. However, the South and West have twice the proportion of "new" units as the Northeast and North Central Regions.*

2. *The pattern of privately owned housing starts, while experiencing severe annual fluctuations, mirrors this regional variation. Since 1973, seven out of ten starts were single-family units, underscoring the dramatic shift in tenure towards owner occupancy.*

3. *The sagging pace of replenishment of the Northeast's residential stock is perhaps characteristic of the broader problem afflicting the region—an aging and increasingly obsolete infrastructure and basic capital plant. This reality also is underscored by its declining share of a contracting public housing start level.*

4. Nonetheless, on a national basis, it is readily apparent that a massive infusion of resources into the housing stock has been taking place. This stands in marked contrast to the nation's industrial and transportation infrastructure, where substantial questions have been raised regarding the adequacy of the pace of capital investment.

Given the scale of new housing construction and the flow of economic resources it represents, it is reasonable to expect significant changes in the quality and the condition of the inventory. Some measures of the reality are considered in the following section.

PHYSICAL CHARACTERISTICS OF THE
NATION'S HOUSING INVENTORY

The process of change in the reservoir of housing in the United States, continuously altered by new starts on the one hand and removals from the inventory on the other, has yielded a very substantial upgrading in housing amenities.

A major illustration is the shifting unit size (rooms per unit) profile (Exhibit 12). In the 1970-to-1976 period, the owner-occupied inventory as a whole increased by 8.0 million units; this occurred despite an absolute reduction of 338,000 units with three or fewer rooms. The major gains comprised larger units—composed of six rooms or more—the net increment of which, 6.2 million units, was three-quarters percent of the total 1970-to-1976 increase.

In the renter-occupied inventory, the changes were much less skewed. There was a decline in the proportion of extreme-sized units, both in the one- and two-room as well as the five rooms or more sectors. It was the three-to-four room category which grew most rapidly; the demographic realities that underlie and support this transition will be discussed in the following section. Suffice it to note here that the full import of these changes can be realized only in the context of very substantial shrinkages in household sizes. Clearly, the role of the rental sector, at least for the more fortunate, in providing long-term, child-rearing environments, has contracted in significance, if not absolute incidence, in light of the increased dominance of larger, owner-occupied units. (The emigration from rental facilities by traditional (husband-wife), family-raising households will be documented subsequently.)

When median unit sizes are partitioned by region and SMSA status (Exhibit 13), there is a remarkable consistency of upgrading (increasing size) for owner-occupied units. This reality holds true for

EXHIBIT 12
UNIT SIZE (ROOMS PER UNIT) OF THE HOUSING INVENTORY: 1970 TO 1976

(Numbers in thousands)

	1970		1976		Change: 1970 to 1976	
	Number	Percent	Number	Percent	Number	Percent
Owner Occupied						
Total	39,886	100.0	47,904	100.0	8,018	20.1
1 room	90	0.2	45	0.1	− 45	−50.0
2 rooms	279	0.7	184	0.4	− 95	−34.1
3 rooms	1,275	3.2	1,077	2.2	− 198	−15.5
4 rooms	5,876	14.7	6,335	13.2	459	7.8
5 rooms	11,394	28.6	13,133	27.4	1,739	15.3
6 rooms	10,720	26.9	13,037	27.2	2,317	21.6
7 rooms or more	10,251	25.7	14,092	29.4	3,841	37.5
Median	5.6	—	5.7	—	—	—
Renter Occupied						
Total	23,560	100.0	26,101	100.0	2,541	10.8
1 room	944	4.0	959	3.7	15	1.6
2 rooms	1,763	7.5	1,654	6.3	− 109	− 6.2
3 rooms	5,381	22.8	6,236	23.9	855	15.9
4 rooms	7,088	30.1	8,451	32.4	1,363	19.2
5 rooms	4,705	20.0	5,074	19.4	369	7.8
6 rooms	2,385	10.1	2,430	9.3	45	1.9
7 rooms or more	1,294	5.5	1,297	5.0	3	0.2
Median	4.0	—	4.0	—	—	—

Note   Numbers and/or percents may not add due to rounding.

Source: U.S. Department of Commerce, U.S. Bureau of the Census, *Current Housing Reports*, Series H-150-76, *General Housing Characteristics for the United States and Regions: 1976*, Annual Housing Survey: 1976, Part A. U.S. Government Printing Office, Washington, D.C., 1978.

EXHIBIT 13

MEDIAN ROOMS PER UNIT, BY REGION AND SMSA STATUS: 1970 AND 1976

	Total		INSIDE SMSAs						Outside SMSAs	
			Total		In Central Cities		Not in Central Cities			
	1970	1976	1970	1976	1970	1976	1970	1976	1970	1976
Owner Occupied										
United States Total	5.6	5.7	5.7	5.8	5.6	5.7	5.8	5.9	5.4	5.5
Northeast	6.0	6.1	6.0	6.1	5.8	5.8	6.1	6.2	6.0	6.0
North Central	5.5	5.8	5.6	5.8	5.5	5.7	5.6	5.9	5.5	5.7
South	5.4	5.6	5.6	5.8	5.6	5.8	5.9	5.8	5.2	5.3
West	5.4	5.6	5.5	5.6	5.5	5.7	5.6	5.6	5.1	5.4
Renter Occupied										
United States Total	4.0	4.0	3.9	3.9	3.8	3.8	4.1	4.0	4.3	4.2
Northeast	3.9	3.9	3.9	3.9	3.8	3.8	4.0	4.1	4.4	4.2
North Central	4.2	4.1	4.1	4.0	4.0	3.9	4.2	4.1	4.5	4.3
South	4.1	4.1	4.0	4.0	3.9	3.9	4.2	4.2	4.3	4.3
West	3.8	3.8	3.8	3.8	3.5	3.6	4.0	3.9	4.1	4.0

Note: Numbers and/or percents may not add due to rounding.

Source: U.S. Department of Commerce, U.S. Bureau of the Census, *Current Housing Reports*, Series H-150-76, *General Housing Characteristics for the United States and Regions: 1976*, Annual Housing Survey: 1976, Part A, U.S. Government Printing Office, Washington, D.C., 1978.

EXHIBIT 14
ALL-YEAR ROUND HOUSING UNIT MEASURES OF HOUSING INADEQUACY

	1976	1970	1960	1950	1940
Percent lacking some or all plumbing	3.4	6.5	16.8	35.4	45.2
Percent dilapidated or needing major repairs	NA	4.6	6.9	9.8	17.8
Percent substandard:					
Dilapidated or lacking plumbing	NA	9.0	18.2	36.9	49.2

Note: NA—Not applicable.

Source: Decennial Censuses of Housing, U.S. Department of Commerce, Bureau of the Census; and the Annual Housing Survey, U.S. Department of Commerce, Bureau of the Census; and U.S. Department of Housing and Urban Development.

metropolitan and nonmetropolitan areas as well. Similarly, there is little regional variation in changes in the size of rental units from 1970 to 1976 or across the metropolitan geographies.

Condition of Housing. Size is merely one criterion of housing quality. Simple measurements of the latter have long evaded researchers. Using extant Census Bureau criteria as a guide, however, it can be concluded that there has been a very substantial upgrading, particularly over the long term. Exhibit 14, for example, presents selected measures of housing inadequacy by decade from 1940 to 1970, as well as data for 1976. It is difficult to realize that as late as 1940, 45.2 percent of America's all-year-round housing units lacked some or all plumbing facilities. The latest data (1976) indicate a reduction of such deficiencies to 3.4 percent of the total inventory.

While the criteria used for rating housing as dilapidated or needing major repairs have been highly controversial, clearly the shrinkage in the incidence of such units has been dramatic—from 17.8 percent in 1940 to 4.6 percent in 1970. Indeed, even if the categories of dilapidated and/or lacking plumbing are aggregated together (substandard), by 1970 these units represented less than 9.0 percent of the stock—in 1940 they comprised nearly half (49.2 percent).

Regional Variations in Housing Quality. The upgrading of America's housing stock has swept across all of its regions. As shown in Exhibit 15, units lacking some or all plumbing facilities have declined in every regional and metropolitan category from 1970 to 1976. By the terminal year only 2.4 percent of the Northeast's housing units, and 1.5 percent of the West's, did not have an adequate quota of

EXHIBIT 15

ALL-YEAR ROUND HOUSING UNITS, LACKING SOME OR ALL PLUMBING FACILITIES, BY REGION AND SMSA STATUS: 1970 AND 1976

(Numbers in Thousands)

| | Total | | INSIDE SMSAs | | | | Outside SMSAs | |
| | | | In Central Cities | | Not in Central Cities | | | |
	1970	1976	1970	1976	1970	1976	1970	1976
United States Total	4,398	2,661	716	492	778	430	2,904	1,739
Northeast	576	419	192	167	171	88	212	164
North Central	1,069	591	216	127	183	98	670	366
South	2,395	1,417	197	134	347	189	1,851	1,093
West	358	234	110	63	77	54	170	116
Percent of Total Occupied Units								
United States Total	6.5	3.4	3.2	2.0	3.3	1.5	13.4	6.8
Northeast	3.6	2.4	3.1	2.7	2.5	1.2	6.5	4.3
North Central	5.7	2.8	3.6	2.1	3.0	1.3	10.3	5.0
South	11.5	5.5	3.2	1.9	6.4	2.6	19.9	9.7
West	3.0	1.6	2.6	1.3	1.5	0.8	6.6	3.6

Note: Numbers and/or percents may not add due to rounding.

Source: U.S. Department of Commerce, U.S. Bureau of the Census, *Current Housing Reports*, Series H-150-76, *General Housing Characteristics for the United States and Regions: 1976*, Annual Housing Survey: 1976, Part A. U.S. Government Printing Office, Washington, D.C., 1978.

such facilities. However, the South still lags the rest of the nation, particularly in its rural (nonmetropolitan) and suburban (outside central cities) contexts. Overall, failure to meet this standard is much more of a problem in rural areas—outside SMSAs—than of central cities. Nationally, in the latter case, only 2.0 percent of the units are deficient, while in the former it is 6.8 percent.

The Changing Pattern of Home Heating Equipment and Fuel Requirements. As the costs of energy soar ever higher, the pattern of fuel use becomes an increasingly vital issue. But well before our own era there were equally important—if not more pressing— elements, concerning the ease, convenience, cleanliness and labor imputs required to keep winter at bay. The data presented in Exhibit 16 provide insight into these matters. As late as 1950, it was coal or coke which was the single most common home heating fuel; more than a third (34.6 percent) of America's occupied housing units secured its heating from such sources. Gas accounted for a little more than a quarter (26.6 percent), with fuel oil, kerosene, etc., at 22.6 percent. Electricity played a very minor role, with only 0.7 percent of America's housing units utilizing it as energy for heating.

By 1976—a quarter of a century later—gas had assumed a dominant role—55.7 percent of all housing units employ it for heat. Oil, which peaked in utilization in 1960 (32.4 percent), returned to its 1950 level. The largest declines were experienced by the most primitive forms of heating—coal, coke, wood and other fuel. Such sources had heated nearly half (44.9 percent) of America's occupied housing units in 1950. By 1976 they were down to the 2.0 percent level. In contrast, electricity showed the biggest proportionate gain, moving up to a heating role for one out of nine (13.7 percent) of the total occupied dwelling units. Clearly the efficiences and virtues embodied in the shift away from coal and wood may be reversed by the issues of relative cost. At least currently, however, American home heating is substantially dependent upon the availability and cost of petroleum and natural gas.

The rapid shifts in fuel installation types are indicated by the fact that as recently as 1970 electricity as the primary heating fuel was installed in 28 percent of the one-family units completed in that year; by 1977 it was fully 50 percent (Exhibit 17). Gas, on the other hand, diminished from a 1970 installation figure of 62 percent to 38 percent for units completed in 1977. Oil was reduced to under the 10 percent mark.

EXHIBIT 16

HEATING FUELS FOR OCCUPIED UNITS: 1950 TO 1976

(in thousands, except percent)

Item	1950	1960	1970	1976	PERCENT DISTRIBUTION			
					1950	1960	1970	1976
Occupied Units, Total	42,826	53,024	63,445	74,005	100.0	100.0	100.0	100.0
House Heating Fuel:								
Utility gas	11,387	22,851	35,014	41,219	26.6	43.1	55.2	55.7
Fuel oil, kerosene, etc.	9,686	17,158	16,473	16,451	22.6	32.4	26.0	22.2
Electricity	283	933	4,876	10,151	.7	1.8	7.7	13.7
Bottled, tank, or LP gas	787	2,686	3,807	4,239	1.8	5.1	6.0	5.7
Coal or coke	14,828	6,456	1,821	484	34.6	12.2	2.9	.7
Wood and other fuel	4,855	2,460	1,060	998	11.3	4.6	1.7	1.3
None	999	478	395	463	2.3	.9	.6	.6

Source: U.S. Bureau of the Census, *Census of Housing, 1960*, Vol. I, No. 1; *Census of Housing, 1970*, Vol. I; and *Current Housing Reports*, Series H-150, Annual Housing Survey, Part A, *General Housing Characteristics for the United States and Region*.

EXHIBIT 17

PERCENT OF NEW PRIVATELY OWNED COMPLETED ONE-FAMILY HOUSES WITH VARIOUS CHARACTERISTICS: 1970 TO 1977

Characteristic	1970	1974	1975	1976	1977
Total Houses (1,000's)	793	940	875	1034	1258
Floor area (sq. ft.)	100	100	100	100	100
Under 1,200	36	24	25	22	20
1,200-1,597	28	29	30	29	30
1,600-1,999	16				
2,000-2,399		34	34	37	38
2,400 and over	21	13	11	12	13
Bathrooms	100	100	100	100	100
1 or less	32	22	24	20	17
1½	20	18	17	13	13
2	32	40	40	45	47
2½ or more	16	21	20	22	23
Heating fuel	100	100	100	100	100
Electricity	28	49	49	48	50
Gas	62	41	40	39	38
Oil	8	9	9	11	9
Other	1	1	2	2	2
Central air condition	100	100	100	100	100
With	34	48	46	49	54
Without	66	52	54	51	46
Parking facilities	100	100	100	100	100
Garage	58	68	67	72	73
Carport	17	10	9	8	7
No garage or carport	25	22	24	20	19

Note: Data beginning 1974 show percent distribution of characteristics for all houses completed (includes new houses completed, houses built for sale ccompleted, contractor-built and owner-built houses completed, and houses completed for rent). Data for 1970 cover contractor-built, owner-built and houses for rent for year construction started and houses sold for year of sale. Percents exclude houses for which characteristics specified were not reported.

Source: U.S. Bureau of the Census and U.S. Department of Housing and Urban Development, *Construction Reports*, Series C25, *Characteristics of New One Family Homes* (a joint publication).

As Americans at this writing face a very uncertain energy future, it is worthwhile to appreciate the sharp rise in the level of amenity which has taken place in recent years, much of which has direct relevance to energy consumption. Some indication of these amenities are revealed by further data in Exhibit 17, which indicate the percentage of new, privately owned one-family houses with various characteristics completed in the several years from 1970 to 1977. In 1970, for example, 37 percent of the newly completed houses had 1,600 or more square feet; by 1977, it was 51 percent. In the earlier year, 48 percent of the homes had two or more baths; by the latter, it was 70 percent. Central air conditioning increased from 34 percent to 54 percent, and the provision of garages from 58 percent to 73 percent.

The decline of minimal housing is indicated particularly by the square footage parameters. In 1970, 36 percent of the newly completed homes contained under 1,200 square feet. While this total figure may have been inflated by relatively inexpensive federally financed housing units under the 235 program, it was still at the 24 percent level in 1974. Three years later, in 1977, it was only 20 percent. Certainly the quality standards of new one-family construction could shrink substantially from the terminal figure shown here without marking a major regression from relatively recent standards.

SUMMARY

Coinciding with the rapidly paced growth of the housing inventory have been substantial improvements in its physical attributes.

1. *The owner-occupied sector has experienced a sharp rate of attrition in small units and secured major additions of large units (as measured by rooms per unit).*
2. *The renter-occupied sector is trending toward a more standardized configuration—three to five rooms—with extreme size facilities, both small and large, declining in relative proportion.*
3. *By all extant quality and condition indicators, (or measures of housing adequacy), there has been a long-term pattern of sustained improvement, with little sign of abatement.*
4. *The amenities packaged within newly completed single-family homes—absolute size (square footage), the number of bathrooms and the incorporation of central air conditioning, for example—have grown continuously throughout the present decade.*

The major question arising from this process of upgrading is its effect on basic cost structures, our next subject of concern.

HOUSING COSTS IN CONTEXT

The tides of inflation are making Americans of all economic classes more and more apprehensive about their capacity to afford the symbols of the good life. Nowhere has this concern achieved more visibility than in the housing domain. The virtual month-by-month escalations in the selling price of new single-family homes, the soaring cost and uncertainty of the simple availability of home heating fuel, the property tax revolt, and landlord-tenant tensions in the context of rent regulation—either applied or proposed—are all real manifestations and potent symbols of the dilemmas at hand. What are the basic cost realities attached to such interrelated housing elements?

While income levels and their direct relationship to housing costs are evaluated in subsequent sections, the overall dollar pressures are evidenced in Exhibit 18. Calibrated upon a baseline of 100 as of 1967, the data indicate the escalating pace of inflation. From 1960 to 1965, the "all items" index increased by a mere 6.5 percent. Over the ensuing five years, 1965 to 1970, the index jumped by 32.1 percent. From 1970 to 1975, the pattern of increase was maintained, with the index soaring by 38.6 percent. While the 1975-to-1978 change stands at 21.1 percent, early measurements of the 1979 experience, if continued, promise to make the 1975-to-1980 increment at least equivalent to that of the preceding five years.

But the constitutent market basket elements of the consumer price index (CPI) have not ascended uniformly. The homeownership component, for example, has consistently risen at a pace far more rapid than the overall CPI. From 1960 to 1970, homeownership costs increased by 48.9 percent, while the all items index grew by 31.1 percent; from 1970 to 1978, an eight-year period, the homeownership index soared 76.8 percent, compared to a 68.0 percent rise in the overall CPI. Rent levels, on the other hand, have tended to lag. From 1960 to 1970, the increase of 20.1 percent was only two-thirds that of the all items index, and barely 40 percent of the homeownership increment. The pattern from 1970 to 1978, though more muted, is similar, with a 49.0 percent increase in rent compared to 68.0 percent for the all items index, and 76.8 percent for homeownership. This lag occurred despite very substantial increases in operating costs particulary in terms of energy. Fuel oil and coal increased 170.9 percent in the 1970-to-1978 period alone, while gas and electricity experienced a 116.8 percent rise.

EXHIBIT 18

CONSUMER PRICE INDEX, UNITED STATES, SELECTED ITEMS: 1960 TO 1978

Year	All[1] Items	Home Ownership	Rent	Fuel Oil and Coal	Gas and Electricity
1960	88.7	86.3	91.7	89.2	98.6
1965	94.5	92.7	96.9	94.6	99.4
1970	116.3	128.5	110.1	110.1	107.3
1971	121.3	133.7	115.2	117.5	114.7
1972	125.3	140.1	119.2	118.5	120.5
1973	133.1	146.7	124.3	136.0	126.4
1974	147.7	163.2	130.6	214.6	145.8
1975	161.2	181.7	137.3	235.3	169.6
1976	170.5	191.7	144.7	250.8	189.0
1977	181.5	204.9	153.5	283.4	213.4
1978	195.4	227.2	164.0	298.3	232.6

Percent Change

Period					
1960 to 1970	31.1	48.9	20.1	23.4	8.8
1960 to 1965	6.5	7.4	5.7	6.1	0.8
1965 to 1970	23.1	38.6	13.6	16.4	7.9
1970 to 1978	68.0	76.8	49.0	170.9	116.8
1970 to 1975	38.6	41.4	24.7	113.7	58.1
1975 to 1978	21.2	25.0	19.4	26.8	37.1

Note: 1. Overall CPI.

Source: Bureau of Economic Analysis, U.S. Department of Commerce, *Survey of Current Business*, (Washington, D.C.: U.S. Government Printing Office, Annual).

Rents on this basis clearly have lagged both the consumer price index generally and the homeownership component most specifically. Given the variance in prices, conventional market analysis would suggest that homeownership should increasingly give way to rental facilities. Certainly, as the data presented earlier indicate, this has not been the case in the last several years. Instead, the pattern has been one of increased demand for single-family housing, undoubtedly in substantial part as a buffer against inflation. But it also may be due to the narrow band of experience documented by the consumer price index.

Weaknessess of the Consumer Price Index. The consumer price index has served as a basis for a variety of housing research and legislation. This has been done frequently without an appropriate appreciation of its shortcomings. The CPI attempts to establish the changing parices of standardized goods over time. Thus, within the limitations of the art from, it is a house or apartment of consistent amenity the price of which is being ascertained and gauged over a period of years. When this approach, however, is matched to the initial conceptual apparatus—the ever changing reservoir of housing—its limitations become obvious. From the consumer's point of view, this is particularly the case since the modular dwelling unit employed by the CPI may, over the course of time, be a decreasingly significant part of the stock. As earlier discussed, housing standards, particularly for new construction, have increased very markedly; at the same time, there has been a very significant reduction in rental configurations particularly at the lower end of the market. The overall housing supply, therefore, is characterized by significant shifts in quality and price levels.

In order to capture these variations, in Exhibit 19 data is presented for median gross rents for the total inventory of rental housing as of 1970 and 1976 (the last year for which this data set is currently available). The disparities are very clear and striking. From 1970 to 1976, for example, the consumer price index for rent went up by 31.4 percent. The medians of the two pools of rental housing—those of 1970 and 1976—compared over time yield a rental increment of 54.6 percent.

The module used in the CPI no longer is representative of the real changes in the universe of rental facilities.

Indeed, by this criterion, given the compositional changes in the rental housing stock as well as increments in unit-to-unit costs, rent levels, based on Exhibit 19, have escaled much faster than the all items CPI index (the latter evidencing a 46.6 percent gain from 1970 to 1976).

The implications of these data are substantial. The owner-operator of the same rental facilities from 1970 to 1976 has probably not had rent increments comparable to the level of increase which has taken place in the CPI, and certainly not equivalent to the surge in energy costs. The long-term tenant typically will have had rent increases which lag those of the total consumer price index.

From the viewpoint of the pools of tenant aspirations, i.e., the universe of rental facility seekers in 1970 versus a similar universe in 1976, there will be very different impressions, i.e., cost of differentials substantially in escess of the nominal CPI. The implications of these data in terms of supply and demand interactions will be explored subsequently.

Regional Variations in Median Gross Rents. On an absolute basis, as of 1976, the highest rent levels in the nation were in the Northeast Region ($182), the lowest were in the South ($151). See Exhibit

EXHIBIT 19

MEDIAN GROSS RENT, BY REGION AND SMSA STATUS: 1970 TO 1976

| | Total | | INSIDE SMSAs | | | | Outside SMSAs | |
| | | | In Central Cities | | Not in Central Cities | | | |
	1970	1976	1970	1976	1970	1976	1970	1976
United States Total	$108	$167	$107	$165	$130	$195	$84	$132
Northeast	110	182	106	177	127	205	99	159
North Central	110	162	108	155	136	195	90	138
South	93	151	97	153	123	194	70	113
West	119	178	118	177	132	189	95	143

PERCENT CHANGE

	1970 to 1976	1970 to 1976	1970 to 1976	1970 to 1976
United States Total	54.6%	54.2%	50.0%	57.1%
Northeast	65.5	67.0	61.4	59.6
North Central	47.2	43.5	43.4	53.3
South	62.3	57.7	57.7	61.4
West	49.6	50.0	43.2	50.5

Note: Numbers and/or percents may not add due to rounding.

Source: U.S. Department of Commerce, U.S. Bureau of the Census, *Current Housing Reports,* Series H-150-76, *General Housing Characteristics for the United States and Regions: 1976,* Annual Housing Survey: 1976, Part A. U.S. Government Printing Office, Washington, D.C., 1978.

19. When interregional rent shifts over time are considered, caution in interpretation must again be observed. Changes over time are a complex phenomenon, the product of a number of distinct processes which should be reiterated: changes attached to those sectors of the supply existing both at the initial and terminal points of the period under consideration; changes as a consequence of deletions and losses; and shifts resulting from the characteristics of new additions. These three causal elements—survivors, deaths and births (analogs to conventional demographic terminology)—have varying importance across the nation's diverse regions.

While rents in the Northeast were increasing most rapidly, this may well be the result of high regional scrappage rates—inventory losses—which occur most frequently in the lower rent sectors. Strikingly enough, however, second only to the Northeast was the South, with rent increments of 62.3 percent. This may result from the relatively rapid buildup of new rental units as a proportion of total within that region (as shown previously in Exhibit 6). This pattern of regional variation is largely carried through to the central cities, suburban areas and outside SMSA territories of each region.

In general, absolute rent levels in central cities tended to be approximately 15 to 20 percent below those found in suburban areas. On the other hand, at least as of 1976, the lowest median rents were outside SMSAs entirely and tended to be at levels approximately 10 to 15 percent below those found in central cities.

New Units Added Versus the Rent Levels of the Reservoir. The entry streams of new rental facilities are characterized by substantially higher rent levels than those of their predecessors—the extant stock. In Exhibit 20, for example, are indicated the 1976 rents of all rental units constructed from 1970 to 1976 versus the 1976 rents for the total supply of the geographic subset in question. For the United States as a whole, the newer facilities had rents 127 percent of those of all units, $212 versus $167.

It is interesting to observe the possibility (and size of sample limitations permit definitive generalizations to be made only with great temerity) that rent levels seem to be increasing somewhat faster outside SMSAs than inside them and, at least based upon the data shown here, in the South. But this is in part a tribute to the relatively low rent levels in the total stock within these areal sectors.

As noted in more detail in the contributions to this volume, America is suffering a very high level of scrappage in its older rental facilities. *Clearly based upon the rent levels of new construction, their replacements are coming onstream at relatively high cost levels.*

EXHIBIT 20

1976 MEDIAN GROSS RENT OF UNITS CONSTRUCTED 1970 TO 1976, BY SMSA STATUS AND REGION

	Total 1978	New Construction 1970 to 1976	Ratio of New Construction to 1976 Total
United States			
Total	$167	$212	1.27
Inside SMSAs	178	219	1.23
In Central Cities	165	202	1.22
Not in Central Cities	195	232	1.19
Outside SMSAs	132	172	1.30
Region (Total)			
Northeast	182	231	1.27
North Central	162	209	1.29
South	151	204	1.35
West	178	220	1.24

Note: Numbers and/or percents may not add due to rounding.

Source: U.S. Department of Commerce, U.S. Bureau of the Census, *Current Housing Reports*, Series H-150-76; *General Housing Characteristics of the United States and Regions: 1976*, Annual Housing Survey: 1976, Part A. U.S. Government Printing Office, Washington, D.C., 1978.

Caught in between are the tenants who, while they may well desire the amenities typically available in the new construction and deplore their lack in the old, find the latter disappearing while the resources to pay for the former are very difficult to secure.

HOUSING VALUES AND PRICES

There may be a significant variation between housing values and sales prices. The latter represent the reality of the market as reflected by actual transactions at a particular moment of time. Collectively, however, sales prices may or may not represent the value of the pool of extant housing, i.e., there is no assurance that the housing which is being sold is necessarily representative of the total universe of housing from which it originates. The historic thrust of analysis has been devoted to price. The data are readily available and a great deal of its functional utility revolves around economic realities at a time of ownership transfer, which in turn typically generates price information. It is this facet, for example, which operationalizes the requirements of mortgage financing and is used as a very substantial measuring stick with which to gauge the competence of individuals to trade up in the new housing market.

In more recent years, housing value, i.e., the measurement of the stored capital of the units comprising the pool of single-family housing, regardless of whether they are sold—and the value realized— or merely latent, has become more significant. This is reflected in the enormous growth of the remortgage concept, i.e., the drawing down of the accumulated equity in a house, over and above extant mortgages, through either a second mortgage or roll-over financing. There is a second aspect which also is becoming noteworthy, the variation in consumer behavior based upon changes in stored wealth, holding other income constant. The measurement issue in this sector, is to assess changes in housing values, without current sales as a guide, i,e., capital accumulation derived through passive homeownership.

In order to distinguish house value from sales price or construction costs, two sets of data have been provided. The first of these is based upon the *Annual Housing Survey* which gives insight into occupant-defined housing value. These results are shown in Exhibit 21, which indicate median house value by region and SMSA status for 1970 to 1976. For the nation as a whole, there was an increase in owner estimated housing value in the six years in question of 88.9 percent. This increase was not reflected uniformly across the nation's regional partitions. The South (102.2 percent) and West (89.3 percent) secured the greatest gains—the Northeast (85.6 percent) and North Central (82.6 percent) experienced the smallest.

The pattern within central cities was one of slightly more modest value gains. The national central city increase (79.2 percent) again exceeded that of the cities of the North Central (66.0 percent) and Northeast (75.3 percent) regions. Suburban areas, while showing increases in excess of those in the central cities, still lagged the national figure. Again, the South and West were the regional leaders. The largest increases were in housing values outside SMSAs. With the exception of the Northeast, every one of the regional areas showed an increase of well above 100 percent. For the nation as a whole, it was 113.9 percent.

Part of this ebullient pattern reflects the change in the inventory of housing from 1970 to 1976. Some indication of this variation is shown by the 1976 value of units constructed from 1970 to 1976 as compared to all owner-occupied units in 1976 (Exhibit 22). The differentials indicate that the relatively newer homes were generally

EXHIBIT 21

MEDIAN HOUSE VALUE, BY REGION AND SMSA STATUS: 1970 TO 1976

	Total		INSIDE SMSAs						Outside SMSAs	
			Total		In Central Cities		Not in Central Cities			
	1970	*1976*	*1970*	*1976*	*1970*	*1976*	*1970*	*1976*	*1970*	*1976*
United States Total	$17,100	$32,300	$19,000	$35,100	$16,400	$29,400	$20,800	$38,300	$12,200	$26,100
Northeast	19,500	36,200	20,500	37,600	16,200	28,400	22,000	39,800	16,400	31,900
North Central	16,700	30,500	18,700	33,000	16,200	26,900	20,600	36,600	11,900	25,200
South	13,600	27,500	15,700	30,500	14,100	26,200	17,400	34,100	10,600	23,500
West	20,600	39,000	22,000	41,200	20,700	38,200	22,800	43,200	14,300	31,200

PERCENT CHANGE

	Total	INSIDE SMSAs			Outside SMSAs
		Total	In Central Cities	Not in Central Cities	
	1970 to 1976	*1970 to 1976*	*1970 to 1976*	*1970 to 1976*	*1970 to 1976*
United States Total	88.9%	84.7%	79.2%	84.1%	113.9%
Northeast	85.6	83.4	75.3	80.9	94.5
North Central	82.6	76.4	66.0	77.7	111.8
South	102.2	94.3	85.8	96.0	121.7
West	89.3	87.2	84.5	89.5	118.2

Note: Numbers and/or percents may not add due to rounding.

Source: U.S. Department of Commerce, U.S. Bureau of the Census, *Current Housing Reports*, Series H-150-76, *General Housing Characteristics for the United States and Regions: 1976*, Annual Housing Survey: 1976, Part A. U.S. Government Printing Office, Washington, D.C., 1978.

EXHIBIT 22

1976 MEDIAN HOUSE VALUE OF UNITS CONSTRUCTED 1970 TO 1976, BY SMSA STATUS AND REGION

	Total 1976	New Construction 1970 to 1976	Ratio of New Construction to 1976 Total
United States			
Total	$32,300	$42,300	1.31
Inside SMSAs	35,100	46,200	1.32
In Central Cities	29,400	43,000	1.46
Not in Central Cities	38,300	47,200	1.23
Outside SMSAs	26,100	36,200	1.39
Region (Total)			
Northeast	$36,200	$46,100	1.27
North Central	30,500	45,000	1.48
South	27,500	37,300	1.36
West	39,000	46,400	1.19

Note: Numbers and/or percents may not add due to rounding.

Source: U.S. Department of Commerce, U.S. Bureau of the Census, *Current Housing Reports*, Series H-150-76, *General Housing Characteristics for the United States and Regions: 1976*, Annual Housing Survey: 1976, Part A. U.S. Government Printing Office, Washington, D.C., 1978.

valued approximately 30 percent higher than the total inventory. The lowest valued new construction was found in nonmetropolitan areas as well as in the South. Over all other geographic areas, the value of new construction is remarkably consistent.

Certainly Americans who were fortunate enough to be homeowners during this period could generally congratulate themselves on the increments in the nominal investment value of their dwellings. However, they may be less sanguine when they confront the sales prices of new one-family houses sold. The data presented in Exhibit 23 detail the median sales price of new one-family houses sold in the United States and its four constituent regions from 1963 to 1978. Sales prices for new one-family homes advanced at a relatively modest pace (30 percent) between 1963 and 1970. For the 1970-to-1978 period, the increase soared to more than four times that rate—137.6 percent. By 1978, median sales price nationally had more than tripled (208.8 percent), from $18,000 in 1963 to a level in excess of $55,000.

There are distinct variations and shifts taking place within the several regions of the United States. The most striking change occurred in the Northeast. In the initial time period, from 1963 to 1970, the median sales price of new one-family homes increased

EXHIBIT 23

MEDIAN SALES PRICE OF NEW ONE - FAMILY HOUSES SOLD: UNITED STATES AND REGIONS: 1963 TO 1978

Year	United States	Northeast	Region North Central	South	West
1963	$18,000	$20,300	$17,900	$16,100	$18,800
1964	18,900	20,300	19,400	16,700	20,400
1965	20,000	21,500	21,600	17,500	21,600
1966	21,400	23,500	23,200	18,200	23,200
1967	22,700	25,400	25,100	19,400	24,100
1968	24,700	27,700	27,400	21,500	25,100
1969	25,600	31,600	27,600	22,800	25,300
1970	23,400	30,300	24,400	20,300	24,000
1971	25,200	30,600	27,200	22,500	25,500
1972	27,600	31,400	29,300	25,800	27,500
1973	32,500	37,100	32,900	30,900	32,400
1974	35,900	40,100	36,100	34,500	35,800
1975	39,300	44,000	39,600	37,300	40,600
1976	44,200	47,300	44,800	40,500	47,200
1977	48,800	51,600	51,500	44,100	53,500
1978 [1]	55,600	58,000	59,100	50,200	61,300
Percent Change					
1963 to 1970	30.0%	49.3%	36.3%	26.1%	27.7%
1970 to 1978	137.6	91.4	142.2	147.3	155.4
1963 to 1978	208.8	185.7	230.2	211.8	226.1

Note: 1 Preliminary

Source: U.S. Department of Commerce, Bureau of the Census, *Construction Reports*, "New One-Family Houses Sold and For Sale," Series C25-78-10 (Washington, D.C.: U.S. Government Printing Office, December 1978). Also: Series C25-71-9, November 1971; C25-78-12, February 1978.

by nearly half (49.3 percent), far in excess of the experience elsewhere in the nation, and this, despite an absolute base level ($20,300) considerably higher than that of other regions or the nation as a whole. However, a clear-cut transformation is evidenced in the 1970-to-1978 period. The increment in the Northeast (91.4 percent) is less than two-thirds that experienced by the balance of the nation. The shift that has taken place is emphasized when contrasted with the experience in the West. In virtually every year through 1976, the median sales prices of new homes in the West were substantially below those of the Northeast. But the gap closed rapidly in the mid-1970s. By 1978, the median sales price in the West, and now also for the first time in the North Central states, was in excess of that in the Northeast. And the South, which has long enjoyed the lowest new house prices in the nation, now appears to be converging toward the levels of the other regions.

The pattern of changes in prices of new one-family housing shown here has contributed to the debate on whether or not the Northeast's relatively high cost of living is meliorating as other regions enjoy an even more rapid increment. Certainly, the new housing prices as shown in Exhibit 23 would tend to lend some level of support to the thesis that says it is so.

But this is a complex arena within which to make generalizations. For example, in Exhibit 24 are shown the median sales prices of existing single-family homes sold in the United States and its regions from 1970 to 1978. Again, the pattern is one of a very rapid general increment in sales price, though at a slightly more modest level (111.7 percent) than held true of new one-family homes (137.6 percent). While the Northeast again has registered the smallest gains (90.1 percent), the West far outdistanced (174.5 percent) the rate of increase secured by other areas.

Based on these data, from 1976 on, the median sales price of existing single-family homes increased nationally by more than $10,000, with the West at double the level, and the South slightly under it. In the Northeast, by contrast, the gain was barely $6,000. The case again can be made for the fact that the Northeast's housing costs, which at one time were far in excess of the balance of the country's—and thus increasing the cost of living—have now substantially dampened, reducing the impetus or rationale for the out-migration of people and economic growth.

From the viewpoint of nominal accumulated wealth, however, based upon this standard, occupants of the other regions of the country may well congratulate themselves on being on a faster moving train. To the degree that in a post-shelter society, increments in housing values and housing costs are to be sought rather than to be avoided, the relative modesty of increments in the Northeast may not be as positive in overall impact as classic theory once would have held.

SUMMARY

The benefits associated with a rapidly expanding supply of housing—and of shelter of increasing quality and amenity—have not been achieved in a vacuum. Accompanying these benefits has been an ever rising matrix of costs.

EXHIBIT 24

MEDIAN SALES PRICES OF EXISTING SINGLE-FAMILY HOMES SOLD, UNITED STATES AND REGIONS: 1970 TO 1978

			Region		
Year	United States	Northeast	North Central	South	West
1970	$23,000	$25,200	$20,100	$22,200	$24,300
1971	24,800	27,100	22,100	24,300	26,500
1972	26,700	29,800	23,900	26,400	28,400
1973	28,900	32,800	25,300	29,000	31,000
1974	32,000	35,800	27,700	32,300	34,800
1975	35,300	39,300	30,100	34,800	39,600
1976	38,100	41,800	32,900	36,500	46,100
1977	42,900	44,400	36,700	39,800	57,300
1978	48,700	47,900	42,200	45,100	66,700

Percent Change

| 1970 to 1978 | 111.7% | 90.1% | 110.0% | 103.2% | 174.5% |

Source: National Association of Realtors, *Existing Home Sales* (Washington, D.C.: Economics and Research Division, May 1979).

1. *The costs of homeownership and rental occupancy have soared, particularly for new entrants into the market.*

2. *While the rental component of the Consumer Price Index (gauged within a context of constant quality accommodations) has lagged the overall CPI, the rent levels attached to the total inventory (as measured by the Annual Housing Survey) show much greater levels of escalation across all geographic partitions.*

3. *At the leading edge of the cost matrix are not only homeownership costs in general, but the sales prices of new one-family homes in particular. The latter phenomena is taking place (perhaps in response to, as will be considered subsequently) at a time of unparalleled production rates and soaring operating costs, particularly in the energy sector.*

While the latter appears to violate the traditional tenets of supply-demand economics, the elaboration of the demand profile lends at least partial explanation to the trends in force. It is to this task that emphasis in now directed.

Housing Demand

INTRODUCTION

The United States, in terms of housing policy, has had more than a generation in which demand was practically accepted as given—housing shortages, at least conceptually, were ever present. The basic impetus of the limited delivery systems of the Depression and World War II, coupled with an enormous expansion in household formation, increments in purchasing power and classic rural-to-urban migration patterns provided an enormous demand flywheel. Over time, however, these patterns are changing, and changing quite rapidly.

A number of demand-related events have transpired in the past decade. For example, media accounts covering the invasion of the bastions of family-raising culture—single-family homes—by single persons or other "unusual" household configurations have become commonplace. Indeed, one of the more visible aspects of social change has been the challenge to the classic hegemony of child-rearing families dominating traditional suburbia. But beneath the surface of such emerging events are evolutionary tides the long-term impact of which promises even more complex change. While such forces can be discerned from the data accounts at hand, their inter-relationships—the products of reinforcing and conflicting trendlines—are difficult to specify.

Nonetheless, this section attempts to synthesize some of the basic forces which shape the inputs into the "pull" or demand sector of the housing market. The major partitions center very roughly around population dynamics, household transformations and last, but far from least, income realities. The major trendlines can be summarized as follows:

1. *The rate of population growth in the United States over the past twenty-five years has decelerated markedly, a consequence of sustained fertility rate declines.*

2. *Variations of fertility in the past—steady reductions in the first four decades of this century, a brief but powerful rise in the ensuing twenty years, and abrupt declines thereafter (post-1960, have been etched deeply into the nation's age structure contours.*

    a) *The major residual is the baby-boom generation, whose presence will be marked throughout the remainder of this century by its bulging age cohorts. In the 1970-to-1985 period, its presence has been, and will be, evidenced within the 25-to-44 years of age sector.*

  b) *A second impact is being made by the progeny of the baby bust, an abrupt indentation in the age structure profile immediately contiguous to the baby-boom bulge. At present, the leading edge of the bust is entering the 18-to-24 years of age sector.*

  c) *The former provides a base for a continuing demand and market target, if only by virtue of its sheer size parameters. The latter, however, has introduced the concept of shrinkage—often quite painfully—into future projections.*

3. *The demand for shelter is not simply a consequence of population per se; the translation of population into household quanta is the essential linkage. The dynamics in effect have tended to amplify the housing ramifications of the baby boom, and may serve to partially mitigate the potentially ominous consequences of a maturing baby bust.*

  a) *The size dimension of America's households has been marked by unabated shrinkage, with the process showing signs of acceleration rather than slowing.*

  b) *The phenomenon is such as to give the impression that households are formed as rapidly as the housing inventory can expand, with population immediately diffusing into any net additional increments in supply. However, housing availability may be considered a facilitator, permitting the working out of the process of household evolution.*

5. *The latter transformation is marked by two driving forces. Most obvious is the role of low levels of fertility—many households are simply characterized by fewer children. But equally significant is the process of changing household configuration:*

  a) *The slowest growing household sector comprises husband-wife families; the fastest growing sectors are one-person configurations, those composed of two or more unrelated individuals, and female-headed families (two or more related individuals). What were once considered "atypical" households are gaining increased presence; the fabled modular configuration (husband-wife, child-rearing units) is declining in relative importance.*

  b) *A process of fragmentation as well as fertility declines, then, is generating an evolving profile of household types.*

Large households—seven persons or more—are virtually disappearing.

6. *Effective housing demand, however, is manifested by the confluence of income resources and household needs and desires. And there is not only a direct relationship between household configurations and income levels, but also between the latter variables and tenure status (owner versus rental).*

   a) *Husband-wife families are the most income affluent household type, particularly in the subset where both marriage partners are employed. Female-headed families, in contrast, are the most income deficient.*

   b) *Standing intermediate are primary individual households (households comprising single persons and two or more unrelated individuals).*

   c) *The more affluent household types—particularly husband-wife families—are shifting from renter status to owner occupancy. Expressed somewhat differently, the rental sector is losing the more income competitive households, while experiencing substantial growth mainly in household types less well endowed in terms of income resources.*

   d) *But atypical households also have experienced ownership gains. The rate of growth of single-person households in the owner-occupied sector is comparable to that in the rental sector.*

POPULATION

Population, and population forecasts, in the United States have been the subject of a variety of conventional "wisdoms." Until only a very few years ago, for example, the vision generally held of the future was one of sustained, inevitable growth, of a population surging past the 300 million person or more level by the year 2000. More currently, the image has been sharply revised to one of a nation dominated by the elderly remnants of the post-World War II baby boom, desperately being supported in their old age by a relatively small youthful productive population.

From the persepective of the housing industry, it is essential that these views, if not reconciled, be at least placed within an investment context. And clearly, within that context, there are significant dynamics at work. The data in Exhibit 25 provide the broader contours

EXHIBIT 25

ESTIMATES OF THE POPULATION OF THE UNITED STATES: JANUARY 1, 1950 TO JANUARY 1, 1979

(Numbers in Thousands)

POPULATION LEVEL

Year	Population Estimate [1]
1950	151,135
1955	164,588
1960	179,386
1965	193,223
1970	203,849
1975	212,748
1979	219,530

POPULATION CHANGE

Period	Number	Percent
1950-1955	13,453	8.9
1955-1960	14,798	9.0
1960-1965	13,837	7.7
1965-1970	10,626	5.6
1970-1975	8,899	4.4

Note: 1 Total population, including Armed Forces overseas.

Sources: U.S. Bureau of the Census, *Statistical Abstract of the United States: 1975* (Washington, D.C.: U.S. Government Printing Office, 1975), p. 11; U.S. Bureau of the Census, *Current Population Reports*, Series P-20, No. 307, "Population Profile of the United States: 1976" (Washington, D.C.: U.S. Government Printing Office, April 1977).

of population change. While there has been an enormous increase in population from 1950 to the present (1979)—70 million people— the dominant process has been one of a *deceleration* of national growth. The pattern, over the twenty-nine years, is one of a very intensive growth in the earlier part of the era under consideration, with sustained decreases, both in absolute and percentage incre- ments, in each of the ensuing five-year periods.

Much of the variation shown here is a function of the declining number of births. An indicator of the underlying process is the *total fertility rate*, a synthetic measure gauging the number of births a typical woman would experience over her reproductive life span were she to experience all of the age specific birth rates extant at a particular point in time. The long-term dimensions and immediate exigencies of fertility are encompassed in the data in

EXHIBIT 26

TOTAL FERTILITY RATE: 1920 TO 1978

Year	Rate	Period	Rate	Period	Rate
1978	1,795[1]	1970	2,480	1955-59	3,690
1977	1,826	1969	2,465	1950-54	3,337
1976	1,768	1968	2,477	1945-49	2,985
1975	1,799	1967	2,573	1940-44	2,523
1974	1,857	1966	2,736	1935-39	2,235
1973	1,896	1965	2,928	1930-34	2,376
1972	2,022	1965-69	2,636	1925-29	2,840
1971	2,275	1960-64	3,459	1920-24	3,248

Note: 1 Provisional estimate.

Source: The rate for 1978 is estimated by the Bureau of the Census; for 1940 to 1977, National Center for Health Statistics, *Vital Statistics of the United States* and Monthly Vital Statistics Report (various issues); for 1920-24 to 1935-39, U.S. Bureau of the Census, *Current Population Reports*, Series P-23, No. 36.

Exhibit 26 (which are expressed per thousand women of child-bearing age). The long-term trend is marked by several fluctuations. In the period from 1920 to 1924, the fertility rate was at the 3.248 level. It declined very abruptly through the balance of the 1920s and precipitously so during the Depression era (1930-1939). By the 1935-to-1939 period, it was down to a little more than the 2.2 mark, just slightly over the 2.110 level, which represents replacement level fertility. The subsequent increase culminated in the baby-boom peak during the 1955-to-1959 period, when the rate reached a half-century high of 3.69, i.e., a typical woman of that year would have borne 3.69 children over her reproductive lifetime. The following twenty years, up to the present date, have seen a nearly consistent decline. By 1972, the rate descended below the replacement level and in the subsequent years has languished at approximately the 1.8 level.

Recurrently, there are assertions that this is merely a transient situation, that women will have children later than has historically been the case, i.e., that a delayed birth wave would ensue and the like. An alternative perspective suggests that the long-term trend has been one of consistent steady decline, altered only by the aberrants of the Depression, World War II and the resultant aftermath. The latter would suggest the present fertility rate as the basic expectation for the future. Nonetheless, whatever the future case, it is clear that over the past twenty-five years, one of the key inputs into the decline in overall population growth as shown in Exhibit 25 has been the reduction in the fertility rate.

But future ramifications must be viewed within the context of the shifting age structure for the population as a whole. The fertility rate may have dropped for women, but to the degree that for any of a variety of reasons there are more women within the fertile age period—or less—than was heretofore the case, the actual birth production will vary. And indeed, depending upon the aging of the population as well as overall survival rates, there will be significant variations in the number of deaths. (The sum of births and deaths is equal to net natural increase.) As shown in Exhibit 27—the components of population change—the number of births increased over the 1973-to-1976 period, a time of continued decline in the fertility rate (Exhibit 26). This result was the consequence of the expansion of the number of women of childbearing age. Thus, the actualities of births were different from those yielded by the fertility level alone. Moreover, it is striking to see the significant role that net civilian immigration has played throughout the 1970s, making up approximately 20 percent of the total increase.

The overall data on increases in the population, then, tend to mask the underlying dynamics in terms of age sectors, whose influences are particularly pertinent to general population growth and, in turn, housing demand forecasts. As shown in Exhibit 28, there have been dramatic changes in the age structure of the population of the United States during the 1970s. Three key phenomena are extant—the baby bust, the baby boom and the growth of the elderly—all of them are the end products of past shifts in fertility and mortality rates, and all of them are permanently etched into society's contours. The baby bust, the after-effect of the decline in fertility in the last twenty years, is marked by the abrupt decline in the number of children under the age of fourteen years, in excess of 7.1 million people. This shinkage has been more than counterbalanced by the baby-boom bulge, evidenced by a 35 percent increase (or 8.8 million) in individuals from 25-to-34 years of age—a peak age of home buying—and an 18.4 percent gain (4.5 million) in individuals 18-to-24 years of age. Nearly as dramatic has been the 20 percent increase (4.1 million) in individuals sixty-five years and over. Clearly, the phenomena both of the rapid growth of retirement communities and nursing homes on the one hand, and a tremendous demand for single-family homes on the other (despite shrinking numbers of children), can be viewed through the spectrum of age sector growth.

As the 1978-to-1985 period is projected, these three cohorts continue to dominate the changes in the nation's age structure. They are joined by a new phenomenon—the baby-boom echo—the

EXHIBIT 27

ESTIMATES OF THE COMPONENTS OF POPULATION CHANGE FOR THE UNITED STATES: JANUARY 1, 1970 TO JANUARY 1, 1979

(Numbers in thousands—includes armed forces overseas)

Calendar Year	Population at Beginning of Period	Total Increase[1]	COMPONENTS OF CHANGE DURING YEAR			Net Civilian Immigration
			Net Natural Increase			
			Increase	Births	Deaths	
1979	219,530	–	–	–	–	–
1978	217,785	1,745	1,403	3,328	1,925	343
1977	216,057	1,728	1,412	3,313	1,901	315
1976	214,446	1,611	1,258	3,168	1,910	353
1975	212,748	1,699	1,251	3,144	1,894	449[2]
1974	211,207	1,541	1,225	3,160	1,935	316
1973	209,711	1,496	1,163	3,137	1,974	331
1972	208,088	1,623	1,293	3,258	1,965	325
1971	206,076	2,012	1,626	3,556	1,930	387
1970	203,849	2,227	1,812	3,739	1,927	438

Notes:

1 Includes estimates of overseas admissions into and discharges from the Armed Forces and for 1970, includes error of closure between censuses.

2 Includes about 130,000 Vietnamese refugees who entered the United States during 1975.

Source: Data consistent with U.S. Bureau of the Census, *Current Population Reports*, Series P-25, No. 793. Estimates of births and deaths (with an allowance for deaths to Armed Forces overseas) are from the National Center for Health Statistics. Estimates of net civilian immigration are based partly on data from the Immigration and Naturalization Service.

EXHIBIT 28

AGE STRUCTURE OF THE POPULATION OF THE UNITED STATES: APRIL 1, 1970 AND JULY 1, 1978

(Numbers in thousands—includes armed forces overseas)

Age	Population		Percent Distribution		Population Change 1970 to 1978	
	April 1, 1970	July 1, 1978	April 1, 1970	July 1, 1978	Number	Percent
AGE						
All ages	204,335	218,548	100.0	100.0	14,213	7.0
Under 5 years	17,163	15,361	8.4	7.0	− 1,801	−10.5
5 to 13 years	36,675	31,378	17.9	14.4	− 5,297	−14.4
14 to 17 years	15,854	16,639	7.8	7.6	785	4.9
18 to 24 years	24,455	28,944	12.0	13.2	4,489	18.4
25 to 34 years	25,146	33,936	12.3	15.5	8,791	35.0
35 to 44 years	23,214	24,383	11.4	11.2	1,170	5.0
45 to 54 years	23,254	23,184	11.4	10.6	− 70	− 0.3
55 to 64 years	18,603	20,668	9.1	9.5	2,066	11.1
65 years and over	19,972	24,054	9.8	11.0	4,082	20.4
Median age . . . (years)	27.9	29.7	—	—	—	—

Source: U.S. Bureau of the Census, *Census Population Reports*, Series P-25, No. 800.

EXHIBIT 29

AGE STRUCTURE OF THE POPULATION OF THE UNITED STATES: JULY 1, 1978 TO JULY 1, 1985

(Numbers in thousands)

Age	POPULATION			PERCENT DISTRIBUTION			POPULATION CHANGE, 1978 to 1985			
	July 1, 1978	July 1, 1985		July 1, 1978	July 1, 1985		Number		Percent	
		Series II	Series III		Series II	Series III	Series II	Series III	Series II	Series III
All Ages	218,548	232,880	228,879	100.0	100.0	100.0	14,332	10,331	6.6%	4.7%
Under 5 Years	15,361	18,803	16,235	7.0	8.1	7.1	3,442	874	22.4	5.7
5 to 13 Years	31,378	29,098	27,665	14.4	12.5	12.1	− 2,280	− 3,713	− 7.3	−11.8
14 to 17 Years	16,639	14,392		7.6	6.2	6.3	−2,247		−13.5	
18 to 24 Years	28,944	27,853		13.2	12.0	12.2	−1,091		− 3.8	
25 to 34 Years	33,936	39,859		15.5	17.1	17.4	5,923		17.5	
35 to 44 Years	24,383	31,376		11.2	13.5	13.7	6,993		28.7	
45 to 54 Years	23,184	22,457		10.6	9.6	9.8	− 727		− 3.1	
55 to 64 Years	20,668	21,737		9.5	9.3	9.5	1,069		5.2	
65 Years and Over	24,054	27,305		11.0	11.7	11.9	3,251		13.5	
Median Age	29.7	31.5	32.0	—	—	—	—	—	—	—

Source: U.S. Bureau of the Census, *Current Population Reports,* Series P-25, No. 704.

magnitude of which is as yet uncertain. The latter, already emerging despite a relatively stable fertility rate, is a consequence of the sheer rise in the number of women of childbearing age—the result of the maturation of the baby boom. The wide potential variation in scale of the "echo" is evident in Exhibit 29, which presents two alternative Census projections—Series II and Series III—for the period in question. The increase in the number of children under five years of age will range between 870,000 (Series III) and 3.4 million (Series II), depending on the level of fertility which ultimately ensues. The implications for the allocation of financial resources to housing, as well as particular shelter configurations and formats, are evident.

The leading edge of the baby bust will have reached 18-to-24 years of age by 1985; this age sector will decline by 3.8 percent or 1.1 million individuals from 1978 to 1985, with attendant ramifications for the rental market—at the least, potential diminution in the number of first-time renters. In contrast, the bulk of the baby-boom progeny will have aged to the 35-to-44 years of age category and this group will expand by 7.0 million persons or 28.7 percent. The trailing edge will be situated in the 25-to-34 years of age sectors, which will grow by 17.5 percent—5.9 million individuals. What this may portend is an increasing demand for single-family homes, particularly in the upper strata of quality, if the baby-boom bulge desires to trade in first homes for higher priced ones. Will a "demand-pull" phenomenon afflict housing prices at an even greater level than in the recent past? Will builders cater to this obvious and/or apparent market bulge to the neglect of other sectors? Or does it give support to the return-to-the-city movement—whose dimensions are as yet uncertain—particularly in the potential context of sustained low fertility patterns? These are compelling questions, the resolution of which will certainly be manifested in the marketplace as the decade of the 1980s is encountered.

Spatial Variation. Spatial redistribution may amplify or attenuate the immediacies of the preceding demand elements. Within the United States, several dominant geographic contours give shape to the population landscape—the accelerating regional shifts, metro-politan-nonmetropolitan tensions, and expanding intrametropolitan differentials. As the 1970s draw to a close, these swings in population settlement become etched ever more deeply.

The regional dimension is marked by slow growth and stagnation afflicting the older Northeast and North Central regions, with the South and West securing the bulk of the national population growth

EXHIBIT 30

POPULATION OF THE UNITED STATES BY METROPOLITAN-NONMETROPOLITAN RESIDENCE AND RACE AND SPANISH ORIGIN: 1978 AND 1970

(Numbers in Thousands)

Race and Residence	1978[1]	1970[2]	Change, 1970 to 1978	Percent Change 1970 to 1978	Percent Change 1960 to 1970[3]	Average Annual Percent Change[4] 1970 to 1978	Average Annual Percent Change[4] 1960 to 1970[3]
All Races	213,467	199,819	13,648	6.8	13.3	0.8	1.3
Metropolitan areas[5]	143,046	137,058	5,988	4.4	16.6	0.5	1.5
In central cities[6]	59,723	62,876	− 3,153	− 5.0	6.5	−0.6	0.6
Outside central cities	83,324	74,182	9,142	12.3	26.7	1.5	2.4
Nonmetropolitan areas	70,421	62,761	7,660	12.2	6.8	1.4	0.7
White	184,806	175,276	9,530	5.4	11.9	0.7	1.1
Metropolitan areas[5]	121,650	118,938	2,712	2.3	14.0	0.3	1.3
In central cities[6]	44,511	48,909	− 4,398	− 9.0	0.1	−1.2	−
Outside central cities	77,140	70,029	7,111	10.2	26.1	1.2	2.3
Nonmetropolitan areas	63,156	56,338	6,818	12.1	7.8	1.4	0.8
Black	24,757	22,056	2,701	12.2	19.7	1.4	1.8
Metropolitan areas[5]	18,463	16,342	2,121	13.0	31.6	1.5	2.7
In central cities[6]	13,687	12,909	778	6.0	33.2	0.7	2.9
Outside central cities	4,776	3,433	1,343	39.1	26.4	4.1	2.3
Nonmetropolitan areas	6,294	5,714	580	10.2	− 5.3	1.2	−0.5

EXHIBIT 30 (CONTINUED)

Race and Residence	1978[1]	1970[2]	Change, 1970 to 1978	Percent Change		Average Annual Percent Change[4]	
				1970 to 1978	1960 to 1970[3]	1970 to 1978	1960 to 1970[3]
Spanish Origin[7]	11,789	8,988	2,801	31.2	(NA)	3.4	(NA)
Metropolitan areas[5]	9,961	7,409	2,552	34.4	(NA)	3.7	(NA)
In central cities[6]	5,886	4,646	1,240	26.7	(NA)	3.0	(NA)
Outside central cities	4,074	2,764	1,310	47.4	(NA)	4.9	(NA)
Nonmetropolitan areas	1,829	1,578	251	15.9	(NA)	1.8	(NA)

Notes:

1 Five-quarter annual averages centered on April from the Current Population Survey.

2 For comparability with data from the Current Population Survey, figures from the 1970 census have been adjusted to exclude inmates of institutions and members of the Armed Forces living in barracks and similar types of quarters.

3 Based on total 1970 and 1960 census populations, including the categories not covered in the Current Population Survey, except for Black, which is based on a 1-in-1,000 sample for 1960.

4 Based on the method of exponential change.

5 Refers to the 243 standard metropolitan statistical areas (SMSAs) as defined in 1970 census publications.

6 1978 and 1970 data for the central cities refer to their 1970 corporate boundaries and exclude areas annexed since 1970; 1960 data refer to 1960 corporate boundaries.

7 Persons of Spanish origin may be of any race.

Source: U.S. Bureau of the Census, *1970 Census of Population*, Vol. 1. *U.S. Summary*, and State parts; PHC(2), *U.S. Summary*, and State parts; *1960 Census of Population*, Vol. I, States parts; and unpublished Current Population Survey data.

during the present decade. The metropolitan-nonmetropolitan framework is increasingly important because of a second transformation, the resurgence of nonmetropolitan areas. Reversing the historical secular trendline—metropolitan areas as the dominant national growth poles—the post-1970 experience has been one of decentralized growth on a vastly amplified scale. Concurrently, the 1970s have seen the central city-suburban gap deepen—an expanding intrametropolitan differential—as the nation's central cities in total have experienced net declines in population for the first time.

The data which underscores these population shifts are presented in Exhibit 30 and require little elaboration. Indeed, their correlation with the comparable partitions employed in the housing supply section, as should be expected, is substantial. This is particularly the case as the black and Spanish sectors of the population are beginning to replicate the patterns of their white forebearers—the former two groups are the fastest growing sectors of the suburban population. Even though they may be building from a relatively low absolute base, current information indicates that this process is accelerating. The only area in which white population growth exceeded that of blacks was in nonmetropolitan territories.

Thus, the absolute pressure of population on the housing market seemingly has declined or abated within central cities, while slowing down but still expanding at a substantial rate within suburbs, and clearly accelerating rapidly in nonmetropolitan areas. This is a pattern that is markedly dissimilar from that of the 1960s—central cities were then still growing at a pace comparable to that of nonmetropolitan areas, while the classic suburban expansion was at full crest. The earlier period was further distinguished by the relative expansion of black populations within central cities—a pattern which has now abruptly slowed.

HOUSEHOLD TRANSFORMATIONS

The broad sweep of demographic data earlier presented, from the viewpoint of the housing market, must be further refined into its household counterparts. By very definition these are the demand units for the vast bulk of America's housing. Since it is population pressure expressed in household quanta that is the major stimulus of the housing market as a whole, the pattern of household sizes therefore is a key variable. Indeed, as will be noted in more detail later, in recent years the shrinkage in size of typical households has been much more significant as a housing demand generator than the absolute growth in population per se.

EXHIBIT 31

HOUSEHOLD SIZE SHIFTS: 1950 TO 1976

(Persons per Household)

Year	Size
1950	3.37
1955	3.33
1960	3.33
1965	3.29
1970	3.14
1971	3.11
1972	3.06
1973	3.01
1974	2.97
1975	2.94
1976	2.89
1977	2.86
1978	2.81

Source: U.S. Bureau of the Census, *Statistical Abstract of the United States: 1978* (Washington, D.C.: U.S. Government Printing Office, 1978).

The pattern of change is summarized in Exhibit 31. In 1950 the average household size in the United States was 3.37 persons. By 1978, it was down to 2.81. To place this within a housing demand context, it should be noted that with a population of 220 million persons (assuming all in households), an average household size of 3.37 persons implies 65.3 million households; an average household size of 2.81 persons translates into 78.3 million households. The 13 million differential provides some idea of the impact of household size shifts.

It should further be observed, however, that the very decline in the size of household, with its nominal generation of increased demand for housing units, may in turn be a consequence of the availability and costs of housing units generally. We know that in societies in which housing buying power has degenerated, all things being equal, the size of household may well increase, as youthful couples simply cannot find adequate facilities away from the parental hearth and as the elderly generation perforce continues to be sheltered by the same roof as their progeny. Thus the decline in the size of household, stimulated certainly as it has been by a variety of demographic and societal-cultural changes, is at least in part also dependent upon the availability of housing units which permit extended family dissolution.

The overall decline in household size is not merely the result of the fertility changes earlier discussed, but also reflects basic compositional variations. In Exhibit 32, for example, are shown households—by type and number—for 1960, 1970 and 1978. In both time periods—1960 to 1970 and 1970 to 1978—there was an increase in total households of approximately 20 percent. Family households (two or more related individuals sharing a housing unit) as a group grew at a much more conservative level—14.6 percent from 1960 to 1970; 10.7 percent from 1970 to 1978. Within the family context, the single major growth sector was that of female-headed households (no husband present). Its 1970-to-1978 growth rate (46.1 percent) stands in marked contrast to that of traditional husband-wife families (5.9 percent). Indeed, the latter represented 74.3 percent of all households in 1960; by 1978, they accounted for only 62.3 percent. What has all to casually been considered as the modular American household unit—husband-wife families—while not about to become extinct, is clearly declining in relative importance at a substantial pace.

The major sector increase was that of nonfamily households (one or more unrelated individuals), which grew by more than half in each of the time periods for which data is presented. In 1960, there were 6.9 million nonfamily householders living alone. By 1978, there were than 16.7 million. An even faster pace of growth—though at a lower absolute level—was in the category of householders with non-relatives present. There were under 1 million such configurations in 1960, but by 1978, they were approaching the 2.4 million level. What were once considered atypical households are gradually gaining increasing mass. The pattern of diversity is not substantial, replicating nationally what was once characteristic only of a few cosmopolitan urban centers.

One of the by-products of the processes at work has been a major decline in the number and proportion of large households. This is particularly significant given the great difficulties of providing shelter for such configurations when combined with low incomes. The vision of housing shortages of the 1950s typically was one of severe overcrowding, and this, only in part because of the limitations of size of the unit. Much more characteristically, it was a function of the number of individuals crowded within it. Thus the data shown in Exhibit 33 are particularly pertinent; indicated are household size distributions both for owner- and renter-occupied facilities for 1970 and 1976. In terms of households comprising seven persons or more, the reduction has been most abrupt. In owner-occupied facilities, for example, the decline in the six-year period under

EXHIBIT 32

HOUSEHOLDS BY TYPE AND SIZE: 1978, 1970 AND 1960

(Numbers in thousands–noninstitutional population)

HOUSEHOLDS	1978		1970		1960		Percent Change	
	Number	Percent	Number	Percent	Number	Percent	1970 to 1978	1960 to 1978
Total Households	76,030	100.0	63,401	100.0	52,799	100.0	19.9	20.1
Family Households	56,958	74.9	51,456	81.2	44,905	85.0	10.7	14.6
Husband-wife	47,357	62.3	44,728	70.5	39,254	74.3	5.9	13.9
Male householder, no wife present	1,564	2.1	1,228	1.9	1,228	2.3	27.4	—
Female householder, no husband present	8,037	10.6	5,500	8.7	4,422	8.4	46.1	24.4
Nonfamily households	19,071	25.1	11,945	18.8	7,895	15.0	59.7	51.3
Householder living alone[1]	16,715	22.0	10,851	17.1	6,896	13.1	54.0	57.4
Householder with nonrelative(s) present	2,356	3.1	1,094	1.7	999	1.9	115.4	9.5

Note: 1 One-person household.

Source: U.S. Bureau of the Census, *Current Population Reports*, Series P-20, Nos. 324 and 327, and unpublished Current Population Survey data.

EXHIBIT 33

PERSONS PER HOUSEHOLD (HOUSEHOLD SIZE): 1970 TO 1976 UNITED STATES TOTAL

(Numbers in Thousands)

	1970		1976		Change: 1970 to 1976	
	Number	*Percent*	*Number*	*Percent*	*Number*	*Percent*
Owner Occupied						
Total	39,886	100.0	47,904	100.0	8,018	20.1
1 person	4,762	11.9	6,278	13.1	1,515	31.8
2 persons	12,010	30.1	15,098	31.5	3,088	25.7
3 persons	6,985	17.5	8,677	18.1	1,692	24.2
4 persons	6,925	17.4	8,786	18.3	1,861	26.9
5 persons	4,554	11.4	5,075	10.6	521	11.4
6 persons	2,468	6.2	2,341	4.9	− 127	− 5.1
7 persons or more	2,182	5.5	1,649	3.4	− 533	−24.4
Median	3.0	—	2.8	—	—	
Renter Occupied						
Total	23,560	100.0	26,101	100.0	2,541	10.8
1 person	6,389	27.1	8,560	32.8	2,171	34.0
2 persons	6,773	28.7	7,929	30.4	1,156	17.1
3 persons	3,923	16.7	4,036	15.5	113	2.9
4 persons	2,875	12.2	2,846	10.9	− 29	− 0.1
5 persons	1,643	7.0	1,443	5.5	− 200	−12.2
6 persons	915	3.9	688	2.6	− 227	−24.8
7 persons or more	1,043	4.4	599	2.3	− 444	−42.6
Median	2.3	—	2.1	—	—	

Notes: Numbers and/or percents may not add due to rounding.

Source: U.S. Department of Commerce, U.S. Bureau of the Census, *Current Housing Reports*, Series H-150-76, *General Housing Characteristics for the United States and Regions: 1976.* Annual Housing Survey: 1976, Part A, U.S. Government Printing Office, Washington, D.C., 1978.

consideration was 24.4 percent—533,000 households. In renter-occupied facilities, the change was more drastic: in six years, 42.6 percent (400,000) of all seven-person-or-more households disappeared. The alleviation of the large family trauma in renter facilities was further accentuated by an additional loss of 427,000 households at the five-and six-person level. The decline of large size households in America is one of the major unpublicized phenomena in the nation today.

The growth area in terms of household numbers has been in the one- and two-person configurations. The increase of more than 3 million such households among renters exceeds the total increase of all renters, i.e., the negative balance is made up by a decline in larger-scale households. Even in the owner-occupied sector, the same basic trend is evident, with an increase of 4.6 million one- and two-person households.

The level of alleviation of overcrowding and of basic demand for large-scale facilities is most important. It permits either a reduction in the scale of new housing units coming on stream, or a vast upgrading of the number of rooms per individual, or both. As has been shown previously and will be given further attention subsequently, it is the latter event which predominates.

The change in household size has taken place nearly universally through the United States. As detailed in Exhibit 34, it is a constant regardless of region or SMSA status. While there are slight absolute regional variations in the size of household, the diminition is pervasive.

Household Composition and Tenure Patterns. The level of market penetration of renter- versus owner-occupied units within various household types has been changing very dramatically in the United States. This has been substantially to the *disadvantage* of the rental sector. As suggested previously, the issues of rising operation and maintenance costs of renter-occupied facilities, as well as the relative dearth of non-governmentally-aided housing starts in this sector, consciously or otherwise reflects largely the price toll of inflation. But this also must be coupled with realities of the shifts of tenure within household categories.

The section which follows focuses on household compositional shifts for both renter- and owner-occupied units from 1970 to 1976. Subsequently examined are the income linkages which make the former such a vital input into changing housing demand formats.

The data in Exhibit 35 presents household configuration by age of head, for renter-occupied units in 1970 and in 1976. As is evident, there is a substantial shrinkage in the number of male-headed house-

EXHIBIT 34

MEDIAN HOUSEHOLD SIZE, BY REGION: 1970 TO 1976

| | Total | | INSIDE SMSAs | | | | Outside SMSAs | |
| | | | In Central Cities | | Not in Central Cities | | | |
	1970	1976	1970	1976	1970	1976	1970	1976
Owner Occupied								
United States Total	3.0	2.8	2.8	2.6	3.3	3.0	2.7	2.6
Northeast	3.1	3.0	2.9	2.7	3.3	3.1	2.9	2.9
North Central	2.9	2.8	2.8	2.5	3.4	3.2	2.5	2.6
South	2.8	2.7	2.8	2.7	3.1	2.9	2.7	2.5
West	2.9	2.7	2.8	2.7	3.2	2.8	2.7	2.6
Renter Occupied								
United States Total	2.3	2.1	2.1	1.9	2.4	2.1	2.6	2.2
Northeast	2.2	2.0	2.2	2.0	2.3	2.0	2.4	2.1
North Central	2.3	2.0	2.1	1.8	2.4	2.1	2.5	2.1
South	2.5	2.2	2.3	2.0	2.5	2.2	2.8	2.4
West	2.2	2.0	1.9	1.9	2.3	2.1	2.5	2.2

Note:　Numbers and/or percents may not add due to rounding.

Source:　U.S. Department of Commerce, U.S. Bureau of the Census, *Current Housing Reports*, Series H-150-76, *General Housing Characteristics for the United States and Regions: 1976*, Annual Housing Survey: 1976, Part A. U.S. Government Printing Office, Washington, D.C., 1978.

Exhibit 35

Renter Occupied Units Household Composition
by Age of Head
1970 and 1976

(Numbers in Thousands)

Household Composition by Age of Head	1970	1976	Change: 1970 to 1976 Number	Percent
Total Renter Occupied	23,560	26,101	2,541	10.8
2-or-More-Person Households	17,171	17,541	370	2.2
Male Head, Wife Present	12,759	11,291	−1,468	−11.5
Under 25 Years	2,282	2,210	− 72	− 3.2
25 to 29 Years	2,408	2,440	32	1.3
30 to 34 Years	1,531	1,459	− 72	− 4.7
35 to 44 Years	2,154	1,722	− 432	−20.1
45 to 64 Years	3,148	2,332	− 816	−25.9
65 Years and Over	1,236	1,127	− 109	− 8.8
Other Male Head	1,143	1,730	587	51.4
Under 65 Years	1,010	1,642	632	62.6
65 Years and Over	132	88	− 44	−33.3
Female Head	3,270	4,520	1,250	38.2
Under 65 Years	2,899	4,130	1,231	42.5
65 Years and Over	370	391	21	5.7
1-Person Households	6,389	8,560	2,171	34.0
Under 65 Years	4,109	5,803	1,694	41.2
65 Years and Over	2,279	2,757	478	21.0

Note: Numbers and/or percents may not add due to rounding.

Source: U.S. Department of Commerce, U.S. Bureau of the Census, *Current Housing Reports*, Series H-150-76, *General Housing Characteristics for the United States and Regions: 1976*, Annual Housing Survey: 1976, Part A, U.S. Government Printing Office, Washington, D.C., 1978.

holds (with wife present) within the overall universe of rental facilities. In the six-year period this sector lost 1.5 million households, a decrease of 11.5 percent. The largest losers were those in the age categories between 35 and 64 years. A significant portion of the total growth in renter households was accounted for by female-headed configurations, whose number expanded by 1.3 million (38.2 percent); the other significant growth sector comprised one-person households, which grew by 34 percent (2.2 million).

The variance in the household composition of owner-occupied units is most striking. The latter in total expanded by 20.1 percent with male-headed households (wife present) nearly matching this growth rate (17.2 percent). Indeed, the husband-wife configurations, on an absolute base, represented more than 60 percent of the total growth. Within it, the fastest growing age sectors were among the relatively youthful (under the age of 35). But even among the more mature, (65 years of age and over), there was a substantial growth increment—23.2 percent. The contrast with the 8.8 percent decline among similar households in renter-occupied units is most significant. *As we will later discuss in more detail, the husband-wife configuration is the most well endowed in terms of income (compared to other household types). Thus the rental sector is losing that portion of its tenantry that has the ability to absorb the escalation in rents arising from inflationary pressures on operating and maintenance costs. The rental market is being "cream skimmed"—it is losing its competitive status for the more affluent households as owner occupancy gains greater market penetration.*

Underlying the shifts in tenure-related household composition are the associated income statistics; it is to a presentation of the principle parameters within this arena that attention must now be directed.

INCOME AND HOUSEHOLD CHARACTERISTICS

A plethora of debate has evolved on the issue of changing relationships between housing costs and income, particularly in the post-1970 period. In this context, the traditional plight of low-income households has received but secondary attention; a new "crisis" has captured not only the fancy of the popular media, but housing scholars as well—the issue of the affordability of homeownership by first-time homebuyers. Certainly, the sheer critical mass of the maturing baby-boom cohort has provided the impetus for this shift in focus, as its huge market impact takes shape. In particular, in this context, there has been a battle of baselines, of initiating longitudinal comparisons in a relatively low cost/price housing year (such as 1970, for example, when a surge of subsidized housing came on stream), which yields a much higher imbalance in the ratio between housing costs and incomes as compared with the results when a longer historical time frame is used. The issue also has been raised, both from an economic and political persepective, as to the "appropriate" relationship between rents and/or housing price and incomes, and

EXHIBIT 36

OWNER OCCUPIED UNITS HOUSEHOLD COMPOSITION BY AGE OF HEAD 1970 AND 1976

(Numbers in Thousands)

Household Composition by Age of Head	1970	1976	Change: 1970 to 1976 Number	Percent
Total Owner Occupied	39,886	47,904	8,018	20.1%
2-or-More-Person Households	35,124	41,626	6,502	18.5
Male Head, Wife Present	30,806	36,108	5,302	17.2
Under 25 Years	800	1,069	269	33.6
25 to 29 Years	2,252	3,186	934	41.5
30 to 34 Years	2,938	4,069	1,131	38.5
35 to 44 Years	7,097	7,512	415	5.8
45 to 64 Years	13,230	14,743	1,513	11.4
65 Years and Over	4,490	5,530	1,040	23.2
Other Male Head	1,298	1,629	331	25.5
Under 65 Years	974	1,251	277	28.4
65 Years and Over	324	378	54	16.7
Female Head	3,019	3,889	870	28.8
Under 65 Years	2,159	2,922	763	35.3
65 Years and Over	860	967	107	12.4
1-Person Households	4,762	6,278	1,516	31.8
Under 65 Years	2,075	2,677	602	29.0
65 Years and Over	2,688	3,602	914	34.0

Note: Numbers and/or percents may not add due to rounding.

Source: U.S. Department of Commerce, U.S. Bureau of the Census, *Current Housing Reports*, Series H-150-76, *General Housing Characteristics for the United States and Regions: 1976*, Annual Housing Survey: 1976, Part A, U.S. Government Printing Office, Washington, D.C., 1978.

whether or not adustments and corrections should be made for the relative impacts of inflation, capital accumulation and a host of other variables.

Much of this discussion has been predicated on measures of centrality, particularly in terms of income. The usual approach has been to compare median family income with equivalent median data for housing costs of various kinds. *The limited insights based upon this type of analysis have led to a consistent understatment of the demand for home ownership and a persistent overestimate*

EXHIBIT 37

MEDIAN FAMILY INCOME AND CONSUMER PRICE INDEX,
UNITED STATES: 1950 TO 1977

Year	Median Family Income Actual Dollars	Constant 1977 Dollars	Consumer Price Index All Items
1950	$ 3,319	$ 8,356	72.1
1955	4,418	9,999	80.2
1960	5,620	11,500	88.7
1965	6,957	13,362	94.5
1970	9,867	15,399	116.3
1975	13,719	15,447	161.2
1977	16,009	16,009	181.5

Period	Gain in Real Income (constant 1977 dollars)
1950 to 1960	$3,144
1950 to 1955	1,643
1955 to 1960	1,501
1960 to 1970	3,899
1960 to 1965	1,862
1965 to 1970	2,037
1970 to 1977	610
1970 to 1975	48
1975 to 1977	562

Source: U.S. Bureau of the Census, Statistical Abstract of the United States: 1978, Washington, D.C., 1978.

of the demand for rental facilities. While in part this is accounted for by omitting the impacts of inflation on consumer preference, a good deal of this confusion has resulted from a failure to partition the data, particularly for income, and thus to distinguish between the household sectors which are capable of competing within the market as presently structured and those whose shelter-buying capacities are less vigorous. In the section which follows, an attempt is made to provide some insight into the dilemma.

What has happened to real incomes in America? The data in Exhibit 37 detail the shifts of median family incomes which have taken place in the United States from 1950 to 1977, both in actual dollars as well as in constant 1977 terms. On the former basis, there was nearly a five-fold increase in the 27-year period under consideration (from $3,319 to $16,009), while in constant dollars, there was but a doubling (from $8,356 to $16,000). These increments, however stated, were not secured at a uniform rate during the period in question. From 1950 to 1960, for example, on a $8,356 dollar

EXHIBIT 38

INCOME CHANGES: FAMILIES, UNRELATED INDIVIDUALS AND
HOUSEHOLDS (U.S. TOTAL), 1970 TO 1977; AND
1977 INCOME BY FAMILY CONFIGURATION

Unit	1970	1977	Change: 1970 to 1977	
			Number	Percent
Families	$9,867	$16,009	$6,142	62.2%
Unrelated Individuals	3,137	5,907	2,770	88.3
Households	8,734	13,572	4,838	55.3

Family Configurations	1977
Total Families	$16,009
Male Head Total	17,517
Married, Wife Present	17,616
Wife in Paid Labor Force	20,268
Wife Employed	20,534
Wife Unemployed	13,855
Wife Not in Paid Labor Force	15,063
Other Marital Status	14,518
Female Head	7,765

Source: U.S. Bureau of the Census, *Current Population Reports*, Series P-60, No. 118, "Money Income in 1977 of Families and Persons in the United States," U.S. Government Printing Office, Washington, D.C., 1979.

base (in 1977 dollars) there was a real income gain of $3,144. The next ten years saw an even greater absolute real increase ($3,899), but one which was secured from a larger base ($11,500). The contrast with the 1970-to-1977 period is striking—in those seven years there was a real income gain of only $610. The pattern of growth in increments in real income in the three five-year periods from 1955 to 1970 now seemingly has aborted. Preliminary data on the 1979 experience indicates that even the small level of growth in the early 1970s is currently at risk.

But the data shown in Exhibit 37 reflect only one household configuration—families (defined as two or more related individuals occupying the same housing unit), the most affluent of household types. When analysis is undertaken of unrelated individuals, who, as earlier indicated, comprise a growing segment of the housing market, the absolute and comparative gaps become all too evident (Exhibit 38). While family income as of 1977 had penetrated the $16,000 level, that for unrelated individuals was still under $6,000. Even though the latter showed significant increases since 1970 (88.3

EXHIBIT 39

HOUSEHOLD INCOME BY GEOGRAPHIC LOCATION, U.S. TOTAL: 1970 TO 1976

	1970	1976	Change: 1970 to 1976 Number	Percent
Owner Occupied				
TOTAL	$ 9,700	$14,400	$4,700	48.5%
Inside SMSAs	11,000	16,200	5,200	47.3
In Central Cities	10,100	14,200	4,100	40.6
Not in Central Cities	11,600	17,300	5,700	49.1
Outside SMSAs	7,500	11,700	4,200	56.0
Renter Occupied				
TOTAL	6,300	8,100	1,800	28.6
Inside SMSAs	6,700	8,500	1,800	26.9
In Central Cities	6,100	7,500	1,400	23.0
Not in Central Cities	7,700	10,100	2,400	31.2
Outside SMSAs	5,300	7,100	1,800	34.0

Note: Numbers and/or percents may not add due to rounding.

Source: U.S. Department of Commerce, U.S. Bureau of the Census, *Current Housing Reports*, Series H-150-76 *General Housing Characteristics for the United States and Regions: 1976*, Annual Housing Survey: 1976, Part A. U.S. Government Printing Office, Washington, D.C., 1978.

percent), clearly these are very limited dollars with which to buy shelter. (The household data in Exhibit 38 are the sum of families and those unrelated individuals not in group quarters.)

Even the rubric of families needs further disaggregation, as detailed at the bottom of the exhibit. Male-headed families, for example, had 1977 incomes of over $17,000; when in addition there was a wife present who was in the paid labor force, the income shifts upward past the $20,000 mark. But if the wife was not in the labor force, the median income declines to the $15,000 level. For female-headed families, an increasingly important segment of American society and of rental occupancy, the median income drops to an extremely low level ($7,765).

Thus within the overall context of "families", there is an income range of approximately $13,000, from $7,765 to $20,534. The most affluent tend to be male-headed families with employed wives; the least prosperous are female-headed families.

But cross sectional variations in household incomes establish only a partial description; tenure is another variable whose entrance into the equation is mandatory. There is a significant linkage between income, household configuration and tenurial status. The general relationship between income and tenure status is shown in Exhibit 39. Households who are owner occupants in 1976 had incomes of $14,400, 78 percent higher than those of renters ($8,100). And this gap has been widening over time; in 1970 the equivalent relationship stood at 54 percent. From 1970 to 1976, the income of owners increased by 48.5 percent, while that of renters increased by only 28.6 percent. These differentials persisted on the same general pattern across the various metropolitan and nonmetropolitan demarcations of the United States.

It is essential to note in this context, that the pools of owners and renters do not function as closed systems over time; substantial streams of households flow between the two pools. The data in Exhibits 35, 36 and 40 suggests that there has been a significant creamskimming of the rental market with the more affluent renters within each of the several household classifications shifting into ownership status. The combined impacts of inflation, progressive income tax brackets, tax benefits as well as the forced savings implicit in mortgaged housing have combined to provide this result.

It is the less fortunate in our society who increasingly predominate the rental housing inventory.

And this reality is manifested for each of the household configurations so far isolated. These are summarized by the data in Exhibit 40, which define the relationship between household configuration, income and tenure status. For each household type, with the exception of a single aberrant (one-person households), it is the owner-occupied sectors which have the higher income levels. The highest relative incomed renter household sets (as compared with owner equivalents) are the age and household configurations which are most rapidly succumbing to the allure of owner occupancy (as established in Exhibits 35 and 36).

Thus much of the financial stress of multifamily rental housing, which is increasingly drawing public attention, relates to the income shortfalls of the tenantry as well as to the overall inflationary impact upon the operating parameters of the facilities themselves.

EXHIBIT 40

OWNER AND RENTER OCCUPIED HOUSEHOLD INCOME, BY HOUSEHOLD CONFIGURATION, U.S. TOTAL: 1976

	Owner Occupied	Renter Occupied	Renter/ Owner Ratio
Total Households	$14,400	$ 8,100	.56
2-or-More-Person Household	15,900	9,500	.60
Male Head, Wife Present	16,800	11,600	.69
Under 25 Years	12,800	9,800	.77
25 to 29 Years	16,200	12,600	.78
30 to 34 Years	17,900	13,000	.73
35 to 44 Years	19,700	13,200	.67
45 to 64 Years	18,600	12,600	.68
65 Years and Over	8,400	6,600	.79
Other Male Head	14,300	8,500	.59
Under 65 Years	15,800	8,600	.54
65 Years and Over	9,000	6,000	.67
Female Head	9,100	5,600	.62
Under 65 Years	9,600	5,700	.59
65 Years and Over	7,100	5,100	.72
1-Person Households	5,100	5,500	1.08
Under 65 Years	8,600	7,800	.91
65 Years and Over	4,200	3,400	.81

Note: Numbers and/or percents may not add due to rounding.

Source: U.S. Department of Commerce, U.S. Bureau of the Census, *Current Housing Reports*, Series H-150-76 *General Housing Characteristics for the United States and Regions: 1976*, Annual Housing Survey; 1976, Part A. U.S. Government Printing Office, Washington, D.C., 1978.

Demand Supply Interrelationships

INTRODUCTION

The static and dynamic interrelationships between the population arrangements expressed in household units (as well as their ancillary economic capacities and social desires) and the supply of shelter (and its parameters and economic thresholds) are the generators, as well as the very definition, of housing markets. *While patterns of demand may emanate from lifestyle desires accompanying broader shifts from a mature industrial to post-industrial society, their physical expression depends upon the capacity of the supply system to accommodate such desires. Indeed, the availability of cost competitive residential accommodations may not merely reflect but also shape the profiles of demand.* The analogy to roadway congestion levels may be appropriate in this context, i.e., new highways tend to generate, at least within given limits, additional traffic such that the level of nominal congestion is only partially relieved. In turn, however, the production of housing units, in a circular network of cause and effect, is most directly impacted by realities of demand.

It is the market arena wherein the population of households is matched to the housing stock. The functioning of the market—its effective allocation of shelter to those requiring or desiring it—is revealed by a select set of indicators detailing the intersection of supply and demand variables. However, such "sensors" are not abundant in number, nor are they entirely comprehensive in terms of coverage. Nonetheless, they are probably sufficient to gauge at least the proximate contours of the broader market landscape.

In this section, three major variables will be examined. Vacancy rates (a measure of the slack capacity of the market) are the quotient of vacant available housing units divided by the total available supply—changes in such rates over time gauge the relative rates of changes in the supply of housing versus the effective demand for it. Persons per room (a measure of internal housing density or crowding) is the quotient (at the micro scale) of household size divided by unit size (in rooms) which provides an index of the fit (quantity of space) of a household to its housing accommodations. Income, cost/price/value relationships, relate the cost of consuming housing to resource (income) availability. The evolution of these indicators over the past several years is briefly summarized below.

1. *While the population of the United States increased by 5.0 percent over the 1970-to-1976 period, the number of households increased by 16.6 percent. In absolute increments, both increased by approximately 10 million. Although not one and the same, for every person added to the population, a household was concurrently formed.*

2. *The production of housing over this period was such as to exceed the net household additions by more than 1 million units (net). The interaction of these two events is documented by a slight rise in the vacancy rate. Nonetheless, the seemingly relentless pace of household formation gives little indication of a slack-*

ening of the demand pressure on the overall supply system, despite the fact that record rates of housing production occurred over the period in question.

3. *According to the vacancy rate indicators, then, there is in general a satisfactory match of households and housing units. At the same time, there appears to be a better fit of individual households to housing units, if the latter is defined by greater quantities of housing per household (persons per room). The nation's population is diffusing itself into an expanding supply network, resulting in diminished levels of overcrowding and much lower levels of internal housing unit density.*

4. *The quantitative "improvements" that the preceding indicators gauge have been achieved at a price—greater shares of income must be surrendered to meet basic shelter costs. Both rent-income and value/price-income ratios have deteriorated (increased) over the 1970-to-1976 period. In the aggregate income gains have lagged the increases attached to the cost/value parameters.*

5. *Partitioning the latter experience by houshold configuration, however, reveals basic market dichotomies. Husband-wife households—which as we have seen previously secured the greatest income gains throughout the 1970s—have been virtually insulated from escalating cost thresholds. In contrast, the female-headed households (two or more persons) have experienced much greater housing cost pressures on their more limited income resources. To a more limited degree, single-person households are afflicted by similar economic strains.*

In the broad then, the basic indicators reveal a market successfully allocating quantities of housing to the household demand sector. However, select household configurations—particularly those resulting from accelerating fragmentation (i.e., divorce and initial household formations)—are beset by an inadequate match of income capacity and shelter costs. Given a much wider level of income dispersion relative to housing cost variation, what is indicated is not so much a "housing problem or crisis" per se, but an income distribution problem. The detailed analyses which follow underscore this basic tendency.

EXHIBIT 41

**POPULATION, HOUSEHOLDS AND HOUSING UNIT CHANGE:
1970 TO 1976**

(Numbers in Thousands)

	1970	1976	Change: 1970 to 1976	
			Number	Percent
Population [1]	204,878	215,142	10,264	5.0
Households [2]	63,401	72,867	9,466	14.9
All Year-Round Housing Units [3]	67,699	79,316	11,617	17.2
Occupied Housing Units [3]	63,445	74,005	10,560	16.6

Notes: 1 As of July 1; includes Armed Forces abroad and inmates in institutions.
2 As of March of the respective years.
3 April 1, 1970 to October 31, 1976.

Source: U.S. Bureau of the Census, *Statistical Abstract of the United States: 1978*, Washington, D.C., 1978.

POPULATION, HOUSEHOLD AND INVENTORY GROWTH

The first order of business before entertaining the direct mergers of supply-demand parameters is a brief recapitulation of the broader trends of growth in population, households and housing units. The basic data in this regard are collected in Exhibit 41. Between the July 1 benchmarks of 1970 and 1976, the population of the nation increased by 10.3 million people, or 5.0 percent. During an equivalent six-year span, but estimated as of March of the respective years, the number of households expanded by 9.5 million or 14.9 percent. To revert to a point made previously, the growth in the number of households is proceeding at such a rate that for every individual added to the population, a household is concurrently formed.

A small problem of comparability arises due to a further variation in benchmarks within the basic data accounts. The *Annual Housing Survey* employs October 31 for current measurements, and April 1970 (the decennial census) as the baseline. Consequently, the housing unit totals are tallied over a slightly longer time frame (6.5 years) in this analysis. Therefore, the 11.6 million unit increase (17.2 percent) in the supply of all-year-round housing units overstates the differential—2.1 million (11.6 million minus 9.5 million)—with the household growth increment. This inconsistency can be mitigated by employing occupied housing units from the *Annual Housing Survey* as a surrogate for independent household tabulations. As a result of extending the accounting period six months, another 1.1 million households (10.6 million versus 9.5 million) are secured, and the household-housing unit differential narrows (11.6 million housing units versus 10.6 million households).

Nonetheless, over the 1970-to-1976 period, the basic trendlines hold. Despite reflections of period inconsistencies, the rate of growth of the housing supply (17.2 percent) is substantially in excess of the pace of growth of demand units—households (16.6 percent or 14.9 percent)—as well as the rate of population growth (5.0 percent).

While this six-year analytical span is only of moderate duration, it still may tend to give the impression of trendlines approximating smooth gradients. As was detailed previously, however, abrupt annual fluctuations marked the supply production function (housing starts). To capture such variations quantitatively, it is necessary to evaluate the relevant data on vacancy rates—a major indicator gauging the demand-supply intersection.

VACANCY RATES

As is the case with a number of the market variables used in this section, vacancy rates have a legislative heritage in measuring market performance. For example, in many instances the justification for rent control is predicated on the basis of a legislative determination of vacancy rates. If the rate falls below a specified level, it is deemed that a housing emergency exists—supply in inadequate to meet housing need (or demand)—and thus a malfunctioning market puts consumers at an extreme disadvantage. With little slack capacity in the inventory, occupants have limited mobility; therefore the market fails to provide an adequate pricing mechanism. There is no inhibition to raising rents when the supply is scarce, hence public regulation is required. (A curious dilemma can arise from such controls, however, if their effect is to hold rents below free market thresholds and requirements. In the latter case, the accommodations represent bargains relative to uncontrolled contests, thereby establishing incentives to tenant stability in place, and in turn serving to maintain a low vacancy rate. The circularity inherent in this process may be enhanced if regulation further discourages new construction activity. A series of reinforcing responses may be actuated, perpetuating supply and demand imbalance.)

In any case, a basic perspective on vacancy rate behavior is provided by the data in Exhibit 42. The pattern over the 1960-to-1977 period reveals an abrupt decline in vacancy rates in the decade of the 1960s, from a total rental vacancy rate in the base year of 8.1 percent to the 5.3 percent level by 1970. The process of change since then has been much more erratic. An increase to the 6.2 percent mark by 1974 was followed by a consistent reduction to the present date. Preliminary data (not shown here) indicates an early 1979 vacancy rate in rental facilities of approximately 4.8 percent, lower than at any time in the last twenty years.

There are significant regional variations, however, within these overall trendlines. The Northeast historically has had vacancy rates less than half those of the West and barely 60 percent of the national level. This situation has changed quite markedly in the post-1970 period. By 1977, the Northeast vacancy rates were comparable to those of the nation as a whole. In 1970, rental vacancy rates in the United States were 5.3 percent, in the Northeast, 2.7 percent; by 1977, they evolved to 5.2 and 5.1 percent, respectively.

The metropolitan-nonmetropolitan rental vacancy rates also evidence a pattern of divergence. Nonmetropolitan areas historically have had the highest level of vacancies; but by 1977, their rate (5.2 percent) fell below that of metropolitan territories (5.3 percent), representing a reversal of demand pressures. Concurrently, despite limited construction activity in central cities, their vacancy rates have continually remained at a level higher than those of their encompassing suburbs.

Throughout the period under discussion vacancies in the owner-occupied sector have been very low, with little in the way of areal variation. The one exception to this latter generalization is in the South, which maintained a rate virtually double that of the balance of the nation—perhaps a tribute to the very rapid pace of new housing construction in that region.

The analysis of vacancy rates across these macro-geographic partitions indicates, at least in very broad measures, that in terms of absolute numbers the expansion of the housing supply has been adequate to meet the growth in demand. Alternatively, reversing the causal sequence, it can be suggested that the supply expansion has been such as to facilitate the formation of comparable demand by enabling the process of household formation to continue unabated.

Nonetheless, were micro-geographic disaggregations available, the satisfactory match of supply and demand evidenced above could well

EXHIBIT 42

VACANCY RATES FOR TOTAL UNITS, BY AREA: 1960, 1965 TO 1977

Area	1960	1965	1966	1967	1968	1969	1970	1971	1972	1973	1974	1975	1976	1977
RENTAL VACANCY RATE														
United States	8.1	8.1	7.7	6.8	5.9	5.5	5.3	5.4	5.6	5.8	6.2	6.0	5.6	5.2
Inside SMSAs	7.0	8.0	7.0	5.9	5.1	4.8	4.9	5.1	5.4	5.7	6.2	6.1	5.7	5.3
In central cities	(NA)	8.1	7.1	6.2	5.5	5.3	5.3	5.4	5.7	6.2	6.8	6.6	6.2	5.7
Outside central cities	(NA)	7.8	6.8	5.5	4.5	4.0	4.3	4.5	4.8	5.0	5.2	5.4	5.1	4.6
Outside SMSAs	10.8	8.8	9.2	8.7	7.7	7.1	6.4	6.4	6.1	6.1	6.2	5.7	5.1	5.2
Northeast	4.9	5.6	5.3	4.8	3.7	3.0	2.7	3.0	3.3	3.9	4.2	4.1	4.7	5.1
North Central	8.3	7.2	6.5	5.7	5.4	5.7	5.8	5.7	6.1	5.9	6.1	5.7	5.6	5.1
South	9.5	9.0	8.5	8.0	7.5	7.2	7.2	7.3	7.0	7.1	8.0	7.7	6.4	5.7
West	11.0	11.9	10.9	8.9	7.1	6.1	5.6	5.7	6.0	6.3	6.2	6.2	5.4	5.0
HOMEOWNER VACANCY RATE														
United States	1.3	1.5	1.4	1.3	1.1	1.0	1.0	1.0	1.0	1.0	1.2	1.2	1.2	1.2
Inside SMSAs	1.3	1.6	1.6	1.3	1.0	0.9	1.0	1.0	1.0	1.1	1.2	1.3	1.2	1.0
In central cities	(NA)	1.5	1.5	1.2	1.2	1.1	1.1	1.1	1.3	1.2	1.3	1.4	1.4	1.2
Outside central cities	(NA)	1.5	1.4	1.3	0.9	0.8	0.9	0.9	0.8	1.0	1.2	1.3	1.1	1.0
Outside SMSAs	1.4	1.6	1.3	1.4	1.3	1.1	1.1	1.0	1.0	1.0	1.1	1.1	1.2	1.4
Northeast	1.0	1.0	0.9	0.7	0.8	0.8	0.8	0.7	0.4	0.6	0.8	1.0	1.0	0.9
North Central	1.2	1.2	1.0	1.0	1.0	0.9	1.0	0.9	1.0	1.0	1.0	1.0	1.0	0.9
South	1.6	2.0	1.8	1.7	1.4	1.2	1.2	1.2	1.1	1.2	1.5	1.5	1.6	1.7
West	1.4	1.9	2.1	2.0	1.3	1.2	1.1	1.2	1.2	1.4	1.5	1.5	1.2	0.9

Note: NA-Not available.

Source: U.S. Bureau of the Census, *Current Housing Reports*, Series H-111-77-5 "Vacancy Rates and Characteristics of Housing in the United States: Annual Statistics 1977," U.S. Government Printing Office, Washington, D.C., 1978.

abort. Within central cities, for example, substantial vacancy rate variations may occur, with demand exceeding supply in select neighborhoods, while less desirable areas may be so weak as to generate inventory losses (abandonment). Manhatten and the South Bronx stand, respectively, as prototypical examples within New York City, realities which are obviously obscured when the aggregate central city indicators are studied.

In any case, vacancy rates at best only indicate the match of broad supply-demand modules. They provide no revelation as to the adequacy of housing accomodations to the households they shelter. To secure at least a general grasp of the latter concern, it is necessary to examine the intersection of unit and household size—indicators of overcrowding and internal housing unit density.

OVERCROWDING: INTERNAL UNIT DENSITY

One measure of market "fit" is the quantity of housing delivered to its occupants, traditionally gauged by measures of overcrowding. The degree to which overcrowding exists provides some indication of the adequacy of the expansion of supply as compared to need and/or demand established from population and household growth. Within this context, the intersecting trajectories of the demand and supply parameters, with little qualifications, have shown substantial positive results throughout recent history. The shrinkage in household size—a slow-growing population rapidly dividing into burgeoning numbers of household configurations—coinciding with increasing units sizes, and an overall housing inventory expanding at a pace at least equivalent to household formations, has generated a diminished level of overcrowding and rising quantities of housing per occupant.

While this phenomenon is certainly not new—analytically, it has acquired a patina of age over the last two decades—the pace of improvement during the 1970-to-1976 period has been substantial. The data in Exhibit 43 reveal, both for owner- and renter-occupied facilities, the profile of the persons per room for the United States as a whole as well as within several geographic subsets. The criterion of overcrowding has tended to grow more stringent as expectations rise. Presently the standard has been elevated to 1.01 or more persons per room. The six years from 1970 to 1976 witnessed virtual halving of the proportion of owner-occupied units with such levels of internal density (6.4 percent to 3.7 percent) within the United States, with a comparable decline experienced in the renter-occupied sector (10.6

EXHIBIT 43

PERSONS PER ROOM, PERCENTAGE DISTRIBUTION, OWNER AND RENTER OCCUPIED UNITS: U.S. TOTAL BY GEOGRAPHIC AREA: 1970 AND 1976

| | Total | | INSIDE SMSAs | | | | | | Outside SMSAs | |
| | | | Total | | In Central Cities | | Not in Central Cities | | | |
	1970	1976	1970	1976	1970	1976	1970	1976	1970	1976
Owner Occupied										
Total	100.0%	100.0%	100.0%	100.0%	100.0%	100.0%	100.0%	100.0%	100.0%	100.0%
.50 or less	53.0	58.1	51.7	57.7	54.8	60.9	49.5	55.9	55.5	58.8
.51 to 1.00	40.6	38.2	42.3	38.8	39.0	39.4	44.4	40.8	37.4	37.0
1.01 to 1.50	5.2	3.1	5.0	3.0	5.0	3.2	5.0	2.9	5.5	3.3
1.51 or more	1.2	0.6	1.0	0.4	1.1	0.4	1.0	0.5	1.7	0.9
Renter Occupied										
Total	100.0%	100.0%	100.0%	100.0%	100.0%	100.0%	100.0%	100.0%	100.0%	100.0%
.50 or less	45.0	53.8	45.6	53.8	46.1	53.3	44.8	54.5	43.0	53.9
.51 to 1.00	44.4	40.0	44.7	40.5	43.7	40.3	46.3	40.8	43.6	38.4
1.01 to 1.50	7.3	4.6	6.8	4.3	7.1	4.8	6.4	3.7	8.7	5.4
1.51 or more	3.3	1.6	2.8	1.4	3.1	1.6	2.4	1.0	4.7	2.4

Note: Numbers and/or percents may not add due to rounding.

Source: U.S. Department of Commerce, U.S. Bureau of the Census, *Current Housing Reports*, Series H-150-76, *General Housing Characteristics for the United States and Regions: 1976*, Annual Housing Survey: 1976, Part A. U.S. Government Printing Office, Washington, D.C., 1978.

percent to 6.2 percent). This general pattern is consistent and pervasive in each of the geographic subsets shown in the exhibit.

In a complementary development, for both owner- and renter-occupied facilities across all geographic partitions, more than 50 percent had .50 persons or less per room by 1976. The consumption of increasing quantities of housing space is clearly a major dynamic of our time.

It is significant to note in this context that the incidence of over-crowding in central cities falls below that extant in nonmetropolitan areas. The problem has not been extinguished by any means but clearly the order of impact has decreased substantially. By 1976, for example, only 1.6 percent of all central city renter-occupied housing units had 1.51 or more persons per room. Even allowing for some level of population undercount, the basic trendlines evident in the data are clearly operable. The quantity of housing delivered to the nation's population and households is cuh as to shift to the periphery major concern on inadequate space allocations.

RENT/VALUE-INCOME RATIOS

Two alternative conceptualizations of the forces underpinning the demand-supply nexus have been advanced to this point. One suggests that the rapid expansion of the supply sector has stimulated and facilitated the process of household formation, in effect serving to escalate demand. The alternate interpretation envisions a relentless sequence of additions to the inventory, a constant struggle to maintain parity with an ever burgeoning demand function, as the nation's population resettles itself into even smaller household configurations. This dichotomy, however, is undoubtedly artificial—to search for a discrete one-way linear causal linkage is large futile. The reality may be more of a circular (stimulus-response) connective chain—comprising both elements suggested above. In our view, it is rather one taking the form of a spiral in which the driving forces reinvigorate one another and gain momentum as they move through time. And the dynamic that is forged receives an additional impetus as other variables are entered into the equation—income capacities, occupancy costs and endemic levels of inflation—the major economic parameters.

Shelter Costs And Income. The nominally excess supply of housing units created from 1970 to 1976 (over and above the growth both of population and household numbers) did not serve to retard the escalation of the basic cost matrix. Summary data in this regard are

EXHIBIT 44

RENTER AND OWNER OCCUPIED UNITS, INCOME, RENT AND UNIT VALUE RELATIONSHIPS, U.S. TOTAL: 1970 TO 1976

			Change: 1970 to 1976	
	1970	1976	Number	Percent
Renter Occupied Units				
Median Gross Rent	$ 108	$ 167	$ 59	54.6%
Median Income	$6,300	$8,100	$1,800	28.5%
Median Rent/Income Ratio[1]	20%	24%	4%	20.0%
Owner Occupied Units				
Median House Value	$17,000	$32,000	$15,200	88.9%
Median Income	9,700	14,400	4,700	48.5
Value Income Ratio[1]	1.7	2.2	0.5	29.4

Note: 1 Published Ratios.

Source: U.S. Department of Commerce, U.S. Bureau of the Census, *Current Housing Reports*, Series H-150-76, *General Housing Characteristics for the United States and Regions: 1976*, Annual Housing Survey: 1976, Part A. U.S. Government Printing Office, Washington, D.C., 1978.

shown in Exhibit 44. Median gross rents, for example, increased by 54.6 percent; median incomes of renter households grew by a much more modest 28.5 percent. In turn, the 20 percent gross rent-income ratio (the proportion of income allotted to shelter) in 1970 shifted to the 24 percent mark by 1976. At this writing preliminary estimates indicate the relationship to have reached the 25 percent threshold. It is striking to see how rapidly the nominal public policy commitment to subsidy for those paying more than 25 percent of their incomes for shelter have been rendered obsolete.

There is no simple analog to rent-income ratios available to summarize the intersection of costs and incomes in the owner-occupied sector. One indication however is shown in the lower half of Exhibit 44, which compares median house values and median incomes from 1970 and 1976. The value to income ratio has degenerated quite sharply over the period in question, increasing from 1.7 in 1970 to 2.2 by 1976.

Certainly, these simple descriptions could serve as preliminary evidence of an impending "crisis", particularly within the rental sector. While the potential of the latter should not be understated, it is possible to indicate two mitigating circumstances. First, to the degree the rising value-income ratio accounts for the experience of those households who were within the ownership market throughout the period in question, it actually translates into a form of capital accumulation or equity buildup. This is by now a well known and appreciated phenomenon. And second, to the degree that the decline in the persons-per-room ratio is a consequence not only of fewer children but of unencumbered household formation, then the greater quantitative consumption of housing on a per household basis implies that housing costs should increase faster than income. That is, income is being stretched thinner through greater consumption of housing space and amenity.

Detailed Rent-Income Ratios. But the use of simple measures of centrality in describing such complex phenomena tend to obscure as much or more than they reveal. Public policymaking requires a grasp of the dispersion or spread of data, the relative importance of the extremes. In Exhibit 45, categories of gross rent income ratios are presented via a variety of partitions. In 1970, slightly less than 40 percent of America's renters were paying 25 percent or more of their incomes for rent; by 1976 the equivalent figure was 46.5 percent. Indeed, in central cities the proportion at the latter point of time neared the 50 percent level. Again, as stated earlier, the change in rent-income ratios basically relates to two different pools of renters at the two moments in time for which the data are presented. As earlier discussed, there has been a consistent withdrawal of more affluent tenantry into homeownership. Thus, while rents have been increasing, the pool of renters represents an increasingly impoverished proportion of American's households. Regardless of the causal factors at work, the pressures that are evolving are evident.

The singular stress of rent on income as a function of household configuration is also key to appropriate insight into the broad market. Data on this point for 1976 are shown in Exhibit 46. Within the universe of two-or-more-person households (male-headed with wife present), only the elderly—those 65 years and over—had rent-income ratios over the 25 percent mark. Indeed, this was the only subset within the husband/wife group significantly over the 20 percent mark.

It is the other household configurations,—those generally of smallest size—particularly those which are female-headed, that must surrender the largest proportions of their incomes for rents. In one-person households the ratio for the more youthful—under 65 years of age—is well below the 25 percent level. For the elderly, however, it rises to 38.1 percent.

It is striking in this context to notice the relative homogeneity of rent levels as indicated in the exhibit. The one exception is one-person

EXHIBIT 45

GROSS RENT AS A PERCENTAGE OF INCOME, UNITED STATES TOTAL: 1970 AND 1976

| Specified Renter Occupied | Total | | INSIDE SMSAs | | | | | | Outside SMSAs | |
| | | | Total | | In Central Cities | | Not in Central Cities | | | |
	1970	1976	1970	1976	1970	1976	1970	1976	1970	1976
	100.0%	100.0%	100.0%	100.0%	100.0%	100.0%	100.0%	100.0%	100.0%	100.0%
Less than 10%	9.8	6.5	8.9	5.7	9.3	5.9	8.3	5.4	13.0	9.5
10 to 14%	19.3	14.7	18.9	14.2	18.5	13.8	19.6	14.8	21.0	16.7
15 to 19%	18.4	17.3	18.6	17.4	17.6	16.4	20.3	18.9	17.6	16.8
20 to 24%	12.9	14.9	13.2	15.1	12.7	14.3	14.2	16.3	11.6	14.3
25 to 34%	14.3	17.9	14.6	18.2	14.5	18.2	14.7	18.0	13.1	17.2
35% or More	25.3	28.6	25.7	29.5	27.3	31.5	23.0	26.5	23.7	25.6
Median	20	24	21	24	21	25	20	23	19	22

Note: Numbers and/or percents may not add due to rounding.

Source: U.S. Department of Commerce, U.S. Bureau of the Census, *Current Housing Reports,* Series H-150-76, *General Housing Characteristics for the United States and Regions: 1976,* Annual Housing Survey: 1976, Part A. U.S. Government Printing Office, Washington, D.C., 1978.

EXHIBIT 46

RENTER OCCUPIED UNITS, BY HOUSEHOLD CONFIGURATION, U.S. TOTAL, INCOME AND RENT RELATIONSHIP: 1976

Household Configuration	1976 Median Income	1976 Monthly Median Gross Rent	1976 Annual Median Gross Rent	1976 Median Rent as a Percent of Median Income
2-or-More-Person Households	$ 9,500	$179	$2,148	22.6%
Male Head, Wife Present	11,600	183	2,196	18.9
Under 25 Years	9,800	166	1,992	20.3
25 to 29 Years	12,600	192	2,304	18.3
30 to 34 Years	13,000	193	2,316	17.8
35 to 44 Years	13,200	195	2,340	17.7
45 to 64 Years	12,600	184	2,208	17.5
65 Years and Over	6,600	163	1,956	29.6
Other Male Head	8,500	186	2,232	26.3
Under 65 Years	8,600	188	2,256	26.2
65 Years and Over	6,000	144	1,728	28.8
Female Head	5,600	167	2,004	35.8
Under 65 Years	5,700	168	2,016	35.4
65 Years and Over	5,100	141	1,692	33.2
1-Person Households	5,500	142	1,704	31.0
Under 65 Years	7,800	155	1,860	23.8
65 Years and Over	3,400	108	1,296	38.1

Note: 1. No nonrelatives present.

Source: U.S. Department of Commerce, U.S. Bureau of the Census, *Current Housing Reports*, Series H-150-76, *General Housing Characteristics for the United States and Regions: 1976*, Annual Housing Survey: 1976, Part A. U.S. Government Printing Office, Washington, D.C., 1978.

EXHIBIT 47

MEDIAN SALES PRICES OF NEW ONE-FAMILY HOUSES SOLD AND MEDIAN FAMILY INCOME, UNITED STATES: 1954 TO 1977

Year	Median Sales Price	Median Family Income	Ratio of Sales Price to Income
1954	$12,300	$ 4,173	2.95
1955	13,700	4,421	3.10
1956	14,300	4,783	2.99
1959	15,200	5,417	2.81
1963	18,000	6,249	2.88
1964	18,900	6,569	2.88
1965	20,000	6,957	2.87
1966	21,400	7,532	2.84
1967	22,700	7,933	2.86
1968	24,700	8,632	2.86
1969	25,600	9,433	2.71
1970	23,400	9,867	2.37
1971	25,200	10,285	2.45
1972	27,600	11,116	2.48
1973	32,500	12,051	2,70
1974	35,900	12,836	2.78
1975	39,300	13,719	2.86
1976	44,200	14,958	2.95
1977	48,800	16,009	3.05
1978	55,600	NA	

Source: U.S. Bureau of the Census, Department of Commerce, *Construction Reports*, New One-Family Houses Sold and For Sale," Series C25-78-10 (Washington, D.C.: U.S. Government Printing Office, December 1978). Also: Series C25-71-9, November 1971 and C25-78-12, February 1978. U.S. Bureau of the Census, Department of Commerce, *Current Population Reports*, Series P-60, No. 116 "Money Income and Poverty Status of Families and Persons in the United States: 1977" (Advance Report), U.S. Government Printing Office, Washington, D.C., 1978.

households 65 years and over with rents at $108. Excluding this group, the lowest rent is for female-headed household 65 years and over, which is slightly over $140. The highest rents are the province of male-headed households (with wife present) which, depending on age characteristics, vary somewhat but peak at $195. The contrast with incomes is clear; while the extremes of rents are separated by only 38 percent ($141 to $195), including one-person households, the extremes of incomes are 158 percent ($5,100 to $13,200).

Certainly, as can be gleaned from the data presented here, as well as CUPR field observations, there is a relatively high minimum threshold within which rental housing can typically be provided regardless

EXHIBIT 48

**OWNER OCCUPIED UNITS, BY HOUSEHOLD CONFIGURATION,
U.S. TOTAL, INCOME AND HOUSE VALUE RELATIONSHIP: 1976**

Household Configuration	1976 Median Income	1976 House Value	House Value- Income ratio
2-or-More-Person Household	$15,900	$33,400	2.1
Male Head, Wife Present	16,800	34,300	2.0
Under 25 Years	12,800	25,400	2.0
25 to 29 Years	16,200	31,800	2.0
30 to 34 Years	17,900	37,000	2.1
35 to 44 Years	19,700	38,000	1.9
45 to 64 Years	18,600	34,900	1.9
65 Years and Over	8,400	28,100	3.3
Other Male Head	14,300	30,000	2.1
Under 65 Years	15,800	31,900	2.0
65 Years and Over	9,000	23,100	2.6
Female Head	9,100	25,900	2.8
Under 65 Years	9,600	26,600	2.8
65 Years and Over	7,100	23,300	3.3
1-Person Households	5,100	23,500	4.6
Under 65 Years	8,600	25,700	3.0
65 Years and Over	4,200	21,900	5.2

Note: 1. No nonrelative present.

Source: U.S. Department of Commerce, U.S. Bureau of the Census, *Current Housing Reports*, Series H-150-76, *General Housing Characteristics for the United States and Regions: 1976*, Annual Housing Survey: 1976, Part A. U.S. Government Printing Office, Washington, D.C., 1978.

of tenant rent-paying capacity. The heavily impacted renters pay rent nearly as high, at least as gauged by medians, as do the more fortunate. One can generalize from this and say that the problem is essentially an income problem, or conversely, a requirement for a completely new conceptualization of how rents are to be met.

The Costs of Ownership. A semi-metaphysical debate has long been underway on the trends in affordability of pre- and post-inflation homeownership. Without entering into the fray, Exhibits 47 and 48 provide some of the key data. The first of these compares the median sales price of new one-family housing with equivalent data for family income, deriving the sales price (value) to income ratio. The pattern is one which has altered quite markedly over time. At the beginning of the 24-year cycle shown, the ratio was approximately 3.0, i.e., median sales price to median family income. It descended to a low of

2.37 in 1970 (in part, undoubtedly as a result of a surge of sub-sidized housing under the Section 235 program becoming available at that time). But since then it has returned abruptly to the same levels as prevailed in the mid-1950s. More current preliminary data, in early 1979, indicates a further degeneration of the ratio to an even higher level.

Clearly this is merely one measurement of the changing housing buying power of Americans. Further elements which would have to be factored into it would be operating costs, the impact of pro-gressive income taxes and the like.

Regardless of the outcome of this debate, it is important to focus on the realities of owner-occupied units by household configurations. Again simple measures of centrality, of median income and its equivalent in house value, provide insights when appropriately partitioned by household configuration (Exhibit 48). While the data are not directly comparable to those presented in Exhibit 47, they do indicate the adjustments, as a function of income related household configurations, to the housing market. The data parallel very closely the rental counterparts discussed in Exhibit 46. It is the elderly- and female-headed households that exhibit the greatest level of imbalance between income and their house values. Thus measures of subsidy are much more intimately related to age/household demographic functions than has as yet been fully integrated into our policymaking.

Summary

The intersection of supply and demand has limited descriptors: In turn generalizations must be made with equivalent modesty. One has to be imbued with some sense of misgiving as to the adequacy of indicators detailing the market demand parameters. Some of the limitations are alleviated by several of the more in-depth probes contained within the papers of this volume; the partitions are sharp-ened and market imperfections are adequately highlighted. Nonethe-less, we are prisoners of our data resources. This is only partially countered by detailed empirical case studies the generalizability of which to broader contexts are always beset by some level of un-certainty. Yet, certain conclusions can still be asserted with a degree of confidence.

　　*1. The delivery of housing resources to America's citizenry has
　　been improving markedly despite some evidence of uneveness*

in regards to select household configurations and to certain geographic subareas.

2. *This has been particularly the case in terms of the addition of relatively abundant quantities of housing of generally excellent physical condition to the nation's inventory. Despite wide-spread fears of an impending "shut down" of the escalator leading to ever higher living standards—or as a consequence of it—there has been little abatement in the expansion of the shelter package secured by the bulk of America's housing consumers.*

But other admonitions must be invoked which are much more chastening.

3. *Levels of consumer expectations do not diminish—they take the form of a one-way ratchet the reversal of which could cause political reverberations sufficient to shake the very foundations of America. The potency of this phenomenon, rather than minimized by the unprecedent expansion in supply throughout the 1970s is accentuated. Success breeds hunger. How are the demand pressures of the 1980s to be met?*

4. *There has been an over-allocation of the nation's resources to housing in order to achieve the shelter success of the 1970s. Perhaps the "laws of housing physics" are beginning to assert themselves. The sheer outpacing of income by the matrix of housing costs may be a consequence of the magnitude of the nation's wealth allocated to housing; the complement of this phenomenon—the inadequate replenishment of the nation's economic infrastructure—then tends to undermine the growth of personal income resources (as a result of stagnating economic productivity). This feedback, in turn, may well serve to abort or terminate the housing improvementss evidenced to date.*

Making such prognostications is hazardous. The limitations of such an undertaking cannot be over-emphasized—the challenges, however, require acknowledgement.

THE LIMITS TO PROGNOSTICATION

Inventing the future is an art form the foundations of which is past experience. Our vision of what is to come is limited by history. No matter how well we cloak this limitation, regardless of whether we use regression analysis, basic trend extrapolation, or some variant

of "gut intuition," the foundation is historical. But the choice of
time frame—of position on the learning curve—within the overall
cluster of human experience varies substantially. When we attempt
to examine a phenomenon such as the return to the city, for example,
we can choose a persepective within the pattern of post-World War
II America. This, as we have seen, was a period of very rapidly rising
real incomes, of a reversal of the decline in fertility rates which had
characterized the 1920s and 1930s and which indeed, in a twenty-
five year time span, resulted in a near 50 percent increase in total
population, and of seemingly never ending increases in housing
buying power and personal transportation advances. Brief interruptions in these phenomena were of such a transient nature as to
barely dimple the remorseless trendline.

Alternately we can seize from the past one of its few immutable
lessons as summarized in a variety of languages and anecdotes but
captured by the simple phrase "and this too shall pass!" (or to put
it into stock market wisdom, "nothing goes up forever!"). Within
this context, a seeming dialectic arises, of older settlements, central
cities aging—and badly—of migration to hitherto relatively virgin
areas, ultimately leading to their corruption and a relative leveling
off of their virtues and competitive competence. Ultimately this
yields a synthesis of relative stability between old and new or alternately a return, not, perhaps, to the central city of yore, but to the
creation of new equivalents either geographically coterminous with
them—or new distinct areal constructs. Perhaps an even more cogent
analog in the practically infinite number of visions that are available—and all within the context called history—is the adoption of
patterns of migration that are shaped by economic events for use as
potential blueprints for the future. Within this context a most striking
precedent is the aborting of the drive toward suburbanization in the
United States which characterized the 1920s, epitomized by an
automobile production level in 1929 in excess of 5 million units—a
level which was not to be reached again for seventeen years. The
abrupt economic downturn which we call the Depression resulted
in a recompaction of population within the central city (as well as
a return to the land). People simply could not afford the suburban
lifestyle which up to then had seemingly advanced as a sure-fire
pattern to the future. The populations of major central cities, many
of which had faltered in the previous decade, actually gained in the
period of the 1930s.

But the same stream cannot be entered twice. The United States,
as we approach the 1980s, is not and cannot ever be again that of

the 1920s, nor any other specific period. Indeed, there is some very significant question as to whether or not it can resemble the United States of a more recent past. What we can learn from history is only that it can be cited to justify any of a variety of forward visions. And this is most strikingly the case when the basic motor forces which have moved an era suddenly stutter, their flywheels falter, and the postulates and unquestioned axioms upon which policy and projection have been based lose coherence until new—and for the moment once again seemingly immutable—elements take their place.

Forecasting the potential of the return to the city requires competence to forecast the shape and taste of our future society; we need the tools with which to measure its economic vigor, to penetrate the psyches of Americans in terms of their fearfulness or confidence in the future, and with it, their taste for risk taking; perhaps even more important, we would have to have a better grasp of the role, competitive status, and appetite for living of the United States within a world economy. The setting no longer is one of western hegemony, and the United States as the dominant figure in this relationship, but increasingly one in which the juxtaposition of the players is most unclear.

The choice of futures by forecasters may be much more a reflection of the current spirit (or dispirit) of the moment, more a time/emotion bound framework than the product of broader thought processes. The rationalization all too frequently invoked are merely cloaks for the dominance of immediate subjectivities.

Within that macrocosmic setting there are a very few rules of the game, a handful of basic parameters, which are reasonably sure at least in the short-run future, and which are most pertinent in reshaping the future. Five should be stressed in advance; others will be made both implicit and explicit in the course of the papers which follow.

1. There will be no mass "return" to central city housing because of love or sudden awakening of the virtues of major urban concentrations, but rather by default of the wherewithal for less developed means of settlement.

2. The demographic parameters of the here and now will continue to shape our lives. The elements of the baby boom, the baby bust which succeeded it, and the increasing numbers of elderly Americans continue to provide the basis upon which all extrapolation has to be made. Within this demographic sector, the impact of migration and its selective nature must be factored.

3. Ours is a post-shelter society and this is perhaps a condition unique in its depth to our own time. Housing in America is much more important as a form of investment, as a form of forced savings, and as a refuge from inflation rather than from the elements. This by no means is to infer that all Americans are well housed—all too many of them are not. It does indicate, however, that the "safe, sound, sanitary" provisions of a generation ago no longer have relevance to the house search by middle America—the bulk of the voters—of today. Long-term, chronic inflation of the duration and extent which we are undergoing alters behavior with equivalent vigor. Its ultimate resolution is far from clear.

4. The process, cloaked by the pompous phrase "the resolution of cognitive dissonance," i.e., of making a virtue of necessity—and indeed, over-time derogating the no longer feasible alternative as unworthy, of rationalizing necessity, is enormously powerful. It can alter lifestyles, reproductive rates and family patterns seemingly within a decade. The acceleration of change possible through the impact of the media clearly differentiates our era from the past.

5. Subject to economic limitations we see the beginning of a major splitting up of the mass popular markets that dominated lifestyles— and housing—in the recent past. There will be much more need for market segmentation, for specific matching of housing configuration costs and areal setting to particular elements within the society, than ever before. This may be obscured by the last wave of the baby boom. But, again, subject to major recession, it will soon dominate the housing field.

The Post-Shelter Society

George Sternlieb
James W. Hughes

A milestone passed virtually unnoticed at the end of 1976. In the first six years of the decade of the 1970s, the nation's housing inventory secured a net addition of approximately 11.5 million units, a level of increase surpassing that of any *full* intercensal decade in the nation's history. Subsequently, in 1977 and 1978, over 4 million additional private-housing starts were initiated—including near-record annual totals of single-family units—thus ensuring the destiny of the 1970s as the most prolific housing decade ever.

Not only have large *absolute* quantities of housing been delivered over the present decade, but also by all extant measures the quantity of housing delivered *per household* and/or *per person* has increased. Coupled with ever-increasing amenity packages—the housing industry's major market failure was the "stripped-down" single-family home—and substantive qualitative improvements, this nation's housing product should be, and is, the envy of the world.

So the housing industry is rich, and it is strong. But why, despite the track record, are the industry and all the people involved with housing as insecure as they are?

Certainly, it cannot be due to the impending demographics. It is readily apparent that the nation is in the middle—the beginning middle not the mature middle—of the biggest demand for housing that it has ever had and probably ever will enjoy. This is the result of the heralded "maturation of the baby boom." (Remember babies? It was a long time ago—for those young enough not to recall, they are tiny people.) The babies of yesteryear are aging into their prime home-buying years. Between 1978 and 1985 there will be 13 million more Americans added to the 25-to-44 year-old age bracket, an increment replicating that of the 1970-to-1978 period. And with the household-size parameters shrinking ever smaller, the surge in demand appears sure. The baby boom generation will be looking for housing; it will be looking to the housing industry for housing. So why is the housing industry worried?

Inventing the future is an art form whose foundation is past experience. Our vision of what is to come is limited by history. No matter how well we cloak this limitation, regardless of whether we use regression analysis, basic-trend extrapolation, or some variant of "gut-intuition"—the foundation is historical. It is useful, therefore, to examine briefly how things were in the past, and what is happening today, and then explore the apprehensions that are associated with an uncertain future.

What did "history" do right? First of all, there was cheap land throughout our experience up until the early 1970s. The cost of land as a percentage of the selling price of a house was in the vicinity of 12 percent. There was such inexpensive land that, periodically, overseas investors would come to the United States and be overwhelmed by the bargains. Shrewd brokers would take them on tours, point to the land values, and foreign investors couldn't wait to put up their pounds, or francs, or marks, as the case would be. In general, they got skinned and boned—because they couldn't believe how cheap and plentiful our land was.

There was also plenty of cheap money. Whether it was in industry or whether it was in housing, money and risk capital were inexpensive. There was a belief in the dollar—not great fear about lending it for long periods of time. Some may remember the 4 percent mortgage. Some may even remember the days of FHA and 3 percent mortgages. A lot more may remember the "Magic Fives." Those were five-year,

5 percent Treasury notes and they were magic. There there were the "Sexy Sixes"—those were six-year, 6 percent notes. They came a year or two later—and they were magic. And now we have the not-too-glamorous, going-on-10-percenters.

What did the housing industry do right? It understood American consumers and was able to provide a product they wanted. It was able to improve the product, trade-up the product, give details to that product, and impart tremendous value to that product. These were values that the consumers could see, taste, feel, and use; they were not hidden values but consumer values. They were not great planning values, maybe not great elite values, maybe not esthetic values, but they were consumer values. It is not difficult to recall the early era of the tract house when the intelligentsia used to joke about it. The classic *New Yorker*-type cartoon was a harried commuter, a little bit under the weather, trying to come home to his Levitt house or equivalent and not being able to remember which of the many identical houses was his. On the other hand, when he found it, he *loved* it.

There was also a relationship between shelter costs and incomes which permitted an enormous escalation of housing standards. People moved upwards from the house that Levitt and a great many other people made famous shortly after World War II—an 800 square foot house, with one-and-a-half baths, and a second floor that was only roughed out (and in some cases, it was pretty rough). By the mid-1950s, the newly built houses in America had a median size of 1100 square feet. Currently, it exceeds 1600 square feet. The middle class moved from a house that was "stripped-down" to a house that was a finished machine for living. The industry detailed that house—let us repeat again—*in a fashion that made sense to the consumers.* They were given value that they could use and see and believe in. Americ's middle class was made, in terms of housing, the envy and the bewilderment of the world. Only the very rich in most countries could live as well in terms of housing as our middle class was living. The United States evolved from a country which before World War II was largely one of renters (most of us have forgotten that) to one in which two out of three households are now owners.

Despite the deterioration of many of these attributes in the decade of the 1970s, the performance of the housing industry—its output—reached unprecedented levels. But this expansion was based on fears as well as needs, and therein lies the problem.

The Pyramiding of Fears

What fears? The 1970s have rapidly given birth to a new pheno-menon—the era of the scared American. There is an increasing belief that the future is not going to be as good as the past. It is an insecurity that manifests itself in the question, "What does America do so uniquely well that it can live as well as it does? Why this national insecurity?

The first and foremost reason is the condition of the dollar, that once-fabled currency. The real essence of genius is distinguishing short-term dislocations from long-term shifts: "Have we caught cold or do we have cancer?" Is the dollar's illness, for example, a momen-tary abberation, or does this mark the end of the American era in which we could do anything better than anybody else? The answers to such questions express a growing negativism which manifests itself in a variety of fashions. An appropriate analogy to them occurs in England where the pet phrase that evolved over the last generation is, "I'm all right, Jack." In other words, "I've got mine. You take care of yourself. I'm going to hang on to mine because it's not going to get better. I'm going to take my chips from the table as best I possibly can and just hang on."

Paradoxically, it is this mood which has been the major prop of the short-term prosperity of the housing industry. Housing invest-ment increasingly has become the preferred vehicle in the flight from the dollar, with levels of implicit and explicit leverage expanded not merely through formal mortgage instruments, but also through con-sumer overextension in terms of share of income resources devoted to housing investment. But there is a "feedback" mechanism at work here. For at the same time, overinvestment in housing serves as a crucial factor in undermining savings and investment. A decade ago, speculators in high-technology stocks and the buyers of mutual funds were the providers of the wherewithal that made industrial-investment costs relatively cheap in the United States. Now he or she is increas-ingly devoting his or her assets to housing. The issue of pre-emption of growth-productive dollars by housing investment becomes in-creasingly worrisome.

Indications are beginning to surface that there has been an over-allocation of the nation's resources to housing in order to achieve the success of the 1970s. Perhaps the "laws of housing physics" are beginning to assert themselves. The outpacing of income by housing costs may be a consequence of the magnitude of the wealth

the nation allocates to housing; the complement of this phenomenon—
the inadequate replenishment of the nation's economic infrastructure—then tends to undermine the growth of personal-income
resources (as a result of stagnating economic productivity). This
"feedback," in turn, may well serve to abort or terminate the
housing improvements evidenced to date.

The willingness of consumers to devote almost extraordinary shares
of income to home ownership—creating, at least until the present,
virtually insatiable demand—has in itself directly served to escalate
the upward surge in housing costs (a demand-pull phenomenon). This
dimension of the flight from the dollar breeds a mood of personal
"fiscal conservatism" that is a poor setting for investment and growth.
Owning housing is to Americans as gold Napoleons in the mattress
were to the French. Scared people are not risk takers except in ultimate desperation. Scared people say, "Stop the world, I want to get
off—the risk factor is too high." And this attitude is also affecting
the housing industry from the production or supply side, with a
cost-push factor reinforcing the dynamics established by demand.

A major dimension of the latter phenomenon is skyrocketing land
costs. Land now accounts for 25 percent of the value of the finished
house in America; it is not because there is less land than there used
to be, it is because there is *less developable* land. Not only have a
variety of stipulations been written into land-use regulation, but
there is a more important factor—enormous uncertainty even after
a piece of land is purchased. Title is taken to that land, money and
improvements are put into it, and at any stage of the game one can
discover that the nominal rights of usage have been vitiated.

The developed piece of land must pay for the risk factor, the delay
factor, and for the builder's failures with other parcels; and the
number of failures is enormous. City councils and planning boards,
in general, have more staying capacity than developers. There is one
community in New Jersey, a town of 6,000 people, which has generated legal bills of $300,000 in order to stop a development. It is
not certain that if the city fathers (or mothers) had approached the
electorate and said, "From each and every one of you, we are going
to take $50," whether they would have gone through the legal
struggle or not, but that's what they are paying. The developer, in
this particular case, has an investment of over $7 million. And
though ultimately he may win, "ultimately" is a long time. In the
meantime, money costs money and uncertainty costs money. The
consumer of the finished product will have to pay those costs.

Short of legal entanglements, the municipal tactics center on "frontloading." Developers must create a residential infrastructure that is virtually armor-plated, that assumes the burden of *all* future risks of growth. No matter that access to the development is an ancient two-lane county highway and the probabilities of additional public burden minuscule, the development must be a completely self-contained package in the broadest of senses. The same fear that fuels such requirements shows itself in consumer's willingness to pay any price to secure a stable port for the future. Little question is raised of the trade-offs: Would the future be served better if the resources consumed by this phenomenon were invested in more productive enterprises?

What the housing industry did very well in the decades prior to the 1970 was sneered at by planners, was an absolute anathema to economists, but made pretty good economic sense to consumers: It built stripped-down developments. It was not the house that was stripped-down, it was the infrastructure, the basic support elements. The development may have started off with septic tanks and ultimately it would need sewage facilities. There may not have been appropriate provision for schools, fire stations, police, and the like. And, from an economist's point of view, that's poor planning. But over the course of the years, these amenities were added. All enlightened observers said how inefficient this lag process was. *What was not appreciated was that such a process of building and adding to housing and development was done in a fashion commensurate with the consumer's income life-cycle.*

People of relatively moderate incomes were permitted to buy into a stripped development. That stripped development had to be added to—and it was added to. Additions were costly—and people complained. But at the same time their incomes were growing; they were young people and hopefully just at the beginning of the rise in their own income cycle. And it worked.

Now we are "frontloading" all of our uncertainties. Dedication of land is required as if every little development were going to end up being New York City. The developments are better, and they are going to last a long time. The only problem is that fewer and fewer people can afford them!

The uncertainties of the process have caused a basic split in the industry. The backbone of building in America used to be the developer/builder who worked on a relatively small scale. But the uncertainties of land use cause a specialization of functions. On the one hand, there are people who develop raw land into finished lots —by fighting with zoning boards, hiring consultants, taking risks— and who have a half-dozen land parcels going at once, so that if one aborts they still have something to sell. Builders, on the other hand, buy these finished lots. *What results are two overheads, two profits, a relative level of inefficiency—and we're paying for that.*

Fragmentation, Consensus, and the Merchandising of Virtue

A consensus used to exist: The bulk of Americans and their representatives believed in housing for the middle class and for the working class, and society was willing to put aside other interests in that cause. Some place down the road, the consensus was lost, and now the issue is whether it can be put together again.

To replace fragmentation with consensus is a very difficult task. As matters are now in the Dance of the Seven Veils that is the relationship between the developer and the community, there seem an infinite number of gyrations, each threatening the project's life.

Let us say that a community takes in a major office park with 6,000 workers. The community is zoned for 3.5-acre (minimum) residential lots. Suit is brought by a prospective housing developer who owns 1,000 acres of residential land with such zoning, on the grounds that it violates whatever municipal regulatory rights exist under the police power. The courts respond: "You're absolutely right!" The attorney for the municipality, questioned by the press as he is leaving the courthouse after the suit (which has, by the way, dragged on for six years), responds: *"We are going to hire an environmentalist."*

What has evolved is environmentalism as a play-for-pay profession and, in its less sanitary fashions, as a version of *This Gun for Hire*. The most unlikely places in the world are discovered to be aquifers, or tracts Indians had traversed in some distant past. That is not to deny the significance and the importance of environmental or archeological considerations. It is to indicate that a world that is looking for weapons will find them, use them, and misuse them. The issue of subdivision controls and building codes of one kind or another are troublesome enough. But with zoning getting buffeted somewhat in the courts, new veils, if you will—new ways to curtail development—are being discovered.

The issue of land clearance in North Carolina illustrates some of the problems. The citizens of one North Carolina community were asked if they wanted smoke in the air, and their answer was quite appropriately, "No, I don't want smoke in the air." With this endorsement the municipality passed a "no-burn" ordinance, because the electorate had said that they did not want any smoke. The only problem 'was that the cost of land clearance increased by $4,000 an acre. If four units per acre are being built, this represents $1,000 in front-end money per unit. Nobody went to the electorate, and said, "Which would you opt for—housing that is going to cost $1,000 a unit more or no-burn?"

What happened was the merchandising of a single dimension of virtue—not a choice between rival virtues. The real problem in a democratic society with an electorate sensitized as is our own, is "How are complex questions merchandised?" It should be reiterated that the issue is not sin versus virtue. We are all, one hopes, in favor of virtue; the real problem is the costing-out of alternative virtues. Now that is a very real problem. Not very much help is coming from anybody, and certainly not from the federal government, which is contributing to the problem by funding only one side of the debate.

How do we put together a housing consensus? There is one school of though that says, "We can't." Now that the nation has housed the bulk of Americans pretty well, they say, it's very difficult to put together anything for the remnant. Let us hope that is not the case.

The problems are particularly exacerbated in large-scale developments. Consider, for example, a planned-unit development in six-stage construction. For the people who move in initially, there is tremendous satisfaction. By the time the third stage of the development is attempted and final approval is required, the same people who were housed in the first two stages are saying "Enough is enough, we like it the way it is."

A Post-Shelter Society

Again, this is a by-product of a scared America. *What has transpired is the shift from housing as shelter to housing as investment.* Ours is now a post-shelter society and this is perhaps a condition unique in its depth to our own time. Housing in America is much more important as a form of investment, and of forced savings (and tax savings), and as a refuge from inflation than as a refuge from the elements. This by no means is to imply that all Americans are well-housed—all too many of them are not. It does indicate, however, that the "safe, sound, sanitary" provisions of a generation ago no longer have relevance to the house search by middle America —the bulk of the voters—of today.

Long-term, chronic inflation of the duration and extent which we are undergoing alters behavior with equivalent vigor. The first question asked by the home buyer in a good many areas is not "Do I like the house?" That was a question of a previous era. But rather "If I buy it, will I be able to sell it? And if I am able to sell it, will I be able to keep pace with inflation? Because if I fall off the train and make the wrong housing buy—or, God help me, buy in the wrong side of town, or worse yet, buy in the wrong town—it may be a good shelter but I'll never be able to get out from under it. I'd be immobilized forever." The fear of "falling off the train," strengthened by the whole new housing picture that has evolved, is part of the flight from the dollar.

Historically when three new houses were built, two of them went to first-time home buyers, one of them to a current homeowner. Currently when three new houses are built, two are secured by trade-ups (current owners), with only one to a first-time home buyer. Who is the trade-up household? It tends to be one that, in terms of family life-cycle (the number of progeny and the like) does not need a bigger house. It is somebody who is saying,"You know, we paid down the mortgage on the old place, the stock market is no good, and the last fellow who invested in a mutual fund hung himself the other day, so we will buy more housing."

Now, like a good many things in life, that is a generally positive thing—positive if there is only some of it—but it can be calamitously destructive if there is too much of it. One of the reasons for inflation in housing costs, as we have suggested, is this desperate feeling that "I've got to have something real." For the middle class in America, there is nothing more real than a house. In an age of inflation, they may even be right.

The Coming Assault on Housing

But even the best of things must come to an end. Housing was once the preferred weapon in fiscal balancing, a principal interventionary stick with which to rap an over-heated economy back into its appropriate place. Yet over the last half-dozen years, since the fiasco of 1974-75, it has been increasingly buffered by the vagaries of the Federal Reserve and banking system. The creation of the certificate of deposit, at indexed interest rates, provided an abundant stream of money. And the increasing liquidity given to mortgages through a variety of governmental and near-governmental resale options seemingly gave *this* housing boom immortal life. The Federal Reserve, however, with its Saturday night bombshell signaled retreat. The cost of borrowing for speculation generally—and housing unquestionably—must, in its view, be brought to a level higher than inflation; a real cost is to be attached to "nonproductive investment."

The federal government is in the role of the "sorcerer's apprentice" —now attempting to curb the very housing demand that it created and was responsible for. Earlier failures to cope with the declining value of our currency—and all the other elements that are sometimes over-simplified in the expression "inflation"—have driven the American investor to the sanctuary of housing investment. This flight now is to be curbed, or at least efforts will be made to this end, pending the onslaught of political realities.

The clash between the desperate drive to provide some backbone and bottom to the dollar and the cost that this process requires will have many manifestations. One of the most affected groups will be the overextended, overmortgaged, over-housing-priced middle class, lured into this game only to find the ballon of expectation endangered by deliberate policy. The threat of housing costs and mortgage costs to the first-time house purchaser/aspirant has been highlighted. Underplayed, however, is the much more powerful fear aroused by a possible decline in the equity that the majority of the American electorate feels is now its right as a function of its present homeownership. The number of homeowners in the United States, nearly 70 percent of all households, far exceeds the legions of organized labor, and a far greater proportion of the voting public is represented there. Much of America's future politics will be determined by the housing picture in the 1980s *not* housing as shelter, but housing as investment.

Housing and Shelter Costs:
The Schizoid Problem of the Central City

George Sternlieb
James W. Hughes

Introduction

The issues of central city housing costs have not received the kinds of detailed analysis and attention which they deserve. In the brief paper which follows, several of the more salient dimensions of the situation are approached. What are the realities of central city housing costs? What are the dynamics of the inventory? And how do they impact the consumer?

The central city housing inventory is nearly 100 times larger than the net annual additions to it. Any analysis of central city housing costs, therefore, which focuses strictly on new construction barely scratches the surface of the primary issues. As the material presented below will indicate, this housing inventory can be viewed as a train, with the last cars (the worst of the inventory) being deleted at a scarcely noted but very important and substantial rate, while their replacements are added to the head of the train in terms of price and quality. This process has permitted a very substantial physical upgrading of the stock, but only at the price of substantial cost increments—and very heavy levels of federal subsidy.

CENTRAL CITY HOUSING INVENTORY: 1970 TO 1976

We cannot design central city housing policy in a vacuum. Optimizing the resources with which to deliver a better living environment requires much more comprehension of the market dynamics that are at work, dynamics which are much more potent in structuring housing costs than is generally comprehended. In Exhibit 1 are shown the broad characteristics of the central city housing inventory for three time periods: 1970, 1973 and 1976.

General Characteristics: Essentially the picture is one of a consistent expansion of the total housing stock, with the number of year-round housing units increasing from 22.6 million in 1970 to 24.5 million in 1976, a gain of almost 2.0 million units or 8.7 percent. There were more than twice as many owner-occupied units added to the stock than was the case for rental equivalents.

It is striking to note in this context that on the single largest percentage change (36.0 percent) was in the number of vacant units, which increased from 1.2 million in 1970 to more than 1.6 million by 1976, a growth of more than 400,000 units. As a consequence the 5.3 percent vacancy rate of 1970 had increased to 6.6 percent by 1976. Although more recent data (not shown here) indicates some shrinkage of the latter figure, clearly this reflects from the tenant's point of view a perhaps greater range of choice. From the owner/operator's point of view, however, it may involve a decline in demand —and with it greater competitive stress which either could lead to lagging rents and/or reduced maintenance and ultimately abandonment. This alternative will be reviewed later in this paper.

Condition of Unit—Plumbing Facilities: We have very few benchmarks for adequately gauging the condition of housing, and those that are extant are much more reflective of physical characteristics rather than adequately describing the shelter environment as a whole. Within the former parameters, however, there is evidence of a substantial upgrading of the inventory. The number of owner-occupied housing units lacking all or some plumbing facilities for example, declined by more than 75 percent from 1970 to 1976, while renter-occupied facilities improved at a slower but still striking 33.8 percent. Again at a later stage of this paper, the question of whether this

EXHIBIT 1

CHARACTERISTICS OF THE CENTRAL CITY HOUSING INVENTORY, 1970, 1973, 1976

(Numbers in Thousands)[1]

	1970	1973	1976	Change: 1970 to 1976 Number	Percent
GENERAL CHARACTERISTICS					
All Year-Round Housing Units	22,584	24,099	24,547	1,963	8.7%
Occupied	21,395	22,493	22,930	1,534	7.2
Owner-Occupied	10,300	11,087	11,349	1,049	10.2
Renter-Occupied	11,095	11,406	11,581	486	4.4
Vacant	1,189	1,605	1,617	428	36.0
PLUMBING FACILITIES					
Owner-Occupied	10,300	11,087	11,349	1,049	10.2%
With All	10,177	11,013	11,319	1,143	11.2
Lacking All or Some	123	74	30	−93	−75.6
Renter-Occupied	11,095	11,406	11,581	486	4.4
With All	10,601	11,036	11,254	653	6.2
Lacking All or Some	494	370	327	−167	−33.8
MEDIAN UNIT SIZE (ROOMS PER UNIT)					
Owner-Occupied	5.6	5.7	5.7	0.1	1.8%
Renter-Occupied	3.8	3.8	3.8	0.0	0.0
UNIT SIZE DISTRIBUTION					
Owner-Occupied	10,300	11,087	11,349	1,049	10.2%
1 and 2 rooms	81	66	40	−41	−50.6
3 rooms	326	315	258	−68	−20.9
4 rooms	1,382	1,352	1,362	−20	− 1.4
5 rooms	3,062	3,150	3,142	80	2.6
6 rooms	3,034	3,399	3,497	463	15.3
7 rooms or more	2,416	2,805	3,049	633	26.2
Renter-Occupied	11,095	11,406	11,581	486	4.4%
1 and 2 rooms	1,659	1,639	1,529	−130	− 7.8
3 rooms	2,919	3,070	3,172	253	8.7
4 rooms	3,213	3,423	3,482	269	8.4
5 rooms	2,004	1,961	2,091	87	4.3
6 rooms	931	965	961	30	3.2
7 rooms or more	369	348	347	−22	− 6.0

EXHIBIT 1 (CONTINUED)

	1970	1973	1976	Change: 1970 to 1976 Number	Percent
MEDIAN HOUSEHOLD SIZE (PERSONS PER UNIT)					
Owner-Occupied	2.8	2.7	2.6	−0.2	− 7.1%
Renter-Occupied	2.1	2.0	1.9	−0.2	− 9.5
HOUSEHOLD SIZE DISTRIBUTION					
Owner-Occupied	10,300	11,087	11,349	1,049	10.2%
1 person	1,372	1,771	1,743	371	27.0
2 persons	3,152	3,398	3,601	449	14.2
3 persons	1,832	2,045	2,120	288	15.7
4 persons	1,699	1,726	1,821	122	7.2
5 persons	1,085	1,093	1,111	26	2.4
6 persons	594	585	549	−45	− 7.6
7 persons or more	566	469	404	−162	−28.6
Renter-Occupied	11,095	11,406	11,581	486	4.4%
1 person	3,544	4,140	4,274	730	20.6
2 persons	3,229	3,311	3,441	212	6.6
3 persons	1,716	1,697	1,617	−99	− 5.8
4 persons	1,180	1,095	1,124	−56	− 4.7
5 persons	655	567	599	−56	− 8.5
6 persons	361	294	289	−72	−19.9
7 persons or more	411	304	237	−174	−42.3
PERSONS PER ROOM					
Owner-Occupied	10,300	11,087	11,349	1,049	10.2%
0.50 or less	5,650	6,495	6,917	1,267	22.4
0.51 to 1.00	4,015	4,092	4,019	4	0.0
1.01 to 1.50	518	422	364	−154	−29.7
1.51 or more	117	78	48	−69	−59.0
Renter-Occupied	11,095	11,406	11,581	486	4.4%
0.50 or less	5,119	5,895	6,173	1,054	20.6
0.51 to 1.00	4,849	4,699	4,667	−182	− 3.8
1.01 to 1.50	785	567	556	−229	−29.2
1.51 or more	342	246	185	−157	−45.9

EXHIBIT 1 (CONTINUED)

	1970	1973	1976	Change: 1970 to 1976 Number	Percent
MEDIAN INCOME					
Owner-Occupied	$10,100	$11,700	$14,200	$4,100	40.6%
Renter-Occupied	6,100	6,900	7,500	1,400	23.0
GROSS RENT					
Specified Renter-Occupied [2]	11,033	11,405	11,581	548	5.0%
Less than $80	2,619	1,680	1,126	−1,493	−57.0
$80 to $99	2,099	1,448	759	−1,340	−63.8
$100 to $149	3,812	3,881	2,790	−1,022	−26.8
$150 to $199	1,525	2,658	3,235	1,710	112.1
$200 to $299	547	1,203	2,697	2,150	393.1
$300 or more	145	266	693	548	377.9
No Cash Rent	284	269	282	−2	0.7
Median	$107	$130	$165	$58	54.2

Notes: 1 Numbers and percents may not add due to rounding.
2 Excludes 1-family homes on 10 acres or more.

Source: U.S. Department of Commerce, U.S. Bureau of the Census, *Current Housing Reports*, Series H-150-76, *General Housing Characteristics for the United States and Regions: 1976*, Annual Housing Survey: 1976, Part A. U.S. Government Printing Office, Washington, D.C., 1978.

represents an upgrading of existing units or their disappearance and replacement with newer facilities will be considered in detail.

Unit Size: The median size of housing units both for owners and renters changed very little over the 1970 to 1976 period. But, the medians conceal a substantial redistribution which has occurred within the universe as a whole. In the owner-occupied supply, for example, there was a substantial reduction in small scale dwelling units. In the renter-occupied equivalent, there was a bimodal distribution, with very small units—one and two rooms—suffering an attrition of 7.8 percent; similarly, the very large rental facilities —those with 7 rooms or more—declined by 6.0 percent.

The Occupants of Central City Housing—Household Size: America's households are shrinking—and the central city is an integral participant in the national trend. As shown in Exhibit 1, the median size of household in owner-occupied units shrank by 7.1 percent; among renters, the decline was nearly 10 percent.

Much of the historical problem in the provision and cost of central city housing facilities has been related to large scale households. It is most significant in this context to see the substantial shrinkage in the larger household configurations.

Indeed, among renter households, only one and two person configurations increased in number. The decline is most striking (−42.3 percent) in households comprising seven persons or more, and secondarily (−19.9 percent) in six person configurations. Thus the great pressure for provision of rental facilities for large-scale families —which in general have been most scarce and most costly— has substantially abated.

However, the pressure and demand for total number of housing units has increased much more than the total population growth increment in central cities would indicate.

The number of people has increased just slightly; the number of housing units required per thousand inhabitants has increased much more substantially. Smaller households mean more households even within a population constant in absolute numbers; in turn this means increased pressure over and above the gross demographics of the housing market.

Overcrowding: Persons Per Room: Traditional investigations of absolute housing deprivation in central cities have focussed upon the overcrowded household—the vision of large families living in inappropriately small facilities. As shown in Exhibit 1, this phenomenom also is much less significant than historically has been the case. The number of owner-occupied housing units with 1.51 persons or more per room has shrunk by more than one-half (−59.0 percent) in six years—the renter equivalent by −45.9 percent. If we isolate the 1.01 to 1.50 persons per room category, there has been a shrinkage of more than 29 percent in both the renter- and owner-occupied sectors.

Median Income: The enormous increase in the quality of housing inventory has been achieved in the face of relatively lethargic increases in the incomes of central city inhabitants over the 1970 to 1976 period. While owner-occupied units have household incomes that increased by 40.6 percent to the $14,200 mark, the corresponding gain for renter households was 23.0 percent. Indeed, in 1976, central city renters as a group had median household incomes of $7500. The national median household income at the same time (1976) stood at $12,686.

Gross Rent: The income data for central city households is particularly noteworthy in the context of the changes that have taken place in rent levels. In 1970, the median gross rent was $107; by 1976, it increased by $58 to $165, a percentage gain of 54.2 percent. In sum, while incomes of renter households increased 23 percent in the six years under consideration, gross rents moved up 54.2 percent.

The changes in rent distributions are harshly evident: the number of units renting for under $100 decreased by over 60 percent while the number of units in the $100 to $149 category showed an attrition of more than one in four (−26.8 percent). At the same time, the number of units renting for $200 to $299 increased by 393.1 percent, and those for $300 or more by 377.9 percent.

SUMMARY: THE BASIC INVENTORY CHANGE

The central city housing inventory has experienced a marked change in profile over the first six years of the decade of the 1970s.

1. *Virtually 2.0 million net additions were added to a 1970 base of 22.6 million units. However, approximately nine out of every ten units in 1976 were part of the pre-existing 1970 inventory.*

   a) *The net growth of renter-occupied units (486,000) was less than half that of owner-occupied units, (1,049,000). The total number of occupied units in 1976 comprises owner and renter sectors of virtually identical size.*

   b) *The total number of vacant units increased by 428,000 or 36.0 percent. The vacancy rate in 1976, 6.6 percent, was considerably greater than that of 1970, 5.3 percent.*

2. *The condition of the overall supply improved markedly. Over three-quarters (75.6 percent) of the owner-occupied units lacking all or some plumbing facilities were removed from the 1970 inventory, as were one-third (33.8 percent) of the renter-occupied facilities.*

3. *Although the overall median number of rooms per unit changed only marginally, there was a net shrinkage in the number of smaller (four rooms and under) owner-occupied units, and a net decline in both very small (one and two rooms) and very large (seven rooms or more) renter-occupied units.*

4. *The contraction of household size, a prominent national phenomenon, was clearly evidenced in central city housing markets.*

    a) In the rental sector, only one and two person households showed absolute gains.

    b) There was a large scale attrition in the number of larger households (6 persons or more) in both the renter- and owner-occupied sectors, with renter households showing more pronounced declines.

5. *As a consequence, it appears that household and housing unit configurations have achieved an increasingly satisfactory match —a considerable reduction in overcrowding. The number of units characterized by more than 1.01 persons per room has experienced significant erosion.*

6. *Increases in median gross rent (54.2 percent) have far outpaced the income gains attached to either renters (23.0 percent) or owners (40.6 percent). While the number of units with monthly gross rents under $100 declined by 60 percent—a loss of 2.8 million such units—the increase in the number over $200 monthly totaled 2.7 million units—over four times that extant in 1970.*

7. *Therefore, the overall improvement in the housing inventory, as well as the reduction in overcrowding, has taken place not only in the context of lagging income gains, but also has been associated with the reduction in the supply of low cost rental housing.*

THE REMOVAL OF LOW RENT HOUSING FROM THE INVENTORY

The process of upgrading the housing stock described in the previous section is very largely the result of demolition rather than rehabilitation.

In Exhibit 2, the 1973 characteristics are shown for those housing units which were extant in central cities as of 1973 but which were removed by 1976. The materials presented here as in the previous exhibit depend upon the *Annual Housing Survey*. While this is a most substantial effort, it is open to some level of error. The basic trends and the phenomena they depict can be assumed to be reasonably dependable, however.

General Characteristics: In the brief three years from 1973 to 1976, three percent of the 1973 housing stock in central cities was *removed from the inventory.* The causes range from demolition, the consolidation of small scale units into larger ones, and the utilization of hitherto residential facilities for nonresidential purposes. However, regardless of the cause from the viewpoint of a person searching for housing accommodation, there was a physical removal of 725,000 units. The bulk of them were facilities that has been renter-occupied—470,000 units or 4.1 percent of the 1973 base. Nearly one in ten of the units which were vacant in 1973 had been removed from the inventory by 1976.

Condition of Unit—Plumbing Facilities: In general, this attrition focussed most heavily (proportionally) on deficient units. More than one in six of all the renter-occupied dwelling units lacking all or some of their plumbing facilities in 1973 were removed from the stock by 1976.

Unit Size: The size distribution of the units removed from the inventory tended to impact the smaller units of the owner-occupied sector. In the renter-occupied sector, it was at the two extremes, with one and two room facilities reduced by over 6 percent, accompanied by the seven room or more units with an equivalent percentage loss.

Household Size: This in turn was paralleled by the size of the households occupying the removed facilities; the renter housing distribution was most heavily impacted in the one person and five persons or more categories. Indeed in this latter category, nearly one in fourteen of the renter-occupied housing units with five persons or more in 1973 had disappeared by 1976.

Persons Per Room: In general, it has been the most overcrowded units which experienced the most substantial losses. For example, one in twelve of the renter-occupied facilities with more than one person per room disappeared from the stock in the brief period under consideration.

Median Income and Gross Rent: In general, the units that disappeared were occupied by the poor. For the total set of owner-occupied facilities, for example, the median household income in 1973 was $11,700; the units removed from this base were occupied by owners with incomes of $8100. This was paralleled in the case of renter-occupied facilities, with the units which were removed from the inventory occupied by households with a median income of $4800 in 1973, barely two-thirds of the 1973 income levesl for all renter-occupied facilities ($6900).

EXHIBIT 2

1973 CHARACTERISTICS OF HOUSING UNITS REMOVED FROM THE CENTRAL CITY INVENTORY: 1973 TO 1976

(Numbers in Thousands) [1]

	Total 1973	Removals: 1973-1976	Removals: Percent of 1973 Total
GENERAL CHARACTERISTICS			
All Year-Round Housing Units	24,099	725	3.0%
Occupied	22,493	582	2.6
Owner-Occupied	11,087	111	1.0
Renter-Occupied	11,406	470	4.1
Vacant	1,605	144	9.0
PLUMBING FACILITIES			
Owner-Occupied	11,087	111	1.0%
With All	11,013	108	1.0
Lacking All or Some	74	3	4.1
Renter-Occupied	11,406	470	4.1
With All	11,036	406	3.8
Lacking All or Some	370	64	17.3
MEDIAN UNIT SIZE (ROOMS PER UNIT)			
Owner-Occupied	5.7	4.9	
Renter-Occupied	3.8	3.8	
UNIT SIZE DISTRIBUTION			
Owner-Occupied	11,087	111	1.0%
1 and 2 rooms	66	2	3.0
3 rooms	315	19	6.0
4 rooms	1,352	27	2.0
5 rooms	3,150	20	0.6
6 rooms	3,399	19	0.6
7 rooms or more	2,805	25	0.9
Renter Occupid	11,406	470	4.1%
1 and 2 rooms	1,639	100	6.1
3 rooms	3,070	95	3.1
4 rooms	3,423	126	3.7
5 rooms	1,961	95	4.8
6 rooms	965	31	3.2
7 rooms or more	348	23	6.6

EXHIBIT 2 (CONTINUED)

	Total 1973	Removals: 1973-1976	Removals: Percent of 1973 Total
MEDIAN HOUSEHOLD SIZE (PERSONS PER UNIT)			
Owner-Occupied	2.7	2.4	
Renter-Occupied	2.0	2.0	
HOUSEHOLD SIZE DISTRIBUTION			
Owner-Occupied	11,087	111	1.0%
1 person	1,771	34	1.9
2 persons	3,398	25	0.7
3 persons	2,045	17	0.8
4 persons	1,726	10	0.6
5 persons	1,093	8	0.7
6 persons or more	1,054	18	1.7
Renter-Occupied	11,046	470	4.1%
1 person	4,140	187	4.5
2 persons	3,311	91	2.7
3 persons	1,697	59	3.5
4 persons	1,095	41	3.7
5 persons	567	39	6.9
6 persons or more	598	52	8.7
PERSONS PER ROOM			
Owner-Occupied	11,087	111	1.0%
0.50 or less	6,495	69	1.1
0.51 to 1.00	4,092	30	0.7
1.01 to 1.50	422	10	2.4
1.51 or more	78	3	3.8
Renter-Occupied	11,406	470	4.1%
0.50 or less	5,895	205	3.5
0.51 to 1.00	4,699	199	4.2
1.01 to 1.50	567	46	8.1
1.51 or more	246	21	8.5
MEDIAN INCOME			
Owner-Occupied	$11,700	$8,100	
Renter-Occupied	6,900	4,800	

EXHIBIT 2 (CONTINUED)

	Total 1973	Removals: 1973-1976	Removals: Percent of 1973 Total
GROSS RENT			
Specified Renter Occupied [2]	11,405	469	4.1%
Less than $80	1,680	124	7.4
$80 to $99	1,448	78	5.4
$100 to $149	3,881	138	3.6
$150 to $199	2,658	78	2.9
$200 to $299	1,203	28	2.3
$300 or more	266	6	2.3
No Cash Rent	269	17	6.3
Median	$130	$108	

Notes: 1 Numbers and percents may not add due to rounding.
           2 Excludes 1-family homes on 10 acreas or more.

Source: U.S. Department of Commerce, U.S. Bureau of the Census, *Current Housing Reports*, Series H-150-76, *General Housing Characteristics for the United States and Regions: 1976*, Annual Housing Survey: 1976, Part A. U.S. Government Printing Office, Washington, D.C., 1978.

In the three years from 1973 to 1976, one in fourteen of all the units which rented for less than $80 in the base year were removed from the stock. More than one in 20 of the units renting between $80 and $99 were similarly taken out of residentail use as well as a far from insignificant one in 30 of the units at the $100 to $149 rent level. Much of the decline in low rent facilities for the total rental housing stock therefore represents not so much an escalation in basic rent levels, but the actual physical disappearance of the housing units in question. It is attrition of the inexpensive housing stock as well as inflation which accounts for the increases in central city housing costs.

How effective has new construction been in replacing this level of decline?

SUMMARY–REMOVALS FROM THE INVENTORY

The 1973 characteristics of the units removed from the central city housing inventory over the 1973 to 1976 period show disproportionate losses of inexpensive, less quality housing.

1. *Three percent of the 1973 all year-round housing units were lost, as was 4.1 percent of the renter-occupied sector, and 9.0 percent of the vacant units.*

2. *The housing units impacted most heavily were the following:*

   a) *Owner- and renter-occupied units lacking all or some plumbing facilities.*

   b) *Small owner-occupied units and both very small and very large renter-occupied units.*

   c) *Rental facilities with low monthly gross rents.*

3. *The following household types were disproportionately represented in the units that were removed:*

   a) *Both very small and very large owner and renter household configurations.*

   b) *Lower income households.*

   c) *Households which experienced overcrowding (1.01 persons per room or more).*

NEW CENTRAL CITY HOUSING CONSTRUCTION: 1970 TO 1976

In the previous sections of this paper, we have considered the gross changes in the total inventory of central city housing as well as the removals from the stock. In this section, the profile of new construction will be examined.

General Characteristics: In the six year period detailed in Exhibit 3, 2.6 million all year-round housing units were constructed, a total equivalent to 10.6 percent of the 1976 residential base. Newly built renter-occupied facilities, 1.4 million units, exceeded their owner-occupied counterparts (984,000). Significantly, new construction accounts for 13.7 percent of the total vacancies in 1976.

Plumbing Facilities and Unit Size: Practically all of the newly constructed units met the test of adequate plumbing facilities. In general they matched the extant size distribution for owner-occupied facilities but were weighted toward the large configurations. Similarly, there was a skew towards three and four room units in terms of the rental units which were constructed.

Household Size and Persons Per Room: The differences in the profiles between the occupants of newly constructed housing units and the total inventory parallel the variations in the size of the newly constructed and existing stock. Owners were skewed towards three

EXHIBIT 3

1976 CHARACTERISTICS OF NEW CONSTRUCTION IN CENTRAL CITIES: 1970 TO 1976

(Numbers in Thousands) [1]

	Total 1976	New Construction: 1970 to 1976	New Construction: Percent of 1976 Total
GENERAL CHARACTERISTICS			
All Year-Round Housing Units	24,547	2,599	10.6%
Occupied	22,930	2,378	10.4
Owner-Occupied	11,349	984	8.7
Renter-Occupied	11,581	1,394	12.0
Vacant	1,617	221	13.7
PLUMBING FACILITIES			
Owner-Occupied	11,349	984	8.7%
With All	11,319	982	8.7
Lacking All or Some	30	2	6.6
Renter-Occupied	11,581	1,394	12.0
With All	11,254	1,394	12.4
Lacking All or Some	327	–	–
MEDIAN UNIT SIZE (ROOMS PER UNIT)			
Owner-Occupied	5.7	5.9	
Renter-Occupied	3.8	3.7	
UNIT SIZE DISTRIBUTION			
Owner-Occupied	11,349	984	8.7%
1 and 2 rooms	40	4	10.0
3 rooms	258	20	7.8
4 rooms	1,362	124	9.1
5 rooms	3,142	243	7.7
6 rooms	3,497	262	7.4
7 rooms or more	3,049	332	10.9
Renter-Occupied	11,581	1,394	12.0%
1 and 2 rooms	1,529	147	9.6
3 rooms	3,172	441	13.9
4 rooms	3,482	479	13.8
5 rooms	2,091	232	11.1
6 rooms	961	77	8.0
7 rooms or more	347	20	5.8

EXHIBIT 3 (CONTINUED)

	Total *1976*	*New Construction:* *1970 to 1976*	*New Construction:* *Percent of 1976 Total*
MEDIAN HOUSEHOLD SIZE (PERSONS PER UNIT)			
Owner-Occupied	2.6	3.3	
Renter-Occupied	1.9	1.9	
HOUSEHOLD SIZE DISTRIBUTION			
Owner-Occupied	11,349	984	8.7%
1 person	1,743	102	5.9
2 persons	3,601	210	5.8
3 persons	2,120	224	10.6
4 persons	1,821	239	13.1
5 persons	1,111	126	11.3
6 persons	549	46	8.4
7 persons or more	404	36	8.9
Renter-Occupied	11,581	1,394	12.0%
1 person	4,274	499	11.7
2 persons	3,441	509	14.8
3 persons	1,617	184	11.4
4 persons	1,124	120	10.7
5 persons	599	48	8.0
6 persons	289	20	6.9
7 persons or more	237	14	5.9
PERSONS PER ROOM			
Owner-Occupied	11,349	984	8.7%
0.50 or less	6,917	491	7.1
0.51 to 1.00	4,019	459	11.4
1.00 to 1.50	364	28	7.7
1.51 or more	48	6	12.5
Renter-Occupied	11,581	1,394	12.0%
0.50 or less	6,173	809	13.1
0.51 to 1.00	4,667	548	11.7
1.00 to 1.50	556	33	5.9
1.51 or more	185	5	2.7
MEDIAN INCOME			
Owner-Occupied	$14,200	$18,300	
Renter-Occupied	7,500	9,800	

EXHIBIT 3 (CONTINUED)

	Total 1976	New Construction: 1970 to 1976	New Construction: Percent of 1976 Total
GROSS RENT			
Specified Renter Occupied[2]	11,581	1,394	12.0%
Less than $80	1,126	122	10.8
$80 to $99	759	45	5.9
$100 to $149	2,790	105	3.8
$150 to $199	3,235	400	12.4
$200 to $299	2,697	539	20.0
$300 or more	693	170	24.5
No Cash Rent	282	13	4.6
Median	$165	$202	

Notes: 1 Numbers and percents may not add due to rounding.
              2 Excludes 1-family homes on 10 acres or more.

Source: U.S. Department of Commerce, U.S. Bureau of the Census, *Current Housing Reports*, Series H-150-76, *General Housing Characteristics for the United States and Regions: 1976*, Annual Housing Survey: 1976, Part A. U.S. Government Printing Office, Washington, D.C., 1978.

to five person households, leading to a larger median household size (3.3 persons per units) in newly constructed units as compared to the overall owner-occupied inventory (2.6 persons per units). Among renters, the skew was toward smaller household configurations. Generally, in turn, this yielded relatively uncrowded facilities.

Median Income and Gross Rent: There is a very substantial variation, however, when the income of occupants who utilize this new construction is analysed. Among owner-occupants of new central city housing, for example, median incomes stood at $18,300. For renter-occupied facilities, it was $9,800. Both income levels are substantially higher than their equivalents for the total 1976 inventory ($14,200 and $7,500, respectively).

It is striking to compare the median incomes (presented earlier) for the households who occupied 1973 housing units which had been demolished (owners: $8,100; renters: $4,800) with the 1976 incomes for occupants of new housing (owners: $18,300; renters: $9,800). Even allowing for the three-year time lag in the data does not measurably reduce the gap between the two.

Essentially the housing which was demolished was occupied by the poor. The new housing which has been added to the stock is occupied by the much more affluent.

The median rent of the newly constructed units by the terminal year (1976) exceeded the $200 level. This stands in marked contrast to the median gross rent of the total inventory ($165). Once again, a comparison with the vanishing stock is most fruitful.

There was a greater level of demolition of units renting for $150 or less in the three years 1973 to 1976 than was erected at equivalent prices from 1970 to 1976. The rate of attrition of low-rent facilities is double the level of new construction.

SUMMARY—NEW CONSTRUCTION

The 1976 profile of units constructed from 1970 to 1976 in central cities is marked by the following tendencies:

1. *Newly constructed units constituted 12.0 percent of the total renter occupied stock in 1976, 8.7 percent of the owner-occupied sector, and 13.7 percent of all vacancies.*

2. *The units generally possess all plumbing facilities and are heavily concentrated in high rent categories. Owner-occupied units are larger in size than the overall base, while newly constructed rental units are concentrated in the middle size (three and four rooms) sectors.*

3. *Newly constructed units have proportionally less overcrowding, and are occupied by households substantially more affluent than those occupying the total inventory.*

CHANGES IN THE HOUSING INVENTORY OF THE LARGER CITIES

The housing characteristics for the nation's central cities in total do not reveal the great variation which occurs in specific cities. In Exhibit 4, a group of major central cities for which data is available from the *Annual Housing Survey* has been isolated.

There are two basic phenomena that dominate the housing shifts. The first and most positive is the enormous level of improvement in housing quality as measured by the criteria of plumbing, kitchen facilities and crowding. The second, and far less positive from the viewpoint of housing costs, is the absolute level of attrition in total housing inventory.

EXHIBIT 4

INDICATORS OF HOUSING QUALITY (SELECTED U.S. CITIES - 1970-1976)

IN CENTRAL CITY City and Years	Lacking Some or All Plumbing	No or Shared Bathroom	No or Shared Kitchen Facilities	More Than 1.0 Persons/ Room	Total No. of Year-Round Housing Units
Boston					
1974	8,000	11,300	6,400	10,500	224,800
1970	12,900	16,700	8,000	15,700	232,400
Percent Change	-38.0	-32.3	-20.0	-33.1	-3.3
Detroit					
1974	11,300	14,300	14,400	22,300	507,700
1970	14,500	18,200	15,400	36,300	529,000
Percent Change	-22.1	-21.4	-6.5	-38.6	-4.0
Washington, D.C.					
1974	4,300	6,600	5,400	16,500	272,400
1970	4,600	5,800	5,200	31,400	278,400
Percent Change	-6.5	+13.8	+3.8	-47.5	-2.2
Los Angeles-Long Beach					
1974	13,300	19,700	31,200	75,500	1,277,400
1970	20,200	27,700	36,200	93,600	1,277,200
Percent Change	-34.2	-28.9	-13.8	-19.3	4.1
Philadelphia					
1975	13,100	17,600	12,400	26,100	651,700
1970	13,700	26,600	12,600	38,100	673,400
Percent Change	-4.4	-33.8	-1.6	-31.5	-3.2
Chicago					
1975	29,900	40,800	31,600	75,700	1,144,300
1970	47,300	61,900	37,900	108,200	1,206,900
Percent Change	-36.8	-34.1	-16.6	-30.0	-5.2

EXHIBIT 4 (CONTINUED)

IN CENTRAL CITY

City and Years	Lacking Some or All Plumbing	No or Shared Bathroom	No or Shared Kitchen Facilities	More Than 1.0 Persons/ Room	Total No. of Year-Round Housing Units
Atlanta					
1975	2,700	3,700	4,800	9,000	169,400
1970	3,400	4,600	3,000	17,100	170,900
Percent Change	−20.6	−19.6	+60.0	−47.4	−0.9
San Francisco-Oakland					
1975	21,200	40,300	30,400	18,800	463,000
1970	27,900	32,200	32,900	29,900	457,000
Percent Change	−24.0	+25.2	−7.6	−37.1	1.3
Houston					
1976	4,300	5,300	7,100	30,900	508,200
1970	8,700	11,600	8,100	39,400	427,500
Percent Change	−50.6	54.3	−12.3	−21.6	18.9
Baltimore					
1976	3,300	4,700	4,700	6,800	287,900
1970	4,800	8,200	5,000	6,400	305,200
Percent Change	−31.3	−42.7	−6.0	6.3	−5.7
Buffalo					
1976	2,200	2,500	3,500	3,000	157,700
1970	4,800	6,400	5,300	7,300	166,100
Percent Change	−54.2	−60.9	−34.0	−58.9	−5.1
Cleveland					
1976	5,600	6,900	8,000	9,100	251,000
1970	6,700	9,400	5,200	17,700	264,200
Percent Change	−16.4	−26.6	−55.8	−48.6	−5.0

Source: Annual Housing Survey, Select Metropolitan Area Reports.

Four of the cities shown here lost 5 or more percent of their total housing stock *after allowance of new construction.* While Houston had an increase of 18.9 percent in the total supply of all-year-round housing units—or 80,000 units in the six years from 1970 to 1976 —Cleveland lost 13,000 units, Buffalo 9,000 and Baltimore nearly 20,000.

The attrition in the extant of housing stock has reduced the number of substandard units, but at a price. What can city and state governments do to manage their inventories in such a fashion as to continue the upgrading without reducing the supply?

The classic approach to reducing costs in America's market oriented society is to increase supply. This process is highly imperfect when we deal with rental facilities in central cities. The reduction in price through competition may lead to a short-run reduction or stabilization of rents. But in the long run, it also leads to an erosion of the stock as owners no longer find it profitable to care for and maintain their buildings. Thus, increased competition through new construction and/or reduction in demand through declining population and household formation, in the long run present procedures, may lead to increased shelter costs as the low end of the market literally goes out of business.

This is exemplified by the increasing levels of housing abandonment which are beginning to characterize many of our older cities, as well as municipalities finding themselves literally by default the owners and operators of last resort.

While this may permit the hiding of the subsidy mechanism through the absorption of subsidies by the cities in question, clearly what is required is a complete rethinking through of municipal policies in terms of code enforcement, rent controls both defacto and dejure, of relationships with welfare department housing procedures and the whole issue, most strikingly, of the future of low income private rental housing facilities.

CHANGING VALUE OF OWNER-OCCUPIED FACILITIES IN CENTRAL CITIES VERSUS SUBURBS

There is a very real dilemma of central city housing policy which revolves around the issues of housing as shelter versus housing as investment. If we wish to optimize shelter, clearly we want to foster a market in which prices remain modest. On the other hand, as housing increasingly becomes the major vehicle for the working class in America to accummulate capital and to combat the impacts of inflation, it becomes increasingly important that investment in housing, whether in central city or suburbia, be a good investment —and increase in price. If we are concerned only with the very poor, for whom capital accumulation may be a luxury beyond current means, we have one set of procedures to follow. We must be concerned however, also with people who want to invest in central city housing—whether blue-collar workers or the more affluent—and this involves another set of considerations. In the exhibits which follow, data which illustrate the problem are presented.

The value of central city owner-occupied housing has moved from a 1970 median of $16,400 to $22,300 in 1973 and to $29,400 by 1976—a six-year increment of 79.3 percent or $13,000. There has been an enormous shrinkage in the number of units valued at under $25,000 in the period under consideration. While such units made up 80 percent of the 1970 central city inventory, by 1976 they comprised less than half. Increments, both in absolute values and proportions, have been even more striking outside of central cities, increasing in nominal value by 81.4 percent. Again, the attrition at below the $25,000 mark—in 1976 dollars—is most striking.

In general, central city owner-occupied housing, in terms of owner specified value, has not increased as rapidly as their non-central city counterparts. The value of central city units, as of 1976, was barely three-quarters that of owner-occupied facilities outside central city. In addition, a portion of the upward shift in central city values for owner-occupied facilities has been the result of demolition. As shown in the last sections of Exhibit 5, a number of lower priced facilities were lost.

The removals that took place from 1973 to 1976 had a median value in the base year of $16,200—more than 20 percent less than that of the universe of owner-occupied central cities facilities of 1973.

NEW CONSTRUCTION

In the place of deletions, the value of new construction, in a sad tribute to inflation, was at much higher levels that that of pre-existing housing. As pointed out earlier, the extant stock in central cities in 1976 had a median value of barely three-quarters of that of non-central cities. The value of new construction which took

EXHIBIT 5

VALUE OF CENTRAL CITY AND NON-CENTRAL CITY (WITHIN SMSA) HOUSING INVENTORY: 1970, 1973 AND 1976; AND 1973 VALUE OF CENTRAL CITY HOUSING UNITS REMOVED FOR THE INVENTORY: 1973 TO 1976

(Numbers in Thousands)[1]

	1970	1973	1976	Change: 1970-1976 Number	Percent
IN CENTRAL CITIES					
Specified Owner-Occupied[2]	8,543	9,240	9,453	910	10.7%
Less than $5,000	239	133	78	− 161	−67.4
$5,000 to $9,999	1,350	619	402	− 948	−70.2
$10,000 to $14,999	2,102	1,371	759	−1,343	−63.9
$15,000 to $19,999	1,916	1,793	1,278	− 638	−33.3
$20,000 to $24,999	1,214	1,499	1,076	− 138	−11.4
$25,000 to $34,999	1,044	2,091	2,389	1,345	128.8
$35,000 to $49,999	444	1,184	1,983	1,539	346.6
$50,000 or more	234	549	1,488	1,254	539.9
Median	$16,400	$22,300	$29,400	$13,000	79.3
NOT IN CENTRAL CITIES					
Specified Owner-Occupied[2]	13,516	15,135	16,431	2,915	21.6%
Less than $5,000	312	131	78	−234	−75.0
$5,000 to $9,999	1,097	476	247	−850	−77.5
$10,000 to $14,999	2,069	996	555	−1,514	−73.2
$15,000 to $19,999	2,880	1,792	938	−1,942	−67.4
$20,000 to $24,999	2,526	2,241	1,331	−1,195	−47.3
$25,000 to $34,999	2,665	4,279	3,755	1,090	40.9
$35,000 to $49,999	1,316	3,313	4,886	3,570	271.3
$50,000 or more	653	1,907	4,642	3,989	610.9
Median	$20,800	$29,500	$38,300	$17,500	84.1

IN CENTRAL CITIES	1973	Removals: 1973-1976	Removals: Percent of of 1973 Total
Specified Owner-Occupied[2]	9,240	65	0.7%
Less than $5,000	133	10	7.5
$5,000 to $9,999	619	11	1.8
$10,000 to $14,999	1,371	11	0.8
$15,000 to $19,999	1,793	6	0.3
$20,000 to $24,999	1,499	9	0.6
$25,000 to $34,999	2,091	6	0.3
$35,000 to $49,999	1,184	11	0.9
$50,000 or more	549	2	0.4
Median	$22,300	$16,200	

Notes: 1 Numbers and percents may not add due to rounding.
          2 Limited to 1-family homes on less than 10 acres and no business on property.

Source: U.S. Department of Commerce, U.S. Bureau of the Census, *Current Housing Reports*, Series H-150-76, *General Housing Characteristics for the United States and Regions: 1976*, Annual Housing Survey: 1976, Part A. U.S. Government Printing Office, Washington, D.C., 1978.

EXHIBIT 6

1976 VALUE OF CENTRAL CITY AND NON-CENTRAL CITY NEW CONSTRUCTION: 1970 TO 1976

(Numbers in Thousands) [1]

	Total 1976	New Construction: 1970 to 1976	New Construction: Percent of 1976 Total
IN CENTRAL CITIES			
Specified Owner Occupied [2]	9,453	733	7.8%
Less than $5,000	78	–	–
$5,000 to $9,999	402	3	0.7
$10,000 to $14,999	759	5	0.7
$15,000 to $19,999	1,278	14	1.1
$20,000 to $24,999	1,076	37	3.4
$25,000 to $34,999	2,389	164	6.9
$35,000 to $49,999	1,983	266	13.4
$50,000 to $74,999	1,049	171	16.3
$75,000 or more	439	76	17.3
Median	$29,400	$43,000	
NOT IN CENTRAL CITIES			
Specified Owner Occupied [2]	16,431	2,509	15.3%
Less than $5,000	78	4	5.1
$5,000 to $9,999	247	8	3.2
$10,000 to $14,999	555	19	3.4
$15,000 to $19,999	938	40	4.3
$20,000 to $24,999	1,331	98	7.4
$25,000 to $34,999	3,755	399	10.6
$35,000 to $49,999	4,886	844	17.3
$50,000 to $74,999	3,247	730	22.5
$75,000 or more	1,395	368	26.4
Median	$38,300	$47,200	

Notes: 1 Numbers and percents may not add due to rounding.
          2 Excludes 1-family homes on 10 acres or more.

Source: U.S. Department of Commerce, U.S. Bureau of the Census, *Current Housing Reports*, Series H-150-76, *General Housing Characteristics for the United States and Regions: 1976*, Annual Housing Survey: 1976, Part A., U.S. Government Printing Office, Washington, D.C., 1978.

place in the six years preceeding that date was within 10 percent of the level of non-central city units.

This tends to indicate that new construction simply cannot or has not been provided within a cost framework comparable to the values which central cities once could provide versus non-central city areas.

The new central city construction which occurred from 1970 to 1976 had a median value of $43,000 in the terminal year. Again, the contrast with the removals becomes most striking—the latter, as of 1973, had a median value of $16,200. Very little of the new central city construction—barely one in twenty units—was valued under $25,000.

OWNED HOUSING THAT DOES NOT GO UP IN PRICE IS EXPENSIVE HOUSING

The actual cost of housing ownership in America must have factored into it the level of inflation in housing value. If, for example, one owns a house which increases in value by 12 percent a year, the real carrying costs of the house in terms of financing—even with a ten percent mortgage, are negative. All that is occurring is a substitution of a stream of monthly payments into a form of capital accumulation. This has sustained the American homebuying boom despite the rigors of cost structures. In turn, at least according to a good many observers, it has made ownership of housing relatively inexpensive.

Once again this presents a significant problem of public policy. If we want to make housing inexpensive for the present central city owners or owner aspirants, its must go up in price! If it does not go up in price proportionately to suburbia, the real cost may be higher than in an affluent suburb—though the nominal cost may have an appearance opposed to this reality.

In Exhibit 7, for example, are shown changes in housing prices for all houses which had bona-fide transfers, in the years indicated, for two classic central cities of New Jersey contrasted with two older but affluent suburbs.

There are several prominent elements presented here. The first is indicated by changes in mean selling price. For the older cities of Newark and Jersey City, the increase in mean sales prices between 1970 and 1977 stand at 52.4 percent and 35.6 percent respectively. For the suburbs, the increases are close to the 70 percent level. Perhaps even more significant is the level of irregularity across the price spectrum. Practically all of the suburban housing, even that of relatively modest price (the 10th and 25th percentiles), secured very substantial increments. In the central cities, the pattern was quite otherwise, with the low end (10th percentile) of the housing stock stagnating in the seven year period under consideration. However, the 90th percentile increased in price much more rapidly.

EXHIBIT 7

SALES PRICES FOR SELECT NEW JERSEY MUNICIPALITIES 1970 AND 1977

OLDER SUBURB: SUMMIT

	1970	1977	Percent Change 1970 to 1977
Mean	$51,011	$ 86,151	68.9%
Percentiles			
10	27,400	50,800	85.4
25	35,000	62,000	77.1
50	44,500	75,000	68.5
75	65,000	101,250	55.8
90	83,800	136,600	63.0

CENTRAL CITY: NEWARK

	1970	1977	Percent Change 1970 to 1977
Mean	$18,286	$ 27,860	52.4%
Percentiles			
10	8,900	8,980	0.9
25	13,500	17,771	31.6
50	18,000	27,000	50.0
75	22,700	36,500	60.8
90	27,000	45,500	68.5

OLDER SUBURB: PRINCETON BOROUGH

	1970	1977	Percent Change 1970 to 1977
Mean	$52,834	$ 89,682	69.7%
Percentiles			
10	16,505	43,300	162.3
25	32,750	62,125	89.7
50	46,500	83,375	79.3
75	72,500	97,500	34.5
90	86,560	154,400	78.4

CENTRAL CITY: JERSEY CITY

	1970	1977	Percent Change 1970 to 1977
Mean	$20,640	$ 27,984	35.6%
Percentiles			
10	11,000	12,000	9.1
25	15,650	19,500	24.6
50	20,500	28,000	36.6
75	25,000	35,000	40.0
90	29,000	43,460	49.9

Source: Unpublished sales files, State of New Jersey.

This latter situation portrays a basic fact of life in many of our older cities. One part of the city is literally going out of business; the more desirable part is flourishing. In addition, the two central cities under discussion have had significant abandonment which has not been reflected in the exhibits, but which in turn would cause a general deflation of the level of increments. There is a much more riskful pattern of investment here as contrasted with the affluent suburbs. In the latter practically all the levels of housing shown have significant price gains. Housing investment in risk situations should be more profitable than holds true for suburbia. That simply is a function of the uncertainty of gain illustrated in the exhibit. The reality is the reverse of this case.

Owner housing as shelter in central cities is available at much lower absolute cost then in affluent suburbia. The real costs after allowing for the effects of inflation—and the risks of wipe-out through abandonment and neighborhood change phenomena—may be much more comparable if not higher in the core.

SUMMARY– HOUSING VALUES, CENTRAL CITIES AND SUBURBS

The evolution of the value and selling price of central city and suburban housing is characterized by the following tendencies:

1. *The median value of central city owner-occupied housing increased by $13,000 or 79.3 percent over 1970 to 1976 period; the suburban equivalent was $17,500 or 84.1 percent. The median central city value ($29,400) in 1976 was but three-quarters (76.8 percent) of that of non-central cities ($38,300).*

2. *Within both areas, there was an enormous shrinkage in the number of units valued under $25,000. This was not only the result of inflation, but also the physical removal of lower valued properties from the inventory. The median 1973 value of central city removals from 1973 to 1976 was $16,200. The 1973 median value of all central city owner-occupied units was $22,300.*

3. *Units constructed over the 1970 to 1976 period had a 1976 median value of $43,000 in central cities. This stands in sharp contrast to median value ($29,400) of the total inventory.*

4. *The value of newly constructed central city units ($43,000) did not differ markedly from their non-central city counterparts ($47,000). Very few low value units were constructed.*

5. *Actual property transactions in select New Jersey cities and suburbs over the 1970 to 1977 period reveal the following patterns of change in sales prices:*

   a) *The increase in mean value of central city sales (owner-occupied units) ranged between 35.6 and 52.4 percent. The suburban equivalent approached 70 percent.*

   b) *Only the upper end of the central city market demonstrated strong increases in value. The lower end showed virtual stagnation.*

   c) *The strong increase in suburban selling price was characteristic of the entire value spectrum.*

6. *A basic fact of life in older central cities is portrayed: one part of the city is literally going out of business while the more desirable not only survives, but flourishes.*

Some Economic Effects of Recent Migration Patterns on Central Cities

George Sternlieb
James W. Hughes

  The impact of selective migration from central cities in the United States has long been a topic of study. The bulk of the effort, however, has concentrated upon the sociological ramifications, initially of white flight—and then of the more general shift of the middle class. In recent years a counter element has been introduced—the potentials both positive and negative of gentrification, of the return of the middle class to selected areas. Somewhat slighted in these analyses have been the aggregate result of these flows of population in terms of their impact on resident incomes and purchasing power within central cities. And it is this element which provides motive power for much of the primary/secondary economic activity, and with it employment opportunities, that conventionally have been focused in urban areas.

  In the paper which follows, demographic data are analyzed in an effort to secure a current reading on the situation. Has the departure of the middle-class ceased? Has the rise of the defacto new town intown, peopled by the more affluent, offset the earlier out-migration trends? Are there longer term dynamics underway in terms of household configuration which give insight into probable futures for the urban core?

Population Losses

The central cities of the United States are losing population; in this retrenchment, it is the very largest of them—those central cities in metropolitan areas with a million or more population—which are the heaviest losers. As shown in Exhibit 1, while the total population of the United States from 1970 to 1977 grew by 6.4 percent, the central cities in total lost 4.6 percent of their residents. The experience of the central cities in the largest metropolitan areas was a decline of 7.1 percent. In the central cities of smaller metropolitan areas, losses of 1.6 percent were evidenced.

Racial Population Shift

The overall data mask significant shifts in racial character. Central cities as a whole, in the seven-year period under consideration, lost nearly one in 12 of their whites (-8.1 percent). Indeed, in the large metropolitan areas, the central city equivalent was nearly a one in eight (-12.3 percent). But gains in black population only partially offset these losses, thus creating the absolute decline. For example, in central cities in metropolitan areas of one million or more, the increase in the number of blacks was only 2.3 percent. The latter resulted from the enormous level of out-migration of central city blacks to suburbia. Current census data indicate, for example, that in the last two years for which data is available (1976 to 1978), this amounted to a net out-migration of some 400,000 people. This process is mirrored by the fully one third (33.9 percent) increase of blacks in suburban areas of our SMSAs.

Household Shifts

Yet within this pattern of population decline there is remarkably little equivalent shrinkage in the need for housing, at least as measured by total units. As shown in Exhibit 2, the number of households has continued, to grow even in the central cities most characterized by absolute population losses. It is particularly striking in this con-

EXHIBIT 1

POPULATION BY TYPE OF RESIDENCE: 1970 AND 1977

(Numbers in Thousands, 1970 Metropolitan Definition)

	TOTAL (ALL RACES)		Change: 1970 to 1977		WHITE		Change: 1970 to 1977		BLACK		Change: 1970 to 1977	
	1970	1977	Number	Percent	1970	1977	Number	Percent	1970	1977	Number	Percent
U.S. Total	199,819	212,566	12,747	6.4	175,276	184,335	9,059	5.2	22,056	24,474	2,418	11.0
Metropolitan Areas	137,058	143,107	6,049	4.4	118,938	122,177	3,239	2.7	16,342	18,048	1,706	10.4
Central Cities	62,876	59,993	−2,883	−4.6	48,909	44,951	−3,958	−8.1	12,909	13,451	542	4.2
Suburban Areas	74,182	83,144	8,932	12.0	70,029	77,226	7,197	10.3	3,433	4,596	1,163	33.9
Central Cities in Metropolitan Areas of 1 Million or More	34,322	31,898	−2,424	−7.1	25,007	21,939	−3,068	−12.3	8,664	8,863	199	2.3
Central Cities in Metropolitan Areas of Less than 1 Million	28,554	28,095	− 459	−1.6	23,903	23,012	− 891	− 3.7	4,245	4,588	343	8.1

Source: Center for Urban Policy Research Analysis of Data Presented in: U.S. Department of Commerce, Bureau of the Census, *Current Population Reports*, Special Studies P-23, No. 55, "Social and Economic Characteristics of the Metropolitan and Nonmetropolitan Population: 1977 and 1970," November 1978.

EXHIBIT 2

HOUSEHOLDS BY TYPE OF RESIDENCE: 1970 AND 1977

(Numbers in Thousands, 1970 Metropolitan Definition)

	TOTAL (ALL RACES)		Change: 1970 to 1977		WHITE		Change: 1970 to 1977		BLACK		Change: 1970 to 1977	
	1970	1977	Number	Percent	1970	1977	Number	Percent	1970	1977	Number	Percent
U.S. Total	63,447	74,142	10,695	16.9	56,609	65,353	8,744	15.4	6,178	7,776	1,598	25.9
Metropolitan Areas	43,851	50,414	6,563	15.0	38,622	43,649	5,027	13.0	4,733	5,981	1,248	26.4
Central Cities	21,401	22,741	1,340	6.3	17,254	17,712	458	2.7	3,833	4,566	733	19.1
Suburban Areas	22,450	27,672	5,222	23.3	21,368	25,937	4,569	21.4	900	1,415	515	57.2
Central Cities in Metropolitan Areas of 1 Million or More	12,056	12,246	190	1.6	9,230	8,914	−316	−3.4	2,625	3,025	400	15.2
Central Cities in Metropolitan Areas of Less than 1 Million	9,344	10,494	1,150	12.3	8,024	8,798	774	9.6	1,207	1,541	334	27.7

Source: Center for Urban Policy Research Analysis of Data Presented in: U.S. Department of Commerce, Bureau of the Census, *Current Population Reports*, Special Studies P-23, No. 55, "Social and Economic Characteristics of the Metropolitan and Nonmetropolitan Population: 1977 and 1970," November 1978.

text to note the 15.2 increase in the number of black households within the central cities of larger metropolitan areas. This is seven times the increase (2.3 percent) in absolute population growth of this group. As we will note, this represents both a very positive tribute to upgrading in housing—but also a far less salubrious fragmentation of households.

Part of the process of household growth in the context of population stability and decline is the actual shrinking size of families, as shown in Exhibit 3. So very much of the housing trauma of the post World War II era involved the difficulties of housing large-scale families that it is now particularly heartening to see the diminishing need shown in Exhibit 3, both in the average size of families and most significantly, in those families in central cities with five persons or more.

But this is not merely a consequence of a declining birth rate, it is also the drastic change in the configuration of households, most importantly, that of the single-spouse family.* In Exhibit 4 are shown data on this point for the nation as a whole, all central cities and central cities in metropolitan areas of one million or more people. Primary families as a group in central cities are shrinking both relatively and in absolute numbers. The case is most strikingly evident in terms of the decline (-965,000 or -7.6 percent) of husband-wife families for all central cities over the 1970-1977 period. For central cities in the larger metropolitan areas, a decline of 12.0 percent or 813,000 families was experienced. In the latter case, husband-wife families have now (1977) achieved minority status, with only 48.8 percent of households in this configuration.

Fully one out of seven (14.8 percent) of all households in the central cities in major metropolitan areas are female-headed (no husband present); moreover, the configuration is the dynamic growth element, with an increase of 22.9 percent in such incidence from 1970 to 1977. Indeed, if we were to sum primary individual households headed by females with families headed by the equivalent sex, they would represent virtually one in three of all central city households.

*Households are generally of two types: primary families and primary individuals. Primary families comprise two or more related individuals and are usually subdivided into three types—husband-wife families, male head (no wife present) and female head (no husband present). Primary individual households comprise either a single person living alone or two or more unrelated individuals. They are usually subdivided into male and female-headed sectors. The Census Bureau, however, plans to replace the term "head" with "householder."

EXHIBIT 3

FAMILIES BY SIZE AND TYPE OF RESIDENCE: 1970 AND 1977

(Numbers in Thousands, 1970 Metropolitan Definition)

	U.S. Total		Change: 1970 to 1977		All Central Cities		Change: 1970 to 1977		Central Cities in Metropolitan Areas of 1,000,000 or more people		Change: 1970 to 1977	
	1970	1977¹	Number	Percent	1970	1977¹	Number	Percent	1970	1977¹	Number	Percent
TOTAL FAMILIES	50,967	56,710	5,743	11.3	15,816	15,529	−287	− 1.8	8,621	8,144	−477	− 5.5
2 persons	18,139	21,530	3,391	18.7	6,033	6,334	301	5.0	3,362	3,336	− 26	− 0.7
3 persons	10,618	12,472	1,854	17.5	3,407	3,497	90	2.6	1,866	1,837	− 29	− 1.6
4 persons	9,649	11,483	1,834	19.0	2,798	2,888	90	3.2	1,498	1,468	− 30	− 2.0
5 persons	6,107	6,209	102	1.7	1,700	1,471	−229	−13.5	897	762	−135	−15.1
6 persons	3,328	2,800	−528	−15.9	936	720	−216	−23.1	497	387	−110	−22.1
7 persons or more	3,126	2,216	−910	−29.1	943	619	−324	−34.4	502	353	−149	−29.7
Average Size of Family	3.57	3.38			3.47	3.30			3.44	3.31		

Note: 1. 1977 family data include a relatively small number of secondary family heads who are not household heads.
2. Numbers may not add due to rounding.

Source: Center for Urban Policy Research Analysis of Data Presented in U.S. Department of Commerce, Bureau of the Census, *Current Population Reports*, Special Studies P-23, No. 55, "Social and Economic Characteristics of the Metropolitan and Nonmetropolitan Population: 1977 and 1970," November 1978.

EXHIBIT 4

HOUSEHOLDS BY TYPE AND RESIDENCE: 1970 AND 1977

(Numbers in Thousands, 1970 Metropolitan Definition)

	U.S. Total		Change: 1970 to 1977		All Central Cities		Change: 1970 to 1977		Central Cities in Metropolitan Areas of 1,000,000 or more people		Change: 1970 to 1977	
	1970	1977	Number	Percent	1970	1977	Number	Percent	1970	1977	Number	Percent
TOTAL	63,447	74,142	10,695	16.9	21,401	22,741	1,340	6.3	12,056	12,246	190	1.6
Primary Families	50,967	56,472	5,505	10.8	15,816	15,444	−372	−2.4	8,621	8,092	−529	−6.1
Husband-Wife Family	43,717	57,471	3,754	8.6	12,478	11,783	−965	−7.6	6,783	5,970	−813	−12.0
Male Head (No Wife Present)	1,621	1,461	−160	−9.9	587	499	−88	−15.0	360	304	−56	−15.6
Female Head (No Husband Present)	5,629	7,540	1,911	33.9	2,480	3,161	681	27.5	1,478	1,817	339	22.9
Primary Individuals	12,480	17,669	5,189	41.6	5,584	7,298	1,714	30.7	3,435	4,155	720	21.0
Male	4,597	6,971	2,374	51.6	2,139	2,971	832	38.9	1,376	1,747	371	27.0
Female	7,883	10,698	2,815	35.7	3,445	4,327	882	25.6	2,059	2,408	349	16.9
TOTAL	100.0	100.0			100.0	100.0			100.0	100.0		
Primary Families	80.3	76.2			73.9	67.9			71.5	66.1		
Husband-Wife Family	68.9	64.2			59.6	51.8			56.3	48.8		
Male Head (No Wife Present)	2.6	2.0			2.7	2.2			3.0	2.5		
Female Head (No Husband Present)	8.9	10.2			11.6	13.9			12.3	14.8		
Primary Individuals	19.7	23.8			26.1	32.1			28.5	33.9		
Male	7.2	9.4			10.0	13.1			11.4	14.3		
Female	12.4	14.4			16.1	19.0			17.1	19.7		

Source: Center for Urban Policy Research Analysis of Data Presented in: U.S. Department of Commerce, Bureau of the Census, *Current Population Reports*, Special Studies P-23, No. 55, "Social and Economic Characteristics of the Metropolitan and Nonmetropolitan Population: 1977 and 1970," November 1978.

Central city populations, then, are increasingly dominated by household types which, as will be shown subsequently, are characterized by relatively low incomes, a major problem which cuts across racial partitions.

Race and Household Configuration

The decline in primary families is largely a white phenomenon, undoubtedly in part as a function of select migration. The whites who are increasing in number and proportion in the central city are largely in primary individual households. Indeed, husband-wife families declined both among whites and blacks in central cities with the former showing a loss of nearly a million, the latter approximately 150,000 (Exhibit 5). The only family type expanding in number within central cities among whites was female-headed (no husband present), with an increase slightly under 250,000. The faster growing incidence of this phenomenon among blacks, however, is indicated by the 432,000 increase in black female-headed (no husband present) families. Nearly 60 percent of the total growth of black households over the 1970-to-1977 period was in this format.

Thus, the white population of central cities is decreasingly that of primary families, increasingly that of single individuals. The sum of these produce a relatively minor increase in total household numbers. Among blacks there is an equivalent decline of husband-wife families to a level where they represent only 38.2 percent of total households—and are nearly matched by a female-headed (no husband present) 29 percent incidence—nearly triple that of white central city households. One out of three (33.0 percent) white households now is in the primary individual sector. The incidence among blacks is nearly as high at the three in ten level (29.7 percent).

The vigor of the shift in household formation in terms of the percentage of primary families headed by females is emphasized by Exhibit 6, which shows the ratios of such households in 1977 versus 1970. There is significant growth both for whites and for blacks; the level of absolute gain, however, in the latter group is nearly double that of the former. Indeed, in all central cities, the growth ratio for the seven years under consideration among blacks is at the 1.34-1.35 level.

By 1977 more than four in ten of all black primary families in central cities were headed by a female.

EXHIBIT 5

CENTRAL CITY HOUSEHOLD TYPE BY RACE: 1970 AND 1977

(Numbers in Thousands, 1970 Metropolitan Definition)

	WHITE		Change: 1970 to 1977		BLACK		Change: 1970 to 1977	
	1970	1977	Number	Percent	1970	1977	Number	Percent
TOTAL	17,254	17,712	458	2.7	3,833	4,566	733	19.1
Primary Families	12,665	11,870	−795	− 6.3	2,917	3,212	295	10.1
Husband-Wife Family	10,667	9,730	−937	− 8.8	1,891	1,744	−147	− 7.8
Male Head (No Wife Present)	439	340	− 99	−22.6	136	146	10	7.4
Female Head (No Husband Present)	1,559	1,800	241	15.5	890	1,322	432	48.5
Primary Individuals	4,589	5,842	1,253	27.3	916	1,354	438	47.8
Male	1,688	2,289	601	35.6	409	631	222	54.3
Female	2,901	3,553	652	22.5	507	723	216	42.6
TOTAL	100.0	100.0			100.0	100.0		
Primary Families	73.4	67.0			76.1	70.3		
Husband-Wife Family	61.8	54.9			49.3	38.2		
Male Head (No Wife Present)	2.5	1.9			3.5	3.2		
Female Head (No Husband Present)	9.0	10.2			23.2	29.0		
Primary Individuals	26.6	33.0			23.9	29.7		
Male	9.8	12.9			10.7	13.8		
Female	16.8	20.1			13.2	15.8		

Source: Center for Urban Policy Research Analysis of Data Presented in: U.S. Department of Commerce, Bureau of the Census, *Current Population Reports*, Special Studies P-23, No. 55, "Social and Economic Characteristics of the Metropolitan and Nonmetropolitan Population: 1977 and 1978," November 1978.

EXHIBIT 6

PERCENTAGE OF PRIMARY FAMILIES HEADED BY FEMALES, BY RACE AND TYPE OF RESIDENCE: 1970 AND 1977

(1970 Metropolitan Definition)

TYPE OF RESIDENCE	TOTAL (ALL RACES)			WHITE			BLACK		
	1970	1977	Ratio 1970-1977	1970	1977	Ratio 1970-1977	1970	1977	Ratio 1970-1977
U.S. Total	11.0	13.4	1.22	9.2	10.7	1.16	28.0	36.8	1.31
Metropolitan Areas	11.7	14.6	1.26	9.7	11.6	1.21	28.9	37.7	1.30
Central Cities	15.7	20.5	1.31	12.3	15.2	1.24	30.5	41.2	1.35
Suburban Areas	8.4	10.6	1.26	7.9	9.6	1.21	22.2	27.9	1.26
Central Cities in Metropolitan Areas of 1 million or more	17.1	22.5	1.32	13.1	16.0	1.22	30.8	41.7	1.35
Central Cities in Metropolitan Areas of less than 1 million	13.9	18.3	1.32	11.5	14.4	1.25	30.0	40.1	1.34

Note: Ratios computed for unrounded percentages.

Source: Center for Urban Policy Research Analysis of Data Presented in U.S. Department of Commerce, Bureau of the Census, *Current Population Reports*, Special Studies P-23, No. 55, "Social and Economic Characteristics of the Metropolitan and Nonmetropolitan Population: 1977 and 1970," November 1978.

Income and Family Configuration

There appears to be a significant relationship between low incomes and female-headed households. This holds true both for whites as well as blacks, but is much more compelling for the latter group. As shown in Exhibit 7, for example, all families in central cities in 1977 had money incomes of slightly under $14,000. Families with female heads, however, had incomes of less than half that, $6,658. For white families with female heads total money income was $7,914. For blacks it was an abysmally low $5,125. And these ratios are degenerating over time, when contrasted with equivalent data for suburban areas.

For every category shown, the ratio between central city and suburban incomes from 1970 to 1977 has declined sharply. All central city families, regardless of their configuration, have incomes which are not keeping pace with equivalent configurations in suburbia, as well as declining in absolute dollars over time.

Female-headed households in central cities have shown the most marked decline in real income over time. The selective migration of blacks to suburbia undoubtedly underlies, at least in part, the one substantial increment (and again these are data in constant dollars) of income accruing to families from 1970 to 1977: total black families in suburbia experienced an income gain of almost $1,300 from $10,745 in 1970 to $12,037 in 1977. The black income decline in the central city is clearly linked with the selective migration of husband/wife families and the residual dominance of female-headed households.

The Increasing Trauma of Rental Housing

In another context, reference has been made to the increasing problem of rental housing in central cities—the issues of delinquency and foreclosure, particularly in HUD held guaranteed mortgages.* Within this context, it is important to focus on the data shown in Exhibit 8, which shows median incomes of household types in central cities by race and tenure for 1973 and 1976. (These are not constant dollars.)

*See George Sternlieb and Robert W. Burchell, "Multifamily Housing Demand: 1975-2000." A Study prepared for the use of the Subcommittee on Priorities and Economy in Government of the Joint Economic Committee, Congress of the United States. (U.S. Government Printing Office, Washington D.C., 1978.)

EXHIBIT 7

TOTAL MONEY INCOME IN 1969 AND 1976
FAMILIES BY SEX, RACE, AND TYPE OF RESIDENCE
(in constant 1976 dollars, families as of March 1977 and April 1970)

	Central Cities	Suburban Areas	Ratio of Central City to Suburban
Total All Races			
All Families			
1970	$14,566	$17,160	.85
1977	13,952	17,101	.82
Families with Female Head			
1970	7,586	9,351	.81
1977	6,658	8,539	.78
White			
All Families			
1970	15,601	17,413	.90
1977	15,069	17,371	.87
Families with Female Head			
1970	9,014	9,842	.92
1977	7,914	8,985	.88
Black			
All Families			
1970	10,188	10,745	.95
1977	9,361	12,037	.78
Families with Female Head			
1970	5,494	5,425	1.01
1977	5,125	5,789	.89

Note: 1970 Metropolitan definition.

Source: Center for Urban Policy Research Analysis of Data Presented in U.S. Department of Commerce, Bureau of the Census, *Current Population Report*, Special Studies P-23, No. 55, "Social and Economic Characteristics of the Metropolitan and Nonmetropolitan Population: 1977 and 1970," November 1978.

Certainly there has been much more vigor of income growth among owners than holds true of renters, with the level of growth in the former triple that of the latter. And this holds true for blacks as well, but is much more extreme. Among the two or more person black households who are owners, incomes increased 21.2 percent. Despite the declining value of the dollar over time, black renters experienced only a 1.5 percent increase.

EXHIBIT 8

MEDIAN INCOME OF HOUSEHOLD TYPES IN CENTRAL CITIES BY RACE: 1973 AND 1976

(1970 Metropolitan Definition)

	TOTAL (ALL RACES)		Change: 1973-1976		Black		Change: 1973-1976	
	1973	1976	Number	Percent	1973	1976	Number	Percent
Owner Occupied								
2 or More Person Household	$12,900	$15,800	$2,900	22.5	$10,400	$12,600	$2,200	21.2
Male Head, Wife Present	13,600	17,000	3,400	25.6	11,700	14,700	3,000	25.6
Other Male Head	12,800	14,000	1,200	9.4	11,300	11,000	−300	− 2.7
Female Head	8,000	9,200	1,200	15.0	7,000	7,200	200	2.9
1 Person Households	4,400	5,900	1,500	34.1	3,900	4,100	200	5.1
Renter Occupied								
2 or More Person Household	$ 8,300	$ 8,800	$ 500	6.0	$ 6,500	$ 6,600	$ 100	1.5
Male Head, Wife Present	9,600	11,500	1,900	19.8	8,400	10,400	2,000	23.8
Other Male Head	8,300	8,200	−100	−1.2	5,900	7,900	2,000	33.9
Female Head	5,800	5,300	−500	−8.6	5,300	4,700	−600	−11.3
1 Person Households	4,600	5,500	900	19.6	3,500	4,400	900	25.7

Notes: 1. 1976 income is that received in 1975.
        2. 1973 income is that received in 1972.

Source: U.S. Department of Commerce, Bureau of the Census, *Annual Housing Survey,* 1973, 1976.

The latter ratio was very largely the result of a declining real income among renter families headed by females. For this category there was an absolute decline of 11.3 percent in incomes. And this obviously would be the more accentuated if it were in constant dollars.

Increasingly the central city is the focal point of the poor. Selective migration, and limited economic opportunites for advancement have produced this result.** It is mirrored in the next set of data to be presented here—that on poverty status.

Poverty Status

Nationally poverty is declining in incidence. In the 1970-to-1977 period under consideration, there was a decline of 2.2 million persons who met the poverty criteria. Exhibit 9 presents the data on individuals by family status who fell below the poverty level.

Every category was reduced except for females who were heads of families; in this group there was an absolute increase of 710,000 individuals, nearly 40 percent. Indeed almost a third of all females who head families fall into the poverty category.

The basic problem is much more clearly focused when the analysis is limited to central cities as shown in Exhibit 10. Unlike the national pattern, there is an *absolute* increase in the number of persons in central cities who fall below the poverty line. While the total central city population declined by 4.6 percent, those in poverty status increased by 2.5 percent. This occurred despite a decline in poverty status among males who headed families and their wives. This gain was completely obliterated—and practically all of the total loss accounted for—by the increase in females who headed families—and their children as well. In central cities female family heads who were under the poverty line increased by 44.7 percent over the seven-year period. By 1977, 37.1 percent of such individuals were below the poverty line.

Male-headed families and wives are climbing out of poverty. Female-headed families increasingly are subjected to all of its limitations and strictures.

**See analysis in : George Sternlieb and James W. Hughes, "The Wilting of the Metropolis," Hearings before the Committee on Banking, Currency, and Housing, U.S. House of Representatives, *Toward a National Urban Policy* (U.S. Government Printing Office, Washington, D.C., 1977).

EXHIBIT 9

POVERTY STATUS IN 1976 AND 1969, PERSONS BY FAMILY STATUS, U.S. TOTAL ALL RACES[1]

(Numbers in Thousands)

Family Status	1970	1977	Change: 1970 to 1977		Percent Below Poverty Level	
			Number	Percent	1970	1977
All Persons	27,204	24,975	−2,229	− 8.2	13.8	11.8
In Families	21,250	19,632	−1,618	− 7.6	11.7	10.3
Head	5,500	5,311	− 189	− 3.4	10.8	9.4
Male	3,667	2,768	− 899	−24.9	8.1	5.6
Female	1,833	2,543	710			
Wives	3,438	2,606	− 832	−24.2	7.9	5.5
Related Children under 18 years	10,560	10,081	− 479	− 4.5	15.3	15.8
Other Family Members	1,752	1,634	− 118	− 6.7	9.8	7.1
Unrelated Individuals	5,954	5,344	− 610	−10.2	37.1	24.9
Male	1,913	1,787	− 126	− 6.6	29.9	19.7
Female	4,041	3,557	− 484	−12.0	41.9	28.7

Notes: 1. Families and unrelated individuals as of March 1977 and April 1970. Excludes unrelated individuals under 14 years old, members of the Armed Forces living in barracks and college students in dormitories.

Source: Center for Urban Policy Research Analysis of Data Presented in: U.S. Department of Commerce, Bureau of the Census, *Current Population Reports*, Special Studies, P-23, No. 55, "Social and Economic Characteristics of the Metropolitan and Nonmetropolitan Population: 1977 and 1970," November 1978.

EXHIBIT 10

POVERTY STATUS IN 1976 AND 1969, PERSONS BY FAMILY STATUS, CENTRAL CITIES, ALL RACES [1]

(Numbers in Thousands)

Family Status	1970	1977	Change: 1970 to 1977		Percent Below Poverty Level	
			Number	Percent	1970	1977
All Persons	9,247	9,482	235	2.5	14.9	15.8
In Families	6,852	7,302	450	6.6	12.5	14.3
Head	1,755	1,961	206	11.7	11.1	12.6
Male	928	764	−164	−17.6	7.0	6.2
Female	827	1,197	370	44.7	33.5	37.1
Wives	861	718	−143	−16.6	6.7	6.1
Related Children under 18 years	3,692	4,017	325	8.8	18.4	23.9
Other Family Members	544	606	62	11.4	8.7	8.8
Unrelated Individuals	2,396	2,180	−216	− 9.0	33.1	24.6
Male	801	796	− 5	− 0.6	27.1	20.6
Female	1,594	1,384	−210	−13.2	37.3	27.7

Notes: 1. Families and unrelated individuals as of March 1977 and April 1970. Excludes unrelated individuals under 14 years old, members of the Armed Forces living in barracks and college students in dormitories.

Source: Center for Urban Policy Research Analysis of Data Presented in: U.S. Department of Commerce, Bureau of the Census, *Current Population Reports*, Special Studies, P-23, No. 55, "Social and Economic Characteristics of the Metropolitan and Nonmetropolitan Population: 1977 and 1970," November 1978.

The incidence of such groups, in turn, has strikingly impacted the fiscal vigor of central cities—while increasing the stress on the social services provided to them. And, this is increasingly a problem which is impacting the black citizens of central cities. As shown in Exhibit 11, the number of black persons in families in poverty status in central cities grew by more than one in nine (10.9 percent) from 1970 to 1977. Among unrelated individuals, there was an increase of one in six (17.7 percent). While there was a significant reduction of male heads and wives in poverty, it was more than overcome by the single largest poverty status growth group—that of female heads of families, which increased by nearly a quarter of a million (57.1 percent).

By 1977 more than half (51.1 percent) of the black females who headed households were below the poverty line. In turn, they substantially accounted for the 42.1 percent of all black related children under 18 years within families who also met the poverty designation.

The urban crisis is not over—it is rather entering on its most fearful challenge. The demographic shifts within our society have left major urban areas increasingly the focal point for the distressed—not merely the impoverished, but the increasingly inpoverished. A thin facade of office structures, of swinging new groups, distracts the eye from the functional reality.

The Aggregate Impact

In Exhibit 12, data are shown indicating the personal income loss in central cities due to net migration from 1970 to 1974, and 1975 to 1977. Whether it is families or unrelated individuals the pattern is similar. The more affluent are leaving, the newcomers are less well endowed fiscally. From 1970 to 1974 there was a reduction in aggregate resident income within central cities of $29.6 billion due to migration. In the two years from 1975 to 1977, the equivalent figure was a loss of $18 billion.

In Exhibit 13, these data have been converted into constant dollars (interpolating for 1974 to 1975, for which data are not available). This indicates an average annual net change (between 1970 and 1977) in 1976 dollars of $9.3 billion. Since these data are cumulative, by 1977 there has been a loss, in 1976 dollars, of $64.8 billion. So in the latter year, if no migration had occurred, $64.8 billion more in annual incomes would have accrued to central city households than was actually received.

EXHIBIT 11
POVERTY STATUS IN 1976 AND 1969, PERSONS BY FAMILY STATUS, CENTRAL CITIES, BLACKS[1]

(Numbers in Thousands)

Family Status	1970	1977	Change: 1970 to 1977		Percent Below Poverty Level	
			Number	Percent	1970	1977
All Persons	3,726	4,167	441	11.8	29.1	31.0
In Families	3,196	3,543	347	10.9	27.7	30.2
Head	725	908	183	25.2	24.9	28.0
Male	290	223	−67	−23.1	14.3	11.7
Female	436	685	249	57.1	49.1	51.1
Wives	260	194	−66	−25.3	13.9	11.3
Related Children under 18 years	1,940	2,081	141	7.3	36.5	42.1
Other Family Members	271	360	89	32.8	18.9	19.8
Unrelated Individuals	530	624	94	17.7	41.7	36.4
Male	197	274	77	39.1	32.6	31.6
Female	333	350	17	5.1	50.0	41.4

Notes: 1. Families and unrelated individuals as of March 1977 and April 1970. Excludes unrelated individuals under 14 years old, members of the Armed Forces living in barracks and college students in dormitories.

Source: Center for Urban Policy Research Analysis of Data Presented in: U.S. Department of Commerce, Bureau of the Census, *Current Population Reports*, Special Studies, P-23, No. 55, "Social and Economic Characteristics of the Metropolitan and Nonmetropolitan Population: 1977 and 1970," November 1978.

EXHIBIT 12

INCOME LOSSES IN CENTRAL CITIES DUE TO NET MIGRATION: 1970 TO 1974 AND 1975 TO 1977

(1970 Metropolitan Definition)

Income in 1973 of Families and Unrelated Individuals 14 Years Old and Over Who Migrated to and From Central Cities Between 1970 and 1974.

Subject	Living in Cities in 1970	Moved Out of Cities Between 1970 and 1974	Moved Out of Cities Between 1970 and 1974	Net Change Between 1970 and 1974
Families (thousands)	16,823	3,363	1,563	− 1,800
Mean Income (Dollars)	$13,349	$14,169	$12,864	−$1,305[1]
Aggregate Income (billions of dollars)	$ 224.6	$ 47.7	$ 20.1	− 27.6
Unrelated Individuals (thousands)	6,975	1,066	926	− 140
Mean Income (dollars)	$ 6,143	$ 7,099	$ 6,092	−$1,007[1]
Aggregate Income (billions of dollars)	$ 42.8	$ 7.6	$ 5.6	−$ 2.0

Income in 1976 of Families and Unrelated Individuals 14 Years Old and Over Who Migrated to and From Central Cities Between 1975 and 1977.

Subject	Living in Cities in 1970	Move Out of Cities Between 1970 and 1974	Moved Out of Cities Between 1970 and 1974	Net Change Between 1970 and 1974
Families (thousands)	16,359	2,003	985	− 1,018
Mean Income (dollars)	$16,120	$15,986	$14,992	−$ 994[1]
Aggregate Income (billions of dollars)	$ 263.7	$ 32.0	$ 14.8	−$ 17.2
Unrelated Individuals (thousands)	8,812	994	940	− 54
Mean Income (dollars)	$ 7,388	$ 8,055	$ 7,612	−$ 443[1]
Aggregate Income (billions of dollars)	$ 65.1	$ 8.0	$ 7.2	−$ 0.8

Note: 1. Simple unweighted difference.

Source: U.S. Department of Commerce, Bureau of the Census, *Current Population Reports*, Special Studies P-23, No. 55, "Social and Economic Characteristics of the Metropolitan and Nonmetropolitan Population: 1974 and 1970," September 1975.

EXHIBIT 13

DERIVATION OF INCOME LOSSES (1976 DOLLARS)
IN CENTRAL CITIES DUE TO MIGRATION:
1970 TO 1977
(1970 Metropolitan Definition)

Average Annual Net Change, 1970 to 1974:	−$7.4 billion (1973 dollars)[1]
Ratio of 1976 to 1973 Consumer Price Index	$\dfrac{170.5}{133.1} = 1.28$ [2]
Average Annual Net Change, 1970 to 1974	−$9.4 billion (1976 dollars)[3]
Average Annual Net Change, 1975 to 1977	−$9.0 billion (1976 dollars)[4]
Net Change, 1974 to 1975	−$9.2 billion (1976 dollars)[5]
Total Change: 1970 to 1977	−$64.8 billion (1976 dollars)[6]
Average Annual Net Change: 1970 to 1977	−$9.3 billion (1976 dollars)[7]

Notes: 1. Derived from Exhibit 12.
                    2. U.S. Bureau of Labor Statistics, *Monthly Labor Review.*
                    3. 1.28 x $7.4 billion = $9.4 billion.
                    4. Derived from Exhibit 12.
                    5. Mean of annual averages of two periods.
                    6. Sum of annual averages of all periods.
                    7. −$64.8 billion ÷ 7 years = −$9.3 billion.

Source: CUPR Analysis.

The ramifications of these losses are of very significant magnitude. If we were to use the conventional rule-of-thumb of 25 percent of income alloted to rent, this represents a departure in excess of $16 billion. If we were to further view this decline in rent paying capacity in terms of its impact on housing values, the results are evident. Assume that an efficient, well managed apartment house sells for five times its gross rent roll: the loss of $16 billion in rent paying capacity translates into a $80 billion reduction in residential real estate values—and with it a proportionate decline in municipal income derived from real property taxation. There are equivalent implications, which need little elaboration, on basic retailing and service industries as well. The pattern of empty stores, of old fading central business districts, and of vacated downtown department stores, is a reflection of this declining residential income base.

As best as we can analyze the data, this has been a sustained dynamic process with little sign of abatement. While much has been made of the relatively few cases of middle-class stabilization and/or return to the city—i.e., the "Capital Hill" phenomena and the like—as yet these are relatively trivial. A witness to the phenomenon is the accompanying data in Exhibit 14 on the median annual income of families and individuals (in constant dollars) for renter households in the boroughs of New York City. The decline since 1969 in all cases has been most substantial, with the overall city median declining from $6,500 to $4,800 over the 1969-to-1977 period. This pattern was largely paralleled from 1974 to 1977, with losses of one-seventh of total income in the brief three-year period. The only exception is a relatively minor 1.9 percent increase (again in constant dollars) in Manhattan. A new town may be evolving intown—the gentrified neighborhood—but it is a relatively slender ray of light, much too limited to support and bring back with it the aging entities that we call central cities.

Conclusion

The future implications of the poverty concentrations mirrored in the data presented earlier are far from precisely definable at this writing. Clearly, in the past, we have had a demographic equivalent of Gresham's Law—the presence of the poor tends to oust the more fortunate in our society. The decline in housing buying power of middle America that is clearly occurring may well cause the aborting of this phenomenon in the future. The decade of the 1970s however, has given little promise of mass revival in the major central cities.

EXHIBIT 14

MEDIAN ANNUAL INCOME OF FAMILIES AND INDIVIDUALS, BY BOROUGH, IN CONSTANT (1967) DOLLARS, FOR RENTER HOUSEHOLDS, NEW YORK CITY, 1964, 1967, 1969, 1974 AND 1977

Characteristics	1964	1967	1969	1974	1977	Percent Change 1974 to 1977
Total New York City	$5,900	$6,000	$6,500	$5,400	$4,800	−11.1%
Borough						
Bronx	$5,600	$5,700	$6,000	$4,700	$4,000	−14.9%
Brooklyn	5,800	5,800	6,000	4,900	4,200	−14.3
Manhattan	5,500	5,600	6,100	5,400	5,500	+ 1.9
Queens	7,100	7,500	8,100	7,000	5,800	−17.1
Richmond	7,100	6,800	7,700	7,100	6,100	−14.1

Source: Peter Marcuse, *Rental Housing in the City of New York* (New York: Housing and Development Administration, 1979).

Back to the Central City: Myths and Realities

George Sternlieb
James W. Hughes

Introduction

As the decade of the 1980s opens, and with a new national energy policy soon to be operationalized, it is an appropriate time for an overview on the potential futures of the central city. This is the subject that has been characterized more by wishful thinking—erecting positive but hazy future abstractions—on the one hand, and despair—invoking ominous forebodings—on the other, than by factual analysis. While past and current trendlines *have been* and *are* ominous, there are recurrent rumors and tentative, but visible stirrings of a more positive note—of an urban middle-class resurgence, of areas revitalized through brownstoning, and of obsolete industrial lofts converted suddenly into residential space. All this is capsulized by the new urban catch phrase "gentrification," making long somnolent areas live once again.

The vacating of an aging manufacturing infrastructure, symbolized by empty multifloored industrial parcels in cities such as New York

153

and Philadelphia, have to some observers signalled the end of the functional role of the city in manufacturing—the termination of the historic linkage between manufacting activity and urban location. Yet the rise of new office facilities and the growth of educational, cultural and service establishments have been viewed as potential offsets at the very least, and possibly, the beginnings of new and ever greater activity.

The overall dynamics at work are difficult to quantify. Complex crosscurrents are obscured by major tides such as the net out-migration of population from metropolitan areas as captured by standardized data accounts. This makes it difficult to observe any detailed subpopulation inmigration. Moreover, the serious observer is frequently distracted by the surrogates of population growth and activity demand—the rise of new bricks and mortar on the urban landscape, or its converse, the shattered remnants of residential and commercial abandonment. They are observable and frequently detailed in popular media. Underlying them, however, is a requirement for statistical rather than anecdotal baselines.

This article brings together available statistical data for speculation on the urban future. The primary focus is on demographic trends and their policy implications. The future demand for central city transportation is a function of its resident population (and its reflection in housing demand), of non-resident workers (particularly as linked to employment change), and last but far from least, non-residents attracted to the city for a variety of non-job related purposes. Available data sources are currently much more definitive for the first of these elements, somewhat less for the second, and all too inadequate for the last. Within these limitations however, a reasonably clear-cut profile is emerging.

A Demographic Overview

The nation's central cities contribute to and are vitally affected by demographic swings characterizing late 20th-century America.[1] The intersection of demographic forces with the basic attributes of central cities will, to a large extent, define the future potential of urban areas. To secure an appropriate baseline for analysis, a brief synopsis of the dynamics in effect is useful; the following summary also interjects a few preliminary observations related to housing demand, as well as some initial commentary on the implications for central cities.

DECELERATING POPULATION GROWTH

The rate of population growth in the United States over the past twenty-five years has decelerated markedly, a consequence of sustained fertility rate declines. As a result, migration is thrust into a more prominent role in population change. High rates of fertility tend to justify and confirm the vitality of established places, serving to mask the realities of declining areas or at least to obscure the necessity of acknowledging them. Central cities are now facing the harsh realities of this phenomenon. The net natural population increase is not of sufficient magnitude to counterbalance out-migration losses.

Variations of fertility in the past—steady reductions in the first four decades of this century, a brief but powerful rise in the ensuing twenty years, and abrupt declines thereafter (post-1960)—have been etched deeply in the nation's age structure contours.

Characteristic Age Structure. The major residual is the baby boom generation, whose presence will be marked throughout the remainder of this century by its bulging age cohorts. In the 1970-to-1985 period, its presence has been, and will be, evidenced within the 25-to-44 years-of-age sectors. Can the central city attract this growth cohort?

A second impact is being made by the progeny of the baby bust, foreordained to travel in the wake of the baby boom—an abrupt indentation in the age structure profile immediately contiguous to the baby boom bulge. At present, the leading edge of the bust is entering the 18-to-24 years-of-age sector.

Age Structure Influences. The baby boom generation provides a base for a continuing demand and market target, if only by virtue of its sheer size parameters. Sharply reduced population growth, however, has introduced the concept of shrinkage in future projections, and often quite painfully.

The central city both reflects and contributes to these age structure dynamics. Even within a context of overall decline there are distinct age sectors characterized by growth.

CHANGING HOUSEHOLD FORMATIONS

Housing comprises one of the more visible symbols of central cities' trying to reassert themselves. Hence it is important to stress that demand for shelter is not simply a consequence of population per se; the translation of population into household quanta is the essentail linkage. The dynamics in effect have tended to amplify the housing ramifications of the baby boom and may serve to partially mitigate the potentially ominous consequences of a maturing baby bust.

Changing Household Numbers. The size of America's households has been marked by unabated shrinkage, with the process showing signs of acceleration rather than slowing. The phenomenon is such as to give the impression that household growth is driving a rapid expansion of the housing inventory. However, housing availability may be considered a facilitator, permitting the working out of the process of household evolution.

In any case, areas of population or decline or stability may still experience a net growth of households, establishing continued pressures for housing accommodations beyond that implied by population alone.

This transformation in household size and number is marked by two powerful forces. Most obvious is the role of the low levels of fertility—many households are simply characterized by fewer children. But equally significant is the process of changing household configuration:

Changing Household Configuration. The slowest growing household sector comprises husband-wife families (families are defined as two or more related individuals); the fastest growing sectors are nonfamily households—one-person configurations and those composed of two or more unrelated individuals—as well as female-headed families. What were once considered "atypical" households are gaining increased presence; the fabled modular configuration (husband-wife-child-rearing units) is declining in relative importance.

A process of fragmentation as well as fertility declines is thus generating an evolving profile of household types. Large households (seven persons or more) are virtually disappearing. The classic urban housing problem of sheltering large families, of limited economic means, is on the verge of becoming a historical artifact.

Smaller households with fewer offspring tend not to be constrained to specialized housing environments, such as suburban, child-oriented domains. The central city potential share (or penetration) of the market is enhanced by its vitality as a workplace, as well as the degree to which its social and physical milieu is attractive to the baby boom generation.

Increasing Female Participation in Labor Force. Accompanying the shifts in household configuration has been the escalating rate of female labor force participation. This is one of the underlying economic forces facilitating the very process of household form-ation, manifesting itself both in female-headed households and two-worker families. In the latter context, job availability for both spouses may well supplant childbearing environments within the residentail decisionmaking process.

With these nationwide tendencies as a backdrop, the settings of central city population change, both in regional and metropolitan contexts, is the first subject examined. Basic central city parameters will then be analyzed in some detail.

Synthesis: Demographic, Metropolitan and Regional

Central city population trends are enveloped within a matrix comprising a number of causal dimensions—demographic, regional and metropolitan-nonmetropolitan.[2] The demographic sector is marked by the increasing importance of migration, compared to net natural increase, as a determinant of local growth. The regional axis is evidenced by high growth rates in the South and West, and a relative stagnancy in the aging Northeast and North Central states. The metropolitan partition shows a marked resurgence of non-metropolitan territories, aborting a trendline that had been in effect for over half a century. Data in Exhibit 1 encompass the broader attributes of these three phenomena.

POPULATION CHANGE DETERMINANTS

For the United States as a whole, deceleration of population growth is gauged by an average annual compound growth rate in the 1970-to-1977 period (0.9 percent) significantly less than that (1.3 percent) of the preceding ten years from 1960 to 1970. The major determinant of population change in this context is the decline in net natural population increase (births minus deaths) over the two periods indicated, while net migration held relatively constant. And it is the increasing relative importance of the latter that translates into spatial shifts, one dimension of which centers on metropolitan clusters.

Metropolitan Population Changes. The decade of the 1960s was one in which the relative concentration of America's population in metropolitan areas probably reached its pinnacle. While metropolitan areas, for example, experienced average annual growth increments of 1.6 percent, nonmetropolitan counties lagged considerably (0.4 percent). Within the metropolitan average growth increment, there was only minor variation as a function of size, with growth rates of the largest metropolitan areas (over 3 million people) generally comparable to metropolitan areas in total. Within nonmetropolitan counties, those increasing in population at the most rapid rate typically were closest to metropolitan centers, as evidenced by the commutation profile indicated in Exhibit 1.

Population Change in Nonmetropolitan Areas. When the focus shifts to the 1970-to-1977 period, an abrupt change in trendline appears. The annual growth rate of nonmetropolitan counties (1.2 percent) experienced a remarkable upswing to almost twice the level characterizing metropolitan areas (0.7 percent). Within the latter category, it was the largest metropolitan areas (over 3 million people) that were suddenly transformed into virtual no growth contexts, with a barely discernable growth of 0.1 percent per year. While counties that have the heaviest incidence of commuting to more concentrated areas were at the forefront of the nonmetropolitan resurgence, their growth rates were nearly matched by noncontiguous areas. Even nonmetropolitan counties in which less than 3 percent of workers commuted to metropolitan areas secured gains at ten times the rate of the previous decade.

NET MIGRATION AS A CRITERION

Even more salient are the net migration data of Exhibit 1. Migration is a telling criterion of location shift by choice, indexing the locational preferences of Americans. Population gains secured via migration are, in effect, immediate gains of economic markets; population growth through net natural increase does not directly produce job holders, homebuyers, or immediate fare payers, at least within short-run contexts. Migrational patterns, therefore, can be viewed as signals of market shifts, pointing to locations of eventual economic vacation (net out-migration) or of expanding support thresholds (net in-migration).

The shifting patterns in this regard are reasonably clear-cut. From 1960 to 1970, nonmetropolitan counties lost considerable population

EXHIBIT 1

POPULATION AND COMPONENTS OF CHANGE FOR SELECTED GROUPS OF METROPOLITAN AND NONMETROPOLITAN COUNTIES: 1960, 1970, AND 1977

(Numbers in Thousands)

| | Population | | | Average Annual Percent Change[1] | | | | | |
| | | | | Population | | Natural Increase | | Net Migration | |
Metropolitan areas, nonmetropolitan counties, and regions	July 1, 1977 (provisional estimate)	April 1 1970 (Census)[2]	April 1 1960 (Census)[3]	1970 to 1977	1960 to 1970	1970 to 1977	1960 to 1970	1970 to 1977	1960 to 1970
United States	216,351	203,305	179,311	0.9	1.3	0.7	1.1	0.2	0.2
Metropolitan[4]	158,550	150,291	128,328	0.7	1.6	0.7	1.1	0.1	0.5
Over 3,000,000	53,260	52,864	45,766	0.1	1.4	0.6	1.0	−0.5	0.4
1,000,000 to 3,000,000	42,035	39,341	32,403	0.9	1.9	0.7	1.2	0.3	0.8
500,000 to 1,000,000	24,088	22,548	19,386	0.9	1.5	0.7	1.2	0.2	0.4
250,000 to 500,000	20,051	18,262	15,838	1.3	1.4	0.8	1.2	0.5	0.2
Less than 250,000	19,116	17,276	14,935	1.4	1.5	0.8	1.2	0.6	0.3
Nonmetropolitan counties by commuting to metropolitan areas[5]	57,802	53,014	50,982	1.2	0.4	0.6	0.9	0.6	−0.6
20 percent or more	4,549	4,013	3,663	1.7	0.9	0.5	0.8	1.2	0.1
10 to 19 percent	10,039	9,209	8,607	1.2	0.7	0.5	0.8	0.7	−0.2
3 to 9 percent	14,796	13,644	12,944	1.1	0.5	0.6	0.9	0.5	−0.4
Less than 3 percent	28,418	26,148	25,768	1.1	0.1	0.6	1.0	0.5	−0.9

EXHIBIT 1 (CONTINUED)

Northeast	49,299	49,061	44,678	0.1	0.9	0.4	0.9	-0.3	0.1
Metropolitan	42,140	42,481	38,609	-0.1	1.0	0.4	0.9	-0.5	0.1
Nonmetropolitan	7,159	6,580	6,069	1.2	0.8	0.4	0.8	0.8	–
North Central	47,941	56,593	51,619	0.3	0.9	0.6	1.0	-0.3	-0.1
Metropolitan	40,221	39,661	35,073	0.2	1.2	0.7	1.2	-0.5	0.1
Nonmetropolitan	17,719	16,932	16,546	0.6	0.2	0.4	0.8	0.2	-0.6
South	69,849	62,813	54,961	1.5	1.3	0.8	1.2	0.7	0.2
Metropolitan	44,907	40,032	32,755	1.6	2.0	0.8	1.3	0.8	0.8
Nonmetropolitan	24,942	22,782	22,206	1.2	0.3	0.6	1.0	0.6	-0.8
West	39,263	34,838	28,053	1.6	2.2	0.9	1.3	0.8	1.0
Metropolitan	31,281	28,118	21,891	1.5	2.5	0.8	1.3	0.7	1.3
Nonmetropolitan	7,981	6,720	6,162	2.4	0.9	1.0	1.2	1.5	-0.4

Notes:

1. Based on the method of exponential change.
2. Includes officially recognized corrections to 1970 census counts through 1976.
3. Adjusted to exclude 12,520 persons erroneously reported in Fairfax County, Va. (Washington, D.C.–Md.–Va. SMSA).
4. Standard Metropolitan Statistical Areas (SMSAs) or, where defined, Standard Consolidated Statistical Areas (SCSAs) and county equivalents of SMSAs in New England (NECMAs); as defined by the Office of Federal Statistical Policy and Standards, Dec. 31, 1977.
5. Classification based on 1970 census data on percent of workers reporting place of work who commuted to metropolitan territory as defined in 1977 (see footnote 4). Of the total 2,455 nonmetropolitan counties, the four groups specified included 178, 331, 479 and 1,467 counties, respectively.

Source: U.S. Bureau of the Census, *Current Population Reports,* Series P-20, No. 336, "Population Profile of the United States: 1978." U.S. Government Printing Office, Washington, D.C., 1979.

through out-migration to areas of greater concentration—the metropolitan nodes. The pattern was most accentuated in those areas in which commuting to the latter was the least significant. In contrast, major metropolitan areas benefited from net in-migration. This period may well have represented the terminal point in the shift of population from the land as a function of the final stages of the agricultural revolution.

Implications for Transportation. The reality documented by the 1970-to-1977 data has rendered obsolete long held spatial conventions. The migration ledgers of metropolitan areas in total were in virtual balance. However, the aggregate totals mask the growing variation as a function of size. While larger metropolitan formations experienced either net out-migration or diminished levels of in-migration, the smaller metropoli (under 500,000 people) actually experienced positive migration gains. Concurrently, nonmetropolitan areas were transformed from origins to destinations in the overall migration process, with the scale of the transition largely correlated with the proportion of workers in the non-metropolitan region who commute to metropolitan areas.

It is clear that the nation has shifted to a new phase of growth as the decade of the 1970 reaches its end. The emerging growth poles are nonmetropolitan areas and smaller metropolitan places. Certainly, part of the nonmetropolitan phenomena may be subsumed under the label of exurbanization. One can view this process as merely a continuance of the dispersion from the core city, first to suburbia and subsequently to more peripheral patterns of settlement. From a transportation perspective, however, given the scale of processes at work, there are a number of issues that are raised. Evident among a wide spectrum of implications is the impact of greater spatial distance on non-journey-to-work trips to the central core.

The central city's pulling power can be interpreted as a function of the frictions inherent in transportation versus the unique lures that are available in the city center. To the degree that the data on spatial diffusion suggests longer trips, in the absence of new transportation facilitators, clearly frictions are increased. Secondly, as population expands further from historic population concentrations, it reaches critical mass, providing the threshold for alternative developments competitive to central city attractions. Indeed this may well intensify that which has already occurred in terms of regional suburban shopping centers, multi-cinema units, large-scale suburban hospitals, and the like. Recent attention on peripheral transportation and on the growth and impact of circumferential highways, is merely a reflection of the thickening of the population concentration in areas adjacent and contiguous to metropolitan regions. Concurrently, however, there is, or will be, an escalation of transportation demands by the newly burgeoning noncontiguous areas (defined as counties in which less than 10 percent of the population commutes to a metropolitan area).

It is also evident from the data shown here that the largest metropolitan areas—those that have the greatest absolute potential for intensive mass transportation—also have shown the least vigorous growth. At least through 1977, the smaller and more dispersed the metropolitan concentration, the greater the trendline of growth.

Regional Population Variance. Changing regional population parameters intersect the above phenomena and generate an additional axis of variation (See Exhibit 1). The Northeast and North Central Region shifted to a net out-migration position in the 1970s with declining net natural increase just sufficient in magnitude to maintain overall population stability. The South, in contrast, secured sharp gains both in migration and total population, while the West retained its position as regional growth leader, although it failed to replicate its level of performance in the 1960s.

Within this context, the metropolitan areas of the Northeast in the 1970s lost population while those of the North Central Region are rapidly approaching stability in size. Only in the South and West are there substantial positive annual growth rates—in part perhaps as a function of annexation that may obscure the basic centrifugal forces at work even in those regions.

The Central City

Within the evolving pattern of metropolitan and regional dynamics, there is another relatively recent occurrence—the absolute population decline in central cities. In the decade of the 1960s, when public attention on the "urban crisis" peaked, the central cities (in total) of the United States still experienced overall population growth. As other "crises" have come to dominate the national consciousness, central cities have quietly shifted to new phases of decline. Data relevant to this phenomenon are presented in Exhibit 2.

EXHIBIT 2

POPULATION BY PLACE OF RESIDENCE: 1970 AND 1977

(Numbers in thousands, 1970 metropolitan definition)

	1970	1977	Change: 1970 to 1977		Percent Distribution	
			Number	Percent	1970	1977
U.S. Total	199,819	212,566	12,747	6.4	100.0	100.0
Metropolitan Areas	137,058	143,107	6,049	4.4	68.6	67.3
Central Cities	62,876	59,993	− 2,883	− 4.6	31.5	28.2
Suburban Areas	74,182	83,144	8,932	12.0	37.1	39.1
Nonmetropolitan Areas	62,761	69,459	6,698	10.7	31.4	32.7
Central Cities in Metropolitan Areas of 1 Million or More	34,322	31,898	− 2,424	− 7.1	17.2	15.0
Central Cities in Metropolitan Areas of Less than 1 million	28,554	28,095	− 459	− 1.6	14.3	13.2

Notes: The metropolitan and nonmetropolitan totals differs from Exhibit 1 due to different date of metropolitan delineation (Exhibit 1, 1977; Exhibit 2, 1970).

Source: Center for Urban Policy Research Analysis of Data Presented in: U.S. Department of Commerce, Bureau of the Census, *Current Population Reports*, Special Studies P-23, No. 55, "Social and Economic Characteristics of the Metropolitan and Nonmetropolitan Population: 1977 and 1970," November, 1978.

SHRINKING POPULATION AND SHIFTING IMPORTANCE

Central cities in the United States experienced a population loss of nearly 2.9 million people (4.6 percent) over the 1970-to-1977 period.[3] Suburban areas over the same time interval increased by nearly 9 million people or 12 percent. It is striking to note that nonmetropolitan areas, which in 1970 had a population comparable in magnitude to that of central cities, by 1977 exceeded the latter by nearly 10 million individuals.

The population loss of central cities was concentrated within major metropolitan areas, relatively slow-growth contexts. But it was far from exclusive to that domian. Central cities in smaller, faster growing metropolitan areas also were afflicted with population declines.

The shifting importance of the central city within the profile of residence places between 1970 and 1977 is revealed by the percentage distributions of Exhibit 2. By 1977 central cities as a whole included only 28.2 percent of the nation's population. Seven years before, they had accounted for 31.5 percent.

Despite media attention lavished on examples of the return to the central city by various population subgroups such as the middle class, and despite some fear on the part of minority groups, as well as some representatives of government, on the displacement impact as a result of such instances of gentrification, the documented statistical profiles appear to evidence a different reality—one of increasing population deconcentration. But further analysis is required of the constituent sectors of this population in order to secure more appropriate insights.

AGE STRUCTURE SHIFTS

The surge in births in the aftermath of World War II took place as its progenitors fled the central cities to the then unquestioned lures of suburbia. Paradoxically, it is now the maturing baby boom cohorts and their residential choices that will shape the central city of the 1980s.

Nationally, the baby boom clustered in the 18-to-35 years-of-age sectors during the 1970s. Its impact within central cities and suburbs is highlighted in the data of Exhibit 3, which indicates age structure patterns of those two spatial constructs for 1970 and 1977. Within the context of overall population decline, central cities have partaken, though to a lesser degree, in the national baby boom surge, reflecting a strong growth component in the 25-to-34 years-of-age sector.[4]

EXHIBIT 3

POPULATION, BY AGE FOR CENTRAL CITIES AND SUBURBAN AREAS: 1977 AND 1970 (NUMBERS IN THOUSANDS, 1970 METROPOLITAN DEFINITION)

	Central Cities		Suburban Areas		Percent Change 1970 to 1977	
	1977	1970	1977	1970	Central Cities	Suburban areas
Total	59,993	62,876	83,114	74,182	− 4.6	12.0
Under 14 years	12,705	15,887	18,887	21,009	−20.0	−10.1
14 to 17 years	4,273	4,506	6,730	6,114	− 5.2	10.1
18 to 24 years	8,304	7,779	10,553	7,659	6.7	37.8
25 to 34 years	9,367	7,855	13,148	9,532	19.2	37.9
35 to 44 years	5,960	6,802	9,831	9,242	−12.4	6.4
45 to 64 years	12,542	13,407	16,961	14,922	− 6.5	13.7
65 years and over	6,842	6,640	7,004	5,704	3.0	22.8

Source: Center for Urban Policy Research Analysis of Data Presented in: U.S. Department of Commerce, Bureau of the Census, *Current Population Reports*, Special Studies P-23, No. 55, "Social and Economic Characteristics of the Metropolitan and Nonmetropolitan Population: 1977 and 1970," November, 1978.

Can the central city hold its youthful adult population? Or will the pattern of migration that seemingly has swept the ranks of those within the 35-to-64 years-of-age range limit its future? It is important to note that the current census forecast for 1978 to 1985 indicates that the greatest level of population growth to be in the 25-to-44 years-of-age sector. The gradual aging of the baby boom will produce a net increment of nearly 13 million people within this age span. Can the city secure more penetration of this growth sector adequate to sustain its future? Much of the demand and future utilization of transportation within central cities is dependent on the answer.

CENTRAL CITY HOUSEHOLDS

Age structure segmentation reveals only one link in the complex chain of demographic shifts. Another phenomenon of relevance to the central city is the attentuation of the nation's population into an expanded format of household types. As a result of declining fertility and increasing fragmentation, the number of households are expanding at a rate much faster than the overall population base. The implications of this sustained process for central cities are depicted in the data in Exhibit 4.

While the nation's central cities lost 2.8 million people (−4.6 percent) between 1970 and 1977, they concurrently secured a 6.3 percent increase in the total number of households (approximately 1.3 million). Thus population retrenchment is not accompanied by a shrinkage in the demand for shelter; quite the contrary, the reality is one of increasing housing demand in central cities.

However, not all household types are expanding in number in central cities. The growth sectors are nonfamily households and female-headed families. In contrast, family households (including husband-wife configurations) are experiencing an absolute level of attrition. While this may give the impression of a shift to a more varied cosmopolitan array of urban households, there is a less sanguine aspect of this development. The most rapidly expanding configurations (female-headed families and nonfamily households) are those least well endowed in terms of income resources. In contrast, the household types contracting in number, particularly husband-wife families, are at the upper rungs of the income ladder. The sheer growth in household numbers tends to obscure an ominous reality of constrained income capacities.

EXHIBIT 4

HOUSEHOLDS BY TYPE FOR CENTRAL CITIES AND SUBURBAN AREAS: 1970 AND 1977

(Numbers in thousands, 1970 metropolitan definition)

	Central Cities		Suburban Areas		Percent Change 1970 to 1977	
	1977	1970	1977	1970	Central Cities	Suburban areas
Total Households	22,741	21,401	27,672	22,450	6.3%	23.3%
Family Households	15,444	15,816	22,330	19,065	− 2.4	17.1
Husband-Wife	11,783	12,748	19,433	16,973	− 7.6	14.5
Male Householder, no Wife Present	499	587	541	485	−15.0	11.5
Female Householder, no husband present	3,161	2,480	2,356	1,608	27.5	46.5
Nonfamily Households	7,298	5,584	5,342	3,385	30.7	57.8

Source: Center for Urban Policy Research Analysis of Data Presented in: U.S. Department of Commerce, Bureau of the Census, *Current Population Reports*, Special Studies P-23, No. 55, "Social and Economic Characteristics of the Metropolitan and Nonmetropolitan Population: 1977 and 1970," November, 1978.

INCOME SHIFTS

Despite the gain in household numbers, the outward flow of
income resources has yet to be inhibited. There are more people
and households moving out of central cities than moving into them
(with the city's net growth in households a result of household
formations originating from the non-moving population); those
that move out have higher incomes than their replacements.

In Exhibit 5, data are shown indicating the personal income
loss due to migration from 1970 to 1974, and 1975 to 1977.
Whether it is families or unrelated individuals (roughly comparable
to nonfamily households), the pattern is similar. The more affluent
are leaving, the newcomers are less fiscally well endowned. From
1970 to 1974 there was a reduction in aggregate resident income
within central cities of $29.6 billion due to migration. In the two
years from 1975 to 1977, the equivalent figure was a loss of $18
billion.

In Exhibit 6, these data have been converted into constant dollars
(interpolating for 1974 and 1975, for which data is not available).
This indicates an average annual net change (between 1970 and
1977) in 1976 dollars of $9.3 billion. Since these data are cumu-
lative, by 1977 there was a loss, in 1976 dollars, of $64.8 billion.
If no migration had occurred by the latter year, $64.8 billion more
in annual incomes would have accrued to central city households
than was actually received.

The ramifications of these losses are of very significant magnitude.
If we were to use the conventional rule of thumb of 25 percent of
income alloted to rent, this represents a diminution of rent-paying
capacity in excess of $16 billion. The transportation implications
are equally compelling. Transportation expenses typically account
for approximately 10 percent of personal consumption expenditures.
Therefore, a departure of $6.5 billion in transportation expenditure
capacity is implied due to migration. Such a level of attrition in the
personal income base stands at variance with the image of a widespread back-to-the-cities movement.

EMPLOYMENT TRENDS

One of the great limitations to urban analysis is the paucity of
employment data for central cities.[5] On a national basis, generalizations are presently limited to cities that are coterminous with

EXHIBIT 5

INCOME LOSSES IN CENTRAL CITIES DUE TO NET MIGRATION: 1970 TO 1974 AND 1975 TO 1977

(Numbers in thousands, 1970 metropolitan definition)

Income in 1973 of families and unrelated individuals 14 years old and over who migrated to and from central cities between 1970 and 1974.

Subject	Living in Cities in 1970	Moved out of Cities Between 1970 and 1974	Moved to Cities Between 1970 and 1974	Net Change Between 1970 and 1974
Families (thousands)	16,823	3,363	1,563	− 1,800
Mean Income (dollars)	$13,349	$14,169	$12,864	−$1,305[1]
Aggregate Income (billions of dollars)	$ 224.6	$ 47.7	$ 20.1	− 27.6
Unrelated Individuals (thousands)	6,975	1,066	926	− 140
Mean Income (dollars)	$ 6,143	$ 7,099	$ 6,092	−$1,007[1]
Aggregate Income (billions of dollars)	$ 42.8	$ 7.6	$ 5.6	−$ 2.0

Income in 1976 of families and unrelated individuals 14 years old and over who migrated to and from central cities between 1975 and 1977.

Subject	Living in Cities in 1975	Moved out of Cities Between 1975 and 1977	Moved to Cities Between 1975 and 1977	Net Change Between 1975 and 1977
Families (thousands)	16,359	2,003	985	− 1,018
Mean Income (dollars)	$16,120	$15,986	$14,992	−$ 994[1]
Aggregate Income (billions of dollars)	$ 263.7	$ 32.0	$ 14.8	−$ 17.2
Unrelated Individuals (thousands)	8,812	994	940	− 54
Mean Income (dollars)	$ 7,388	$ 8,055	$ 7,612	−$ 443[1]
Aggregate Income (billions of dollars)	$ 65.1	$ 8.0	$ 7.2	−$ 0.8

Note: 1. Simple unweighted difference.

Sources: U.S. Department of Commerce, Bureau of the Census, *Current Population Reports*, Special Studies P-23, No. 55, "Social and Economic Characteristics of the Metropolitan and Nonmetropolitan Population: 1974 and 1970," September 1975.

U.S. Department of Commerce, Bureau of the Census, *Current Population Reports*, Special Studies, P-23, No. 75 "Social and Economic Characteristics of the Metropolitan and Nonmetropolitan Population: 1977 and 1970," November 1978.

EXHIBIT 6

DERIVATION OF INCOME LOSSES (1976 DOLLARS) IN CENTRAL CITIES DUE TO MIGRATION: 1970 TO 1977

(1970 metropolitan definition)

Average Annual Net Change, 1970 to 1974:	−$7.4 billion (1973 dollars)[1]
Ratio of 1976 to 1973 Consumer Price Index:	$\frac{170.5}{133.1} = 1.28$ [2]
Average Annual Net Change, 1970 to 1974	−$9.4 billion (1976 dollars)[3]
Average Annual Net Change, 1975 to 1977	−$9.0 billion (1976 dollars)[4]
Net Change, 1974 to 1975	−$9.2 billion (1976 dollars)[5]
Total Change: 1970 to 1977	−$64.8 billion (1976 dollars)[6]
Average Annual Net Change: 1970 to 1977	−$9.3 billion (1976 dollars)[7]

Notes: 1. Derived from Exhibit 5.
2. U.S. Bureau of Labor Statistics, *Monthly Labor Review.*
3. 1.28 X $7.4 billion = $9.4 billion.
4. Derived from Exhibit 5.
5. Mean of annual averages of two periods.
6. Sum of annual averages of all periods.
7. −$64.8 billion ÷ 7 years = −$9.3 billion.

Source: CUPR Analysis.

counties, the smallest geographic partition for which employment information is released by federal government agencies. Exhibit 7 is inclusive of the major cities meeting this criterion. Data for major New Jersey cities (not coterminous with counties) secured by the state are also presented in Exhibit 7.

Briefly, central city employment has lagged that of the nation, implying much stronger rates of economic growth in suburban and nonmetropolitan jurisdictions. And, the aging urban centers of the Northeast not only lag the general nationwide expansion, they also have experienced severe absolute shrinkage. But even in the latter, particulary in Manhattan, the casual urban observer cannot help but note the rise of substantial new commercial and office edifices, implying a vitality completely at odds with the statistical ledgers. How can one account for this apparent paradox?

There are deceptive phenomena at work in central cities; attention is often riveted to new hotels, office buildings and commercial emporiums rising in the "new" downtowns. These are very im-

EXHIBIT 7

EMPLOYMENT TRENDS, SELECT CITIES: 1970 TO 1977

Area	1970	1975	1977	Change: 1970 to 1975		Change: 1975 to 1977	
				Number	Percent	Number	Percent
U.S. Total[1]	86,922,000	92,331,000	97,849,000	5,409,000	6.2%	5,518,000	6.0%
Philadelphia	1,000,172	882,216	873,440	− 117,956	− 11.8	− 8,776	− 1.0
Boston	573,312	525,203	523,738	− 48,109	− 8.4	− 1,465	− 0.3
San Francisco	550,695	548,241	548,568	− 2,454	− 0.4	327	0.0
New Orleans	324,998	339,982	348,253	14,984	4.6	8,271	2.4
Indianapolis	427,777	433,792	455,503	6,015	1.4	21,711	5.0
Denver	364,133	379,705	399,975	15,572	4.3	20,270	5.3
New York City[2]	3,317,200	3,378,700	3,157,500	− 438,500	− 11.5%	− 221,200	− 6.5%
Newark[3]	191,595	162,569	139,204	− 29,206	− 15.1%	− 23,365	− 14.4%
Jersey City	73,804	64,850	58,450	− 8,954	− 12.1	− 6,400	− 9.9
Paterson	49,360	48,726	39,445	− 634	− 1.3	− 9,281	− 19.0
Camden	41,683	36,835	31,366	− 4,848	− 11.6	− 5,469	− 14.8

Notes: 1. U.S. Department of Commerce, Bureau of Economic Analysis (BEA); Total Employment, including wage and salary government and proprietors; annual average.
2. U.S. Department of Labor, Bureau of Labor Statistics (BLS): Wage and salary employment including government; March of each year.
3. State of New Jersey, Covered Employment: Wage and Salary Employment, excluding government; March of each year.

Source: Center for Urban Policy Research Analysis of Data Presented in: U.S. Department of Commerce, Bureau of the Census, *Current Population Reports*, Special Studies P-23, No. 55, "Social and Economic Characteristics of the Metropolitan and Nonmetropolitan Population: 1977 and 1970," November, 1978.

portant and very positive in and of themselves, but all too frequently they serve to mask the limits of growth within the municipality as a whole.

Changing Employee/Floor Area Ratios In many cases, such new facilities replace older amenities, with little attendant job generation. In general, the process is one of consolidation of facilities previously dispersed within the urban center.

The amount of space per employee in new office structures tends to be much higher than in the old. Thus the employee multiplier of a given floor area is not as substantial as historic ratios would indicate.

Concentration of Employment Generators The physical locations of the new amenities tend to be concentrated in the visible "prestige" sectors of the city most often frequented by outside visitors. Shrinkage, on the other hand, tends to be in lesser sites, the old industrial sectors and aging hostelry zones. There is little glamour, few visitors and even less comment as these facilities are slowly drained of activity.

The recentralization of shrinking or stable central city employment, of concentration within an ever smaller "winner's circle," and of increased levels of compaction through higher density facilities, presents whole new dimensions of transportation problems and potentials. In the midst of an overall static or even sagging transportation demand function, there may be an unprecedented level of peaking at a very few sites and an ominous shrinkage for many of the more outlying ones.

Conclusion

The ultimate shadow of energy costs and shortages have the potential to deflect the seemingly remorseless process of spatial diffusion. However, until the restructuring implied by this admonition is asserted on the metropolitan landscape, certain conclusions cannot be avoided.

It is premature to extrapolate from isolated success stories a wide ranging back-to-the-cities movement. There has been little, if any, abatement in the broader centrifugal forces depleting the urban arena.

It is always possible that the thin entering edge of select revitalization may be wedge shaped. The full significance of phenomena in their early stages tend to be obscured by the broader system of data accounts. But at this time it is difficult not to acknowledge the harsh reality that a new town may be evolving intown—the gentrified neighborhood—but at most it is relatively slender, much too limited to support and bring back with it the aging entities that we call central cities.

The preconditions for urban renaissance are not easy to attain. Urban resettlement appears to occur only in unique economic contexts (central city economies characterized by high-paying white-collar positions for large and expanding numbers of young white-collar workers) coinciding with unique residential environments—an emenity-rich housing stock, or alternative parcels of unique attributes, amenable to restoration efforts. And these two elements, if not spatially contiguous, must have strong transportation linkages.

In conjunction with the unique residential environment condition, the cultural dimension is of significance. In select locations subpopulations oriented toward various facets of the arts have achieved critical mass, fashioning neighborhood revitalization. The Soho district in Manhattan, however, is of considerably less magnitude than the South Bronx.

There are indications of a broader demographic partitioning of a select set of American cities. Groups of special interests and common proclivities are moving to specialized national loci rather than merely a neighborhood or subarea of a specific city. The regional city, which once served as a magnet for various individuals who could not find others of equivalent sympathies in peripheral small towns and rural areas, is increasingly giving way to the specialized national city. These serve not merely a region but the nation. An example is the enormous complex of youth and near-youth (and those who want to be near-youth) that characterizes Boston. There are equivalent cities emerging both for this group and for others throughout the country. In turn this unique character serves with its corollaries to generate a whole new scale of tourist traffic, of those who may not participate in the specifics of the settlers, but find such areas worthy of being visited. The tremendous flow of tourists to San Francisco is in part an attribute to its natural site, but also to a unique ambiance that it has developed. The colonies of retirees, artists and near artists that have generated substantial population growth for Sante Fe and Albuquerque epitomize this trend toward specialization as part of function, but with image and pulling power as well.

The dominant growth phenomenon of the 1970s, at least through the period preceding the 1979 energy crisis, has been the resynthesis of the metropolitan activity system to the outer fringe—adjacent to the circumferential transportation band. More dispersed, peripheral nonmetropolitan population growth may in part be considered "surrogate" metropolitan growth, dependant on transportation links to the new circumferential metropolitan economy. The spatial form of the latter (exurbia) often appears as undocumented metropolitan extensions or outcroppings along new or improved transportation routes.

Subject to limitations of energy and financial resource, the central city core transportation issue is largely being blunted not by new means of transit but rather by decline in need.

Notes

1. For a more detailed overview, see: George Sternlieb and James W. Hughes, *Current Population Trends in America*, (New Brunswick, N.J.: Rutgers University, Center for Urban Policy Research, 1978).

2. See: George Sternlieb and James W. Hughes, *Post-Industrial America: Metropolitan Decline and Inter-Regional Job Shifts* (New Brunswick, N.J.: Rutgers University Center for Urban Policy Research, 1976); George Sternlieb and James W. Hughes, "The New Metropolitan and Regional Realities of America," *Journal of the American Institute of Planners* (July 1977); and George Sternlieb and James W. Hughes, *Revitalizing the Northeast: Prelude to an Agenda* (New Brunswick, N.J.: Rutgers University, Center for Urban Policy Research, 1978).

3. Migration data for central cities is more limited in scope. Yet the following evidence is available:
   Between 1970 and 1975, central cities lost 13,005,000 persons five years old and over and only gained 5,987,000 persons, for a net loss of 7,018,000. In contrast, suburbs had a net immigration of 5,423,000 of persons five years old and over.
   Between 1975 and 1978, central cities lost 9,915,000 persons three years old and over and only gained 5,987,000 persons, for a net loss of 4,628,000. Suburbs had a net immigration of 3,527,000. Based on this data, it appears that net out-migration has actually increased in scale in the post-1975 period. See: U.S. Bureau of the Census, *Current Population Reports*, Series P-20, No. 285, "Mobility of the Population of the United States: March 1970 to March 1975" (U.S. Government Printing Office, Washington, D.C., 1975); and, U.S. Bureau of the Census, *Current Population Reports*, Series P-20, No. 331, "Geographical Mobility: March 1975 to March 1978" (U.S. Government Printing Office, Washington, D.C., 1978).

4. For an analysis of the potential impact see; James W. Hughes and George Sternlieb, *Jobs and People; New York City 1985* (New Brunswick, N.J.: Rutgers University Center for Urban Policy Research, 1978).

5. For a detailed explanation of sources, see: Michael R. Greenberg, Donald A. Krueckeberg and Connie O. Michaelson, *Local Population and Employment Projection Techniques* (New Brunswick, N.J.: Rutgers University Center for Urban Policy Research, 1978).

The "Two-Cities" Phenomenon

George Sternlieb
James W. Hughes

Introduction

American cities have always been an amalgam of the rich and the poor, both straddling an uneasy middle class, separate and distinct from each of them. The functioning of the city in its many facets—particularly as a manufacturing nexus, a role which dominated the economics of so many cities—found place and utility for each of these groups. Entreprenuer and distributor, basic factory hand and unskilled labor, all were hitched to the urban manufacturing dynamo. As Wilbur Thompson aptly stated the case:

> "We did not, for the most part, build great cities in this country; manufacturing firms agglomerated in tight industrial complexes and formed labor pools of half a million workers. This is not the same thing as building great cities; our great industrial transformation has left us with a large number of overgrown 'factory towns'."

177

The stresses between the several groups were never trivial and frequently bubbled to the surface; as witness stands the long history of urban riots and labor warfare. But within this context, there was a logic and economic rationale which tended to provide common denominators.

An evolving post-industrial world has shattered that balance. We are still coping with the necessity of putting together a new Realpolitik consonant both with the limitations and new potentials of our "overgrown factory towns." In part, the birth of this required symbiosis is hindered by a failure to comprehend the irrevocable changes both in demographics and economic functions which must be accepted for a successful shaping of the future. The city as we have known it, and the forms of social and economic organization which have characterized it, are simply irrecoverable. From the viewpoint of the poor, the city of goods production, of large-scale relatively unskilled employment, has become the city of redistribution—of transfer payments and welfare. For the elite there is a city—far from new, but increasingly vigorous—of information processing and economic facilitation, of consumption rather than production. Lost between these two poles and fast disappearing are the middle groups who find both the lifestyles and economic opportunities of suburbia (and increasingly exurbia) affordable and much more fulfilling.

The Two Cities

Thus the vision of the city becomes strikingly bipolar: on the one hand the city of the poor with anywhere from a quarter (Boston) to a seventh (New York) of the population on welfare; of crime rates that stagger the imagination even when appropriate allowance is made for their vagaries; of truancy levels (vastly understated by official reporting techniques), which make a mockery of the traditional role of public education as a homogenizing influence and ladder upward for the urban proletariat.

Separate and distinct from this—indeed, though very frequently in physical proximity, but psychologically and fiscally at a vast distance—is the city of the elite. Varying in scale from a very few select blocks in some municipalities, to substantial and growing population thresholds in others, is the city whose inhabitants are matched to the new job base, peopled by groups who do not require or utilize the impacted local service base.

Typically, they are either childless or sending their children to selected private schools, never to be found in the overcrowded municipal hospitals, and certainly not dependent on the welfare provisions of the city. While their actual numbers may be relatively few, they inhabit the city of the tourist and the visitor. Since they are relatively novel, as distinct from the overstudied masses, they attract perhaps more attention than their numbers warrant from observers both amateur and learned. Indeed so vigorous are the numbers of studies of such individuals as to magnify their importance and in turn to generate a new buzz word of "gentrification".

The functional reality of new cities is easily summarized: there are a select number of nonsmokestack cities which bear the visible signs of compatibility with a post-industrial economy. This is evidenced by the dominance of major service production facilities—the massive office buildings which characterize the new downtowns. Their tight clustering attain even more visible mass with the appearance of the increasingly vigorous central city hotel-convention phenomenon. The latter represents in part an increase in accommodations but, rather more strikingly, a replacement of old, no longer adequate facilities geared for lower income groups, with new highly visible structures whose patronage is divided between serving as an accessory to production services and information processing on the one hand, and the city as elite consumption hub on the other.

In select cities, complementary residential appendages have arisen, paralleling this economic growth. Again, in turn, these represent more of a recompaction of the more affluent central city strata from crumbling neighborhoods than they do a net in-migration.

In the very act, however, of bringing these groups together, a critical mass of appeal is generated which in turn fosters a greater pulling power of the center city as alternative life style. It is this phenomenon which has given birth to the image of urban revitalization, with the imperial city of Washington, D.C., given its unparalled center city job base in the van, with New York City certainly, and Philadelphia, if less so, showing remarkable vigor.

But the dimensions of this phenomenon should not be exaggerated. If the migrational flows to and from central cities are examined over the 1975-to-1978 period, it is found that substantial net migration losses occurred, particularly among the higher-income sectors (Exhibit 1). For every family whose income was over $15,000 that migrated to the city, three departed. This pattern is certainly not indicative of a widespread process of gentrification and is of sufficient magnitude to dim the emergence of the new "vibrant kernels".

EXHIBIT 1

CENTRAL CITY MIGRATION BY FAMILIES: 1975 TO 1978

Family Income	Number of Families[1]	Central City to Suburbs	Movers From:		Central City Net Change
			Suburbs to Central City	Abroad to Central City	
Under $5,000	295	46	32	20	+ 6
$5,000 to $9,999	905	175	81	70	− 24
$10,000 to $14,999	1,407	244	104	36	−104
$15,000 to $24,999	2,983	692	245	48	−399
$25,000 and over	2,049	423	168	25	−230
Total	7,639	1,580	630	199	−751

Note: [1] Number of husband-wife families with head 14 to 54 years of age, residing in central cities in 1978. (Numbers in thousands)

Source: U.S. Bureau of the Census Current Population Reports, Series P-20, No. 331, "Geographic Mobility: March 1975 to March 1978," U.S. Government Printing Office, Washington, D.C., 1978.

In terms of employment, the passing of the age of manufacturing has not been fully compensated by the rise of in-city service industry replacements. The recent development of automation within the office sector—of the rationalization of labor intensive white collar activities—is perhaps even more striking than its predecessors in manufacturing. The absolute scale of central city employment, with few exceptions, is at best constant, and more commonly, shrinking. The gap between the skills, work habits and acceptance accorded the poor—in particular, the minority poor—and the requirements of the new occupations has resulted in a mismatch between the bulk of central city residents and the jobs proximate to their homes. Thus one finds very high levels of unemployment cheek by jowl with basic shortages of skilled clerical personnel. And on a more mundane level, the savage attrition which has taken place in central city resident incomes as a function of selective migration has reduced the opportunities for small-scale service operations. From 1970 to 1977, for example, the flows of in-migration and out-migration to and from central cities yielded an annual average net reduction in resident incomes of 9.3 billion dollars per year. In this context the potential for resident services provided by fledgling entrepreneurs must endure a most hostile incubator.

The existence of the "two cities" phenomenon, and the extreme disparity between the human elements that characterize the segments, is shown in Exhibit 2. This provides data on a variety of parameters for the universe of New York City renters compared with the new elite inhabiting the much publicized converted buildings and new private structures constructed under recent tax incentive provisions. The new elite are characterized by their relative youthfulness, high incomes and concentration in the new prestige occupations (including the burgeoning artistic professions) as compared to the overall city renter profile.

Housing and Budgetary Confrontations

There is an enormous difference in goal structures between the two groups—the poor and the elite—who increasingly dominate the urban political arena. It has many aspects but is perhaps most easily characterized in terms of attitudes toward housing and municipal expenditures. In the former regard, the poor seek inexpensive shelter. They look toward the city either to provide housing directly, or to manage the private market so as to assure low rents and minimal

EXHIBIT 2

OCCUPANT CHARACTERISTICS OF NEW RESIDENTIAL STRUCTURES NEW YORK CITY, 1977

Category	New York City Total[1]	New Structures (Tax Incentives)	Converted Buildings Apartments	Lofts
Household Income	$8,395	$26,302	$21,479	$22,253
Occupation				
Professional/ Technical	13.6%	41.7%	38.2%	33.2%
Manager/ Administrator	7.8	26.0	21.3	18.7
Artist	2.1	8.8	15.7	35.0
Clerical	27.1	4.4	3.7	2.3
Craftsman/ Operative	25.2	1.4	1.1	2.3
Median Age	44.4 years	33.6 years	29.6 years	34.0 years

Note: [1] 1975 data.

Source: Kristina Ford, *Housing Policy and the Urban Middle Class* (New Brunswick, N.J.: Rutgers University, Center for Urban Policy Research, 1978).

increments in shelter costs. Indeed the extreme difference with the elite is captured by the stress on housing as *shelter*. To the elite caught up in a post-shelter society, housing increasingly is viewed as a form of investment. To them, the goal is capital enhancement through increase in housing value. They have the resources for housing purchase either in fee simple, or condominium/cooperative forms of ownership. They have the tax status that, within our inflationary society, practically demands housing ownership. Thus to the affluent group, housing as shelter from the elements is far less important than housing as a tax shelter and while the poor are victimized by housing cost/price increases, to the affluent they are the justification for investment. Indeed a very good case can be made that truly inexpensive housing—again within our inflationary context—can only be housing which goes up in value, with capital increases serving as a offset to operating costs.

Thus municipal politics increasingly has as one of its irritants the rival demands of the two groups: the one seeking neighborhood improvement, and a reduction in the number of housing units and structures which might reduce values or limit their increases in price; the other fearful that any reduction in structure number or increase in housing for the affluent might very will set up a speculative run on their own facilities which will result in cost increases. While the situation sketched here is far from perfectly defined—as witnessed by the love affair of the affluent renters with rent control—the schism is becoming increasingly evident.

The variants in housing policy goals are paralleled by attitudes toward the municipal budget. To the poor, municipal expenditures on health, education and welfare are among the few rays of light in an otherwise dismal environment. To the new elite groups in the cities, these are extraneous. In their place are rather environment-enhancing—and real estate price-increasing—investments in parks, recreational facilities, libraries and the like. The yin-yang of this conflict dominates—sometimes quietly, sometimes turbulantly—budget meetings in every major city in America.

But these are merely two facets of a struggle which is increasingly securing definition: The rival roles of the city as the port of last resort for those who have fallen off, or who were never able to secure passage on the economic train, versus the city as an entity whose care and enhancement, by very definition, requires a re-structuring in order to recapture the affluent. In the latter case, for example, fiscal zoning rapidly dominates (the provision of a variety of incentives for land use activities which will generate more in the way of revenues than costs) and becomes a primary virtue. However, it sometimes conflicts with the provision of amenities and necessities for the poor and, perhaps even more strikingly, with their sense of priorities.

Reconciliation

Is there a potential reconciliation between these two elements? Are we doomed to have a city of Manhattan—and a city of the rest of New York? A city of North Michigan Avenue—and a city of the rest of Chicago? Indeed are there possibilities of a political as well as functional split?

The real necessities which we believe will emerge are very simple—
at least in our more socially advanced areas. Much of the services
upon which the poor are dependent are linked to the fiscal vigor
of the city which is called on to provide them. From this point of
view each new downtown ratable, rather than being at best unimportant—at worst a potential threat to the poor—is rather a triumph.
Cities can only provide adequate social services within our political
environment if they are cities of vigor. There is no flow of transfer
payments from state or federal governments, at least currently on
the horizon, which will obviate this basic reality. Bankrupt cities
reduce services first. The lessons of municipal cutbacks are all too
clear cut in this regard. National funding is an inadequate surrogate
given the variance in costs and the increasing voter predominance of
relatively socially conservative regions.

If cities are to be reconstructed, what is going to be required is
a reconciliation between the two warring parties. The poor need the
rich. if nothing more, the history of the last twenty years indicates
what happens when the cities become wards of the state, for the state
is far less generous; the quality of social services are far more limited.

The poor need the city of resource. In order for cities to flourish,
however, they must secure flexibility of land use, a capacity to entice
truly significant levels of the affluent to stay, and, hopefully, even to
return to them. The myth of gentrification as a large-scale phenomenon has created alarm well in advance of any commensurate
reality. The "two cities" are increasingly dominated by the poor yet
there are potentials for positive rebirth. These may well abort. The
cooperation of the bulk of the extant population is essential.
America's urban future requires many inputs—but certainly not
least among them is forestalling the adversary relationship which
is evolving between the "two cities".

Physical Revitalization Strategies: Adaptive Reuse

Robert W. Burchell
David Listokin

Introduction

The purpose of this paper is to describe the *physical* redevelopment strategies that may be employed by a municipality, given the availability of surplus land in various types of declining neighborhoods. This kind of activity comprises the *physical* implementation stage of adaptive reuse planning—a process that seeks to (1) anticipate, (2) interimly-control, (3) acquire, and (4) plan for, the reuse of real property which currently exhibits only marginal economic value.

The strategies presented here represent close to 25 years experience with urban renewal and a decade's experience with neighborhood perservation. Important lessons have been learned from each of these precursors. In the first instance, it has been shown that the most realistic path to renewal is to take an uncharacteristically hard line on the short-run probability of successful redevelopment of a declining neighborhood; in the second, we have found out that what can be done must be attempted within the confines of acknowledged low levels of both fiscal resources and regularly-funded, support personnel.[1]

Thus, adaptive reuse recognizes that neighborhoods, possibly awaiting a new function, take time to turn around. Rather than doing nothing and hoping that long-run panaceas will emerge in the future, immediate, small-scale, redevelopment activities can be initiated which will improve the quality of life in the short-run and not take away from the long-run reuse potential of either properties or structures.[2]

Strategies are targeted to different types of neighborhoods,[3] based on type of neighborhood (stage of decline), required capital commitment, and potential risk of this committment. It should be realized however, that circumstances unique to a particular geographic area or fiscal climate weigh heavily on the physical reuse strategy to be employed and thse must be taken into account in the choice of an appropriate strategy.

Background

The physical reuse strategies that will be discussed represent the culmination of local adaptive reuse planning. Reuse planning attempts first, to *anticipate and inventory* surplus real property.[4] This is accomplished through survey and tabulation of existing surplus properties and, using this information about structures and their respective neighborhoods, predicting the type, magnitude and location of residential and nonresidential property abandonment.

A second activity of reuse planning is to secure *interim control* of the deteriorating properties before deterioration is so pronounced as to render them unavailable for reuse. Municipal control of owner-abandoned, vacant/occupied properties is typically achieved through receivership actions or emergency repair/hazardous building laws.

Once controlled, decisions have to be made *to retain in the long-run (rehabilitation), retain in the short-run (boarding and sealing) or dispose of (demolishing and clearing) surplus structures.* While these decisions are being made about the structure, *long-term legal control* is being sought for the entire property (structure and land) through foreclosure, donation, condemnation or lease-purchase agreements.

Subsequent to legal control, the more traditional planning aspects of adaptive reuse 'planning' begin. Decisions are made as to what properties will remain in public versus private control, those that will be slotted for short-term or long-term reuse, etc., and various property disposition strategies and land banking/storing measures are put into effect in support of these decisions.

An adaptive reuse plan/program emerges as an element of the local master plan or as a component of CDBG filing procedures, Neighborhood Strategy Area designation requirements, UDAG justification documents or other local/state program authorizations. The form and aegis of the adaptive reuse plan, a foster child of both public urban renewal and provate-public neighborhood preservation redevelopment philosophies, varies considerably from city to city. It is amazingly consistent, however, in its component activities. Property reuse is always involved with the tabulation, control and disposition of surplus properties.

The culmination of the property gathering, control, clearance and disposition measures are the specific *physical redesign and reuse activities*. Several involve both structure and the land parcel; the bulk, however, involve only the land parcel. The physical reuse strategies that are the end product of the adaptive reuse process are:

Unique Residential Revitalization—Residential residences converted from surplus (1) private non-residential (commercial/industrial) lofts or (2) public (railroad, school) spaces.

Unique Non-Residential Revitalization—Commercial or industrial spaces converted from surplus (1) structures (specialty stores, pottery barns, leather tooling businesses) or (2) vacant land (peddlar's rows, flea markets, open air produce markets).

Intensified Public Services—Lot redesign and/or municipal/private special service arrangements to permitt off-street loading, rear property solid waste removal and/or additional street lighting, for properties in areas of special need.

Transportation System Upgrading—Street realignments and road expansions made possible by the acquisition of land available from municipal surplus property assemblages and, where applicable, improvements in mass transit facilities service.

Neighborhood Parking—Street-level and other parking alternatives developed on surplus property sites in thinning neighborhoods.

Active/Passive Recreation Use—Providing both active facilities (e.g., tot lots and vest pocket parks) and passive facilities (e.g., flower gardens and grassed areas) on previously abandoned or underutilized vacant lots.

Interior Lots/Lotsteading—The creation of less dense, immediate space and structure-related lawns and gardens through the acquisition of neighboring surplus property.

Land Banking/Urban Gardening—Long term land holding measures for abandoned properties that will not have structures built upon them in the forseeable future.

Adaptive Reuse and Neighborhood Condition

While each redevelopment situation is unique unto itself there are definite development contexts for which specific reuse strategies appear more appropriate.[5] Different redevelopment contexts are linked to significantly different rates and stages of real property deterioration. Over the last decade there have been a number of attempts to classify neighborhoods according to stage of decline.[6] Usually, a five category classification scheme is developed. In this type of classification two stages of neighborhoods are not in decline —these are growing and stable neighborhoods. Three stages of *declining* neighborhoods also flow from the classification schemes. They are frequently termed areas of *selective, moderate* and *rampant* neighborhood decline. The definitions below describe the structural and real property characterisitics of these types of neighborhoods.

Selective Decline—Poor upkeep of structures and surrounding properties; emerging structure vacancy, occasional vandalism to unoccupied properties. Scattered parcels of surplus vacant land.

Moderate Decline—Visible deterioration of occupied and unoccupied properties, increasing number of unoccupied structures; substantial share of unoccupied structures abandoned or vandalized. Moderate aggregates of surplus vacant land due to past structure demolition.

Rampant Decline—Significant disrepair of most structures. Numerous structures vacant/abandoned. Obvious vandalism and arsonous fires. Significant cleared contiguous land areas due to past demolition.

As is indicated by Exhibit 1, the most productive locations for adaptive reuse intervention are neighborhoods where decline is just *beginning*. These are areas of growing vacancy, scattered structure

EXHIBIT 1

PHYSICAL ADAPTIVE REUSE STRATEGIES AND
NEIGHBORHOOD CONDITION

	NEIGHBORHOOD CONDITION		
ADAPTIVE REUSE STRATEGY	*Rampant Decline*	*Moderate Decline*	*Signs of Selective Decline*
Unique Residential Revitalization			X
Unique Nonresidential Revitalization			X
Intensified Public Services: Off-Street Commercial Docks			X
Intensified Public Services: Off-Street Solid Waste Removal		X	X
Intensified Public Services: Transportation System Upgrading	X		
Neighborhood Parking		X	X
Active/Passive Recreation		X	X
Interior Lots Adopt-a-Lot		X	X
Vegetable Gardens	X	X	
Land Banking	X		

Definition: *Selective Decline*—Poor upkeep of structures and surrounding properties; emerging structure vacancy, occasional vandalism to unoccupied properties.

Moderate Decline—Visible deterioration of occupied and unoccupied properties; increasing number of unoccupied structures; substantial share of unoccupied structures abandoned and vandalized. Moderate aggregates of surplus, vacant land due to past structure demolition of once-occupied properties.

Rampant Decline—Significant disrepair of most structures; numerous structures vacant/abandoned; obvious vandalism and arsonous fires. Significant cleared areas due to past demolition.

Source: Rutgers University Center for Urban Policy Research.

abandonment and the emerging appearance of surplus cleared property. They provide sites where *unique residential and commercial revitalization* may be attempted and where efforts at *intensified public services* have the greatest longevity or potential for success. These are also areas where individual investments in *lotsteading* and *adjacent property purchase* (to increase density and provide offstreet loading/services) are undertaken to augment or enhance residential and commercial revitalization efforts. They are further locations of potential public investment for *street level parking* and *active/passive recreation uses.*

Areas of *moderate decline* present the potential for using contiguous vacant property sites for redevelopment. Yet these locations of decreasing occupancy and increasing property abandonment and disinvestment, oft times, are not locations where modest residential and commercial revitalization efforts can flourish. Instead, these are areas where *adjacent lots* may be claimed to decrease local density, where *active/passive recreation uses* may be developed in selected locations and, if in the early stages of moderate decline, where additional *street level parking* and off-street, solid waste removal may be attempted. Moderately declining neighborhoods, due to the presence of contiguous abandoned lots also provide unique opportunity for initial attempts at *urban gardening.*

In neighborhoods of *heavy decline* fewer adaptive reuse strategies can be employed. Yet adaptive reuse definitely has a role in such neighborhoods. This type of neighborhood characterized by heavy structure abandonment, significant amounts of contiguous surplus property and only long-run redevelopment potential, provides ideal locations for road realignments to improve traffic flow, sites for land bank assemblages that may be brokered as a package to clients desiring access to superior urban mass transit systems, and locations for urban truck farming at a significant scale. These neighborhoods are also the sites/opportunities for unconventional renewal—the once-in-a-lifetime airport development, sports arena, etc. whose natural transportation/communication advantages override the negative effects of immediately peripheral neighborhoods.

Adaptive Reuse Strategies

The following measures are physical adaptive strategies which may be used in neighborhoods where properties have only marginal economic value. As the term 'adaptive reuse' indicates these are strategies which assume an alteration of the original purpose of the land for the proposed use to have any value at all. The strategies represent a response to Urban Renewal fantasy and Neighborhood Preservation immobility. They are realistic, achievable, redevelopment activities which, for the most part, are supported or subsidized by operative, federal and state programs.

Unique Residential Revitalization

Limited residential revitalization is often possible in situations where unique location, structural configurations, or legal mechanisms allow development alternatives not usually available on the open market. Recent publications such as *New Profits From Old Buildings,*[7] *Revitalizing Urban Neighborhoods*[8] and *Recycling Buildings: Renovations, Remodeling, Restorations and Reuses*[9] have discussed different opportunities for this type of rehabilitation and conversion.[10] Examples of these situations include: industrial loft residential-retro-fitting, condominium conversion of previous rental housing units, and elderly/senior citizen housing from surplus school/railroad structures. In the first case, garment, printing and metal processing industrial lofts which have limited industrial or commercial potential in thinning central city areas may have unnatural residential potential due to their close-in locations or established communications networks. New York City, for example, has experienced a wave of loft conversions in previously industrial neighborhoods such as Soho, Noho, and Tribeca in Manhattan, the Atlantic Avenue corridor in Brooklyn and Long Island City in Queens[11] (see Exhibit 2 for further examples). The nonresidentail to residential conversion must be recognized as legal by the applicable zoning ordinance, as conversion usually requires a reasonably-expensive fixturing commitment (kitchen, baths, lighting systems, etc.) that will not be made unless a legal certificate of *residential* occupancy can be granted.

Condominium conversion from previous rental housing units assumes that the potential of the recipient neighborhood is sufficiently strong to allow the future debt retirement/occupancy costs of each unit to be two to three times the current rent. This increase reflects mortgage costs for rehabilitation and maintenance outlay which includes operating costs, insurance and taxes. Condominium conversion is a strategy often employed in the stronger neighborhoods of cities which have rent control. Prominent examples include Park Slope in New York City, Hyde Park in Chicago, and Capital Hill in Washington, D.C. In these cities, rent level increases are limited by legislative fiat; conversion circumvents rent control and new residents pay market price for the units that they occupy.

The potential for conversion of a railroad or school space depends jointly on the structure and its location.[12] Surplus school space, almost always elementary schools, is found predominantly in residential areas. Location thus initially favors residential construction:

EXHIBIT 2

UNIQUE RESIDENTIAL REVITALIZATION:
APPLICATION AND SUPPORTIVE PUBLIC STRATEGIES

STRATEGY:

UNIQUE RESIDENTIAL REVITALIZATION

One hundred and twenty (85%) of the 150 cities with structure aban-donment. Selected examples include: Arlington, Va., Atlantic City, N.J., Carbondale, In., Chester, Pa., Chicago, Il., Cumberland, Md., Lynn, Ma., Gloucester, Ma., High Point, N.C., Ithaca, N.Y., Joliet, Il., New Castle, De., Mt. Vernon, N.Y., New York, N.Y., Richmond, Mn., Terre Haute, In., and Washington, D.C.

SELECTED CASE DESCRIPTIONS:

Chicago, Il., Extensive conversion of rental buildings to condominiums. Similar activity is taking place in nearby Evanston, Il.

Gloucester, Ma., Central Grammer School converted to moderate income, rental housing.

Ithaca, N.Y., DeWitt High School converted to multi-use complex containing housing, offices and shops.

New York, N.Y., Numerous instances of loft conversions in Soho, Noho, Tribeca and other formerly-industrial, Manhattan neighbor-hoods. Conversions also taking place in similar outer borough areas such as Long Island City, in Queens and the Atlantic Avenue cor-ridor in Brooklyn.

New York, N.Y., Growing volume of rental buildings converted to condominiums. This process is affected by rent control and con-dominium conversion regulations (e.g., fuel overcharges to basic rent price and level of tenant agreement required before conversion is allowed).

Washington, D.C., Increasing instances of rental buildings converted to condominiums. Volume of conversion is also influenced by local rent control and condominium conversion statutes.

SUPPORTIVE PUBLIC STRATEGIES:

State:

The most common form of *state* adaptive reuse assistance is aid for residential rehabilitation—*all* states (25) with adaptive reuse pro-grams offer low-cost loans, technical assistance or other subsidies/ encouragement for residential rehabilitation.

Federal:

The most common form of *federal* adaptive reuse assistance is also residential rehabilitation support. There are 11 such programs (out of a total of 30 federal adaptive reuse programs) which encourage rehabilitation by providing mortgage insurance, loan guarantees, mortgage writedowns, etc.

To illustrate, the abandoned Gloucester (Massachusetts) Central Grammar School, located in a single-family neighborhood, was successfully converted to single-family, attached housing.[13] (This project sparked a similar conversion of another nearby educational facility.[14]) Where market and structural characteristics of the surplus property allow, commercial adaptation is possible. Ithaca's unused DeWitt High School was converted to a commercial complex containing shops, offices and apartments.[15] Dallas' Central Middle School is now used as a neighborhood shopping center. Abandoned schools in Manhattan are presently being converted to multiple uses including art galleries and museums.[16]

The neighborhoods for residential revitalization activities must be both unique and only in the early stages of nonresidential economic decline. Structure investment is usually tied to believed, future neighborhood stability once the conversion takes place.

UNIQUE NONRESIDENTIAL REVITALIZATION (EXHIBIT 3)

Limited commercial revitalization in *declining* areas is often possible in situations where unique structural or locational advantages permit. In *healthier* areas one can count on routine replacement of a commercial use that has failed due to one or several of the more conventional business maladies, i.e., misreading of the market, mismanagement, personal tragedy of owner, etc. This is usually not the case in declining areas. Except for a limited number of necessary convenience goods outlets (drug store, candy store, liquor store, etc.), successor commercial uses in declining areas depend heavily on the uniqueness of the site or commercial endeavor.[17] Flea markets, open air produce markets, surplus property outlets, peddlars' rows, are the types of unique and nomadic activities which depend on central locations or access to major thoroughfares; specialty stores, primitive/ novice art distribution centers, pottery/handcraft aggregates, etc., frequently need a structure of significant size or architectural significance to merchandise their goods.

Nonresidential adaptive reuse frequently capitalizes on the changing economic function and markets in the central city. To illustrate, many urban communities have experienced a decline in basic manufacturing activity and hence a softening in the value/price of old lofts and factories. The very fact that these structures can now be purchased inexpensively permits their reuse for new commercial purposes. In Rochester, New York, for example, Lawyers Cooper-

EXHIBIT 3

MODERATE CONVERSION OF EXISTING MIXED USE FACILITIES
TO CREATE NEW COMMERCIAL USES

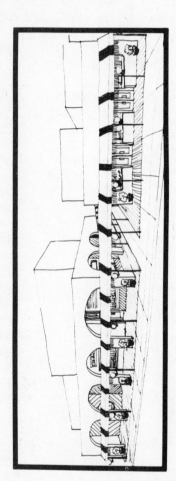

Source: F. Gradilone, Rutgers University Center for Urban Policy Research, 1979.

EXHIBIT 4

UNIQUE NONRESIDENTIAL REVITALIZATION: APPLICATION AND SUPPORTIVE PUBLIC STRATEGIES

STRATEGY:	UNIQUE NONRESIDENTIAL REVITALIZATION
MUNICIPAL APPLICATION (Selected Examples):	Twenty-five cities (16%) of the 150 cities evidencing structure abandonment. Examples include: Akron, Oh., Baltimore, Md., Boston, Ma., Charleston, S.C., Dallas, Tx., Gary, In., Indianapolis, In., Louisville, Ky., Maynard, Ma., New Castle, Pa., New Orleans, La., Rochester, N.Y., San Francisco, Ca., Sherman, Tx., Youngstown, Oh., York, Pa.
SELECTED CASE DESCRIPTIONS:	*Charleston, S.C.*, Eastside solid waste incinerator converted to municipal office and library.
	Dallas, Tx., Cumberland High School converted to commercial office building.
	Maynard, Ma., Digital Equipment Co., Inc. conversion of out-dated textile mill to office space.
	Rochester, N.Y., Refurbishing of an old mill to 125,000 square feet of office space by Lawyers Cooperative Publishing Co.
	San Diego, Ca., Mansion (Heilborn House) converted to bank branch office of San Diego Federal Savings and Loan.
	San Francisco, Ca., Foremost Ice Cream factory converted to 65,000 office building by McGraw-Hill, Inc.
	York, Pa., City purchase of abandoned department store with UDAG funds. The former department store after transfer to a private developer, was converted to a modern office/retail facility.
SUPPORTIVE PUBLIC STRATEGIES:	
State:	About half of the states (25) with adaptive reuse programs offer technical/financial assistance for nonresidential revitalization.
Federal:	An increasing level of federal assistance is available—11 programs are now offered (the same number as for residential revitalization). The most important federal, non-residential programs are HUD's Urban Development Action Grant and the EDA's Title I and Title II loan/grant programs.

ative Publishing Company decided to remain in the city because it could inexpensively purchase an abandoned old mill that was suitable for conversion to office space. Digital Equipment Co., Inc. similarly purchased an outdated textile mill in Maynard, Massachusetts and subsequently converted the building to office space and display showrooms (see Exhibit 4 for further examples).

Unique nonresidential revitalization will often accompany unique residential revitalization. This relationship is much more symbiotic than accidental. Loft conversions to apartments generate demand for convenient retail and service facilities (e.g., stores and day care centers), themselves often usually housed in former lofts. The provision of this new retail-service network, in turn, encourages further residential conversion of lofts—activity stimulating a second round of nonresidential revitalization. This cycle is vividly displayed in Soho and Noho in Manhattan. The conversion of lofts to residence has encouraged a mushrooming of loft conversions to stores and cultural-recreational centers. These additions have strengthened and encouraged continued Soho-Noho residential revitaliztion.

The neighborhood for commercial revitalization is keyed to the amount of permanency of the planned investment. For vacant lot-based flea markets/peddlars' rows, neighborhood conditions may be as deteriorated as moderate decline; for structure-based, specialty store activities or office space conversion, the neighborhood must be much more stable, i.e., just beginning or only 'signs' of selective decline.

INTENSIFIED PUBLIC SERVICES—OFF-STREET COMMERCIAL DOCKS (EXHIBIT 5)

A significant problem for older urban areas is the traffic congestion and snarls, on minor arterials, occasioned by the streetside loading and unloading of commercial vehicles.[18] This situation frequently exists because insufficient loading space was allocated to these structures at the time of their original development. This, quite possibly reflected both the primacy of space and a different view of ultimate land use at the time of the original construction. Retail commercial space was highly in demand and expensive; thus most fronting spaces had to be allocated to rent paying tenants with little or no wastage. Further, the types of stores ehich once occupied these spaces may not have required truck delivery of bulk items—again occasioning omission of street-side loading space.

EXHIBIT 5

MINOR STRUCTURE CLEARANCE TO PROVIDE OFF-STREET COMMERCIAL DOCKS

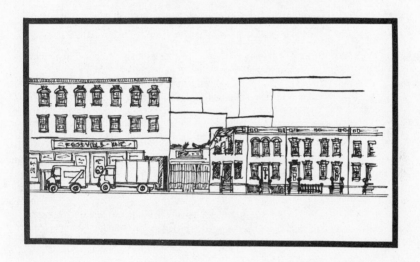

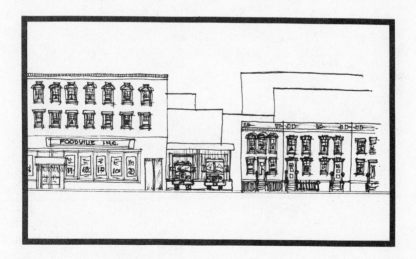

Source: F. Gradilone, Rutgers University Center for Urban Policy Research, 1979.

EXHIBIT 6

INTENSIFIED PUBLIC SERVICES–OFF-STREET COMMERCIAL DOCKS: APPLICATION AND SUPPORTIVE PUBLIC STRATEGIES

STRATEGY:

INTENSIFIED PUBLIC SERVICES–OFF-STREET COMMERCIAL DOCKS.

MUNICIPAL APPLICATION (Selected Examples:)

Fifteen cities (10%) of the 150 cities with structure abandonment. Examples include: Ashland, Ky., Buffalo, N.Y., Dallas, Tx., Des Moines, Ia., Lansing, Mi., New Castle, Pa., Paramount, Ca., San Bernardino, Ca., Wilmington, De., and York, Pa.

SELECTED CASE DESCRIPTIONS:

Buffalo, N.Y., CDBG funds used to demolish eight abandoned row houses to provide loading space in rear of produce distribution market.

Dallas, Tx., Demolition to improve truck unloading for converted Cumberland High School (see Unique Nonresidential Rehabilitation).

Lansing, Mi., CDBG funds used in Washington Square Annex Project to demolish deteriorated single-family homes impeding loading/unloading at neighborhood factory.

White Plains, N.Y., Abandoned buildings to rear of avenue with commercial stores demolished in order to improve off-street access.

York, Pa., Codorus Creek Project included demolition of abandoned houses to rear of commercial buildings in order to improve truck delivery.

SUPPORTIVE PUBLIC STRATEGIES:

State:

Only two states–Georgia and Texas–have specifically targeted programs for local public service upgrading.

Federal:

Two HUD programs, UDAG and CDBG, can be used for land clearing/demolition to assist commercial reuse/redevelopment.

As the demand for non-convenience, commercial facilities in the central core lessened due to suburban or regional competition, this occasioned vacant/abandoned commercial storefronts. The opportunity to crop out one or two shells, in a row of structures, obviously presents itself. The subsequent demolition of buildings, adjacent to commercial uses regularly serviced by large trucks, enables space to be created so that loading and unloading may take place off-street. Exhibit 5 presents graphic portrayal of just such a reuse strategy and Exhibit 6 describes illustrative examples.

Demolition to improve access is often a component of a larger commercial-industrial revitalization strategy. To illustrate, to facilitate truck delivery, York, Pennsylvania's Codorus Creek Renewal Project demolished abandoned houses to the rear of a commercial district. In Lansing, Michigan, the Washington Square Annex Project demolished a row of deteriorated single-family homes impeding loading/unloading at a neighborhood factory. Eight row houses were demolished in Buffalo, New York to improve access to a new produce distribution market.

Structure clearance to provide off-street commercial docks must take into account the potential longevity of the commercial facilities needing the loading space. Obviously, if the businesses which occupy the retail space are only economically-marginal, significant public investment should not be undertaken for this purpose. Thus, the scattered abandonment neighborhood or downtown area with, at least, short-run stability should be looked to as a possible site for the provision of off-street access. The most successful examples to date have been urban grocery stores, metal fabricating activities, printing businesses, etc., which appear to retain demand for their goods/ services long after other forms of retailing have passed from the scene.

Another form of off-street loading may take the form of pooled spaces for small specialty clients or for multiple members of a large, flea market. For these types of activities, space reserved for loading need not be much more than the space itself. Heavy investment in platforms/stairways is not necessary, as the main purpose is to keep adjacent traffic moving by removing regular delivery vehicles from the streets.

INTENSIFIED PUBLIC SERVICES—
TRANSPORTATION SYSTEM UPGRADINGS (EXHIBIT 7)

In the development of a neighborhood, street patterns and lot configurations occur as much from existing use as they do from planning. This combination frequently yields imperfect results. Triangular or semi-circular intersections, discontinuous streets, streets of varying pavement width, odd shaped lots, lots of excessive or reduced size, often emerge as fixed elements of the cityscape.

In declining areas, as the demand for land decreases, property may become available which may be redesigned to eliminate all or some

EXHIBIT 7
MODERATE STRUCTURE CLEARANCE TO IMPROVE TRAFFIC FLOW

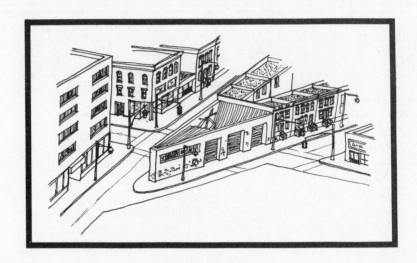

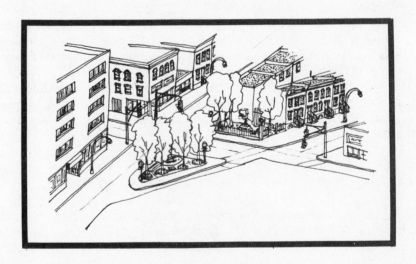

Source: F. Gradilone, Rutgers University Center for Urban Policy Research, 1979.

EXHIBIT 8

TRANSPORTATION SYSTEM UPGRADING: APPLICATION AND SUPPORTIVE PUBLIC STRATEGIES

STRATEGY: TRANSPORTATION SYSTEM UPGRADING

MUNICIPAL APPLICATION (Selected Examples:) Nine cities (6%) of the 150 cites with structure abandonment. Examples include: Berkeley, Ca., Bronx, N.Y., Detroit, Mi., Evanston, Il., Holyoke, Ma., Kansas City, Ka., New London, Ct., St. Louis, Mo., and Reading, Pa.

SELECTED CASE DESCRIPTIONS: *Bronx, N.Y.,* Both Charlotte Street and St. Ann redevelopment proposals include demapping several streets and realignment of others.

Detroit, Mi., Abandoned buildings demolished in Elmwood Park rehabilitation project in order to construct new roads and to realign existing streets.

Kansas City, Ka., The 5th and Minnesota Avenue renewal project included realignment of two thoroughfares made possible by using surplus land—Washington Boulevard and Minnesota Avenue.

New Brunswick, N.J., Downtown redevelopment includes multiple cases of road system upgrading in order to improve ingress/egress to CBD.

St. Louis, Mo., CDBG funds used in Franklin Industrial Park Redevelopment to realign several connecting streets between Franklin Park and CBD.

Hoboken, N.J., Mass transportation center refurbished using UMTA funds.

SUPPORTIVE PUBLIC STRATEGIES:

State: Three quarters of all (25) states with adaptive reuse assistance provide both technical and financial assistance for transportation system upgrading.

Federal: Two programs—HUD CDBG and DOT Title 23—can be used to finance land clearing/demolition resulting in improved residential/commercial access. Another source of support is UMTA's Title 3-Section 3-Urban Initiatives program.

of the negative conditions mentioned above.[19] Land may be cleared to obtain proper street alignment or more consistent street widths; lots may be combined or shaved to improve lot dimension consistency; curb surface area may be expanded for safety purposes; curb cuts may be introduced to provide ramps for the handicapped, elderly, etc. Finally, standard width, two land arterials (no parking either side) may be cut and redesigned to allow for non-restrictive bus loading/unloading.

Since street redesign is often costly, experience has shown that projects must be designed that may be funded either as exclusive local capital investments or as capital additions whose funding will be augumented through intergovernmental transfers. In most instances, this translates into either modest local redesign endeavors or more encompassing, intergovernmentally-shared activities.

Street realignment is one of the few strategies that is ideal for badly deteriorated neighborhoods. It is in just such locations that significant amounts of surplus property becomes available; sufficient to allow street and right-of-way design considerably different from what already existed. To illustrate both the Charlotte Street and St. Ann Revitalization Projects in the South Bronx will demolish abandoned properties in order to realign important connector streets. In New Brunswick, N.J. an abandoned factory on the periphery of the CBD was demolished to provide badly-needed realignment of a major state road. (See Exhibit 8 for further examples.)

NEIGHBORHOOD PARKING (EXHIBIT 9)

Deteriorating neighborhoods of older, second order cities or in outlying areas of major cities, have transportation demands/preferences that occasion automible use much more so than was the case when these areas were originally developed. This is due to a combination of factors such as changing occupational characteristics of residents and decentralization of employment activities away from the major nodes once served by mass transit. In these locations, streets are characterized by dual side, bumper to bumper parking on thoroughfares that were designed for single-side parking and much less intensity of use. This creates problems from the regular cleaning and repair of streets, snow removal during the winter season, and additionally, imposes a forced parking search for neighborhood residents at the close of each working day.

In areas that have moderate levels of structure abandonment it is possible to aggregate contiguous parcels of land for additional

EXHIBIT 9

MAJOR STRUCTURE CLEARANCE TO PROVIDE PROXIMATE OFF-STREET PARKING

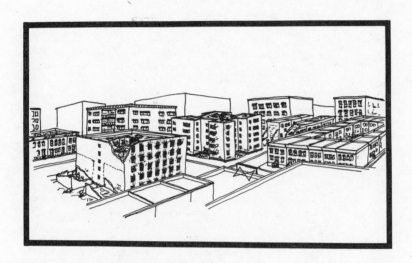

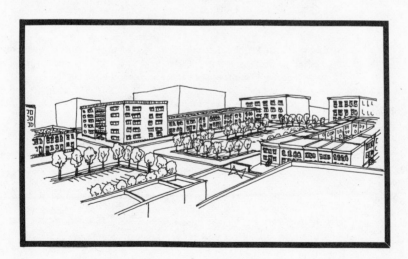

Source; F. Gradilone, Rutgers University Center for Urban Policy Research, 1979.

EXHIBIT 10

NEIGHBORHOOD PARKING:
APPLICATION AND SUPPORTIVE PUBLIC STRATEGIES

STRATEGY:	NEIGHBORHOOD PARKING
MUNICIPAL APPLICATION (Selected Examples):	Ten cities (8%) of the 150 cities with structure abandonment. Examples include: Bronx, N.Y., Detroit, Mi., Evanston, Il., Hoboken, N.J., Kalamazoo, Mi., New Brunswick, N.J., New London, Ct., Lansing, Mi., and Superior, Wi.
SELECTED CASE DESCRIPTIONS:	*Bronx, N.Y.*, Charlotte Street redevelopment proposal includes conversion of abandoned lots to neighborhood parking areas.

Detroit, Mi., Abandoned buildings demolished in West Side Industrial rehabilitation project to provide both access and parking for revitalized industrial park.

Hoboken, N.J., Abandoned structures near-PATH terminal demolished in order to provide street level commuter parking.

Kalamazoo, Mi., City purchased abandoned state amory with CDBG funds and demolished structure to provide parking. In the South Mall area, the city purchased abandoned lots and buildings with CDBG funds, demolished on-site buildings, and created 600 space parking lot.

New Brunswick, N.J., Never used, cleared urban renewal sited converted to parking lot for nearby new twin office towers. A similar use is planned for proposed convention center-hotel complex.

New London, Ct., Abandoned lots acquired on Bank Street for police department and post office parking.

SUPPORTIVE PUBLIC STRATEGIES:	
State:	No specific form of state assistance for this adaptive reuse objective.
Federal:	HUD CDBG and UDAG funds can be used for demolishing buildings to create parking lots adjacent to residential or nonresidential buildings.

street-level parking.[20] Cleveland, Ohio assembled 20 abandoned lots to provide a 200 space parking lot at a key location near the CBD. New London, Connecticut reused tax foreclosed lots for additional police department parking (see Exhibit 10). This supplemental parking provided in these communities will potentially alleviate thoroughfare congestion created by double parking, provide longer term, off-street parking, and free street-side spaces for shorter-term convenience uses. As there is less overall demand for parking space, schemes such as alternate side parking or "cleaning period non-utilization" may be instituted to gain access to curbside positions for cleaning, maintenance, emergency snow removal, etc. Street level parking usually involves grading and paving of multiple land parcels and the installment of street lighting at the edges of the parking area.

It should be noted that areas must be chosen carefully to avoid creating neighborhood foci or undue maintenance and/or security problems. The area must have sufficient overall property abandonment to allow significant property assemblages to be obtained yet must be reasonably intact so that the demand for street level parking is still strong. Areas of moderate decline, i.e., those with noticeable amounts of abandoned structures and cleared, vacant land appear to be the most appropriate sites for this proposed reuse.

ACTIVE/PASSIVE RECREATION USE (EXHIBIT 11)

Residential neighborhoods in urban areas often lack on-site active or passive recreation space for both young and old. *Active* open space areas permit such uses as tot lots with durable playground equipment, roller skating flats (both permanent and portable), handball/tennis backstops, etc. *Passive* open space areas emphasize flower gardens and grassed areas with pathways/benches strategically spaced to allow use without damaging either laws or planted spaces.

McKeesport, Pa., for example, demolished two abandoned commerical buildings and created a 15 acre, combined active/passive recreation center. On a smaller scale, Camden, N.J. demolished an abandoned drug store to form a small, passively-oriented vest pocket park (see Exhibit 12 for other examples).

Passive-oriented open spaces in urban neighborhoods, if not carefully planned, may serve as future locations of loitering for the unemployed, addicts, physically/mentally disabled and the downtrodden elderly. As such, passive open space is either located im-

EXHIBIT 11

MINOR STRUCTURE CLEARANCE TO CREATE
TOT LOTS/VEST POCKET PARKS

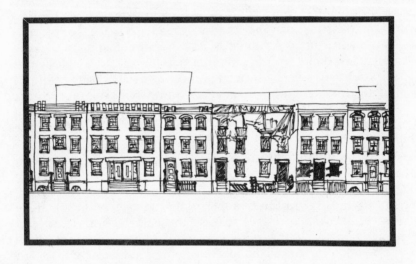

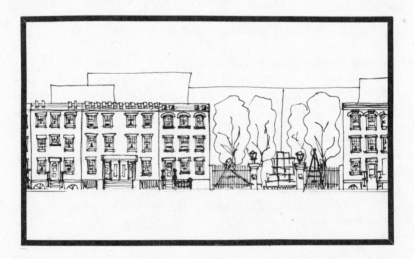

Source: F. Gradilone, Rutgers University Center for Urban Policy Research, 1979.

EXHIBIT 12

ACTIVE-PASSIVE RECREATION USE:
APPLICATION AND SUPPORTIVE PUBLIC STRATEGIES

STRATEGY: ACTIVE-PASSIVE RECREATION

MUNICIPAL APPLICATION (Selected Examples): Fifteen cities (10%) of the 150 cities with structure abandonment. Examples include: Camden, N.J., Charleston, S.C., Fitchburg, Ma., Mckeesport, Pa., New Brunswick, N.J., Oakland, Ca., Pontiac, Mi., Port Arthus, Tx., Somerville, Ma., Springfield, Il., and Wilmington, De.

SELECTED CASE DESCRIPTIONS: *Camden, N.J.*, Abandoned drug store demolished—land converted to vest pocket park maintained by adjacent church.

Charleston, S.C., Municipal use of funds from Heritage Conservation Recreation Service and private foundation to develop small park near Fort Sumter.

Fitchburg, Ma., Parking lot of abandoned branch bank converted to vest pocket park. CDBG funds used to purchase playground equipment.

McKeesport, Pa., Two abandoned commercial buildings, vacant six years, demolished—site converted to 15 acre park.

New Brunswick, N.J., Urban renewal lands, with minimal redevelopment potential, converted to vest pocket parks.

Springfield, Il., 200 highway right-of-way (encompassing 13 acres) developed into buffer zone-park by municipal development of walking areas and tot lots.

Wilmington, De., Regular disposal of city owned lots, by donation or sale, to community groups that will refurbish with recreational equipment and provide ongoing supervision.

SUPPORTIVE PUBLIC STRATEGIES:

State: Twenty of the twenty-five states that provide adaptive reuse assistance offer assistance in the form of categorical park or recreational aid.

Federal: CDBG funds available for demolishing buildings for reasons of safety or future redevelopment plans. Several federal programs assist the purchase/donation of land for parks including: HUD's Section 414 Grants and the Section 203(k) Surplus Property Transfers administered by HEW, GSA, and the Heritage Conservation and Recreation Service (Dept. of the Interior). Aid for equiping or refurbishing vest pocket park-tot lots is available from the Urban Park and Recreation Recovery Program administered by the Heritage Conservation and Recreation Service.

EXHIBIT 13

MODERATE STRUCTURE CLEARANCE TO PROVIDE REAR YARDS AND OFF-STREET REFUSE PICK-UP

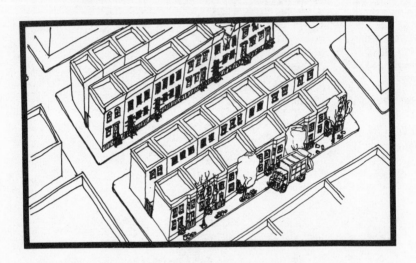

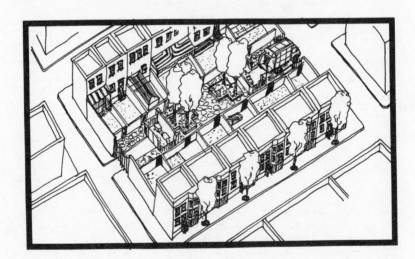

Source: F. Gradilone, Rutgers University Center for Urban Policy Research, 1979.

EXHIBIT 14

INTERIOR LOTS/LOTSTEADING:
APPLICATION AND SUPPORTIVE PUBLIC STRATEGIES

STRATEGY:	INTERIOR LOTS/LOTSTEADING

MUNICIPAL APPLICATION (Special Examples):   Seventeen cities (11%) of the 150 cities with structure abandonment. Examples include: Albany, N.Y., Ashville, N.C., Baltimore, Md., Covington, Ky., Cumberland, Md., Dallas, Tx., East St. Louis, Il., Elizabeth, N.J., High Point, N.C., Louisville, Ky., Minneapolis, Mn., Jersey City, N.J., Philadelphia, Pa., Port Arthur, Tx., and Wilmington, De.

SELECTED CASE DESCRIPTIONS: *Baltimore, Md.*, City has employed successful homesteading program with ancillary lotsteading strategy.

Camden, N.J., Tax foreclosed lots, as they become available, offered by city to requesting lotsteaders.

Philadelphia, Pa., As in Baltimore, city has expanded homesteading to include lotsteading to requesting residents.

Port Arthur, Tx., Several abandoned 50' x 150' lots transferred to adjacent churches, etc.

Wilmington, De., City sells vacant lots to adjacent property owners for $1. Neighborhood groups are also encouraged to adopt and maintain vacant land parcels.

SUPPORTIVE PUBLIC STRATEGIES:

State: Eighty percent of the 25 states with adaptive reuse programs have operable programs which assist the development of interior lots/lotsteading.

Federal: Three federal programs are available. Community Development Block Grants may be used for structure demolition to decrease density of adjacent buildings. Lot *improvements* may also be funded by the CDBG program. The remaining two federal programs—HUD Section 414 and GSA Section 203(k) provide for the transfer of surplus federal lands for inner city municipal/resident reuse.

mediately proximate to exclusively controlled users (elderly, handicapped etc.) or is extensively patrolled to avoid damage to plantings
or pathways caused by vandals, unsupervised children, etc.

Neighborhoods of light to moderate residential abandonment
appear as the most likely recipients of this reuse strategy. Alternative
sites are available given noticeable amounts of structure deterioration
and cleared land yet neighborhoods where demand for such facilities
is still strong. The new recreation spaces upon completion, become
part of a reasonably stable, geographic area.

INTERIOR LOTS/LOTSTEADING (EXHIBIT 13)

A constant in *urban* life is reduced light/air and immediate exterior
physical space usually necessitated by maximizing the utilization of
highly priced land. In residential urban areas seldom is there enough
unoccupied space for multi-directional exposures and exterior gardens, lawns, interior courts, sitting areas, etc.

In specific neighborhoods, where the demand for land is diminished, currently unoccupied space adjacent to occupied parcels may
provide the opportunity for the construction of additional windows
and to expand the grassed area of a building site. The terms "adopt-
a-lot" and "lotsteading" refer to the actions of residential landowners
who acquire adjacent surplus real property to open them up to light
and air or to reduce the density of their immediate environs.[22]

In many instances cities with homesteading programs (e.g., Wilmington, Philadelphia and Baltimore) have added "lotsteading" as
an additional neighborhood supportive activity. The approach of
both programs is quite similar—surplus property is obtained from
municipal offices (oft-times bordering owners have priority in these
parcels) and become a part of the legal description of the plot of
the opting adjacents provided the new owners satisfy occupancy/
maintenance requirements. (See Exhibit 14 for examples of lotsteading).

Two interested property owners occasionally equally divide or
"Share-a-lot." A benefit accruing to such division is that if the property is currently occupied by a structure, increased light and air is
then available to both neighboring properties after structure is
removed. In addition, lawns and gardens are created and then become native to the cityscape much as they are an integral part of
the more traditional suburban community. Some type of fencing
or natural border frequently is created to avoid subsequent tres-

EXHIBIT 15

MAJOR STRUCTURE CLEARANCE FOR SHORT-TERM LAND BANKING

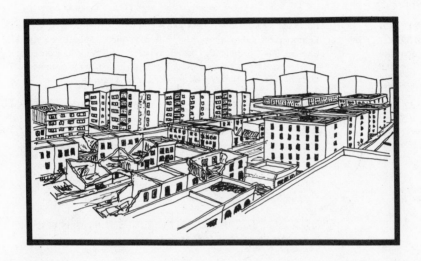

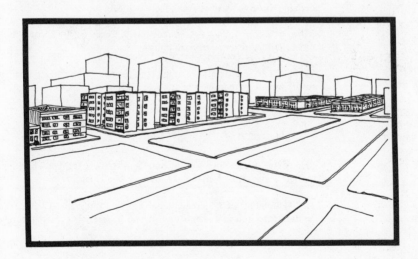

Source: F. Gradilone, Rutgers University Center for Urban Policy Research, 1979.

EXHIBIT 16

LAND BANKING:
APPLICATION AND SUPPORTIVE PUBLIC STRATEGIES

STRATEGY: LAND BANKING

MUNICIPAL   Fourteen cities (14%) of the 150 cities with structure abandonment.
APPLICATION   Examples include: Alexandria, Va., Baltimore, Md., Bay City, Mi.,
(Selected   Chelsea, Ma., Cleveland, Oh., Hempstead, N.Y., Lackawanna, N.Y.,
Examples):   Lower Merion, Pa., New Haven, Ct., Milwaukee, Wi., Ossining, N.Y.,
      Philadelphia, Pa., Winston-Salem, N.C., and York, Pa.

SELECTED CASE   *Baltimore, Md.*, Southeast Land Bank assists rehabilitation/home-
DESCRIPTIONS: steading activities.

      Cleveland, Oh., City land banks parcels taken via accelerated tax
      foreclosure.

      Milwaukee, Wi., City land banks foreclosed and donated lands to
      assist public and private reuse.

      Philadelphia, Pa., Philadelphia Industrial Development Corporation
      land banks vacant industrial parcels.

      St. Louis, Mo., St. Louis Land Reutilization Authority uses land
      banking for large scale redevelopment projects.

      Winston-Salem, N.C., Land banking used to encourage construction
      of low/moderate income rental housing.

      York, Pa., Major parcels are being land banked in Southeast area for
      future inner-city redevelopment.

SUPPORTIVE
PUBLIC
STRATEGIES:

      State: Five states offer primarily technical assistance for land banking:
      Massachusetts, Michigan, New Jersey and Rhode Island.

      Federal: The Community Development Block Grant Program (CDBG) can
      be used for municipal acquisition of real property for planned future
      uses.

passing or use of this space by neighborhood residents other than the specific owners themselves.

This type of adaptive reuse strategy is most appropriate for beginning or moderately declining neighborhoods. Demolition and clearing costs usually prohibit its application in areas of rampant decline.

LAND BANKING/URBAN GARDENING (EXHIBIT 15)

The social and economic conditions of deteriorating neighborhoods may be such that there exists widespread structure and property abandonment with little or no development interest on the part of the future public or private property holders. Once cleared of structures, there is land for which there is no short-term use.[23]

Communities faced with the problem of growing inventories of surplus properties such as Newark, St. Louis, Kansas City and Cleveland have turned to landbanking as a recycling mechanism (see Exhibit 16 for other examples).

Land banking consists of intake, holding and reuse components. Land becomes part of the "bank, " i.e., is transferred from private to public ownership through sale, condemnation, donation or lease-purchase agreements. Only certain land parcels are selected for land banking; criteria for selection include: economic value/noneconomic value to other public or quasi-public agencies, presence of adjacent bankable land parcels, levels of serious structure deterioration in the immediate neighborhood, projected redevelopment schedule for the area, etc. Land is withdrawn from the bank through various forms of municipal property disposition.

Land banking recognizes the necessity to actively control land while planning for its reuse. The operator of the land bank; i.e., municipal surplus property manager, independent land use authority, etc., must make decisions as to: (1) which land will be retained in public control versus transfer to private ownership; (2) which immediate, limited uses must be deferred fro longer term, more encompassing uses; (3) what will be the most realistic land use assignment for lands which obviously have no value under existing classifications.

URBAN GARDENING (EXHIBIT 17)

Also in neighborhoods were limited future development potential exists, growing numbers of community residents have turned to vegetable and flower gardening on the cleared vacant land tracts.[24]

EXHIBIT 17

URBAN GARDENING–INNER - CITY VEGETABLE GARDENS: APPLICATION AND SUPPORTIVE PUBLIC STRATEGIES

STRATEGY: URBAN GARDENING–INNER-CITY VEGETABLE GARDENS

MUNICIPAL   Sixteen (10%) of the 150 cities with structure abandonment. Ex-
APPLICATION   amples include: Atlanta, Ga., Baltimore, Md., Boston, Ma., Chicago,
(Selected   Il., Cleveland, Oh., Detroit, Mi., Houston, Tx., Jacksonville, Fl., Los
Examples):   Angeles, Ca., Memphis, Tn., Milwaukee, Wi., Newark, N.J., New
                     Orleans, La., New York, N.Y., Philadelphia, Pa., and St. Louis, Mo.

SELECTED CASE: *Cleveland, Oh.* 2500 individual urban gardens at 68 sites throughout
DESCRIPTIONS: the city. Gardens are loaned to individuals upon recipt of signed
                     waver of liability from gardener—average plot size 10' x 20'.

                     Los Angeles, Ca., 40 community and individual gardens. Gardens
                     leased from city for $1 annually. Community garden size 400-600
                     ft.^{2}; individual gardens approximately 250 ft.^{2}.

                     Newark, N.J., Over 1500 individual urban gardents currently being
                     tilled. Gardens are rented for $1 annually from city—average plot
                     size 30' x 30'.

                     Philadelphia, Pa., 236 'vacant lot' gardens for community and in-
                     dividual purposes. Community garden size averages 50' x 100';
                     individual gardens 15' x 15'. City grants permission for one years'
                     use via letter which includes waiver of liability.

                     St. Louis, Mo., Close to 600 urban gardens: 2 community, 524 family
                     (backyard), 240 individual. Average family garden 12' x 25'; mini-
                     gardens 10' x 10'. Must send letter to Community Development
                     Office to petition.

SUPPORTIVE
PUBLIC
STRATEGIES:

   State: No state programs specifically targeted for urban gardening adaptive
                     reuse objectives.

   Federal: U.S. Department of Agriculture "Urban Gardens Demonstration
                     Program", provides technical and limited financial assistance to cities
                     desiring to establish urban gardening programs.

Gardens exist at the community, family and individual scale. For these three types of gardens average size is 50 feet x 100 feet, 20 feet x 25 feet and 10 feet x 15 feet respectively. Land is obtained for gardens from the city usually by signature of the prospective gardener on a waiver of municipal liability. Lands are loaned or rented to individuals for one year frequently at token cost.

Urban gardens, most of which produce truck farming vegetables, may be found in Newark, N.J., St. Louis, Mo., Cleveland, Oh., and Philadelphia, Pa.

Conclusion

Adaptive reuse planning is a sensible approach to neighborhood revitalization. It is an integrated strategy for the inventory, control, assembly and reuse of surplus real property. The reuse phase presents multiple *physical* land use alternatives whose selection and application depend upon existing neighborhood conditions. Thus, there are physical reuse strategies which appear more or less appropriate for beginning, moderately declining or heavily deteriorating neighborhoods.

The physical reuse strategy, regardless of neighborhood application, recognizes limited value associated with the current use designation of land. Various private-public partnerships emerge which attempt to slightly alter the land's use to enhance its or neighboring properties' value. This is the essence of adaptive reuse —a strategy of central city redevelopment whose objectives are tempered by the reality of limited property potentials and diminished meliorative resources.

Notes

1. See Roger S. Ahlbrandt and Paul C. Brophy, *Neighborhood Revitalization: Theory and Practice* (Lexington, Mass.: Lexington Books, 1975); Michael Agelasto *Neighborhood Conservation Through Housing Rehabilitation* (Washington, D.C.: Congressional Research Service, 1976) Report No. 76-154.

2. Donald Ball, "There's Even Hope for Housing in Detroit," *Planning*, Vol. 45, No. 7 (July 1979) pp. 20-24; David B. Carlson, *Revitalizing North American Neighborhoods: A Comparison of Canadian and U.S. Programs for Neighborhood Preservation and Housing Rehabilitation.* (Washington, D.C.: Urban Institute, 1978). Peter Lane and Anthony Zahn, *Recycling Inner City Real Estate* (New York: Practicing Law Institute, 1976).

3. George Sternlieb and James W. Hughes, "Analysis of Neighborhood Decline in Urban Areas," in U.S. Department of Housing and Urban Development, *Housing in the Seventies Working Papers* (Washington, D.C.: Government Printing Office, 1976), pp. 1117-1180; U.S. Department of Housing and Urban Development, *Neighborhood Preservation Catalogue* (Washington, D.C.: Government Printing Office, 1976).

4. See Chapter Thirteen in this monograph.

5. Donald Cannon *et al.*, "Identifying Neighborhoods for Preservation and Revival," *Growth and Change*, Vol. 8 (January, 1971), pp. 35-38.

6. See footnote 3 and Public Affairs Counseling, *HUD Experimental Program for Preserving the Declining Neighborhood: An Analysis of the Abandonment Process* (San Francisco: Public Affairs Counseling, 1973); B. Goldstein, *Neighborhoods in the Urban Economy: The Dynamics of Decline and Revitalization* (Lexington, Mass.: Lexington Books, 1979).

7. Raynor M. Warner *et al.*, *New Profits From Old Buildings: Private Enterprise Approaches to Making Preservation Pay* (New York: McGraw Hill, 1978).

8. U.S. Department of Housing and Urban Development, Office of Program Planning and Evaluation. Urban Housing Committee Region, IV (Atlanta, Georgia), *Revitalizing Urban Neighborhoods: Programs Around the United States* (Atlanta, 1979).

9. Elizabeth Thompson (ed.), *Recycling Buildings: Renovations, Remodeling, Restorations and Reuses* (New York: McGraw Hill, 1977).

10. See also, Michael D. Rancer, "New Uses for Old Buildings: Options for Recycling," *Municipal Innovations*, No. 18 (May 1977), entire issue; Gene Bunnell, *Built to Last: A Handbook on Recycling Old Buildings.* (Washington, D.C.: Preservation Press, 1977); "Recycling for New Uses," *Buildings*, Vol. 70 (June 1960), entire issue.

11. Kristina Ford, *Housing Policy and the Middle Class* (New Brunswick: Rutgers University Center for Urban Policy Research, 1978).

12. Judith N. Getzels, "Recycling Public Schools", *ASPO Planning Advisory Service*, (August 1976), Report No. 319.

13. *Ibid.*

14. *Ibid.*

15. *Ibid.*

16. For further discussion of reuse potential and strategies, see Sherban Cantacuzino, *New Uses for Old Buildings*, (London: The Architectural Press, 1975); Giorgio Cavaglieri, "Design Adaptive Reuse," *Historic Preservation*, Vol. 26, (January-March 1974), pp. 12-17; "The Challenge of Underused Church Property and the Search for Alternatives." The Proceedings of the First International Conference on. . . ., May 13-14, 1975 (Cambridge, Mass.: The Cheswick Center, 1975); Educational Facilities Laboratories, *Reusing Railroad Stations* (New York: Educational Facilities Laboratories, 1974); Educational Facilities Laboratories, *Surplus School Space: Options and Opportunities.* (Washington, D.C.: Government Printing Office, 1976); U.S. Conference of Mayors, *Railroad Land Revitalization*, Vol. 1, No. 1, (1979).

17. Cambridge Seven Associates, Inc. "An Old Brewery Complex and River Site Will Become an Art and Transportation Museum with Waterfront Promenades," *Progressive Architecture*, (January 1979), p. 74.+; Praynor M. Warner *et al.*, *Business and Preservation: A Survey of Business Conservation of Buildings and Neighborhoods* (New York: INFORM, 1978); Emanuel Berk, *Downtown Improvement Manual* (Chicago: American Society of Planning Officials, 1976); Benjamin Goldstein, "Revitalization of Commercial Areas in Urban Neighborhoods," *Practicing Planner*, Vol. 6 (June 1976), p. 33-36; Walter C. Kidney, *Working Places, The Adaptive Use of Industrial Buildings* (Pittsburgh: Overpark Press, 1976); Marie Nahikian, "Here's One City Where Commercial Rehab Works," *Planning*, Vol. 43 (July 1977), p. 14-15; W.P. O'Mara, "Adaptive Use of Older Buildings: New Interest in an Existing Opportunity," *C.I.I. News and Views*, Technical Report 5, (February 1979), p. 14.

18. Stanley Abercrombie, "Adaptive Reuse" *Urban Design*, Vol. 8 (Summer 1977), pp. 34-37; "Adaptive Reuse: The Key to Born Again Central Cities," *Mortgage Banker* (December 1978), pp. 57-59; Denre, R. Lwo & Sharon Ryan eds. "Managing Urban Decline: An Urban Conservation Report from Dayton," *Nation's Cities*, Vol. 14 (March 1976), p. 17; Roger Ahlbrandt, "Public Policies for the Preservation of Capital in Older Areas," *American Real Estate and Urban Economics Association Journal*, Vol. 5 (Spring 1977), pp. 68-84.

19. Stanley Abercrombie, "Adaptive Re-use," *Urban Design* Vol. 8 (Summer 1977), pp. 34-37; "Recycling for New Uses," *Buildings*, Vol. 70 (June 1976).

20. Gordon Bender, *Multiple Use Facilities. Staff Report for Federal Architectural Task Force* (Washington, D.C.: Federal Architectual Project, National Endowment for the Arts, 1974).

21. " 'Port-a-Parks' Halt Vacant Lot Blight: Colorful Small Parks Planted in Downtown Winniped, Canada Provide Shopper an Oasis Until Developers Arrive," *The American City and County* (February 1979), p. 68+.

22. Helen Macre, "Urban Homesteading & Today's Frontier," *HUD Challenge*, Vol. 8 (December 1977), pp. 8-12; Michael Molyneux, "A California Experiment in Urban Homesteading," *Western City*, Vol. 53 (May 1977), pp. 20-22; Urban Systems Research, *The Urban Homesteading Catalogue*, 3 Volumes. (Washington, D.C.: Government Printing Office, 1977).

23. Craig Davis, "Issues in Municipal Public Land Banking," *Annals of Regional Science* (November 1976), pp. 55-56; John Linner, "Cleveland is Banking Tax Delinquent Land," *Practicing Planner*, Vol. 7 (June 1977), pp. 9-13; Joseph Rosenblum, "Land Banking" National Council for Urban Economic Development Information Service, No. 15 (June 1978) entire issue; Joseph Rosenblum, "Land Banking," *National Council for Urban Economic Development Information Service*, No. 15 (June 1978), entire issue.

24. C. Bearre, "Detroiters Turn Vacant Lots/Gardens" *The Sun*, (Detroit) 4 (6): 3 Apr. 8, 1976; L. Brauer, "Garden on the Move (urban gardening education)." *Ext. Serv. Rev. Coap. Ext. Serv.* 49(1): 14-15, Jan/Feb. 1978. NLA Code No. 1EX 892 EX.; Cheryl Brickner, "Detroiters Dig

Growing Roots." *Extension Service Review.* 49(1): 4-5 Jan/Feb. 1978; Robert Frausto, "Guerilla Gardens Blossom As City Folks till the Earth." Planning *ASPO* 42 (10): 20-21 1976; "Get Growing: Adopt a Lot. *Management Information Service Report.* April 1977, entire issue. Allison Hallingby, "Urban Gardens: Weed'em and Reap." *Nation's Cities* 15 (7)L 4-5 Jl. 1977.

Multifamily Housing Demand: 1975-2000

George Sternlieb
Robert W. Burchell

INTRODUCTION

Multifamily housing and indeed rental housing generally is the stepchild of government attention to shelter requirements. While just prior to World War II less than half of all American households owned their own residences, the positive relationship between housing acquisition costs, operating elements and incomes has permitted a vast expansion of ownership.

The massive shift from a predominantly renter society to one of ownership is shown in Exhibit 1. From 1890 to 1930 the proportion of total housing units occupied by renters stayed between the 52 and 54 percent level. The enormous toll taken in America's household incomes in the Depression is reflected by an abrupt increase to 56 percent renters in 1940. Forced saving of the World War II years, combined with vigorously productive government policies, made possible rapid shift to ownership after this period. In 1950, there were 4 million more owner-occupied housing units than renter

219

EXHIBIT 1
OCCUPIED HOUSING UNITS BY TENURE (U.S. TOTAL, 1975)
[Units in thousands]

Year	Total occupied units	Owner occupied		Renter occupied	
		Number	Percent	Number	Percent
1890	12,690	6,066	47.8	6,524	52.2
1900	15,964	7,455	46.7	8,509	53.3
1910	20,256	9,301	45.9	10,954	54.1
1920	24,352	11,114	45.6	13,238	54.4
1930	29,905	14,280	47.8	15,624	52.2
1940	34,855	15,196	43.6	19,659	56.0
1950	42,826	23,560	55.0	19,266	45.0
1960	53,024	32,797	61.9	20,227	38.1
1970	63,450	39,885	62.9	23,565	37.1
1973	69,337	44,653	64.4	24,684	35.6
1974	70,830	45,784	64.6	25,046	35.4
1975	72,523	46,867	64.6	25,656	35.4

SOURCE: U.S. Department of Housing and Urban Development, "HUD Statistical Yearbook, 1976" (Washington, D.C. Government Printing Office, 1977), p. 261.

equivalents; by 1975, nearly two-thirds of all American households lived in their own facilities. In the 5 years from 1970 to 1975, the United States added 7 million net new owner-occupied housing units compared with barely 2 million units for renters—and this despite the very brisk upsurge in the latter as a function of Government subsidy implementation. In turn, rental housing, particularly large-scale multifamily facilities, has been seen as a largely transitional provision for a good many of its occupants until they can reach the new appropriate standard—a house of one's own.[1] Indeed, one of the major objections to the large central city was that this latter type of provision simply could not be met there—and that often occupants in such areas had no choice but the "inferior" rental housing.[2]

Homeownership has been the beneficiary of positive attention from practically all groups within our society. As indicated by poll after poll it is the keystone of the good life for most Americans. Thus the literature on homeownership, both popular and technical, is vast.[3]

Large-scale multifamily housing on the other hand has uniquely been undertaken by the professional developers and managers. These relatively specialized individuals are competent to deal with the increasing role of Government both directly and indirectly in its provision.[4] The bulk of these interventionary mechanisms is by no means the province of the federal government. While convential tract developers bemoan the increasing load of locally mandated requirements; minimum lot size, subdivision controls and the like; acquisition of land for individual dwellings, though frequently costly, has been far more popularly accepted than equivalent provision for multifamily units. Even at luxury rent levels the latter are frequently barred from suburban locations.[5] Multifamily housing is viewed as the city, as crowding, as changing the nature of the suburban-exurban setting of the homeowner. When the development incorporates low-income housing, the situation is even further accentuated.[6] The post World War II shift of the basic shelter ethic of the United States from rental accommodations to those offering home ownership has reinforced this feeling. The resulting stress, as reflected in the escalation of the costs of land appropriately zoned for multifamily housing in desirable locations has been enormous.[7]

In the last several years the real housing buying power of American households has been substantially reduced. Inflation in land, in building cost and, most of all, operating elements have begun to far outstrip post-tax incomes.[8] Despite this situation, Americans continue to pursue one-family homeownership with increased vigor. Some observers believe this represents the desperation of buyers who desire homeownership at any price today, fearing that tomorrow it will be even further out of their reach. Such a condition is by definition precarious. *While we may hope for the abatement of housing cost inflation, the changing demographic characteristics of America's population, together with a vast level of internal mobility, reinforces the belief that renewed attention to the multifamily housing development area is past due.*

Sequence Of the Paper

This paper has as its prime target the definition of future demand for multifamily housing. In order to achieve this, the presentation will turn first to data on who lives in rental housing partitioned by the type of structure they occupy. By matching these characteristics to future projections of America's population (which is undertaken in the section that follows), a preliminary profile of future rental demand emerges. This is refined by unit size configuration to reflect only multifamily (five units or more) rental housing. This in essence raises the question, "If all elements other than changing demographic characteristics of the population are equal, what would be the demand for multifamily rental housing?"

Clearly, however, these stable conditions rarely are maintained. Thus, the third section of the study looks at the supply elements and the factors which impact upon them. This, in turn, reflects upon some of the underlying dynamics which may well significantly alter the demand silhouette generated in the preliminary approach. The last section of the study concludes with a summary of basic findings together with their implications for national housing policy.

I. WHO LIVES IN RENTAL HOUSING: A MARKET PROFILE

INTRODUCTION

Practical forecasting requires a firm foundation in the present. Rental housing, particularly in larger structures, appeals to certain segments of our population. This section of the study is devoted to defining these elements. Some tenants are there by choice— others by necessity, some are long-term residents and some are transients, either in hope or reality, on thier way to one-family facilities. In any case, this type of profile when applied to future demographics provides a first rough estimation as a basis for more refined subjective elements.

HOUSING AND POPULATION CHARACTERISTICS: HOUSEHOLD SIZE BY STRUCTURE

There were more than 25 million renter households in the united States as of 1975. Typically these were relatively small households in terms of the number of people within them, indeed the median figure for all renter households was 2.1 Slightly less than one-third are one-person households, with a nearly matching proportion containing two persons. Households with five or more persons make up only one in nine of all renter units.

See Exhibit 2.

Most renters do *not* live in large-scale structures.[1] Approximately one-third live in facilities with only one unit (i.e., one-family rental units), with an additional one-fourth in structures with two-to-four units. *Indeed, if we were to limit the definition of large-scale*

EXHIBIT 2
RENTAL HOUSING—HOUSEHOLD SIZE
BY STRUCTURE SIZE (U.S. TOTAL, 1975)
[In thousands]

Persons	Total (U.S.) renter	Structure size						Mobile home or trailer
		1 unit	2 to 4 units	5 to 9 units	10 to 19 units	20 to 49 units	50-plus units	
Total	25,656	8,432	6,772	3,028	2,514	2,058	2,332	519
1	8,262	1,589	2,175	1,119	1,019	936	1,279	145
2	7,733	2,313	2,153	966	832	665	650	153
3	4,187	1,630	1,181	443	377	261	189	106
4	2,719	1,293	724	343	155	116	113	75
5	1,392	740	318	130	81	45	53	25
6 or more	1,364	867	221	127	51	35	48	16
Median (United States)	2.1	2.7	2.1	1.9	1.8	1.6		2.3

	Northeast	North-Central	South	West
Regional rental units (total)	6,690	5,938	7,763	5,254
1 unit	982	1,918	3,610	1,922
Mobile/trailer	46	98	272	103

SOURCE: U.S. Department of Commerce, Bureau of Census, "Annual Housing Survey (1975)," table V-53-45 (unpublished).

multifamily housing to those structures with 20 or more apartments, the total of 4.3 million would make up barely one-sixth of all rental units.

In general, household size decreases with the scale of the structure. Thus, for structures with one-rental unit the median size is 2.7, for the five-to-nine unit structure it is 1.9, for the 20-to-49 unit structures 1.6; in structures with 50 or more units, over half of the apartments have only one person. There are less than 200,000 families with five or more persons in large-scale structures—those with 20 or more units [a rather substantial proportion of these are probably public housing]. In sum, therefore, *the most important configurations in the world of renter shelter are small-scale structures and these are particularly skewed toward smaller households, con-trary to common perception.* This latter element is particularly the case in large-scale rental structures (five units or more) which are substantially the domain of small households rather than large sized families.[2]

REGIONAL VARIATION

At the bottom of Exhibit 2 is shown data by region for rental housing and some of its elements. There is an unfounded belief that it is the Northeast which is the dominant province of rental shelter. Clearly, as shown in the data, this is not the case. The South actually has more rental housing units than the other regions shown, with the Northeast second, and the West last.

Included is further information indicating the number of rental units which are in one structure as well as mobile homes or trailers. The resulting skew in regional allocation is evident. The Northeast has the smallest number of one-unit rentals as well as the smallest number of mobile homes or trailers used for residence. These two groups combined make up less than one-sixth of the total rental units in the region. In the South, on the other hand, more than half of all rental facilities are in one-unit structures, mobile homes, or trailers. The equivalent for the North-Central and Western States is roughly one-quarter and one-third, respectively. *Thus it is the Northeast which, by far, has the greatest number of multifamily rental structures. In that region structures with two or more units shelter a total of more than 5½ million individuals to the South's less than 3 million.*[3] [4] *The other two regions are intermediate.*

HOUSEHOLD TYPE

The data on number of persons per household earlier presented mask a substantial skew of sex distribution within households. Rental housing is much more the province of female-headed households, for example, than holds true of owner-occupied units. As shown in Exhibit 3, one out of six of all renter housing units in the United States is occupied by a female-headed household; in owner-occupied facilities, the equivalent is one in nine. Less than one-quarter of these rental facilities is occupied by husband and wife plus children under the age of 18 and, as would be guessed, the bulk of these are in small-scale structures. When examination was undertaken of female-headed households with two or more persons, there was little in the way of a regional skew.

In sum, husband and wife households represent a minority of the occupants of rental housing. This is particularly the case in large-scale units with barely one-third of the households in 20-or-more unit structures having this configuration.

EXHIBIT 3
RENTAL HOUSING—HOUSEHOLD TYPE
BY STRUCTURE SIZE (U.S. TOTAL, 1975)
[In thousands]

Household composition	Total (U.S.) renter	Structure size						Mobile home or trailer
		1 unit	2 to 4 units	5 to 9 units	10 to 19 units	20 to 49 units	50-plus units	
1-person households	8,262	1,589	2,175	1,119	1,019	936	1,279	145
2-or-more person household	17,394	6,843	4,597	1,909	1,495	1,123	1,053	375
Husband and wife	11,632	4,992	2,911	1,173	313	688	693	263
(With own children under 18)	(6,069)	(3,025)	(1,473)	(598)	(377)	(238)	(197)	(161)
Other male head	1,463	471	370	184	154	143	98	43
Female head	4,299	1,380	1,316	552	428	291	262	70

	Northeast	North-Central	South	West
1-person households	2,215	2,041	2,226	1,780
2-plus-person households, female headed	1,179	922	1,349	850

SOURCE: U.S. Department of Commerce, Bureau of Census, "Annual Housing Survey (1975)," table(s) V-53-4 to V-53-7 (unpublished).

RACE

While blacks make up 10 percent of total American households, they occupy 1 in 6 of all rental units.[5] Indeed, in the South more than one-quarter of all rental units are so occupied. There is significant regional variation along this line. In the West, blacks occupy 1 in 12 of the rental units, in the North Central States 1 in 7, and in the Northeast 1 in 6.

As shown in Exhibit 4, the distribution of blacks to whites as a function of structure size has little consistent variation until we turn to the structures of 50 or more units. Here blacks make up fully 19 percent of the occupants—this is probably due to the inclusion of large-scale public housing facilities within this structure size grouping.

EDUCATION

There are few more inclusive socioeconomic indicators in a society such as ours than education. In this context it is particularly noteworthy to view the educational level of the occupants of rental housing of all kinds in 1975 as shown in Exhibit 5. For all the heads of household in rental units, the median figure is 12.4, i.e., slightly over the high school level. This compares with 12.2 for homeowners as a group.

EXHIBIT 4
RENTAL HOUSING — RACE BY STRUCTURE
SIZE (U.S. TOTAL, 1975)
[In thousands]

Race	Total (U.S.) renter	Structure size						Mobile home or trailer
		1 unit	2 to 4 units	5 to 9 units	10 to 19 units	20 to 49 units	50-plus units	
Total	25,656	8,432	6,772	3,028	2,514	2,058	2,332	519
White	20,788	6,852	5,521	2,411	2,027	1,715	1,771	481
Black	4,252	1,428	1,164	514	412	264	436	34
Other	616	142	88	103	75	79	124	5

	Northeast	North-Central	South	West
Regional rental units (total)	6,690	5,938	7,763	5,254
Black	1,036	804	1,979	433
Other	143	69	88	315

SOURCE: U.S. Department of Commerce, Bureau of Census, "Annual Housing Survey (1975)," table V-53-1 (unpublished).

There is little variation among renters in educational attainment as a function of structure category. There is some indication that, in general, a higher level of formal schooling tends to be found in the larger developments. The lowest level of educational attainment, 12.2 median years of school completed, is found in one-unit mobile home and trailer rentals.

On the bottom of the Exhibit is shown median education of renters by region. This is roughly in accord with national trends. In any case it shows relatively slight variation.

Thus, large-scale rental housing currently is skewed toward small household sizes with a disproportionate number of them female-headed and a somewhat higher proportion of blacks than is the case for ownership housing. It should be kept in mind, however, that households in all forms of rental units, while representing some measure of dispersion, are well within the mainstream of American households generally.

EXHIBIT 5
RENTAL HOUSING—YEARS OF SCHOOL COMPLETED

| Years of school completed | Total (U.S.) renter | Structure size | | | | | | Mobile home or trailer |
		1 unit	1 to 4 units	5 to 9 units	10 to 19 units	10 to 49 units	50-plus units	
Total	25,656	8 432	6,772	3,028	2,514	2,058	2,332	519
No school	260	143	59	9	16	3	29	1
Elementary:								
Less than 8 yrs	2,858	1,300	695	272	155	166	222	47
8 yrs	2,184	765	611	205	165	129	251	58
High school:								
1 to 3 yrs	4,240	1,531	1,189	501	331	284	288	177
4 yrs	8,062	2,540	2,271	932	799	635	679	206
College:								
1 to 3 yrs	4,051	1,155	1,033	572	525	395	309	61
4 yrs or more	4,000	998	915	536	522	446	553	30
Median	12.4	12.2	12.4	12.6	12.7	12.7	12.6	12.2

	Northeast	North-Central	South	West
Median education by region	12.3	12.5	12.3	12.7

SOURCE: U.S. Department of Commerce, Bureau of Census, "Annual Housing Survey (1975)," table 53-51 (unpublished).

II. HOUSEHOLD FORMATION AND THE FUTURE DEMAND FOR MULTIFAMILY HOUSING

INTRODUCTION

The rough base of the demand figures to be generated for future multifamily housing demand at its initial level is a projection of population growth by age and sex segment. This, in turn, when multiplied by headship rates[1] (the proportion of people within each age and sex group who are heads of households) yields the number of renter households. Once this has been established such renter households are allocated to structure of various sizes.

HOUSEHOLD TYPE AND STRUCTURE SIZE

In Exhibit 6 data by age of head are presented for various configurations of household in 1975. These are further partitioned into structure size categories.

By using the ratio of the number of households headed by an individual within each of the sets to the total population of that same category, we secure a ratio of households to population for each

EXHIBIT 6
HOUSEHOLD TYPE AND
STRUCTURE SIZE (U.S. TOTAL, 1975)
[In thousands]

Household composition by age of head	Total (U.S.) renter	1 unit	2 to 4 units	5 to 9 units	10 to 19 units	20 to 49 units	50-plus units	Mobile home or trailer
Total	26,656	8,432	6,772	3,028	2,514	2,058	2,332	519
One-person households	8,262	1,589	2,175	1,119	1,019	936	1,279	145
Under 65 yrs	5,559	1,000	1,472	850	748	682	700	106
65 yrs and over	2,703	589	703	269	271	254	578	38
Two-or-more-person household	17,394	6,843	4,597	1,909	1,495	1,123	1,053	375
Male head, wife, present no nonrelatives	11,517	4,912	2,895	1,167	913	682	688	260
Under 25 yrs	2,299	811	642	279	249	146	74	97
25 to 29 yrs	2,555	1,008	698	301	237	143	103	65
30 to 34 yrs	1,416	681	327	137	104	76	57	35
35 to 44 yrs	1,741	911	362	165	96	81	97	29
45 to 64 yrs	2,398	1,102	599	198	135	145	187	32
65 yrs and over	1,109	399	268	87	91	90	169	4
Other male head	1,578	551	386	190	154	150	102	45
Under 65 yrs	1,469	508	353	188	150	139	85	45
65 yrs and over	109	43	33	1	4	10	17	0
Female head	4,299	1,380	1,316	552	428	291	262	70
Under 65 yrs	3,918	1,238	1,199	504	404	273	232	68
65 yrs and over	381	142	117	48	24	19	30	2

SOURCE: U.S. Department of Commerce, Bureau of Census, "Annual Housing Survey (1975)," table A-1 (unpublished).

of the several categories. For example, in 1975 there were a total of 5,559,000 one-person households under age 65. The total population from 18 to 65 at that time was 124,880,000. Thus the ratio of household headship was 0.045 (heads of household under the age of 18, a very small proportion of all households, have been excluded). By then using the U.S. Department of Agriculture projections for equivalent age groups for 1980, 1990 and the year 2000, respectively, multiplied by the household headship rate as of 1975, we secure the equivalent number of renter households for each particular category. Thus, in 1980 there will be 6,085,000 one-person households under the age of 65, in 1990, 6,701,000, and in the year 2000, slightly over 7 million.

By summing the total future renter households for each of the categories a first approximation of future demand is secured. *From 1975 to 1980 the increase in total renter households is approximately 2.5 million units (from 25,656,000 to 28,226,000). In the decade of the 1980, using procedures described above, an increase of an additional 2.9 million renter households is observable. In the 10 years from 1990 to 2000, the increase slackens to under 2 million households.* See Exhibit 7.

EXHIBIT 7
FUTURE RENTER HOUSEHOLDS 1980-2000— USING SERIES II POPULATION PROJECTIONS AND CONSTANT 1975 HOUSEHOLD-TO-POPULATION RATIOS

Type of household	1975 Households	1975 Population in comparison category	Ratio of households to population in comparison category	1980 Households	1980 Population in comparison category	1990 Households	1990 Population in comparison category	2000 Households	2000 Population in comparison category
1-person household:									
Under 65	5,559	[1] 124,880	0.045	6,086	135,252	6,701	148,913	7,181	159,578
65-plus	2,703	[2] 22,405	.121	3,016	24,927	3,609	29,824	3,850	31,822
2-or-more-person household:									
I. Male head (wife present, no nonrelatives):									
Under 25 (males 18 to 25)	2,299	13,910	.165	2,448	14,838	2,092	12,678	2,058	12,475
25 to 34 (males)	3,971	15,348	.259	4,660	17,993	5,290	20,424	4,435	17,124
35 to 44 (males)	1,741	11,149	.156	1,959	12,560	2,802	17,964	3,161	20,261
45 to 64 (males)	2,398	20,834	.115	2,423	21,069	2,558	22,244	3,296	28,659
65-plus (males)	1,109	9,176	.121	1,223	10,108	1,452	11,999	1,539	12,717
II. Other male head:									
Under 65 (males 18 to 65)	1,469	61,239	.024	1,595	66,460	1,759	73,311	1,884	78,519
65-plus (males)	109	9,176	.012	121	10,108	144	11,999	153	12,717
III. Female head:									
Under 65 (females 18 to 65)	3,918	63,642	.062	4,265	68,791	4,687	74,603	5,265	34,927
65-plus (females)	381	13,228	.029	430	14,819	517	17,824	554	19,105
Total future renter households	25,656			28,226		31,611		33,376	

SOURCE: "Annual Housing Survey (1975)," Rutgers University Center for Urban Policy Research, spring 1978.

[1] Total population 18 to 65.
[2] Total population 65-plus.

It must be stressed that this approach is at best a first approximation with a number of very specific limitations. Principal among them is the issue of future population growth. At least through the year 1990, however, this plays a relatively small role with all but a very few of the heads of households through that year presently countable—if subject to attrition. Even when the projection is taken to the year 2000, the vast bulk of the heads of household similarly are presently countable.

In addition, however, there is the proportion of individuals in the various age and sex cohorts who will form households. Second, within the total growth of households, will the proportion who turn to rental facilities as against ownership remain reasonably constant? *Much of the housing demand since 1950 has been a function of higher headship rates—of the high proportion of individuals willing and capable of initiating new households. There is evidence that this process, particularly for large-scale facilities, has run its course. Thus, it is felt that the 1975 rates are appropriate.*[2]

THE FIRST APPROXIMATION OF FUTURE RENTER HOUSING NEED

The number of new renter households is not directly equivalent to the number of additional rental housing units required. The principal additions lie in the issues of replacement, i.e., the loss either by demolition or conversion of extant rental units, as well as the level of vacancies that must be maintained in order to provide reasonably market fluidity. Neither of these elements is without controversy in terms of appropriate proportions.

The *replacement ratio* is a particularly controversial one. There is a substantial shift of rental units into the ownership stream through such processes as condominium conversion, the movement of partially seasonal rental housing into full-time ownership residences and the like. Offsetting this, on the other hand, are the uncounted numbers of units that shift from ownership into the rental market.[3] Examples of the latter are conversion of single large units into two or more smaller rental facilities. The last section of this study will turn to some of the potentials in the conversion realm. For the moment it will be assumed that the inflow and outgo by conversion into the rental pool are relatively balanced.

The Attrition Problem

There is a substantial leakage from America's housing stock in the form of abandonment and demolition. In the 5 years from 1970 to 1975, the loss in structures with five or more dwelling units approximated the 2½ percent level.[4] *Much of this, based on somewhat incomplete data, was concentrated in the older cities of the Northeast. The complement of population decline, and the out-migration of the more affluent, combined with some level of provision of competitive alternative housing units elsewhere was responsible in large part for this occurrence*

It should be noted in this context, that the overall housing unit attrition level hovers close to the 1 percent mark, thus indicating the significant stress on larger scale structures.[5]

For the purposes of this study, a 2 percent future attrition level has been projected. This indicates as average longevity of 50 years for the multifamily stock. It assumes that while the unnatural attrition level of recent years may continue in the central cities, it will be somewhat blunted as a national statistical phenomenon by the increasing level of multifamily housing which is either relatively new and/or constructed in areas of substantial housing demand.

Vacancy levels are the essential lubricant of the market. There is no generally accepted definition of a "market" which is an appropriate balance between supply and demand. Alaska, for example, has defined a housing market with less than a 3 percent vacancy rate as being of undue rigor.[6] The FHA, and at least in more stable areas the housing field as a whole has used a 5 percent vacancy figure as an appropriate one.[7] [8] The 5 percent figure is used in terms of the *additional* units required by future renter households in order to provide fluidity and a competitive market.

Exhibit 8 summarizes, by type of household—(1) the number of future renter households, (2) a vacancy figure which adds 5 percent to this marginal increment, and (3) a replacement figure of 2 percent. This latter has as its base the midperiod level of units (i.e., 1975, 1985, 1995) for each of the projected time periods.

For one-person households, under the age of 65, in 1980, therefore, the figures would indicate (1) a future renter household number of 527,000 (see Exhibit 7 for the origin of this figure), (2) a vacancy figure of 5 percent—or an additional 26,000 units—and (3) a 2 per-

EXHIBIT 8

FUTURE DEMAND FOR RENTAL HOUSING—1980-2000 (ADDITIONAL UNITS)

[U.S. total, by household type, in thousands]

Type of household	1980 (1975-80)			1990 (1980-90)				2000 (1990-2000)				
	Future renter households (1)	Vacancy (5 percent of future renter household) (2)	Replacement (2 percent of existing number of units) (3)	Total	Future household (1)	Vacancy (2)	Replacement (3)	Total	Future household (1)	Vacancy (2)	Replacement (3)	Total
1-person household:												
Under 65	527	26	582	1,135	615	31	1,278	1,924	480	24	1,435	1,940
65-plus	313	16	286	615	593	30	1,662	1,285	241	12	770	1,023
2-or-more-person household:												
I. Male head (wife present, no nonrelatives):												
Under 25	149	7	238	394	−356		454	98	−34		412	378
25 to 34	689	34	432	1,155	630	32	996	1,658	−855		888	33
35 to 44	218	11	186	415	843	42	476	1,361	359	18	632	1,009
45 to 64	25	1	240	266	135	7	498	640	738	37	660	1,435
65-plus	114	6	116	236	229	11	268	508	87	4	308	399
II. Other male head:												
Under 65	126	6	152	284	164	8	336	508	125	6	376	507
65-plus	12	1	10	23	23	1	26	50	9		30	39
III. Female head:												
Under 65	347	17	410	774	422	21	896	1,339	578	29	1,054	1,661
65-plus	49	2	40	91	87	4	94	185	37	2	110	149
Total additional rental demand	2,569	127	2,692	5,388	3,385	187	5,784	9,356	1,765	132	6,676	8,573

SOURCE: Rutgers University Center for Urban Policy Research, spring 1978.

cent replacement requirement (582,000 housing units) based on the number of renter households within this category as of the midperiod prior to project. This yields a grand total of 1,135,000. For each of the household types, and for each of the several intervals through the year 2000, the data are presented in Exhibit 8. At the very bottom of the exhibit are shown the totals for all types of rental demand using this approximation procedure. Thus, for the period from 1975 to 1980, by these calculations, nearly 5.4 million additional rental units will be required. For the decade of the 1980s the equivalent figure is close to 9.4 million; for the 1990-2000 period it is over 8½ million additional rental units.

It is interesting to note the impact of both the baby boom and the baby bust in the data array.[9] The first is shown by the single largest sector increment in 1975-80 period; it is in the 25-to-34 age category for male-headed households with wife present. In the next decade it is shared by the 24-to-34 and 35-to-44 year groups while in the decade of the 1990s it moves to the 45-to-64 year bracket. The baby bust, on the other hand, is shown by the two areas of decline in the decade of the 1980s and 1990s, respectively. In the first it is the male-headed household, wife present, under the age of 25; in the second, as a refection of the age cohort advancing in time, it is the same category of household, but now aged to the 25-to-34 year mark.

It is equally important to note the striking increment in female-headed households under the age of 65 with two or more persons. This distinctive group requires more than 700,000 additional rental housing units from 1975 to 1980, over 1,300,000 in the following decade, and by the 1990s it is the single largest of the renter household categories.

THE SHARE OF THE RENTAL HOUSING MARKET TO BE SECURED BY MULTIFAMILY UNITS

The data shown above are for all rental housing units but as shown in Exhibit 9A-9C, there are substantial variations in the proportion of households of various configurations in terms of the types of rental structures in which they live. *In the material which follows, incidence within various structure categories as of 1975 by household characteristic is used to prorate the future demand for multifamily, renter-occupied units distinct from the total universe of rental housing.*

EXHIBIT 9-A.—

FUTURE DEMAND FOR MULTI-FAMILY (5 UNITS OR MORE) RENTAL UNITS—1980

(1975-80) (U.S. TOTAL—BY SIZE CONFIGURATION)

[In thousands]

Type of household	Total future demand for rental housing (all structure and size configurations) (columns a-g)	Total future demand for multifamily housing (5 or more units per) (columns c-f)	Structure size multifamily units						
			1 unit (a)	2 to 4 units (b)	5 to 9 units (c)	10 to 19 units (d)	20 to 49 units (e)	50-plus units (f)	Mobile home or trailer (g)
1-person households:									
Under 65 yrs.	1,137	610	204	301	174	153	140	143	22
65 yrs or older	617	314	134	160	62	62	58	132	9
2-or-more-person households:									
I. Male head—wife, present no nonrelatives:									
Under 25	395	129	139	110	48	43	25	13	17
25 to 34	1,154	336	491	298	127	99	64	46	29
35 to 44	415	105	217	86	39	23	20	23	7
45 to 64	266	74	122	67	22	15	16	21	3
65 or older	235	92	85	57	18	19	19	36	1
II. Other male head:									
Under 65	283	108	98	68	36	29	27	16	9
65 or older	23	7	9	7	0	1	2	4	0
III. Female head:									
Under 65	775	280	245	237	100	80	54	46	13
65 or older	91	29	34	28	11	6	5	7	0
Total additional multifamily rental demand	5,391	2,084	1,778	1,419	637	530	430	487	110

SOURCE: Rutgers University, Center for Urban Policy Research, spring 1978.

EXHIBIT 9-B.—
FUTURE DEMAND FOR MULTI-FAMILY (5 UNITS OR MORE) RENTAL (1980-90) (U.S. TOTAL—BY SIZE CONFIGURATION) UNITS—1990

[In thousands]

Type of household	Total future demand for rental housing (all structure and size configurations) (columns a to g)	Total future demand for multihousing (5 or more units per) (columns c to f)	Structure size multifamily units						
			1 unit (a)	2 to 4 units (b)	5 to 9 units (c)	10 to 19 units (d)	20 to 49 units (e)	50-plus units (f)	Mobile home or trailer (g)
1-person household:									
Under 65	1,926	1,033	346	510	294	260	237	242	37
65 or older	1,286	654	280	334	129	129	121	275	18
2-or-more-person household:									
I. Male head—wife, present no nonrelatives:									
Under 25	98	32	35	27	12	11	6	3	4
25 to 34	1,656	482	705	428	182	143	91	66	41
35 to 44	1,362	344	712	283	129	75	64	76	23
45 to 64	640	178	294	160	53	36	39	50	8
65 or older	508	200	183	123	40	42	41	77	2
II. Other male head:									
Under 65	508	194	176	122	65	52	48	29	16
65 or older	50	15	20	15	0	2	5	8	0
III. Female head:									
Under 65	1,340	484	423	410	173	138	94	79	23
65 or older	186	58	69	57	23	12	9		1
Total additional multifamily rental demand	9,560	3,674	3,249	2,475	1,102	900	755	920	173

SOURCE: Rutgers University, Center for Urban Policy Research, spring 1978.

EXHIBIT 9-C.—
FUTURE DEMAND FOR MULTI-FAMILY (5 UNITS OR MORE) RENTAL UNITS—2000 (1990-2000) (U.S. TOTAL—BY SIZE CONFIGURATION)
[In thousands]

Type of household	Total future demand for rental housing (all structure and size configurations) (columns a to g)	Total future demand for multifamily housing (5 or more units per) (columns c to f)	1 unit (a)	2 to 4 units (b)	5 to 9 units (c)	10 to 19 units (d)	20 to 49 units (e)	50-plus units (f)	Mobile home or trailer (g)
1-person households:									
Under 65 yrs.	1,942	1,042	349	514	297	262	239	244	37
65 yrs and over	1,022	519	223	266	102	102	96	219	14
2-or-more-person households:									
I. Male head-wife, present no nonrelatives:									
Under 25	377	123	133	105	46	41	24	12	16
25 to 34	34	10	14	9	4	3	2	1	1
35 to 44	1,010	255	528	210	96	55	47	57	17
45 to 64	1,437	399	660	359	119	80	88	112	19
65 or older	400	157	144	97	31	33	32	61	2
II. Other male head:									
Under 65	507	194	175	122	65	52	48	29	16
65 or older	38	11	15	12	0	1	4	6	0
III. Female head:									
Under 65	1,660	599	525	508	214	171	115	98	28
65 or older	142	45	53	43	18	9	7	11	1
Total addtional multifamily rental demand	8,569	3,354	2,819	2,245	992	809	703	823	151

SOURCE: Rutgers University, Center for Urban Policy Research, spring 1978.

The data earlier discussed in this paper for household incidence by housing type make it possible to further refine and secure a projection for the various configurations of structure which will be required to incorporate the rental units. Again it must be stressed that these projections depend upon 1975 equivalence, i.e., respective categories and preferences similar to those of the specific base year. The projections which are shown in Exhibits 9-A, 9-B and 9-C incorporate both the vacancy rates and replacement ratios earlier discussed.

They show that in the 5 years from 1975 to 1980, a total additional multifamily rental demand slightly in excess of 2 million units—2,084,000 or approximately 416,000 units per year. For the 10-year period from 1980 to 1990, the equivalent is 3,674,000 units—of just slightly over 367,000 per year. In the decade of the nineties, the multifamily demand (5 units or more) declines again to the 335,000 mark per year.

It is the scrappage and replacement level rather than new household demand which is the major factor. Thus, the success of efforts at multifamily structure rehabilitation or other forms of preservation becomes the crucial variable in assessing future needs.

III. SUPPLY AND DEMAND FACTORS IN MULTIFAMILY HOUSING

THE PHYSICAL DEMAND OF CONSTRUCTION

Neither the projected number of gross rental housing units nor the proportion of them allocated to multifamily structures is such as to cause alarm over the delivery capacity of the American building industry. *The target figures shown, even extending them substantially, are well within our grasp.*

America's delivery capacity in multifamily housing is evidenced by its experience from 1969 through 1977 as shown in Exhibit 10. The peak year was the 917,000 units in such configurations, started in 1972. This undoubtedly reflects the substantial impetus of Section 236 funding.[1] The trough is in the recession of 1975 with starts at 208,000 during this year decreasing to barely 20 percent of the peak level.[2] *For the 7 years from 1969 to 1975, we started more than 4 million multifamily units or an average slightly in excess of 600,000 per year.*

EXHIBIT 10

TOTAL (PRIVATE AND PUBLIC) MULTI-FAMILY (5 UNITS OR MORE)
HOUSING UNIT STARTS, 1969-77

	Total (private and public) multifamily or more)	Federally subsidized	
		Total (5 units or more)	Percent of total starts
Year:			
1969	590, 100		
1970	558, 000		
1971	798, 500		
1972	917, 000	[1] 1, 045, 370	
1973	800, 300		
1974	386, 800		
1975	208, 100		
Total (1969–75)	4, 258, 800	1, 045, 370	24. 5
1976	292, 200	54, 340	18. 5
1977	415, 200	179, 430	43. 2

[1] Cumulative, 1969-75

NOTE: Limitations of data do not permit precise count of the number of multifamily units in nonrental forms. Even using the gross numbers of cooperative and condominium construction, shown in exhibit 13, would not alter the conclusions, however. The approximate number of multifamily (5 units or more) condominium starts was: 1974, 104,000; 1975, 26,000; 1976, 38,000; 1977, 57,000.

SOURCE: U.S. Department of Commerce, Bureau of Census, "Construction Reports (C20-78-1)—Housing Starts," January 1978; 10th Annual Report in National Housing Goals, January 1978, Washington, D.C., GPO, 1978, p. 40.

BARRIERS TO MEETING DEMAND

High Rate of Government Subsidy and Inflation. In more recent years, a slow but increasingly significant post-recession upsurge has started with the 292,000 starts of 1976 followed by 415,000 in 1977 and somewhere on the order of 550,000 to 600,000 anticipated for 1978. *It should be noted here that the new vigor is substantially a reflection of an increased level of explicit government subsidy. Practically all of the increase from 1976 to 1977, for example, was the result of Federal subsidization.*[3]

The need for this level of Federal input is a result of the growing imbalance between rent paying capacity and the rents required for unaided new multifamily units. In Exhibit 11, is shown data on the evolving picture of new major structure construction together

EXHIBIT 11
INFLATIONARY INDEXES PERTAINING
TO THE HOUSING INDUSTRY, 1972-77

	Consumer Price Index (CPI)		Boeckh Index—cost of new construction (percent increase) [1]
All items	All items (percent increase)	Housing (percent increase)	
1972	125.3	129.2	100.0
1973	133.1	135.0	105.9
1974	147.7	150.6	115.8
1975	161.2	166.8	127.2
1976	170.5	177.2	137.3
1977	[2] 177.1	[3] 184.1	149.9

[1] Apartments, hotels, and office buildings.
[2] 41.3 percent increase over 1972.
[3] 42.5 percent increase over 1972.

NOTE: CPI—1967 equals 100; Boeckh Index—1972 equals 100.

SOURCE: U.S. Department of Housing and Urban Development "1976 Statistical Yearbook—HUD," p.258; U.S. Department of Commerce, "Construction Review," November 1977, p. 47.

with an equivalent time series for housing costs generally as well as the changes in the cost of "all items." It is the first of these which has risen most dramatically. The cost of new major structures has gone up by nearly half [49.9 percent] from 1972 to 1977. During the same period the "all items" index rose 41.3 percent, general housing costs rose 42.5 percent.[4]

It is most striking to note that this level of inflation was undented by the massive recession in multifamily starts in 1975 which saw a precipitous downturn of nearly 80 percent. While perhaps a longer period of recession might curb the cost elements, the secondary ramifications do not make this an appealing prospect.

Land Zoning and High Interest Rates. Principal among the cost elements involved are those of land and money. The problems of zoning and the increasing flight from the dollar into land speculation have made sites which are both suitable and legally available for multifamily housing a relative scarce commodity in areas of high demand.[5]

The consequence in terms of the impact on the rent level requirements needs little amplification. While a number of states have made slight overtures toward a broadening of land use elements, these have been relatively minor. Many of the issues of zoning for multifamily housing, therefore, have ended up in the courts, a procedure which is both costly, time consuming, and scarcely generalizable.

Obtaining land zoning through the courts is both uncertain and very expensive. The construction of multifamily housing, therefore, has become a highly riskful venture. It has not been aided by a variety of environmental protection requirements, many of which have been misused as a second line of defense by local authorities in order to avoid high density housing.

The Federal entry into land use regulation has been miniscule. While there have been occasional urges by A–95 Review Agencies to take the lead in this regard, there has been little backing when these middle level review groups come under fire from local communities and citizenry.

The cost of money, a commodity whose cheapness in the United States made our housing the envy of the world, has been rising across the board. It should be noted, moreover, that despite this overall increase, *the financing of multifamily housing is not considered a desirable venture on the part of major sophisticated lenders.*[6]

At this writing, insurance companies are actively competing for shopping center properties. Indeed, the capitalization rate on some of the very best of these has been driven down to the 7½ percent level. At the same time, the proportion of total loans by such companies in multifamily housing has declined—and the rates of return required are escalating rapidly. Current capitalization rates, for example, on prime apartment house construction are currently reaching the 10 percent level.[7] Much of this stems from the operating imbalance endemic to this form of housing.[8]

Operating Costs Escalation and the Fear of Rent Control. The increased pressures on operating costs of multifamily housing are far from unique. They are felt in a broad spectrum of American life and industry. Within the homeownership domain, however, they can be at least partially offset by a combination of a do-it-yourself and don't-do-it-at-all approaches. The homeowner can absorb some of the increases by doing more work within his residence than would otherwise be the case and simply not think of it as as expense, or otherwise reduce the levels of maintenance or resident comfort, i.e., if one's fuel bill is too high, decrease the heat level. In industry as well as shopping center operation, there have been substantial efforts to utilize a variety of capital intensive investments to reduce operating costs. Multifamily housing has not yielded to equivalent procedures. Operating standards are largely set by a combination of the market and local housing codes. *There has been little in the way of innovational frontend investment to replace current practices of building operations.*[9]

At most, we see a drive toward reducing or transferring the burden of costs through separately loading operating costs. Examples of the latter include the decentralization of air-conditioning, making it incumbent upon each of the tenants to pay for his own usage, separate metering for utilities, etc. These provide automatic pass-alongs but, if anything, increase the gross rents since, in general, such provision is less efficient than centralized equivalents.

Since 1970 there has been a steady rise in rent to income ratios. In part, this resulted from a shift of the more affluent renters into homeownership; in part, however, it is a reflection of the increased rents required to meet operating costs.

In 1970, for all rental housing, gross rent as a percentage of income was 20 percent. By 1975, it had risen to 23 percent. In that year rent-income ratios were highest in large-scale multifamilay housing, with the median at approximately the 24 percent level, as shown in Exhibit 12. While the cost squeeze is far from unique to rental housing (increases in costs of homeownership have been higher than those of rental housing) homeownership costs have been offset by the capital gains resulting from inflation. The real costs of homeownership, at least for the more fortunate occupant, have been decreased by the increases in housing value. Thus homeownership has been sustained, despite the cost-income squeeze in this arena, by its speculative nature; by the capital value increments which have abated the pressures of annual carrying costs.

The same does not hold true for rental housing. There is no equity buildup, the hard-pressed consumer simply finds a larger share of his or her income going for rents.

The imbalance, in a variety of areas, has brought either the reality or the threat of *rent control*. In turn, this has had a very strong chastening influence upon lender and builder willingness to become involved in the multifamily rental housing industry except under the most favorable circumstances.[10] These largely revolve around luxury construction, the possibilities of condominium construction, and/or, essentially, a bailout Government mortgage. In this last case, the builder's profit comes not from operating the structure, but rather from its construction. The price, in turn, has been a massive wave of Government guaranteed multifamily mortgages which are

EXHIBIT 12
RENTAL HOUSING — GROSS RENT AS A PERCENT OF INCOME (1975)

Rent as a percent of income	Total (U.S.) renter	1 unit	1 to 4 units	5 to 9 units	10 to 19 units	20 to 49 units	50-plus units	Mobile home or trailer
Total	24,959	7,736	6,772	3,028	2,514	2,058	2,332	519
Less than 10 percent	1,710	629	484	184	137	122	125	30
10–14 percent	3,599	1,215	987	426	350	266	313	41
15–19 percent	4,055	1,261	1,114	490	466	321	377	66
20–24 percent	3,572	1,018	900	454	406	304	431	59
25–34 percent	3,990	1,076	1,121	547	447	365	354	80
35 percent or more	6,556	1,668	1,935	867	660	614	680	132
Not computed	1,437	869	231	61	49	66	51	111
Median	23	22	24	24	23	25	24	26

	Northeast	North Central	South	West
Gross rent as a percent of income by region (median)	24.0	23.0	22.0	24.0

SOURCE: U.S. Department of Commerce, Bureau of Census, "Annual Housing Survey (1975)," table 0-53-53 (unpublished).

in deep difficulty. *As of late 1977, approximately 1 in 5 of the nearly 7,000 projects currently under Federal subsidy in the United States were either in a state of mortgage default or assignment, or the projects themselves have been acquired by HUD through foreclosure.*[11]

In the privately financed areas, the situation is not nearly as serious—but there is some indication of an increased level of mortgage delinquency. The drive toward condominium conversion bears strong witness to the reluctance of private operators to continue despite preferential tax legislation.

Cooperative and Condominium Conversion. The growth of the condominium and cooperative form of housing, particularly the former, is shown in Exhibit 13. In 1970, there were only 85,000 condominium units in the United States. In the 5 years from 1970 to 1975, more than 1 million new units were constructed. In addition, there were 100,000 conversions. While the pattern in cooperatives clearly shows a preference for conversions, it also indicates new construction equal to 20 percent of the base in the 5 years from 1970 to 1975. By 1975, condominiums made up 1.85 percent of all occupied housing units of all configurations and cooperatives an additional 0.65 percent. While many of these were in townhouse configurations, as shown in the exhibit, a substantial proportion were high-rise and garden configurations, i.e., within the multifamily domain.[12]

EXHIBIT 13

CONDOMINIUM AND COOPERATIVE HOUSING STOCK (U.S. TOTAL)

[In thousands]

	Existing, 1970	New construction, 1970–75	Conversion, 1970–75	Removals, 1970–75	Inventory	Percent of all occupied units, 1975
Condominiums........	85	1,078	100	11	1,252	1.85
Cooperatives..........	351	70	25	7	439	.65

DISTRIBUTION OF CONDOMINIUMS BY STRUCTURE TYPE

[In percent]

	Northeast	North-Central	South	West	United States
Townhouse...............	55	35	40	55	45
Garden...................	35	40	40	40	40
Highrise..................	10	25	20	5	15
Total..................	100	100	100	100	100

SOURCE: U.S. Department of Housing and Urban Development, "HUD Condominium/Cooperative Study, Vol. 1—National Evaluation." p. III-2, 1974; III-25.

Will the condominium or co-op replace the necessity for additional rental units? Certainly the preference for ownership strongly supported both by inflationary considerations and the tax code is substantial.

Broader public policy is caught on the horns of a dilemma: on the one hand, resident ownership has definitively been linked with positive conditions such as the maintenance and care of structures. On the other hand, given the mobility required by a technological society, one would have to view the potential shift toward the relative immobility of homeownership with some measure of concern. Rental housing for those without the required downpayment for home acquisition, for those in transit to more permanent location, and for those individuals who require the delegation of all the managerial function of ownership to others, should not pass from the scene—and, given its key nature and scale of its incidence, undoubtedly it will not.

CONCLUSIONS

The need for multifamily housing is a function of both household formation, and the share of those households who will find this type of shelter most appropriate to their needs and resources. Given a continuance of the 1975 market share by household type, we can forecast (after appropriate allowance for vacancy and demolition), a demand for multifamily housing well within our production capacity. *Indeed, the production anticipated for 1978 is nearly 1½ times the annual requirement for 1975-80, slightly more than that ratio for the years in the decade of the 1980s and nearly twice as much as required in the 1990s. The "housing problem" has shifted from the provision of gross number of units to a struggle for controlling their costs.*

However, we caution that the aforementioned problems—high level of Government subsidy, high rate of inflation, high interest rates, escalating operating costs, the fear of rent control and condominium conversions—are indeed serious and pose potential problems to the delivery of new multifamily units.

We have a significant need for increased provision of mulitfamily rental housing. We have the experience, the skilled manpower and the competence to construct it. We have yet to attack the issues of the costs and with them the adequacy of existing housing programs to deal with the problem.

The Federal efforts to decrease housing costs have largely revolved around cheapening the cost of money through subsidizing interest rates and/or extending the longevity of mortgages and thus reducing amortization. Despite efforts in this regard, the imbalance between rent and incomes has continued.

Under HUD Section 8, we have approached the problem differently, in essence grouping all of the subsidy mechanisms into a rent allowance.[13] *By making the manifold stream of subsidies explicit and amassing them into one figure, we may have created a politically self-defeating program.*[14] The large scale of the annual subsidies involved raises some concern as to their potential longevity. We still have not come to grips with the basic cost issues in multifamily shelter, neither in land acquisition, construction, nor most significantly, in operation. In this last area, while there was an aborted attempt by HUD to develop a national training program and research activity, it is noted for its lack of accomplishment.

The gap between our production capacity and future need provides an opportunity to refine our approaches to providing new housing as well as offering a significant potential for additional upgrading of existing housing—increasing the demolition ratio.

National data can be misleading. A vacancy in New York City does not provide housing opportunity for the family which has moved to Houston. Much of the challenge of the future must involve a selective pruning of archaic and faulty multifamily structures from areas of declining need, while maintaining an appropriate fiscal maintenance balance for the remainder. At the same time, however, the responsibility for developing new facilities for regions of high growth will be substantial. The increased trend toward government financing of multifamily housing indicates a weakness in their market viability—an inadequate balance between construction costs, financing, operating costs and rents. However, there is strong reason to believe that unless there is a significant shift out of one-family housing, a very strong and critical review should be required of major incentive programs to increase the flow of multifamily units in any substantial measure in excess of the target figures presented here.

We have been coping with housing production in a relatively short-term frame of reference. Even the 10-year projections of a decade ago, and the famous 26 million unit figure which resulted, failed to grasp the longevity of housing. [15]

Large-scale shelter structures make sense only with long-term utility. The apartment house built today must have utility for a minimum of 35 to 40 years, otherwise its real "costs" both to its developer and to the Nation as a whole may be completely inordinate. In turn, this basic arithmetic indicates the necessity for market projections certainly through the year 2000 and beyond.

ADDENDA

I. THE COMPETITIVE FINANCIAL DISADVANTAGE OF MULTIFAMILY HOUSING

In our paper we have pointed to the inbalance between current capitalization rates for multifamily housing (in most areas of the country now in excess of 10 percent) versus the equivalent for shopping centers with recently consummated sales at the 7½ percent mark. They are both forms of income property and historically have partaken of the same financial markets. They both represent avenues for highly leveraged investment through the use of long-term debt financing. Why the difference?

The variation lies primarily in the relative ease with which the shopping center leasing format adjusts to inflation. Typical leases involve a base rent charge with a percentage override past certain minimal sales volume. Assume that the physical volume of goods—the number of units and the quality thereof remains constant. Strictly as a function of inflation, once the minimal rent threshold is reached, the owner of a shopping center will receive additional rents as a percentage of the inflation in total dollar sales. *The escalators are automatic; they do not require renegotiation but rather take place immediately.*

While the depreciation aspects of investments in shopping centers have been somewhat altered over time through changes in the tax code, with additional limitations periodically under discussion, in a world troubled by inflation the shopping center looks relatively safeguarded. Thus, not only is the owner's equity relatively secure against the erosion of the dollar, but so is the collateral base of the mortgage holder.

In addition, there has been a rapid evolution of the variety of financial mechanisms used to underwrite such facilities with participation loans increasingly prevalent. A typical financing currently involves not merely a fixed yield mortgage but also some measure of upward flexibility, either some equity participation, a potential percentage rent override on sales past a certain level, or the equivalent. Leases with individual store tenants typically call for an instant passthrough of increased costs such as taxes. The services provided by the shopping center are precisely enumerated as are the requirements of the tenantry.

The contrast with the multifamily market is evident. Rents nationally have tended to lag the overall consumer price index, and indeed, have even more substantially lagged the costs of homeownership. Despite this there is substantial consumer resistance to rent increases commensurate with inflation. Time lags through more or less long-term leasing arrangements are not uncommonly built into the contractual arrangement.

More formidable, however, is the fear, either real or latent, of rent controls. These have tended to put a damper on increases. In a study, for example, conducted by Goldman-Sachs (the investment banking firm), the finding was made that rents generally would have to increase on the order of 20 to 25 percent before multifamily housing could be viewed as an appropriate investment vehicle for its clients.

In a sense, some multifamily housing has been the victim, at least in part, of a variety of federally of locally supported mortgage cost lowering schemes of the past. These have permitted initial financing at relatively lower interest charges than would have been required by free market rent levels. However, when mortgages are recast in order for owners to recapture equity, subsidized mortgages may not be available. An enormous gap then opens up between the capacity of the current rent levels to carry free market debt service requirements. For example, assume a building is financed under a below market rate mortgage at the 6 percent level, with the mortgage five times the rent roll of the building. In the course of time, the mortgage is paid down, and the owner wishes to recapture his equity by rolling over the indenture, i.e., refinancing it. Current market interest rates are at the 10 percent interest level. Again we will calculate the mortgage as five times the rent roll.

The difference in interest charges, very roughly calculated, is the 4 percent rate difference multiplied by five times the rent roll or 20 percent of the annual rent. While this illustration overstates the case—rents, for example, may well have gone up since the initial mortgage was taken out—it illustrates the problem of moving from a subsidized market to a nonsubsidized one. The level of equity buildup in subsidized, rent limited structures, thus may be vastly overstated if just the level of amortization is viewed.

In the case of the shopping center, the disjuncture on refinancing is much less. While influenced by the overall increase in interest charges, there are very few that were the beneficiaries of subsidization.

The situation is further complicated by the archaic nature of operating patterns in multifamily housing. There has been little in the way of technological innovation, little in the way of labor saving devices or organizational formats which will produce real savings in operating costs. The historic capacity of the middle class to live in multifamily housing without subsidization was in very large part a tribute to the availability of inexpensive labor, of janitors and superintendents paid trivial sums of money plus perhaps a marginal basement apartment in return for a 60-hour workweek. The rapid unionization of this sector in some areas, the disappearance in all areas of equivalent adequate labor, imposes a very substantial operational stress. It has resulted with dissatisfaction toward the level of services on the part of tenants on the one hand and/or increased operating costs on the other.

The rent levels in multifamily housing are also limited by the tax benefits and investment opportunities available through alternative forms of housing. There is substantial evidence of a cream-skimming procedure—a shift of more affluent tenantry over time to the one-family market. While this may be attuned to national objectives, *it leaves the remnant tenant pool much more limited in rent paying capacity* (and for that matter, will).

It should be noted, in this latter context, that while a variety of Government aid programs for renters trigger in at 25 percent of income (less appropriate allowances for scale of family, et cetera), there is substantial evidence that occupants of one-family housing are paying substantially higher proportions of their incomes for this privilege—thus indicating relative preference in the marketplace for the latter shelter format.

In sum, therefore, sophisticated investors view the multifamily structure, except under unique circumstances and unique locations, as a relatively riskful, noninflation proof investment.

We have had substantial involvement in interviewing on an off-the-record basis, both major mutual savings banks and insurance companies which were once major investors in this form. Suffice it to say that, in general, it is now only of marginal interest.

II. THE FUTURE OF SECTION 8

The history of Section 8 and the stipulations (subsequently generally violated) of the original enabling legislation and administrative requirements illustrates the frustrations, limitations and learning about housing of a whole generation of programs. The legislation was an effort to take the Federal Government out of the real estate business—out of the production subsidy business, out of the locational problems and move rather to a revival of the low income market through direct subsidies to consumers. Its ideal was mixed income housing and the stimulation of construction and rehabilitation through the strengthening of demand. The increasing reality is one in which all or nearly all the tenants in a building are under Section 8, of a constellation of aid programs used concurrently, with Section 8 essentially sitting uneasily on top of them. And this is in direct contravention of its original intent as a replacement of such programs. It is one in which Section 8 is increasingly used as a takeout mechanism for poorly conceived and/or financed governmental housing efforts of the past. In this latter regard, it is being utilized to relieve the fiscal pressures of FHA and state housing finance agency projects which would otherwise require refinancing.

Thus in a significant measure Section 8 merely involves the propping up of older forms of Government subsidization by new forms of Government assistance rather than their replacement.

The program is enormously costly. At a time when median rental levels in New York City, for example, hover at around the $200 per month mark, the fair market rents for new construction and substantial rehabilitation in elevator buildings within that city range from $491 for an efficiency apartment to $873 for a four-bedroom unit. For extant housing, the equivalent figures are $223 and $390. There is increasing evidence that the nominal maximums, particularly for new construction, become the minimums. There is additional evidence that there is much questionable rehabilitation being offered—and subsidized—by the program.

Certainly some of these programs are the results of administrative difficulties to be encountered by any new, complex approach to an area as varied as America's housing. However, the track record now is long enough to raise serious question.

At a minimum it will require much more in the way of supervision. We would suggest further that the unit costs are so high, the number of individuals covered by the programs so very large, as to limit its extent in the future. It does nothing to attack the basic operating cost problem, nor does it provide adequate stimulus for operational and/or construction efficiencies. The program conceptually is commendable—operationally we would view it as questionable.

III. FUTURE ADDITIONS OR REDUCTIONS OF THE RENTAL HOUSING STOCK THROUGH CONDOMINIUM CONVERSION OR SUBDIVISION OF ONE-FAMILY UNITS

The rental housing industry of the United States gives substantial indication of moving away from its unique operating pattern to one much closer to the European—particularly the French version; the condominium or co-op. In the basic paper we have cited the data which is available on condominium conversion. There is great variation in the rate at which this is taking place within the United States as a whole—and within the economic categories of tenantry as well. There is no question that for the more affluent members of our society, given current tax laws and the inability to pass through that portion of rents which go for local property taxes (an issue which is currently being raised by New York State) the condominium—co-op format has increasing post-tax virtues. These are further compounded by the possibilities it offers as a possible haven for inflation-fleeing dollar investments. We would suggest, however, that given the present income levels of the Nation's renters, the level of conversion, unless aided by some form of Government financing, will be relatively slow over time.

In terms of new construction of multifamily units, the pattern is much more forcefully toward condominiums. It should be noted that the data in these areas must be viewed with some measure of trepidation. Studies that we have undertaken in Florida, for example, indicate that a number of nominal condominium units, depending upon the vagaries of the market and specific ownership patterns, are available for rent. The flow between these various forms of tenure is quite abrupt and probably at least in part, avoids the Census count net. To the degree, therefore, that condo co-op replaces straight rental housing, there will be a decrease in the number of such units available.

The other side of the ledger, however, is the conversion of one-family private homes into two or more units. Though it has attracted much less attention, it may be equally forceful. Much of this is undertaken outside normal, legal procedures. Indeed, in a great many jurisdictions in which it is occurring, it is specifically illegal. We have undertaken a comparison of Census data over time which indicates far more two-family homes than can be accounted for in terms of nominal permits and starts. The answer is conversion.

The median size of household since 1970 in the United States has gone from 3.14 persons down to the 2.8 level. The increase in home-ownership costs as a percentage of income has been equally dramatic. Given these elements combined with the extraordinary number of four- and five-bedroom units, particularly in split-level configurations, this yields a highly probable flow of conversion in the future. Field studies undertaken by the Center for Urban Policy Research at Rutgers University, for example, in a classic post World War II suburban area—Bergen County, N.J.—very specifically indicate that this process is well underway. It should be stressed that this is not merely a phenomenon of poor or central city areas, but rather one which is also taking place in the suburbs.

Thus two conflicting elements are at work. The first, condominium conversion reducing the number of rental units, the second conversion of one-family homes into two or more units, increasing their availability. A side note should be entered in this reckoning which indicates some of the fiscal pressures which are at work. One of the more popular configurations of New York City housing now—and one which dominates the unaided housing starts—is the so-called "illegal three." This is the term which is used in *official* city counts to denote structures which are nominally built and licensed for two-family occupancy but which incorporate as a matter of course a third unit. Given current real estate costs, this merely exemplifies the pressures to secure some measure of income in order to support ownership.

IV. RECOMMENDATIONS

1. HUD HAS A RESPONSIBILITY FOR ALL THE NATION'S HOUSING STOCK

The bulk of HUD programming, executive focus, and research has been devoted to the low rent-income end of the housing stock. There has been inadequate focus on the long pipeline which lies behind it, and on the enormous national investment in the general multifamily housing stock which simply cannot be replicated. Federal action, in terms of stemming the tide of abandonment and housing decay, has tended to intersect too little and too late in the process. In general, it has been based upon an inadequate comprehension of the overall dynamic. HUD simply must broaden its attention span.

2. WITHIN FHA THE LEVEL OF DATA MAINTENANCE AND COMPREHENSION ON MULTIFAMILY HOUSING IS TOTALLY INADEQUATE

While operating statements are required under a variety of FHA programs, they are rarely, if ever, audited, poorly reviewed, inadequately administered and standardized. Second, there is no overall attempt at analysis, at developing operating cost data, trend analysis, etc. In the absence of such devices abrupt and very costly crises which may have been long in the making come as unexpected surprises. *We cannot afford the sloppiness involved. Nowhere in the United States is there adequate, impartial data on operating costs and the like for multifamily housing. We are collecting the raw elements required for such analysis but simply not closing the loop in terms of appropriate structuring and quantification.*[1]

3. TAX TREATMENT OF RENTS

The issue of the deductability by tenants of that portion of their rent which essentially flows through the landlord's hands to local jurisdictions in terms of real estate taxes must be reviewed. The situation is already coming to a head in New York and rather than a perfunctory acceptance or rejection of the concept a rigorous analysis of the future role of rental housing and the issue of its tax treatment should be undertaken.

4. THE FEDERAL ROLE IN RENT CONTROL

There should be no hesitation or reluctance to override local rent control ordinances when the latter impact the fiscal vitality of federally financed or guaranteed projects. The "on again-off again" of practice in this area has brought into question the whole validity of HUD rent guidelines. It has endangered both private and public multifamily investment and, most importantly, has left the courts and the electorate without a nonpartisan yardstick.

5. CONVENTIONALLY CONSTRUCTED MULTIFAMILY HOUSING IS TOO EXPENSIVE TO USE FOR SHORT-TERM CRISES

The scrappage rate (losses from the stock) are so high, the foreclosure and mortgage delinquency data so ominous, as to provide reason for apprehension. We have been much readier with subsidy mechanisms to launch multifamily housing, i.e., through mortgage subsidies and the like, than we have been to grasp the full-life cycle and the issues of refinancing.

There is currently substantial pressure to broaden out those provisions of Section 223 which permit refinancing for rehabilitation of multifamily housing. Given the relative weakness of the market this may well end up with Uncle Sam becoming the owner of structures which come under the program by default of owners. The latter will liquidate their investment at nominal face values which simply overstate their market worth. *The principle of supporting conversion is essential. Its operating mechanisms, however, require much more attention.*

6. THERE IS AN ENORMOUS NEED FOR OPTIMIZATION OF
   MANAGEMENT AND OPERATING PROCEDURES IN
   MULTIFAMILY HOUSING

The Federal track record in this sphere is notable by its absence. While early experience in attempting to support an operational management research activity has been sadly disappointing, re-examination of the entire area is called for. The payoffs could be most considerable. *Considering the fact that government at all levels is de facto the largest single owner of multifamily housing— and there is some indication if anything, the stock in its possession will increase—there is both a broad as well as a parochial necessity for such programming.*

7. MOST IMPORTANTLY OF ALL, IN THE LIGHT OF THE
   INFLATIONARY BONANZA THAT HAS BEEN ATTACHED TO
   HOMEOWNERSHIP, THE DEMAND FOR MULTIFAMILY HOUSING
   AS INDICATED IN THE BASE PAPER WILL NOT INCREASE

Estimates given current levels of market penetration by household characteristics multiplied by the numbers of households forecast in each of the several sectors considered, indicate that substantial conservatism must be the order of the day.

This is a very harsh reality particularly in terms of immediate need. There is a contraction in the availability of such facilities. *But we are not dealing with a transient good. The only way such structures make sense is in terms of a long and useful lifetime. The costs of over-optimism in this sphere could be enormous.*

NOTES

1. See Fisch, Oscar, "Dynamics of the Housing Market," *Journal of Urban Economics* (October 1977).

2. Sternlieb, George and Robert W. Burchell, *Residential Abandonment: The Tenement Landlord Revisted* (New Brunswick, N.J.: Rutgers University, Center for Urban Policy Research, 1972).

3. See for instance: Marcuse, Peter. *The Financial Attributes of Home Ownership for Low and Moderate Income Families* (Washington, D.C., The Urban Institute, 1972); Struyk, Raymond J., *Urban Homeownership; The Economic Determinants* (Lexington, Mass., Lexington Books, 1976); Burnbawn, Howard and Rafael Weston, "Homeownership and the Wealth Position of Black and White Americans" (Cambridge, Mass.: Program on Regional and Urban Economics, Howard University, 1972); Heald, David, "The American Dream: Fact or Fiction," *Real Estate Appraiser* (July-August 1977).

4. U.S. Department of Housing and Urban Development. *HUD Condominium Cooperative Study* (Washington, D.C.: Government Printing Ofice,1974); James, Franklin, *The Return to the Central City* (Washington,D.C.: The Urban Institute, 1978); Sternlieb, George and Kristina Ford, *Loft Conversion in New York City* (New Brunswick, N.J.: Rutgers University, Center for Urban Policy Research,1978).

5. See Williams, Norman, Jr. and Thomas Norman, "Exclusionary Land-Use Controls: The Case of Northeastern New Jersey;' *Syracuse Law Review*, Vol. 22 (1971), "Suburban Snobbery," *The New Republic* (June 26, 1971).

6. Masotti, Louis H. and Jeffrey K. Hadden, *The Urbanization of the Suburbs* (Beverly Hills, California: Sage Publications, Inc., 1973); Sternlieb, George, *The Garden Apartment Development; A Municipal Cost-Revenue Analysis* (New Brunswick, N.J.: Bureau of Economic Research, 1964).

7. Williams and Norman, op. cit., Babcock, Richard F., "The Courts Enter the Land Development Marketplace," *City* (January/February 1971); Mandelker, Daniel R., "Controlling Land Values in Areas of Rapid Urban Expansion," *University of California at Los Angeles, Law Review*, Vol. 12, p. 734.

8. Sternlieb, *et al.*, "The Private Sector's Role in the Provision of Reasonably Priced Housing," *Federal Home Loan Bank Board Journal* (Spring 1976).

9. Kristof, Frank S., "Urban Housing Needs Through the 1980's" (Washington, D.C.: U.S. National Commission on Urban Problems Research No. 10, 1968).

10. Ibid.

11. For comparison purposes "multifamily rental structures" are used here as structures for rent with *two units or more*. In a subsequent portion of this paper this will be narrowed to the more traditional definition of structures of *five units or more*.

12. Sternlieb, George and James W. Hughes, *Revitalizing the Northeast* (New Brunswick, N.J. Rutgers University, Center for Urban Policy Research, 1978).

13. Sternlieb, George and Robert W. Lake, "Aging Suburbs and Black Home-ownership," *The Annals of the American Academy of Political and Social Science*, Vol. 42 (November 1975).

14. Frieden, Bernard J. and Arthur P. Solomon, *The Nation's Housing: 1975-1985* (Cambridge, Mass.: Joint Center for Urban Studies, 1977).

15. *Ibid.*

16. Sumichrast, Michael J. and Maurey Seldin, *Components of Future Housing Demand* (Washington, D.C.: National Housing Center, 1966).

17. Comparison of 1970 multifamily (5 units or more) housing units plus annual, multifamily housing starts (1970-1975) to multifamily housing units in 1975.

18. U.S. Department of Agriculture, Forest Service, *Projections of Demand for Housing by Type of Unit and Region* (Washington, D.C.: U.S. Government Printing Office, May 1972).

19. See Lett, Monica R. *Rent Control: Concepts, Realities and Mechanism* (New Brunswick, N.J.: Center for Urban Policy Research, 1976), p. 40.

20. This is a shade less than the current rental vacancy data. While there is some regional variation, with vacancy rates typically higher in areas with substantial construction rates (the South and West *versus* the North), there has been an increasing tendency to leveling across the Nation.

    Thus the future total vacancy rate projected here is the sum of the current rate plus the provision made for new units.

21. U.S. Department of Housing and Urban Development, *FHA Techniques of Housing Market Analysis* (Washington, D.C.: U.S. Government Printing Office, August, 1970).

22. De Leeuw, Frank, *The Demand for Housing: A Review of Cross-Sectional Evidence* (Washington, D.C.: The Urban Institute, 1971).

23. *Housing and Community Development Act of 1968*, "Section 236 Interest Subsidy Program."

24. See Sternlieb, George and James W. Hughes, *Current Population Trends* (New Brunswick, N.J.: Rutgers University, Center for Urban Policy Research, 1978).

25. See also Priest, Donald E., "The Uncharted Trend Toward Increased Public-Private Cooperation of Housing Development," *American Real Estate and Urban Economics Association Journal* (Summer 1977); Ira G. Kawaller, "The Role of Federal Subsidies in the Construction of Multi-

26. U.S. Department of Commerce, Bureau of Domestic Commerce, *Construction Review*, December Volume 1967-1977.

27. Williams and Norman, op.cit.

28. See Stegman, Michael A., "Multifamily Distress and the Conservation of Older Neighborhoods: A Cause for National Concern" (Washington,

D.C.: U.S. Department of Housing and Urban Development, Office of Policy Development and Research, February, 1978).

29. Information secured from Goldman Sachs investment research, Spring 1978.

30. For further elaboration, see addenda.

31. See Seidel, Stephen R. *Government Regulation and Housing Cost* (New Brunswick, N.J.: Rutgers University, Center for Urban Policy Research, 1978).

32. Tobier, Emanuel, *et al., Mortgage Financing and Housing Markets in New York State: A Preliminary Report* (Albany, New York: New York State Legislature, May 1977).

33. Baron, Richard D., Beverly B. Huchman and Robert Kolodny, *Preserving HUD. Assisted Multifamily Housing: An Affirmative Role for the Area Office* (Working Submission to the U.S. Department of Housing and Urban Development, November 1977); see also HUD, *Budget, Justification for 1979*, Part 1, G2.

34. For elaboration on this issue, see addenda.

35. *Housing and Community Development Act of 1974*, "Section 8 Housing Assistance Payment Program."

36. For elaboration on this issue, see addenda.

37. *Housing and Urban Development Act of 1968.*

38. A possible guide would be the operating data for multifamily buildings gathered under contract for New York City by the BLS.

The Uncertain Future of Rental Housing

George Sternlieb
James W. Hughes

Introduction

It is only within the post World War II era that America moved from a nation of renters to one of homeowners. As late as 1940, only 43.6 percent of the nation's dwelling units were owner occupied. Currently, two-thirds of all Americans own their own homes. The shrinkage in rental tenure and its replacement by homeownership has been viewed as a principal symbol of an affluent society—the triumph of the rise of real incomes and housing purchasing power on the part of most Americans. Yet as the cost of homeownership increases, as real housing buying power diminishes and as demographers point to the wave of youthful households emanating from the baby boom generation (as well as an increasing number of elderly), there has been an expectation that rental housing would once again assume a more formidable position within America's housing production system. This expectation, however, has been far from realized; indeed, construction statistics indicate that non-govern-

257

mentally aided multifamily rental housing starts have approached the lowest levels of the post World War II years.[1]

What makes this construction "shortfall" ominous is the fact that, concurrently, rental vacancy rates have reached unprecedented low levels, striking a sudden awareness that the private rental housing industry of the United States is in trouble. Why is there this growing gap between nominal expectation and reality? Why has the market failed to respond to low vacancy rates as traditional housing economics would apparently require? What new factors have been ushered into prominence in this regard?

Throughout the decade of the 1970s, the cumulative effects of a number of forces have melded together to produce a dynamic whose momentum increasingly challenges the historic assumptions underpinning rental housing markets. For the purposes of this paper, we have isolated five of the more significant phenomena.

1. The emergence of a *Post-Shelter Society*.
2. The *"cream-skimming"* of the rental inventory.
3. The escalation of rental *cost structures* in an inflation ridden, energy scarce era.
4. The institutionalization of *rent control* and the proliferation of *condominium conversions*.
5. The prospective coming of age of the *"baby bust"* generation.

As these forces mature and self reinforce one another, there is growing doubt not only about the future viability of the private rental housing industry, but also its capacity to survive in its more traditional forms.

A Post-Shelter Society

A dominant rationale for housing choice in America today is no longer shelter from the elements but rather housing as investment, as a form of tax shelter and as one of the few successful refuges from an inflationary environment. This has completely restructured the realities of the market, though not perhaps our rhetoric nor the thinking of many housing planners. We have become a post-shelter society. Excluded from this new society are those lacking the means— capital resources and taxable incomes—to secure membership. Yet, as we will note subsequently, the fallouts are rapidly slipping from the domain of the private housing market.

The inflation in housing costs for homeowners is essentially counterbalanced by a parallel inflation in real or conjectured capital values. In terms of cash flow immediacies, homeowners—particularly newcomers to the market—seemingly are willing to devote unprecedented portions of their incomes to supporting housing acquisition. The alleviatory elements are nominally tax coverage and capital gains potential. Thus, when homeownership is employed as a leveraged investment, its support can be accepted quite realistically as the sum both of nominal shelter costs plus the surrogate quanta of funds which would once have gone into more traditional forms of investment—private insurance, savings accounts and the securities market.

The rental housing situation is quite different; there are no tax advantages to the tenantry; rents must be paid from post tax income.[2] Moreover, there is no compensatory investment element offsetting rents. The rental market and its soaring cost structures—both in terms of development and operation—must compete within an environment devoid of the incentives attached to homeownership.

But such rationalizations have by now assumed the status of an established convention. Indeed, it probably has become a dominant folk wisdom of our time. What has not been fully appreciated, however, is its residual impact on the rental market—it has generated a very marked cream-skimming of higher incomed households out of the potential pool of renters.

The Dynamics of Cream-Skimming

Within the overall context of the growth of personal incomes in the United States, there are very significant differences as a function of household configuration. As shown in Exhibit 1, families, for example, as of 1977 had incomes nearly triple those of unrelated individuals.[3] Within the total family set, moreover, there is a wide range of income variation, which may well exemplify a new class partition within the United States; households with one versus two or more persons working. For example, male-headed households having a wife in the paid labor force had median incomes in excess of $20,000, fully a quarter higher than that for all families. Female-headed households (no husband present), on the other hand, had incomes ($7,765) less than half that for all families.

The ramifications of these partitions are amplified when the occupant characteristics of owned versus rented units are reviewed (Exhibit 2). Male-headed households (with wife present), which include the most affluent household types, increased by 5.3 million over the 1970-to-1976 period in the owner-occupied sector; in contrast, the renter-occupied sector lost 1.5 million such households.

EXHIBIT 1

INCOME CHANGES: FAMILIES, UNRELATED INDIVIDUALS AND HOUSEHOLDS (U.S. TOTAL), 1970 TO 1977; AND 1977 INCOME BY FAMILY CONFIGURATION

Unit	1970	1977	Change: Number	1970 to 1977 Percent
Families	$9,867	$16,009	$6,142	62.2%
Unrelated Individuals	3,137	5,907	2,770	88.3
Households	8,734	13,572	4,838	55.3

Family Configuration	1977
Total Families	$16,009
Male Head Total	17,517
Married, Wife Present	17,616
Wife in Paid Labor Force	20,268
Wife Employed	20,534
Wife Unemployed	13,855
Wife Not in Paid Labor Force	15,063
Other Marital Status	14,518
Female Head	7,765

Source: U.S. Bureau of the Census, *Current Population Reports*, Series P-60, No. 118, "Money Income in 1977 of Families and Persons in the United States," U.S. Government Printing Office, Washington, D.C., 1979.

Other male-headed households had a rate of increase in rental facilities double that of the owner-occupied sector. Similarly, female-headed groups had a far higher rate of growth in rental units than held true in owner-occupied accommodations. This variation in market penetration by household type means that rental facilities are increasingly the refuge of household configurations of lower income—those characterized by more substantial resources are increasingly attracted to homeownership.

Even when disaggregation is undertaken by age sector within various household configurations, it is those with far less income who occupy rental facilities (Exhibit 3). In sum, therefore, the market penetration of rental units increasingly captures the lower incomed households of American society. Tenant incomes have significantly lagged those of owners.

EXHIBIT 2

RENTER AND OWNER OCCUPIED UNITS:
HOUSEHOLD COMPOSITION
1970 AND 1976

(Numbers in Thousands)

Household Composition by Age of Head	1970	1976	Change: 1970 to 1976 Number	Percent
Total Owner Occupied	39,886	47,904	8,018	20.1%
2-or-More-Person Households	35,124	41,626	6,502	18.5
Male Head, Wife Present	30,806	36,108	5,302	17.2
Other Male Head	1,298	1,629	331	25.5
Female Head	3,019	3,889	870	28.8
1-Person Households	4,762	6,278	1,516	31.8
Total Renter Occupied	23,560	26,101	2,541	10.8
2-or-More-Person Households	17,171	17,541	370	2.2
Male Head, Wife Present	12,759	11,291	−1,468	−11.5
Other Male Head	1,143	1,730	587	51.4
Female Head	3,270	4,520	1,250	38.2
1-Person Households	6,389	8,560	2,171	34.0

Note: Numbers and/or percents may not add due to rounding.

Source: U.S. Department of Commerce, U.S. Bureau of the Census, *Current Housing Reports*, Series H-150-76, "General Housing Characteristics for the United States and Regions: 1976," Annual Housing Survey: 1976, Part A, U.S. Government Printing Office, Washington, D.C., 1978.

Cost Structures and Income Lags

The end result of this process of cream-skimming is revealed by the data of Exhibit 4. From 1970 to 1976, median gross rents increased by 54.6 percent. The median incomes of rental occupants, however, increased by only 28.5 percent. Within the owner-occupied sector, median incomes increased by 48.5 percent, more than one and a half times as fast as that for renters. While median house values increased even more abruptly (88.9 percent) than rents, to those who were homeowners throughout this period, this escalation, rather than being ominous, served to rationalize their homeownership decision. For those who became owners—or wish to become owners—the 88.9 percent increment is a justification for assuming relatively high cost burdens.

EXHIBIT 3

OWNER AND RENTER OCCUPIED HOUSEHOLD INCOME, BY HOUSEHOLD CONFIGURATION, U.S. TOTAL: 1976

	Owner Occupied	Renter Occupied	Percent
Total Households	$14,400	$ 8,100	.56
2-or-More-Person Households	15,900	9,500	.60
Male Head, Wife Present	16,800	11,600	.69
Under 25 Years	12,800	9,800	.77
25 to 29 Years	16,200	12,600	.78
30 to 34 Years	17,900	13,000	.73
35 to 44 Years	19,700	13,200	.67
45 to 64 Years	18,600	12,600	.68
65 Years and Over	8,400	6,600	.79
Other Male Head			
Under 65 Years	15,800	8,600	.54
65 Years and Over	9,000	6,000	.67
Female Head			
Under 65 Years	9,600	5,700	.59
65 Years and Over	7,100	5,100	.72
1-Person Households			
Under 65 Years	8,600	7,800	.91
65 Years and Over	4,200	3,400	.81

Note: Numbers and/or percents may not add due to rounding.

Source: U.S. Department of Commerce, U.S. Bureau of the Census, *Current Housing Reports*, Series H-150-76, "General Housing Characteristics for the United States and Regions: 1976," Annual Housing Survey: 1976, Part A. U.S. Government Printing Office, Washington, D.C., 1978.

Among renters, the median rent/income ratio moved from 20 percent in 1970 to 24 percent in 1976. At this writing, there is some indication that it is over the 26 percent level. The capacity of tenants to absorb higher rent levels is questionable—the level of inflation in operating and construction costs is far in excess of their income increases.

Consequently, the long progression of increased proportions of multifamily housing starts which are governmentally aided is not a temporary aberrant; it is merely one manifestation of a new split in the housing market. With the exception of luxury apartment houses,

EXHIBIT 4

RENTER AND OWNER OCCUPIED UNITS, INCOME, RENT AND UNIT VALUE RELATIONSHIPS, U.S. TOTAL: 1970 TO 1976

	1970	1976	Change: 1970 to 1976 Number	Percent
Renter Occupied Units				
Median Gross Rent	$ 108	$ 167	$ 59	54.6%
Median Income	$ 6,300	$ 8,100	$ 1,800	28.5
Median Rent/Income Ratio[1]	20%	24%	4%	20.0%
Owner Occupied Units				
Median House Value	$17,100	$32,300	$15,200	88.9%
Median Income	9,700	14,400	4,700	48.5
Value Income Ratio[1]	1.7	2.2	0.5	29.4

Note: 1. Published Ratios.

Source: U.S. Department of Commerce, U.S. Bureau of the Census, *Current Housing Reports*, Series H-150-76, "General Housing Characteristics for the United States and Regions: 1976," Annual Housing Survey: 1976, Part A. U.S. Government Printing Office, Washington, D.C., 1978.

and development which have aspirations toward condominium conversion, there will continue to be increasing proportions of America's rental facilities which are supported directly or indirectly by government. Adding significant pressure in this direction is the continued ratcheting of energy costs to even higher thresholds, rendering the investment economics of the private rental housing package increasingly dubious.

Rent Control and Condominium Conversion

Other byproducts of sustained inflationary pressures are the attempts by local governments to buffer (and pacify) their constituencies via one of the few avenues open to them—rent control.[4] The classic elements of property rights have changed abruptly from a concentration on landlord privileges to the protection of the tenantry. Regardless of the equities involved this has made investment in rental property riskful. As the uncertainties of securing acceptable cash flows in rent regulated environments mount, the enthusiasm of private investors has continued to diminish.

Such strictures, in conjunction with the desire to capture part of the withdrawal of more affluent tenantry—and to capitalize on the momentum of "homeownership as investment"—have led to the phenomenon of condominium conversion, the shift of units of rental tenure to ownership status. Regardless of the dynamics at work— conversion as a takeout mechanism for survival and/or as a very lucrative investment strategy—the end effects are similar, a reduced potential for expansion of the private rental housing inventory.

The Baby Bust and Future Demand

The preceding elements can all be viewed as an outgrowth of high endemic levels of inflation and a flight from currencies in general and the dollar in particular. As they converge, a dynamic has been forged whose consequences are increasingly ominous to rental housing markets. Yet another independent stricture must be factored into the basic equation—a perception of the coming to age of the baby bust generation.

The sharp declines in fertility in the past two decades have forced the necessity of acknowledging shrinkage as a basic component of future projections. As the nation proceeds through the balance of the century, there will be sharp contractions in population first in the 18-to-24 years-of-age sectors and subsequently in the 25-to-34 years old categories.[5] Thus, as the baby bust generation matures, the number of initial household formations will decline, and with it, seekers of rental accomodations. The perception of this impending lag raises significant doubts on the use of investment—which requires long periods of time to justify its existence—to meet and satisfy relative short-term needs.

As the housing buying power of Americans declines, and the one-family unit syndrom—at least for newcomers to the field—becomes more elusive, there will be a growing requirement for alternative mechanisms. Private rental housing, at least in large-scale development, has become the victim of inflation and tax policy. Can it—and should it—be reshaped for the future?

Notes

1. See: "Housing in the United States: An Overview," the first essay in this volume.
2. The Internal Revenue Service has recently disallowed attempts by New York State to amend its real property tax law to entitle renters to an itemized deduction for property tax levies (included in their rent payment).
3. Households are generally of two types: primary families and primary individuals. Primary families comprise two or more related individuals and are usually subdivided into three groups—husband-wife families, male head (no wife present) and female head (no husband present). Primary individual households comprise either a single person living alone or two or more unrelated individuals.

   In Exhibit 1, the data for unrelated individuals include persons in group quarters (not in households). The household data comprise both families and those unrelated individuals residing in households (primary individual households).

   The data in Exhibits 2 and 3, secured from the *Annual Housing Survey*, are solely for households. However, male head (wife present) configurations are by definition, families. Other male head, or female head, can either be families or primary individual households.
4. See: George Sternlieb and James W. Hughes, "Rent Control's Impact on the Community Tax Base," *The Appraisal Journal*, Volume XLVII, Number 3 (July 1979), pp. 381 to 395.
5. For a detailed analysis, see: George Sternlieb and James W. Hughes, *Current Population Trends in the United States* (New Brunswick, N.J.: Rutgers University, Center for Urban Policy Research, 1978) and George Sternlieb and Robert W. Burchell, *Multifamily Housing Demand: 1975-2000*, A Study Prepared for the Joint Economic Committee, Congress of the United States, U.S. Government Printing Office, Washington, D.C., 1978.

Rent Control's Impact on the Community Tax Base

George Sternlieb
James W. Hughes

Synopsis

The impact of rent control on a community's fiscal base is a critical but often unclear phenomenon. This results from the considerable time lag between the institution of rent control and the actual registration of its impact within the affected community's formal property assessments. The detailed experience of Fort Lee, New Jersey is empirically analyzed in this regard. The events experienced to date suggest that rent control is a subsidy the cost of which ultimately must be born by the balance of the property taxpayers of the municipality.

Introduction

The seemingly endemic inflation of the post-1970 era has generated renewed interest in the subject of rent control. While there were earlier abortive ventures, rent regulation in the United States dates back to the days of World War II. Within two years after the conclusion of the war, however, except for New York, it has been largely relegated to history.

Despite efforts within a few communities to revive rent control mechanisms, the first major implementations largely had as their foundation the wage and price freeze instituted by President Nixon in 1971. Rents under Phase I of the program were frozen as were prices of all other goods. After this initial freeze, some measure of flexibility was instituted under Phase II. On the latter's demise, a number of communities either decided to continue or shortly thereafter reinstituted them.

First-era controls were a response to transient wartime exigencies, of massive population shifts in the face of a virtual cessation of housing activity.[1] Typically first-era controls involved a very specific finding of immediate emergency, usually tied to a specific vacancy level.[2]

The proliferation of second generation controls (which have flourished particularly in New Jersey with more than 130 communities regulating rents in some form or other), has been predicated on a situation construed as much more chronic in nature, an effort by local communities to buffer their constituencies from inflation within the limited sphere of action open to municipal government. The supermarket shelves would quickly empty out if food prices were controlled on a local level; gas stations would stop pumping fuel if subjected to local price restrictions. Such goods are particularly mobile and footloose—apartment structures, however, are fixed in place.

The arguments both for and against rent control are enormously varied and will not be discussed at length in this paper.[3] Typically they encompass the issues of consumer protection on the one hand versus the rights of property on the other—essentially a two-party contest between landlords and tenants. Much broader issues, endowed with a much greater level of political potency, are those surrounding the interests of parties outside the immediate debate. These include future potential tenants—and whether or not the market will continue to provide new rental accommodations within a regulated environment. Indeed the question has been raised as to whether or not financial institutions, as well as entrepreneurs, are willing to invest and build within this context.

The second and increasingly significant issue is the impact on the municipal fiscal system. Do controls merely represent a curbing of landlord profits so as to limit unfair rent increases? Or do they represent a broader subsidy to tenants which ultimately must be paid for in significant part by other segments of the community? Crucial to the evaluation of this issue is the impact of rent control on the municipal property tax base (property assessments) and the subsequent effect on municipal incomes.[4] If the value of income-producing property is by definition a function of the income stream it generates, and if rent control limits income, then does the value of the parcel in question decline over time and/or fail to keep pace with inflation? And if so, how is this reflected in the assessment base? If there is a negative impact, who pays?

These are compelling questions. The impact of rent control on a community's fiscal system is a critical but often unclear phenomenon. This results from the time lag between the institutionalization of rent control and its ultimate ramifications for the property tax base. The detailed experience of one community which is analyzed in this article provides insight into the dynamics which are involved.

Serving as the western terminous of the George Washington Bridge, Fort Lee, New Jersey for most of its history has served as a suburb of New York City. Over the 1960-to-1972 period, approximately 5900 new apartment units were constructed, mostly on the Palisades overlooking the river and the skyline of Manhattan.[5] By the latter date, apartments had come to dominate the assessment base of the community.

Fort Lee is a useful laboratory of investigation. The apartment presence is such that any changes they experience are clearly felt by the municipality as a whole; it is relatively small in scale—the effects of rent regulation are not obscured to the extent of a large, more complex setting. And municipal rent control has been extant in Fort Lee since 1972, a sufficient span of time to enable externalities to surface—the events currently (1978) in motion have sufficiently evolved so that at least some tentative answers to the questions raised above are available. Before turning to the specifics of this particular case, however, it is useful to explore the broader environment of rent control—the realities of rental increases in the context of inflation and family income changes.

The Broader Environment of Rent Control

At least up through 1970, the United States has been relatively unique in the relative stability of prices which it has enjoyed. As indicated in Exhibit 1, the overall consumer price index (CPI) rose by 31.1 percent between 1960 and 1970, or a compound annual growth rate of 2.75 percent. While disturbing to conservative groups

EXHIBIT 1

CONSUMER PRICE INDEXES: 1960 TO 1977

Absolute Value (1967=100)

Commodity	Year		
	1960	1970	1977
All Items (Overall C.P.I.)	88.7	116.3	181.5
Homeownership	86.3	128.5	204.9
Rent	91.7	110.1	153.5
Fuel Oil and Coal	89.2	110.1	283.4
Gas and Electricity	98.6	107.3	213.4

Percentage Change

	1960 to 1970	1970 to 1977
All Items (Overal C.P.I.)	31.1%	65.2%
Homeownership	48.9	59.5
Rent	20.1	39.4
Fuel Oil and Coal	23.4	157.4
Gas and Electricity	8.8	98.9

Source: U.S. Department of Commerce, Bureau of Economic Analysis, *Survey of Current Business*, Vol. 58, No. 6, Part 1 (June 1978), pp. 5-8

U.S. Department of Commerce, Bureau of Economic Analysis, *Survey of Current Business*, Vol. 51, No. 7, Part 1 (July 1971), pp. 5-8.

at the time, in retrospect this experience appears relatively benign. Within this broader parameter, the cost of homeownership was increasing at a decade rate of 48.9 percent, while rents lagged considerably, with an increase of 20.1 percent over ten years, or 1.85 percent per year compounded annually. In part, the latter was made possible by the comparative modesty of the charges in the costs of energy (as shown in the exhibit).

This situation changes quite dramatically in the seven years which followed. Between 1970 and 1977, the overall consumer price index soared by 65.2 percent, representing a compound annual rate of growth of 7.43 percent, more than twice the annual increments of the previous decade (2.75 percent). Within this context, however, once again the pattern of rent changes (39.4 percent) was in the vincinity of 60 percent of the "all items" index despite the very dramatic escalation in energy costs. Fuel oil and coal, for example, increased by 157.4 percent over this seven-year period.

EXHIBIT 2

MEDIAN FAMILY INCOME: 1960 TO 1977

Year	Income
1960	$ 5,620
1970	9,867
1977	16,009

Percent Change

1960 to 1970	75.6%
1970 to 1977	62.2

Source: U.S. Bureau of the Census, *Current Population Reports*, Series P-60, No. 116, "Money Income and Poverty Status of Families and Persons in the United States: 1977" (Advance Report), U.S. Government Printing Office, Washington, D.C., 1978.

The corresponding changes in median family income for these two periods amplify the shift that has taken place (Exhibit 2). From 1960 to 1970, income gains (75.6 percent) exceeded by a wide margin the increase in the consumer price index (31.1 percent). Since 1970, however, this favorable relationship has aborted, with gains in median family incomes (62.2 percent) lagging the increases in the consumer price index (65.2 percent). Nevertheless, "real rent buying power" has maintained a positive note. From 1960 to 1970, incomes expanded at a rate of more than three times that of rents (75.6 percent versus 20.1 percent). The gap between the two rates narrowed but the basic relationship persisted from 1970 to 1977. when income growth (62.2 percent) was more than one and one half times that of rent (39.4 percent). While higher taxes as a function of the progressivity of IRS codes as well as changes in the social security law may serve to mute the conclusion, it is evident that rents have not increased as rapidly as the total consumer price index—and have become relatively "cheaper" within the context of at least median family incomes. (Certainly, different income groups may well have had varied experiences.)

If we view rents as having primacy among family expenditures therefore, they should represent a smaller segment of the family budget. But this is a family budget which is now under stress in a variety of directions, with food, transportation and service expenditures growing markedly. The temptation to make rents not a focal point of family fiscal planning but a relatively low pressure element within the inflationary milieu of this decade is policially beguiling. As noted earlier, there are limited powers available to municipal governments for controlling the inflationary stresses on their residents. Singularly immobile and therefore most susceptible to local government intervention is rental housing.

The Fort Lee Experience

The economic environment depicted above, although set in the framework of national parameters, clearly bounds the Fort Lee experience. After a brief outline of the evolution of rent control in this local setting, the implications for the internal operation of a prototypical high rise structure in Fort Lee are closely reviewed.

THE EVOLUTION OF RENT CONTROL

Municipal rent control was enacted in Fort Lee in January, 1972. Determining that rent gouging in multifamily dwellings created a public emergency, the governing body prohibited rent increases in excess of the percentage increase in the Consumer Price Index (CPI).[6] Subsequently, in November, 1974, a modified rent control ordinance was adopted. Although nominally still linking rent increments to the percentage change in the CPI, a provision of the legislation prohibited rent increases above 2.5 percent. In the context of the economic conditions of the time, the practical effect was a 2.5 percent ceiling on rent increases.[7] However, landlords were permitted to pass through to tenants, in the form of a tax surcharge, increases in property taxes above their 1972 level (base year). Both of these legislative formulations precipitated a number of legal appeals by affected landlords.[8]

Another major revision in the Fort Lee rent control system was enacted in June, 1976. The 2.5 percent ceiling was replaced by a "maximum annual percentage" (MAP) index, linked to increases in operating costs as guaged by property tax changes and specified weighted components of the CPI. However, the MAP formula was not to become effective until the final disposition of previously instituted appeals.[9] At the same time, effective immediately, the tax surcharge or pass-through was repealed. (This section of the ordinance became known as the "tax surcharge repealer".)[10] Hence, the only immediate effect was to prohibit tax pass-throughs, shift the burden of real estate taxation from the tenant to the landlord and limit annual rent increases to 2.5 percent.

While the preceding description oversimplifies a very complex chain of events, through 1976 the rent control system of Fort Lee became increasingly restrictive. The cap or ceiling on rental increases evolved from the change defined by the CPI, to an effective 2.5 percent limitation (with the tax pass-through permitted) to a 2.5 percent limitation without the tax pass-through. The latter was obstensibly an interim provision, but remained operational through late 1978.[11] Consequently, throughout the period under analysis in this paper, the rental income flows of apartment parcels in Fort Lee were constrained to an increasing degree.

IMPACT ON MULTIFAMILY STRUCTURE[12]

There is always considerable difficulty in generalizing the operating parameters of multifamily housing—configurations are varied, financing complex and operations inconsistent. In the course of the Fort Lee litigation, detailed operating histories of 35 multifamily buildings were prepared by a certified public accountant, representing a unique body of longitudinal and cross sectional data.[13] A specific building was selected and accepted by all parties involved in the suit as being typical of the operating experience within the community.

The prototype, Mediterranean Towers I, is an efficiently managed luxury highrise building comprising 483 units. Construction was initiated in 1964 and a certificate of occupancy was granted in 1966; the average monthly rental in 1976 was $360. The operating history of this parcel is indicated in Exhibit 3.

In 1970 it had a total income flow of $1,968,243; 41 percent of this was consumed by expenses, leaving a net income ratio of 59 percent—or a net operating income of $1,161,421.[14] To secure an estimate of the building's income producing value, the conventional approach of capitalizing net operating income can be employed.[15] While there is always some spectrum in captialization rates, we have utilized the historical capitalization rates compiled for conventional apartments by the American Life Insurance Association (A.L.I.A.)[16] Using the 1970 rate of 10.4 percent, the capitalized value would be $11,167,509.

By 1973 the total income of the building had increased by 11.9 percent to $2,201,965; in contrast, total expenses increased by 17.9 percent. Nonetheless, the net operating income of the building increased by 7.7 percent to $1,250,661, since the absolute dollar value of the increase in income exceeded that of total expenses. This did not prohibit the degeneration of the expense and income

EXHIBIT 3

MEDITERRANEAN TOWERS I
OPERATING STATEMENT: 1970 TO 1976

	1970	1973	1976
TOTAL INCOME	$ 1,968,243	$ 2,201,965	$ 2,353,175
Net Rental Income	1,736,493	1,951,732	2,082,644
Garage and Other Income	231,750	250,233	270,531
TOTAL EXPENSES	$ 803,822	$ 951,304	$ 1,331,940
Utilities (energy)	63,323	109,574	199,278
Real Estate Taxes	264,820	309,335	476,682
Administration	113,301	133,326	173,549
Maintenance	129,137	117,500	160,921
Other Operating & Miscellaneous	236,241	281,569	321,510
NET OPERATING INCOME	$ 1,161,421	$ 1,250,661	$ 1,021,235
Expense Ratio	41.0	43.2	56.6
Net Income Ratio	59.0	56.8	43.4
CAPITALIZATION RATE	10.4	9.4	10.3
Capitalized Value	$11,167,509	$13,304,904	$ 9,914,903

	Percent Change	
	1970-1973	1973-1976
TOTAL INCOME	11.9%	6.9%
Net Rental Income	12.4	6.7
Garage and Other Income	8.0	8.1
TOTAL EXPENSES	17.9	40.0
Utilities (energy)	73.0	81.9
Real Estate Taxes	16.8	54.1
Administration	17.7	30.2
Maintenance	− 9.0	37.0
Other Operating & Miscellaneous	19.1	14.2
NET OPERATING INCOME	7.7	−18.3
Expense Ratio	5.3	31.0
Net Income Ratio	− 3.7	−23.6

Source: Sternlieb & Company, *Special Report for the Fort Lee Property Owners and Taxpayers Committee*, Hackensack, N.J., November 1977.

ratios; the former increased to 43.2 percent while the latter decreased to 56.8 percent. The increasing proportion of income consumed by expenses was in part a tribute initially to Phase I and Phase II federal wage and price control efforts as well as to the built-in lag generated by long-term or multi-year leases.

Despite the restrictions on its income stream, the building's rental gains were still sufficient to insure that its capitalized value did not deteriorate. The capitalization rate for comparable properties derived by A.L.I.A. had declined to 9.4 percent by 1973; in conjunction with a higher net operating income, this yielded a nominal capitalized value of $13,304,904.

The very end of 1973 was marked by fuel crisis and the abrupt escalation of energy costs. In substantial measure as a function of these events, combined with inflation in other operating costs, expenses increased by 40.0 percent between 1973 and 1976; the cost of utilities alone soared by 81.9 percent while real estate taxes expanded by 54.1 percent. Total income, however, constrained by the municipally-enacted control mechanisms detailed earlier, increased by only 6.9 percent to $2,353,175. The impact of these differential growth rates on net operating income was considerable— a decline of 18.3 percent to $1,021,235. The net income ratio thus had moved from 59.0 percent in 1970 to 56.8 percent in 1973, and hence to 43.4 percent in 1976. Expenses, 41.0 percent of income in 1970, consumed 56.6 percent by 1976.

In the latter year, with the capitalization rate for comparable structures at 10.3 percent, the capitalized value of the parcel therefore dipped to $9,914,903—or a reduction of $3,390,001 over a three-year period. Thus control constraints on Mediterranean Towers' income stream over the six-year period under consideration, in the context of unrestrained increased in operating costs, appear to have adversely affected its market value as gauged by capitalized net operating income.[17] Another way to highlight the declining fiscal posture of the building is the change in the gross income multiplier—capitalized value divided by total income. In 1970, the gross multiplier stood at 5.67; by 1976, it had declined to 4.21.[18]

Rent Control and the Property Tax Base of the Community

There are significant problems in measuring the short-run impact of rent control upon the real estate values of affected multifamily parcels and ultimately upon their encompassing communities. There are relatively few municipalities that practice annual reassessment. Even in those cases, the absence of comparable sales upon which to base valuations of large-scale rental facilities poses a difficult problem. While the law of large numbers tends to provide an adequate base for single-family units, the same does not hold true, certainly never in as adequate a fashion, for multi-family parcels. In communities that practice reassessment only at longer intervals—and in many areas of the United States this typically is either on a five- or ten-year base—the situation is even more difficult to analyze. Rent control or other value-inhibiting or enhancing activities may thus be under way for a significant period of time without formal acknowledgment within the assessment base. The long-term process of appeal and abatement procedures may impose significant time lags.

In the Fort Lee case, assessments on existing properties from 1970 to 1976 were based upon a municipal-wide revaluation undertaken in 1970. The community does not practice spot reassessement. Thus while assessments are nominally at full market value, the vagaries of changes in market values distorted this relationship over time. In 1977 Fort Lee undertook a total revaluation.

There are three basic models with which to analyze the impact of rent control on the property tax base of a municipality:

1. The market value (and therefore the assessment) of rent control parcels keeps pace with the changing levels of value of all properties in the community. Assume that a municipality in a pre-control base year has 50 percent of its property tax base composed of apartment properties. Assume further that the market values of these parcels continue to exhibit the same levels of inflation as all other real property in the community. At some future date, therefore, the property tax burden borne by the rent controlled apartments will remain at 50 percent. From the viewpoint of the owners of other forms of real property, particularly single-family homeowners, this would be, at a minimum, an ideal situation. It presumes, however, that the imposition of rent control has no deleterious effect on the market values of rental housing (multi-family) within the municipality and/or that this is not reflected in the ultimate level of assessment.

2. The rent controlled apartments are permitted (and secure in the market with) a constant net operating income equal to that extant in the year prior to the enactment of rent control. Assume that the capitalization rate extended by the market remains constant; thus the capitalized (market) value of the affected buildings re-

mains constant. In turn assume that the buildings' assessments are directly proportionate to this capitalized value. If the values of other properties within the municipality remained constant, the rent controlled sector would continue to account for the same proportion of the total assessment base. Given the levels of inflation, however, which have affected real property over the last ten years, and assuming that the "values" of the real property of the community were enhanced by this inflation, the proportion of the total municipal property tax bill which would be supported by the rent controlled sector would decrease. The other categories of real property in the municipality therefore would bear an increased burden within the property tax system.

3. From the viewpoint of other property owners, the most ominous possible case is one in which the net operating income declines as a function of rental restrictions; even assuming a constant capitalization rate, the market (capitalized) value of the parcel would consequently be reduced. Assuming further that municipal assessments are ultimately a direct function of market value shifts, the assessed values of the rent controlled properties will erode. Consequently, the remaining categories of real property within the community, assuming their values are at best constant, or at worst reflect extant inflation, will account for an increasing share of the total property valuations of the community. And thus their tax burdens will be significantly greater than would be the case otherwise.

Note in this analysis that we have assumed capitalization rates which are constant regardless of the presence or absence of rent control. This, in all probability, will not be the case. In part, capitalization rates for income producing property, particularly in times of inflation, presume the capacity to advance rates. If there is rent control, by definition there is a limit on future rent mobility. Thus an increased level of risk is introduced and there is a strong probability of a somewhat higher capitalization rate than would otherwise be the case. Endangered income simply is more riskful and therefore must yield a higher rate of return in order to attract investment.

There is yet another stipulation which should be entered into this equation: the issue of additional capital investment in multifamily rental facilities in the presence of rent control. There is indication based upon previous studies that lending institutions are loathe to grant mortgages and entrepreneurs somewhat less interested in constructing such facilities, within a controlled context. If a community does not want apartment construction, this issue may be moot, or indeed well may serve as an endorsement of rent control as a perhaps less controversial line of defense than exclusionary zoning. If, on the other hand, a municipality views apartments as an appropriate addition to its developmental pattern—and in light of fiscal impact analysis very well may view them as providing some measure of alleviation to the overall tax burden—rent control may result in foregone opportunities. Again, these are issues which are not addressed in the analysis which follows.

EXHIBIT 4

FORT LEE VALUATION BY LAND USE CATEGORY AND PROPORTIONAL SHARES 1970 TO 1977

Category	1976 Assessed Valuation	Percent of Total	1977 Assessed Valuation	Percent of Total
Vacant Land	$ 16,376,010	3.73%	$ 27,580,310	3.59%
Residential	140,185,765	31.95	251,152,300	32.71
Commercial	50,417,830	11.49	94,865,505	12.36
Industrial	5,351,600	1.22	10,300,200	1.34
Apartment	226,382,545	51.60	383,822,800	50.00
Total	$438,713,750	100.00	$767,721,115	100.00

Source: Fort Lee Assessor's Office
Division of Taxation, New Jersey Department of the Treasury
Bureau of Government Services, New Jersey Department of Community
Affairs

THE FORT LEE EXPERIENCE

In Exhibit 4 is shown the assessed valuation of the various categories of real property in Fort Lee for 1976 and 1977. The earlier year represents a continuation of the assessments originated in 1970, with the appropriate adjustments entered for new construction and successful appeals. As is shown in the exhibit, apartments accounted for 51.6 percent of the total valuation as of 1976. A community-wide revaluation was undertaken in 1977 which resulted in an approximate 80 percent increase in the total assessed valuation. The apartment's

EXHIBIT 5

APARTMENT APPEALS, FORT LEE
1973 THROUGH 1977

	1973	1974	1975	1976	1977
Value of Appeal (Assessment Reduction Sought)	$ 25,519,200	$ 38,808,300	$ 77,759,360	$ 86,388,610	$192,242,419
Total Valuation	392,255,465	415,190,765	437,869,620	438,713,750	767,721,115
Appeals as Percent of Total Valuation	6.5%	9.3	17.8	19.7	25.0
Apartment Valuation Total	180,714,900	199,506,200	226,673,100	226,382,545	383,822,800
Appeals as Percent of Apartment Valuation	14.1%	19.3	34.3	38.2	50.1
Assessed Tax Rate	.0257	.0264	.0299	.0397	.0245
Potential Tax Impact of Reductions[1]	655,843	1,024,539	2,325,005	3,429,628	4,709,939

Note: 1. Tax rate x Appeal Valuation

Source: Fort Lee Assessor's Office

share of total valuation was reduced to 50 percent, thus initally indicating a somewhat higher level of inflation in other forms of realty than in the multifamily stock.

However, in New Jersey the process of municipal reevaluation can be any of three conventional techniques—cost, market data and income approaches. For multifamily parcels in Fort Lee, the cost (depreciated reproduction) approach was employed—establishing the value of the vacant land plus the present cost of reproducing the building minus depreciation from all sources. Its underlying logic assumes a rate of return and yield based not on original value, but rather on competition with newly created stock. By very definition this newly created stock must bear a rate of return and consequently rent levels appropriate to the current market. In the case of Fort Lee, however—with rent control stipulations—this was not the case. The rent levels were—at least according to the owners—substantially less than would be justified by the current costs of reproduction (less depreciation) or for that matter the historic ratios of operating yields.

Consequently, the outcome of the 1977 revaluation brought with it a sharp increase in appeals for assessment reductions. Since the advent of rent control, the latter have increased considerably in magnitude over time. As shown in Exhibit 5, $192,242,419 in reduced apartment assessments were sought in 1977, 50.1 percent of total apartment valuations. The tax impact of these potential reductions totaled $4,709,939.

In New Jersey, if appeals are not resolved at the municipal level, they move successively to County Boards of Taxation and to the New Jersey Division of Tax Appeals of the Department of the Treasury (and if need be, to the Appellate Division of Superior Court). In early 1978, the Bergen County Tax Board granted $96,153,173 of the total 1977 appeal of $192,242,419. While Fort Lee is appealing this ruling with the State Division of Tax Appeals (with tax monies held in reserve), the ultimate impact (if upheld) at this time is shown in Exhibit 6. With the reduction in apartment valuations to $287,669,627, the latter represents only 42.83 percent of the total assessed value of real property within the community. In essence, this reduction represents the capitalization of the missing rent dollars, i.e., the gap between controlled rents (and the rate of return secured with them) and the rent potential within a noncontrolled market. This in turn is the conceptual basis of the cost approach employed in the revaluation process.

THE STAKE OF THE COMMUNITY

Put at its simplest, the following formulation is at work: rental income supports market value, which in turn is the basis for assessments within the property tax system. And in a housing market where supply and demand are in equilibrium and income is not regulated, there should be substantial congruence between income-supported value and depreciated reproduction costs. However, in Fort Lee, the gap between free market and controlled rents has been opening for nearly seven years and with it, an equivalent divergence between the market values of the parcels in question and their depreciated reproduction costs. The Bergen County Tax Board, in closing this gap—in recognizing the decline in the income-producing capacities of the affected buildings—was merely acknowledging the realities.

The consequences however, are far from limited to landlords and tenants. Apartment structures in Fort Lee were projected by the municipal authorities to account for 50 percent of the total municipal revenues derived from real property taxation. They now will support only 42.83 percent, or a reduction of 14.34 percent. This in turn, assuming that property tax levies hold constant, requires the balance of the real property within the community to bear an increased tax burden in order to compensate for the rent control derived gap.

In Exhibit 6 the tax implications of the initial situation for the community as of 1977 are also shown. The assessed property tax rate, which is the quotient of the property tax levy divided by the assessed valuation, is .0245. For the sake of clarification, we have projected out the impact on a typical single-family unit assessed at $60,000. As orignially anticipated, based upon the initial revaluation ($767,721,115), the taxes to be borne would have been $1,470. Based upon the adjusted valuation ($671,467,942), i.e., after the successful appeal to the County Tax Board, the tax rate increases to .0280. The property tax levy on the same single-family unit therefore shifts to $1,680, a net increase of $210 or 14.29 percent.

Exhibit 7 shows the changes for the total residential and apartment sectors within the community. Under the initial situation with apartments in total assessed at $383,822,800, the tax rate, as derived previously, was .0245. The apartment sector therefore should have borne a $9,403,659 tax levy. At the same time, other forms of residential property were assessed $6,153,231 in property taxes.

EXHIBIT 6

THE IMPLICATIONS OF THE ASSESSMENT REDUCTIONS

Reduction in Apartment Assessment: $96,153,173   (1977)

Adjusted Valuation Structure   (1977)

Category	Assessed Valuation	Percent of Total
Vacant Land	$ 27,580,310	4.11%
Residential	251,152,300	37.40
Commercial	94,865,505	14.13
Industrial	10,300,200	1.53
Apartment	287,669,627	42.83
TOTAL	671,567,942	100.01

1977 Initial Situation: Tax Implications

$$\frac{\text{Assessed}}{\text{Tax Rate}} = \frac{\text{Property Tax Levy}}{\text{Assessed Valuation}} = \frac{\$ 18,809,167}{\$767,721,115} = .0245$$

Property Tax Levy on Single-Family Unit   ($60,000 assessed value)

.0245   ($60,000)   = $1,470

1977 Adjusted Situation: Tax Implications

$$\frac{\text{Assessed}}{\text{Tax Rate}} = \frac{\text{Property Tax Levy}}{\text{Assessed Valuation}} = \frac{\$ 18,809,167}{\$671,567,942} = .0280$$

Property Tax Levy on Single-Family Unit   ($60,000 assessed value)

.0280   ($60,000)   = $1680

Percent Change in Tax Rate

$$\frac{.0280 - .0245}{.0245} = \frac{.0035}{.0245} = 14.29 \text{ percent}$$

Source: Fort Lee Assessor's Office
Division of Taxation, New Jersey Department of the Treasury
Bureau of Government Services, New Jersey Department of Community Affairs

In the adjusted situation, with apartments now assessed only on $8,054,750 tax levy, i.e., a reduction of $1,348,909, the tax rate increases to .0280. The property taxes on other forms of residential property increase by $879,033 to $7,032,264. The balance of this shift must be carried by the remaining categories of real property within the community.

In essence, therefore, rent control represents more than a transfer of resources between landlords and tenants. It is not a two-party

EXHIBIT 7

TAX APPEALS AND SHIFTS IN RELATIVE TAX BURDENS

1977 Initial Situation

Property Tax Levies on Residential and Apartment Properties

Residential
.0245 ($251,152,300) = $6,153,231

Apartment
.0245 ($383,822,800) = $9,403,659

1977 Adjusted Situation

Property Tax Levies on Residential and Apartment Properties

Residential
.0280 ($251,152,300) = $7,032,264

Apartment
.0280 ($383,822,800 − $96,153,173)
.0280 ($287,669,627) = $8,054,750

transaction but rather a three-party concern, with the third party—all other property taxpayers within the community—having to bear the ultimate costs of the rent control subsidy.

If we assume that in the long run the market values of income-producing properties are a function of income and that assessments ultimately reflect market values, then the share of the burden transfered to other sectors of the community will be equivalent roughly to the portion of the foregone rent roll which is normally absorbed by real property taxes. Thus in a community in which real estate taxes represent approximately 20 percent of the rent roll of the building, approximately 20 cents out of every dollar gap between nominal market and controlled rents will be carried by the third party.

Such ramifications surface only after a considerable period of time elapses following the imposition of rent control. In areas such as New Jersey, changes in the market value of properties are not automatically registered within the assessment base (the formal determinations of market values at a specific point in time for the purposes of municipal property taxation). Adjustments and alternations of this base between community-wide revaluations—with the exception of new construction and deletions—face a lengthy appeal process where final resolutions may take several years. The sluggish responsiveness of the assessment system to reflect changing market realities virtually precludes large-scale, cross-community analyses of the impact of rent control at this time. Published municipal valuation data still do not reflect the massive caseload embedded within the appeal process.

Indeed, even in Fort Lee, the formal registration of the changes detailed above have been held in abeyance pending the municipality's appeal of the County Tax Board's ruling. (However, the municipality has had to assess property taxes sufficient to cover the taxation shifts of the Tax Board's decision. These monies are presently held in reserve.) Consequently, analyses of the impact of rent control on the market value of income-producing properties which do not integrate the time lag factor are of limited utility.

Notes

1. Monica R. Lett, *Rent Control: Concepts, Realities, and Mechanisms* (New Brunswick, N.J.: Rutgers University, Center for Urban Policy Research, 1977).
2. A good post-war case in point would be the rent controls instituted in Alaska as a function of the pipeline construction. The state swarmed with construction workers generating enormous but transient levels of housing demand. Automatically abrogating rent controls were enacted, with a trip mechanism set at the 3 percent level. When vacancy rates reached that point, the control mechanism was to be automatically lifted.
3. While typically rent regulation is thought of in terms of the limited budgets of the poor, it is most striking to note that second generation rent control has been most successfully implemented in middle class and more affluent communities. Not uncommonly the arguments espoused, i.e., the powerlessness of tenants and the like, are derived from the rhetoric of poverty areas. Increasingly, however, rent controls are employed to buffer middle and upper-middle class groups.
4. The terms *assessment base* and *property tax base* are used interchangeably. They refer to the total assessed valuation (valued for tax purposes) of real taxable property within a community. The following definitions are appropriate to the New Jersey property tax system, the context of this study:

> An ad valorem tax. The local property tax is measured by property values and is apportioned among taxpayers according to the assessed value of taxable property owned by each taxpayer. The tax applies to real estate and tangible personal property of telephone and telegraph companies.

A local tax. The property tax is a local tax assessed and collected by municipalities for the support of municipal and county governments and local school districts. No part of it is used for support of state government.

Amount of tax (a residual tax). The amount of local property tax is determined each year, in each municipality, to supply whatever revenue is required to meet budgeted expenditures not covered by monies available from all other sources. School districts and counties notify municipalities of their property tax requirements. Municipalities add their own requirements and levy taxes to raise the entire amount. As a residual local tax, the total property tax is determined by local budgets and not by property valuations or tax rates.

Property assessment (the tax base). All taxable property is assessed (valued for taxation) by local assessors in each municipality. Assessments are expressed in terms of "taxable value."

Taxable Valuation. The taxable valuation of a municipality is commonly referred to as the ratable base and comprises real property and business personal property. These elements, in turn, are defined as follows:

Real Property. The value of real property is the total taxable value of agricultural, residential and industrial land (excluding railroad property which was removed from the local real property tax base, effective in 1967), and the improvements thereon (e.g., buildings).

Business Personal Property. This category refers to such property as machinery and production facilities. In New Jersey, only the business property of telephone, telegraph and messenger system companies is assessed at the local level and taxes at the local rate, since the taxation of other business personal property was transferred to the state in 1968. After that date, "personal property used in business (other than the business of telephone, telegraph and messenger system companies) is subject to a uniform state tax instead of the local tax. Nonbusiness personal property is no longer subject to any property tax and inventories of all businesses were excluded from property taxation."

See: New Jersey Department of the Treasury, Division of Taxation, *Annual Report* (Trenton, annual).

5. The surge of apartment construction can be construed in part as an expansion of the Manhattan CBD, transforming a suburban node into a virtual "neighborhood" of New York City.

6. On April 5, 1973, the New Jersey Supreme Court upheld municipalities' power to enact such ordinances regulating rental increases. *Inganamort* v. *Borough of Fort Lee*, 62 N.J. 521 (1973).

7. It should be noted that the Consumer Price Index (for the New York-Northeastern New Jersey) increased from 137.5 in 1973 to 150.9 in 1974,

a change of 9.7 percent. For the preceding three years, the average annual percentage change was 4.8 percent.

8. After an immediate challenge in trial court (A-163, *Helmsley* v. *Borough of Fort Lee*), the landlords were permitted to increase rents up to the percentage change in the CPI, but any increases greater than 2.5 percent were to be placed in escrow during the appellate process.

9. *Helmsley* v. *Borough of Fort Lee*, 75 N.J. 31 (1977), cert. granted.

10. As a point of interest, it should be noted that this modification was enacted shortly after the public disclosure of the 1976 tax rate, which increased over the 1975 rate by approximately 34 percent. This represented a sharp upward thrust compared to the experience of the preceding years.

11. *Helmsley* v. *Borough of Fort Lee*, No. A-163/164/165/166/167-77 (N.J., decided Oct. 17, 1978).

12. For the purposes of this paper, we use the terms "multifamily units," "apartments" and "rental units" interchangeably.

13. "The 35 buildings in the survey contain 7,542 apartments, or units; they comprise approximately 85 percent of all rental units in the borough. Fifteen buildings with 4,958 units were classified as highrises, 11 buildings with 2,053 units as lowrises, and 9 buildings with 531 units as garden apartments. The survey included buildings whose landlords were not plaintiffs in this litigation. For each building the landlord supplied detailed financial data for the years 1970 through 1976, including financial statements, utility and fuel bills, real estate tax bills, payroll and income tax returns, insurance and mortgage information, monthly rent rolls, and any applications for hardship relief." *Helmsley* v. *Borough of Fort Lee*, No. A-163/164/165/166/167-77 (N.J., decided Oct. 17, 1978).

14. Net operating income is known also as "net operating profit," "contribution to debt, depreciation and profit" and "net operating profit (available to interest and depreciation)." It is the difference between incomes received and direct operating and maintenance expenses. The net income ratio is defined as net operating income divided by total income; the expense ratio is the complement of the net income ratio.

15. For descriptions of this approach, see: Charles B. Ackerson, *Capitalization Theory and Techniques* (Chicago: American Institute of Real Estate Appraisers of the National Association of Realtors, 1975).

16. *The Appraiser*, September 1976, p. 4.

17. The prototypical nature of Mediterranean Towers' operating experience is reflected in the data below for a group of 22 multifamily structures built prior to 1970 in Fort Lee.

Net Operating Income in 1976 as a Percentage of 1973 Level

Class	Range	Median
Highrise	76.6-103.9%	94.5%
Lowrise	93.2-104.3%	99.1%
Garden	77.6-102.2%	99.6%

For each structure class, net operating income as a percentage of its level in 1973 has declined. This is the most marked in the highrise category, where the median case stands at 94.5 percent.

The following data on expense ratios for the same sample of structures amplifies the causes of decline.

Expense Ratio in 1973 and 1976

Class	1973		1976	
	range	median	range	median
Highrise	.425–.594	.475	.529–.661	.566
Lowrise	.397–.554	.416	.472–.585	.521
Garden	.353–.577	.415	.443–.678	.505

For the highrise sector, the median expense ratio in 1973 had increased from .475 to .566, indicating the sharp increase in the proportion of income consumed by expenditures.

A further measure of generalization is available from a special survey conducted in New York City by the Bureau of Labor Statistics for the purpose of providing a basis for rent increments permitted for multi-family rent stabilized structures within New York City.

Year	NYC Index*	% Increase	CPI	% Increase
1967	100.0		99.3	
1968	103.5	3.5	102.9	3.6
1969	107.6	4.0	109.7	6.6
1970	116.6	8.4	117.7	7.3
1971	132.2	13.4	124.6	5.9
1972	139.7	5.7	130.4	4.7
1973	150.8	7.9	137.5	5.4
1974	179.7	19.2	150.9	9.7
1975	191.3	6.5	163.7	8.5
1976	203.5	6.4	174.3	6.5
1977	219.5	7.9	183.7	5.4

*The NYC Index is determined in April of each year. For comparability, the CPI in the table is the New York-Northeastern New Jersey "All Items" index for April of each year.

The NYC index went from a 1970 base of 116.6 to 150.8 in 1973, an increase of 29.3 percent; by 1978 the index reached 203.5, an increase over 1973 of 34.9 percent. Operating costs of multifamily housing based upon the New York City data have far outpaced the consumer price index, reaching a 1977 level of 219.5 in 1977 (based on 1967 as 100). The CPI moved from 99.3 percent in the 1967 base year to 183.7 by 1977. (The data has been extracted from; *Helmsley* v. *Borough of Fort Lee*, No. A-163/164/165/166/167-77 (N.J., decided Oct. 1978).

18. If we assumed a constant capitalization rate of 10.4 percent, the following capitalized values for the respective years would result:

1970	$11,167,509
1973	$12,025,586
1976	$ 9,819,567

The gross income multipliers would then take the following values:

1970:	5.67
1973:	5.46
1976:	4.17

19. As the time span beyond the base valuation increases, the general tendency is for the gap to widen between assessments and market values. According to the date of assessments among municipalities, a number of independent valuation systems may exist which are not in synchronization with one another. If inflation affects all properties within a single jurisdiction equally, that gap then poses little difficulty for property taxation at the municipal scale. (At higher scales of operation—regional school and county taxes, for example—county and state determined equalization ratios can transform individual municipalities' assessment totals into comparable equalized (market) valuations.) Moreover, new additions of real properties normally are assessed according to the economic criteria of the base valuation.

Where certain property sectors experience market value changes at variance with the general community pattern, problems arise. The appeal process is extended and laborious; when added to the span of time required to firmly establish market value shifts (pre-appeal), it is not surprising that the actual registration of the latter in the assessment system lags the onset of rent control by a considerable period of time.

Condominium Conversion Profiles: Governmental Policy

George Sternlieb
James W. Hughes

Introduction

Condominiums and condominium conversions have become a phenomenon of significant proportions in recent years. Changing demographic profiles of the nation's population—increasing numbers of nonfamily-raising households, emerging economic strictures buffeting the single-family home market, the dissolution of the rental market via rent control limitations, etc.—have all congealed into a force favoring the condominium mode of residential development. Yet the very magnitude of the current trends and the changes they evoke have brought cries for increased public regulation.

This paper is based on a study performed for Washington, D.C., an area experiencing a debate over conversion regulation after the externalities of the process had been highly publicized.[1] The problem, however, is much more complex than simply impeding or facilitating conversion. The objective here is to examine the demographic and economic profiles of the households affected by the condominium

289

conversion process, and, based upon these findings, to sketch out the policy implications attached to them.

The data comprise a set of 200 structured interviews with households enveloped in the conversion process.[2] From cross-tabulations of these data, it was possible to draw a series of generalized household profiles, sharpening the authors' perception of conversions impact. While certain partitions of the data may have limited statistical reliability, it is felt that the broad brush strokes of the phenomenon are adequately captured.

The Basic Framework

The starting point in formulating policy directed toward the regulation of condominium conversions is the profiling of the major residential actors affected by the process. This paper will focus on two:

1. The *Purchasers* of converted condominium units and
2. The *Conversion Move-outs*, who had been tenants in buildings subsequently converted to condominium status, and who decided to move out rather than purchase.

Of the latter, it is important not only to determine their *demographic characteristics*, but also their *move-out rationale*: why did they move and how is this motivation linked to their demographic profiles? Isolation of these variables should enable policymakers to gauge the possible hardships fostered by the condominium conversion process.

The profiling of the purchasers has a somewhat different objective. Here it is important to gain a perspective on the *size of the potential market* for converted condominium residences. If the purchasers' demographic characteristics indicate that they represent a *unique subgroup* of the general population, then there may be a limited demand and proposed public regulation could be overreacting. However, if the profile indicates a potential *large supply* of such consumers, then perhaps an extensive set of ground rules should be formulated to regulate a potentially large phenomenon, particularly if the move-outs give evidence of bearing substantial hardships.

For each of these household categories, three modular household types tend to emerge. Consequently, six profiles overall have been constructed: principal, secondary, and tertiary types for both the move-outs and the purchasers.

The evaluation of market subgroups is made easier conceptually if one has an evaluative framework indicating who lives where and why. Basic to this task are the various paradigms of the family life cycle and their relationship to specific housing types. For example, both apartment renters and condominium purchasers stand at variance from the widely prevalent conceptualization of the modular American family, i.e., a husband/wife/two children configuration residing in a single-family dwelling. Of much smaller size and with age characteristics tending toward the extremes (both young and old households) are the resident types found in most rental and condominium units. These unique household types bound the modular family, as they are in the pre- and post-childrearing stages of the family life cycle.

In order to grasp this situation better, particularly since the profiles highlight the uniqueness of the parties affected by condominium conversion, the authors hypothesize the following sequences in changes in residential status as a household ages.

Combining these two typologies, one can see that the parties probably enveloped within the condominium conversion process are households generally "before and after" family raising as well as a unique subset which has foregone the option of children. These are families that are simply not immersed in the single-family home alternative.

It is this framework which provides a background for viewing the household types involved in condominium purchase or conversion move-out. The authors have found that the conversion move-outs form a distinctly smaller and older household than that prevalent for typical apartment dwellers. This helps to establish strongly the elderly nature of the population moving out of converted buildings. At the same time, the condominium purchaser tends to manifest demographic characteristics similar to those of apartment dwellers as a whole, but is substantially more affluent.

The distinct profiles are summarized below, presenting the principal, secondary, and tertiary profile types, respectively, for the conversion move-outs and the condominium purchasers.

Before proceeding, one additional explanatory note is warranted. In order not to become overly muddled in a welter of detail, the household profiles present the pre- and post-conversion housing cost comparisons without explicitly recognizing the various implications of income tax deductions, equity buildup assumptions, and opportunity cost considerations of condominium ownership. Consequently these are computed separately and follow the presentation of the profiles. The conversion move-outs are examined first.

The Conversion Move-outs

PRINCIPAL MOVE-OUT PROFILE

1. An elderly household with a head whose median age is over 60 years.
2. The household is relatively small, predominantly comprised of one or two members, with a median size of 1.25 persons. This is an empty nester, in the post-childrearing stage of the life cycle.
3. The median household income approaches $8,500 with the largest concentration being below $10,000.
4. The principal source of income appears to be social cecurity and pensions, a result of retirement and not being active in the labor force.
5. The length of residence in the unit before conversion often far exceeded five years.
6. The former unit was typically small—efficiencies and one-bedrood types—and the gross rent was under $200 monthly. This rent appeared appropriate to the basic income resources.
7. The condominium changeover would have forced an increase in basic housing costs to a point where they would have consumed almost 53 percent of income, i.e., $4,500 ($375 monthly) out of a median annual income of $8,500 would have had to be devoted to the shelter function. Under rental status, the household was charged $2,184 in annual gross rent ($182 monthly), representing 25.7 percent of income.
8. The households in this module exhibited very strong attitudes against conversion of rental apartments to condominiums in general.
9. Their reaction was also unfavorable towards conversion of their particular building to condominium status.
10. Those few who remained were the ones move-outs saw as unable to move because of physical, emotional, or other factors.

11. The rationales put forth by the principal move-out profile group for not staying were:

   a. The unit was too expensive.
   b. They did not want to buy.
   c. They felt they were too old to buy.

12. All three responses had hearly the same frequency of occurence; there was a slight tendency towards stressing financial considerations, reflecting thier economic situation.

13. The reasons "not wanting to own" and "too old" reflect the stage in the life cycle of the subgroup—empty nesters and the elderly who neither need nor want the investment potential and responsibility that goes with homeownership.

14. After relocation, their new unit has a median rent of $182 monthly. Interestingly enough, this is exactly the same median total that prevailed for the units which underwent condominium conversion. So our principal profile did not experience any appreciable cost increases, as defined by rent, by moving to a new rental unit.

15. Their new dwelling location evidenced the tendency to maintain residence within Washington, D.C., although the conversion engendered a neighborhood change.

SECONDARY MOVE-OUT PROFILE

1. An elderly household with a head whose median age is in the late 50s.

2. The household is relatively small, predominantly comprised of one or two members, with a median size of 1.25 persons. This is an empty nester, in the post-childrearing stage of the life cycle.

3. The secondary move-out prototype differs from the above counterpart in terms of socioeconomic resources. This subpopulation generally has an income exceeding $15,000, with a median of $25,000.

4. The principal source of income is from employment in professional and technical occupations.

5. The length of residence in the unit before conversion again exceeded five years.

6. The former unit was typically large, generally encompassing two or three bedrooms, and the gross rent often exceeded $200 and (many times) $300 monthly. Again, this rent appeared within the scope of the tenants income resourses.

7. The shift to ownership status would have increased the cost of shelter substantially. When renting, the median annual income of $25,000 was not burdened significantly by the $3,672 annual ($306 monthly) rent payment, the latter accounting for only 14.7 percent of household income. However, purchasing the unit as a condominium would have meant incurring housing costs of $7,823 annually ($652 monthly), necessitating the expenditure of 31.3 percent of income on housing. For such households, purchase would not have been rendered an impossibility by economic strictures, particularly since many future costs, such as that involved with the education of children, had already been borne. Only the prospect of imminent retirement appears to serve as a negative inducement.

8. The attitude of the middle aged/elderly households in general bulked very strongly against the conversion of rental apartments to condominiums.

9. Their reaction was also unfavorable towards conversion of their particular building to a condominium.

10. Despite their relatively affluent income, their rationale tended more toward economics, and less toward not wanting to buy and being too old to buy.

11. The predominant reason, then, that the subgroup did not buy reflected their tendency not to want to tie up capital resources in the structure, especially with retirement on the horizon.

12. This type 2 partition subsequently moved to a new rental unit with a median rent of $325 monthly. This represents a slight increase over the $306 median which prevailed in the former residence before conversion. Again, the relocation process did not serve to impose a substantial increase in the rent burden applied to this household.

13. This new residence is within Washington, D.C., but in a different neighborhood.

TERTIARY MOVE-OUT PROFILE

1. Young households, not yet entered into the family-raising stage of the life cycle. The household head is generally under 30 years of age.
2. The household again is very small, overwhelmingly comprised of units of one or two persons.
3. Generally a moderate income household, falling between the boundaries established by the primary and secondary prototypes. Although outside the purview of the formal survey, the authors would hypothesize limited accumulations of capital resources.
4. Employment in professional and technical occupations.
5. Predominantly a short term residence (under 36 months) in the converted unit.
6. The former unit typically consisted of one or two bedrooms costing below $300 monthly. This again appears commensurate with the extant income flow.
7. Only 24.3 percent of income—$2,880 annually ($240 monthly) out of a median yearly income of $11,875—had to be devoted to rent under the pre-conversion arrangement. By shifting to the condominium format, yearly housing costs would have jumped to $6,221 ($518 monthly), accounting for over 52 percent of the household's income resources. Although a young, small household—one which may possess substantial future income potential—is being affected by these parameters, it is also a family unit which may not have accrued a substantial capital base, and one which faced many unknown costs accompanying future childrearing and family responsibilities. Ownership may not have been appropriate at the time of conversion, even if the economic blackages demonstrated above did not present themselves.
8. These households, not yet entered into the family raising stage of the life cycle, felt very strongly against the conversion of rental apartments to condominiums.
9. Their reaction was unfavorable towards the conversion of their particular building to a condominium.
10. The overwhelming rationale exhibited by this profile for not purchasing was economic in nature. A secondary emphasis was "not wanting to own."

11. Young households not only have modest incomes but limited accumulations capital resources which constrains their ability to buy the unit. This factor clearly molded their particular attitudes.
12. The post relocation median rent totals $245 monthly, and represents only a slight increase over the extant $240 monthly rent in the vacated unit.
13. While the two former groups indicated they will remain renters in the future, the tertiary profile ultimately hopes to enter into ownership. At present, however, they are renting in Washington, D.C., in a different neighborhood than the conversion.

Conversion Move-outs—Policy Considerations

It appears, then, that the previous residential arrangements before condominium conversion reflected a well-functioning housing market, striking a balance between demand and supply. But the cost implications of condominium conversion on those who chose to depart the structures appear to have been quite substantial. The shift in the character of supply—the cost increase attendant to a unit whose shelter function remained constant—visibly altered the market, with the emerging economic reality forcing the move-out process in a number of instances. This affected both the younger households (insufficient accumulation of capital resources) and the elderly households (insufficient current income stream). Moreover, those not bound by economic strictures per se (late middle-aged) wanted to keep their capital reserves liquid, especially with retirement approaching. Consequently, age or economics or both made condominium ownership inappropriate, and, in fact, made the decision to move out a very rational one indeed.

While the move itself represents some degree of hardship (when any type of change is induced into a stable residential situation, disruptions and dislocations are inevitable by-products of the transition process), there is little evidence to suggest that the market was not able to absorb the move-outs at rents comparable to those charged before the condominium conversion occurred. Moreover, they shifted to units comparable in size and quality to those vacated, and most of these were still within the city, although in a different neighborhood than the converted structure. Thus, a substantial flux of movement was occasioned, a process where long term neighborhood residents were displaced to other neighborhoods. And the costs of moving, in terms of out-of-pocket expenses, are far from trivial.

Undoubtedly, these are hardships, but nowhere near the magnitude of the selected vignettes highlighted by the popular media. Moreover, the assertion is not borne out that there are not equivalent rental facilities either extant or being generated at a pace sufficient to provide accommodations at reasonable prices for the oustees. Yet the retired elderly subset may be in need of protection; the vigor which they can bring to the very process of apartment search and moving may be minimal indeed. The energies required in fixing up and growing accustomed to new facilities and neighborhoods may be beyond their muster. These are the elements which form the critical focus of governmental policy regarding the regulation of condominium conversion.

The Condominium Purchasers

The second major group of households participating in the condominium conversion process are the purchasers. Their profiles are analogous to the move-outs in reference to size, but overall they are substantially younger and much more affluent. Moreover, in a number of cases, they represent an in-migration to the city, both from the immediate suburbs and from other metropolitan areas, thus displacing less affluent city households. Depending upon the perspective taken, this represents either a beneficial or undesirable chain of events. This question will be subsequently addressed after the prototypical households are presented.

PRINCIPAL PURCHASER PROFILE

1. A young household with a head whose median age is in the low 30s.
2. The household is relatively small, predominantly composed of one or two members, with a median size of 1.17 persons. This is a household in the pre-childrearing stage of the life cycle.

3. The median household income approaches $19,400, with a significant number earning above $25,000 and a similar sized segment at between $10,000 and $15,000.
4. The principal source of income is from employment in professional, technical, and managerial occupations.
5. The length of residence in their previous unit before condominium purchase ranged between 13 and 36 months.
6. Their former unit typically rented for $174 monthly. This rent appeared appropriate given the basic income resources.
7. Their condominium purchase generally comprised one and two bedroom units, with a median price level of $29,412. The condominium cost appears within the scope of the current income resources.
8. The condominium purchase was associated with an increase in basic housing costs to the point where they consumed 23 percent of income; i.e., $4,425 ($369 monthly) out of a median annual income of $19,375 would have had to be devoted to the shelter function. Under their former renter status, the household was paying $2,088 in annual gross rent ($174 monthly), representing only 8.3 percent of income. The purchase of the condominium unit did not appear to strain the household's budget significantly.
9. The condominium purchase represents an extension of the constancy of limited space needs associated with a young household not childrearing. Previously, this subgroup was an almost exclusive rental apartment dweller, and came primarily from Washington, D.C., and secondarily from its suburban areas. Their search process typically engendered an informal contact network comprised of friends and acquaintances. Their predominant concern in choosing the condominium unit was locational and accessibility attributes, with these variables perhaps representing surrogates for the future potential value of the unit. Their search focus tended toward emphasizing neighborhood rather than the building per se. This subgroup expresses the most concern for the current tax implications of ownership vis-a-vis rental.

SECONDARY PURCHASER PROFILE

1. An elderly household with a head whose median age is the mid-60s.
2. The household is again relatively small, predominately comprised of one or two members, with a median size of 1.17 persons. This household can be characterized as an empty nester, in the post-childrearing stage of the life cycle.
3. The median household income is approximately $25,000.
4. The principal source of income appears to be social security and pensions.
5. Their length of residence at their previous dwelling typically exceeded five years.
6. The former unit typically rented at $242 monthly, a rent level relatively modest in comparison to their basic income resources.
7. Their current condominium unit generally comprises two or three bedrooms, and had an offering price of $46,667. Their current cost of shelter appears appropriate to their current income flow.
8. The shift to ownership status increased the cost of housing substantially, but did not result in the consumption of an inordinate proportion of the household budget. When renting, the median annual income of $25,000 was associated with a former annual rent payment ($150 monthly) or $1,800, The latter accounting for only 7.2 percent of household income. The purchase of the condominium unit jumped this cost threshold significantly to where the annual cost of housing approached $6,873 ($573 monthly) but this still only necessitated the expenditure of 27 percent of current income on housing. Again the purchase represented cost increases, but increases of the nature that could be borne by their current income flow.*
9. Their former residence place was typically a rental unit; however, a certain proportion were former private home-owners. There appears to be a mixed proportion of both former owners and renters coming from both Washington,

*Note that we have excluded the opportunity costs involved in the down payment.

D.C. and its suburban areas. Thus, their movement patterns represent both an inter-city and suburban-to-city migration pattern. But predominantly these purchasers were inner city renters. Access was a main criterion of choice of the particular unit, perhaps indicating their limited mobility. Given their proclivity not to be in the labor force, it is not surprising that the tax deductions associated with ownership were not rated highly by this group. Thus, the elderly demonstrate less interest in the investment function of condominiums, and they are more concerned with the amenities of the specific parcel as well as its locational and accessibility attributes. This was the only profile group to rank unit and building amenities very high, again reflective of their limited mobility.

TERTIARY PURCHASE PROFILE

1. A unique set of middle-aged families not in the process of childrearing. The household head has a median age in the vicinity of 50 years.
2. The household is again very small, overwhelmingly comprising units of one or two persons.
3. This is an affluent household, in its prime earning years, as evidenced by a median income of $35,000.
4. The principal source of inomce is from employment in professional, technical, and managerial occupations.
5. Their length of residence in their former unit was a long term one, generally exceeding five years.
6. Their former unit rented for $242 monthly, certainly commensurate with the extant income flow.
7. Their current condominium unit is generally comprised of two bedrooms and costs in the vicinity of $47,500. The cost of shelter does not put any burden upon the household's annual income.
8. Only 8.3 percent of income—$2,904 annually ($242 monthly) out of a median income of $35,000—had to be devoted to rent under their prepurchase arrangement. In the shift to condominium format, yearly housing costs increased to $6,965 ($580 monthly), but still accounted for only 20 per-

cent of the household's income. In this case, considering that these are households in their peak earning years, purchase of the condominium unit made very good economic sense.

9. They previously resided in rental units, with a small subset having been single-family unit owners. Their previous geographic location was principally Washington, D.C., and also the suburban areas, with renters and owners not tied exclusively to either of these geographical locations. Their search process was underlaid by an informal informational network tied strongly to friends and personal contacts. The search focus again emphasized neighborhood, with locational and accessibility requirements the dominant selection criteria. They viewed the tax savings occasioned by ownership as not quite as important as the principal profile group, but much more important than did the secondary group.

RENTAL VS. CONDOMINIUM OCCUPANCY COSTS

The overall cost impact on the housing consumer of the condominium purchase can best be presented in the following tabular summary. Included are four modular income levels, the former annual gross rents associated with these incomes, the condominium sales prices, and the gross annual cost estimates of the condominium format. For each of the income levels, the gross annual cost estimates reveal that the shelter costs of ownership increase substantially above those extant in the rental market, ranging from $1,500 in the case of the $20,000 income level to almost $3,800 in the case of the $50,000 income level. However, these are gross estimates and do not include such variables as equity buildup, tax deductions, and opportunity costs. These are computed on average annual bases and deducted from the gross annual costs. The final column—Refined Cost Estimate—compares very favorably with the former rental parameters. For the $20,000 income level, the refined annual condominium cost of $2,980 stands below the former annual gross rent. A similar relationship holds for each of the model types.

Moreover, the maximum benefits of condominium ownership accrue to those at the highest income levels, as the tabular material shows. For the $50,000 income household, linked with a $60,000 condominium unit, the actual cost to the housing consumer is $400 less than the former rent payment. Consequently, if the entry thresholds are met (i.e., an annual gross income in the vicinity of

EXHIBIT 1
RENTAL VS. CONDOMINIUM OCCUPANCY COST

	Rental		Condominium	
Income Level	Former Annual Gross Rent	Sales Price	Gross Annual Cost Estimate	Refined Cost Estimate *
$20,000	$3,000	$30,000	$4,500	$2,980
$30,000	$3,900	$40,000	$5,960	$3,627
$40,000	$4,500	$50,000	$7,420	$4,216
$50,000	$5,100	$60,000	$8,879	$4,718

* Considering equity buildup, tax deductions, and opportunity cost (Average Annual Parameters based on Mortgage Life).

$20,000), then it is possible to enter into condominium ownership without increasing shelter costs. Moreover, in an inflation-ridden world, the potential increase in the value of the property are most evident. There should be no question as to the benefits of condominium ownership to the affluent. However, severe entry conditions must be met before such benefits can accrue to prospective purchasers. These center about the prerequisite income levels necessary to gain the tax benefits and sufficient capital resources to cover downpayment requirements.

CONDOMINIUM PURCHASERS POLICY CONSIDERATIONS

The purchaser profiles strongly suggest that it is erroneous to view the condominium conversion process as fostering a torrent of family-raising households pouring in from the suburbs to displace elderly and less affluent housing consumers. The purchasers ccomprise very small households, not in the process of childrearing, and possessing substantial income resources. But while these purchasers make up a very small sector of the housing consumers in Washington, D.C., the authors would hesitate to suggest that they represent a limited phenonmenon.

Indeed, the dynamic growth sector of American society is the 25 to 34 age group, expected to increase by almost 12 million people (46.1 percent) during the decade of the 1970s. This is happening while

the total United States population is increasing by 19 million or
9.4 percent. Thus, this age sector will account for 63 percent of the
country's growth. Moreover, over 80 percent of the growth in households between 1970 and 1973 constituted one- and two-person "non-
modular" households—young unmarried couples without children,
divorcees, empty nesters, and senior citizens.[4]

Consequently, the purchasers are embedded in a national demographic shift which will see their numbers bulk larger and larger. If
the severe income thresholds can be met, and if the condominium
conversion process is attractive to a good proportion of the households characterized by the profile, then it is clear that the phenomenon
may not be of limited proportions. A large supply of such consumers
require regulation, particularly if the benefits they engender are
outweighed by the costs they impose. The former comprise the net
additive purchasing power brought into the jurisdiction by affluent
purchasers, as well as the upgrading of the municipal fiscal position
by virtue of increased assessments on the converted parcels. At the
same time, these must be matched against the substantial hardships
borne by the move-outs. Thus many competing interests, costs, and
benefits must be carefully weighed. It is to these questions that this
paper now turns.

Policy Alternatives

A jurisdiction is often faced with the problem of regulating condominium conversion after the externalities of the process have been
highly publicized. A substantial political head of steam can build up
as the problems of tenants, forced to move as a consequence of conversion, gain the attention of the media. In Washington, D.C., for
example, many newspaper accounts focused on elderly individuals
whose life styles were substantially impacted by this phenomenon.
Another motivating factor which enters into the scene is the assertion
that there are not equivalent rental facilities either extant or being
generated at a pace sufficient to provide accommodations at reasonable prices for the oustees. Despite the nervous frenzy these factors
engender, the starting point in determining alternatives must be a
consideration of the objectives of regulation.

WHAT IS THE OBJECTIVE OF CONDOMINIUM REGULATION?

The answer to this somewhat rhetorical query can either be a very brief, or very complex. It is relatively easy to say that the objective is to provide protection to tenants and buyers. Once these elements are left, however, one is faced with the broader question which is one more of policy than of administrative procedures: "Does the jurisdiction wish to encourage the process of condominium conversion or discourage it?"

The costs and benefits of each alternative must be carefully weighed and balanced. Certainly, if a jurisdiction wishes to stall conversion, it can do so. The capacity to encourage the process is more limited, however, since the basic conversion activity depends very largely on market demand, financing, and the like. While conceivably municipal loan programs and a variety of other efforts could affect demand and financing, as yet this has not been done.

RELATIONSHIP BETWEEN RENT CONTROL AND CONDOMINIUM CONVERSION

The basic objectives of condominium regulation take on substantial complexity if the jurisdiction is also involved in rent control.

The imposition of rent controls finds as its natural complement the conversion of rental units into condominiums. The pressure on landlords to escape from control mechanisms obviously will vary with the flexibility of these same mechanisms to defect the realities of operating cost changes. Certainly, however, their imposition makes the ownership of rental facilities a more riskful, less promising investment. The response is to attempt to sell out. Since private buyers for the parcel as a whole are faced with the same drab picture as the prospecitve seller, this is not a particularly promising avenue except when a structure is recapitalized down (i.e., the sale price is lowered to reflect the altered profit potential [whether real or imaginary] within the market mechanism).

What is left, therefore, is the condominium conversion process. Since the building now is to be sold among a variety of individuals each of whom becomes the owner of his own apartment, the strictures on rent level are irrelevant. In addition, given the favorable treatment accorded homeowners (as compared with renters) in terms of taxes, it is frequently possible for the owner to secure from the individual buyers a higher than pre-control price for the sum of the apartment units within the converted structure.

From the tenant's point of view, however, rent controls diminish one of the primary objectives of homeownership—and with it condominium unit purchase—and that is some protection against the onslaught of inflation. Fear of the declining value of the dollar in housing is reflected really in two separate streams. On the one hand, there is the allure of buying a condominium at a low price level and preserving the real value of the dollars concerned regardless of an inflation in real prices which may diminish money kept in the bank. On the other hand, there is the possibility of preserving oneself through ownership from the inflation of rents as a function of heightened yield to rental property operators.

Rent control makes this latter issue moot, since it insures the rental occupant against dependence on the owner/operator's goodwill to minimize rent increases. In some cases, at least, its implementation means that even real increases in operating costs will be (unwillingly!) subsidized by the owners through a reduction of the capital value of the plant, rather than being reflected, at least immediately, in the rent dollars paid.

As the gap between the free market rents potential and the control levels increases, one perceives the growth of a new phenomenon which must be considered as one views the condominium process.

THE UNBUNDLING OF PROPERTY

The term unbundling used here is similar to that employed by the courts when they instructed IBM to set up separate schedules for programming, servicing of machines, and the machines themselves— taking what hitherto was thought of as a single product and separating it into a variety of ownerships. That is what has occurred in the field of real property. Part of the problem one has in conceptualizing the condominium conversion process is the time lag between beliefs as to what constitutes reality and the current actualities. A prime example of this gap lies in the area of the right to dispose of property. If there is any one essential attribute which clear title has always possessed, it is the right of disposition, i.e., sale. Why then the growing constraints against owners' selling? These arise from the fact that what has been against owners' selling? These arise from the fact that what has been formulated are tenant property rights in the physical premises which he occupies. In essence, the owner's rights in the property—despite the legal fiction of clear title in the old sense, i.e., of a title that is not beclouded by other claimants in a formal sense—are now limited by the new tenants' rights.

THE RISE IN THE STATUTORY TENANT

Typically, the rights of tenantry have been embodied and limited by leases, written agreements on rights and obligations between landlords and tenants. The new division of property rights, however, can (and frequently does) bypass this format. The classic example would be the rights and privileges of the tenant-in-occupancy to remain so, even in the face of normal eviction procedures. Genreally, most rent control legislation, for example, embodies some anti-eviction procedures. These are typically generated with the belief that otherwise the tenants would be subject to a variety of landlord harassment if they should complain of rent increases or other punitive procedures. There is substantial variation on grounds for eviction in rent control ordinances, but increasingly these may involve lengthy periods of time. Even when evicion is desired for the purposes of demolishing a building and erecting an alternative in its place, the rights of possession of the tenant in occupancy must be observed— and this without written lease. The clearest test of this tenant property interest is the fact that it can, and frequently is, recognized by a cash payment.

Again, as the gap between free market rents and controlled rents expands (as it must if controls do not permit elevation of rent levels corresponding to the inflation in building costs) the implicit value of the tenants' property right to maintain his protected rent level clearly increases. Indeed, even if the rents for the unit being converted and alternative rental facilities were equal (that is, if there were a variety of alternative accommodations and straight rental facilities equivalent to, and located within the neighborhood, market, region, etc., of the about-to-be-converted building), there would be a basic interest on the part of at least some tenants in maintaining their extant facilities. The costs of moving, of discomfort, and of the particular difficulties of immobile elderly, are significant.

As one reviews this latter element, it is clear that there are certain elements of property interest which can be recognized by cash payments. Other elements (particularly in the case of the elderly) must be reckoned in their time and level of discomfort and are simply not reconcilable by cash. The latter may be thought of essentially as terminal occupancies.

When a landlord unilaterally attempts to convert his building, therefore, he is not merely proposing to dispose of his classic title to the parcel. He may be making this effort without recognition of the fact of the implicit tenant-in-occupancy property interests. It is irrelevant to comment that the latter may not be recognized in the classic courses in property taught at law school; they are evident much more significantly in the realities of politics, as witness the strictures set up against conversion in a variety of municipalities. How is this conflict to be resolved, and what is the municipality's stake?

THE CITY'S ECONOMIC STAKE

Outright rejection of the conversion process has serious fiscal implications for the implementing jurisdiction. Condominium conversion often is accompanied by a significant upgrading of older parcels through substantial rehabilitation on the part of the landlord. Clearly, it is in a municipality's best interest to see the maintenance and improvement of its own standing stock of structures, i.e., what may realistically be considered its capital plant.

In addition, the sale of condominium units cumulatively entails a substantial increase in the previous value of the property. This, in turn, is reflected by a significant upgrading of the assessment base of the structure and therefore the municipality's revenue. The authors' surveys of the relationship between the nominal assessments before and after conversion indicate a potential upgrading of 50 to 60 percent with no increase in the municipal expenditures required to service the parcel.

Given the harsh limitation of every city's current capacity to secure additional funds for servicing those of its citizens who have very limited incomes, every dollar secured in this fashion is of prime importance. Therefore, *from a strictly fiscal point of view, one can view the condominium conversion process as significantly upgading the taxpaying capacity of middle and upper middle income housing, thus providing the wherewithal for financing the needs of less fortunate residents.*

To sum up this area as succinctly as possible, if the fiscal implication of condominium conversion were the only one to be considered, every jurisdiction should be enthusiastically encouraging the process. But this procedure entails, as the move-out profile suggests, a significant measurd of problems, discomfort, and, in some cases, substantial out-of-pocket expenditures for those for whem the conversion process means displacement. How can these two conflicting interests be resolved? Detailed below are several approaches to a compromise between these two positions.

Differential treatment as a function of age. The problem of conversion is far greater among the elderly than it is among more youthful households. It might be desirable, therefore, to have some level of protection against the process specifically for the elderly in residence. Developing cut-off points for this process and the legal base might be difficult, but it probably can be done.

This may have to be coupled with some form of tax relief or incentive to continue the housing of such households. One of the problems that arises from special protection for the elderly is that the landlords of rental units may (even though not currently thinking in terms of conversion processes) be disinclined to rent to them for fear of later inhibiting such a process. Cushioning this with some form of tax support may make it packageable.

Income limitations. The appeal of the condominium is largely confined to those whose incomes (and, consequently, income taxes) are set at a relatively high level. These households can best take advantage of the tax implications of the condominium process. The condominium as a tax form is far less attractive to those with more modest incomes. Unfortunately, these individuals are typically those who have the least flexibility in terms of finding alternate accommodations, in off-setting the costs of moving, and the like.

The present era has been fairly casual about imposing means tests on the poor, and generally has rigorously avoided them for the middle class. Inhibiting condominiums is a process which is quite costly to a municipality; it provides a subsidy, through foregone tax increases, for those who can continue in rental facilities because of municipal intervention. One approach would be to impose a means test. This would provide protection for those of limited resources while permitting the process to continue for the affluent renter, thus allowing the enhancement of the jurisdiction's fiscal base.

This approach becomes particularly significant when one considers the disparity in income levels between the move-outs and the purchasers. Even among the elderly there are those of affluence and, with it, a substantial propensity to buy into the building. Therefore, what might be considered is both an age and income protection feature.

Longevity in the building. Should more in the way of recompense be made for those who are long term residents in a building? The move-out profiles indicate a substantial deviation in length of previous tenure. Most of the elderly, for example, were long term residents. A substantial proportion of the more youthful occupants of the converted building lived there for a much shorter period of time. Should this variation be recognized in controlling the condominium process, and compensating those who are to be moved? While arguments can be made that the recent mover has most currently faced the expenses of moving and the like, certainly the psychological stake of the long-term occupant is much more substantial.

A geographic division. There are sections of every jurisdiction which would very substantially benefit from the possibilities of owner occupancy. Indeed these areas, if they do not secure this type of stability, may well face the prospect of generalized decline. Other sections (perhaps those which *currently* are most in demand for the condominium process) may be relatively stable, and here the policy of promoting the condominium process, at least from this perspective, holds little benefit. Should one view, then, the permission of condominiums (or, for that matter, even their enthusiastic initiation) in certain geographic areas as part of a master plan for maintaining the vatality and overall ecology of a jurisdiction?

Most efforts at neighborhood stability have focused on the physical elements of housing; much more attention undoubtedly should be placed on the tenurial arrangements: of ownership, management, and the like. Should a municipality use the condominium process as a flexible toold in this regard?

THE MINIMUM THRESHOLD REQUIREMENTS FOR THE TENANTS IN OCCUPANCY

Regardless of the specific stipulations imposed and the variations in the impact permitted under municipal jurisdiction of this process, there may well be a number of minimal across-the-board arrangements which should be secured for all tenants in residency. While the exact quantity of them may perhaps be made dependent upon their specific status or other variations as outlined above, they must be fed into the mix of thinking.

Relocation benefits or aid. Should landlords be required to find specific apartments for the displacees? Or, for the sake of simplicity, can one simply quantify this relocation aid in terms of a lump-sum payment?

Substantial prior notice. Interestingly enough, the bulk of the authors' respondents were not too upset by the rather casual notice which many of them received of the impending conversion of their buildings. Certainly, in order to avoid any undue hardship, there should be a substantial period between formal initiation of condominium process and loss of residency status. This may, however, if inordinately long, impose significant financial stress on the condominium process. For example, if notice is required 20 months in advance of conversion, and a tenant in occupancy moves quite promptly, the owner of the building may be burdened with the costs of maintaining an empty apartment until all the legal requirements of conversion are cleared. An appropriate compromise obviously is required here.

First preference and discounts for tenants in occupancy. Certainly the first part of this approach would meet with little resistance on the part of landlords. Discounts may be less popular. They do, however, acknowledge the tenant property interests which were discussed earlier. There is some question whether they would meet the full measure of the gap involved in the finances of going from renter to condominium owner. In some cases, certainly, it might provide the wherewithal for the downpayment, or some major piece of it.

Conclusion

This paper has attempted to suggest briefly some of the policy areas for consideration by municipalities facing the dilemmas of condominium conversion. These areas have emerged from a detailed analysis of the demographic and economic profiles of the conversion move-outs and condominium purchasers. Certainly, far more space than that already used can be occupied by additional alternatives covering a host of matters. But any basic policy decision must take account of *all* the players, the broad public interest as well as the displacees, the potential buyers, the owners; the poor as well as the rich and the middle class. How are these to be balanced by a jurisdiction? The decision is far more complex than simply a question of facilitating or impeding the process.

Notes

1. George Sternieb and James W. Hughes, *Washington Condominium Survey* (New Brunswick, New Jersey: Center for Urban Policy Research, Rutgers University, 1975).
2. Sternlieb and Hughes. The extensive array of cross-tabulations obviously cannot be presented in this paper. Their full exposition and synthesis into profile types is available in the main report.
3. Chester Rapkin and William G. Grisby, *Residential Renewal in the Urban Core* (Philadelphia: University of Pennsylvania Press, 1960). George Sternlieb and James W. Hughes, "Profiling the High Rent Center City Market," *Real Estate Review*, III, No. 3 (Fall 1973), pp. 86-91; and George Sternlieb, *et al.*, *Housing Development and Municipal Costs* (New Brunswick, New Jersey: Center for Urban Policy Research, Rutgers University, 1973).
4. Anthony Downs, "The Real Estate Outlook Through Mid-1976." *Real Estate Review*, V, No. 2 (Summer 1975), p. 27.

The Impact of Local Government Regulations on Housing Costs and Potential Avenues for State Meliorative Measures

Robert W. Burchell
David Listokin

Introduction

The purpose of the paper which follows is to detail the differing housing costs associated with various forms of governmental regulation as a prelude to defining the state's role in mitigating these costs. Thus the paper has two parts—Part I-*The Housing Costs of "Excess" Governmental Regulation* and Part II-*Meliorative Strategies for State Intervention*.

In Part I, the reader is introduced to the local land development process and the specific local regulatory controls which affect development. At each step the "excess" cost of governmental control is defined, related to the applicable regulation, and dollar/percent figures of purchase price impact are specified.

Part I provides the groundwork for Part II. The second part of the paper classifies state intervention strategies into three broad forms of local influence: *Enabling/Informational, Coordinating and Control.* These forms of intervention vary by the degree to which state actions override local development and regulatory prerogatives. Within each

313

of these categories representative state experience is discussed. This provides the necessary background material to begin to pair appropriate state actions with areas of government regulation where significant potential cost savings have been found to exist. This two part identification process—(1) Where savings can be made in land development activities, and (2) the type of activities that can bring about these savings—is essential to maintain appropriate means-end perspectives. Why, for instance, should those concerned with housing people at the lowest possible costs view energy conservationists and their derivative energy codes as "the " problem when the effect of energy conservation measures are only moderately cost-inducing in the short run and even less so over a longer time period? Rather, the culprit well may be the local zoning ordinance which requires a minimum building size twenty-five percent greater than what is found in either equivalent ordinances nationally or in model codes, and resultantly, adds five percent "up front" to the purchase price of a new house.

Furthermore, what are the alternatives for state action with regard to this situation? Does the state attempt to promulgate an unrestrictive model zoning code and encourage local governments to adopt it, or does it mandate a fair share housing plan, which in order to house low-income families, requires the dissolution of any minimum building size requirements in existing local ordinances. These are the types of issues with which the state must deal—this is the framework within which choices must be weighed.

Part I–The Housing Costs of "Excess" Government Regulation

Background

During the latter part of the 1960s there was great concern that increases in housing costs were outstripping the housing consumer's ability to pay—that rents or carrying costs were escalating faster than resident incomes.

B. Bruce Briggs in an article in the *Public Interest*[1] explored the housing cost "problem" of that era. His findings are reflected in Exhibit 1. What he found was that over the period 1960 to 1970, head of household income in rental units increased by approximately 5.4 percent annually; rents or the amount paid to occupy these units during that same period increased, on average, by only 2.3 percent annually. It was clear also that the direction of the relationship and the significant edge of income increases over those of rents held for serveral measures of housing purchasability.

EXHIBIT 1

PRE-1970 RELATIONSHIPS OF HOUSING COSTS AND RESIDENT INCOME INCREASE

Financial Characteristics	Median Structure Value, Median Contract Rent and Head of Household Income (1960)					Median Structure Value, Median Contract Rent and Head of Household Income (1970)					Annual % Change 1960-1970 (Simple)				
	U.S.	N.E.	N.C.	S.	W.	U.S.	N.E.	N.C.	S.	W.	U.S.	N.E.	N.C.	S.	W.
Head of Household Owner Occupied (1)	$ 5,800	$ 6,500	$ 5,900	$ 4,800	$ 6,500	$ 9,700	$10,900	$10,000	$ 8,200	$10,700	6.7%	6.8%	6.9%	7.1%	6.2%
Renter Occupied (2)	$ 4,100	$ 4,700	$ 4,400	$ 3,100	$ 4,400	$ 6,300	$ 6,900	$ 6,700	$ 5,400	$ 6,500	5.4%	6.8%	5.2%	7.4%	4.8%
Structure Value Owner Occupied (3)	$11,900	$13,300	$12,100	$ 9,500	$13,700	$17,100	$19,500	$16,700	$13,600	$20,600	4.4%	4.7%	3.8%	4.3%	5.0%
Contract Rent Renter Occupied (4)	$ 71	$ 72	$ 75	$ 59	$ 76	$ 89	$ 92	$ 91	$ 72	$ 107	2.3%	2.8%	2.1%	2.2%	4.1%
Increase in Rent to Increase in Income (4÷2)	—	—	—	—	—	—	—	—	—	—	.42	.41	.40	.30	.85
Increase in Value to Increase in Income (3÷1)	—	—	—	—	—	—	—	—	—	—	.66	.69	.55	.60	.82

Source: See Exhibit 2

In 1974, the authors of this paper presented a paper at the Federal Home Loan Bank Board Conference on "Housing" (San Francisco)[2]. Using information from the *Annual Housing Survey*, it was shown that the situation described by Briggs for the 1960s had reversed itself during the early 1970s. Over the period 1970 to 1973, rents not only increased faster than income, (Exhibit 2), but, in addition, where they had once lagged income increases by a factor of 1 to 2, they now led income by almost the same margin (2 to 1). Contract rent over the period 1970 to 1973 increased at a rate of 10 percent annually; income increases for this same period were slightly under 5 percent.*

The previous analyses monitored income-housing cost trends in the existing *multifamily* housing stock. Other more recent queries concentrated on the affordability of new *single-family* housing. Frieden and Solomon in *The Nation's Housing 1975-1978*[3] note that the price of new single-family housing increased by 10.5 percent annually over the period 1970-1976, whereas median family incomes increased at an annual rate of slightly under 8 percent. John Weicher in an article in the *AREUEA Journal*[4] disagrees with Frieden and Solomon and notes that over the period 1949-1969 new single-family housing has been priced at approximately three times resident family income and has been relatively constant over this time period. In fact, the ratio decreased slightly to 2.5 from 1970 to 1972 and returned to the 3.0 level in 1975.

Thus, while some may argue about the extent of the gap, it is at least clear that in the decade of the 1970s, as opposed to that of the 1960s, incomes are certainly not gaining ground on housing costs. To the contrary, repeated evidence shows that over the most recent monitoring periods *housing costs* are increasing faster than incomes for most forms of housing.

---

*Anthony Downs in a recent article in *Real Estate Review*[5] uses BLS average rental housing costs for "low budget urban families of four" and the Consumer Price Index for *rent* to refute both the direction and magnitude of post-1970 differences in renter housing costs and renter incomes. This approach suffers from comparing growth in renter and *owner* incomes to growth in solely renter expenses. If those who currently occupy owned housing chose to occupy rental housing, the position of those who currently occupy rental housing would be further worsened.

EXHIBIT 2

POST-1970 RELATIONSHIP OF HOUSING COST AND RESIDENT INCOME INCREASES

Financial Characteristics	Median Structure Value and Median Contract Rent (1973)					Annual % Change 1970-1973 (Simple)				
	U.S.	N.E.	N.C.	S.	W.	U.S.	N.E.	N.C.	S.	W.
Family Income Owner Occupied (1)	$11,500	$12,600	$11,700	$ 9,800	$12,700	6.2%	5.2%	5.7%	6.5%	6.2%
Renter Occupied (2)	$ 7,200	$ 7,800	$ 7,400	$ 6,600	$ 7,500	4.8%	4.3%	3.5%	7.4%	5.1%
Structure Value Owner Occupied (3)	$24,100	$29,400	$22,800	$19,800	$27,800	13.6%	17.1%	12.2%	15.2%	11.7%
Contract Rent Renter Occupied (4)	$ 116	$ 123	$ 113	$ 94	$ 132	10.1%	11.2%	8.0%	10.2%	7.8%
Increase in Rent to Increase in Income (4÷2)	—	—	—	—	—	2.1	2.6	2.3	1.4	1.5
Increase in Value to Increase in Income (3÷1)	—	—	—	—	—	2.2	3.3	2.1	2.3	1.9

Source: U.S. Department of Commerce, U.S Bureau of the Census. Current Housing Report Series H-150. *Annual Housing Survey, Parts A-D General Housing Characteristics for U.S. and Regions. 1973.* U.S. Census of Housing. *Financial Characteristics of Owner Occupied and Rental Vacant Housing Special Report. 1960.*

Several factors have been pointed out as contributing to this shift. Among these are rapid escalation in the price of land[6]; less, but nonetheless significant, increases in the costs of housing materials[7] and last, increases in cost associated with both (1) unnecessarily increased quality in the basic housing envelope and (2) delay/denial of the regular production of most forms of housing.[8] The paper which follows concentrates on two of three of this last category of housing cost inflators: unnecessarily mandated housing quality and delay associated with delivery of the basic housing structure. This paper differs slightly from the theme of the papers of Einsweiller and Banta in that it defines regulatory impact on housing costs as a more encompassing problem than can be countered by the meliorative remedy of simplification and consolidation. There is a significant aspect of the housing cost/government regulation problem that does not have to do with streamlining of regulations but instead with their *elimination*, as they unnecessarily overspecify the quality of the land/structure development end-product.

This paper further differs from Einsweiller and Banta in that it recognizes private housing production as almost totally controlled by *local* regulations and ordinances with influence from the state taking the form of *indirect* "carrot and stick" activities which locals, in most instances, will attempt to avoid. As such, Part II of this paper is as concerned with action measures which *force* housing (fair share plans, HAP requirements, etc.) as it is with the technical assistance measures of regulatory simplification.

Definitions

The first portion of this paper will deal with specific *excess* regulatory costs associated with various stages of development. *Excess regulatory cost is defined as those costs which emanate from regulations which specify a development standard above and beyond what is necessary for protection of the basic health, safety and welfare of the occupants of this housing.* This is a very stringent definition of "excess" as it includes many regulatory requirements which fall into the housing improvement category of "nice, but not necessary."

The specifications of potential impact on housing costs which would accrue from regulatory reform, i.e., simplification or elimination of excessive regulation, is divided into three categories. These vary by their percent impact on the current purchase price of a new single-family dwelling unit.

Regulatory reform will have a *significant* impact if the simplification or elimination of regulations will reduce the purchase price of single-family home by 2 to 5 percent; it will have a *moderate* effect if it causes a reduction of 1 to 2 percent; it will have only a *slight* effect if potential purchase price reductions due to regulatory reform are less than 1 percent.

Cost impact will be specified within specific sectors of the land development process. The production of a single-family home is viewed as going through three stages: *development, construction and pre-occupancy*.[10] The entire process is summarized in Exhibit 3, which is the key reference exhibit for both parts of this paper.

The *development* stage includes all necessary processing and land improvements to convert a parcel of raw land to a developable lot ready for structural improvement. These consist of feasibility, engineering, and impact studies, preliminary and final plat approval specifications for and final site improvements, hook-ups to municipal infrastructure, etc.

The *construction* stage includes all processing requirements and improvements necessary to *erect* a completed single-family home. These consist of permits/approvals related to the structural frame, interior systems (plumbing, electrical, heating), interior finish and final site preparation.

The *pre-occupancy* stage deals with the necessary procedural steps to occupy a completed house. These consist of performance of title examinations, acquisition of hazard insurance, meeting closing requirements and the costs/procedures associated with the house search process. Regulations which have formalized these procedures do not directly affect the cost to *produce* a house. Rather, they add significantly to the cost to *purchase* a house.

The empirical analyses which were used to base percentage impact estimates have been derived from the "Afterword" of Stephen Seidel's[11] *Government Regulations and Housing Costs* put together by the authors and Professor Kristina Ford of the Rutgers University Center for Urban Policy Research. Empirical analyses relating to housing cost impact, culled from various sources by Seidel over the period 1965 to 1975, have been standardized and updated to 1978 through the application of the Consumer Price Index.

The house to which impact is specified is a three-bedroom-single-family, detached house of 1200 square feet on a half acre, developed in the Northeast at a mid-1978 cost of $50,000. It is developed in a community of strong local regulatory control—one which evidences most of the "popularly-held" innovative development controls. All

EXHIBIT 3

GOVERNMENT REGULATIONS WHICH AFFECT THE HOUSING DEVELOPMENT PROCESS

Regulation	Definition of Excess Cost	Potential Impact on Housing Costs	Role "Category" of State (see Part II of this paper)	State Mitigation Strategy (see Part II of this paper)
		A. Excess Costs Related to Regulations Affecting the *Development* Stage of Housing		
Development Stage				
I. *Zoning Regulations*				
A. Single Family: Rezoning	Additional Processing time related to in-appropriate or dated use specification of potentially develop-able land	Significant	Enabling and inform-ational; Controlling	Provide zoning and planning enabling legis-lation; encourage regular review of existing proposed land use by strengthening link between zoning and comprehensive plan; recommend/develop model zoning ordin-ance or state land use plan; review, via A-95, local sensitivity to single-family housing need; adopt statewide fair share plan.
B. Single Family: Minimum lot Size	Excessive lot sizes in suburban, develop-ing communities (greater than ¼ acre)	Moderate	Coordinating; Controlling	Same as 1A.
II. *Growth Controls*	Reduced flow of land based on previous five year averages of annual land conversion rate	Moderate	Enabling and informational	Review and provide guidance to develop-ment and adoption of regional growth control plans; include in model land use laws greater-than-local growth strategies which are keyed to realistic land conver-sion rates

EXHIBIT 3 (CONTINUED)

Regulation	Definition Excess Cost	Potential Impact on Housing Costs	Role "Category" of State (see Part II of this paper)	State Mitigation Strategy (see Part II of this paper)
III. *Environmental Review-Site Plan/Subdivision Processing*	Additional processing time due to lack of coordination of environmental and subdivision review or inefficiencies in subdivision review process	Significant	Enabling and informational; Controlling	Provide subdivision/site plan review enabling legislation; publish model subdivision regulations; include realistic time maximums for review in model or state land use law; enact critical area or "little NEPA" environmental review process; encourage state-federal coordination in environmental control and assessment
IV. *Subdivision/ Site/Plan Requirements* A. Vegetation Burning Prohibited	In developing subdivision process, requirement to bulldoze/haul to replace on-site vegetation burning	Moderate	Coordinating; Controlling	Coordinate and interpret air quality standards as they relate to future development; enact realistic air quality requirements; define broad areas where negative effect of ambient air far exceeds potential from point-source contributors

B. Excess Costs Related to Regulations Affecting the *Construction* Stage of Housing

Construction Stage

V. *Building Codes*	"Nice but not necessary" structural improvements	Significant	Enabling and informational; Controlling	Provide guidance in code standards by publishing optimal model building code (excluding unnecessary structural improvements and allowing performance standards); adopt a mandatory state-wide "maximum" building code

EXHIBIT 3 (CONTINUED)

Regulation	Definition Excess Cost	Potential Impact on Housing Costs	Role "Category" of State (see Part II of this paper)	State Mitigation Strategy (see Part II of this paper)
VI. Energy Codes	Adoption of ASHRAE Code	Slight	Coordinating	Provide *incentives*, not requirements, for energy saving devices
VII. Zoning Ordinance	Minimum building size for 3 bedroom house in excess of 1000 Ft²; for garden apartment in excess of 600 Ft²	Significant	Enabling and informational; Coordinating; Controlling	Provide zoning enabling legislation; recommend ranges of acceptable minimum building size within zoning ordinances; review, via A-95, local progress to reduce unnecessary requirements

C. Excess Costs Related to Regulations Affecting the *Occupancy* stage of Housing

Occupancy Stage				
VIII. Settlement Costs	17% over face charges	Moderate	Controlling	Reduce hidden, duplicate and unnecessary front-end costs through better regulation of real estate and finance industry; allow innovative mortgage instruments

Source: Rutgers University, Center for Urban Policy Research, Summer 1978

controls are assumed to be triggered via the development of this land parcel—no specific aspect of control is waived by a particular regulatory authority.

Development Stage

The regulatory controls affecting housing cost during the development stage are:

1. *Zoning ordinances* which govern the type and intensity of development,
2. *Growth controls* which govern the pace and mix of development,
3. Environmental controls which protect natural areas from detrimental development,
4. *Subdivision regulations* which determine the level of public infrastructure which must accompany development.

ZONING ORDINANCE

As indicated in Exhibit 3, zoning regulations most often affect (a) the supply of land, and (b) the number of housing units which may be built on that land.[12] Land is typically not zoned for its most appropriate use given both regional and local demand for that land. The classic suburban case is the overzoning for industrial land and underzoning for residential purposes.

The time involved for the necessary *rezoning* of land for residential use occasions "holding" costs to the developer. These consist of interest charges on the mortgaged land, interim property taxes and unrealized opportunity costs on the portion of capital necessary to convince a lender to mortgage the remaining value of a raw land parcel.

Using an average delay time of five to six months and current standards for the cost of capital and taxes on unimproved land, the typical "excess" cost of the rezoning process on the purchase price of a $50,000 home ranges from $400-$600 or approximately one percent of final consumer cost. By previous definitions of percent impact of regulatory constraints, it is said to have a *moderate* effect on housing costs.

Minimum lot size or the smallest parcel upon which a housing structure may be erected also affects housing cost. Excess cost in this is associated with developable land parcels in suburban locations whose zoning requirements mandate lot size greater than one-quarter acre. The one-quarter acre standard is chosen as a compromise size adequate to provide distance and aesthetic considerations for housing consumers, acceptable municipal service loads for municipalities/school districts and reasonable development densities for builders. (See Seidel, Chapter 8.)

The house which is being developed in this example is on a half acre. Excess costs are then associated with the raw land purchase price of the extra one-quarter acre. Through survey, this has been deemed to be approximately $800-1200 on a $50,000 house.* As such, the impact of lot size is said to be *significant* (2 to 5 percent of purchase price).

GROWTH CONTROLS

Growth controls limit, schedule, or channel new population according to the capacity of necessary public services or according to a desired maximum community size.[13] These regulations are sewer or building moratoria, population caps, capital facilities schedules, etc. (See Seidel, Chapter 9.) The original intent of growth controls was to pace and channel, not to slow, development within a community. The primary housing cost impact of these controls is inflated land values in areas proximate to the municipality with growth controls, i.e., this land is now worth more due to the inherently shorter processing time. These external costs will not be considered here, only the costs associated with the specific land parcel— the cost of owning the land but not being able to improve it. While there is a benefit to controlling both the tempo and sequence of development, any delay or holding time caused by reduced flows of land to the land conversion process via a growth controlled system (based on previous annual averages) will be considered excessive.

For the single-family home subdivision, it will be assumed that the amount of land converted with growth controls lagged non-growth control land conversion rates by 25 percent. This was sufficient to cause a landholder a six-month delay awaiting his land to be channeled for development. The unnecessary development delay multiplied by the holding costs of land upon which the $50,000 single-

---

*The difference in cost between a half and a quarter acre lot size is relatively slight as both offer the capacity to build only one single-family dwelling unit.

family home is developed amounts to $400-600—a *moderate* (1-2%) impact on housing costs.

SUBMISSION CRITERIA/PROCESSING
(Preliminary Engineering, EISs, Market Analysees, Fiscal Impact Statements, Site Plan/Subdivision Processing)

Submission criteria typically constitute "non-hardware" preconditions to preliminary plat approval.[14] EIS, fiscal impact analyses preliminary engineering designs, allow the community to anticipate and plan for the local economic effects of forthcoming development. Often these requirements, imposed by different layers of government (local, county, region, state) cause scheduling delays. While many offices attempt concurrent processing, most non-local agencies prefer an initial sift of unfeasible proposals at the local level to reduce their workload. They consequently add their requirements *after* the local processing steps necessary to determine initial project feasibility (Seidel, Chapter 10). The result is direct costs to the consumer in the form of passed-on, land-holding expenses for their period of delay.

In the example at hand, a state-imposed, Coastal Zone EIS requirement delayed average subdivision processing time (6 months) by 3 months. Land holding costs per month, multiplied by the three-month delay period, add approximately $200-300 to the purchase prices of the house—and thus have a *slight* (less than 1 percent) impact on resulting housing costs.

SUBDIVISION REQUIREMENTS

Subdivision requirements ensure that land improvements are made to a given standard of quality and that the new subdivision "ties-in" correctly to the existing community.[15] Further, they provide mandatory steps which a developer must meet to secure for future residents the necessary electricity, heating fuel and water, which comes from local public suppliers. Finally, they enable the development to be viewed as "complete" from the community's standpoint whether or not all developable lots are sold. This is accomplished by requiring that a developer post a bond covering the cost of all "on-site" improvements which the community may exercise in the event that the developer defaults on improvement obligations.

There are three main categories of subdivision requirements—land clearing obligations, street-frontage-related improvements and design requirements (Seidel, Chapter 7). Excess consumer housing costs relate, in the first case, to prohibition of on-site burning of vegetation and the resultant necessity to bulldoze and haul; in the second case, to lot widths in excess of 80 feet which unnecessarily inflate the requirements for sanitary sewers, storm drain pipes, water distribution systems, curbs and gutters, sidewalks and pavement; and in the third case to overdesign—the mandatory provision of underground untilities, sidewalks on two rather than one side of the street, excess pavement widths and rights-of-way, landscaping requirements and land dedication or in-lieu fees. Excess costs in these latter two cases are a function of frontage requirements. In this example, it is assumed that local subdivision regulations call for 100 foot frontages, 20 feet in excess of the average 80 foot requirement found normally with quarter acre lots. Each of these categories of excessive subdivision requirements adds approximately $1,000 to the price of a $50,000 single-family home. Subdivision requirement categories are thus both individually (2 percent) and collectively (6 percent), said to have a *significant* effect on housing costs. Total costs of excess governmental regulation relating exclusively to the development stage of this example are approximately $5,000 or 10 percent of final purchase price.

Construction Stage

Government controls which affect the price of housing during the construction phase are:

1. *Building codes* which specify minimum standards for various materials used in erecting a house,
2. *Energy conservation regulations* which require improvements to reduce the amount of fuel and electricity necessary to occupy the house,
3. *Zoning ordinances* which require minimum floor areas or building size.

BUILDING CODE

A building code provides a structure development standard to which incremental additions to a community must adhere.[16] Several aspects of the building code system are responsible for increased housing costs. In many cases the administration of the code is uncoordinated and enforcement is at the discretion of local building officials. The code itself may require safety and quality features which are in excess of what can reasonably be defined as *minimum* requirements.

There is a large body of literature which lists excessive requirements associated with the construction of the structural frame and provision of interior systems (i.e, electrical or plumbing) for a residential structure. Improvements which have recurringly been deemed as "nice, but not necessary" by researchers and confirmed by national safety organizations are of the following type: ground fault interrupters, smoke detectors, fire wall between garage and living area, copper wiring, shut-off controls at rear of stoves, underground cast-iron and copper pipe, unnecessary framing material and siding quality. While these provide qualitative assets to the housing shell, they are unnecessary when the *sole* consideration is minimum safety of housing occupants and resultantly, *base price of shelter.*

In most instances these excess costs vary with the size of the structure. The aggregate amount of excess cost in the example single-family home represents the per square foot costs of each of the unnecessarily required items times the difference between the zoning ordinance mandated building size (1200 square feet) and the average size of a three-bedroom-single family home (1040 square feet). In the example, the above requirements add approximately $900 to the cost of a single-family home—they thus have a *moderate* effect on housing costs.

ENERGY CODE

The purpose of a community initiating an energy code for new single-family housing is to provide long-run energy savings which accrue to (1) society as a whole in the form of reduced energy use, and (2) the individual vis-a-vis lower utility bills.[17] This is accomplished through more complete insulation, storm or double pane windows on all exterior glass surfaces, heating inspections to check furnace efficiency, zone heating for different locations of the house, automatic shut-offs on range and oven pilot lights, etc.

Yet each of these measures occasion a definite short-run cost to the housing consumer. The definition of excess in this case is local adoption of comprehensive energy conservation measures (the ASHRAE code, for instance) which call for most of the above listed improvements for single-family homes. For the example house these requirements (again based on house size) add approximately $300 to the resulting purchase price. As such, they are said to have a *slight* effect on housing costs. (See Seidel, Chapter 6.)

ZONING ORDINANCE: MINIMUM BUILDING SIZE REQUIREMENTS

Perhaps one of the single largest contributors to excess housing costs is a mandatory requirement of housing space of a certain square footage. Far in excess of any health requirement, the device is used to guarantee a certain quality of house (in terms of structure value) and, by extension, a similar quality of neighborhood. Standardizing for the neighborhood variable, large house size usually guarantees expensive housing. The increase in building size requirements further reflects consumer preference—the public, since 1950, has been demanding increasingly larger structure sizes.

Excess costs in the example are defined as mandated house size in excess of the national average of three-bedroom homes (1040 square feet) times the cost per square foot to construct the building envelope. In this case the latter figure is assumed to be $20 a square foot. As such, an ordinance requirement which specifies 1200 square feet rather than 1040 square feet adds approximately $3200 to the purchase price. The minimum building size requirement thus adds *significantly* to the cost of housing.

Excess governmental costs related to the *construction* stage of housing total $4400. This is close to 9 percent of purchase price and only 1 percent less than the percent impact of inflationary cost regulations associated with the *development* stage.

Pre-Occupancy Stage

SETTLEMENT COSTS

Settlement fees are the costs to the purchaser for assuming ownership of a house. The settlement phase of purchasing a house has evolved from a complex system of laws governing the transfer and purchase of real property.[19] It includes *title examination* to ensure both lender and purchaser that the seller owns what is being conveyed; *title insurance* which guarantees that the title examination is done properly; *origination fee* to compensate lenders for expenses incurred in making a loan; *prepaid expenses* such as real estate taxes, hazard insurance premiums and special assessments to reduce the chance of early delinquency and foreclosure; *loan discount payments* to cover processing costs of below-market-interest-rate loans; and finally, *brokerage fees* associated with advertising the property and bringing together an acceptable buyer and seller. The banks, title insurance companies, appraisers, realtors and other various private and government participants in the process operate in an atmosphere increasingly confusing to the housing consumer.

Settlement fees have recently received attention because of their relatively high cost. These fees usually approximate 8 to 12 percent of the purchase price of a house, although the most expensive houses do not have proportional costs. Through marketable title laws, lower attorney fees, lower title insurance enabled by extensive analysis of risk and better regulation of title insurance companies, savings of approximately one-sixth could possibly be gained. Since most settlement costs are tied to a structure's value, settlement costs reflecting Northeastern averages have been tallied for the example single-family home. One-sixth of these aggregate costs are taken as potentially reclaimable if improvements to this system are made and are thus considered excess. At approximately $600 per $50,000 home, excessive settlement regulations are said to have a *moderate* effect on resulting housing costs.

Summary—Part I

Exhibit 4 summarizes the potential impact of regulatory reform/ elimination, by affected regulation, for the various stages of the land development process. What is clear from this exhibit is that the traditional local land development controls, i.e., the zoning ordinance, subdivision regulations and building code, so dominate local land development processing that they become, by default, the most fertile area of potential regulatory reform. It is in the (1) *zoning ordinance*, which controls the supply of raw land, the use to which that land will be put and the size of the structure to be erected upon it; (2) *subdivision regulations*, which govern the range and quality of site improvements; and, (3) *building code* which controls the range and quality of structural improvements, where advances must be made. Improvements in these controls alone would account for 75 percent of the potential savings in all regulatory reform. If all excess costs imposed by these documents alone were eliminated, the purchase price of the example home would be reduced by close to 15 percent.[20]

EXHIBIT 4

EXCESS COSTS RELATED TO REGULATIONS AFFECTING THE VARIOUS STAGES OF HOUSING DEVELOPMENT

Development Stage	Impact	Construction Stage	Impact	Pre-Occupancy Stage	Impact
I. Zoning Ordinance	Moderate-Significant	V. Building Codes	Significant	VIII. Settlement Costs	Moderate
II. Growth Controls	Moderate	VI. Energy Conservation Regulations	Slight		
III. Environmental/Review Subdivision Processing	Significant	VII. Zoning Ordinances	Significant		
IV. Subdivision Requirements	Moderate-Significant				
TOTAL	10% (A)	TOTAL	9% (B)	TOTAL	1% (C)

TOTAL EXCESS COSTS OF REGULATIONS AFFECTING HOUSING PRODUCTION
(A+B+C) = 20% OR APPROXIMATELY $10,000 ON A $50,000 HOUSE

Source: Rutgers University, Center for Urban Policy Research, Summer 1978

Part II—Meliorative Strategies for State Intervention

Future Role of the State

In theory, state government is sovereign with respect to land use control. Local jurisdiction are creatures of the state and exercise land regulations at its pleasure. The U.S. Supreme Court discussed this relationship:[21]

Neither their (local government) charter, nor any law conferring governmental powers, or vesting in them property to be used for governmental purposes, or authorizing them to hold or manage such property . . . constitutes a contract with the state within the meaning of the Federal Constitution. The state, therefore, at its pleasure may modify or withdraw all such powers . . . . In all these respects the state is supreme . . .

In practice, most states have allowed localities considerable latitude in formulating land use policy.[22] They have enacted enabling legislation authorizing local units of government to control development through such means as zoning and subdivision regulations. While states nominally had the authority and obligation to review whether or not the local controls conformed with enabling legislation and indeed served the public welfare, in practice they assumed a hands-off attitude;[23] local regulations were imbued with a statutory and administrative presumption of validity.

The local perspective may have furthered the needs and desires of community residents, but, it often yielded short-sighted results that worked to the detriment of regional interests and the housing consumer.[24] Beginning in the late 1960s, the legal land use field in the persons of John Reps,[25] Daniel Mandelker,[26] Fred Bosselman[27] and others argued for the termination of the "ancient regime of purely local control."[28] While Reps suggested that local units of government should perhaps be denied zoning power,[29] others felt that local authority should be retained but supplemented by greater state scrutiny of local actions and by limited direct state control in areas of critical social or environmental concern.[30] The last few years we have witnessed various categories of intervention. They are summarized below:

ENABLING AND INFORMATIONAL STATE ROLE

1. *Tighten enabling framework and administrative procedure.* States still provide enabling legislation for zoning, but some mandate that local controls follow and further local comprehensive planning. States also have attempted to reduce the uncertainty and delay of local processing of development applications by taking such actions as designating a maximum time limit for local decisions and allowing one-stop permitting.
2. *Provide information and model statutes.* To further help guide local controls, states have published model subdivision, building code and other model legislation.
3. *Provide general framework for development.* Numerous states are embarking on state planning and are publishing plans to provide guidance as to where growth is most suitable.

COORDINATING STATE ROLE

4. *Coordinate funded activities.* Through their A-95 power, state clearinghouses are attempting to insure that federally funded actions follow federal and state development and programmatic guidelines.
5. *Allocate local housing goals.* A few states have developed fair share plans which allocate housing production goals for localities.

CONTROLLING STATE ROLE

6. *Provide direct controls.* States have enacted direct controls such as little-NEPA, coastal and wetlands regulations.

OTHER ACTIONS

7. *Authorize regional authorities and fiscal reform.* States have made other efforts to "rationalize" development by such means as authorizing and encouraging regional planning bodies and modifying a fiscal structure which traditionally has encouraged restrictive fiscal zoning.

Three Levels of State Intervention

These emerging activities represent different levels of state intervention. The first strategy—providing enabling legislation and information—is passive; it represents a mild form of state action where efforts are made to improve the basic rationality and effectiveness of planning and zoning. By tightening the enabling framework, states hope to insure that localities are behaving appropriately—adopting regulations according to a local plan and processing applications for development in a predictable and timely fashion. Improved local regulation also is encouraged through the dissemination of model statutes and by the state providing a general framework for development via a state plan.

A second and stronger state role is labeled coordinative. In this case a direct and more forceful attempt is made to convince localities to adopt less stringent and more flexible development regulations. Examples include the use of A-95 review power to scrutinize local zoning and development of specific fair share quotas for localities. New Jersey, for example, has attempted to make state aid to municipalities contingent upon local good faith efforts to allow the construction of fair share goals of low and moderate income housing.

A third and even more forceful role is assumed when the state imposes direct controls. This intervention may take various forms. Some states have imposed mandatory building codes. Many have enacted detailed regulations for development in coastal plains, flood plains, wetlands and similar environmentally fragile locations. And most states have a little-NEPA statute which requires and governs the preparation of environmental impact statements.

These emerging future state roles have implications for reducing the cost of housing. The following section discusses their potential.

Enabling and Informational State Role

FUTURE STATE ROLE: TIGHTEN ENABLING FRAMEWORK AND ADMINISTRATIVE PROCEDURE

Local planning and the preparation of the master plan, in theory, should precede and provide the empirical basis for formulating local zoning ordinances.[31] This process allows communities to regulate development in a manner that meets needs and yet is sensitive to social and environmental constraints. In practice, planning is often omitted, is done perfunctorily, or in other ways does not influence the final growth strategies which are adopted.[32]

This state of affairs clearly does not allow for optimal land use control. It can adversely affect development costs because local zoning may not reflect housing demand nor the most desirable planning criteria. Communities may not allow multifamily housing and may require excessive lot size—two areas of price increasing government regulations—because they have not considered the planning benefits of more innovative and flexible zoning which might lower government capital improvement expenditures.

Development costs are not only affected by the tradition-tied nature of local zoning regulations, but also by the manner in which these rules are administered.[33] While zoning procedure is governed by state law, actual administration is uniquely shaped by local rules and customs. As noted by Norman Williams:[34]

> In zoning as elsewhere, the actual remedies are thus matters of the highest importance. . . . In many instances special characteristics of the local procedure strongly influence the availability of any of these remedies. In a few instances, peculiarities of local procedure have a major influence on the availability of remedies in the state and even upon the substantive law.

Inadequate local zoning administration can increase development costs by delaying hearings and rulings, requiring developers to make similar presentations before different boards, etc. The uncertainty of the entire process is a further problem that discourages entry by potential builders (thereby limiting competition) or development of other than traditional land and housing patterns.

States have recognized these substantive and procedural deficiencies and some have attempted to address their drawbacks by specifying and tightening the planning-zoning relationship and implementation. California requires that cities and counties prepare a plan which includes housing, land use and open space considerations.[35] The Local Government Comprehensive Planning Act requires Florida communities to plan and to consider specific elements ranging from land use and housing to utility and intergovernmental coordination.[36] Oregon's much heralded land use reforms include a planning act imposing mandatory local as well as county and state planning.[37]

Some states have attempted to strengthen the planning-zoning link by mandating that local regulations follow and further the comprehensive plan. California's 1971 consistency/compatibility legislation provided that zoning and subdivision approval coincide with adopted general plans.[38] The California Attorney General has interpreted this legislation strongly, commenting that "the general plan is, in short, a constitution for all future development in the city."[39]

States have also attempted to systematize and rationalize land use procedure. The New Jersey Land Use Law of 1975[40] set forth [41]

uniform and regular requirements for administrative procedures that may be followed locally. These procedural sections cover for, meetings of municipal agencies, hearings, notice of hearings. . . appeals to the governing body, as well as several other technical matters of procedure.

Some of the above reforms have been inspired by the ALI's Model Land Development Code.[42] The code emphasizes planning; in Fred Bosselman's view that new proposals are consistent with the growing dissatisfaction with the "traditional concept of the plan as an advising document with no legal effect."[43] The code also encourages changes that will reduce uncertainty and delays. Part Four of Article II, for example, allows a developer to ask for a consolidated hearing rather than appearing before multiple local or extra-local agencies to request a permit.

COST-REDUCING POTENTIAL OF STATE ENABLING FRAMEWORK AND ADMINISTRATIVE REFORMS

The aforementioned changes, by making zoning a more rational and predictable process, can reduce housing costs. As shown in Exhibit 1, increased zoning for multifamily units—a possible outcome of a more formal planning-zoning link—has a significant potential impact on housing prices. Other possible byproducts, such as reduced building size or lot requirements, would further moderate unit shelter costs. Procedural changes are especially welcome from a cost-reduction perspective. The New Jersey Municipal Land Use Law, for example, specifies time limits on actions to be taken by planning boards, (e.g., from forty-five to ninety days for site plan review) and also provides a "one-stop service" for developers.[44] Planning boards or boards of adjustment can individually approve development plans, thus obviating the need for separate though similar appearances by the developer at each board.

The practical limitations of these reform measures to reduce housing costs must be recognized, however. In many instances the actual changes induced by the state actions are not as sweeping as they might appear. Numerous states still do not require that local zoning follow local planning or more commonly are not monitoring localities' observance of planning and adopted comprehensive master plans. In this regard it is important to note that the ALI code does *not* require municipalities to base land use controls on local land development plans.[45] The code offers certain incentives to communities that do but the bonuses offered (e.g., the power to allow PUDs, to develop "precise plans" and to acquire land for such precise plans) are not very alluring. Moreover, as pointed out by George Raymond, the code might discourage localities from adopting a plan, for once they take such action, all of their land use policies are subject to state review, while not accepting a plan would limit state adjudication to "critical areas."[46]

There are also loopholes in some of the state planning requirements. The New Jersey Land Use Law, for example, while nominally requiring that zoning ordinances "be substantially consistent with the land use plan element of the master plan or designed to effectuate such plan element,"[47] allows communities to ignore this mandate if the governing body votes to do so.[48]

Even were states to vigorously enact and enforce mandatory planning and require that land use regulations follow the planning element, this strategy would not insure that communities would necessarily eliminate cost-increasing regulations. Localities could go through the motions of planning or else could plan in an inflexible or parochial manner. It is not difficult to justify the prohibitions discussed in the first part of this paper on environmental or fiscal grounds. More stringent action is needed, such as states requiring that localities take into account the regional need for lower cost housing when they enact local zoning rules. These strategies are described shortly.

PROVIDE INFORMATION AND MODEL STATUTES

To further encourage localities to adopt innovative and more flexible land use controls, states have served as clearinghouses for basic planning information and legislation. A 1976 study by the American Institute of Planners[49] indicated that most states provided this service. The New York Division of State Planning and Community Affairs gives technical assistance on such matters as planning and zoning, personnel management and community development—activities typical of comparable agencies in other states.

Another tactic is the development and promulgation of model development ordinances that hopefully will be adopted by local units of government. Oregon's Land Conservation and Development Commission not only engages in state planning such as designating areas of critical concern, but also is obliged to prepare model zoning, subdivision and other ordinances.[50] The New Jersey Department of Community Affairs has made available numerous publications on planned unit development, transfer of development rights, etc., in order to inform and encourage localities to adopt these innovative land use strategies.[51]

The preparation and publication of model building codes is a widespread state effort to influence local controls. The legal authority to enact building regulations is derived from the police power of the state but most have chosen to delegate this authority to local units of government.[52] In turn, local jurisdictions often have enacted disparate rules of a narrow specification rather than performance nature—regulations accused of stifling innovation and adding to the uncertainty of housing development.

States have attempted to encourage localities to adopt more uniform and reasonable building regulations by writing model building codes. Georgia and Maryland, for example, have published such voluntary codes (as opposed to mandatory state requirements, discussed below). While many state models merely summarize portions of various already available national model codes (e.g., voluntary codes have been influenced by the BOCA basic, BOCA mechanical, BOCA Plumbing and National Electrical Model Codes), states hope that the separate publication and dissemination by them will prove more influential on localities.

Cost-Reducing Potential Of State Information Role

Local development regulation can appreciably inflate the price of housing. Excessive local subdivision rules, such as those concerning lot width, design/dedication requirements, block length, etc., all add to development delays. Archaic building codes can especially increase construction costs. They often prohibit less expensive materials (e.g., plastic pipe); require additional equipment/features such as extra ducts, extra thickness gypsum, masonry chimneys, etc.; and disallow innovative and cost-reducing techniques such as preassembled electrical-plumbing harnesses.

States can encourage innovation and reduced costs by publishing model codes, subdivision procedures,[53] zoning standards, and in other ways acting as an information source and an agent for stimulating local flexibility. Such steps may prompt localities to adopt more uniform and reasonable regulations and standards.[54]

States already have a track record in encouraging some local regulatory reform. Numerous New Jersey municipalities adopted PUD regulations after state publication of a model code and a guide for local evaluation of the fiscal and environmental impacts of planned unit developments. State model building codes also have had some impact; surveys by Ventre-ICMA, National Bureau of Standards, Rutgers University Center for Urban Policy Research and others have indicated that numerous localities have based their building codes on state model standards.[55]

An information-clearinghouse role is still quite passive and often ignores state suggestions on model ordinances, for example. In other instances they may begin with a state model ordinance but so modify it with added local requirements and procedures that the cost-saving potential of the state statute is lost. The harmful effect of excessive local overlay is seen dramatically in building codes. Localities often use the recommended state code as a minimum (rather than maximum) threshold and then add their own prohibitions/specifications.

PROVIDE A GENERAL FRAMEWORK FOR DEVELOPMENT

State planning had its origins in the 1930s when state equivalents of the federal National Planning Board were created.[56] These federally inspired bodies considered such matters as housing, transportation and municipal finance. The end of the Depression and the exigencies of World War II and the early post-war period saw the eclipse of state planning, however. The hiatus lasted for about fifteen years, until the early 1960s when amendments to the 701 program and new legislation (e.g., the 1965 Water Resources Planning Act) sparked a revival of activity.

The last decade has witnessed a new range and intensity of state planning. This blossoming has been discussed in such recent publications as *State Planning: Intergovernmental Policy Coordination, Land Use and the States, State Land Use Activity, and Land-State Alternatives for Planning and Management.*[57] One outproduct of the more active role is the formation of a state development plan to suggest to private developers and local units of government where and what type of growth is most suitable. The sentiment for such a plan was summarized by the State Council of Governments.[58]

[Growing] recognition that a basic function of the state planning process is coordination of policy formulation and program design has revised interest in plan documents. Effective coordination requires a policy framework. Purposes must be defined to guide governmental entities at both state and regional levels along compatible paths. . . . A state comprehensive plan theoretically fills this need.

In a few isolated cases the State comprehensive plan is adopted by the legislature and serves as a formal guide and policy framework for coordination. Hawaii's Growth Policies Plan, Vermont's Capability and Development Plan and Rhode Island's State Guide Plan are three examples of the more formal documents.[59]

More common are state plans which are not binding but rather serve as a device to communicate where the state believes different types and intensity of development should occur. (These are termed by Healy as "guider plan" approaches.)[60] Connecticut's State Plan for Conservation and Development is one such example.[61] It specifies areas deemed most suitable for open space, limited development or more intense urban development, taking into consideration such restraints as the water and sewer infrastructure and desired future land use relationships. The plan is directed at state agencies, local units of government and private developers. Connecticut attempts to use "moral suasion and wide publicity"[62] to induce compliance but the plan is not binding. The recently published New Jersey State Development Guide similarly identifies corridors of development and areas recommended for light or nonuse such as the environmentally fragile Pinelands.[63]

COST REDUCING POTENTIAL OF STATE PLANNING ROLE

By providing a source of information for and framework of development, state planning and the publication of a state plan, can help induce some local regulatory reform. Communities located in designated high-growth centers may rethink local prohibitions against more intense forms of development. This relaxation was one of the goals of New Jersey's Development Guide—to encourage suburbs in growth corridors to remove barriers to multifamily housing, and developments of a non-traditional nature, such as PUDs.

The practical cost-reducing potential of this strategy is very limited, however:

1. A voluntary plan conveys a *general* sense of state recommended growth types, location and concentration. It is therefore had to relate to specific local regulations.
2. The state growth plan may not adhere to other state policies concerning environmental protection and more dispersed housing opportunity. This confusion lessens its local influence.
3. The plan is often not updated on a regular basis, thus making it practically less implementible.
4. State plans often have little more significance than a prestigious recommendation. They may not be formally adopted by the legislature or executive branches and do not carry incentives for adherence nor do they impose sanctions on those who ignore their policies.

It is interesting to note the contrast with the type of state plan envisioned by the ALI code.[64] This document would be prepared by the central state land planning agency (SLPA). It would be formally adopted, updated at a five-year interval and would be coordinated with state transportation environment and other strategies. Additionally, while it would not be binding on local plans and actions, it would probably serve as a much more influential document than current "framework" state plans.

Coordinative State Role

REVIEW FUNDED ACTIVITIES

This group of state strategies attempts to influence local decisions concerning growth in a more direct and forceful manner than the policies already described. A-95 review is the most significant for it gives the state considerable potential leverage to help monitor and influence local actions. It is described below.

The Office of Management and Budget (OMB) issued circular A-95 in 1969 in an effort to guide the review required by Section 204 of the Demonstration Cities Act, Title IV of the Intergovernmental Cooperation Act and other legislation.[65] The circular called for the designation of multijurisdictional bodies called "clearinghouses." State, regional and metropolitan clearinghouses were to be established. The state agency was the comprehensive planning authority designed by the governor; the regional agency was the nonmetropolitan areawide agency designated by the governor; and the metropolitan agency was recognized by the OMB.

These multijurisdictional bodies were to consider and comment on how local applications for federal aid related to and harmonized with statewide or areawide comprehensive plans submitted to executive agencies. The clearinghouses also were to consider such matters as the extent to which proposals duplicated or ran counter to other projects or activities and the environmental impact of the proposal.

Circular A-95's review scope has been expanded since its adoption in 1969. In 1972 clearinghouses were directed to consider the civil rights implications of proposed actions and in that year OMB extended the review provisions of twenty-two HUD programs for Housing Production and Mortgage Credit. In 1975, A-95 coverage was expanded even further; it now encompasses almost two hundred federal aid programs.[66]

A-95 can be an important resource for states wishing to influence local development policies. State clearinghouses could comment negatively on local applications for sewer, water processing and purification plants, highways, road improvements, etc., if these facilities would be used to service only single-family housing in these communities designated in the state plan as best suited for intensive development. The A-95 process can significantly increase the real importance of the state plan for it can give this document official import as a guide that will be considered by state clearinghouses.

A-95 review also gives states a "stick" strategy to force localities to adhere to fair share plans and other efforts to increase the supply of lower cost housing. (Fair share is separately discussed below). Governor Byrne of New Jersey, for example, issued Executive Order No. 35 specifically directing the State Clearinghouse to consider fair share progress.[67]

State officials participating in regional planning activities and regional clearinghouse review and comment decisions on municipal and county applications for federal funding shall take into account whether a municipality or group of municipalities is meeting or in the process of meeting a fair share of low- and moderate-income housing.

State officials administrating state and federal programs providing grants and loan aid and technical assistance to municipalities and counties shall, in accordance with existing law and for purposes of providing incentive aid consistent with the objectives of this Executive Order, give priority where appropriate to cooperating municipalities.

The A-95 program has significant potential for influencing local housing policies for Local Housing Plans (HAPs) reviewed by A-95 clearinghouses. The Community Development (CD) program has become one of the most significant sources of funding for community development, public facilities, housing, etc. Applicants for community development assistance must submit a HAP which summarizes local housing conditions, the number of persons that need assistance and the optimal location for subsidized units. HAPs must be considered by A-95 clearinghouses and these bodies could use their review power to negatively evaluate those HAPs which do not consider the need for lower cost housing and which do not specify how such units would be encouraged locally.

COST REDUCING POTENTIAL OF STATE REVIEW ACTIVITIES

This state strategy, best typified by A-95 program, has considerable potential for inducing municipalities to reduce excessive building requirements. As shown in Exhibit 3, A-95 can be a factor in moderating prohibitions against multifamily housing or requirements for large lot zoning. (A-95 has been utilized by numerous *regional* planning entities to help reduce barriers to multifamily and lower cost units.)

In practice, state review authority often has proved a paper program. This is best illustrated by A-95's shortcomings. Many clearinghouses have not taken their responsibilities seriously and executive agencies receiving their clearinghouse reports have not paid the evaluations much heed. A General Accounting Office report (1975) indicated widespread noncompliance or minimal compliance with A-95 requirements.[68] Potomac Institute, HUD and Brookings Institution reports similarly concluded that the A-95 review process has been *pro forma* and largely ineffectual.[69]

Clearinghouses have been extremely reluctant to critically use their review power as a wedge against local housing restrictions. The *Hartford* decision highlighted review body inaction.[70] In this regard it is interesting to note that New Jersey's Executive Order 35 was far from being as effective as it could be.

The A-95 program has become more effective in recent years. Major improvements have been summarized in the ACIR's recent study, *Regionalism Revisited.*[71] But the clearinghouse review of requests for federal aid still has not become fully operational or meaningful. Given this overall drawback and the specific hesitation by states to use their A-95 power to forcefully convince localities to revise their housing regulations, state review of funded activities has severe limitations as a policy to reduce housing costs.

ALLOCATE LOCAL HOUSING GOALS

All the strategies discussed thus far represent attempts to increase local sensitivity to the need for providing a greater mix of housing and some entry of lower cost units. A few states have used fair share plans to allocate specific magnitudes of lower priced housing that communities would not accept.

Two states, Massachusetts and New Jersey, have the most extensive fair share strategies. Massachusetts "anti-snob" zoning law was enacted in 1969.[72] While it did not allocate exact counts of housing for each local unit of government, it did establish minimum and maximum goals. The program operated through an appeals process. Sponsors of low and moderate housing would file a single comprehensive permit request with the local board. Should the latter reject the proposal, the developer could appeal to the state board, the Housing Appeals Committee of the Department of Community Affairs. This committee reviews proposals and comes to a decision by balancing local planning objectives against regional need for low- and moderate-income housing. The Massochusetts statute requires the Committee to uphold a local board's rejection of a permit if the locality has met the following statutory minimum production of low- and moderate-income housing.

a) 10 percent of a town's housing units are subsidized for low- or moderate-income persons, or

b) such housing exists in the community on sites constituting 1.5 percent of the total land area, excluding public land.

The lesser of these quotas, rules. And a local board need not approve a permit for construction of housing on sites comprising .3 percent of the town's land area, or 10 acres, whichever is larger, in any one year.

New Jersey has the most extensive state fair share program. Its intellectual origins date from 1969 when a bill was introduced requiring local land use regulations to reflect the "need for various types of housing for all economic and social groups in the municipality and in the surrounding region."[73] The bill required every planning board to set aside housing sites for various economic and social groups into it master plan and stated that the powers of land use and planning should not be used in any way to exclude any economic, racial, religious or ethnic group. The prognosis of this bill was described by Paul Ylvisaker as follows:[74]

Political reaction was swift and blazing. With unprecedented unanimity, half a dozen Republican candidates for Governor opened their campaign by saying they would never support the Bill and, if elected, would forthwith fire the Commissioner who had proposed it—one of the rare campaign promises that was later honored.

In November 1972, Assemblyman Albert Merck introduced a bill[75] establishing a voluntary fair share plan; it was an effort toward a-chieving the balanced housing plan called for by the Governor William Cahill. This effort also failed. The administration had difficulty convincing legislators to sponsor the measure and the proposal never came close to adoption; in fact, the sponsor of the land use package was defeated in the next election. State Senator Raymond Bateman described the reaction:[76]

The legislators of both parties are not about to become involved in something the overwhelming mass of [the] people they represent are violently opposed to . . . . The general public feels the legislation is an attempt at state control of zoning and local land use, and people are home rule oriented in New Jersey.

The defeat of Cahill's housing measures did not deter subsequent reform efforts but the focus of activity somewhat shifted from the legislature to the executive branch. In April 1976, Governor Byrne issued Executive Order 35 calling for the determination of local fair share goals and the financial penalization of municipalities that continued to practice restrictive land use controls. Initial local fair allocations was released in December 1976 but Byrne voiced his displeasure with the methodology employed. A revised plan was released in May 1978 which allocated a total of 520,000 units to be built over a 12-year period.[77] About a week later the New Jersey Senate passed its own version of fair share and an attempt currently is being made to reconcile the executive and legislative fair share approaches.

COST-REDUCING POTENTIAL OF STATE ALLOCATION

A state allocation approach addresses itself to alleviating numerous local housing prohibitions. It often establishes goals for multifamily units and lower cost single-family dwellings—configurations often prohibited at the local level (see exhibit 3). Fair share can also temper some of the excessive building restrictions of local growth control plans; as discussed in the *Mount Laurel* decision,[78] an allocation approach is compatible with a local growth plan as long as the latter considers the need for lower-cost housing and provides for its construction, though at a controlled pace.

Fair share is a stronger and more direct and specific state strategy than the others previously discussed. It sets an exact housing goal, specifies that localities must meet this allocation and often provides penalities for communities that ignore the quota. While the approach has been adopted by only two states, it has received strong judicial backing that may induce more widespread implementation. The New Jersey *Madison*[79] and *Mount Laurel* decisions broke early legal ground, and other state courts have recently supported the fair share standard. Pennsylvania's State Supreme Court, for example, in *Sorrick v. Zoning Board of Upper Providence,*[80] specifically adopted a fair share principle in ruling against a local prohibition of multifamily housing.

Fair share is a strong potential state strategy but it remains to be seen whether or not it can succeed as a device to lower housing costs. There are technical questions concerning what are appropriate distribution formulas. More critical is the focus and will of fair share bodies. Many implementing agencies have concentrated on the allocations of state and federally subsidized units. They have not considered the more general class of unaided housing the cost of which can be reduced by modifying restrictive local land use regulations. Thus fair share has not been used as a housing cost reduction strategy. (The New Jersey Supreme Court ruling in *Oakwood at Madison v. Township of Madison*[81] might spur greater emphasis for state action to lower the cost of housing by mandating that communities do not preclude the opportunity for "least cost housing.")[82]

More crucial is the question of the willingness of agencies designing fair share plans to strongly implement such strategies. New Jersey is a good case in point. Executive Order 35 clearly stated that the state would take strong action against localities not adhering to their allocation, but this rule has not been effectively implemented. New Jersey has been unwilling to take the politically unpalatable step of denying state or federal aid to localities.

State Control

PROVIDE DIRECT CONTROLS

One of the major aspects of the "Quiet Revolution" in land use is the growing number of cases where the state (or some other regional body) directly controls some aspects of development. Most attention has focused on Hawaii, Florida and a few other jurisdictions where a large measure of regulation has been passed by the state. The efforts of some states to control growth in specified areas such as New York's Adirondack Park and Delaware's Coastal Zone prohibitions also have been well documented.[83]

There are other less well known instances of direct state control. Building codes are one such example. About ten states including Connecticut, Massachusetts and New Jersey have mandatory general building codes.[84] To illustrate, in 1969 the Connecticut legislature enacted Public Act 443 (Chapter 354, Sections 19.395-402).[85] This legislation authorized a mandatory statewide code and established a rigorous program for the training and certification of local building officials. Persons seeking to become building officials were required to have a minimum of five years experience in construction design or supervision. Additionally, such individuals would have to take a state-run training program developed by the State Building Codes Standard Committee and would then have to pass both written and oral examinations.

About forty states have adopted binding state rules controlling industrialized housing.[86] Many are cooperating to develop a nation-wide system for the certification of factory-assembled housing components. These efforts should eliminate some of the barriers to industrialized construction.

Many states impose direct environmentally-related controls such as environmental impact statement requirements and standards for construction in coastal zones, wetlands and marshlands. States also have set standards for air, water, noise pollution, etc. and have en-acted regulations to reduce energy consumption in housing. These efforts often have been inspired by federal action. Environmental Impact Statements were first required by the National Environmental Policy Act of 1969 (NEPA). By 1973 about 17 states had adopted "little NEPA" legislation.[87] A recent survey conducted by the Center for Urban Policy Research[88] indicated that as of April 1978 about 38 states had acted legislatively or administratively to establish NEPA equivalents.

COST-REDUCING POTENTIAL OF DIRECT STATE ACTION

Some of the aftermentioned activities do have a significant ability to reduce costs. A state building code which allows performance standards and establishes requirements for tighter administration and improved personnel can reduce construction expenditures. A state code also means that building rules will be uniform now throughout the state, a change which may encourage more mass production.

Certain direct state controls probably will *increase* costs, however, by creating an added layer of prohibitions and regulatory review. Coastal zone construction rules, by limiting the amount of developable land, increase housing prices.[89] Wetlands and flood plain prohibitions can have a similar impact. "Little NEPAs" can require additional EIS preparation and review over and above what is specified by the federal government.

The goal of much direct state action is enhanced environmental sensitivity and protection. The price of this objective often means increased housing development and construction costs. This tradeoff is likely inevitable. What states can do is to temper and structure their own controls so that they do not unnecessarily increase costs. To illustrate, states can modify their little NEPAs to reduce duplicative work. They can set time limits for processing as established by Washington's Environmental Coordination Procedures Act. States can coordinate with federal agencies so that a combined federal state impact statement is satisfactory or can allow joint federal state processing of environmental permits. This joint procedure is followed now in Florida. State and federal agencies also can agree to use uniform definitions of critical areas, exchange environmental inventory information banks, establish parallel review schedules and allow reciprocity of review.[90]

States can further encourage regional information systems so that the basic data needed to prepare EIS are available centrally and do not have to be spearately derived for each statement. States also can urge that the EIS be "analytical" rather than "encyclopedic"—a step which can reduce the cost of preparation.

Other State Actions

States can help reduce housing costs in other ways. Encouraging the formation of regional bodies is one important strategy for these agencies often have more influence on local actions than the state itself. Many regional bodies have enacted fair share plans; the allocation strategies of the Miami Valley Regional Plan Commission and Metropolitan Council (Twin Cities) are nationally famous.[91] Some regional bodies have attempted to reduce environmental assessment and evaluation costs by creating central data banks. The Northeastern

Illinois Planning Commission attempted to develop a natural resource information system (NARIS) for this reason.

Some regional authorities specifically have addressed the question of government regulations and housing costs. The Metropolitan Council, with the assistance of the Association of Metropolitan Municipalities, has issued guidelines to help reduce housing costs by allowing "minimum cost" units.[92] It recommended that local ordinances: 1) should not require garages; 2) should not require lot sizes for single-family detached homes any larger than 6,000-8,000 square feet or a density of five-to-seven units per acre in all or portions of sewered communities; and, 3) should not include a house size requirement. To give these guidelines greater weight, the Council stated it would consider the local reaction to those recommendations when reviewing comprehensive plans or applications for federal housing assistance.

States can lessen the intensity of local ratable zoning by reforming the public finance structure. Norman Williams has repeatedly emphasized that the state's financial power is one of it strongest land use controls and that fiscal reform is needed to induce more sensible land use.[93] Some states have allowed regional tax sharing reforms. Minnesota, for example, enacted the Fiscal Disparities Act[94] while New Jersey allows tax sharing in the Hackensack Meadowlands district.

Other meliorative state actions include:

1. *Integrating state capital budgeting with its planning efforts.* This strategy has been adopted by numerous states such as Michigan and Vermont.[95] The latter state, for example, adjusts its capital plan to the Land Capability and Development Plan. More sensible State capital placement and timing can act as a growth control device which channels new development in appropriate locations.

2. *Encourage local or regional development management systems.* States can encourage sensible growth management which takes into account regional housing need. Some examples include the Twin Cities and Montgomery County (Maryland) approaches.

3. *Replace selected direct controls with incentive systems.* Instead of states mandating that all development contain certain specifications, they can provide an incentive system. Current efforts to encourage energy conservation is one such example. Many states have adopted the energy conservation standards suggested by the American Society of Heating, Refrigeration and Air

Conditioning Engineers, commonly referred to as ASHRAE–95.[96] States have gone beyond a standard approach and are offering and allowing incentives for the installation of innovative energy systems. Some examples:[97]

Arizona exempts devices used for production of nonfossil fuel energy from property taxes and allows a one-quarter income tax credit against the cost of a solar energy system.

Nevada allows property owners to deduct the difference between the assessed value of a property with and without solar energy installation.

Colorado provides that all solar systems be assessed at 5 percent of their original systems.

Maryland, Massachusetts, Michigan, New Jersey and other states provide a property tax exemption for solar energy systems.

This type of legislation does not mandate that new types of heating/cooling plants be installed, a requirement which would raise the initial purchase price of a home. Instead it provides incentives, either actual tax reductions or else protection from upward reassessment, for those who do opt for energy saving systems.

4. *State Financing Controls.* It has been suggested that states take stronger action to reduce settlement and financing costs. This intervention might include adopting marketable title statutes,[98] scrutinizing title insurance fee schedules (especially in cases of recertification);[99] and allowing more flexible mortgage instruments[100] such as variable rate, graduated payments and non-amortized loans. Some of these reforms, such as offering a more marketable title offer some potential for cost reduction. Others, however, would not work to shave consumer outlays but rather would make financing more readily available. This is true of many of the flexible mortgage strategies. While some, e.g., the graduated payment mortgage, would reduce initial dollar outlays, others, such as VRMs may very possibly increase costs as interest rates would rise with inflation.

Forces Negating A Strong State Role to Reduce Housing Costs

There is obvious popular appeal for state strategies to lower consumer housing prices. At the same time certain counter forces exist which may impede such action.

Financining Restraints. The Federal 701 funds have been one of the prime forces encouraging greater state planning and intervention. Recent appropriation cutbacks in the 701 program may temper further state involvement; since 1975, overall 701 assistance has dropped by 30 percent and targeted aid to state planning agencies has declined by an ever greater amount.

The level of federal aid flowing to states and then to localities as opposed to direct federal to local disbursement has also been cut precipitously. As discussed by Richard Nathan:[101]

> [T] here is now a widespread awareness that basic changes are taking place. I refer specifically to the dramatic growth in federal grants-in-aid paid directly to local governments . . .
>
> In 1979, one-third of the $84 billion in federal grants budgeted for states and localities will be paid to local units. If we put to one side welfare-type programs (AFDC and Medicaid), . . . then half of all remaining federal grants to states and localities currently go to local governments . . .
>
> This is a threefold increase in the local proportion of federal grants over a decade.

This increasing importance of direct federal assistance to localities has the affect of diminishing the monetary control and therefore the influence of states over localities to adopt less restrictive and more flexible housing regulations.

The Environmental Imperative. Starting in the early 1970s, states began to add their own environmental safeguards and regulations to the standards set by the federal government. This added regulatory overlay reflects a conceptual view that the states should strongly intervene to protect the environment and cannot rely on federal safeguards. The burgeoning state environmental regulation is not conducive to reducing housing costs linked with government. While the added expenditures resulting from coastal zone, mini-NEPA and similar state intervention can be reduced by pruning excessive prohibitions and improving coordination with the federal government, the state environmental thrust represents a move toward *added*, not reduced, housing expenditures.[102]

Summary—Part II

The state has a variety of potential strategies that it might employ to reduce housing costs. These strategies span the range of substantive answers to regulatory problems and may be implemented with varying degrees of persuasive force. Since force occasions resistance as the amount of force applied increases, the range of potential applications narrows.

The state, in an enabling or informational role, is able to reach a broad audience on a variety of topics. This includes promulgation of model statutes, ordinance drafting assistance and the like. State exposure is limited, yet so too is the chance for substantive reform.

If the state adopts a more coordinative role through a regional agency such as A-95 review or HUD regional offices which might encompass review of zoning ordinances or local HAP, Fair Share Plans, the state's exposure is increased, yet so too is the potential for uniformly unrestrictive zoning ordinances and meaningful HAP and Fair Share quotas.

If the state adopts direct controls such as those of the "Critical Area" or Coastal Zone programs, local prerogatives are clearly under challenge. For substantive areas of desired control, the state is at war with its subordinate political subdivisions. This decision must be made very carefully as the state cannot wage "war" on multiple fronts.

Obviously, a policy of mix and match must be employed which attempts to apply levels of persuasion which are tempered by the political reality of achievable results. This mix and match of strategies is just as appropriate for attempting to introduce the same regulatory reform at multiple locations as it is for multiple regulatory reform in the same location.

Conclusions

The preceding analyses indicate that state interventionary attempts in the local development process have the greatest potential for impact if they concentrate on the three traditional local ordinances which control local land development—*zoning ordinance, subdivision regulations, and the building code*. It is in the development steps which are controlled by these ordinances where the greatest gains in housing cost reduction may be achieved.

The paths of state intervention also become clear when these agents of housing cost inflation are isolated. The state, through its enabling legislation and informational role, must promulgate technically efficient and adaptable model local zoning ordinances, subdivision regulations and building codes.

Local governments must be encouraged to adopt such regulations in order to adequately fulfill Fair Share, HAP, or other statewide mandated housing plans. If compliance is not forthcoming, state-to-local intergovernmental revenue transfers may be stopped and/or municipal officials may be held liable personally for inappropriate conduct which occupying elective office.

In substantive regulatory areas which require coordinated statewide policy, i.e. "Critical Areas," Coastal Zone, etc., the state should get (and has gotten) into the land regulation business directly, establishing through state permitting or other form of regulatory measure *solely* state authority for the development of certain categories of land. Control of development in these areas must be completely wrested from local influence. This type of direct intervention should be kept to a minimum, however.

Thus, not startlingly, if we were to recommend an integrated strategy of state interventions in local development processing for the purpose of attempting to reduce housing costs due to excessive regulation, the recommended strategy would not be terribly dissimilar from what is already taking place in the field, piecemeal.

An integrated strategy for an attack on housing costs is little more than an aggregation, synthesis and organization of the cost-saving activities currently ongoing in states across the nation. Part II of this paper, presented in a format of *substantive* concerns, is the closest thing to a shopping list for such a strategy.

Notes

1. B. Bruce Briggs, "The Cost of Housing," *The Public Interest* (Summer 1973), pp. 34-42.
2. George Sternlieb, Robert W. Burchell and David Listokin, "The Private Sector's Role in the Provision of Reasonably Priced Housing," in *Resources for Housing* (San Francisco: Federal Home Loan Bank Board, 1976).
3. Bernard J. Frieden and Arthur P. Solomon, *The Nation's Housing 1975-1985* (Cambridge, Mass.: Joint Center for Urban Studies, 1977).
4. John C. Weicher, "The Affordability of New Homes," *Journal of the American Real Estate and Urban Economics Association.* Vol. 5, No. 2 (Summer 1977). See also Bernard Frieden and Arthur P. Solomon, "The Controversy Over Homeownership Affordability," *Journal of the American Real Estate and Urban Economics Association*, Vol. 5, No. 3 (Fall

1977), p. 355; John Weicher, "Response to Frieden and Solomon," *Journal of the American Real Estate and Urban Economics Association*, Vol. 5, No. 3 (Fall 1977), p. 360.

5. Anthony Downs, "Public Policy and the Rising Cost of Housing," *Real Estate Review*, Vol. 8, No. 1 (Spring 1978), p. 27.

6. Urban Land Institute "Single Family Raw Land Price Trends, Jacksonville Florida." Chart in detailed workshop report on research related to the "Effects of Environmental and Land-use Regulations on Housing Costs," unpublished (November 22, 1976).

7. Boris Lang, "The Rising Cost of Housing Materials" (Washington, D.C.: National Association of Homebuilders Research Paper, unpublished, 1977).

8. See Bernard J. Frieden, *The War On Housing* (New York: The Free Press, 1979 forthcoming).

9. See Tom Muller and Franklin J. James, "Environmental Impact Evaluation and Housing Costs," *AREUEA Journal* (Spring, 1977).

10. Robert W. Burchell, James W. Hughes and George Sternlieb, *Housing Costs and Housing Restraints* (New Brunswick, N.J.: Rutgers University, Center for Urban Policy Research, 1969).

11. Stephen R. Seidel, *Housing Costs and Government Regulations: Confronting the Regulatory Maze* (Rutgers University, New Brunswick, N.J.: Center for Urban Policy Research, 1977).

12. See, for example, Norman B. Williams, Jr., *American Land Planning Law*, Vol. I (Chicago, Illinois: Callaghan and Co., 1975).

13. Michael Gleeson, *et al.*, *Urban Management Systems*, Planning Advisory Service Report No. 309-310. (Chicago, Illinois: American Society of Planning Officials, 1975).

14. See, for instance, Robert W. Burchell and David Listokin, *The Fiscal Impact Handbook: Measuring the Costs of Land Development* (New Brunswick, N.J.: Rutgers University, Center for Urban Policy Research, 1978).

15. Robert H. Freilich and Peter S. Levi, *Model Subdivision Regulations—Text and Commentary* (Chicago, Illinois: American Society of Planning Officials, 1975).

16. Richard L. Sanderson, *Codes and Code Administration* (Chicago: Building Officials Conference of America, Inc., 1969).

17. Harrison Fraker and Elizabeth Schacker, *Energy Husbandry in Housing: An Analysis of the Development Process in a Residential Community, Twin Rivers, N.J.* (Princeton University, Center for Environmental Studies—Report No. 5, 1973), p. 45.

18. See, for example, Charles Haar, "Zoning for Minimum Standards: The Wayne Township Case," *Harvard Law Review*, 66 (1953), p. 1051.

19. U.S. Department of Housing and Urban Development and Veterans Administration, *Report on Mortgage Settlement Costs* (Washington, D.C.: U.S. Government Printing Office, 1972).

20. See Kristina Ford, "Afterword" in Seidel, *Housing Costs and Government Regulations*, p. 355.

21. *Hunter v. Pittsburgh*, 207 U.S. 161, 178-179 (1907).

22. Marion Clawson, "A Capsule History of Land in the United States," in *America's Land and Its Uses* (Washington, D.C.: Resources for the Future, 1975); Seymour Toll, *Zones American* (New York: Grossman Publishers, 1969); S.J. Malielski, Jr., *The Politics of Zoning: The New York Experience* (New York: Columbia University Press, 1966); John Delafons, *Land Use Controls in the United States* (Cambridge, Mass.: M.I.T. Press, 1969), p. 39.

23. See Richard Babcock, *The Zoning Game: Municipal Practices and Policies* (Madison: University of Wisconsin Press, 1966); Charles Haar, "Regionalism and Realism in Land Use Planning," *University of Pennsylvania Law Review*, Vol. 105 (1957), p. 526; "State Police Power-Zoning—Validity of Local Ordinance Depends on Considerations of Regional Not Merely Local General Welfare," *Vanderbilt Law Review*, Vol. 25 (1972), p. 472; "Notes: The Responsibility of Local Zoning Authorities to Nonresidential Indigents," *Stanford Law Review*, Vol. 23 (1971), p. 774.

24. See Norman Williams, Jr. and Edward Wacks, "Segregation of Residential Areas Along Economic Lines: Lionshed Lake Revisited," *Wisconsin Law Review*, Vol. 27 (1969), p. 827; Urban Land Institute, *Fair Housing and Exclusionary Zoning*, Research Report No. 23 (Washington, D.C.: National Committee Against Discrimination in Housing and the Urban Land Institute, 1974); Lawrence Sager, "Tight Little Isalnds: Exclusionary Zoning, Equal Protection, and the Indigent," *Stanford Law Review*, Vol. 21 (1970), p. 767; Norman Williams and Thomas Norman, "Exclusionary Land Use Control: The Case of Northeastern New Jersey," *Syracuse Law Review*, Vol. 22 (1971), p. 475.

25. John Reps, "Requiem for Zoning," in *Planning 1964* (Chicago: American Society of Planning Officials, 1965).

26. Daniel Mandelker, "The Role of Zoning in Housing and Metropolitan Development," in U.S. Congress, House Committee on Banking and Currency, Papers Submitted to Subcommittee on Housing Panels and Housing Production, *Housing Development and Developing a Suitable Living Environment*: Part 2, 92nd Cong., 1st sess., (Washington, D.C.: Government Printing Office, 1971).

27. Fred Bosselman and David Callies, *The Quiet Revolution in Land Use Controls* (Washington, D.C.: Government Printing Office, 1972).

28. *Ibid.*, p. 1

29. See footnote 25.

30. Robert H. Freilich, "Awakening the Sleeping Giant: New Trends and Developments in Environmental and Land Use Controls," in the Southwestern Legal Foundation, *Proceedings of the Institute on Planning Zoning and Eminent Domain* (New York: Matthew Bender and Co., 1975).

31. Charles Haar, "In Accordance with a Comprehensive Master Plan," *Harvard Law Review*, Vol. 68 (1954), p. 1154. See also, "Twenty Years After—Renewed Significance of Comprehensive Plan Requirement," *Urban Law Annual*, Vol. 9 (1975).

32. *Ibid.*

33. Norman Williams, Jr. "Administrative Aspects of Zoning" in *American Planning Law-Land Use and the Police Power*, Vol. 5 (Chicago: Callaghan and Company, 1975), p. 1.

34. *Ibid.*

35. California Government Code, §65560(d), 65561(d), 65563, 65566, 65567, 65860(a), 65910.

36. Robert G. Healy, *Land Use and the States* (Baltimore: John Hopkins Press, 1976), p. 202.

37. John Volkman, "Oregon's LCDC Funded" in *Land Use Law and Zoning Digest*, Vol. 27, No. 9 (1975).

38. Cal. Gov't Code ΣΣ 65869, 6647.5, 66474 (1976).

39. 59 OP. Cal. Att'y Gen. 129 (1976). Cited in Daniel J. Curtin and K.L. Shirk, Jr., "Land Use, Planning and Zoning," *The Urban Lawyer*, Vol. 9, No. 4 (1977), p. 726.

40. New Jersey Law of 1975, ch. 291.

41. William Miller, "The New Jersey Land Use Law Revision: A Lesson for Other States," *Real Estate Law Journal* Vol. 5, No. 2 (Fall 1976), p. 129.

42. Americal Law Institute, *A Model Land Development Code*, Tentative Draft No. 3 (April 1971).

43. Fred P. Bosselman, George M. Raymond and Richard A. Persico, "Some Observations on the American Law Institute's Model Land Development Code," *The Urban Lawyer*, Vol. 8, No. 3 (1976), p. 477.

44. See Miller, "The New Jersey Land Use Law Revision." See also "The Municipal Land Use Law," *New Jersey Municipalities* (March 1976), p. 6.

45. Bosselman, Raymond and Persico, "Some Observations on the American Law Institute's Model Land Development Code," p. 488.

46. *Ibid.*

47. Act Σ 49; c. 40:55D-62.

48. Miller, "The New Jersey Land Use Revision," p. 141.

49. American Institute of Planners, *Survey of State Land Use Planning Activity* (Washington, D.C.: Government Printing Office, 1976). See also Leonard V. Wilson and L.V. Watkins, "State Planning: Problems and Promises," *State Government*, Vol. 48 (Autumn 1975), p. 240; Kenneth Pearlman, "State Environmental Policy Acts: Local Decision Making and Land Use Planning," *Journal of the American Institute of Planners*, Vol. 43, No. 1 (January 1977), p. 42.

50. Volkman, "Oregon's LCDC Funded."

51. New Jersey Department of Community Affairs, *Evaluating The Fiscal Impact of Planned Unit Development* (Trenton: New Jersey Department of Community Affairs, 1976).

52. See Seidel, *Housing Costs and Government Regulations.* Raymond Myers, "State Building Code Profile," *Construction Review* (March 1977).

53. See Robert H. Freilich and Peter S. Levi, *Model Subdivision Regulations* (Chicago: American Society of Planning Officials, 1975).

54. For discussion on the performance concept in building construction, see U.S. National Bureau of Standards, *The Performance Concept: A Study of Its Application to Housing* (Washington, D.C.: Government Printing Office, 1969); U.S. National Bureau of Standards, Bruce Foster, ed. *Performance Concept in Buildings; Vol. I—Invited Papers. Proceedings of a Symposium* (Washington, D.C., March 1972).

55. See footnote 52.

56. Council on State Governments, *State Planning: Intergovernmental Policy Coordination* (Washington, D.C.: Government Printing Office, 1976), Appendix I.

57. Council of State Governments, *Land: State Alternatives for Planning and Management.* (Lexington, Ky.: Council of State Governments, 1975); see footnotes 49 and 56.

58. Council of State Governments, *State Planning, Intergovernment Policy Coordination*, p. 16.

59. *Ibid.*, p. 25.

60. Healy, *Land Use and the States*, p. 202.

61. American Institute of Planners, *State Land Use Activity*, p. 1.

62. Healy, *Land Use and the States*, p. 148.

63. *Star Ledger*, May 26, 1978.

64. See George Raymond, "ALI Model Code is Concerned with Planning and the Physical Development of the Land," *AIP Newsletter*, Vol. 9, No. 5 (May 1974), p. 12.

65. See Bureau of National Affairs, *Housing and Development Reporter*, reference file, Vol. 1, p. 09:0021; Melvin Mogulof, "Regional Planning Clearance and Evaluation: A Look at the A-95 Process," *Journal of the American Institute of Planners*, Vol. 37, No. 6 (1971), pp. 418-22.

66. Advisory Commission on Intergovernmental Relations, *Regionalism Revisited: Recent Areawide and Local Responses* (Washington, D.C.: Government Printing Office, 1977).

67. State of New Jersey, Executive Order, No. 35, April 2, 1976.

68. Norman Beckman, *et al.*, "National Urban Growth Policy: 1974 Congressional and Executive Action," *Journal of the American Institute of Planners*, Vol. 41, No. 4 (July 1975), pp. 235-37.

69. Potomac Institute, *The Housing Assistance Plan: A Non-Working Program for Community Improvement?: A Preliminary Evaluation of HUD Implementation of the 1974 Housing and Community Development Act* (Washington, D.C.: Potomac Institute, 1975); The U.S. Department of Housing and Urban Development, *Community Development Block Grant Program: A Provisional Report* (Washington, D.C.: Government Printing Office, 1975); Richard P. Nathan *et al., Block Grants for Community Development* (Washington, D.C.: Government Printing Office, 1977).

70. *City of Hartford v. Carla A. Hills*, U.S. District Court, District of Connecticut, Civil No. H-75-258, p. 26. The Housing and Community Development Act of 1974 offers many avenues for attack on restrictive land use policies. See U.S. Civil Rights Commission, *Twenty Years after*

"Brown"; Herbert Franklin, "Open Communities Litigation and the Housing and Community Development Act of 1974," in *Exclusionary Land Use Litigation* (Washington, D.C.: National Committee Against Discrimination in Housing, 1975); and Daniel Lauber, "The Housing Act and Discrimination," *Planning*, Vol. 41 (February 1975), pp. 24-25.

71. See footnote 66.

72. Mass. Gen. Laws Ann. Ch. 40B secs. 20-23 (Supp. 1973 inserted by State 1969, Ch. 774).

73. S. 803 sec. 7.1(c) N.J. Leg. Reg. Sess. (1969).

74. Paul N. Ylvisaker and Meg Power, "Planning and Housing USA: Land Reform in New Jersey," *The Planner*, Vol. 61 (May 1975), p. 174.

75. State of New Jersey, Assembly no. 1421, introduced November 13, 1972.

76. *Newark Star Ledger*, February 9, 1972.

77. *Star Ledger*, June 6, 1978.

78. 67 N.J. 151, 336 A. 2d 713 (1975).

79. 117 N.J. Super. 11, 283 A. 2d 353 (1971).

80. See *Land Use Digest* Vol. 11, No. 3 (March 1978).

81. See Jerome G. Rose, "Oakwood and Madison: A Tactical Retreat By the New Jersey Supreme Court to Preserve the Mount Laurel Principle," *Urban Law Annual*, Vol. 13 (1977), p. 189.

82. Jerome G. Rose. "A New Test for Exclusionary Zoning: Does It Preclude the Opportunity for Least Cost Housing," *Real Estate Law Journal*, Vol. 6 (1977).

83. Bosselman and Callies, *The Quiet Revolution in Land Use Controls*; Williams, "State and Regional Land Use Controls," Part 18, *American Planning Law.*

84. See Sternlieb and Listokin, "Building Codes."

85. Charles G. Field and Steven R. Rivkin, *The Building Code Burden*, (Lexington, Mass.: Lexington Books, 1975). George Sternlieb and David Listokin, "Building Codes: State of the Art, Strategies for the Future," Paper prepared for the HUD Housing Task Force, June 1973.

86. For a discussion of the state industrialized housing laws see "How Strong Are the State Factory Housing Laws?" *Professional Builder*, (January 1972), p. 178; "Model Code Approved for Factory Housing," *Engineering News-Record* (April 27, 1972), p. 16; "Factory Built Housing: Statutory Solutions," *University of Chicago Law Review*, Vol. 88 (1971), pp. 793-794; "Analyses of the Probable Impact of the California Factory Built Housing Law," *Stanford Law Review*, Vol. 29 (May 1971), p. 978; "Closing the Low-Cost Housing Gap: The California Factory-Built Housing Law," *Columbia Journal of Law and Social Problems*, Vol. 8 (Summer 1972), p. 469.

87. Robert W. Burchell and David Listokin, *The Environmental Impact Handbook* (New Brunswick, N.J.: Rutgers University Center for Urban Policy Research, 1975).

88. Robert W. Burchell, David Listokin, and Shrikant Sinha, *EIS Update: The Environmental Impact Handbook II* (New Brunswick, N.J.: Rutgers University Center for Urban Policy Research, 1978).

89. Dan K. Richardson, *The Cost of Environmental Protection* (New Brunswick, N.J.: Rutgers University Center for Urban Policy Research, 1976); Melvin B. Molgulof, *Saving the Cost* (Lexington, Mass.: Lexington, 1975).

90. See U.S. Department of Housing and Urban Development, *Final Report of the Task Force on Housing Costs* (Washington, D.C.: Government Printing Office, 1978).

91. David Listokin, *Fair Share Housing Allocation* (New Brunswick, N.J.: Rutgers University Center for Urban Policy Research, 1977).

92. "Housing Guidelines and Developer Competition Encourage Smaller, Less Expensive Homes in the Twin Cities," *PAS Memo* (December 1977), p. 2.

93. See Williams, *American Planning Law.*

94. See John W. Windhorst, Jr., "The Minnesota Fiscal Disparities Law," *Land Use Law and Zoning Digest*, Vol. 28, No. 4 (1976), p. 7.

95. Robert C. Einsweiler, "State/Local Options in Regulatory Reform," Unpublished paper presented for the ULI Regulatory Simplification Seminar, Sea Pines Plantation, South Carolina, Feb. 22-24, 1978, p. 24.

96. Alan A. Hodges, "Do We Have the Energy to Conserve," *Urban Land*, Vol. 36, No. 2 (February 1977), p. 12.

97. Rutgers University Center for Urban Policy Research, *Energy Conservation in New and Built Units* (forthcoming).

98. See U.S. Department of Housing and Urban Development and Veterans Administration, *Report on Mortgage Settlement Costs* (Washington, D.C.: Government Printing Office, 1972).

99. *Ibid.*

100. See D.I. Smith, "Reforming the Mortgage Instruments," *Federal Home Loan Bank Board*, Working Paper No. 11 (April 1976), pp. 2-10; S.R. Stansell and J.P. Millar, "How Variable Rate Mortgages Would Affect Lenders," *Real Estate Review* (Winter 1976) p. 115; Richard Marcis, "Variable-Rate Mortgages: Their Use and Impact in the Mortgage and Capital Markets," *American Real Estate and Urban Economics Association Journal* (Spring 1974), p. 21. See also Federal Reserve Board, *Ways to Moderate Fluctuations in Housing Construction* (Washington, D.C.: U.S. Government Printing Office, 1972).

101. Richard P. Nathan, "The Outlook for Federal Grants to Cities," Unpublished paper, May 8, 1978.

102. For a counter-argument, see Mary E. Brooks, *Housing Equity and Environmental Protection: The Needless Conflict* (Washington, D.C.: American Institute of Planners, 1976).

Design Standards in Developing Areas: Allowing Reduced Cost Housing While Maintaining Adequate Community Development Standards

Robert W. Burchell
David Listokin

Introduction

The purpose of the following paper is to analyze zoning/subdivision/ environmental design requirements, currently in force in fringe or developing communities, as a prelude to developing governmental policy which simultaneously may ensure both adequate community design and minimum price of inclusive shelter. The paper will concentrate exclusively on zoning, subdivision and evironmental design standards. It will not address the various permitting or processing requirements associated with these particular land use controls such as building codes or the various timing measures subsumed under the general rubric of growth control. These are topics of other papers which will be presented elsewhere in this conference.

The paper is divided into five sections:

I. Statement of the Issues Surrounding Design Requirements

The *first section* will overview briefly popular hypotheses regarding land use standards and their impact on housing costs. Questions on the magnitude of the problem, by type of land use control and by subsets of specific controls, will be posed here.

Section II, in presenting the results of a national field survey of municipal land use controls, will attempt to answer the questions developed in *Section I* as well as provide comparisons between existing local ordinance requirements and design standards recommended by various trade associations, professional groups and/or housing support agencies. The object of this section is to provide some measure of common understanding as to how severe community overdesign is, and the specific concentration of overdesign in zoning versus subdivision controls; in engineering various planning-type standards, etc.

Section III presents a formula for combined state and local action to combat overrestrictive design requirements. It alerts communities to the magnitude of their own problems with a checklist of potentially severe zoning, subdivision and environmental design requirements. This portion of the paper further provides a structure for meliorative governmental policy at both the state and local levels.

Section IV provides examples of the program measures discussed above as they exist, for the most part in isolation, in a few specific states and localities. The point of this section is to demonstrate that corrective measures are already being attempted in the field and the bulk of recommended policy is indeed capable of being implemented.

The *final section* of the paper summarizes the literature surrounding design requirements' impact on housing costs. The literature annotations are presented both by particular land use control and by whether they deal with specific costs or are just overviews of the issues related to this control.

I. Background—A Statement of the Issues

Few issues have dominated the housing/land use planning literature to the degree of exclusionary zoning. National commissions have reported results of their investigations to the field on several occasions;[1] recent zoning treatises have devoted entire sections to permutations of this issue;[2] professional organizations have studied and restudied its origins and historical evolution;[3] research institutes have repeatedly sought its causative agents as a prelude to developing corrective policy.[4] This concept, over its more recent history, has been defined as land use controls (zoning ordinances, subdivision regulations, environmental controls, growth control systems) which interfere with the provision of reduced-cost housing, typically at the outer reaches of the metropolitan area wherein adequate land is available for this housing.

A flurry of case law initially zeroed in on local zoning practices, i.e., minimum lot size, minimum frontages, minimum building size, mandatory bedroom ratios and limitations on multifamily development as "the exclusionary zoning problem."[5] A second generation of decisions challenged overrestrictive subdivision regulations, growth control measures and environmental controls as also contributing to "the problem."[6] Finally, an attack has been waged on excessively complicated permitting procedures, development submission requirements and required participation in offsite capital improvements as yet another manifestation of exclusionary land use procedures.[7]

At issue is the denial of lower cost housing due to recurring instances of communities increasing development standards and procedures beyond what is necessary for the minimum protection of health, safety and welfare of housing occupants.

It is further claimed that these are purposeful acts to restrict entrance to communities to all but higher income groups and additionally to assure current residents that they will not bear the municipal servicing costs of future residents.[8]

Within the bevy of literature, however, the specific effects of various exclusionary measures on housing costs are not cleanly presented. For instance, one does not get a feeling for: 1) the validity of the argument of fringe communities' across the board zoning; 2) whether or not this upzoning holds true as well for subdivision and environmental (if any) design requirements; and 3) if unnecessary upgrading pertains only to design standards or, as well, to required off-site improvements or municipal capital facility initiations/expansions.

Obviously, to construct meliorative policy it is critical to be able to make the distinctions noted above. Is there in developing communities a noticeable skew to larger lot sizes/widths, non-zoning for multifamily development/mobile homes? Does this also apply to more frequent requirements for dual sidewalks, street lighting, shade trees, larger rights-of-way/pavement widths, etc? Are design requirements what are overspecified or are they requirements relating to the provision of off-site streets, sewers, land dedication for schools, etc?

Finally, how do these requirements compare to what is believed necessary to achieve a guaranteed level of acceptable development?

II. The Severity of the Design-Imposed Problem By Type of Land Use Control

BASIC DEFINITIONS, THE SAMPLE OF COMMUNITIES

Subsequent analyses will attempt to view the degree to which previously stated hypotheses, related to required design criteria in fringe communities, are applicable to this class of communities.

The analyses will compare zoning and subdivision criteria in both developing and developed communities. In addition, they will briefly glimpse at local environmental compliance procedures in the form of required environmental impact statements (EIS) and critical area legislation, primarily that relating to the coastal zone.

To begin, it is necessary to define what is meant by a "developing" versus "mostly developed" community. The literature surrounding the New Jersey *Mount Laurel* decision is most helpful in this instance. It notes, in its three-part classifications of communities (developed, developing and rural) that a *developing* community should exhibit evidence of most or all of six basic characteristics:[9]

(1) sizable land area,
(2) sizable portion as yet undeveloped,
(3) location outside central city,
(4) location in path of inevitable development,
(5) significant population growth in immediate past,
(6) loss of rural nature of community.

Developed communities are defined as central cities or older built-up suburbs; *rural* areas as undeveloped and likely to continue as such for some time into the future.

While it is beyond the confines of this analysis to apply the *Mount Laural* criteria to city selection, cities selected for analysis are classified into "developing" and "most developed"* due to the amount of land left for development, size, location within the metropolitan area and population growth over the period 1970-1975. A developing community is one which is a non-central city of a standard metropolitan statistical area (SMSA), of more than five square miles in size, that has grown in population by more than 15 percent over the period 1970-1975 and has more than 35 percent of its land yet to be developed. A mostly developed municipality is a central city/older suburb of an SMSA, whose physical size is in excess of one square mile, of positive population growth (less than 5 percent) over the period 1970 to 1975 and, finally, one wherein no more than 10 percent of the municipal land area is currently available for development.

These selection criteria, applied randomly in the largest SMSAs of the four Census defined regions (Northeast, North Central, South, West), yielded two sets of approximately 40 communities each. Both zoning and subdivision regulations were obtained from the bulk of these communities; a questionnaire was administered to the local administrator or planning board director in each community. Information obtained from the ordinances and interviews in 1976, augmented with callbacks in 1978, form the basis of the following analyses.

ZONING DESIGN STANDARDS

Exhibit 1 summarizes design standards found in municipal zoning ordinances throughout the country. According to definitions stated previously, standards are partitioned to those found in developing versus developed communities.

The standards chosen are those which most frequently appear in zoning ordinances as design requirements and also those reported throughout the exclusionary zoning literature as "part and parcel" of the housing unavailability problem. They are: (1) minimum lot size/width, (2) minimum floor areas/building size, and (3) permissible housing types.

Minimum Lot Size and Width. Minimum lot size specification is quite different in developed versus developing communities. Close

---

*The term "developed" will be used to describe a "mostly" developed community for the remainder of this paper.

EXHIBIT 1

ZONING DESIGN STANDARDS IN MUNICIPAL ZONING ORDINANCES

Minimum Lot Size

	Developed (n=41)	Developing (n=42)
Percent Having Available Land with Minimum Lot Size of:		
Less than a quarter acre	62.5%	39.0%
Greater than 1 acre	7.5%	25.6%
(Percent Having Explicit Provisions)	98.0/92.9	

Minimum Lot Width

Percent Having Available Land With Minimum Lot Width of:		
Less than 70 feet	51.2%	23.7%
More than 150 feet	9.8%	26.4%
(Percent Having Explicit Provisions)	98.0/90.5	

Minimum Floor Area

Percent Specifying Floor Areas of Size:		
Less than 1,000 feet	90.0%	33.3%
More than 1,400 feet	5.0%	26.7%
(Percent Having Explicit Provisions)	25.4/35.7	

Permissible Housing Types

For Residential Zones:		
Permit as of Right Other Than Single-Family Detached (Does not include PUD/Cluster Zones)	14.6%	5.1%
Allow as a Special Exception or Permitted Use:		
Explicit Multifamily Development	7.2%	2.6%
PUD or Cluster Development	36.6%	33.3%
Mobile Homes	10.0%	30.0%
(Percent Having Explicit Provisions)	47.7/51.4	

Source: Rutgers University, Center for Urban Policy Research Zoning and Subdivision Ordinance Survey (Fall 1976).

to two-thirds (62.5%) of the ordinances surveyed in *developed* communities had developable land in zoning categories of a quarter acre or less. The same potential to build on this size lot in *developing* communities was found only approximately one-half (39.0%) as often. This is due to the fact that the minimum lot sizes four times the quarter acre size were found in developing communities more than three times as frequently as they were in developed communities. Thus, there is a inherent skew towards the mandating of larger lot sizes in the zoning ordinances of developing versus developed communities.

Essentially the same scenario applies to lot widths. The shorter frontages associated with smaller lots are permitted far less often in developing than they are in developed communities. On the other hand, excessive frontages, twice what are normally found with quarter acre lots, are will represented in the developing class of communities.

Minimum Building Size. Minimum building size or, synonymously, floor area requirements, are much less often specified in both developed and developing municipal zoning ordinances than is the case for lot size and lot width. Whereas virtually all communities, both developed and developing, had ordinance requirements which specified minimum lot size and lot width, only 25 to 35 percent of these same communities impose a minimum building size requirement. It is interesting to note however that, when specified, there are striking differences between developed and developing communities. Of those communities which imposed a minimum building size requirement in developed communities, 90 percent had categories which permitted development of housing units of 1,000 squre feet or less; the same was true for only 33 percent of the ordinances of developing communities. In this latter category of community, fully 26 percent required housing units of floor area greater than 1,400 square feet.

Permissible Housing Types. Probably the most interesting statistics of all are those dealing with permissible housing types. What is very clear from this survey is that, even in developed communities, zoning ordinances specify single-family detached housing almost to the exclusion of all other housing types. Only one in twenty developing communities provide for other than single-family homes as of right. This is one-third the figure for developed communities. Thus, the garden apartment/low-rise "zone" is virtually nonexistent in areas which are characterized by having sufficient available land to support this kind of development. Even as an explicitly stated special exception or permitted use, multifamily development permissions lag similar authorizations for both PUDs and mobile homes.

What is encouraging to see, however, is the growth of PUD and cluster provisions as special exceptions/permitted uses in the zoning ordinances of both developed and developing communities. Although developing communities lag developed communities by about 10 percent, one-third of the former have the potentially innovative PUD and cluster provisions.

ZONING DESIGN STANDARD HYPOTHESES–A SECOND LOOK

In terms of the key hypothese to be tested here, it is clear that developing or fringe areas impose much more severe zoning standards than is the case for non-fringe, developed areas. There also appears to be no rationale for the imposition of these standards relating to protection of health, safety and welfare of community residents or to the prevention of general environmental degradation. In a question unrelated to this specific analysis, when local zoning officials were asked to respond as to why limited growth control measures were imposed, they rejected reasons such as loss of environmental quality or straining capital infrastructures already at capacity, and instead, chose the phrase "to maintain the community as it is" as their most pertinent response.

Two other of the proposed hypotheses also bear scrutiny at this point. The first is that developing areas' zoning ordinances frequently do not include potentially innovative design measures and standard supplanters such as planned unit development (PUD), cluster provisions, etc. This does not appear to be the case.

As noted previously, a significant proportion of both developing and developed communities' zoning ordinances contain provisions for PUD. Yet PUD development has paled nationally, lagging considerably more conventional development. What has happened is evidenced by local community responses shown in Exhibit 2. Less than 40 percent of those communities which have the PUD alternative as a legitimate development vehicle have had more than two developments processed through their associated approval stages. Moving away form the rule of law in conventional zoning to the increased administrative discretion available via PUD or other innovative mechanisms carries with it a much more involved, and thus longer, approval process. These types of developments, often larger than conventional subdivision, further flag the attention of the general

EXHIBIT 2

INDICATIONS OF HOW DEVELOPMENT IS TAKING PLACE

I. For those communities with PUD/Cluster Zones or PUD/Cluster developments allowed as special exceptions/permitted use, what percentage have had more than two developments processed through this vehicle?

	Developed	Developing
More than Two Developments Processed	27.8%	37.0%
(Percent Having Explicit Provisions)	43.9/64.3	

II. During the course of a year, what percent of requests for building permits simultaneously involved filing for rezoning, special exception, permitted use, etc?

	Developed	Developing
Median	9.0%	10.1%
	(mostly rezoning to multifamily)	(mostly special exception, permitting use)
(Percent Responding)	92.7/85.7	

III. On average, how often was relief granted?

	Developed	Developing
Median	62.5%	31.5%

public to a greater degree, thereby contributing to rejection or delay and noncompletion.

The second of the proposed hypotheses is that the zoning ordinances of developing communities usually do not permit, as of right, residential development of other than single-family homes. That is appallingly evident. There is an inherent bias, reflected in zoning ordinance exclusion, of multifamily development in the suburbs, particularly emerging suburbs. In terms of potential cost savings, the continued absence of multifamily zones in developing communities far outweighs any potential savings available through the reduction of minimum development standards associated with traditional single-family homes.

Suburban rental housing occupancy costs are less than two-thirds those associated with ownership of a detached single-family home in comparable communities. With the reduction in household size that has taken place over the last decade, the space typically found in rental facilities is more appropriate to the needs of a vast market of both youthful and elderly childless families. These families are currently forced to occupy more space at significantly higher costs, due to the unavailability of multifamily accommodations in peripheral, developing areas.

SUBDIVISION DESIGN STANDARDS

Exhibit 3 summarizes design standards found in subdivision ordinances of both developing and developed communities. Standards dealing with major hardware (streets, sidewalks, curbs) items are presented by mode of specific design requirement; those which deal with the smaller development appurtenances (street signs, shade trees, etc.) are presented by a tabulation of how often a requirement exists. Design standards are grouped into the following categories: *Streets, Streetscape, Street Hardware, Sewarage Facilities, Drainage/ Storm Sewers, Water Facilities and Public Utilities.*

Scrutinizing this exhibit it is obvious that, except for capital system upgrading, the same kind of overspecification found in the zoning ordinances of developing versus developed communities gnerally does not hold true for subdivision requirements.

Streets, Streetscape, Street Hardware. For *streets*—rights of way, pavement widths and cul-de-sacs' mandated subdivision standards are essentially the same for developing and developed communities. In fact, in developing communities, a *larger* cul-de-sac length is permitted—thus contributing to potential reduction in costs. Pavement width requirements are 10 percent larger for both collector and local streets in developing versus developed communities. One glaring difference between developed and developing communities is the frequency in the latter of the developer having to provide off-site streets and improvements. This requirement was found twice as often in developing as in developed communities.

In terms of the *streetscape* (signs, lighting, trees, off-street parking), the ordinances of developing communities less often mandate these appurtenances than the ordinances of developed communities. The

EXHIBIT 3

SUBDIVISION DESIGN STANDARDS IN MUNICIPAL SUBDIVISION REGULATIONS

	Developed	*Developing*
Streets		
Right of Way		
Collector (Mode)	60'	60'
Local (Mode)	50'	50'
Pavement Width		
Collector (Mode)	30-35'	36'
Local (Mode)	30'	31-39'
Cul-De-Sac		
Radius	50'	50'
Length	500'	500-600'
Off-site Streets/ Improvements (Required)	34.3%	68.3%
Streetscape		
Street Signs (Required)	75.8%	69.0%
Street Lighting (Required)	73.5%	51.4%
Shade Trees (Required)	63.6%	54.1%
Off-Street Parking (Required)	100.0%	94.9%
Street Hardware		
Curbs and Gutters (Required)	67.6%	55.0%
Sidewalks (Required both sides of street)	81.8%	57.1%
Sidewalk Width (Mode)	5'	4'
Block Length (Mode)	400-500'	500-600'
Sewerage Facilities		
Sanitary Sewage (Septic Tanks permitted)	35.3%	69.0%
Minimum Diameter	8"	8"
Overdesign for Sewage Capacity (For "Foreseeable" future)	65.6%	87.8%
Tap-in Fee (Median)	$50	$250
Off-site Sewerage Facilities (Developer responsibility for)	39.4%	67.5%
Manhole Spacing	200-400'	200-400'

EXHIBIT 3 (CONTINUED)

	Developed	Developing
Drainage/Storm Sewers		
Storm Drainage Facilities (Developer responsibility for)	97.1%	97.6%
Off-site Storm Drainage Improvements (Developer responsibility for)	38.2%	52.5%
Water Facilities		
Percent of new subdivisions which had preexisting water mains	87.0%	25.0%
Water Mains (Developer responsibility)	91.4%	100.0%
Water Main Diameter	6"	6"
Water Laterals (Developer responsibility)	94.3%	88.1%
Fire Hydrants (Developer responsibility)	97.1%	92.9%
Fire Hydrant Interval	500'	500'
Off-site Water Facilities (Water main extensions, water treatment plants)	44.1%	61.5%
Public Utilities		
Underground Installations (Mandatory in more than 50% of instances)	62.9%	71.4%
Land Dedication		
For Open Space/Recreation (Mandatory requirement)	17.6%	14.3%
For Schools (Mandatory Requirement)	0.0%	35.9%
For Government Facilities (Mandatory requirement)	9.7%	9.1%
Improved Guarantees		
Surety Bonds (Percent required as principal mode of improvement security)	82.9%	92.9%
Escrow Account (Percent required as Principal Mode)	68.8%	71.4%

Source: Rutgers University, Center for Urban Policy Research (Spring 1979).

most significant difference is in street lighting which is required in developing communities only two-thirds as often as it is in developed communities.

In the case of *street hardware* (blocks, curbs, gutters, sidewalks), again developing communities less frequently require these items across-the-board than is the case for developed communities. Curbs and gutters and sidewalks are madated 20 to 30 percent less often in fringe communities—further, sidewalks are narrower and block lengths are longer. Each of these differences indicate positive sensitivity to less stringent design requirements for less developed communities.

Sewerage Facilities/Drainage Storm Sewers. Sewerage facilities reflect peripheral areas' concern for system upgrading. The direct result of this concern is expressed in developing communities; overdesign for sewage capacity, more frequent requirement for developer provision of off-site sewer facilities and significantly larger sewer tap-in fees. As is evident in Exhibit 3, tap-in fees in developing communities average five times the levy that is found in developed communities (with no indication that this reflects increased costs perculiar to this type of community); overdesign for future expectation regarding end-state holding capacity takes place in developing communities one-third again as much as it does in developed communities; finally, the requirement that the developer provide off-site sewer facilities/improvements takes place twice as often in developing communities. The only potential countervailing trend is the much greater frequency of ordinances in developing communities to allow septic tanks (2:1 versus developed communities) yet this permission usually is associated with lot sizes of ½ acre or more.

The development standard requirements for *drainage/storm sewers* and for *water facilities* also reflect the general observation of subdivision controls as they apply to developing versus developed communities: basic development hardware is required to the same or a lower level in developing communities; major systems are charged out at a significantly higher rate for developing communities. For instance, the provision of storm drainage facilities are required of developers almost uniformly and to the same level in both classes of communities. However, off-site storm drainage improvements are required in developing communities one-third more frequently than they are in developing communities.

Water Facilities—Public Utilities. For water facilities, the necessity to provide water mains, water laterals and fire hydrants as well as requirements for water main diameters and fire hydrant intervals again are essentially the same for both developing and developed communities. The requirement to provide off-site water facilities appears one-third more frequently in developing versus developed communities. Mandatory underground installation (in more than 50 percent of approvals granted) of public utilities (electricity, telephone, etc.) is required 15 percent more often in developing communities. This latter requirement, reflecting primarily aesthetic considerations, is certainly excessive given the limited development of these communities and the inital costs and recurring maintenance requirements of such installations.

Land Dedication/Improvement Guarantees. Improvement guarantees of one form or another (surety bonds, escrow accounts, etc.) are now an almost across-the-board requirement (85-90 percent) of communities (both developed and developing) nationally. In developing communities they are required slightly more often (10 percent) than they are in developed communities.

Land dedication for open space/recreation or for government facilities does not appear to be as frequent a subdivision requirement as one would be led to believe. Only in 10 percent of the ordinances surveyed is there a dedication requirement for municipal government facilities—police outpost, rescue station, municipal administration building, etc. Roughly twice this percentage of communities require land to be dedicated for local (development-oriented) recreational purposes for on-site open space. Essentially equal dedication requirements exist for both developing and developed communities in these instances.

Land dedicated for *schools*, however, is sharply increased and definitely skewed to developing communities. Not only is it a frequent requirement—over one-third of the ordinances surveyed in developing communities—it is almost totally absent as a development requirement in ordinances of developed communities. Again the excess requirement for "system upgrading" is vividly apparent in developing communities.

SUBDIVISION DESIGN STANDARD HYPOTHESES—A SECOND LOOK

The idea that developing or fringe area communities impose severe subdivision design standards on new developments seems not to be true in all cases. Compared to development standards required by developed communities for most *major and minor subdivision hardware items*, fringe area communities' impose equal or less stringent subdivision requirements.

This is not true in the case of *major capital facility development*, however. Developing municipalities require developer participation in major system initiation, significantly more often than is the case for developed communities. This is demonstrated overtly in far higher required participation in off-site street, sewer, drainage and water improvements and in land dedication requirements for schools. It is a much more covert activity in their requirement of more frequent participation in the installation of underground utilities and in the payment of much higher sewer tap-in fees. Further, currently developed communities are not now in the position of having imposed these provisions in the past and once matured to full development, having rescinded them. Rather, for the most part, when currently developed communities were developing, today's, rather than tomorrow's residents bore the cost of community capital infrastructure expansions. Today's currently developing communities have a different philosophy—tomorrow's residents bear an up-front share of current and future capital expansion.

Developers converting raw land in fringe areas are thus not necessarily plagued with: severe requirements for right-of-way and pavement widths, street signs and lighting or shade tree requirements, excessive requirements for curbs and gutters and sidewalks, or manhole and fire-hydrant spacing, water main and sewer diameters, etc., rather they are faced with very heavy participatory requirements in municipal capital facility initiation or upgrading.

DEVELOPING COMMUNITIES AND INDUSTRY—WIDE STANDARDS

A further question to be asked in terms of zoning and subdivision standards in developing communities is, how does field practice compare with standards which have been developed by professional organizations, housing support agencies and trade associations?

Exhibit 4 presents selected zoning and subdivision standards from the American Society of Civil Engineers (ASCE), U.S. Department of Housing and Urban Development, American Planning Association (formerly ASPO), American Public Health Association, Urban Land Institute, Twin Cities Metro Council and others.[10] It should be noted that there is presently a reasonable amount of disagreement as to level of specificity of and the level of "standards" themselves in the several alternative field sources. For instance, for local streets, curbs and gutters may be required or optional, replaced by grassed drainage swales or by asphalt surfaces with graded edges. Further, there is an increasing tendency to move away form explicit specifications of standards in favor of ranges of standards (depending upon desired density, location or geographic area, etc.) or more general statements of the type "what is deemed appropriate by the municipal engineer" or "in accordance with good design practices." Finally, the level of generality frequently increases when one moves from engineering to planning design criteria, i.e., from specification of sidewalk width to whether or not sidewalks should be part of the neighborhood fabric at all.

EXHIBIT 4

ZONING AND SUBDIVISION CONTROL DESIGN STANDARDS
TABULATIONS OF PROFESSIONAL GROUPS, TRADE ASSOCIATIONS, HOUSING SUPPORT AGENCIES

	ICMA[1]	ULI[2]	APHA[3]	KOPPELMAN/ DECHIRA[4]	METRO COUNCIL	SUBURBAN ACTION	HUD
A. Minimum Lot Size (Single-Family) 3 Persons, 3 BR.	7500 ft²	1-5 Units/Acre	5-7 Units/Acre	5000-40,000 ft²	6000 ft²	5-7 Units/Acre	7500 ft²
B. Minimum Lot Width (Single-Family) 3 Persons, 3 BR.	60 ft						60 ft

	ICBD[8]	BOCA[9]	APHA	SOUTHERN[10]	METRO COUNCIL	WISCONSIN[11] REGIONAL PLAN	HUD
C. Minimum Floor Area (Single-Family) 3 Persons, 3 BR.	330 ft²	450 ft²	450 ft²	450 ft²	700 ft²	700 ft²	640 ft²

	ULI	APHA	KOPPELMAN/ DECHIRA	SUBURBAN ACTION	METRO COUNCIL
D. Permissible Housing Types - Densities					
Row Houses	6-14 Units/Acre	16-19 Units/Acre	1000-2000 ft²	8-12 Units/Acre	
Garden Apts.	15-20 Units/Acre	25-30 Units/Acre	500-8000 ft²	20-45 Units/Acre	Up to 20/Acre

SUBDIVISION CONTROL

	ASCE[12]	APA(ASPO)[13]	METRO COUNCIL	HUD
A. Streets				
Rights of Way				
Collector	—	60 ft.	60 ft.	Present & Future Road Widenings
Local	—	50 ft.	50 ft.	—
Pavement Width				
Collector	26 ft	32 ft.	36 ft.	34 ft.
Local	—	50 ft.	30 ft.	—
Cul-de-sac				
Diameter	80 ft.	25 ft. (Radius)	50 ft.	80 ft.
Length		Not 7500 ft.	—	Not 7500 ft.

EXHIBIT 4 (CONTINUED)

SUBDIVISION CONTROL	ASCE[12]	APA(ASPO)[13]	METRO COUNCIL	HUD
B. Streetscape				
Signs	–	$50/Sign	–	–
Lighting	–	Req. (Local Eng.)	–	–
C. Street Hardware				
Curbs/Gutters	Grass Drainage Swales	–	No	Grass Drainage Swales
Sidewalks	None (80 ft. Lot	–	No	If Pedestrian Safety Requires
Sidewalk Width	4 ft	–	–	4 ft.
Block Length	–	–	–	–
D. Sewerage				
Septic Tanks Permitted	–	–	–	No Statement
Sanitary Sewer Pipe (Min. Diam.)	–	6 ft	6 ft.	–
E. Drainage				
Manhole Spacing	500 ft.	–	400 ft. +	At Optimum Intervals
Storm Sewer Pipe (Min. Diam.)	12 in.	–	–	Not less than 15 in.
F. Water Facilities				
Water Main (Min Diam.)	6 ft.	6 in.	6 in.	–
Fire Hydrant Interval	–	–	–	–

Notes: 1-14, see footnote 10.
Source: Rutgers University, Center for Urban Policy Research, Spring 1979.

Zoning. Recommended field standards for zoning—minimum lot size and frontage and minimum building sizes may be found in a variety of sources. *HUD's Minimum Property Standards, ULI's Community Builder's Handbook, ICMA's Principles and Practices of Urban Planning,*[11] publications from Twin Cities Metro Council and so on.

While there are great numbers of partitions by which the information is presented (attached or detached dwelling, number of persons occupying unit, etc.) for a single-family home, recommended minimum lot size frequently falls between 6,000-8,000 square feet, frontages between 50-70 feet and minimum building size from 500-700 square feet. For single-family attached and multifamily dwellings, recommended densities for townhouses range between 12 and 20 units per acre and for garden apartments between 16 and 30 units.

Viewing this range of standards, it is clear that the zoning ordinances of *both* developed and developing communities specify minimum lot and building dimensions far in excess of the trade associations tabulated in Exhibit 4. The better suburban zoning ordinances lag recommended minimums by at least 2:1. This is true for both lot and building sizes. Further, in the few cases where these zoning ordinances allow row houses or multifamily development, permitted densities again are about one-half what is recommended by the trade associations, professional groups or housing support agencies.

An apparently glaring omission from any of the sources of standards is guidelines to communities on the types of residential zones that should be included in ordinances given the community's size, development pace, etc. While there is great detail on densities for types of zones, if present locally, there is almost no listing of what residential zones should be present. Thus, the high potential for the exclusion of multifamily zones from suburban communities remains unchallenged.

Subdivision Control. What is apparent from the comparison of subdivision standards is that on most *major/minor hardware items* practice is in step with professional groups' industry-wide, minimum specifications. For instance, developing communities' required minimums for rights-of-way, pavement width, cul-de-sac radius and length are not too dissimilar from APA (ASPO) *Model Subdivision Regulations,* HUD *Minimum Property Standards*[12] and the Metro Council's recommended minimums. Sewer diameters, water main diameters, sidewalk widths, manhole spacing, fire hydrant intervals, again, for the most part, are on a par with what is suggested as reasonable by AFCE, APA, or the Metro Council.

For *neighborhood design requirements*, (i.e., whether or not to require sidewalks, curbs and gutters, shade trees, etc.), the ASCE/HUD and APA (ASPO) seem to span what is found in the field— ASCE/HUD having minimum requirements somewhat less than what is present in the average developing community's zoning and subdivision ordinances, APA (ASPO) requiring as high or slightly higher than standards at about the same level what is found in this type of community. Little mention is made at all in any of the industry-wide publications as to who should bear the responsibility of off-site improvements or local capital facility expansions. AFCE, HUD, APA do not address this issue directly. As a matter of fact, HUD's *Minimum Property Standards* fail to address the issue of minimum sanitary sewer requirements at all—i.e., whether or not spetic tanks are permitted or if new development must tie into the existing sewer system. Inferences are made in HUD's *Manual of Acceptance Practices* that sewering will be "to the level of what is currently in force locally"—flimsy guidance at best.

ENVIRONMENTAL CONTROLS

The environmental "requirements" that will be touched on in this section are those controls that directly affect the local development process such as: local and state environmental impact requirements (little, mini-NEPAs), State Coastal Zone Programs, critical area legislation (Wetlands, Floodplain Acts),[13] Clear Air Act (as amended 1977) and the Federal Water Pollution Control Act Amendments of 1972.

The presence of these programs in developing or fringe areas versus mostly developed areas varies considerably by program. Developing areas tend to be confronted with development requirements associated with critical area or Coastal Zone Programs; developed areas with those emanating from local compliance with Clear Air or Water Pollution Control Acts. There is also significant regional variation in the imposition of environmental controls as is evidenced by the percentage of developments being impacted in the Southern part of the country at only one-half the rate of those impacted in Western regions.

The impact of environmental control programs on local development is seen primarily in four areas: (1) impact statement costs, (2) permitting costs, (3) increased land costs due to reduced supply and (4) development delay and/or denial associated with procedural compliance. In the few empirical analyses that have been undertaken to date, by far the largest segments of the cost of environmental

regulation are those associated with the delay and denial of development. For the most part, these costs are the subject of other papers
to be presented at this conference. Even so, *aggregate* costs associated
with most of environmental controls have been found to affect the
cost of a single-family home by only 1-4 percent nationally.[14]

A common thread of many of the environmental programs is a
requirement to file an environmental impact statement. Frequently,
a derivative of the original NEPA format, environmental impact
statements are required for both *state* public and publicly-permitted,
private development acts in approximately 40 states. To varying
degrees, this requirement has filtered down and now affects *local*
public and publicly-permitted, private development acts.[15] In the
sample of communities, developing or fringe communities imposed
a local environmental impact statement requirement or mandated
environmental review in two-thirds of the cases—three times the rate
of developed communities. In most instances, the requirement called
for very general descriptive information concerning native wildlife
and vegetation as well as site specific information on potential
environmental degradation if the project was to be implemented.

Another frequent byproduct of environmental controls is development alteration consistent with conservation goals of a protected
area. Local developers responding to a survey by the Center for
Urban Policy Research in 1976,[16] indicated that the two most
frequent effects of critical area controls were density reductions
(in many cases linked to the inclusion of more recreation and open
space) and structure siting alterations.

In the latter case, if a sketch plat was required and agreement
could be reached on siting requirements at this point, the necessity
for major siting changes was greatly reduced. In the former case, in
many instances, it was unclear whether the required density alteration was from an explicit standard or from a negotiable range which
the developer had initially interpreted to his own advantage.

ENVIRONMENTAL CONTROLS IN TODAY'S POLITICAL ENVIRONMENT

Since the beginning of the energy crisis, the environment as an
issue, has been in retreat. A general consciousness on the part of the
public to the reality of limited resources has caused a backlash
against any force delaying or denying the consumer material goods.
Reduced price housing, denied to a potential consumer by excessive
environmental requirements, is causing these requirements to be
viewed with a caustic eye.

This situation and other reasons have caused the Council on Environmental Quality to significantly revise the environmental impact format.[17] Revisons call for an EIS of no more than 50 pages, one which presents 3 to 4 alternatives up-front and allocates to each equal coverage, and finally, one which is heavily analytical and geared to environmental issues which have been agreed upon beforehand as the most important local concerns. Thus the new "standard" of the field is a no-nonsense, streamlined EIS, sensitive to the potential cost-inducing aspects of impact analysis.

The scope of the action to be viewed by the EIS also is changing. HUD's EIS requirements are moving away from project by project assessments, to areawide (neighborhood) analysis, to comprehensive plan (entire community) EISs. Further, the idea that the project EIS should present only site-specific information not on hand as a result of a community-wide Natural Resource Inventory (NRI) is finally emerging in the form of formal governmental policy changes. The burden appears to be shifting from the developer to both the community and the developer. The community must environmentally plan through areawide EISs or Natural Resource Inventories; the developer must augment this general information with specific detail for the particular site that is being developed. This change in philosophy also should carry with it accompying cost reductions.

A new cost-conscious standard likewise is affecting critical area and Coastal Zone environmental requirements. A study, completed by the Real Estate Research Corporation for the Office of Coastal Zone Management, acknowledged the necessity, within the Coastal Zone, to insure that housing potential of inclusive land is not indiscriminantly eliminated.

Innovative zoning measures such as cluster provisions, PUD, TDR are proposed for use in the Coastal Zone to maintain density levels which contribute to the potential for reduced-cost housing. Thus, where feasible, Coastal Zone environmental controls' impact on housing will be to provide guidelines on where housing is permitted and how it should be sited rather than to reduce the quantity of housing or eliminate it entirely.

In sum, the *design* requirements of environmental controls are not sufficiently extensive or abusive to cause great concern. Further, in-house (agency) evaluations have produced, for the most part, a new generation of control sensitive to housing cost reduction.

CONCLUSIONS

The design standard "problem" of fringe communities is *not* uniform across the major subsets of land use regulation. Fringe or developing communities have more severe zoning design standards (minimum lot and structure dimensions) than developed communities and both developing and developed communities have more severe requirements than the various professional or trade associations indicate as adequate.

By far, the most acute problem is not lot and structure dimensions or lack of innovative development alternatives (PUD, cluster provisions, etc.), but rather the exclusion within the zoning plans of developing communities, of multifamily development as of right. Very few suburban zoning ordinances provide for zones of developable land to be converted to multifamily use. An additional problem area is the existing density maximums in the few communities whose ordinances permit multifamily development. For both row house and low-rise-multifamily development, existing communities (developing and developed) typically allow only 50 percent of what is specified as reasonable by the various trade standards. Similarly, very few sources of standards explicitly recommend the inclusion of multifamily zones in the zoning regulations of developing communities. This is the area in which there lies the greatest potential for housing cost savings—yet one which remains virtually untouched by public policy initiatives.

Subdivision design regulations of developing communities, especially those which relate to major and minor engineering-type hardware, do not seem to be as restrictive as the zoning ordinances of these communities. Standards for developing communities for rights-of-way and pavement widths, sidewalk widths, water main and sewer pipe diameters, etc., are generally on a par with *both* those of developed communities when the ruralness of the community clearly dictates reduced need for an extensive development infrastructure.

Yet, in subdivision control, there is also an acute problem which again is not addressed within the confines of most recommended standards. This is the issue of required off-site improvements or contributions to municipal capital facility expansion. Developing communities are characterized by imposing extensive off-site road, water, sewer and drainage requirements on the developer as well as land dedication mandates for public school construction. Thus, for the most part, a developer can anticipate relatively reasonable on-site subdivision requirements in the suburbs—what he must deal with in terms of uncertainty and additional costs are the required off-site improvements and/or capital infrastructure contributions.

Environmental controls seem to be more of a delay and denial development problem than one of excessive standards. While fringe communities impose more environmental controls than developed areas, new federal standards show significant potential for cost reduction.

III. A Blueprint For State and Local Action

The previous section of this paper attempted to order and prioritize what is loosely called the suburban, land use control design problem. The purpose of this section is to use these results in molding a framework for meliorative governmental action—both state and regional and local.

The two levels of governmental action may be looked upon not only as broader and narrower substantive focus but also as a procedural partitioning—i.e., (1) encouraging to do or providing guidance on how to do (state) and (2) actually doing it (local).

NECESSARY STATE/REGIONAL ACTIONS

In theory, state government is sovereign with respect to land use control. Local jurisdictions are creatures of the state and exercise land regulations at its pleasure. In practice, most states have allowed localities considerable latitude in formulating land use policy. They have enacted enabling legislation authorizing local units of government to control development through such means as zoning and subdivision regulations. While states nominally had the authority and obligation to review whether or not the local controls conformed with enabling legislation and indeed served the public welfare, in practice they assumed a hands-off attitude; local regulations were imbued with the classic statutory and administrative presumption of validity.

Regional agencies, such as Councils of Government (COGs), have also generally been very passive with respect to local land use controls. The 1960s and 1970s saw a proliferation of regional planning entities and a general strengthening of county planning boards. These two levels of planning grew in power as they assumed and were assigned development review obligations, most prominently as designated

A-95 clearinghouses. While regional agencies have the right, and in certain instances the obligation, to review local land use ordinances, this became an essentially perfunctory task.

Stronger state and regional agency intervention is needed to induce similarity of objective between various governmental levels' development plans. The keynote of such a strategy is the preparation of a state and regional agency development plan.

Background Studies to and the Preparation of a State/Regional Agency Development Plan. The Standard Zoning Enabling Act requires that zoning should be "in accordance with a comprehensive plan." In practice, the "rational" sequence of ordering objectives, then summarizing the results of these objectives into a comprehensive plan to guide the formulation of local land use controls, has not been followed. The disjointed planning-zoning relationship is aptly portrayed by overrestrictive local zoning and subdivision regulations which ultimately forbid entrance to the community to population groups for whom the master plan is attempting to provide. Communities may not allow multifamily development and may require excessive minimum building size—two areas of price increasing government regulation—yet a goal of the master plan is to provide for the housing needs of the community's young and old populations.

States should require that: (1) communities engage in planning and, (2) that local land use regulations flow from and attempt to implement the objectives of their comprehensive plans. To ensure that this requirement does not merely result in a paper exercise, states should attempt to guide the local planning and land use control process by preparing a state development plan or at least the land use element of such a plan. The development plan would be based on empirical analyses. States should prepare extensive background studies considering future population and employment growth, environmental constraints for critical areas and socioeconomic factors such as reducing the journey-to-work, providing lower cost housing proximate to employment modes, maximizing existing capital facility infrastructures, etc.

The recommendation that a state development plan be prepared is not meant to add a new overlay of regulations which would further complicate the development process, nor is it designed to increase unrealistically the workload of state planning agencies. This state development framework is viewed as a broad set of guidelines recommending corridors of short-, medium- and long-range growth as well as areas to remain in their national state in perpetuity. It would provide development density ranges for specific growth centers depending upon local employment growth, their location, holding capacity, etc. States are currently required by HUD Section 701 Comprehensive Planning Grants to prepare a land use element of the comprehensive plan, albeit many have only begun to satisfy this provision. The land use plan can serve as the "hard product" of a state development framework. Local units of government would be required to consider these state frameworks in their own planning activities and derivative land use controls.

Establish State/Regional Positions on: (1) Recommended Inclusive Housing Types to Achieve Density Goals; (2) Who Should Pay for What Capital Improvements, When; (3) Reduced Development Design Standards to Achieve Lower Cost Housing.

(1) Recommend Inclusive Housing Types to Achieve Density Goals. What was obvious from the foregoing analyses was an absence of multifamily housing from the bulk of developing communities' zoning ordinances. Multifamily units are critical elements in the production of reduced cost housing. They are ideal for occupancy by young and old, childless households, groups which currently exhibit the greatest housing needs in terms of number of households to be satisfied. Yet, suburban communities inherently shy away from this type of housing development. They must be shown by some upper level agency responsible for coordinating development of greater scope than that which is taking place in a single community, what their specific role is in achieving regional and state housing needs and what housing types must be included in their ordinances to fulfill this role.

(2) Who Should Pay, for What Capital Improvements, When? The question of who bears the costs of local capital infrastructure development and improvement is also an integral element of any program to provide for reduced cost housing. In subdivision regulation, the developer is not being "hurt" by overdesign in requirements for a community's basic hardware items, rather his pain is evident in reaction to mandated capital facility contributions. These costs are passed on directly to the new housing consumer both initially, in the form of sales price, and later, in recurring monthly housing costs. The state, within overall objectives for capital facilities planning, must assign responsibility to various echelons of government including procedures which will be used to finance these major additions.

(3) Reduced Development Design Standards to Achieve Lower Cost Housing. The state should review various trade and professional group design standards and develop a set of zoning, subdivision and environmental design standards that reflect the most current ideas that simultaneously provide for reduced cost housing while ensuring acceptable standards of community development. Potential sources to be reviewed are: HUD's *Minimum Property Standards* (Single-family and Multifamily), APA's *Model Subdivision Regulations*, Twin Cities Metropolitan Council's *Modest Cost Housing Standards*, ASCE's *Development Standards*, etc.

A simple list of the type included in Exhibit 5 should be promulgated and distributed to communities in zones of designated short- and medium-range growth. This list will alert developing communities to existing overdesign and to the degree that overdesign exists, provide them with a shopping list of necessary areas of ordinance review.

Reduce Fiscal Incentives for Community Overdesign; Establish Fair Share Measures to Provide Pressure for Design Standard Changes. States and regions must look to revenue sources other than the local real property tax to finance public servicing obligations. In the absence of such revenue shifts, tax base sharing must be implemented to more evenly distribute property tax rewards. These types of measures remove fiscal zoning as a rationale for the imposition of severe local design standards.

Most suburban communities would willingly leave the underhoused in central cities. It has been pointed out, however, that to achieve real capital gains in owned housing, moderate income families must participate in the preferred suburban housing market. Fair Share and other allocation and redistribution strategies serve this end. They should be implemented to establish a push force to local communities to provide an adequate share of lower-cost housing within their geographic bounds.

Require State and Local Environmental Impact Statements to Conform to New CEQ Guidelines for Federal Agencies; Encourage Community-Wide NRIs and Site Specific EISs; Require Critical Area Implementation Efforts to be Sensitive to Housing Needs Within Their Area of Concern.

Streamlined CEQ guidelines now affecting federal EIS submissions should be adopted at state and local levels. The new abbreviated, analytical EIS, dealing with only important local environmental issues, should be used for project level impact evaluations. In addition, states should encourage both areawide EISs and communitywide

EXHIBIT 5

COMMUNITY GUIDE TO POTENTIAL OVERDESIGN IN LOCAL LAND USE CONTROLS (NUMEROUS "NO" RESPONSES INDICATE PROBABLE LOCAL OVERDESIGN)

	Yes (Check)	No

I. **ZONING ORDINANCE**
Does your community permit/acknowledge:

Lot size/width—building size

A. Lot sizes of less than 7500 feet? ___ ___
B. Frontages of less than 60 feet? ___ ___
C. Single-family building size of less than 700 feet? ___ ___

Permissible Housing Types

A. Multifamily development as of right? ___ ___
B. Garden apartment densities of 20-40 units per acre? ___ ___
C. Cluster or PUD development as special exceptions or permitted uses? ___ ___

II. **SUBDIVISION REGULATIONS**
Does your community permit/acknowledge:

Streets

A. Local road rights-of-way of less than 50 feet? ___ ___
B. Local road pavement widths of less than 30 feet? ___ ___
C. Cul-de-sac minimum diameters of larger than 80 feet? ___ ___
D. Municipal responsibility for provision of off-site road improvements? ___ ___

Streetscape

A. Municipal responsibility for provision of street signs, street lighting and shade trees? ___ ___

Street Hardware

A. Grass drainage swales or asphalt w/raised edges in place of curbs and gutters for local roads? ___ ___
B. No sidewalks or sidewalks on only one side of the street? ___ ___
C. Sidewalk widths of 4 feet or less? ___ ___
D. Block lengths longer than 800 feet? ___ ___

EXHIBIT 5 (CONTINUED)

Sewerage

A. Septic tanks where sanitary sewer connec-
     tions are costly or not feasible?   ———   ———
B. Sewer connection pipes of less than 8 inches?   ———   ———
C. Sewer tap-in fees of less than $50?   ———   ———
D. Municipal responsibility for provision of
     off-site sewerage facilities?   ———   ———

Drainage/Storm Sewers

A. Municipal responsibility for provision of
     off-site storm/drainage improvements?   ———   ———
B. Manhole spacing of greater than 500 feet?   ———   ———

Water Facilities

A. Water main diameters of 6 inches or less?   ———   ———
B. Fire hydrant intervals of greater than 500 feet?   ———   ———
C. Municipal responsibility for provision of
     off-site water facilities?   ———   ———

Public Utilities

A. Above-ground utility installation?   ———   ———

Land Dedication

A. Municipal responsibility for provision
     of open space/recreation purposes?   ———   ———
B. Municipal responsibility for provision
     of land for government (non-school)
     facilities?   ———   ———
C. Municipal responsibility for provision
     of land for schools?   ———   ———

III. ENVIRONMENTAL CONTROLS
      Does your community permit/acknowledge?

A. Analytic EISs or less than 50 pages on mutually
     agreed-upon environmental issues?   ———   ———
B. EISs which satisfy local as well as regional
     or state EIS requirements?   ———   ———
C. Density increases in segments of the coastal
     zone immediately peripheral to designated
     critical areas?   ———   ———
D. Transfer of development rights to outside
     of the coastal zone?   ———   ———

Source: Rutgers University, Center for Urban Policy Research (Spring 1979).

NRIs. This will reduce the number of EIS submitted and allow the EIS to contribute site specific information to a community in which environmental planning already exists.

National Coastal Zone initiatives to simultaneously house people and maintain sensitivity to critical environmental areas should be encouraged. Innovative development modes (PUD, Cluster, etc.) which do not impact severely on fragile lands yet maintain the density of development should be emphasized.

NECESSARY LOCAL ACTIONS

The following is a laundry list for local communities desiring to ensure against overspecification of local development regulations:

1. Review local ordinances to ensure that they include housing types which support both regional and state housing goals.
2. Eliminate developer contributions to capital infrastructure if other than development residents will benefit from required improvements.
3. Compare local development regulation standards with state or professional group guidelines for modest-cost housing.
4. Provide incentives (increased density) to developers willing to build modest-cost houisng.
5. Undertake community-wide NRIs or comprehensive plan EISs to minimize the scope of project level EISs.
6. Attempt to link planning and environmental and fiscal objectives via integrated land use controls such as those in impact zoning.
7. Consider national demographic changes which suggest revisions in local housing and land use policy.
8. Periodically review recommendations stated above.

IV. Illustrations of Design Mitigation Program Initiatives Which Exist Nationally

STATE/REGIONAL ACTIVITIES

State Development Plan Background Studies Relating to Design Issues. The last decade has witnessed a new range and intensity of state planning. This blossoming has been discussed in such recent publications as *State Planning: Intergovernmental Policy Coordination, Land Use and the States, State Land Use Activity* and *Land-State Alternatives for Planning and Management.*[18] These reports reveal that most states are already engaging in economic, population, environmental and social analyses which can serve as key empirical base documents in considering design issues. Maryland, for example, has formulated mathematical models showing the relationship between employment opportunities and change in population. These models have been used to project the magnitude and distribution of population in five-year increments to the year 2000. Maryland also has established an automated geographic information system indicating key environmental features, existing land uses and the extant transportation and untility infrastructure.

New Jersey has a long history of preparing background studies to its twenty-year State Housing Plan. Since the early 1970s it has developed and refined economic-population models and has made long-range, economic-demographic projections in such publications as *New Jersey 1980* and *New Jersey Toward the Year 2000*.[19] The State Department of Community Affairs (DCA) conducted one of the first state-wide inventories of existing land use controls, e.g., lot size-frontage and minimum house requirements, extent of multi-family zones, etc. DCA has also repeatedly projected the housing need for all 576 municipalities in the State. These allocations incorporated such factors as extant local housing deterioration and the goal of providing housing proximate to employment centers. DCA, with the State Department of Environmental Protection and Office of Coastal Zone Management has mapped environmentally precarious areas, e.g., wetlands, floodplains, etc. All these analyses were considered in the formulation of the New Jersey Comprehensive Guide Plan.

Most often states already conduct many of the socioeconomic and environmental background studies discussed above.

Planning-Zoning Consistency. Numerous jurisdictions require local planning mandate that the land use regulations which are adopted be consistent with locally-derived and upper level planning objectives. To illustrate, California requires that cities and counties prepare a plan which includes housing, land use and open space considerations.[20] Zoning must be consistent with the goals of the adopted local plan. The California Land Use Law mandates that the "various land uses authorized by the (zoning) ordinance be compatible with the objectives, policies, general land uses and programs specified in such a plan."

Other states have similar legislation. The Local Government Comprehensive Planning Act[21] requires Florida communities to plan and to consider both mandatory and optional state objectives. (Provision of low- and moderate-income housing is a mandatory state objective.) The Act also requires that development by government agencies and local land use regulations "be consistent with the adopted plan." The New Jersey Municipal Land Use Law[22] requires the preparation of a master plan. The plan is not merely a referral document but is supposed to be a current basis for local zoning and planning regulations. It must be periodically updated every six years and must contain a policy statement indicating its relationship to: (1) the land uses of contiguous municipalities; (2) the master plan of the county in which the municipality is located and; (3) the State Comprehensive Guide Plan—a document recommending various growth strategies for different regions of the State.

Some of these reforms have been inspired by the ALI's *Model Land Development Code*.[23] The code emphasizes planning; in Fred Bosselman's view the new proposals are consistent with the growing dissatisfaction with the "tranditional concept of the plan as an advising document with no legal effect."[24] It is important to note, however, that the ALI code does *not* require municipalities to base land use controls on local land development plans. The code offers certain incentives to communities that do, but the bonsuses offered (e.g., the power to allow PUDs, to develop "precise plans" and to acquire land for such precise plans) are not very alluring. Moreover, as pointed out by George Raymond,[25] the code might discourage localities from adopting a plan, for once they undertake such an action all of their land use policies are subject to state review; not accepting a plan would limit state adjudication only to "critical areas."

Formulating a State Development Plan. Requiring planning-zoning consistency offers the advantage of more "rational" and orderly land use controls but numerous states have felt it necessary to additionally influence the pace and direction of development by adopting state development plans. Most common are state plans which are not binding but rather serve as a device to communicate where the state believes different types and intensity of development should occur. (These are termed by Healy as "guider plan" approaches.)[26] Connecticut's State Plan for Conservation and Development is one such example. It specifies areas deemed most suitable for open space, limited development, or more intense urban development, taking into consideration such restraints as the water and sewer infrastructure and desired future land use relationships. The plan is directed at state agencies, local units of government and private developers. Connecticut attempts to use "moral suasion and wide publicity" to induce compliance—the plan is not binding. The recently published New Jersey Comprehensive Guide Plan similarly identified corridors of development and areas recommended for light or nonuse such as the State's environmentally fragile Pinelands. As noted, communities are required to consider the Guide Plan in formulating their own master plan.

In a very few cases the state development plan or framework is more than just an advisory document. Oregon's Land Use Law[27] requires that cities and counties prepare a comprehensive plan and that local and county zoning, subdivision and other regulations be designed to implement the plan. A State Land Conservation and Development Commission is also authorized. The Commission establishes statewide planning goals and guidelines, taking into consideration such factors as the location of public facilities and critical environmental areas, e.g., wetland or floodplains.[28] The Commission then reviews state, city, county and special district comprehensive plans and land use controls to see if they comply with the state criteria. If they do not, the Commission may prescribe and modify such plans and controls.

Some regional agencies have also formulated development plans. The Twin Cities Metropolitan Council is mandated by Minnesota Law to prepare comprehensive guides which "consist of a compilation of policy statements, goals, standards, programs and maps prescribing guides for an orderly economic development, public or private, of the metropolitan area."[29] The Metropolitan Council has responded to this charge by preparing and refining the Metropolitan Development Guide.[30] The Guide delineates a Metropolitan Urban Service Area (MUSA) as the region within which residential development is actively encouraged. All communities within MUSA are given the responsibility for providing housing to satisfy both local need and the needs of "persons of a range of incomes." The Guide additionally specifies different development strategies for the subareas within MUSA (e.g., center cities, fully developed suburbs, areas of planned urbanization, freestanding growth centers, etc.) in terms of what type of housing and land use policies should be emphasized.

The Development Guide has served as a working document. The Council's housing strategies, such as fair share, have been encorporated into the plan and the Gude is used for reviewing applications under the A-95 procedure. The Guide even serves as the framework which the Metropolitan Council uses to review local and county comprehensive plans as required by Minnesota's 1976 Metropolitan Land Planning Act.

State Development Plans and Design Standards. While state development plans have not formally specified specific local design standards, some states have recommended less stringent but still reasonable regulations. Florida, for example, recently published *Reducing Housing Costs* which suggested:[31] (1) allowing higher density zoning, e.g., PUDs and accepting smaller houses with fewer amenities; (2) reducing subdivision standards for roads, utility line installation, curbs and gutters and sidewalks; and (3) encouraging cluster development with cul-de-sacs and loop streets which reduce lot costs.

New Jersey has published *A Guide for Residential*[32] *Design Review.* While this document focuses on specifying appropriate local procedural review of subdivision applications, it does suggest less stringent regulations. To illustrate, it indicates that single-family homes be permitted at densities as high as 8 units per acre, townhouses at densities of 12 units per acre, garden apartments at up to 30 units per acre and high-rise construction at 50 units per acre.

The Metropolitan Council has published recommended design standards to encourage "modest cost" housing. Its *Advisory Standards*[33] publication recommends that local ordinances should not: (1) require garages; (2) require lot sizes for single-family detached homes any larger than 6,000-8,000 square feet or a density of five-to-seven units per acre in all or portions of sewered communities; nor (3) include a house size requirement at all, since minimum house sizes are adequately provided for in the state building code (600-700 square feet for 2- and 3-bedroom, single-family homes).

IMPLEMENTATION MEASURES: FAIR SHARE

In recent years, several states and regional planning bodies have enacted fair share plans. Fair share has been fostered by numerous influences such as: (1) advocacy for and growth of regional responses to housing and land use problems; (2) attendant growing federal support for regional planning agencies, e.g., Councils of Government; and (3) support by courts in New Jersey, Pennsylvania, New York and other states for a "fair share" solution to eliminating exclusionary zoning.[34] Since 1974, fair share has been further encouraged by HUD's Housing Opportunity Plan (HOP) which authorizes the allocation of bonus Section 8 and Section 701 funds to jurisdictions with a HUD approved Housing Opportunity Plan—in effect a fair share system.

Two states, Massachusetts and New Jersey, have the most extensive fair share plans. Massachusetts' "anti-snob" zoning law was enacted in 1969.[35] While it did not allocate exact counts of housing for each local unit of government, it did establish minimum and maximum goals. The program operated through an appeals process. Sponsors of low and moderate housing would file a single comprehensive permit request with the local board. It was hoped that consolidation of the approval process would expedite construction of lower cost housing. In the event that the local board would reject the housing applications, the developer could appeal to the state board, the Housing Appeals Committee of the Department of Community Affairs. This committee reviews proposals and comes to a decision by balancing local planning objectives against regional need for low- and moderate-income housing. The Massachusetts statute requires the Committee to uphold a local board's rejection of a permit if the locality has met a statutory minimum production of low- and moderate-income housing.

New Jersey has the most extensive state fair share program. The state has allocated a total of 520,000 housing units to be built over a 12-year period. All 576 local jurisdictions are assigned a housing production goal. The local fair share is determined by taking into account such factors as local housing deterioration and population-employment growth.

The New Jersey courts have recognized fair share as an appropriate housing strategy and the state has attempted to foster implementation by issuing Executive Order 35[36] which links state aid to the level of local implementation of the housing allocation.

Numerous regional planning agencies have also enacted fair share strategies. Prominent examples include allocation plans developed by the Miami Valley Regional Planning Commission ("Dayton Plan"), the Metropolitan Twin Cities Council, Washington Council of Governments (COG) and Puget Sound COG.[37]

How have the allocations plans fared? Only a few, e.g., the Dayton Plan and the Metropolitan Council's effort, have achieved any notable success, albeit far from "opening up the suburbs." The limited success is due to several factors. The plans' allocations of specific numbers of units to local jurisdictions has troubled both the initiators of the strategies and those charged with enforcement (e.g., the courts) as being arbitrary. The focus of the fair share plans is another limiting trait. Most strategies allocate subsidized units only. This narrow purview limits the effectiveness of fair share, especially during periods of federal retrenchment of housing assistance. The enforcement of the fair share allocation is an often undefined or unaccepted obligation. Legislative and executive bodies usually have been hesitant to press for local adherence because of the plan's controversy and conflict with "home rule" sentiments. The courts also have clearly been uncomfortable in "legislating" or enforcing specific fair share plans.

IMPLEMENTATION MEASURES–FISCAL CHANGE

Since the 1960s, many states have substantially increased their intergovernmental assistance to municipalities and school districts, thereby lessening the local tax burden for support of public services. In some cases this change has been prompted by court decisions declaring the financing of schools from the local property tax to be unconstitutional. The *Serrano* decision in California and *Robinson*[38] decision in New Jersey forced both states to substantially increase their allocations to local schools. Other states, e.g., Connecticut and New York are currently under court order to implement similar reforms.

There are more limited instances of regional tax base sharing, a strategy which would similarly reduce the local fiscal pressures resulting from growth. A prominent example is Minnesota's Fiscal Disparities Bill.[39] Enacted in 1971, the bill guarantees every unit of government in the Twin Cities area a share of the total commercial-industrial tax base regardless of where future commercial and industrial growth occurs in the Twin Cities region. Under this plan, each community receives a share of the region's commercial-industrial ratables according to a prescribed formula. Wealthier communities with comparatively high property valuations receive smaller shares than their less affluent counterparts, and larger communities receive more aid than their smaller neighbors. In sum, the formula attempts to allocate to those areas with the most need.

These financing changes would reduce the fiscal pressures which have led communities to require large lot zoning and mandate that developers provide many utility and infrastructure improvements. The financial reform should also make localities more amenable to regional land use schemes, (e.g., fair share, adhering to a state regional land use plan), because regionalism no longer threatens a precarious local fiscal tax base. The existing fair share track record lends credence to the argument that allocation is more palatable when it does not cause a severe local fiscal hardship. Fair share's comparatively easy acceptance in Minneapolis-St. Paul and in the Greater Washington, D.C. area may be attributed, in part, to the fact that, in both areas, most schools costs are paid by extra-local bodies, such as counties. In contrast, one reason for vociferous opposition to regional allocation in New Jersey stems from that state's financing system, which places virtually the full school funding burden on localities.

It is important to realize, however, that increased state funding of local public services would not always eliminate the fiscal reasoning of exclusionary land use policies. For example, under many state school aid programs, affluent districts receive only a token flat grant per pupil. Moreover, the revised programs in states such as California and New Jersey actually reduce the assistance to many wealthy communities. These jurisdictions would have no incentive to allow less stringent land use controls and even might be tempted to require additional developer improvements to reduce the public servicing cost. A more fundamental drawback is that fiscal concerns are only one motivation for existing land use control. Other contributing forces include hostility to multifamily housing and a desire to retain a "rural" atmosphere by allowing only low density housing. Public financing reform does not address these influences on local design standards.

Other fiscal "stick and carrot" strategies, such as reducing state aid to communities who retain restrictive controls or offering additional assistance to cooperating localities perhaps offer greater potential, yet few jurisdictions have enacted or have forcefully implemented such measures. To illustrate, New Jersey's Executive Order 35 was not enforced and, in fact, led to resolutions for state constitutional changes to prohibit such executive actions.

The most potent fiscal stick strategy is offered by the A-95 review program. States and many regional planning agencies are A-95 clearinghouses and as such review local applications for federal aid. A negative comment by a clearinghouse does not automatically invalidate the grant proposal but may hinder or delay its acceptance. Some clearinghouses, such as the Metropolitan Council and MVRPC have effectively used their A-95 power to force local compliance with fair share and other land use reform efforts. Most clearinghouses, however, have declined to take what is clearly a controversial action.

LOCAL ACTIVITIES

Review Land Use Regulations and Provide for a Rational Basis for Zoning. There are some outstanding examples of communities attempting to determine how they will control growth and to search for an empirical, often environmental, basis for local controls. Medford Township, New Jersey, for example, prepared a natural resource inventory and a local capability analysis.[40] This "carrying capacity" study then served to guide preparation of a development control ordinance, a growth management plan and performance design standards.

Duxbury, Massachusetts has adopted the land use control strategy of "impact zoning." The technique relates land use demands to land use capacities, assesses the consequence of proposed land use changes, and provides a legislative and administrative framework for land use management.

Before adopting impact zoning, Duxbury had a minimum of one-acre zoning and a set of conventionally specified subdivision regulations. The community now allows a range of higher density housing (e.g., multifamily and attached single-family at densities of up to six units per acre) and also has adopted performance subdivision regulations. Developers have the right to negotiate with Duxbury concerning which improvements are needed in a specific project (e.g., street width, should sidewalks be provided? etc.) and also how improvement standards can best be met.

It is important to note, however, that while the impact and carrying capacity zoning allows flexible standards, it also sometimes increases developer "front-end" costs in terms of the time land must be held. Additional town-developer negotiations are often the norm and there is greater uncertainty concerning how and what types of development will be allowed. In sum, there is some question whether the potential savings from adopting "empirically based" standards is not offset from added expenditures arising from the more flexible but often less specific land use system.

To encourage less stringent local design standards, some states and regional planning agencies have suggested guidelines for local self-review of land use regulations. The Metropolitan Council has published the following guidelines:[41]

1. Have the cost impacts of the land use regulations been examined? Have the local requirements been compared to national model

codes and to the advisory standards recommended in this report? (Advisory Standards for Land Use Regulations).*

2. Do the zoning and subdivision requirements exceed the lot size, house size and garage standards recommended in this report? In all single-family zoning classifications?

3. If lot size and density exceed the standards, is the need for the local requirements identified as part of specific policy and planning determinations for the community? Are there unique soil, environmental, or planning considerations which require the higher standards?

4. Does the zoning ordinance require a minimum house or dwelling unit floor area? If so, has the community identified why a local requirement is necessary in view of the house size requirement in the Minnesota Uniform Building Code?

5. Does the zoning ordinance require garages for single-family homes? If so, why is this necessary to protect health, safety and welfare or carry out other intents of the community's zoning ordinances?

6. Are housing developers planning and building dwellings according to the minimum standards? Has interest been expressed by developers in building units on smaller lots or smaller homes than are permitted under the current requirements?

7. Are there a significant number of requests made for variances for these zoning and subdivision standards? Are such variances regularly granted for smaller lots, smaller homes or reduction in garage requirements?

8. Does the compreshensive plan contain policy relative to housing needs, costs, types and density?

9. Does the comprehensive plan call for a review or reaffirmation at specific intervals?

Implement Minimum Design Standards. Numerous communities have followed this strategy. As an example, Oshawa, Ontario has adopted lower standards for lot areas and setbacks and increased lot coverage in residential areas.[42] House size requirements were reduced from approximately 1,100 to 750 square feet. Lot size standards also were modified, e.g., townhouses could be built at densities of up to twenty units per acre as opposed to a previous density ceiling of about ten to fifteen per acre.

*See bibliography for full description.

The revised controls are an outgrowth of a study entitled, *Density, Liveability and Cost in Single-Family Detached Housing.*[43] This analysis evaluated the functional need and relationship between existing different design standards and recommended less stringent but still satisfactory zoning and subdivision criteria.[44]

Several communities in New Jersey have revised their land use controls in response to the *Mt. Laurel* (1973) and *Oakwood at Madison v. Township of Madison* (1977) decisions.[45] *Mt. Laurel* emphasized the municipal obligation to provide for a fair share of regional housing need. *Madison* stressed the obligation of developing municipalities to adjust their zoning regulations so as to not preclude the construction of "least cost" housing consistent with health and safety standards. The "least cost" concept establishes an obligation by communities to withdraw or modify stringent land use controls which unnecessarily increase the cost of housing. Such controls might include large lot size and house size requirements, prohibition and limitation of higher density or multifamily housing and unnecessary subdivision regulations.

There has been a cautious local reaction to *Mt. Laurel and Madison*; many communities are waiting further clarification by the courts. The changes in local design requirements have usually taken the form of (1) allowing Planned Unit Development as a special exception or permitted use; (2) permitting construction of single-family attached or condominium units; and (3) downzoning to allow limited construction of smaller single-family homes on reduced-size lots.

V. Design Standards: Bibliography

INTRODUCTION

    A. *Zoning and Subdivision Regulations: Housing Cost and Other Impacts*

    B. *Zoning and Subdivision Regulations: Background, Standards and Current Practice*

    C. *Environmental Controls: Housing Cost and Other Impacts*

    D. *Environmental Controls: Background and Current Practice*

    E. *Innovative Strategies: The Search for A More Effective and Equitable Land Use System*

Part A annotates selected significant studies focusing on how zoning and subdivision regulations influence the cost of housing and the housing delivery process. Part B supplements this discussion by listing important reports considering the evolution and inter-relationship of current design standards or recommending model zoning and subdivision criteria.

The bibliography on environmental controls is organized in an analogous fashion. Part C annotates significant studies considering how environmental impact statement, coastal zone and other environmental requirements affect housing cost. Part D cites reports, studies, etc. which summarize the history, evolution and inter-relationship of the various environmental controls.

Part E concludes the bibliography by providing citations of selected studies dealing with specific innovative land use strategies, such as impact, performance and inclusionary zoning, density bonuses and state and regional agency review of local land use controls.

A. ZONING AND SUBDIVISION REGULATIONS:
HOUSING COSTS AND OTHER IMPACTS

Boeck, Graydon R. *Residential Land Development, Planning, Utilities and Streets.* Report prepared for the Government Regulations Subcommittee, Modest Cost Housing Advisory Committee Minneapolis: Metropolitan Council, October 6, 1979.

Boeck examines existing zoning-subdivision regulations in the Twin Cities region and recommends less stringent but still satisfactory standards. For example, instead of requiring a minimum quarter-acre lot for single-family houses and such subdivision requirements as 80 foot street right of way and 44 foot street collector width, Boeck suggests that 7,500 square foot lots, 60 foot street right of way and 36 foot collector width standards be allowed. The revised criteria would reduce land and improvement costs from approximately $6,400 to $4,000 per lot.

This analysis is an "engineering" approach to examining zoning and subdivision regulations. The less stringent standards which are recommended are justified as being accepted by national regulatory bodies, e.g., professional engineers association, or by "proven" field experience. While limited in applicability to the Twin Cities area, Boeck's study is thorough and clearly attempts to specify what are excess land use control requirements and to what extent they inflate the cost of housing.

Lincoln, James R. J., Dean C. Coddington and John R. Penberty. *An Analysis of the Impact of State and Local Government Intervention in the Homebuilding Process in Colorado.* Denver, Colorado. Bickert, Brown, Coddington and Associates, April 1976.

Study examines regulartory cost impact in Colorado by considering nine case studies of housing development. The analysis concludes that between 1970-1975, new or more stringent government regulations increased the costs of a single-family home by $1,500 to $2,000—an inflation of 3 to 4 percent. Over half of the cost increase results from added site development expenditures, water sewer permit fees and land dedication fees. The remainder is the consequence of unnecessary construction standards and procedures, e.g., requiring smoke detectors and furnace air-intake ducts as a consequence of overrestrictive building codes.

Metropolitan Council. *Advisory Standards for the Land Use Regulation.* Minneapolis, Metropolitan Council of the Twin Cities; *Advisory Land Use Standards for Multifamily Housing.* Minneapolis Metropolitan Council of the Twin Cities, December 1978.

Both reports discuss the factors contributing to the high cost of housing and recommend less stringent local land use regulations. For single-family construction, the analyses suggest allowing a density of five to seven units per acre and eliminating garage requirements. For multifamily construction, the reports recommend allowing densities of up to twenty units per acre (where suitable); (2) not requiring the construction of garages; and (3) not requiring an excess of 1.5 off-street parking spaces per unit.

Both documents are designed to help convince and guide localities to revise their land use regulations to permit less expensive housing. They are the outgrowth of previous empirical investigations such as the *Modest-Cost Housing in the Twin Cities Metropolitan Area.*

Metropolitan Council, Modest-Cost Private Housing Advisory Committee. *Modest Cost Housing in the Twin Cities Metropolitan Area.* Minneapolis, January 15, 1977.

The Council considers the escalating cost of housing in the Twin Cities region and evaluates how government regulations can be modified to reduce housing costs. The main recommendations are to: (1) reduce zoning requirements to allow single-family homes on 7,500 square foot lots; (2) eliminate local building size requirements (building size would be regulated by the Minnesota Building Code— approximately 600 square feet for two-bedroom houses and 700 square feet for three-bedroom houses); and (3) eliminate local requirements for garages. The report estimates that allowing smaller lots could reduce costs by about $2,500 while eliminating garage requirements could save between $3,500 (one-car garage) to $4,750 (two-car garage). (The cost saving potential of eliminating local house size requirements are not specified.)

The Twin Cities report makes other recommendations to reduce costs including: (1) allowing more innovative building codes; (2) modifying public improvements and design specifications; (3) co-ordinating government regulations; (4) charging more reasonable fees; (5) providing incentives (e.g., additional state aid) to communities enacting cost sensitive land use regulations; and (6) having government units (state, county and local) absorb the costs for public improvements when the benefits are areawide.

This analysis is one of the most extensive discussions of strategies to reduce housing costs through allowing less stringent government regulations. It also contains a comprehensive appendix of minimum zoning standards recommended by several different national organizations.

Minnesota Housing Institute. *The Multiplicity of Factors that Contribute to the Cost of Housing.* Minneapolis, April 1974.

The Institute considers a hypothetical subdivision development and examines the cost impact of building codes, municipal charges and fees, land development costs, structural requirements and financing and real estate costs. State and local requirements are often determined to be excessive—not yielding benefits commensurate with the added costs.

The Institute also explores alternative regulatory modification models which offer potential cost savings. The models include variations of lot and house size, setback and frontage standards, ground preparation requirements and presence and absence of a garage. The monograph concludes that structure size is the most significant cost component, followed by land development standards and the presence and absence of a garage. It recommends adoption of less stringent public requirements (e.g., allowing higher density single-family construction).

Real Estate Research Corporation. *Home Construction Cost Increase: St. Louis, County, Mo.* Chicago: Real Estate Research Corporation, September 1975.

Study considers the 1970-75 increase in lot development and building costs in St. Louis County as a result of more stringent government regulations. It projects that new requirements for street lighting, greater collector street widths, higher permit and inspection fees, upgraded electrical systems, etc.; inflated typical tract single-family housing costs by $1,600 to $2,500—an increase of about 5 percent. The analysis does not, however, differentiate between "reasonable" and "excess" government regulations.

Regional Planning Council (Area Housing Council). *Development Regulations and Housing Costs.* Baltimore, September 1975.

The Area Housing Council, an advisory group to the Baltimore Regional Planning Council, examines procedural and substantive housing development requirements in the Baltimore region. This study, an update of the 1973 *Public Improvements Costs* analysis by the Planning Council, expands the earlier report by considering local review and approval procedures, e.g., permitting, sewer and EIS clearance requirements, in addition to subdivision standards. The report recommends simplifying and clarifying government regulations and eliminating repetitive activities.

Regional Planning Council. *Public Improvement Costs for Residential Land Development: A Comparison of Five Counties in the Baltimore Region.* Baltimore: Regional Planning Council, December 1973.

Report utilizes case studies and a "hypothetical building block approach" to detail varying land development requirements and costs for four housing types: low density single-family (one unit per acre);

higher density single-family (four units per acre); townhouses (eight units per acre); and garden apartments (sixteen units per acre). Land development costs include street, storm drain, water, sewer and streetscape improvements.

Land development costs in the five Baltimore Counties, range from $4,100 to $5,000 per unit for low density single-family construction; between $3,400 to $4,600 for higher density single-family projects; $1,900 to $2,500 for townhouses, and $660 to $1,100 for garden apartments.

The Area Council study is descriptive, specifying development expenditures resulting from all government regulations. It notes, however, frequent instances of higher standards which do not "bear any relationship to efficiency and safety considerations." The report recommends more uniform and reasonable public land development regulations.

Sternlieb, George and Lynne Sagalyn. *Zoning and Housing Costs.* New Brunswick, N.J.: Center for Urban Policy Research, Rutgers University, 1972.

Monograph examines the impact of various exclusionary land use controls upon housing costs. It concludes that public policy decisions pertaining to minimum zoning requirements are significant factors in explaining market value. The size of the house, directly affected by the minimum size regulation and indirectly conditioned by minimum lot size requirements, is the single most important factor explaining selling price variation. Lot size and lot frontage specifications are also highly significant. Subdivision regulations are not statistically significant in explaining price variation but the analysis notes that subdivision requirements decrease with increased local zoning standards, which themselves inflate housing costs.

Sternlieb and Sagalyn also consider the impact of allowing less stringent land use regulations. Reducing minimum single-family lot size from one acre to one-quarter acre, permitting 100 foot frontage (instead of 200 feet) and reducing minimum house size from 1,600 to 1,200 square feet would reduce the predicted selling price of a $45,000 single-family home to about $38,000—a saving of approximately 15 percent.

The Sternlieb-Sagalyn study is one of the first empirical investigations of the cost consequences of local zoning and subdivision regulations. It does not focus on "excess" regulations but rather illustrates the considerable affect of the full set of local controls on aggregate selling price.

Seidel, Stephen R. *Housing Costs and Government Regulations.* New Brunswick, N.J.: Rutgers University Center for Urban Policy Research, 1977.

See General Purposes Articles for overall description.

Chapter Seven and Eight and Ten and the Afterword of this study consider the housing cost impacts of excess zoning, subdivision and environmental controls. Seidel cites numerous cases of local design standards which are in excess of basic but acceptable criteria, e.g., quarter-lot size, sidewalks on one side of the street, etc. The influence of EIS, Coastal Zone and other environmental requirements are also traced.

Monograph estimates that excess zoning standards can increase single-family homes cost by about 6.4 percent ($3,200 in additional costs) and excess environmental requirements by .05 percent ($250 additional cost).

This analysis is one of the few attempts to define what is meant by the "excess costs of government regulations." These costs are divided into three categories: direct costs, the costs of delay and uncertainty and the costs of unnecessary or overrestrictive requirements. Seidel also summarizes most of the extant literature examining the costs and other implications of public land use controls.

U.S. General Accounting Office. *Why Are New House Prices So High, How Are They Influenced by Government Regulations, and Can Prices be Reduced.* Washington, D.C.: Government Printing Office, 1978.

See General Purpose Articles for overall description.

Report considers subdivision and zoning requirements in 87 communities and compares these to less expensive alternative criteria approved and recommended by HUD, other government agencies, or professional organizations. It identifies numerous excessive and cost-increasing requirements for site improvements, lot size, land dedication, municipal fees, subdivision review and approval processes. The most restrictive communities required standards which raised street and site improvement costs by as much as $2,700, required land dedications amounting to $850 per single-family home, imposed municipal fees as high as $3,300 per home and had local review and approval processes that took up to twenty-one months. Housing construction standards (as specified by building codes) were judged much less restrictive though still a factor inflating housing prices. There is little discussion of the rationale used to assign cost increases or to identify restrictive standards, however.

The analysis also notes that housing costs have increased as a result of: (1) market demand by buyers desiring larger homes with greater amenities; (2) the belief by builders that more expensive lots necessitate larger, more profitable homes; and (3) continued builder reliance on traditional construction materials and techniques because of preference, familiarity, or consumer demand. These hypotheses are also given only minimal empirical documentation, however.

The Comptroller General recommends that housing prices could be reduced by (1) initiating research to determine what type and size less expensive homes could be marketed; (2) offering tax incentive and other financial credits to builders offering less expensive homes; (3) exploring changes in capital tax gain treatment which might encourage purchase of such housing units; (4) establishing HUD approved land development standards; and (5) providing technical assistance.

U.S. Department of Housing and Urban Development. *Final Report of the Task Force on Housing Costs*, Washington, D.C.: Government Printing Office, 1970.

A very general policy-oriented report detailing potential corrective measures to mitigate increases in housing costs. The analysis first considers the macro forces affecting housing construction; housing industry cycles, national monetary policy, national tax policy, increasing government regulations, unstable money supply, constrained labor markets, resistance to innovation, special housing needs, utility charges, taxes and hazard insurance, and inadequate basic research. It then focuses on three substantive areas: (1) land supply and development; (2) building and technology; and (3) financing money markets and marketing.

The Task Force did not conduct original research but cites relevant current analyses. For example, in considering land availability, reference is made to a report by the ABA noting that 99 percent of the undeveloped land in the New York Metropolitan Area is restricted to single-family and that more than half of Connecticut's vacant land zoned for residential use is for minimum lots of one-to-two acres.

Extensive policy recommendations are made both to address the identified national macro problems (e.g., to review national monetary and tax policies affecting housing) and to meliorate the substantive deficienceis of land supply and development, building and technology, and financing. For instance, the Task Force recommends that more land could be made available through such actions as: (1) developing minimum standards for use by HUD in evaluating local land use controls; (2) developing technical information and advisory guidelines for local regional and state bodies; (3) encouraging sub-state regional councils to develop regional standards in land supply and land use relationships; and (4) supporting these compliance efforts through the disbursement of federal funds.

Weidenbaum, Murray L. "Government Regulations and the Cost of Housing" *Urban Land* Vol. 37, No. 2 (February 1978), pp. 4-5.

Article summarizes different studies specifying increasing housing costs as a result of government regulations. It recommends that (1) government use regulatory controls sparingly and with discretion; (2) developers should voluntarily respond with an improved building package; (3) interest groups must increase their sensitivity to economic factors; and (4) academic research should pursue the specific effect of the broad array of government controls.

B. ZONING AND SUBDIVISION REGULATIONS: BACKGROUND, STANDARDS AND CURRENT PRACTICE

American Public Health Association.
Planning the Neighborhood. Washington, D.C.: APHA, 1960.

American Society of Planning Officials.
Problems of Zoning and Land-Use Regulations. Washington, D.C.: Government Printing Office, 1968. (U.S. National Commission on Urban Problems, Research Report No. 2.)

———————————————.

Street Standards in Subdivision Regulations. Chicago, Ill: ASPO, February 1964. 12pp. (Planning Advisory Service Report No. 183.)

Babcock, Richard F.
The Zoning Game: Municipal Practices and Policies. Madison: University of Wisconsin Press, 1966.

Bergman, Edward M., *et al.*
External Validity of Policy-Related Research on Development Control and Housing Costs. The Center for Urban and Regional Studies, University of North Carolina, Chapel Hill, 1974.

Burns, Leland S. and Frank Mittelbach.
"Efficiency in the Housing Industry," The Report to the President's Committee on Urban Housing, Volume II, *Technical Studies.* Edgar F. Kaiser, Chairman. Washington, D.C.: Government Printing Office, 1968.

Construction Industry Research Board.
Development and Government Approval Process In California. 1976

County of Santa Clara, Planning Department.
Housing Development Cost as Influenced by Government Regulations and Fees: A Study of Four Cities in Santa Clara County. (HUD 701 Study No. 611974), 1974.

Crecine, John, Otto Davis and John Jackson.
"Urban Property Markets: Some Empirical Results and Their Implications for Municipal Zoning," Journal of Law and Economics 19 (1967), p. 76.

DeChiara, Joseph and Lee Koppelman.
Planning Design Criteria. New York: Von Nostrand Reinhold, 1969.

Florida Department of Community Affairs.
Reducing Housing Costs. (Technical Paper Series, No. 3), July 1977.

Freilich, Robert H and Peter S Levi.
Model Subdivision Regulations Text and Commentary. Chicago: American Society of Planning Officials, 1975.

Gaffrey, Mason.
Land as an Element of Housing Cost: The Effects of Public Policies and Practices. Institute for Defense Analysis, 1968.

Hirshon, Robert E.
"The Interrelationship Between Exclusionary Zoning and Exclusionary Subdivision Control," Journal of Law Reform (Winter 1972), pp. 351-360.

HUD, U.S. Department of,
Minimum Property Standards for One and Two-Family Dwellings.

James, Franklin Jr. and Oliver D. Windsor.
"Fiscal Zoning, Fiscal Reform, and Exclusionary Land Use Controls," Journal of American Institute of Planners (April 1976), pp. 130-141.

National Commission on Urban Problems.
"Land Use Controls: Zoning and Subdivision Regulations." in *Building the American City.* Washington, D.C.

National Association of Home Builders.
Cost Effective Site Planning—Single-Family Development, 1976.

——————————————————.

Fighting Excessive Government Regulations—An Information Kit. Washington, D.C., 1976.

——————————————————.

Impact of Government Regulations on Housing Costs: A Selected Annotated Bibliography. Washington, D.C.: NAHB, 1976.

Ohls, James, Richard Weisberg and Michelle White.
"The Effects of Zoning on Land Value," Journal of Law and Economics 17 (1974), p. 429.

Orange County, Cost of Housing Committee.
The Cost of Housing in Orange County, 1975.

President's Committee on Urban Housing. (Kaiser Commission)
A Decent Home. Washington, D.C.: Government Printing Office, 1968.

San Diego Chamber of Commerce.
Final Report of the Joint City Industry Task Force on the Building Inspection Department. (no date)

Seeley, Toor H.
Building Economics: Appraisal and Control of Building Design Cost and Efficiency. London:MacMillanBook Co., Inc., 1972.

Siegan, Bernard.
Land Use Without Zoning. Lexington, Mass: D.C.Heath and Co., 1972.

Solomon, Arthur P.
The Effect of Land Use and Environmental Controls on Housing: A Review, 1976.

Suburban Action Institute.
A Study of Exclusion. Tarrytown, N.Y.: 1973.

Suburban Maryland Homebuilders Association.
High Cost of Housing in Montgomery County, 1976.

Urban Land Institute.
The Community Builders Handbook. Washington, D.C.: Urban Land Institute, 1968.

——————————.

The Effects of Large Lot Size on Residential Development. (Technical Bulletin, No. 32). Washington, D.C., 1958.

ULI and NAHB.
Cost Effective Site Planning/Single-Family Development. Washington, D.C.: Urban Land Institute, 1976.

ULI, NHAB, and ASCE.
Residential Streets—Objectives, Principles, and Design Considerations. Washington, D.C.: Urban Land Institute, 1976.

——————————.

Residential Storm Water Management—Objectives, Principles, and Design Considerations. Washington, D.C.: Urban Land Institute, 1976.

Williams, Norman Jr., and Thomas Norman.
"Exclusionary Land-Use Controls: The Case of Northeastern New Jersey," Land-Use Controls Quarterly, No. 4, p. 1 (Fall 1970).

C. ENVIRONMENTAL CONTROLS:
   HOUSING COST AND OTHER IMPACTS

Brooks, Mary E. *Housing Equity and Environmental Protection.* Washington, D.C.: American Institute of Planners, 1976.

The main thesis of the monograph is that there is no irreconcilable conflict between environmentalists and groups espousing lower cost housing for the poor and minorities, but rather that housing rights and environmental protection are interconnected. Part of the analysis considers case studies detailing the residential costs of environmental protection. Brooks concludes that the direct costs (e.g., preparation of an EIS) of environmental reviews are negligible but that environmental protection programs, by causing delays and other uncertainties, add to the vulnerability of the development process.

The Brooks study is one of the first to stress the need for environmentalists to be sensitive to the cost implication of environmental controls and to argue that there are many common goals shared by both environmentalists and developers. (See also Healy, "Environmentalists and Developers: Can They Agree on Anything" in this bibliography.)

"California Environmental Studies"

California has been a leader in promulgating state environmental review procedures. Many studies have been conducted in this state to compare the benefits versus costs of the environment impact statements, coastal zone requirements and other environmental regulations. The most prominent California analyses are cited below as discussed by the National Association of Home Builders.

Construction Industry Research Board. *Cost of Delay Prior to Construction*, (March 1975).

The California Environmental Quality Act of 1970 demands impact reports for both public and private projects. Costs caused by this review delay are identified in this report to be balanced against the environmental benefits of the review process. Three cost components of time delay between acquisition and construction are identified: holding costs, inflation and overhead costs. The average delay cost is estimated to equal 20 percent of residential single-family project prices.

——————————————————————. *Economic Analysis California Coastal Zone Conservation Act*, (May 1976).

Evaluation of the effect of regulatory commissions charged with the responsibility to implement coastal zone management controls on building activity. During the three years of their operation (1973-1975), the 15 commissions have denied 488 permits at a total value of $439,541,600. Additionally, it is assumed that some unknown percentage of the 618 permits voided during this time were withdrawn due to factors associated with compliance with coastal zone regulations.

Comptroller General of the United States. *Environmental Assessment Efforts for Proposed Projects Have Been Ineffective.* Washington, D.C.: Government Printing Office, 1975.

Critical report of HUD's environmental impact statement (EIS) procedures. Comptroller evaluates HUD preparation and review of environmental impact statements for selected federally insured and guaranteed projects and notes numerous deficiencies including: (1) inadequate consideration of alternatives to the proposed projects and environmental consequences; (2) ambiguity concerning appropriate level of environmental clearance process and/or not preparing a statement where required; (3) inadequate independent environmental assessments; and (4) the failure of environmental impact statements to serve as input for effective policy and decisionmaking. The Comptroller recommends policy improvements including establishing better review procedures and criteria, using outside experts where needed and creating a formal training program for HUD clearance personnel.

The Comptroller analysis does not specify the cost of EIS preparation and review, but stresses the need to streamline the environmental review procedure, eliminate unnecessary "bulk" and make EIS more meaningful and policy oriented. The study is similar to the Commission of Federal Paperwork and Council of Environmental Quality reports cited later in this bibliography.

Healy, Robert G. *Environmentalists and Developers: Can They Agree on Anything.* Washington, D.C.: The Conservation Foundation, 1977.

Healy argues that there are numerous emerging bases for agreement between environmentalists and developers such as the latter, for economic reasons, tending to construct smaller projects which pose less of an environmental impact. The report recommends joint action by the two groups to encourage non-prescriptive planning and more flexible zoning; to reduce unnecessary infrastructure requirements; and to take other measures to encourage affordable, environmentally sound projects.

James, Franklin J. and Thomas Muller.*"Environmental Impact Evaluation, Land Use Planning and the Housing Consumer," Journal of American Real Estate and Urban Economics Association*, Vol. 5 No. 3 (Fall 1977), pp. 279-341.

See General Purpose Articles for overall description.

After describing environmental impact review (EIR) requirements, the article considers EIR cost impact. Expenditures amount to $192 per housing unit in Florida (about .5 percent of the cost of the single-family homes examined) and $115 in California (.3 percent of the cost of a home in this location). Approximately 17 percent of the EIR expense is attributed to the direct cost of preparing the environmental review (e.g., consultant's fees). The remaining expenditure (outside of a negligible amount for public sector review) results from the added delays imposed by the EIR process. Delays are costly in that they increase carrying charge costs for interest payments, property taxes and general overhead expenses.

As an outgrowth of the EIR evaluation described above, the Urban Land Institute published, *State Mandated Impact Evaluations: A Preliminary Assessment (1976)*. This report considers the cost and effectiveness of state mandated environmental impact review in California, Florida, Montana and Wisconsin.

These analyses and the Richardson study, *The Cost of Environmental Protection*, are the most detailed empirical investigations of the cost implications of environmental procedures. All reach similar conclusions—the requirements inflate costs by less than one percent of the housing unit selling price, primarily due to processing associated delays.

Real Estate Research Corp. *Business Prospects Under Coastal Zone Management*. (March 1976).

Focusing on the economic impact of public investment, this study explores the influence of Coastal Zone Management on public expenditures, land values, investment opportunities and business profitability. The information is presented on three sets of matrices.

The study concludes "the economic benefits of CZM in California will, at a minimum, offset non-compensated losses in land value or business opportunity. The positive effects of a more attractive secure physical environment, combined with greater efficiency attained by the elimination of urban sprawl, will outweigh these losses overall."

Richardson, Dan K. *The Cost of Environmental Protection—Regulating Housing Development in the Coastal Zone.* New Brunswick, N.J.: Rutgers University Center for Urban Policy Research, 1976.

One of the first analyses to empirically document the costs of complying with coastal zone management procedures/reviews. It examines twenty-one residential developments in New Jersey and monitors the cost impact of the New Jersey's Coastal Area Facility Review Act (CAFRA).

The study concludes that the expenditures incurred by a developer as a result of the standard regulatory process in New Jersey amount to $4,584 per single-family unit and $2,185 per multifamily unit. As a result of New Jersey Coastal Zone Program compliances, these costs increase to $4,720 for single-family units and $2,310 for multi-family units—an added expense of $136 and $125 respectively.

The Richardson study essentially confirms Muller and James' findings as to the relatively small impact on housing costs of non-permitting related environmental controls. It is further useful in that it provides several alternative models of where and when the state may enter the local review process and the costs of delay associated with these various entry points.

U.S. Commission on Federal Paperwork. *Report on Environmental Impact Statements.* Washington, D.C.: Government Printing Office, 1977.

Report considers the time and "paperwork" consequences of federal environmental impact statement (EIS) requirements. The analysis examines various housing related EIS issues, such as the variations between HUD, FMHA and VA in their specification of project size thresholds when an impact statement must be prepared. Policy recommendations for improving the EIS process are given, including: (1) preparing an areawide EIS; (2) establishing interagency agreements for determining lead and joint agency EIS responsibility; (3) incorporating the draft EIS into initial project planning documents; (4) developing environmental resource inventories; and (5) allowing and encouraging, where appropriate, a summary document instead of a largely descriptive EIS.

U.S. Council on Environmental Quality. *Environmental Impact Statements: An Analysis of Six Years Experience by Seventy Federal Agencies.* Washington, D.C.: Council on Environmental Quality, 1976.

CEQ evaluation of the 1970-1976 experience of federal agency EIS preparation and review. The report concludes that the EIS process has, in general, been successful in improving decisions affecting the environment but has not always been consistent nor as effective as possible. Recommendations are given for improving: (1) EIS triggering—when a statement must be filed; (2) EIS focus—the optimal statement emphasis and format; (3) EIS relevancy—how needless bulk and narrative can be eliminated; (4) EIS timing—what strategies can streamline the procedure; (5) communication of the EIS findings; and (6) interagency cooperation.

D. ENVIRONMENTAL CONTROLS: BACKGROUND AND CURRENT PRACTICE

Ackerman, Bruce L.
"Impact Statements and Low Cost Housing," Southern California Law Review, 46 (1973), p. 754.

Babcock, Richard F. and David L. Callies.
"Ecology and Housing," in Modernizing Urban Land Policy, edited by Marion Clawson. Washington, D.C. Resources for the Future, 1973.

Mogulof, Melvin B.
Saving the Coast. Lexington, Mass: Lexington Books, 1975.

Peevey, Michael R.
"The Coastal Plan and Jobs: A Critique," in The California Coastal Plan: A Critique, p. 93. San Francisco: Institute for Contemporary Studies, 1976.

Urban Land Institute.
Economic Benefits of Coastal Zone Management: An Overview, 1976.

Walter, J. Jackson.
*"A Survey of Permits and Impact Statements Required for a PUD:
A Memorandum,"* Real Estate Law Journal 33: (Winter 1975),
pp. 215-226.

E. INNOVATIVE STRATEGIES: THE SEARCH FOR A MORE
    EFFECTIVE AND EQUITABLE LAND USE SYSTEM

Council on State Government.
State Planning: Intergovernmental Policy Coordination. (Appendix
1). Washington, D.C.: Government Printing Office, 1976.

Gleeson, Michael E., *et al.*
*Urban Growth Management Systems: An Evaluation of Policy-
Related Research.* Chicago: American Society of Planning Officials,
1975. (Planning Advisory Service Report Nos. 309, 310).

Godschalk, David R. and Norman Axler.
Carrying Capacity Applications in Growth Management. Chapel
Hill, N.C., 1977.

Healy, Robert G.
Land Use and the States. Baltimore: John Hopkins Press, 1976.

Heeter, David.
*Toward a More Effective Land-Use Guidance System: A Summary
and Analysis of Five Major Reports.* Chicago: American Society of
Planning Officials, 1969. (Planning Advisory Service Report. No.
250).

Heyman, Ira Michael.
"Innovative Land Regulation and Comprehensive Planning," Santa
Clara Lawyer, 13:2 (Winter 1972), pp. 183-235.

Levin, Melvin R., Jerome G. Rose and Joseph S. Slavet.
New Approaches to State Land-Use Policies. Lexington, Mass:
Lexington Books, 1974.

Marcus, Norman and Marilyn W. Groves, eds.
*The New Zoning: Legal, Administrative, and Economic Concepts
and Techniques.* New York: Praeger Publishers, 1970.

Meshenberg, Michael J.
The Administration of Flexible Zoning Techniques, ASPO, 1976.

Pease, James R. and John Stockham.
*"New Land Use Control Techniques: A Summary Review and
Bibliography."* (Unpublished paper) Land Resources Management

Program, Oregon State University Extension Service, Corvallis, Oregon, 1974. *Performance Standards: A Technique for Controlling Land Use.* Oregon State University, Extension Service, 1974 (Special Report 424).

Rogal, Brian.
"Subdivision Improvement Guarantees," ASPO *Planning Advisory Service*, Report No. 298 (January 1974).

Rose, Jerome G.
"From the Legislatures: The Mandatory Percentage or Moderately Priced Dwelling Ordinance (MPMPD) Is the Latest Technique of Inclusionary Zoning," Real Estate Law Journal 3:2 (Fall 1974), pp. 176-180.

Thompson, Kate.
"A Comparative Study of Three Land Use Controls: Performance Zoning, Timing Ordinances, and Transfer of Development Rights." (Unpublished paper). Harvard Law School, 1975.

Yannacone, Victor J., Jr., John Rahenkamp and Angelo J. Cerchione. *Impact Zoning: Alternative to Exclusion in the Suburbs.* (Unpublished manuscript) Yannacone & Yannacone, Patchogue, N.Y., 1975.

Yurman, Dan.
"Can Density Bonuses Pay Off," Practicing Planner Vol. 6, No. 2 (April 1976), pp. 14-20.

Notes

1. See, for example, President's Committee on Urban Housing, *A Decent Home* (Washington, D.C.: Government Printing Office, 1968, National Commission of Urban Problems, *Building the American City* (Washington, D.C.: Government Printing Office, 1967).

2. See, for example, Norman B. Williams, Jr., *American Land Planning Law.* (Chicago, Illinois: Callaghan and Co., 1975, Volume I).

3. Marion Clawson, "A Capsule History of Land in the United States," in *America's Land and Its Uses* (Washington, D.C.: Resources for the Future, 1975); Seymour Toll, *Zoned American* (New York: Grossman Publishers, 1969); S.J. Makielski, Jr., *The Politics of Zoning; The New York Experience* (New York: Columbia University Press, 1966); John Delafons, *Land Use Controls in the United States* (Cambridge, Mass.: M.I.T. Press, 1969).

4. Urban Land Institute, *Fair Housing and Exclusionary Zoning*, Research Report No. 23 (Washington, D.C.: National Committee Against Discrimination in Housing and the Urban Land Institute, 1974). See also American Society of Planning Officials, *Problems of Zoning and Land Use Regulations* (Chicago: ASPO, 1964).

5. See Norman Williams, Jr. and Edward Wacks, "Segregation of Residential Areas Along Economic Lines: Lionshed Lake Revisited," *Wisconsin Law Review*, Vol. 27 (1969), p. 827; Lawrence Sager, "Tight Little Islands: Exclusionary Zoning, Equal Protection, and the Indigent," *Stanford Law Review*, Vol. 21 (1970), p. 767; Norman Williams and Thomas Norman, "Exclusionary Land Use Control: The Case of Northeastern New Jersey," *Syracuse Law Review*, Vol. 22 (1971), p. 475.

6. Stephen R. Seidel, *Housing Costs and Government Regulations; Confronting the Regulatory Maze* (Rutgers University, New Brunswick, N.J.: Center for Urban Policy Research, 1977); Robert H. Freilich and Peter S. Levi, *Model Subdivision Regulations—Text and Commentary* (Chicago, Illinois: American Society of Planning Officials, 1975).

7. See Richard P. Fishman, *Housing for All Under Law* (Cambridge, Mass.: Ballinger, 1978).

8. See Footnote 1.

9. 67 N.J. 151, 336 A.2d 713 (1975). See also Jerome G. Rose and Melvin R. Levin, "What is a Developing Municipality Within the Meaning of the Mount Laurel Decision," *Real Estate Law Journal*, Vol. 4 (1976).

10. American Public Health Association (APHA) *Planning the Neighborhood* (1960); Joseph DeChiara and Lee Koppelman, *Planning Design Criteria.* (New York: Van Nostrand Reinhold Company, 1969); Urban Land Institute, *The Community Builders Handbook* (Washington, D.C.: Urban Land Institute, 1968); Suburban Action Institute, *A Study of Exclusion*, Vol. 1. (Tarrytown, N.Y.: Suburban Action Institute, 1973); Metropolitan Council, *Modest-Cost Housing in the Twin Cities Metropolitan Area* (Minneapolis: Metropolitan Council, 1976); Urban Land Institute, National Association of Home Builders, and American Society of Civil Engineers, *Residential Streets—Objectives, Principles and Design Considerations* (Washington, D.C.: Urban Land Institute, 1976); Urban Land Institute, National Association of Home Builders, and American Society of Civil Engineers, *Residential Storm Water Management—Objectives, Principles, and Design Considerations* (Washington, D.C.: Urban Land Institute, 1976); U.S. Department of Housing and Urban Development. *Minimum Property Standards Single Family Housing.* Handbook No. 4910.0 (Washington, D.C.: Government Printing Office, 1973); U.S. Department of Housing and Urban Development, *Manual of Acceptable Practices* (Washington, D.C.: Government Printing Office, 1972).

11. *Ibid.*

12. *Ibid.*

13. See Brooks, Mary E., *Housing Equity and Environmental Protection* (Washington, D.C.: American Institute of Planners, 1976); Robert W. Burchell and David Listokin (editors), *Future Land Use* (New Brunswick, N.J.: Rutgers University Center for Urban Policy Research, 1975); Robert W. Burchell and David Listokin *The Environmental Impact Statement Handbook* (New Brunswick, N.J.: Rutgers University Center for Urban Policy Research, 1974).

14. See section V. "Bibliography".

15. See Burchell and Listokin, *Environmental Impact Statement Handbook.*

16. See Seidel, *Housing Costs.*

17. Robert W. Burchell and David Listokin, *Environmental Impact Statement Handbook Update* (New Brunswick, N.J.: Rutgers University Center for Urban Policy Research, 1979).

18. Council on State Governments, *State Planning: Intergovernmental Policy Coordination* (Washington, D.C.: Government Printing Office, 1976), Appendix I; Council of State Governments, Land: *State Alternatives for Planning and Management* (Lexington, Ky: Council of State Governments, 1975); American Institute of Planners, *Survey of State Land Use Planning Activity* (Washington, D.C.: Government Printing Office, 1976); Council on State Governments, *State Planning: Intergovernmental Policy Coordination* (Washington, D.C.: Government Printing Office, 1976).

19. Franklin James, and James Hughes, *New Jersey 1980* (New Brunswick, N.J.: Rutgers University Center for Urban Policy Research, 1977); James Hughes, *et al., New Jersey Towards the Year 2000* (New Brunswick, N.J.: Center for Urban Policy Research, 1977).

20. California Government Code, § 65560(d), 65561(d), 65563, 65566, 65567, 68560(a), 65910; 59 OP. Cal. Att'y Gen. 129 (1976). Cited in Daniel J. Curtin and K.L. Shirk, Jr., "Land Use Planning and Zoning," *The Urban Lawyer*, Vol. 9, No. 4 (1977), p. 726.

21. Florida Local Government Comprehensive Planning Act of 1975. ΣΣ4(4), 4(5) (1975).

22. New Jersey Law of 1975, ch. 291; William Miller, "The New Jersey Land Use Law Revision: A Lesson for Other States," *Real Estate Law Journal*, Vol. 5, No. 2 (Fall 1976), p. 129.

23. American Law Institute, *A Model Land Development Code*, Tentative Draft No. 3, April 1971.

24. Fred P. Bosselman, George M. Raymond and Richard A. Persico, "Some Observations on the American Law Institute's Model Land Development Code," *The Urban Lawyer*, Vol. 8, No. 3 (1976), p. 477.

25. *Ibid.*, p. 488.

26. Robert G. Healy, *Land Use and the States* (Baltimore: John Hopkins Press, 1976), p. 202.

27. Ore. Rev. Stat. Σ197.015 (1973).

28. See C. Little, *The New Oregon Trail* (Washington, D.C.: Conservation Foundation, 1974).

29. See Metropolitan Council, *Housing Plans, Programs and Guidelines* (Minneapolis: Metropolitan Council, 1977).

30. *Ibid.*

31. Florida Department of Community Affairs, *Reducing Housing Costs* (Tallahassee, Department of Community Affairs, 1977).

32. New Jersey Department of Community Affairs, *A Guide for Residential Design Review* (Trenton, N.J.: Department of Community Affairs, 1976).

33. Metropolitan Council, *Advisory Standards for the Land Use Regulation.* (Minneapolis: Metropolitan Council of the Twin Cities, 1977); Metropolitan Law Council, *Advisory Land Use Standards for Multifamily Housing* (Minneapolis: Metropolitan Council of the Twin Cities, 1978).

34. David Listokin, *Fair Share Housing Allocation* (New Brunswick, N.J.: Rutgers University Center for Urban Policy Research, 1976).

35. Mass. Gen. Laws Ann. Ch. 40B secs. 20-23 (Supp. 1973 inserted by State 1969, Ch. 774).

36. State of New Jersey, Executive Order, No. 35, April 2, 1976.

37. See Listokin, *Fair Share Housing Allocation.*

38. David Listokin, *Funding Education* (New Brunswick, N.J.: Rutgers University Center for Urban Policy Research, 1972).

39. See John W. Windhorst, Jr., "The Minnesota Fiscal Disparities Law," *Land Use Law and Zoning Digest*, Vol. 28, No. 4 (1976), p. 7.

40. See Devow Schneider, *et al., The Carrying Capacity Concept as a Planning Tool*, Planning Advisory Service, Report No. 338 (December 1978).

41. See footnote 33.

42. See American Society of Planning Officials, "Planning Agency Ideas for Encouraging Low- and Moderate-Income Housing," *PAS Memo* (December 1977).

43. *Ibid.*

44. Telephone Conversation with Kulbir Singh, Planner, Oshawa Ontario, February 1979.

45. See Jerome G. Rose, Oakwood at Madison: A Tactical Retreat by the New Jersey Supreme Court to Preserve the Mount Laurel Principle, *Urban Law Annual*, Vol. 13.

Racial Transition and Black Homeownership in American Suburbs

Robert W. Lake

Introduction

Accumulation of equity through homeownership is perhaps the most widespread and successful means of wealth generation available to the American middle class. The inflation of housing values in the post World-War II era has been a particular boon to the largely suburbanized homeowning middle-class white population. The nation's black population, however, comprised of renters rather than owners and generally confined to portions of older urban areas that have not experienced the inflation of housing values characteristic of suburbia, has been less able to benefit from the wealth generative potential of suburban homeownership. Recent trends, since 1970, show a slight increase of black population in the suburbs, and a corresponding decrease in the proportion of the black population remaining in the central cities. It is therefore instructive to consider, first, the extent to which increase in the rate of black suburbanization is synonymous with increased homeownership, and secondly, whether

419

black suburban homeownership is synonymous with equity accumulation and the generation of wealth.

In addressing these issues, this paper examines the extent to which racial transition from white to black or black to white occupancy accompanies the turnover of suburban housing units. Analysts have long stressed the importance of existing housing stocks, as opposed to new construction, as a source of homeownership possibilities for blacks and other minorities.[1] The transfer of existing units from white to black occupancy is thus a necessary concomitant of black suburban population growth. The suburban focus is justified since it is there that ownership possibilities are most concentrated.

Data made available through the U.S. Census Bureau's *Annual Housing Survey* permit year to year tracing of unit and household characteristics in a national sample of housing units resurveyed each year.[2] Utilizing data for 1974 and 1975, three aspects of suburban racial and tenure transition are analyzed in terms of their impact on black homeownership in the suburbs.

First, what is the magnitude of transition from white to black occupancy in suburban housing units? Disaggregating this overall transition rate into renter and owner components provides a measure of availability of homeownership opportunities for blacks in the suburbs.

Second, what are the characteristics of suburban housing units acquired by blacks? Here, differentiation between units initially occupied by whites and those units which turn over within the black housing market provides evidence of the significance of white to black transition as a source of quality owner-occupied suburban units. While earlier studies have examined the characteristics of *neighborhoods* or *areas* experiencing white to black racial succession, data on the individual housing units involved have heretofore not been available.[3]

Thirdly, what are the housing market dynamics confronting the suburban black homeowner seeking to recapture stored equity through resale? Earlier studies, not focused primarily on suburbia, have demonstrated that a black-occupied housing unit infrequently reverts to white occupancy.[4] If this pattern is replicated in the suburbs, then black homeowners wishing to sell will be at a distinct disadvantage: adequate market demand is required if homeownership is to function as a path to capital accumulation. The suburban dream will be less golden if otherwise equivalent units owned by blacks and whites are funnelled into dual resale markets leaving blacks with inferior rates of economic return and equity recapture.

Initial findings suggest that white to black transition in suburban rental units far outpaces that in owner occupancy, extending the central city disparity in homeownership rates for whites and blacks into the suburbs. Those black suburbanites who do own their own homes are far more dependent on black replacements than are whites, saddling black owners wishing to sell with the consequences of lesser black buying power. Complicating the picture, however, is the finding that more black-owned suburban units are turned over to whites than to other blacks, suggesting that the market for black-occupied units may be more open in the suburbs than has previously been reported for central city areas.

Property value is found to be a significant feature, with the lowest value black-owned suburban units yielding the least likelihood of equity return upon transfer to another household. The findings suggest the need for policy initiatives aimed at stimulating the demand for black-owned suburban units, for it is only in this way that suburban homeownership will provide blacks with the wealth generative function it has traditionally served for earlier aspirants to the middle class.

In assessing these trends, the following discussion focuses first on the rate of black suburbanization since 1970 and the characteristics of black suburban households. We then address in turn the magnitude of racial transition of individual suburban housing units, the characteristics of those housing units, and the conditions of equity recapture in black-owned housing in the suburbs.

Black Suburbanization Since 1970

The data on black suburbanization during the seventies reveal some slight gains in black representation in the noncentral city portions of SMSAs.[5] The characteristics of these suburban black households show them to differ from both central city blacks and suburban whites.

GROWTH RATES

Suburban black growth rates between 1970 and 1976 have outstripped those for whites, largely as a consequence of the far smaller black population in the 1970 base year. Between 1970 and 1976, the number of black suburban households increased by 49 percent to a total of 1.4 million, compared to a 21 percent increase, to 25.8 million, in white suburban households. Black owner-occupied units in the suburbs increased by 39 percent (compared to 23 percent for whites) while black renter-occupied units increased by 62 percent (compared to 16 percent for whites). Black households constituted some 5 percent of all suburban households in 1976, essentially maintaining a level that prevailed throughout the sixties and early seventies. Finally, a somewhat larger proportion of total metropolitan area black households lived in the suburbs in 1976 (23 percent) than was the case in 1970 (19 percent). Among metropolitan area blacks in owner-occupied units, the suburban share increased marginally from 27 to 28 percent between 1970 and 1976. Among black renter households, the suburban share increased from 14 percent in 1970 to 19 percent in 1976.

CHARACTERISTICS

Two sets of comparisons help clarify the nature of the black suburban niche within the current metropolitan structure. Compared to suburban white households, suburban blacks on average continue to receive short shrift. Compared to central city blacks, however, suburban residence represents a substantial improvement in both housing and neighborhood quality.[6]

Considering tenure and housing type in 1975, for example, just under half (49.4 percent) of black suburban households were owners, compared to almost three-fourths (71.2 percent) of white suburbanites, and about a third (35.4 percent) of black central city households. Conversely, some 17 percent of black suburbanites lived in structures of ten or more units, compared to only 9 percent of white suburban households and 23 percent of black city dwellers. Turning to property value, 11 percent of black suburban households, versus 2 percent of white suburbanites, and 15 percent of black city residents lived in units whose property value was less than $10,000. At the same time, 10 percent of black suburbanites lived in homes valued at $50,000 or more, in contrast to 24 percent of white suburban households, but only 3 percent of black central city residents. In terms of overall housing satisfaction, black suburbanites were only half as likely as white suburbanites, but one and a half times more likely than black city dwellers, to rate their housing unit as excellent. Ratings of overall neighborhood quality are distributed similarly.

Two general conclusions can be drawn from this brief overview. First, compared to white households in the suburbs, black suburban households occupy less satisfactory, lower value units in less desirable neighborhood settings, and have attained lower proportions of owner occupancy. Secondly, the data indicate the extension to the suburbs of patterns previously documented for central cities: it is on average the more affluent, higher status blacks who are the first to move into previously all-white areas, thereby improving their housing and neighborhood quality.

With this brief introduction to the relative characteristics of black suburban households within the metropolitan setting, we turn now to an examination of racial transition in the existing suburban housing stock.

Race and Tenure Change in the Suburban Housing Stock

Data from the *Annual Housing Survey* national samples provide information on 15.9 million suburban housing units for which race and tenure can be identified in both 1974 and 1975. Utilization of this data set permits identification of the magnitude of racial and tenure change within the suburban housing stock, and analysis of changes in household characteristics attendant on turnover in the housing inventory.

TOTAL INVENTORIES

We begin by comparing the racial and tenure characteristics of the suburban inventory in 1974 with the identical units in 1975 (Exhibit 1). As indicated above, the total suburban inventory is divided approximately 70/30 between owner and renter occupancy, and some 5 percent of total units in both years are black. The overwhelming share of units, of course, evidences no change in tenure or race from one year to the next. Relative shifts within this framework, however, provide initial evidence of differences in black and white experiences in the suburban housing market.

First, considering racial transition within the entire suburban inventory, 0.64 percent (101,000) of the entire 1974 supply shifted from white to black in the one-year period. Disaggregating by 1974 tenure, 0.23 percent (26,000 units) of the owner-occupied stock and 1.63 percent of the renter-occupied units (75,000 units) shifted from white to black during the period. This suggests that owner-occupancy units in the white inventory become available to black buyers at a slower rate than do renter-occupancy units.

Secondly, considering tenure change within each racial category, 1.59 percent of the black-occupied inventory (11,000 units) changed

EXHIBIT 1

TENURE AND RACIAL CHARACTERISTICS OF THE SAME-UNIT INVENTORY, U.S. SUBURBS,[a] 1975 BY 1974

(Numbers in Thousands)

| | | 1975 Tenure and Race (Households) | | | | | | | |
| 1974 Tenure and Race (Households) | | Owner Occupied[b] | | | | Renter Occupied[c] | | | |
	Total	Total	White	Black	Other	Total	White	Black	Other
All Units	15,899	11,307	10,793	369	143	4,592	4,136	362	94
White	14,989	10,813	10,757	23	32	4,176	4,050	78	49
Black	692	363	18	345	0	329	48	278	3
Other	218	131	18	1	111	87	38	6	42
Owner-Occupied[b]	11,295	11,099	10,602	360	135	196	178	10	7
White	10,798	10,618	10,569	22	26	180	170	4	6
Black	365	352	15	337	0	13	7	6	0
Other	132	129	18	1	190	3	1	0	1
Renter-Occupied[c]	4,604	208	191	9	8	4,396	3,958	352	87
White	4,191	195	188	1	6	3,996	3,880	74	43
Black	327	11	3	8	0	316	41	272	3
Other	86	2	0	0	2	84	37	6	41

Notes: Columns might not add to totals due to rounding.
[a] U.S. Suburbs = non-central city portions of fifty SMSAs for which intra-metropolitan location of unit is reported on AHS national survey tapes. See footnote 2.
[b] Owner-Occupied = Owner-Occupied + condominium + cooperatives.
[c] Renter-Occupied = Renter-Occupied + Rented. No Cash Rent.

Source: U.S. Bureau of the Census, *Annual Housing Survey*: 1974 and 1975, national sample public use tapes.

from renter to owner occupancy between 1974 and 1975, but 1.88 percent (13,000 units) reverted from owner to renter occupancy. Within the white-occupied inventory, in contrast, 1.30 percent (195,000 units) changed from renter to owner while only 1.20 percent (180,000 units) reverted from owner to renter occupancy. In all, focusing here on tenure changes within each racial inventory and ignoring for the present the extent of racial transition, the 1974 white inventory registered a net gain of 15,000 owner-occupied units while the black inventory registered a net loss of 2,000 owner-occupied units. A larger net share of the original 1974 stock of black units than white units, in other words, shifted out of owner occupancy from 1974 to 1975.

EXHIBIT 2

1974-1975 TENURE CHANGE BY RACIAL CHANGE, SUBURBAN HOUSING UNITS OCCUPIED BY RECENT MOVERS IN 1975, UNITED STATES[a]

(In Thousands of Units)

Tenure Transition 1974-1975[b]	All Units		White-White		Racial Transition 1974-1975 Black-Black		White-Black		Black-White	
	#	%	#	%	#	%	#	%	#	%
All Units	2,250	100.0	2,044	100.0	77	100.0	84	100.0	45	100.0
Own-Own	516	22.9	491	24.0	4	5.2	16	19.0	5	11.4
Rent-Rent	1,506	67.0	1,348	65.9	64	83.1	63	75.0	31	70.5
Own-Rent	133	5.9	116	5.7	6	7.8	4	4.8	7	15.9
Rent-Own	95	4.2	89	4.4	3	3.9	1	1.2	2	4.5

Notes: Columns might not add to totals due to rounding.

      a Suburban units are those in the non-central city portion of fifty SMSAs for which intrametropolitan location of units is specified on AHS national survey tapes. See footnote 2. Recent movers are those households which moved into the unit within the twelve month period prior to 1975 AHS enumeration.

      b Owner-occupied = owner + condominiums + cooperatives.   Renter-occupied units = renter + rented, no cash rent.

Source: U.S. Bureau of the Census, *Annual Housing Survey*: 1974 and 1975, national sample public use tapes.

HOUSING MARKET TURNOVER

Of the 15.9 million suburban units described above, we have identified 2,250,000 units within the white and black suburban housing inventories that turned over between 1974 and 1975 (Exhibit 2). This figure represents a 14.3 percent turnover rate. (We have excluded from further discussion the 218,000 units—1.4 percent of the total—occupied by "other races" in 1974.) Units occupied by a different household in 1974 and 1975 were identified as those which in the latter year survey responded to questions asked only of "recent movers," households that moved in within the twelve-month period preceding the survey. These units form the data base for our analysis of market turnover and racial transition.[7]

Considering turnover by tenure, 5.8 percent of owner-occupied units in 1974 turned over during the year, while the equivalent rate for renter-occupied units was 34.8 percent. Not surprisingly, in other words, rental units in the suburbs change hands at a faster rate than owner-occupied units.

Considering turnover by race, 14.2 percent of white-occupied units and 17.6 percent of black-occupied units changed occupancy between 1974 and 1975. The higher black turnover rate is expected since blacks are more concentrated than whites in renter-occupied units.

Finally, the turnover rate in owner-occupied units is essentially identical for blacks and whites: 6.0 percent of black owner-occupied units and 5.8 percent of white. In the rental market, however, the turnover rate in white renter-occupied units (35.8 percent) exceeds that in black renter-occupied units (30.6 percent). Going somewhat beyond the data, these findings may suggest that suburban rental occupancy for whites is typically a temporary stop en route to homeownership, while it is a far more stable and permanent tenure arrangement for blacks confronted with barriers to home-ownership imposed by downpayment requirements, mortgage restrictions, and discrimination.

RACIAL CHANGE

The final question in this section focuses on the role of racial change within the more general picture of housing turnover. Again drawing on the data in Exhibit 2, four observations can be made.

First, white to black transition still serves as a more important source of suburban housing than does turnover within the black housing market. Of the 161,000 units with a new black occupant in 1975, 84,000 (52 percent) transferrred from white to black occupancy while only 77,000 (48 percent) were already black-occupied in 1974. This finding suggests the relative recency of black arrival in the suburbs and the relatively small base of existing black settlement.

Secondly, white to black transition far outweighs black to white transition in both absolute and relative terms. As noted above, white to black change amounted to 84,000 units; in contrast, only 45,000 suburban units transferred from black to white between 1974 and 1975. Of the resulting net gain of 39,000 new black-occupied units, 10,000 came on as owner-occupied and 29,000 were renter-occupied in 1975.

The third question focuses on the probability of ownership for new black occupants. If a new occupant of a suburban housing unit is black rather than white, the likelihood is greater that the black household will rent rather than buy, regardless of the race of the initial occupant. This finding is revealed by the tenure characteristic of the units within each racial transition category (Exhibit 2). Focusing on the race of household in the *second year*, a transfer within the rental market constitutes 83.1 percent of black-black and 75.0 percent of white-black turnover, but only 70.5 percent of black-white and 65.9 percent of white-white turnover. Combining these figures with those for transfers from ownership to rental status, units rented in 1975 (rent-rent plus own-rent) constitute 86 percent of all turnovers to a new black occupant and only 72 percent of turnovers to a new white occupant.

Finally, what is the probability of a black owner-occupied unit in the initial year remaining within the owner inventory or shifting to rental status during turnover? We find that a black-owned unit is more likely than a white-owned unit to shift to renter-occupancy, again regardless of the race of the new occupant. Of white-owned transition units in 1974, 19 percent of those turned over to a white household and 20 percent of those turned over to a black household shifted to renter occupancy in 1975. Of black-owned units, in contrast, 58 percent and 60 percent of those turned over to, respectively, a white and black household shifted into the rental market. The implications for equity recapture in black-and white-owned suburban units are evident.

SUMMARY OF TRANSITION FINDINGS

The principal findings thus far can be summarized briefly. New black occupancy in the suburbs more often involves a unit shifted out of the white inventory than one transferred from a previous black occupant. Such transition, further, is predominantly a one-way street: white-black transition far outweighs transfers from black to white. Largely due to differential turnover rates, owner-occupied units in the suburbs become available to potential black occupants at a slower rate than rental units. Black units turn over faster than those occupied by whites, largely because blacks are more concentrated in rental units and these turn over faster than owner units. Black rental units, however, turn over at a slower rate than do white rental units, suggesting that black rental occupancy in the suburbs—perhaps due to fewer available options—is less temporary and more stable than white rental. While white-black transition results in a net gain in black suburban owner-occupied units, this gain is in part offset by a loss of owner units through tenure change within the black inventory.

The present data suggest, but do not allow testing, the hypothesis that black owner-occupied units gained through racial transition are subsequently lost by an inability to sustain adequate demand within a dual housing market context. (Further evidence on this point must await data on turnover chains over a longer time period than presently available.) In sum, black suburbanites are less likely than their white counterparts to own their own home, and those who do are more likely than white owners to transfer their unit to rental status in the event of turnover of the unit.

Characteristics of Transition Units

The discussion thus far has focused on the magnitude of turnover and transition within racial segments of the suburban housing market. What of the characteristics of the housing units comprising these racial sub-markets? Are housing units transferred from white to black substantially different from those transferred within the white housing market? Do units in these categories differ in turn from those transferred within the black housing market?

To examine these questions, we compare units in each of the suburban racial transition categories in terms of four basic characteristics: age of structure, median value, median rent, and overall evaluation of housing and neighborhood quality. For this segment of the discussion, we focus on those housing units for which tenure type (own or rent) is maintained both before and after the move. Units that changed tenure type (own to rent, rent to own) are eliminated from further discussion due to small sample sizes and the resulting ambiguity of generalizations based on a relatively small number of observations.

AGE OF STRUCTURE

Transfers within the black suburban housing market tend on average to involve substantially older units than transfers within the white market. White to black turnover appears concentrated in relatively newer units, reflecting perhaps the comparatively greater buying power of those black households who can gain access to the formerly white segment of the suburban market. In contrast, black to white transfers appear generally restricted to both the newest and the oldest suburban units, possibly suggesting that the same process of "gentrification" is at work in the suburbs as has been reported for many central cities.

Among all suburban transition units in 1975, about a third (31.3 percent) of white-white transfers, but only a fourth (26.5 percent) of black-black transfers, were built in the preceding six years (1969-1974). A higher proportion (43.2 percent) of units transferred from white to black were built in this period, as were over half (51.1 percent) of black-white units. Another third (29 percent) of black-white units were built prior to 1939.

Among owner-occupied units, fully two-thirds of the suburban units transferred between black owners were built from 1950 to 1959, making them between 16 and 25 years old. In contrast, well over half (56.7 percent) of the units transferred between white owners were fifteen years old or less—built since 1960. Within the rental market, recently-built units (1969-74) are again underrepresented among black-black transfers (28.9 percent), followed in frequency by turnover within the white market (32.9 percent), from white to black (39.4 percent), and overwhelmingly represented among black-white transfers (72.6 percent). In all, the data suggest that as gauged by age of structure, white-to-black transition results in improvement in the black-occupied suburban housing stock. Some of this improvement is offset, however, since in most cases only the newest (but also some of the oldest) units are transferred from black to white occupancy.

MEDIAN VALUE

The median value of suburban units transferred within the white market was $40,000, compared to a median value of $36,200 for units transferred from black to black. Units transferred from white to black ownership were yet lower in value on average ($30,400). White replacement of a black household is clearly confined to the highest value units, as indicated by a median value of $55,000 for units shifting from black to white.

Transfer of a unit within the black sub-market appears to provide relatively inexpensive housing, as the median value-to-income ratio in this market segment is only 1.8.[8] Black purchase of a previously white-owned unit results in a median value-to-income ratio of 2.4 and the figure for white-white transfers is 2.1. Clearly, black home purchase requires a significantly larger proportion of income when the previous owner is white than when the previous owner is black.

MEDIAN RENT

Suburban rent levels within the all-white market ($175) are the highest among the various market segments examined; conversely, rents in black-black units are on average the lowest ($145). In contrast to the situation in owner occupancy, however, these comparatively low rents in the black rental market are coupled with the highest measure of rent as a percent of income (30.6 percent).[9] Average rent levels are identical in white-black and black-white units ($170). In the former segment, however, this rent level amounts to 27 percent of income, above the 25 percent norm, while in the latter segment the same median rental amounts to only 23 percent of income, below the norm. Indeed, suburban white renters are on average burdened with a 23 percent rent/income ratio regardless of the race of the previous renter, while black renters in the suburbs pay substantially more than a fourth of their income for housing.

Comparing rent levels with rents paid in the household's previous unit, blacks renting a previously white-occupied unit experience the highest increase in rent ($61) over what they were paying in their previous unit. Blacks renting previously black-occupied units experience a rent increase of $47, while whites renting previously white-occupied units increase their rent by only $20.

HOUSING AND NEIGHBORHOOD QUALITY

The distribution of responses on overall ratings of the housing unit and the neighborhood are essentially identical, and therefore can be discussed together. Fully twice the proportion of households in the white-white market (30 percent) as those in the black to black market (15 percent) rated their house and neighborhood as excellent. Black households in previously white units were more likely to offer an "excellent" rating (25 percent) than were black households in previously black units. Similarly, households in black-black units were most likely (40 percent) to evaluate house and neighborhood as only fair to poor. Only 16 percent of whites in previously white units but 26 percent of blacks in previously white units offered this low rating.

SUMMARY

The above discussion furnishes a brief sketch of the housing available in each of the suburban racial sub-markets. Suburban units that turn over from white to white are on average recently built units, of higher value than those transferred to black occupancy, and yield a below average value-to-income ratio. Rental units in the white-white market command the highest rent but nonetheless command the lowest proportion of their residents' income.

A direct contrast is evident in the suburban units that turn over from black to black. Such units are on average older and of lower value than white-white units. Rent levels in this market segment are the lowest but nonetheless constitute the largest percentage of income. Black suburban renters experience the biggest increase in rent over rentals paid in their previous units, regardless of whether the new rental unit was previously occupied by a black or white. Black-black units and their neighborhoods are least likely to be rated excellent by their residents and most likely to be rated fair or poor.

Units transferred from white to black occupy a position somewhere between these two extremes. These are generally newer units, contributing to an upgrading of the black-occupied suburban housing stock. However, owner-occupied units in this category have the lowest median value. Black renters of previously white-occupied units experience the largest increase in rent over their previous unit. While rental levels in white-black units are equal to those in black-white units, this amount represents a larger proportion of income for the former group than the latter. Black-occupied units formerly occupied by whites, however, are more likely than those previously occupied by blacks to receive satisfactory ratings of housing and neighborhood quality.

Finally, units transferred from black to white occupancy are in general among either the newest or the oldest portions of the suburban inventory and command the highest median value and relatively high rent levels.

Black Homeownership and Wealth

The final question posed in our analysis focuses on the efficacy of suburban homeownership as a means of equity accumulation. Numerous studies have pointed to the significance of homeownership as the principal source of savings for the lower and middle income population, and equity accumulated in the home has traditionally served as the launch vehicle for upward mobility among many immigrant ethnic groups.[10] What has been the recent experience of black suburban homeowners?

A direct response to this question would require data on the sales price of equivalent suburban homes sold by white and black owners in equivalent settings. Unfortunately, the *Annual Housing Survey* matched national samples do not contain sufficient cases of turnover of suburban black-owned units to permit adequate comparison. Even if adequate data were available, the question of "equivalence" of housing units and neighborhood settings has by no means been settled. In the absence of such direct evidence, however, substantial insight into black suburban housing market dynamics is provided through several indirect sources: (1) value change in black- and white-owned suburban units; (2) the pattern of racial and tenure change in black-owned units; and (3) the previous tenure of black suburban homebuyers.

VALUE CHANGE

From the standpoint of the aspiring homebuyer, the inflation of housing prices in recent years has caused considerable concern. From the seller's standpoint, however, such inflation simply magnifies the significance of homeownership as an investment. To what extent have black suburban homeowners shared in this equity building inflation of housing prices?

To answer this question, reported property value in owner-occupied suburban units for 1974 was compared to property value in the same units reported in 1975. According to Census Bureau definitions, these value figures represent "the respondent's estimate of how much the property (house and lot) would sell for if it were for sale." The results of this comparison are tabulated in Exhibit 3.

At all levels of housing value, suburban units occupied by blacks in both 1974 and 1975 were less likely to increase and more likely to decrease in value than units occupied by whites. Among the lowest value properties (those valued less than $20,000 in 1974), 41 percent of white-occupied units, but only 25 percent of black-occupied units, had increased in value in 1975. Among the highest value properties (those valued at $50,000 or more), 13 percent of white-occupied but 24 percent of black-occupied units had decreased in value by 1975. At intervening value levels, black-owned units were less likely than white-owned to increase in value and were up to twice as likely to decrease in value. For example, among suburban units valued from $20,000 to $34,999 in 1974, 20 percent of black-owned units, versus 27 percent of white-owned units, had

EXHIBIT 3

1975 PROPERTY VALUE BY 1974 PROPERTY VALUE, IN IDENTICAL BLACK AND WHITE OWNER-OCCUPIED UNITS, U.S. SUBURBS (PERCENTS)

Property Value in 1975	*Less than $20,000*		*Property Value, 1974* $20,000- $34,999		$35,000- $49,999		$50,000 or more	
	White-White	*Black-Black*	*White-White*	*Black-Black*	*White-White*	*Black-Black*	*White-White*	*Black-Black*
Less than $20,000	59.3	75.0	4.9	8.7	0.9	6.7	0.6	12.1
$20,000-$34,999	34.5	20.9	68.4	71.6	9.0	17.1	2.3	0.0
$35,000-$49,999	4.5	4.1	24.6	17.8	67.8	58.5	10.4	11.9
$50,000 or more	1.8	0.0	2.1	1.9	22.3	17.7	86.8	76.0
Total	100.0	100.0	100.0	100.0	100.0	100.0	100.0	100.0
Number of Units (in 1,000's)	(1,123)	(98)	(3,763)	(138)	(2,499)	(47)	(1,857)	(11)

Note: U.S. Suburbs = non-central city portions of fifty SMSAs for which intra-metropolitan location of units is reported on AHS national survey tapes. See footnote 2.

Source: U.S. Bureau of the Census, *Annual Housing Survey*: 1974 and 1975, national sample public use tapes.

increased in value by 1975, while 9 percent of black units, but only 5 percent of white units, decreased in value. Similarly, increases were reported for 22 percent of white-owned but 18 percent of black-owned units valued between $35,000, and $49,999, while 24 percent of black units and 10 percent of white units in this value category decreased between 1974 and 1975.

In sum, when comparing reported property value of identical suburban units at two points a year apart, units owned by blacks in both years were less likely to increase and more likely to decrease in value than white-owned units matched by value in the initial year. If inflation in housing prices is producing windfalls for some, the above data suggest that such beneficial effects are less likely to accrue to a suburban homeowner who is black than one who is white.

THE MARKET FOR BLACK-OWNED UNITS

It is an elementary economic notion that the disproportionate value increase of white-owned and black-owned units may be due to weaker demand for the latter. The data discussed above and summarized in Exhibit 2 suggest several sources of such weakness.

First, the probability that a black-owned suburban unit will turn over to a black household is far higher than that of a white-owned unit. With black households comprising a stable 5 percent of the suburban population, roughly that proportion of housing turnovers should go to blacks in an unbiased market. Indeed, of all 649,000 owner-occupied suburban units that turned over between 1974 and 1975, 4.6 percent were black-occupied in 1975. Disaggregating this total picture by race, however, reveals a significant pattern: fully 46 percent of the suburban *black-owned units* that turned over, but only 3.2 percent of the suburban *white-owned units* that turned over, went to a black household. In short, the probability that a suburban black owner will be replaced by another black is fourteen times that of a white owner. As a result, black home sellers are more likely than their white counterparts to bear the burden of lower black purchasing power.

Secondly, suburban black home buyers acquire white-occupied units more frequently than black-occupied units. As suggested above, this finding indicates both the recency of black arrival in suburbia and also the limited pool of desirable black-owned suburban units that potential black buyers might choose from. The data suggest further that black sellers are at a competitive disadvantage to the extent that they have to compete for buyers with the far more extensive white-owned stock available for sale.

Thirdly, the corollary to the above is that suburban black home sellers are replaced by whites more frequently than by other blacks. This may reflect in part the relative weakness of effective black demand for suburban housing units. More importantly, however, if whites constitute the largest proportion of demand for black-owned units, and white replacement is restricted to the highest value black-owned units, then it is the lower value black suburban units that are most impacted by inadequate demand.

Finally, the weakness of the market is reflected in the higher proportion of black than white owners who are replaced by renter households in the same units. Furthermore, this discrepancy is most pronounced among lower value housing units. Of units valued below $20,000 in 1974 and occupied by a different household in 1975, 9 percent of black-owned units, but only 2 percent of white-owned units, shifted to rental occupancy upon turnover.

PREVIOUS TENURE

If black suburban home sellers are far more dependent on black replacements than their white suburban counterparts, then it follows that the weaker purchasing ability of potential black buyers will impact more negatively on black sellers than on white. Previous tenure impacts on home purchase through the availability of equity to apply to the downpayment. First time homebuyers must be able to draw from personal savings, relatives, or other sources for the downpayment that second time buyers typically obtain from the equity accumulated in the previous unit. Equity accumulated through previous homeownership greatly facilitates home purchase, and racial differences in tenure of previous unit influence downpayment ability.

Fully 60 percent of black purchasers of suburban housing units in 1975, but 49 percent of white purchasers, rented their previous unit. Thus, white homebuyers were substantially more likely than black buyers of suburban units to draw on previous equity to help finance their suburban home purchase.[11]

Further, white suburban homebuyers were more likely to own than rent their previous unit regardless of whether it was located in a central city or a suburb. Among black suburban homebuyers, however, an interesting pattern emerges when location of the previous unit is considered along with tenure. Eight out of ten black suburban homebuyers whose previous residence was in a central city rented that unit; six out of ten already in the suburbs, however, were owners. Thus, while black homebuyers already in the suburbs are somewhat more likely to be previous owners when compared to their white counterparts, this former group constitutes a considerably smaller share of black homebuyers than white. In sum, central city renters comprise the largest share (42 percent) of black suburban homebuyers; another 18 percent were suburban renters, and only 40 percent were owners. Among white suburban homebuyers, in contrast, only 17 percent were central city renters, and 51 percent were previous owners. The implication of these figures for our discussion is straightforward. Black suburban homeowners, more dependent than are whites on finding a black buyer to achieve a sale, are significantly confined to a segment of the market characterized by a weaker asset position as measured by equity accumulated in a previous home.

Summary and Conclusions

A growing share of the nation's metropolitan area black population is located in the suburbs. At first glance, such a shift may be thought to signal a reversal of the racial separation that has marked metropolitan patterns for decades. The evidence presented here, though partial and qualified in many ways, suggests that excessive optimism may be premature. Suburbanization per se is neither synonymous with equal housing opportunity nor will it automatically serve the wealth accumulative function it has provided for previous suburbanizing ethnic groups. Progress toward these goals requires continued monitoring of the housing market conditions governing the black suburbanization process that is underway.

Our initial look at the nature of black suburbanization has focused on three broad elements of the process: the magnitude of white to black transition as a source of suburban housing, the characteristics of the housing units involved, and the potential of homeownership thus achieved as a means of equity accumulation. As of the mid-1970s, we found that rental units become available to blacks at a faster rate than owner-occupied units, that black suburbanites are less likely than whites to own their own homes, and that those who do are more likely than whites to see their units transfer to rental occupancy with subsequent turnover. Compared to suburban units transferred within the white sub-market, units that turn over from white to black are on average older, are of lower value, and are assigned lower ratings of housing and neighborhood quality. Finally, owner-occupied units within the black suburban submarket are less likely to increase in value and more likely to decrease in value than equivalently priced units within the white sub-market.

If these trends continue unchecked, we will have yet further evidence of the disparity between the black experience in America and that of other ethnic and immigrant groups. For the latter, dispersion into the suburbs was synonymous with assimilation, the breaking down of ethnic enclaves, and unfettered upward mobility. Initial evidence to date raises the issue of whether the equivalent process will hold for the suburbanizing black population. The spectre of "two societies" so often hailed to describe black cities and white suburbs may simply be replicated at a new metropolitan scale.

Notes

1. See, for example, John Kain, "Theories of Residential Location and Realities of Race," in *Essays on Urban Spatial Structure* (Cambridge: Ballinger, 1975), pp. 139-40.

2. Our discussion of post-1970 suburban housing characteristics is based on published and unpublished data from the U.S. Bureau of the Census *Annual Housing Surveys* for 1974, 1975 and 1976. The *Annual Housing Survey* comprises a national sample of some 84,000 housing units resurveyed each year and weighted to represent the national housing stock.

The Census Bureau's confidentiality requirements restrict identification of intra-metropolitan location of sampled housing units in some cases. Unless otherwise indicated, our analysis of "suburban" housing units is therefore limited to units in the noncentral city portions of fifty SMSAs for which intrametropolitan location is identified on AHS computer tapes. These fifty SMSAs which contained 74.8 percent of the nation's black metropolitan occupied housing units in 1970 are: Akron, Albany-Schenectady-Troy, Anaheim-Santa Ana-Garden Grove, Atlanta, Baltimore, Birmingham, Boston, Buffalo, Chicago, Cincinnati, Cleveland, Columbus, Dallas, Denver, Detroit, Ft. Worth, Gary-Hammond-East Chicago, Greensboro-Winston Salem-High Point, Honolulu, Houston, Indianapolis, Jersey City, Kansas City, Los Angeles-Long Beach, Louisville, Miami, Milwaukee, Minneapolis-St. Paul, New Orleans, New York City, Newark, Norfolk-Portsmouth, Oklahoma City, Paterson-Clifton-Passaic, Philadelphia, Phoenix, Pittsburgh, Portland (Ore.), Providence-Warwick-Pawtucket, Rochester, Sacramento, St. Louis, San Bernardino-Riverside, San Diego, San Francisco-Oakland, San Jose, Seattle-Everett, Tampa-St. Petersburg, Toledo, and Washington, D.C.

3. For a review of the literature on the characteristics of transition neighborhoods, see Karl E. Taeuber and Alma F. Taeuber, *Negroes in Cities: Residential Segregation and Neighborhood Change* (New York: Atheneum, 1969).

4. For example, Chester Rapkin and William Grigsby, *The Demand for Housing in Racially Mixed Areas*, (Los Angeles: University of California Press, 1960).

5. This discussion, utilizing published data sources, covers the suburban portions of *all* metropolitan areas identified in the 1970 census. See U.S. Bureau of the Census, Current Housing Reports, Series H-150-76, *General Housing Characteristics for the United States and Regions: 1976.* Annual Housing Survey: 1976, Part A, Table A-1 (Washington, D.C.: USGPO, 1978).

6. Data based on a limited sample of suburban housing units. See footnote 2 supra.

7. Discrepancies between totals in Exhibts 1 and 2 result from the procedures utilized to identify housing units occupied by different households in 1974 and 1975. Exhibit 1 includes all suburban housing units for which race, tenure and suburban location could be identified in both 1974 and 1975. Exhibit 2 includes only that sub-set of Exhibit 1 units occupied by "recent movers" at the time of the 1975 survey. As a result, some units shown as having turned over in Exhibit 1 are not identified as "recent movers" in Table 2. "Recent movers" are defined by the Census Bureau as households which moved into the unit during the twelve-month period preceding the survey. Since AHS national surveys are conducted between October and December of each year, some units may be resurveyed as much as fifteen months apart. Some households could thus move into a unit subsequent to the 1974 survey and not be counted as "recent movers" in 1975. Further discrepancies are introduced in cases where the race of the household head changes through marriage, separation, or divorce but the household continues to occupy the same dwelling unit. The effect of

these accounting procedures is to decrease the within-category totals reported in Exhibit 2 compared to Exhibit 1. There is no evidence, however, that relationships between categories in Exhibit 2 are skewed in any systematic way.

8. A long-standing and well-calloused rule of thumb suggests that value should not exceed 2.5 times total family income.

9. An equally hoary rule recommends that rent should be no more than 25 percent of income.

10. See, for instance, John Kain and John Quigley, *Housing Markets and Racial Discrimination* (New York: National Bureau of Economic Research, 1975).

11. U.S. Bureau of the Census, Current Housing Reports, Series H-150-75D, *Housing Characteristics of Recent Movers*, Annual Housing Survey: 1975, Part D (Washington, D.C.: USGPO, 1977).

Housing Search Experiences of Black and White Suburban Homebuyers*

Robert W. Lake

I. Introduction

Despite substantial improvements in black socioeconomic levels since 1960,[1] and despite federal legislation prohibiting racial discrimination in housing,[2] the proportion of metropolitan area blacks living in the suburbs is far below the proportion of whites at equivalent income levels.[3] Given the adequacy of incomes and no evidence for a lack of "taste" among blacks for suburban residence, racial discrepancies in suburban representation may be ascribed to greater costs and/or difficulties in the suburban housing search experience of blacks.

According to this argument, if the costs of search for a new residence (in monetary, psychic, time and effort terms) exceed the costs of remaining in place, then search may be terminated, accompanied by either a downward readjustment of aspirations or increasing dissatisfaction.[4] Systematically greater search costs confronting

439

black potential homebuyers would thus bar substantial numbers of otherwise qualified black households from seeking and/or finding a suburban residence. If this is the case, a growing number of black households are living in sub-optimal housing (i.e., less housing than they need and can afford) amid mounting dissatisfaction.

At least three models of racial differences in housing search can be posited. First, lack of previous experience in the housing market and relatively lower levels of prior ownership may result in greater inefficiency, and therefore higher costs, of black search as opposed to white. Second, overt discrimination by gatekeeper institutions such as real estate brokers and mortgage lenders may curtail the flow of information regarding housing vacancies and borrowing opportunities, thereby increasing search costs for blacks. Thirdly, the expectation of discriminatory treatment may cause black potential homebuyers to approach and use these institutional gatekeepers differently, and less efficiently, than their white counterparts. In this final model, search costs are increased for blacks by the necessity of adapting search behavior to the constraints imposed by having to work with' discriminatory institutions.

This paper assesses the relative importance of each of these models in explaining differences in the housing search experiences of a sample of black and white recent homebuyers in five suburban New Jersey communities.[5] Focusing on the successful homebuyer, the analysis asks whether the search experience of black buyers was more protracted, costly, or inefficient than the search of equivalent white buyers, and if so, whether contextual differences, overt discrimination, or black adaptation better explains observed differences in search experience.

The paper is divided into six further sections. Section II summarizes the basic framework adopted in this analysis for conceptualizing residential mobility and the housing search process, and then presents the three models of racial differences in housing search.

Section III provides an overview of the sample of recent homebuyers, differentiated by race of buyer and the racial composition of the destination neighborhood. This discussion documents the extent to which black and white homebuyers differ in background contextual characteristics (e.g., socioeconomic level, reason for moving, etc.) that might be expected to influence the search process.

In Section IV, we turn directly to the question of racial differences in seach behavior as measured by the length and extensiveness of search, number and type of information sources used, and the like.

The discussion in Sections V and VI employs regression analysis to assess the extent to which racial differences in search remain after controlling for background differences affecting the search process. The policy issue is addressed by estimating the extent to which eliminating contextual differences would decrease discrepancies between white and black search experiences. The final section provides a summary of findings and relevant policy implications.

II. Housing Search Behavior and Race

CONCEPTUALIZING SEARCH BEHAVIOR

The congruence between a household and its housing unit is embodied in the concept of place utility.[6] A utility threshold, unique for each household, can be defined below which the household's present unit is unsatisfactory. This lack of congruence causes stress, and a negative utility threshold is reached when stress (the costs of staying) exceeds the costs of moving.[7] Search costs, measured in monetary, psychic, time, and effort terms, are a component of total moving costs. Stress, or disequilibrium, results from a change in either the household (life cycle, new-job opportunity, aspirations) or the housing unit (condition, maintenance costs, neighborhood conditions).

Three options are available to households confronting rising dissatisfaction with their housing unit. The first is to adjust needs, expectations, or aspirations to bring them back into line with the existing unit. The second is to restructure the unit (e.g., add on rooms, close off rooms, etc.) so as to better fit the household's needs. The third option is to exchange the existing unit for a more satisfactory one. Relative costs determine which option is chosen. Stress caused by deteriorating neighborhood conditions, for instance, may constitute a psychic cost that outweighs any costs of search and moving.[8] Conversely, a household that has initiated search may exhaust its resources of time and effort, discontinue search, and readjust its aspirations downward in order to stay in the existing unit. Most residential moves that are completed tend to be relatively short-distance moves, involving an adjustment of housing needs within the same social area.[9]

The functions of housing search, once initiated, are to locate acceptable alternatives and to develop criteria for evaluating those alternatives.[10] The efficiency of a household's search process depends on the amount and quality of information possessed initially (i.e., prior experience), the information channels available to and utilized by the searcher, and the way in which this information is used by the searcher.[11] Thus, the first-time homebuyer may require additional time (and therefore costs) to develop criteria for evaluation, to identify and learn to use potential sources of information, and to synthesize the information obtained.

Information about housing vacancies is typically disseminated through at least one of four channels: mass media (e.g., newspaper listings), specialized agencies (e.g., real estate brokers), public information displays (e.g., "For Sale" signs), and the seller's personal contact network.[12] A seller or agent controlling a vacancy will use one or another of these dissemination channels depending on the relative cost/effort required and the anticipated or desired audience to be reached. Thus, each channel contains information biases, and utilization by the searcher of one channel over another will yield a spatially and qualitatively biased sub-set of information regarding housing vacancies. For instance, word-of-mouth channels are typically used to disseminate information about either extremely exclusive or extremely deteriorated units. In the former case, audience restriction is of concern, while for deteriorated units cost minimization predominates. Risa Palm has shown that real estate agents tend to be very localized in their recommendations to buyers, so that choice of a particular broker may limit search to that area encompassed by the broker's information field.[13]

To summarize the perspective outlined here, the effort in time, monetary, and other considerations a household will expend in search for a new unit is relative to the costs extracted by staying in place. The search process involves acquiring new information, evaluating it in the light of existing knowledge, and measuring the relative costs of moving to the new unit, continuing the search for further alternatives, or terminating search without moving. The efficiency of a household's search behavior depends on the amount and quality of prior knowledge, the content of information channels available to the household, and the household's ability to utilize those information channels. Systematic differences between black and white homebuyers along any of these dimensions would generate differential search costs by race, effectively reducing access to housing opportunities for the disadvantaged group.

MODELS OF RACIAL DIFFERENCES IN SEARCH EXPERIENCE

Three models are proposed that account for less efficiency and greater costs of search behavior of potential black homebuyers. These models ascribe greater black search costs to either direct or indirect racial discrimination (Exhibit 1).

EXHIBIT 1

MODELS OF SUBURBAN HOUSING SEARCH DISCRIMINATION

Model	Operant	Discriminatory Impact	Policy Response
(1) CONTEXTUAL (Indirect Discrimination)	Searchers differ due to past discrimination: lower education, income, previous ownership; concentration in central cities, etc.	Inexperience in search; lack of knowledge of information sources; use of inefficient sources.	Compensatory affirmative action.
(2) DIRECT DISCRIMINATION			
(2a) Overt Discrimination	Searchers treated differently by intermediaries on account of race: non-cooperation, racial steering, etc.	Unavailability of information on vacancies.	Strengthen and enforce open housing legislation.
(2b) Black Adaptation to Discriminatory Institutions	Searchers behave differently vis-a-vis intermediaries: differential utilization of search mechanisms.	Inefficiency in search; more effort, longer time required to obtain equivalent information.	Develop alternative unbiased information sources.

The *contextual model,* implying indirect effects of historical discriminatory patterns, proposes the existence of significant differences between whites and blacks in background (or contextual) factors influencing residential location and mobility. Thus, lower educational levels, lower income-earning ability, greater concentration in central cities, a low probability of prior ownership, and concentration in rental housing—all legacies of a historical tradition of discrimination—generate disproportionally greater obstacles in the search process of potential black homebuyers. These contextual differences between blacks and whites result in inadequate prior knowledge of the workings of the housing market, an inability to obtain information about housing unit vacancies, and an inability to evaluate and use information effectively.

The contextual model thus suggests that racial differences in search *experience* are due to racial differences in search *behavior*. Less sophisticated than white buyers, blacks use less efficient information sources (e.g., personal networks rather than formal sources) and constrain their search to only a small fraction of available vacancies because of a lack of awareness.

Two additional models contend that racial differences in search experience arise from direct discrimination. The first of these points to *overt discrimination* practiced by institutional gatekeepers such as real estate brokers and mortgage lenders. Such institutional actors can effectively limit the flow of information to black buyers by denying that a particular unit is on the market, by cancelling appointments, failing to appear or claiming to be out of the office, by steering black buyers to particular neighborhoods, and so on. The overt discrimination model therefore argues that blacks are no less adept in search than are whites but that they are treated differently by key intermediaries in the search process.

Instances of overt discrimination may in fact be relatively infrequent.[14] A low incidence of flagrant discrimination, however, is not necessarily an indication of unbiased broker behavior or the efficacy of open housing legislation. Rather, the third model suggests that black homebuyers, sophisticated enough to avoid situations of outright discrimination, adapt their search behavior to account for constraints imposed by a discriminatory market. The *black adaptation model* therefore proposes that racial differences in search experience arise from the way potential black buyers approach and use institutional intermediaries given the expectation of discriminatory treatment. For example, a white buyer might use a real estate agent to obtain information about housing vacancies. An equivalent black buyer, in contrast, expecting minimal cooperation from the agent, might first learn of the vacancy through another source (e.g., "For Sale" sign) and only then approach the agent to inquire about the unit.

To recapitulate (see Exhibit 1), the *contextual model,* based on indirect discrimination, posits the use of different search strategies by whites and blacks due to contextual or background differences in socioeconomic characteristics and experience of the two groups. Direct discriminatory effects underlie both the *overt discrimination model* and the *black adaptation model;* in the former case blacks are seen as treated differently by institutional intermediaries, while the latter model sees blacks using these intermediaries differently given the expectation of discriminatory treatment.

The extent to which differences between black and white search experience are accounted for by each of these models has significantly policy implications. Discrepancies in search due to contextual factors require a policy aimed to compensate for these background differences—the principle behind affirmative action-type programs. Further support for this sort of response might be generated by a finding that blacks are more subject than whites to the negative effects of contextual factors, i.e., if differences are race-based and not simply founded on class/economic distinctions.[15]

In contrast, a finding of a "pure" race effect persisting after controlling for contextual factors requires a different policy response. Evidence of outright discrimination against qualified black home-buyers might justify further strengthening and enforcement of open housing legislation, as in bills currently pending before Congressional committees aimed at broadening the scope of Title VIII coverage and widening HUD's role in administrative enforcement.

Finally, evidence of black adaptation to existing institutions in order to minimize the experience of outright discrimination requires the introduction of alternative unbiased sources of information. Penalties of black adaptation to a discriminatory market include poorer quality information, the requirement of extra time, and a less-efficient search process. The availability of alternative information sources, such as a public multiple listing service, would allow blacks to bypass or lessen their dependence on potentially discriminatory institutions.

III. The Recent Buyers Sample

THE RECENT BUYERS SURVEY

The data for this analysis were obtained during October-December 1978 in a structured telephone survey of 1,004 recent homebuyers in five suburban New Jersey case study communities. The total sample includes 234 black households and 770 white.

The case study communities were selected to represent a range of suburban communities across the state to which black households are currently moving. An earlier analysis of census and school enrollment racial data revealed a typology of suburban communities in the state in which black population has been increasing since 1970.[16] Based on this analysis, five communities encompassing a range of housing prices, income levels, and geographic location within the state were selected for further intensive analysis. Three communities (Franklin Township, Ewing Township, and Peasantville) are adjacent to central cities (New Brunswick, Trenton, and Atlantic City, respectively) and represent the spill-over of central city black population into adjacent inner-suburban areas. The remaining communities (Teaneck Twp. and Montclair) represent dormitory residential communities with relatively higher income and housing price levels.

The total population of New Jersey was 10.7 percent black in 1970, and 6.3 percent of suburban housing units were black-occupied. The corresponding percent black population for the five towns in 1970 ranged from a low of 9.3 percent in Ewing Twp. to a high of 33.0 percent in Pleasantville. By limiting our analysis to these five towns, several components of the suburban black population are not represented. One such element is rural poverty-area black households within metropolitan boundaries. Prior analysis, however, showed that this population group is declining in numbers since 1970 within the state. A second element not represented within the sample is individual wealthy black pioneer households moving into otherwise all-white communities. The survey does include, however, black households moving into all-white neighborhoods within the case study communities.

Computerized records of every arms-length real estate transaction by municipality were obtained from the State Treasury Department.[17] These records include block and lot numbers, sale price, assessed value (land and improvements) and a code indicating property type (single-family residential, commercial, etc.). Block and lot numbers for every single-family housing sale in the five communities were listed out for the three-year period July 1974 through June 1977. These block and lot numbers were matched with records in the five local assessors' offices to identify the buyer's name; telephone numbers were then obtained for this 100 percent sample of recent homebuyers. Telephone interviews averaging 30-40 minutes in length were conducted with a total of 1,004 recent homebuyers. Because of the preponderance of white buyers, a racial screen question was employed and an additional 781 white interviews were terminated. The total of 1,785 contacts represents 44.8 percent of single-family sales in the five towns during the three-year period, and 69.6 percent of the usable sample (disregarding absentee owners, unpublished numbers, etc.).

Within each case study community, four neighborhood categories have been defined on the basis of 1970 census block data by race and the race of new buyers moving into the block during the survey period. These neighborhood categories are as follows:

(1) *All-White:* 1970 census block population less than 5 percent black; only white in-movers. Mean 1970 percent black on these blocks was 0.51.

(2) *Black-Entry:* 1970 census block population less than 5 percent black; black in-movers during the study period. Mean 1970 percent black on these blocks was 0.63.

(3) *Inter-Racial:* 1970 census block population more than 5 percent and less than 80 percent black. Mean 1970 percent black population was 29.3 percent.

(4) *All-Black:* 1970 census block population more than 80 percent black. Mean 1970 percent black population on these blocks was 86.1.

The breakdown for sample whites and blacks by neighborhood category is:

Neighborhood Category	Black	White	Total
All-White	0.0	73.5	56.3
Black-Entry	50.9	12.8	21.8
Inter-Racial	37.6	13.0	18.7
All-Black	11.5	0.7	3.2
Total	100.0	100.0	100.0

CHARACTERISTICS BY RACE OF BUYER AND NEIGHBORHOOD

The mean sale price of homes purchased by this sample of recent buyers ranged from a low of $35,600 for blacks in All-Black neighborhoods to a high of $52,800 for whites in Black-Entry neighborhoods. Differences in mean sale price by race of buyer across neighborhood categories are significant at the .001 level. Given this range of purchase prices, it is reasonable to expect significant differences in the contextual or background characteristics of blacks and whites moving into each of the four neighborhood racial categories.

Socioeconomic Characteristics. (Exhibit A-1 to Exhibit A-4) Black households are larger, on average, than white households in all neighborhood categories, ranging from 3.3 for whites in All-White neighborhoods to 4.0 for blacks in Inter-Racial neighborhoods. The total number employed, however (1.8), is invariant across racial and neighborhood groups, with only black households in All-Black neighborhoods averaging 2.1 employed members. Single-parent households constitute 10 percent of black families in Inter-Racial neighborhoods and 5 percent or less in all other categories. Family-size differences are reflected in the distribution of households with children: husband-wife families with children are more common among black households than white in all neighborhood categories. White household heads are nearly twice as likely as their black neighborhood counterparts to be under 30, and somewhat more likely to be 50 or over. Black household heads, in other words, are more likely than whites in each neighborhood type to be in the prime income-earning years (35-49). Between 18 and 25 percent of all racial and neighborhood groups are employed as managers or administrators, and another 10 to 15 percent of all groups work in sales or clerical positions. Whites in each neighborhood type are somewhat more likely than blacks to be in professional occupations (e.g., 49 percent of whites and 24 percent of blacks in Inter-Racial neighborhoods) while the converse is true for blue-collar occupations (45 percent of blacks and 10 percent of whites in Inter-Racial neighborhoods). Whites have somewhat higher educational levels than blacks in each neighborhood type: 75 percent of whites and 50 percent of blacks in Black-Entry neighborhoods have a college degree or better, while the percentages in Inter-Racial neighborhoods are 69 percent for whites and 33 percent for blacks.

Previous Residence. (Exhibit A-5 to Exhibit A-7) Whites in all neighborhood categories were more likely than blacks to own their previous residence (e.g., 44 percent of whites but 32 percent of blacks in Black-Entry neighborhoods). Blacks buying units in All-Black neighborhoods had the lowest rate of prior ownership (19.2 percent). Turning to location of previous residence, blacks in Black-Entry neighborhoods are clearly new arrivals: less than 1 percent moved within the same neighborhood. In contrast, nearly 11 percent of blacks in Inter-Racial neighborhoods traded housing within the same neighborhood. Whites were more likely than blacks to have lived in a suburban community: 40.9 percent of whites but only 21.4 percent of blacks in Inter-Racial neighborhoods moved from a New Jersey suburb. Similarly, 17.2 percent of whites but only 6.1 percent of blacks in Black-Entry neighborhoods moved from an out-of-state suburb. Blacks, in contrast, were central city residents prior to their move: fully 64 percent of blacks in Black-Entry neighborhoods moved from a central city location. Finally, whites were more likely than blacks to move for job-related reasons. Perhaps reflecting their central city origins, blacks were more likely than whites to move because of dissatisfaction with the neighborhood.

In sum, significant background differences in socioeconomic characteristics, previous tenure, and location of previous residence can be discerned among black and white homebuyers in the sample. The next section assesses racial differences in search experience and the following section examines the relationship between the two.

IV. Racial Differences in Search Behavior

Startlingly little difference is discernable in either the information sources used or found helpful by black and white homebuyers in the sample (Exhibit 2). Well over 90 percent of both blacks and whites used a real estate agent and comparable proportions rated the broker as somewhat or very helpful. Nearly identical proportions of both blacks and whites used the remaining sources listed. This initial finding yields little support for the contextual model that claims that blacks are less experienced or knowledgable than whites in the housing search process.

Two significant differences do emerge from the data, however. First, blacks place somewhat more importance on information obtained from friends: 33.2 percent of blacks but only 25.5 percent of whites say this was "very helpful." Evidently, personal networks are an important information source for black suburban homebuyers who may require assurance that a particular community is hospitable to black entry. As one black participant reported in a videotaped group interview designed as a follow-up to this study: "I wanted to make sure there wouldn't be any crosses burned on my lawn."

Secondly, black homebuyers reveal a greater dependence than whites on "For Sale" signs as a source of information on vacancies: nearly 40 percent of blacks but only 25 percent of whites said this

EXHIBIT 2

SOURCES OF INFORMATION USED AND FOUND HELPFUL, BY RACE OF BUYER
(PERCENTS)

SOURCE USED AND FOUND

Information Source[a]	Very Helpful	Somewhat Helpful	Total Helpful	Not Helpful	Can't Say	Source Not Used	Number of Cases
Talk to Friends[b]							
Black	33.2	23.1	56.3	8.7	0.9	34.1	229
White	25.5	34.2	59.7	6.0	1.3	32.9	765
Talk to Relatives							
Black	20.8	16.9	37.7	5.6	0.0	56.7	231
White	14.5	20.3	34.8	7.4	0.9	56.8	767
Talk to Fellow Employees							
Black	17.2	19.3	36.5	4.7	1.7	57.1	233
White	14.4	21.4	35.8	6.4	0.5	57.3	763
Check Newspaper Listings							
Black	23.1	34.1	57.2	10.9	1.7	30.1	229
White	26.9	33.9	60.8	12.5	0.9	25.9	762
Walk Around							
Black	13.4	17.2	30.6	3.9	0.0	65.5	232
White	14.3	13.1	27.4	4.3	0.5	67.7	761
Drive Around							
Black	42.2	27.6	69.8	4.7	0.9	24.6	232
White	35.7	32.7	68.4	6.2	1.1	24.4	759
"For Sale" Signs[c]							
Black	17.5	21.8	39.3	7.4	0.4	52.8	229
White	10.6	14.1	24.7	8.7	1.3	65.3	758
Real Estate Agent							
Black	76.4	15.9	92.3	2.1	1.3	4.3	233
White	71.6	16.1	87.7	3.1	1.6	7.6	765

Notes: (a)   "Other" sources, including community groups, bank personnel, and builders or contractors, were used by fewer than 15 percent of the sample, with no significant differences found between blacks and whites.

            (b)   Chi-square statistic significant at .01.

            (c)   Chi-square statistic significant at .001.

Source: CUPR Recent Buyers Survey, Fall 1978.

was very or somewhat helpful. Ironically, municipal ordinances banning "For Sale" signs to forestall block-busting may have the unintended consequence of removing a vital information source for black buyers. A pattern emerging from the videotaped group interviews is that black buyers often first identify an available unit through a "For Sale" sign and only then approach a real estate broker for information regarding asking price and access to the unit. This initial evidence may suggest that while both black and white buyers nominally use the same sources, black buyers approach these sources differently and with a different set of expectations for the type of information that will be forthcoming.

Further evidence for the similarity in white and black search experience is found in a comparison of the duration and extensiveness of search (Exhibits 3 and 4). Raw-score comparisons of search activity reveal almost no racial difference in the number of housing units seriously considered (2.2), the number of brokers contacted (2.8), the number of information sources used (5.0) and the number found helpful (4.3). This parity in sources utilized, however, appears to bear less of a pay-off for blacks than for whites: black search appears restricted to fewer housing units and fewer communities while extending over a longer time period.

In Exhibit 4, racial differences on a smaller set of search measures are reported in log form. The log transformation is useful since the difference between, for example, 50 and 60 units looked at is substantively less important than the difference between 5 and 10.

Percent differences in mean log search are reported in the bottom half of Exhibit 4. Blacks spend on average half again as much time as whites thinking about looking for a new unit. Comparing blacks and whites moving into the same neighborhood category, the greatest discrepancy is found in Inter-Racial neighborhoods. Whites moving into these neighborhoods appear to be making the most precipitous moves. Compared to whites moving into All-White neighborhoods, whites in other neighborhoods show no difference in time thinking prior to active search. Blacks, in contrast, spend up to 62 percent more time in pre-move deliberations. These findings may in part be due to the greater likelihood among whites to move because of a job transfer, while blacks are more likely to move because of dissatisfaction with the neighborhood. An additional reason for this discrepancy may also be a greater reluctance among blacks to move from a familiar setting to a potentially inhospitable one.

EXHIBIT 3

RAW-SCORE COMPARISONS OF SEARCH ACTIVITY AMONG EIGHT RACE AND NEIGHBORHOOD GROUPS (MEANS)[a]

Race of Buyer and Neighborhood[b]	Months Thinking of Looking	Months in Active Search	Number of Units Looked At	Number of Units Internally Inspected	Number of Units Seriously Considered Searched	Number of Communities Searched	Number of Brokers Contacted	Number of Banks Contacted	Number of Information Sources Used	Number of Information Sources Found Helpful
All Whites	6.5 (742)	5.6 (761)	22.8 (751)	17.0 (756)	2.2 (769)	3.5 (759)	2.8 (708)	1.9 (671)	4.9 (735)	4.2 (735)
All Blacks	10.2 (213)	5.7 (229)	18.1 (221)	13.9 (225)	2.2 (233)	3.3 (231)	2.8 (223)	1.4 (194)	5.1 (226)	4.5 (226)
All-White Neighborhoods (Whites)	6.1 (522)	6.1 (538)	22.8 (531)	17.3 (534)	2.2 (543)	3.5 (538)	2.8 (503)	1.9 (475)	5.0 (544)	4.3 (544)
Black-Entry Neighborhoods										
Whites	6.1 (92)	4.7 (94)	22.8 (93)	18.1 (94)	2.3 (95)	3.9 (93)	2.6 (89)	2.4 (79)	4.7 (95)	4.0 (95)
Blacks	9.6 (105)	4.7 (114)	21.2 (110)	16.4 (110)	2.3 (115)	3.7 (115)	3.0 (112)	1.4 (99)	5.2 (115)	4.4 (115)
Inter-Racial Neighborhoods										
Whites	8.0 (94)	3.7 (95)	22.2 (93)	13.9 (94)	2.1 (96)	2.8 (95)	3.4 (86)	1.9 (82)	4.8 (96)	4.1 (96)
Blacks	10.9 (79)	6.2 (82)	16.5 (79)	12.9 (82)	2.2 (84)	3.1 (82)	2.5 (82)	1.5 (66)	5.1 (85)	4.6 (85)
All-Black Neighborhoods (Blacks)	11.5 (22)	7.4 (25)	13.2 (24)	9.2 (25)	2.1 (26)	2.3 (26)	2.6 (21)	1.4 (19)	4.8 (26)	4.2 (26)

Notes: (a)   Number of cases indicated in parentheses.
(b)   Neighborhood racial categories do not sum to the total number of whites and blacks because missing racial data for some blocks in the 1970 census prevented assignment of these cases to neighborhood categories.

Source: CUPR Recent Buyers Survey, Fall 1978.

EXHIBIT 4

COMPARISON OF SEARCH ACTIVITY OF EIGHT RACE AND NEIGHBORHOOD GROUPS RELATIVE TO WHITE MAJORITY SEARCH

Race of Buyer and Neighborhood	Months Thinking of Moving (ln)	Months in Active Search (ln)	Number of Units Looked At (ln)	Number of Units Internally Inspected (ln)	Number of Communities Searched (ln)	Number of Banks Contacted (ln)
All Whites	1.2117	1.1705	2.5788	2.2817	.9638	.3978
All Blacks	1.7850	1.4348	2.5393	2.2764	.9670	.2724
All-White Neighborhoods (Whites)	1.2205	1.2549	2.5656	2.2722	.9640	.4177
Black-Entry Neighborhoods						
Whites	1.1369	.9750	2.6774	2.4213	1.0846	.4593
Blacks	1.5595	1.2461	2.6720	2.3973	1.0731	.2684
Inter-Racial Neighborhoods						
Whites	1.2450	1.0154	2.4853	2.0857	.8016	.3791
Blacks	1.9747	1.5276	2.3194	2.0293	.8490	.2580
All-Black Neighborhoods (Blacks)	1.8955	1.6294	2.4447	1.9910	.7794	.2516

EXHIBIT 4 (CONTINUED)

Race of Buyer and Neighborhood	Months Thinking of Moving (ln)	Months in Active Search (ln)	Number of Units Looked At (ln)	Number of Units Internally Inspected (ln)	Number of Communities Searched (ln)	Numbers of Banks Contacted (ln)
Percent Differences:						
All Blacks vs. All Whites	47.3*	22.6*	– 1.5	– 0.2	0.3	–31.5*
Blacks vs. Whites in Black-Entry Neighborhoods	37.2*	27.8*	– 0.2	– 1.0	– 1.1	–41.6*
Blacks vs. Whites in Inter-Racial Neighborhoods	58.6*	50.4*	– 6.6	– 2.7	5.9	–31.9*
Compared to Whites in All-White Neighborhoods:						
Whites in Black-Entry Neighborhoods	– 6.9	–22.3*	4.4	6.6	12.5	10.0
Blacks in Black-Entry Neighborhoods	27.8*	– 0.7	4.2	5.5	11.3	–35.7*
Whites in Inter-Racial Neighborhoods	2.0	–19.1*	– 3.1	– 8.2	–16.9*	– 9.2
Blacks in Inter-Racial Neighborhoods	61.8*	21.7*	– 9.6*	–10.7	–11.9	–38.2*
Blacks in All-Black Neighborhoods	55.3*	29.8*	– 4.7	–12.4*	–19.2*	–39.8*

Note: * = difference between means is significantly different from zero at the .05 level (two-tailed test).

Source: CUPR Recent Buyers Survey, Fall 1978.

Black households also spend substantially more time in active search than do their white counterparts. Black search time is 28 percent higher than that of whites in Black-Entry neighborhoods and 50 percent higher in Inter-Racial areas. Compared to whites in All-White neighborhoods, whites moving into other neighborhood types actually spend on the order of 20 percent *less* time in active search, while blacks spend between 20 and 30 percent *more* time.

Though black housing search extends over a longer period of time, there is little difference in the log number of units looked at or internally inspected. The housing search experience of blacks appears to be less efficient in this regard, since the same number of units are examined but in a longer time period. If anything, blacks actually gain access to *fewer* units though they spend more time in search: compared to whites in All-White neighborhoods, blacks in Inter-Racial neighborhoods look at 10 percent fewer units, and blacks in All-Black areas inspect 12 percent fewer units.

The geographic extent of search is also more constrained for blacks than for whites. Again using whites in All-White neighborhoods as the norm, blacks in Inter-Racial and All-Black areas confine their search to between 10 and 20 percent fewer communities (the difference for blacks in Inter-Racial areas is not statistically significant).

Finally, blacks are substantially more confined than whites in the number of banks they contact for a mortgage. Evident here is that black homebuyers do considerably less "shopping around" for a bank with favorable mortgage terms than do white buyers. A greater propensity among black buyers to use FHA or VA mortgages, obtain financing from a mortgage company, and rely on the real estate broker to arrange the loan explain this finding. The alternative explanation of differential mortgage approval rates for whites and blacks is not supported by the data.

In sum, black housing search appears to be significantly less efficient than that of whites, with the same number or fewer units examined—in fewer communities—over a longer time span. The previous section documented the extent of background differences between whites and blacks that might account for observed differences in search experience. The next section examines this relationship.

V. Unified Regression Equations for Housing Search

The independent effects on search behavior of background characteristics and race are assessed in the regressions reported in Exhibit

5. Variables entered in the equations are those suggested by the conceptualization of search behavior summarized in Section II.

Unit and Buyer Characteristics. Purchase price of the unit, a summation of housing size and quality and a proxy for resources available to the buyer, is directly and significantly related to the extensiveness of search. A higher sale price is associated with a longer period of active search covering more units in more communities. In contrast, age of household head has a constraining impact on search behavior: older household heads spend more time in pre-search deliberation, examine fewer units, and confine their search to fewer communities. Previous ownership has the effect of lessening search time: a move from rental occupancy seems to require greater deliberation and a longer search process in which options are discovered and evaluated. Blue-collar occupation and a high school education (simple $r = .513$) lengthen search time but restrict search to fewer units.

Previous Residence. A move within the same neighborhood appears to involve a fortuitous move to improve housing fit: such movers inspect fewer units and confine their search to essentially a single community. A job-related move allows little time for deliberation or search: households moving for this reason spent 35.7 percent less time in active search than otherwise equivalent households (regression coefficient = $-.4414$ on log scale). The search process for these households is nonetheless quite efficient, since they inspect on average 25.6 percent more units than other households despite the limited time available to them. In contrast, families moving for housing unit or neighborhood reasons engage in proportionally longer search. Since these moves are motivated by dissatisfaction with the present unit, households continue searching until the desired improvement is realized.

Mobility Behavior. A household's selection criteria also independently influence its search behavior. Families for whom the price or characteristic of the unit per se are the primary criteria extend their search over a broader geographic area encompassing more communities. As would be expected, households choosing their unit because of its characteristics have inspected a larger number of units. Conversely, families for whom social criteria are the most important (to some extent a euphamism for racial composition) restrict their housing search to fewer units. Prior knowledge of the community also curtails the extent of search, especially as measured by the number of communities. Time in active search, however, is

EXHIBIT 5
REGRESSION EQUATIONS ON SEARCH MEASURES FOR TOTAL SAMPLE

DEPENDENT VARIABLES

Independent Variables	Months Thinking of Moving (ln)	Months in Active Search (ln)	Number of Units Looked At (ln)	Number of Units Internally Inspected (ln)	Number of Communities Searched (ln)	Number of Banks Contacted (ln)
UNIT CHARACTERISTICS						
Number of Bedrooms	.0473	.0424	.0328	.0657*	.0657**	-.0149
Age of House	-.0007	-.0001	.0017	.0008	.0009	.0001
Land Assessed Value (ln)		.0313			-.6670**	
Community Type (Montclair or Teaneck = 1)	.0396		.0080	.0743		.0366
Sale Price (ln)	.0818	.2859**	.9051***	.9370***	.4925***	-.0231
BUYER CHARACTERISTICS						
Age of Head	.0129***	-.0024	-.0169***	-.0149***	-.0089***	-.0058**
Previous Tenure (Own = 1)	-.1947*	-.1614*	-.0048	-.1204	.0785	-.1042*
Blue Collar Occupation (Yes = 1)	.3098***	.1339				
High School Grad or Less (Yes = 1)			-.1845*	-.1635*	-.0863	-.0742

EXHIBIT 5 (CONTINUED)

DEPENDENT VARIABLES

Independent Variables	Months Thinking of Moving (ln)	Months in Active Search (ln)	Number of Units Looked At (ln)	Number of Units Internally Inspected (ln)	Number of Communities Searched (ln)	Number of Banks Contacted (ln)
PREVIOUS RESIDENCE						
Same Neighborhood (Yes = 1)	.1945	− .0564	− .2204	− .2422*	− .2681***	.0794
Out of State Central City (Yes = 1)	.0358	.0616	− .0042	.0234	− .0251	.0034
Job-Related Move (Yes = 1)	− .4492***	− .4414***	.1309	.2281**	.1038	.0611
Housing Unit Reason (Yes = 1)	− .0070	.1411*	.0396	.0605	− .0280	.0448
Neighborhood Reason (Yes = 1)	.1641	.1887*	.2406*	.2426**	.0608	.0262
MOBILITY BEHAVIOR						
Chose Unit for Financial Reasons (Yes = 1)	− .0022	− .0402	.0293	.0140	.3001***	.0680
Chose Unit for Social Reasons (Yes = 1)	− .1257	− .0858	− .1467*	− .0822	− .0501	.0235
Chose Unit for Housing Unit Reason (Yes = 1)	− .0155	− .0683	.1811	.2261**	.3925***	− .0494
Prior Knowledge of Community (Yes = 1)	− .0461	.1345*	− .1249	− .1362*	− .2622***	− .0341
Real Estate Agent as Most Important Source (Yes = 1)	.0445	− .0253	.2495***	.2662***	.0111	− .0145

EXHIBIT 5 (CONTINUED)

Independent Variables	DEPENDENT VARIABLES					
	Months Thinking of Moving (ln)	Months in Active Search (ln)	Number of Units Looked At (ln)	Number of Units Internally Inspected (ln)	Number of Communities Searched (ln)	Number of Banks Contacted (ln)
FINANCING FACTORS						
Chose Bank for Terms (Yes=1)						.5604***
Chose Bank for Convenience (Yes=1)						.3923***
FHA/VA Mortgage (Yes=1)						-.2281***
RACE (Black=1)	.4312***	.2142***	.0779	.0887	.0281	.0528
Constant	-.1731	-2.1510	-6.8019	-7.6576	-3.1509	.7023
F	5.5002	5.5536	7.9949	10.4947	9.9708	10.0575
R^2	.112	.110	.150	.188	.179	.239
Sample Size	805	831	830	836	841	694
RACE AND NEIGHBORHOOD[a]						
Relative to WAW:						
WBE	.0248	-.2343**	.0349	.0666	.0577	-.0118
BBE	.3316***	.0139	.0639	.0673	.0343	.0419
WIR	.0713	-.2319**	-.0249	-.0554	-.0783	-.0085
BIR	.5930***	.3324**	.1114	.1432	.0218	.0907
BAB	.6099**	.3969*	.3399	.1796	.0141	.1144
R^2	.117	.131	.153	.189	.184	.243
Relative to WBE:						
BBE	.3068*	.2481*	.0291	.0007	-.0234	.0537
R^2	.117	.131	.153	.189	.184	.243
Relative to WIR:						
BIR	.5217***	.5643***	.0865	.1986	.1001	.0992
R^2	.117	.131	.153	.189	.184	.243

EXHIBIT 5 (CONTINUED)

Notes: Significance levels: *** p < .01; ** p < .05; * p < .10

    (a) Race and neighborhood categories:
        WAW   Whites in All-White Neighborhoods
        WBE   Whites in Black-Entry Neighborhoods
        BBE   Blacks in Black-Entry Neighborhoods
        WIR   Whites in Inter-Racial Neighborhoods
        BIR   Blacks in Inter-Racial Neighborhoods
        BAB   Blacks in All-Black Neighborhoods

Source: CUPR Recent Buyers Survey, Fall 1978.

longer, perhaps the converse of the brief search period engaged in by job transferees from outside the local area. Finally, the use of a real estate broker as the most important information source results in 28 percent more units looked at and 31 percent more units internally inspect as compared to other sources of information.

Financing Factors. A separate set of financing factors pertains specifically to the number of banks contacted to obtain a mortgage. Choosing a bank because of advantageous terms resulted in a 75 percent increase in the number of banks contacted, as compared to other reasons for selection (e.g., real estate broker recommendation). In contrast, obtaining an FHA or VA mortgage results in a 20.4 percent decrease in the number of banks contacted, presumably reflecting the importance of broker assistance in obtaining the mortgage in these cases.

Race. All other things equal, black homebuyers spend substantially longer in search of housing than otherwise comparable white buyers. Comparing all blacks with all whites in the sample, the coefficient on a dummy variable for race indicates that black households spent 54 percent more time thinking about moving and 24 percent more time in active search than did white households equivalent in unit and buyer characteristics, previous residence, and mobility behavior. Thus, the search process of black homebuyers extends over a longer period than that of whites even when differences in background contextual factors are controlled for.

Despite the longer duration of black housing search, there is no difference in the number of units looked at or examined or the number of communities searched by whites and blacks when controlling for background differences. This is in accord with the comparison of log search values reported above. However, the finding of racial parity in the number of units examined when controlling for intervening factors refutes the null hypothesis that contextual variables may have concealed racial differences in the extensiveness of search. Finally, differences between whites and blacks in the number of banks contacted disappear when controlling for the reason for selecting the bank and for the type of mortgage obtained.

Further insights into the effect of race on search behavior are obtained by considering neighborhood racial composition as well as the race of the buyer (Exhibit 5). Identical regression equations were run with the single race dummy replaced by separate dummies for each of the race/neighborhood combinations. With the variable for whites in All-White neighborhoods left out of the equation, the independent effect of each of the remaining categories is expressed relative to this norm.

Focusing first on decision time prior to search, neither whites in Black-Entry nor whites in Inter-Racial neighborhoods are appreciably different from whites in All-White neighborhoods. The differences for all black groups, however, are significant, with the difference increasing appreciably with increasing black neighborhood concentration. Compared to whites in All-White neighborhoods, otherwise comparable blacks in Black-Entry neighborhoods spend 39 percent more time in deliberation prior to active search, blacks in Inter-Racial areas spend 81 percent more time, and blacks in All-Black neighborhoods spend 84 percent more time, all other things being equal.

A similar pattern is evident in time in active search. Here, whites in Black-Entry neighborhoods and Inter-Racial neighborhoods spend some 21 percent *less* time in active search than whites in All-White neighborhoods, controlling for background factors. Each black group, in contrast, averages longer search time relative to whites in All-White neighborhoods, and again the difference is greater as the neighborhood percent black increases. Blacks in All-Black areas spend half again as long in active search (48.7 percent) as comparable whites in All-White neighborhoods.

The same regressions run with pertinent neighborhood race dummies omitted allow comparisons of white and black home-buyers within the same neighborhood categories. Blacks in Black-Entry neighborhoods spend 36 percent more time thinking of moving and 28 percent more time in active search than whites moving into the same neighborhoods with the same background characteristics. Blacks in Inter-Racial neighborhoods spend 69 percent more time thinking of moving and 76 percent more time in active search than their otherwise comparable white neighbors.

In sum, regression analysis with a unified sample and dummy race variables reveals that the housing search experience of black home-buyers is significantly less efficient than that of whites with identical background contextual characteristics. While comparable whites and blacks examine equal numbers of housing units, the process for blacks extends over a considerably longer time period, with greater implied costs of time and effort expended and benefits foregone. This finding lends considerable support to the direct discrimination models of racial differences in housing search, since significant impediments to black search remain after contextual differences have been controlled for.

In the next section, we extend the analysis to consider the differential impact of contextual factors on the housing search experience of each race and neighborhood group.

VI. The Differential Impact of Contextual Factors by Race and Neighborhood Group

The unified sample regressions reported above reveal the significance of race in accounting for differences in search experience when contextual variables are controlled. Unanswered by this analysis, however, are (1) to what extent do contextual factors impact blacks and whites differently? and (2) what is the estimated impact of a policy designed to remove the effect of contextual differences?

DIFFERENTIAL EFFECTS

Stratified regression equations by race of buyer and neighborhood permit comparative analysis of factors influencing the search experiences of black and white homebuyers. The equations used for the unified sample, run separately for all whites and all blacks and with race dummies omitted, are reported in Exhibits 6 and 7.

Age of household head extends time in pre-search deliberation for whites but not for blacks. Conversely, previous ownership reduces pre-search thinking for white buyers but has no impact on black deliberations. The longer time required for black buyers to begin active search is evidently less a function of lack of ownership experience than uncertainty about a potentially inhospitable environment. A job-related move accelerates pre-search decision-making far more precipitously for blacks than for whites (white coefficient of $-.3243$ = -27.7 percent; black coefficient of -1.1239 = -67.5

EXHIBIT 6

CONTEXTUAL FACTORS INFLUENCING SEARCH BEHAVIOR OF WHITE HOMEBUYERS

DEPENDENT VARIABLES

Contextual Factors	Months Thinking of Moving (ln)	Months in Active Search (ln)	Number of Units Looked At (ln)	Number of Units Internally Inspected (ln)	Number of Communities Searched (ln)	Number of Banks Contacted (ln)
UNIT CHARACTERISTICS						
Number of Bedrooms	.0417	.0309	.0508	.0706	−.0675*	−.0216
Age of House	−.0016	−.0015	.0015	.0012	.0005	.0004
Land Assessed Value (ln)		.0357			−.0682*	
Community Type (Montclair or Teaneck = 1)	.0724		−.0638	−.0034		.0456
Sale Price (ln)	−.0011	.2813*	.9419*	1.0211*	.4246*	−.0414
BUYER CHARACTERISTICS						
Age of Head	.0137*	−.0038	−.0176*	−.0147*	−.0072*	−.0060*
Previous Tenure (Own = 1)	−.2829*	−.1861*	−.0842	−.2205*	−.1469*	−.1138*
Blue Collar Occupation (Yes = 1)	.1364	.0210				
High School Grad or Less (Yes = 1)			−.1863	−.1802	−.0609	−.0837
PREVIOUS RESIDENCE						
Same Neighborhood (Yes = 1)	.1771	.0400	−.1753	−.1732	.1602	.0852
Out of State Central City (Yes = 1)	−.0994	−.0136	−.0250	−.0043	−.0605	.0452*
Job-Related Move (Yes = 1)	−.3243*	−.4259*	.1622	.2724*	.1578*	.0638
Housing Unit Reason (Yes = 1)	.1002	.1618*	.0388	.0365	.0259	.0572
Neighborhood Reason (Yes = 1)	.3228*	.1986	.3284*	.3043*	.1323	−.0269

EXHIBIT 6 (CONTINUED)

Contextual Factors	Months Thinking of Moving (ln)	Months in Active Search (ln)	Number of Units Looked At (ln)	DEPENDENT VARIABLES Number of Units Internally Inspected (ln)	Number of Communities Searched (ln)	Number of Banks Contacted (ln)
MOBILITY BEHAVIOR						
Chose Unit for Financial Reasons (Yes = 1)	.0507	−.0046	.0711	.0756	.3339*	.0701
Chose Unit for Social Reasons (Yes = 1)	−.0982	−.0681	−.1317	−.0680	−.1395*	.0027
Chose Unit for Housing Unit Reasons (Yes = 1)	−.0311	−.1023	.1724	.2800*	.3998*	−.0844
Prior Knowledge of Community (Yes = 1)	−.0839	.1178	−.1506	−.1351	−.2654*	−.0300
Real Estate Agent as Most Important Source (Yes = 1)	.1281	−.0138	.3322*	.3228*	.0311	−.0057
FINANCING FACTORS						
Chose Bank for Terms (Yes = 1)						.5600*
Chose Bank for Convenience (Yes = 1)						.4077*
FHA/VA Mortgage (Yes = 1)						−.2319*
Constant	.6709	−1.9808	−7.2301	−8.5904	−2.4355	.9116
F	2.5291	3.9768	6.8151	8.9107	9.1943	8.2307
R^2	.065	.097	.154	.192	.197	.237
Sample Size	632	651	653	656	656	552

Note:　* Indicates a coefficient significantly different from zero at the .10 level.

percent). The coefficient for a neighborhood-related move is significant only for the white sub-sample and has no effect on black
decision-making. Blue-collar occupation and central-city residence,
however, impact uniquely on black buyers' time spent thinking of
looking for a house.

Turning to time spent in active search, critical variables in white
search are purchase price (longer search) and previous ownership
(shorter search). Moving for a housing unit reason extends white
search time but is not a significant factor in black search. Instead,
moving within the same neighborhood decreases black search time
by nearly half (−47.3 percent) compared to other black buyers,
and has an insignificant effect on white search. Trading up within
the same neighborhood appears to be a significant means for blacks
to improve their housing without incurring substantial search costs.

Comparing black and white equations for number of units looked
at and inspected, the most significant difference pertains to use of a
real estate agent as the primary information source. Use of a broker
increases the number of units available to whites by some 40 percent
over whites using other primary sources; it has no impact on facilitating the housing search process of blacks.

Previous ownership also influences the number of units inspected
by blacks and whites differently. Previous owners among white
buyers inspect some 20 percent *fewer* units than other whites; among
blacks, previous owners inspect 45 percent *more* units. Ownership of
a previous unit seems to allow whites to be more discerning in their
selection of units to inspect internally. Among black homebuyers, in
contrast, previous ownership seems to impart an appreciation of
housing quality that requires the rejection of the inadequate units
that are often shown to black prospects. First-time black homebuyers,
in other words, may quickly accept the less adequate units made
available to the black sub-market that the more-experienced black
homebuyers reject.

REMOVING CONTEXTUAL DIFFERENCES

Analysis of the unified sample revealed that racial differences in
search remain even after background differences between whites and
blacks have been controlled. Stratifying by race revealed in turn that
background variables effect the housing search experience of blacks
and whites differently. The remaining question, then, is what proportion of the racial difference in search experience would be eliminated by a policy designed to equalize the backgroud characteristics
of white and black homebuyers?

This analysis utilizes the stratified equations for black and white housing search reported above, with the black sub-sample means entered into the white equations and white means applied to the black equation (Exhibits 6 and 7). In this method, the unique black impact of background characterisitcs is applied to the sample of white homebuyers, and the particular dynamics of white search are applied to the black sample. Two estimates are obtained for each search measure: (1) the difference between the mean black score on that measure and the black score estimated with the white equation; and (2) the difference between the mean white score and the white score estimated with the black equation. The weighted average of these two estimates yields the difference between white and black search controlling for the unique impact of background characteristics on the racial sub-samples. The method is extended to differences between neighborhood racial categories using the stratified equations reported in Exhibit A-8.[18]

The effect of eliminating background differences between whites and blacks in this fashion is limited at best. For time thinking prior to search fully 75 percent of the original difference between blacks and whites remains after controlling (Exhibit 8). A somewhat better effect is achieved for blacks versus whites in Black-Entry neighborhoods, yet 64 percent of the original difference still remains. Controlling for contextual factors removes less than 20 percent of the difference between whites and blacks in other neighborhood categories.

The effect on time in active search is even less impressive (Exhibit 9). As in the case of pre-search time, some 72 percent of the original difference between whites and blacks remains. Within particular neighborhood categories, controlling for background differences has no appreciable effect on black-white disparities in search time.

Only in the case of number of banks contacted does an original significant difference disappear (Exhibit 10). The implication here, however, is that the number of banks contacted by whites and blacks would no longer be different if the latter were as able as the former to select a bank because of advantageous credit terms.

EXHIBIT 7
CONTEXTUAL FACTORS INFLUENCING SEARCH BEHAVIOR OF BLACK HOMEBUYERS

Contextual Factors	Months Thinking of Moving (ln)	Months in Active Search (ln)	Number of Units Looked At (ln)	Number of Units Internally Inspected (ln)	Number of Communities Searched (ln)	Number of Banks Contacted (ln)
UNIT CHARACTERISTICS						
Number of Bedrooms	.0708	.1028	− .0585	.0631	.0129	.0145
Age of House	.0049	.0078*	.0042	− .0032	.0024	− .0005
Land Assessed Value *(ln)*		.0446			− .0414	
Community Type (Montclair or Teaneck = 1)	− .1678		.2058	.3522*		− .0218
Sale Price *(ln)*	.3827	.2669	.8367*	.5769*	.6830*	.0954
BUYER CHARACTERISTICS						
Age of Head	.0042	.0015	− .0099	− .0122	− .0106	.0003
Previous Tenure (Own = 1)	.2338	− .0514	.3545*	.3749*	.1237	− .0815
Blue Collar Occupation (Yes = 1)	.6318*	.3632*				
High School Grad or Less (Yes = 1)			− .2439	− .1742	− .0833	− .0760
PREVIOUS RESIDENCE						
Same Neighborhood (Yes = 1)	.4001	− .6409*	− .2701	− .3482	.5981*	− .0211
Out of State Central City (Yes = 1)	.4573*	.1484	.0452	.1769	.0208	.1700
Job-Related Move (Yes = 1)	−1.1239*	.5084*	− .1528	− .1138	.1711	.0878
Housing Unit Reason (Yes = 1)	− .3203	− .0020	− .0272	.1409	− .0525	− .0033
Neighborhood Reason (Yes = 1)	− .3344	.1423	− .0279	.0428	− .1268	.1644

DEPENDENT VARIABLES

EXHIBIT 7 (CONTINUED)

DEPENDENT VARIABLES

Contextual Factors	Months Thinking of Moving (ln)	Months in Active Search (ln)	Number of Units Looked At (ln)	Number of Units Internally Inspected (ln)	Number of Communities Searched (ln)	Number of Banks Contacted (ln)
MOBILITY BEHAVIOR						
Chose Unit for Financial Reasons (Yes = 1)	− .1909	− .2674	− .1331	− .1566	.1759	− .0082
Chose Unit for Social Reasons (Yes = 1)	− .2799	− .2051	− .2423	− .1604	.1963*	.0852
Chose Unit for Housing Unit Reasons (Yes = 1)	.1556	.0693	.3196	.0539	.3967*	.0392
Prior Knowledge of Community (Yes = 1)	.0177	.1781	− .0940	− .1994	− .2959*	− .0809
Real Estate Agent as Most Important Source (Yes = 1)	− .2433	− .0180	− .0085	.1128	− .0130	− .0496
FINANCING FACTORS						
Chose Bank for Terms (Yes = 1)						.4790*
Chose Bank for Convenience (Yes = 1)						.2752*
FHA/VA Mortgage (Yes = 1)						− .1747*
Constant	−2.6056	−2.4475	−5.9184	−3.7825	−5.6195	− .7192
F	2.2835	2.5794	2.5680	3.0917	3.2670	2.4463
R^2	.200	.213	.215	.245	.250	.288
Sample Size	173	180	177	180	185	142

Note: * Indicates a coefficient significantly different from zero at the .10 level.

* EXHIBIT 8

RESULTS OF CONTROLLING FOR CONTEXTUAL FACTORS INFLUENCING MONTHS THINKING OF LOOKING FOR A HOUSE

Race of Buyer and Neighborhood	DIFFERENCE IN MEAN SEARCH		
	Raw Effect (Before Controlling)	Estimated Effect (Controlling for Context) [a]	Estimated Effect as Percent of Raw Effect
All Blacks vs. All Whites	.5702*	.4296*	75.3
Blacks vs. Whites in Black-Entry Neighborhoods	.4226*	.2709*	64.1
Blacks vs. Whites in Inter-Racial Neighborhoods	.7297*	.6337*	86.8
Compared to Whites in All-White Neighborhoods:			
Whites in Black-Entry Neighborhoods	−.0836	.0328	(b)
Blacks in Black-Entry Neighborhoods	.3390*	.2796*	82.5
Whites in Inter-Racial Neighborhoods	.0245	.0109	(b)
Blacks in Inter-Racial Neighborhoods	.7542*	.6180*	81.9
Blacks in All-Black Neighborhoods	.6750*	1.3319*	197.3

Notes: * Indicates difference between means is significantly different from zero at the .05 level (two-tailed test).

     (a) Weighted average of the difference obtained when white means are entered into the black equation, and vice versa, where the weights correspond to the number of whites and the number of blacks, respectively.

     (b) Neither difference is significantly different from zero at the .05 level.

Source: CUPR Recent Buyers Survey, Fall 1978.

EXHIBIT 9

RESULTS OF CONTROLLING FOR CONTEXTUAL FACTORS INFLUENCING MONTHS IN ACTIVE SEARCH

DIFFERENCE IN MEAN SEARCH

Race of Buyer and Neighborhood	*Raw Effect (Before Controlling)*	*Estimated Effect (Controlling for Context)* [a]	*Estimated Effect as Percent of Raw Effect*
All Blacks vs. All Whites	.2632*	.1886*	71.7
Blacks vs. Whites in Black-Entry Neighborhoods	.2711*	.2575*	95.0
Blacks vs. Whites in Inter-Racial Neighborhoods	.5122*	.4875*	95.2
Compared to Whites in All-White Neighborhoods:			
Whites in Black-Entry Neighborhoods	−.2799*	−.2796*	100.6
Blacks in Black-Entry Neighborhoods	−.0088	−.0888	(b)
Whites in Inter-Racial Neighborhoods	−.2393*	−.2099*	87.7
Blacks in Inter-Racial Neighborhoods	.2727*	.2486*	91.2
Blacks in All-Black Neighborhoods	.3745*	.4250*	113.5

Notes: * Indicates difference between means is significantly different from zero at the .05 level (two-tailed test).

(a) Weighted average of the difference obtained when white means are entered into the black equation, and vice versa, where the weights correspond to the number of whites and the number of blacks, respectively.

(b) Neither difference is significantly different from zero at the .05 level.

Source: CUPR Recent Buyers Survey, Fall 1978.

EXHIBIT 10

RESULTS OF CONTROLLING FOR CONTEXTUAL FACTORS INFLUENCING NUMBER OF BANKS CONTACTED

DIFFERENCE IN MEAN SEARCH

Race of Buyer and Neighborhood	Raw Effect (Before Controlling)	Estimated Effect (Con-trolling for Context)[a]	Estimated Effect as Percent of Raw Effect
All Blacks vs. All Whites	−.1254*	.0387	0.0
Blacks vs.Whites in Black-Entry Neighborhoods	−.1909*	−.0043	2.3
Blacks vs. Whites in Inter-Racial Neighborhoods	−.1211*	.0211	0.0
Compared to Whites in All-White Neighborhoods:			
Whites in Black-Entry Neighborhoods	.0416	−.0068	(b)
Blacks in Black-Entry Neighborhoods	−.1493*	−.0352	23.6
Whites in Inter-Racial Neighborhoods	−.0386	−.0453	(b)
Blacks in Inter-Racial Neighborhoods	−.1597*	−.0064	4.0
Blacks in All-Black Neighborhoods	−.1661*	.1720*	NA

Notes: * Indicates difference between means is significantly different from zero at the .05 level (two-tailed test).

  (a) Weighted average of the difference obtained when white means are entered into the black equation, and vice versa, where the weights correspond to the number of whites and the number of blacks, respectively.

  (b) Neither difference is significantly different from zero at the .05 level.

Source: CUPR Recent Buyers Survey, Fall 1978.

VII. Summary and Policy Implications

Little difference is discernable between the housing search experiences of suburban black and white homebuyers when measured on the number of information sources used, the number of real estate brokers contacted, and the number of housing units seriously considered. Evidently, certain basic requirements of search must be met by all homebuyers, on the average, in order to successfully purchase a dwelling unit.

The evidence is strong, however, that black housing search is considerably less efficient—and therefore more costly—than white search. Black homebuyers required substantially more time prior to active search to assess options, consider alternatives, collect information, and overcome hesitations. Black households in the sample similarly spent significantly more time in active search, again accumulating greater costs of time and effort and foregone benefits. Despite the longer time required however, black housing search is at best equivalent in extent to white search and in many cases encompasses fewer units in fewer communities.

The analysis yields little support for the contextual model of racial differences in housing search experience. Regardless of existing differences in the background characteristics of white and black suburban homebuyers, both groups utilize the same information sources with the same frequency, and evaluate these sources equally. Existing differences between black and white search behavior are virtually undiminished when the effects of background differences are controlled. Thus, blacks matched in background characteristics with whites still spend substantially more time in search to find an acceptable suburban housing unit.

The protracted nature of black housing search thus appears to be due to some combination of overt discrimination and black adaptation to avoid discrimination. Use of a real estate agent as the primary information source yields access to a greater array of units for whites but not for blacks. Black searchers, in other words, examine no more units through a broker than they would if they relied solely on newspaper listings or personal networks. Prior ownership among whites facilitates the search process by allowing the searcher to better specify what is desired. Among blacks, prior ownership extends search time by educating the searcher to reject inadequate units offered in the black sub-market. In sum, the findings suggest that the information and options made available to black home seekers are inadequate in both quantity and quality relative to the white experience, requiring a greater expenditure of time and effort to obtain the same end.

The implications for policy point to a combination of strengthening anti-discrimination legislation and the development of an unbiased source of information on vacancies. A publicly-supported multiple listing service, established on a county-wide basis and available to all home seekers for a small fee, would equalize the availability of information. The analysis reported here suggests that this is a potentially fruitful direction to pursue.

Notes

*This paper is excerpted from Robert W. Lake, *Race and Housing in the Suburbs* (New Brunswick; Center for Urban Policy Research, forthcoming). An earlier version was presented in a seminar at the Office of Policy Development and Research, U.S. Department of Housing and Urban Development, Washington, D.C., December 20, 1979. The research is funded by grant No. MH31324 from the National Institute of Mental Health, Public Health Service, U.S. Department of Health, Education, and Welfare. Special appreciation is owed to Dr. George Sternlieb, Director of the Center for Urban Policy Research, to Stephen C. Casey for invaluable comments and assistance throughout the analysis, and to William Dolphin for computer programming.

1. James P. Smith, "The Improving Economic Status of Black Americans," *American Economic Review*, 68 (May 1978), 171-78.

2. Specifically, Title VIII of the Civil Rights Act of 1968.

3. See, for instance, Albert I. Hermalin and Reynolds Farley, "The Potential for Residential Integration in Cities and Suburbs: Implications for the Busing Controversy," *American Sociological Review*, 38 (October 1978), 595-610; John F. Kain and John M. Quigley, "Housing Market Discrimination, Home Ownership and Savings Behavior," *American Economic Review* 62 (June 1972), 263-277.

4. Kevin F. McCarthy, *Housing Search and Mobility* (Santa Monica: Rand Corp., 1979).

5. Recent homebuyers in the five case study communities (N = 1004) were interviewed by telephone during Fall 1978 as part of a larger study funded by DHEW's National institute of Mental Health, examining institutional barriers to black suburban homeownership. Other segments of the study document post-1970 national trends in black suburbanization, examine the magnitude of white-to-black transition in suburban housing units, identify the characteristics of New Jersey suburban communities with increasing black population, and analyze sales price differentials and equity recapture in black-occupied suburban units. Yet additional segments have yielded extensive open-ended interviews with real estate

brokers and videotaped focused group interviews with sub-samples of black and white homebuyers. See Robert W. Lake, *Race and Housing in the Suburbs* (New Brunswick: Center for Urban Policy Research, forthcoming).

6. Julian Wolpert, "Behavioral Aspects of the Decision to Migrate," *Papers of the Regional Science Association,* 15 (1965) 159-172; William Michelson, *Man and His Urban Environment* (Reading, Mass: Addison-Wesley, 1976 revised ed.).

7. Julian Wolpert, "Migration as an Adjustment to Environmental Stress," *Journal of Social Issues,* 22 (October 1966) 92-102.

8. William Michelson, *Environmental Choice, Human Behavior, and Residential Satisfaction* (New York: Oxford University Press, 1977).

9. James W. Simmons, "Changing Residence in the City, A Review of Intra-Urban Mobility," *Geographical Review,* 58 (October 1968) 622-651.

10. Donald J. Hempel, *Search Behavior and Information Utilization in the Home Buying Process* (Storrs, Conn.: Center for Real Estate and Urban Economics Studies, University of Connecticut, 1969).

11. Lawrence A. Brown and Eric G. Moore, "The Intra-Urban Migration Process: A Perspective" in Larry S. Bourne (ed.) *Internal Structure of the City* (New York: Oxford University Press, 1971) 200-209.

12. Eric G. Moore, *Residential Mobility in the City,* Commission on College Geography Resource Paper No. 13 (Washington, D.C.: Association of American Geographers, 1972).

13. Risa Palm, "Real Estate Agents and Geographical Information," *Geographical Review,* 66 (July 1976) 266-280; and _____. *Urban Social Geography from the Perspective of the Real Estate Salesman* (Berkeley: Center for Real Estate and Urban Economics, University of California, 1976).

14. Frederick J. Eggers, *et al.* HUD Housing Market Practices Survey (Washington, D.C.: U.S. Dept. of Housing and Urban Development, 1979).

15. William J. Wilson, *The Declining Significance of Race* (Chicago: University of Chicago Press, 1978).

16. Robert W. Lake and Susan Caris Cutter, "A Typology of Black Suburbanization in New Jersey Since 1970," *Geographical Review* (forthcoming, April 1980).

17. For a full description of survey and sampling methodology see Robert W. Lake, *Race and Housing in the Suburbs* (New Brunswick: Center for Urban Policy Research, forthcoming).

18. The reduced-form estimating equations in Exhibit A-8 were developed to accommodate the reduced sample size in the neighborhood strata. For each search measure, variables were entered in step-wise fashion until the maximum adjusted R^2 value was reached. A smaller subset of variables significant across all strata was then selected from among those entered prior to termination.

EXHIBIT A-1

HOUSEHOLD COMPOSITION, BY RACE AND NEIGHBORHOOD RACIAL COMPOSITION (PERCENTS)

Household Composition	Whites in All-White Neighborhoods	Whites in Black-Entry Neighborhoods	RACE OF BUYER AND NEIGHBORHOOD				
			Blacks in Black-Entry Neighborhoods	Whites in Inter-Racial Neighborhoods	Blacks in Inter-Racial Neighborhoods	Blacks in All-Black Neighborhoods
Single-Parent Household	5.0	3.4	4.8	2.4	10.0	4.8
Husband-Wife, No Children	54.8	47.1	37.5	59.8	21.3	33.3
Husband-Wife, With Children	40.1	49.4	57.7	37.8	68.8	61.9
Total	100.0	100.0	100.0	100.0	100.0	100.0
Number of Cases	496	87	104	82	80	21

Chi-square = 45.736 with 10 d.f. $p < .001$.

Source: CUPR Recent Buyers Survey, Fall 1978.

EXHIBIT A-2

AGE OF HOUSEHOLD HEAD, BY RACE AND NEIGHBORHOOD RACIAL COMPOSITION (PERCENTS)

Age of Household Head	RACE OF BUYER AND NEIGHBORHOOD					
	Whites in All-White Neighborhoods	Whites in Black-Entry Neighborhoods	Blacks in Black-Entry Neighborhoods	Whites in Inter-Racial Neighborhoods	Blacks in Inter-Racial Neighborhoods	Blacks in All-Black Neighborhoods
Less than 30	17.7	18.7	8.7	12.2	7.4	8.7
30-34	33.1	30.8	29.1	34.4	21.0	26.1
35-39	17.5	15.4	28.2	23.3	24.7	21.7
40-49	17.5	18.7	24.3	18.9	37.0	21.7
50 and over	14.1	16.5	9.7	11.1	9.9	21.7
Total	100.0	100.0	100.0	100.0	100.0	100.0
Number of Cases	519	91	103	90	81	23

Chi-square = 39.869 with 20 d.f. p < .01

Source: CUPR Recent Buyers Survey, Fall 1978.

EXHIBIT A-3

OCCUPATION OF HOUSEHOLD HEAD, BY RACE AND NEIGHBORHOOD RACIAL COMPOSITION (PERCENTS)

Occupation	*Whites in All-White Neighborhoods*	*Whites in Black-Entry Neighborhoods*	*Blacks in Black-Entry Neighborhoods*	*Whites in Inter-Racial Neighborhoods*	*Blacks in Inter-Racial Neighborhoods*	*Blacks in All-Black Neighborhoods*
			RACE OF BUYER AND NEIGHBORHOOD			
Professional	47.1	47.3	38.0	48.9	23.8	18.2
Manager, Administrator	23.8	25.3	21.3	22.2	17.5	22.7
Sales, Clerical	10.6	14.3	16.7	13.3	10.0	13.6
Blue Collar	13.5	11.0	20.4	10.0	45.0	36.4
Other	5.0	2.2	3.7	5.6	3.8	9.1
Total	100.0	100.0	100.0	100.0	100.0	100.0
Number of Cases	520	91	108	90	80	22

Chi-square = 72.476 with 20 d.f. $p < .001$

Source: CUPR Recent Buyers Survey, Fall 1978.

EXHIBIT A-4

EDUCATION OF HOUSEHOLD HEAD, BY RACE AND NEIGHBORHOOD RACIAL COMPOSITION (PERCENTS)

Education	RACE OF BUYER AND NEIGHBORHOOD					
	Whites in All-White Neighborhoods	Whites in Black-Entry Neighborhoods	Blacks in Black-Entry Neighborhoods	Whites in Inter-Racial Neighborhoods	Blacks in Inter-Racial Neighborhoods	Blacks in All-Black Neighborhoods
High School Grad or less	19.0	11.7	26.8	19.8	42.4	48.0
Some College	13.8	12.8	22.3	11.5	24.7	28.0
College Grad	32.2	44.7	30.4	34.4	22.4	12.0
Professional or Graduate School	35.0	30.9	20.5	34.4	10.6	12.0
Total	100.0	100.0	100.0	100.0	100.0	100.0
Number of Cases	537	94	112	96	85	25

Chi-square = 76.726 with 15 d.f. p < .001

Source: CUPR Recent Buyers Survey, Fall 1978.

EXHIBIT A-5

PREVIOUS TENURE, BY RACE AND NEIGHBORHOOD RACIAL COMPOSITION
(PERCENTS)

Previous Tenure	RACE OF BUYER AND NEIGHBORHOOD					
	Whites in All-White Neighborhoods	Whites in Black-Entry Neighborhoods	Blacks in Black-Entry Neighborhoods	Whites in Inter-Racial Neighborhoods	Blacks in Inter-Racial Neighborhoods	Blacks in All-Black Neighborhoods
Own	38.0	44.4	31.8	26.6	22.9	19.2
Rent	62.0	55.6	68.2	73.4	77.1	80.8
Total	100.0	100.0	100.0	100.0	100.0	100.0
Number of Cases	527	90	110	94	83	26

Chi-square = 17.170 with 5 d.f. p < .01

Source: CUPR Recent Buyers Survey, Fall 1978.

EXHIBIT A-6
LOCATION OF PREVIOUS RESIDENCE, BY RACE OF BUYER AND RACIAL COMPOSITION OF PRESENT NEIGHBORHOOD
(PERCENTS)

Location of Previous Residence	RACE OF BUYER AND NEIGHBORHOOD					
	Whites in All-White Neighborhoods	Whites in Black-Entry Neighborhoods	Blacks in Black-Entry Neighborhoods	Whites in Inter-Racial Neighborhoods	Blacks in Inter-Racial Neighborhoods	Blacks in All-Black Neighborhoods
Same Neighborhood	9.6	7.5	0.9	9.7	10.7	8.0
Different Neighborhood, Same Town	15.2	14.0	6.1	14.0	17.9	16.0
N.J. Suburb	34.7	21.5	22.8	40.9	21.4	16.0
N.J. Central City	10.7	8.6	13.2	5.4	15.5	20.0
Out-of-State Suburb	6.9	17.2	6.1	4.3	3.6	4.0
Out-of-State Central City	21.0	25.8	50.9	22.6	28.6	36.0
Other	1.9	5.4	0.0	3.2	2.4	0.0
Total	100.0	100.0	100.0	100.0	100.0	100.0
Number of Cases	533	93	114	93	84	25

Chi-square = 95.458 with 30 d.f. $p < .001$

Source: CUPR Recent Buyers Survey, Fall 1978.

EXHIBIT A-7

REASON FOR MOVING FROM PREVIOUS UNIT, BY RACE OF BUYER AND RACIAL COMPOSITION OF PRESENT NEIGHBORHOOD (PERCENTS)

Reason for Moving from Previous Neighborhood	*RACE OF BUYER AND NEIGHBORHOOD*					
	Whites in All-White Neighborhoods	Whites in Black-Entry Neighborhoods	Blacks in Black-Entry Neighborhoods	Whites in Inter-Racial Neighborhoods	Blacks in Inter-Racial Neighborhoods	Blacks in All-Black Neighborhoods
Job-Related Move	21.2	33.3	25.2	21.1	11.9	11.5
Housing Unit Reason	31.0	37.6	25.2	32.6	34.5	26.9
Life-cycle Reason	31.5	21.5	27.8	32.6	34.5	30.8
Dissatisfied with Neighborhood	12.6	5.4	19.1	11.6	17.9	23.1
Other	3.7	2.2	2.6	2.1	1.2	7.7
Total	100.0	100.0	100.0	100.0	100.0	100.0
Number of Cases	539	93	115	95	84	26

Chi-square = 32.927 with 20 d.f. p < .05

Source: CUPR Recent Buyers Survey, Fall 1978.

EXHIBIT A-8

CONTEXTUAL FACTORS INFLUENCING SEARCH BEHAVIOR AMONG SIX RACE AND NEIGHBORHOOD GROUPS

Contextual Factors	RACE OF BUYER AND NEIGHBORHOOD					
	Whites in All-White Neighborhoods	Whites in Black-Entry Neighborhoods	Blacks in Black-Entry Neighborhoods	Whites in Inter-Racial Neighborhoods	Blacks in Inter-Racial Neighborhoods	Blacks in All-Black Neighborhoods
MONTHS THINKING ABOUT LOOKING:						
Sale Price (ln)	-.1043	.1182	.5179	-.0471	.1637	2.4210*
Age of head	.0066	.0088	-.0109	.0223	.0287*	.0155
Job-related move (Yes = 1)	-.4619*	-.5549*	-.3997	-.2598	-1.1634*	-1.4131*
Neighborhood reason (Yes = 1)	.3402*	.7858	.7092*	-.3423	-.3594	-.5084
Chose unit for housing unit reason (Yes = 1)	.0980	-.0035	.1815	-.7031	-.3843	.5565
Constant	2.1415	.3190	-3.6828	1.0780	-.7520	-23.7016
F	6.1246	1.7827	1.7533	1.0895	2.6481	1.5838
R²	.059	.100	.089	.063	.163	.361
N	491	86	96	87	74	20
MONTHS IN ACTIVE SEARCH:						
Sale Price (ln)	.2039	.6223	.2770	.1785	.2494	.7271
Number of bedrooms	.0526	-.0487	.1195	-.1477*	.1915	.0446
Previous Residence in same neighborhood (Yes = 1)	.0406	.6294*	-1.3661*	.0079	-.4992*	-1.3049*
Job-related move (Yes = 1)	-.7340*	-.5716*	-.4833*	-.2433	-1.0249*	-1.4586*
Chose unit for financial reason (Yes = 1)	-.0365	-.5964*	-.3132	.2780	.2942	.0646
Constant	-.9653	-5.5613	-1.9809	-.3359	-1.6094	-5.8595
F	10.3755	4.0415	2.7863	1.2108	2.7514	3.3799
R²	.092	.196	.116	.066	.157	.471
N	521	89	112	91	80	25

EXHIBIT A-8 (CONTINUED)

RACE OF BUYER AND NEIGHBORHOOD

Contextual Factors	Whites in All-White Neighborhoods	Whites in Black-Entry Neighborhoods	Blacks in Black-Entry Neighborhoods	Whites in Inter-Racial Neighborhoods	Blacks in Inter-Racial Neighborhoods	Blacks in All-Black Neighborhoods
NUMBER OF UNITS LOOKED AT:						
Sale Price *(ln)*	.8272*	.3222	.3081	1.2381*	1.4658*	.4616
Number of bedrooms	.0802	.2581*	.0316	-.0407	.0351	.2041
Age of head	-.0211*	-.0016	.0190	.0032	-.0289*	-.0148
Previous residence in same neighborhood (Yes = 1)	-.4752*	.7233	-1.5571	-.7673*	-.0828	.6936
Job-related move (Yes = 1)	.1116	.2670	.1188	.1889	.1056	.2322
Chose unit for social reasons (Yes = 1)	-.1380	-.6751*	-.0649	-.0933	-.1747	-.4823
Constant	-5.7312	-1.5809	-1.4592	-10.5834	-12.0678	-2.3611
F	12.2299	2.7190	1.1167	3.9106	6.1274	1.4005
R²	.132	.175	.069	.231	.358	.393
N	491	84	97	85	73	20
NUMBER OF UNITS INTERNALLY INSPECTED:						
Sale Price *(ln)*	.8388*	-.2017	.1008	1.3206*	1.4785*	.0679
Number of bedrooms	.1032*	.3268*	.0981	-.0894	.0014	.1731
Age of head	-.0244*	.0007	.0206	.0071	-.0251*	-.0329*
Prior knowledge of community (Yes = 1)	-.2856*	-.6130*	-.4254*	.1124	-.1243	-.1279
High school grad or less (Yes = 1)	-.1895	-.6574*	-.1959	-.3916	.1866	-.5839
Community ambience (Montclair or Teaneck = 1)	.0486	-.0898	.3743*	-.0597	-.0271	.2324
Constant	-6.0525	3.7600	.1169	-11.8248	-12.6510	2.2846
F	16.1702	3.6925	2.4142	4.6199	4.9341	2.5235
R²	.162	.213	.139	.253	.294	.502
N	508	89	97	89	78	22

EXHIBIT A-8 (CONTINUED)

RACE OF BUYER AND NEIGHBORHOOD

Contextual Factors	Whites in All-White Neighborhoods	Whites in Black-Entry Neighborhoods	Blacks in Black-Entry Neighborhoods	Whites in Inter-Racial Neighborhoods	Blacks in Inter-Racial Neighborhoods	Blacks in All-Black Neighborhoods
NUMBER OF COMMUNITIES SEARCHED:						
Sale Price (ln)	.1665*	.2687	.3229	.2254	.7564*	.3933
Age of head	−.0113*	−.0011	−.0139	−.0029	−.0085	−.0128
Previous residence in same neighborhood (Yes = 1)	−.3715*	−.2530	−1.0224	−.2858	−.5117*	−.9682*
Job-related move (Yes = 1)	−.1459*	.4376*	.1699	−.0174	.1219	.4782
Chose unit for social reasons (Yes = 1)	−.2511*	−.2949*	.0687	−.4087*	.2171	−.0674
Chose unit for housing reasons (Yes = 1)	.1905*	.4898*	.4265	.2220	.5289*	.0500
Constant	−.3170	−1.8678	−1.9753	−1.3287	−6.9022	−2.6381
F	10.5178	4.3639	1.3057	2.1474	4.6686	1.2551
R²	.114	.254	.077	.140	.289	.334
N	497	84	101	86	76	22
NUMBER OF BANKS CONTACTED:						
Sale Price (ln)	.0614	−.1928	.1089	−.2513	.1350	−.6356
Previous tenure (Own = 1)	−.2206*	−.0856	.0776	−.2705*	−.1487	−.4732*
Chose bank for terms (Yes = 1)	.6192*	.6396*	.5847*	.7340*	.3904	.0834
Chose bank for convenience (Yes = 1)	.4561*	.4120*	.4813*	.2898*	.1462	.3951
FHA or VA mortgage (Yes = 1)	−.2528*	−.2254	−.0078	−.2344	−.2339	−.7921*
Constant	−.4049	2.2771	−1.0836	2.9224	−1.1076	7.5815
F	28.9724	2.6874	7.8235	7.6530	1.2330	4.9625
R²	.256	.171	.340	.350	.112	.693
N	428	71	82	77	55	17

Note: *Indicates a coefficient significant at the .10 level or better.

The Effect of Race on Opinions of Housing and Neighborhood Quality

Stephen C. Casey

Summary of Findings

Simple means or medians of white versus black owners/renters' opinions of structure and neighborhood quality indicate significantly higher white opinions of housing and immediate geographic area than is the case for blacks. These differences range from one-third to one-half of a point on a four point scale.

These racial variations are due to one or both of the following components: (1) the *disparity* in the personal, housing and neighborhood characteristics of blacks versus whites and (2) the difference in attitude between whites and blacks within *similar* housing/neighborhoods. The magnitude of the second component is measured in this research.

Developing regression equations using initially only objective variables to standardize for socioeconomic characteristics and housing features reduces the race effect to a relatively insignificant level of approximately 0.15. Thus, overall, whites and blacks of similar

income, education, housing amenities, etc. report the conditions
of the housing and neighborhood they occupy similarly. This is
true for owners as well as renters. The raw or unrefined race effect
essentially disappears when one standardizes for the nature of the
populations considered.

The small remnant effect, not explained by economic equivalency
of the observed populations, is further scrutinized three ways to
evalute its durability under more intensive analyses. More variables
(now including subjective variables) are included in the regression
equations; geographic locations of the observed population are
taken into account, and finally, one opinion of the respondent
(neighborhood) is allowed to affect the other (structure).

In the first case, additional variables reduce the race effect slightly;
in the second, geographic differentiation further reduces the race
effect and shows that what little effect exists is concentrated in the
Southern and Western suburbs and North Central cities; in the
third case, the race effect except for these areas is swept away
entirely when opinion of neighborhood is allowed to effect opinion
of structure.

In sum, there appears to be no significant differential attributable
solely to race in either owners' or renters' specification on housing
quality. Whites and blacks living in similar conditions evaluate structures and neighborhoods which reflect these conditions similarly.
Thus, this rebuts theories that claim the existence of an inherent
racial bias in expressed opinions of structure and neighborhood
quality.

Introduction

For over four decades economists, planners and public policymakers have sought a consistent and meaningful way to objectively
evalute housing quality.[1] The goal thus far has proved elusive.
While typically we have focused on physical basics, such as complete
plumbing, as an objective index of housing quality, there have also
been significant demurrers—sufficiently so that subjective measures,
opinions of residents, are now being tested for their usefulness and
reliability.

In 1940, the first major attempt at gathering housing data was
initiated. In this Census, two measures of the *state of repairs of the
structure* were used—*not needing major repairs and nedding major
repairs.*[2] These measures said nothing of the original construction

of a structure—a shack and small single family home in an equal state of repair were classified similarly.

In 1950, an emphasis on the *condition* of a structure rather than its state of repairs was seen in the emergence of a new dichotomous classification of "structure condition"—*not dilapidated and dilapidated.*[3] "Condition" of a structure took into account its original construction. A dilapidated unit was defined as one which had one or more serious deficiencies or was of insufficient original construction so that it either (1) provided inadequate shelter or (2) endangered the safety of its' occupants. To provide necessary continuity from one Census to the next, it was assumed that "not needing major repairs" and "not dilapidated" were equivalent and a similar equivalency existed for "dilapidated" and "needing major repairs."

In 1960, a three way classification was used—the 1950 not dilapidated category was divided into two subcategories—*sound and deteriorating.*[4] The division of "not dilapidated" into "sound" and "deteriorating" reflected user interest in meliorative public programs for a portion of the housing stock which might soon become dilapidated. Assessments of the condition of the "not dilapidated" portion were necessary prior to its partitioning.

While housing "condition" was an improvement over the previous "state of repairs" designation, those associated with housing desired a broader measure than condition—one which included a measure of the completeness of a housing unit in terms of meeting basic health criteria. Thus, since 1940, a combination of (1) the structural condition indices and (2) the availability of specified plumbing facilities has been used to indicate housing as either *not substandard or substandard.*[5] Through the 1960 Census, this was the most generally accepted definition of housing quality. A housing unit was "substandard" if it was:

(1) Dilapidated; or
(2) Lacked one or more of the following facilities: hot running water in the structure, flush toilet for private use, bathtub or shower for private use.

This dual emphasis on condition as well as a threshold level of housing "hardware" reflected attempts to eliminate hazards to the "health, safety and welfare" of housing occupants—a basic phrase of most housing legislation of that period.

As a check on reliability, in the late 1960s the Census Bureau attempted to evaluate its enumerators' specifications of housing condition. The results of this report clearly diminished the initial enthusiasm of policymaker with the 1960 Census results.[6]

According to the Census Bureau:

"the statistics are unreliable; our best estimate is that if another group of enumerators had been sent back to rate the housing units of the United States, only about one-third of the units rated as dilapidated or deteriorating by either group of enumerators would be rated the same by both groups of enumerators."

The 1970 Census, reflecting the ambivalence of late-1960 research results, included as a measure of substandard housing: (1) counts of year round housing units lacking some or all plumbing facilities and (2) "estimates" of units with all plumbing facilities but in dilapidated condition.* Estimates were obtained indirectly by combining data on structural condition obtained in the post-Census sample survey of Components of Inventory Change with data on related housing characteristics from the previous decennial Census.

During the 1970s the *Annual Housing Survey* added to the list of potential objective housing quality measures by including a significant number of additional indications of structural condition. They included detailed data on housing defects and breakdowns in equipment, type of dwelling unit, characteristics of occupant households and their expenditures on housing services.[7]

Several analyses were undertaken of the additional objective housing condition measures. The results of these analyses were summarized in a memo from the Chairman, Subcommittee on Housing Quality to the Chairman, Federal Agency Council on the 1980 Census. It stated:[8]

"Analysis of *Annual Housing Survey* did not identify any subsets of variables that appeared to provide a clear basis for development of an operational definition of housing quality."

Following this sobering evaluation, the 1980 Census will contain only information on condition of housing units in the following categories: age of structure, number of toilets, existence of complete kitchen facilities, source of water, sewer disposal and air conditioning.

*Information on the structural condition of housing units was not collected in the 1970 Census because of the evidence of response or unreliability.

The 1980 Census will continue to produce two numerically additive measures of substandard housing (1) a count of units lacking some or all plumbing facilities (2) an extimate of dilapidated housing with all plumbing facilities.[9]

As housers/planners have become increasingly dissatisfied with traditional measures of housing quality there has been a call for more information about housing quality—specified not in terms of missing plumbing, peeling paint or enumerator specification of condition, but rather in terms of the opinions of the people who live in this housing, i.e. residents.

Opinions of both housing and neighborhood were included for the first time in the 1973 *Annual Housing Survey*. The justification for this inclusion was a reflection of paucity or inconsistency of the housing quality information from the decennial Census and a turn towards viewing housing quality "in the eyes of the beholder"—those who actually occupied the structure or lived in the neighborhood.[10]

Several other analyses involving the use of subjective indices of structure quality and quality of the community or neighborhood have also been done in recent years. The scope of the sample, the exact type of question asked and the conclusions involving racial differences have varied across these studies.

Andrews et al.[11] and Campbell et al.[12] have completed studies which are national in scope. Both measured, among other things, general satisfaction with the housing environment and concluded that blacks rated their housing more negatively than whites even when differences in socioeconomic status and some geographic indicators were controlled for.

Two other studies, Burby and Weiss[13] and Nathanson et al.[14] analyzed the evaluations of home and community within seventeen planned communities in the United States. The residents of these communities tend to be younger and have higher income and educational attainment than the populace at large. Thus, the results from these areas cannot necessarily be extrapolated to other locations nationally.

In Columbia, Maryland, Nathanson found a significant relationship between opinion of dwelling unit and race (blacks being more negative) but no relationship between race and attitude toward the community of Columbia. Burby's study, which encompassed more communities, used a seven point scale to measure satisfaction and found blacks somewhat less satisfied than whites in townhouses. On various specific aspects of livability for residents of single family homes, blacks were significantly more satisfied than whites.

Papers by Durand[15] and Lovrich[16] examined black/white evaluations of local public services in the cities of St. Louis and Denver, respectively. Both found that blacks rated the quality of local services more negatively than whites; a difference which could not be explained by differing socioeconomic characteristics of the two racial groups.

Finally, Diaiso et al.[17] did a study involving perception of housing and neighborhood quality of college students in the Pittsburgh area. Although this sample presents some of the same generalizability problems that the studies on planned communities did, the authors claim that their sample is representative of future middle class housing consumers in Eastern cities similar to Pittsburgh.

This study does not deal exclusively with perception variation by race but rather focuses on any possible racial or other variable which might affect evaluation of both housing and neighborhood attributes. Racial effects are measured by allowing all the subjects to rate a set of pictures of various housing types and then comparing black and white responses. After doing this, the authors found a negligible effect of race on perceptions of housing and neighborhood quality.

The *Annual Housing Survey*, with its large national sample and wealth of variables, presents an opportunity to combine the positive aspects of the above-mentioned studies on a broad scale. With the breadth of available variables, controls can be made on socioeconomic status, housing tenure, housing physical features, housing age and housing economics. The size of the sample and its national scope allows inter-regional and intra-regional controls and comparisons.

Preliminary analyses of both the housing and neighborhood quality data reported by residents shows consistently higher ratings of structure and neighborhood by white residents than by blacks. Important insight into the reliability of the resident opinion information can be gleaned if this racial reporting difference can be isolated and subjected to statistical analyses to test its actual presence. This is the purpose of the research which follows.

Methodology

The research design will initially attempt to isolate a "race effect" in evaluations of structure and neighborhood quality in the *Annual Housing Survey* by comparing white and black mean ratings within the major tenurial categories, owner and renter.

If and where a race effect can be isolated its true nature must be investigated. Is there truly a race effect i.e., an independent effect, not explained by differences in socioeconomic status and housing features between whites and blacks? If an independent race effect does exist the valididty of personal subjective evaluation is suspect.

Regression equations will be developed for each race for owner and renter specification of structure and neighborhood quality. Stepwise regression will be used to initially select an array of complete (i.e. provided for all cases) objective variables to explain both white and black opinions of structure and neighborhood.* If the resultant explanatory power of the equations is insufficient, additional objective information not available for all cases will be introduced to the data set. In the end, a regression equation of 9-13 variables will emerge to define black/white opinions of their housing and immediate geographic area.

To test the true nature of the race effect, once the equations are developed, one race will be run in the other's equations—i.e., blacks in the white equations; whites in the black equations.** This process standardizes for differences in socioeconomic status and housing features of the two races. Does the race effect stand up or is it reduced to zero for equivalent populations living in similar housing?

If racial differences in perception of neighborhood and structure condition persist, once differences in socioeconomic and housing status are controlled, other explanatory means will be in introduced to interpret and explain this difference: (1) adding "subjective" predictor variables to the regression equations, (2) narrowing the geographic scope of the analysis and (3) using one "opinion" variable (neighborhood) to explain the other "opinion" variable (structure).

In addition, two analyses of specific variables will be undertaken because of their singular importance. This will be done for *value** of the structure and for the *neighborhood** variable. These latter analyses are contained in Appendices V and VI. Among the objective variables for owners, *value* is by far the most highly correlated with both evaluation of neighborhood and structure quality. *Neighborhood* is the sole evaluation of the immediate geographic area made by the enumerator.

---

*See Appendix I for definitions of these variables
**See Appendix IV for basic regression equations.

What Do The Data Say—Is There a Difference of Opinion on the Part of Whites and Blacks as to Neighborhood Quality That Has to be Analyzed?

THE RESPONSE OF WHITE AND BLACK OWNERS TO STRUCTURE AND NEIGHBORHOOD QUALITY

Structure Quality (House Opinion). The sample of specified owners who have lived in their house for at least three months serves as the data base for owner analyses. Two important variables—value of the house and housing costs—are only given for specified owners. The mandatory residence period serves a dual purpose. First, several structure breakdown variables are only available for the group; second, it provides a reasonable minimum period for residents to base both structure and neighborhood opinions.

Exhibit 1 shows the evaluations of the quality of the structure for both whites and blacks. From this exhibit it is clear that both white and black owners are extremely positive about the condition of their housing. Whites, representing 93 percent of those that own

EXHIBIT 1

SPECIFICATION OF STRUCTURE QUALITY (HOUSE OPINION) FOR OWNERS BY RACE

	Structure Quality				
	(1)	*(2)*	*(3)*	*(4)*	
Race	*Excellent*	*Good*	*Fair*	*Poor*	*Total*
White	16,143	16,999	2,903	204	36,249
	(44.5)	(46.9)	(8.0)	(0.6)	(100.0)
Black	731	1,455	595	68	2,849
	(25.7)	(51.1)	(20.9)	(2.4)	(100.0)
Total	16,874	18,454	3,498	272	39,098

Mean for whites = 1.646; Mean for blacks = 2.000 — white/black difference significant at .001 level.

Notes: 1. Data is weighted and in thousands
          2. In parentheses are the row or *race* percentages.
          3. Numbers on top of columns indicate numeric assignments.

Source: U.S. Department of Commerce, U.S. Department of Housing and Urban Development, *Annual Housing Survey*, 1976.

the housing that they occupy, rate their housing as excellent or good in nine out of ten cases. The figure for blacks, while lower than whites, is still a good to excellent rating in close to eight out of ten cases.

It is interesting to note than while the grouped category excellent/ good is relatively close for both whites and blacks, the percentage of black owners who rate their housing as excellent (25.7 percent) is only 58 percent of the figure for whites (44.5). Further, one-in-five blacks rate their housing as fair and one-in-forty as poor. The proportion of whites reporting these latter categories are only one-third those of blacks.

If numbers are assigned to all responses (1 for excellent, 4 for poor), the mean for whites is 1.65; the mean for blacks if 2.00 (Interpolations of medians yields 1.2 for whites; 1.5 for blacks). A difference of means test applies to the former yields statistically significant differences at the .001 level. Thus, while differences appear small bacause both racial groups, on average, rate their housing good to excellent, whites' average rating of their housing is significantly higher than blacks'.

*Neighborhood Quality (Street Opinion).*Exhibit 2 presents the evaluations of *neighborhood* quality of *owned-housing* occupants, also by race. Although reasonably high ratings are again reported by both whites and blacks, the separation between races on the neighborhood variable is more pronounced than it is on the structure variable. Close to 90 percent of white owners rated their neighborhood as excellent or good, with almost equal representation in the excellent and good categories. About 9 percent of white owners rated their housing as fair; 1 percent as poor. Blacks, on the other hand, were less sanquine about their neighborhood. Les than 70 percent of black owners rated their neighborhoods as excellent of good, with almost one-third of the black owners reporting neighborhood conditions as fair or poor.

If one again assigns numerical ratings to the responses (1 for excellent, 4 for poor), the mean of all responses to neighborhood quality for whites is 1.67; for blacks, it is 2.13. It is noteworthy that the latter figure falls out of the "goo" range, i.e. the average black opinion concerning neighborhood is less than good. A difference of means test again shows that the average rating of neighborhood condition by whites is significantly different than that of blacks at the .001 level.

EXHIBIT 2

SPECIFICATION OF NEIGHBORHOOD QUALITY (STREET OPINION) FOR OWNERS BY RACE

	Structure Quality				
	(1)	*(2)*	*(3)*	*(4)*	
Race	Excellent	Good	Fair	Poor	Total
White	15,991	16,525	3,342	387	36,245
	(44.1)	(45.6)	(9.2)	(1.1)	(100.0)
Black	613	1,363	769	108	2,853
	(21.5)	(47.7)	(27.0)	(3.8)	(100.0)
Total	16,604	17,888	4,111	495	39,098

Mean for whites = 1.672; mean for blacks = 2.131 – white/black differences significant at .001 level.

Notes: 1. Data is weighted and in thousands.
2. In parentheses are the row or *race* percentages.
3. Numbers on top of columns indicate numeric assignments.

Source: U.S. Department of Commerce, U.S. Department of Housing and Urban Development, *Annual Housing Survey*, 1976.

In Sum, on both the indices of structure and neighborhood quality there are observed differences in ratings reported by white and black owners. The differences for white and blacks are more pronounced for neighborhood than structure but both are statistically significant at a conservative level.

THE RESPONSE OF WHITE AND BLACK RENTERS TO STRUCTURE AND NEIGHBORHOOD QUALITY

Structure Quality (House Opinion). The sample of specified renters* who have lived in their residence for at least three months serves as the data base for renter analyses. Exhibit 3 presents *renter* respondent evaluations of structure quality by race. Blacks represent approximately 18 percent of all renters; two and one-half times their representation in owned housing.

Both white and black *renters* are less positive about housing structure quality than are *owners*. Seventy percent of white renters

Specified renters are residents who live in rental housing units excluding single-family homes on 10 acres or more.

EXHIBIT 3

SPECIFICATION OF STRUCTURE QUALITY (HOUSE OPINION)
FOR RENTERS BY RACE

Structure Quality

| | (1) | (2) | (3) | (4) | |
Race	Excellent	Good	Fair	Poor	Total
White	3,888	8,874	4,242	889	17,893
	(21.7)	(49.6)	(23.7)	(5.0)	(100.0)
Black	408	1,549	1,412	509	3,878
	(10.5)	(39.9)	(36.4)	(13.1)	(100.0)
Total	4,296	10,423	5,654	1,398	21,771

Mean for whites = 2.119; mean for blacks = 2.521 – white/black differences significant at .001 level.

Notes: 1. Data is weighted and in thousands.
2. In parentheses are the row or *race* percentages.
3. Numbers on top of columns indicate numeric assignments.

Source: U.S. Department of Commerce, U.S. Department of Housing and Urban Development, *Annual Housing Survey*, 1976.

rate their housing as excellent or good; the equivalent figure for black renters is just over 50 percent. One-in-four white renters state housing quality as only fair; one-in-three black renters report a similar condition. Thirteen percent of blacks report their rental housing as poor.

Assigning numbers to ratings for both racial groups permit tabulation of a mean for white *renter* responses to structure quality of 2.12; for blacks the figure is 2.52. Thus, both white and black renters' average opinions of structure quality fall below the "good" range. The rating differences between whites and blacks, 0.40, is slightly larger than that observed for white versus black *owners* on structure quality, 0.35. The difference of means for white versus black renters is statistically significant at the .001 level.

The two components of the renter population, "cash rent" and "no cash rent", are very similar in results. (The former component represents 93 percent of the renter category). "No cash renters" are slightly more positive about structure quality than is the case for "cash renters," yet white-black differences are similar (See Appendix III.).

Neighborhood Quality (Street Opinion). Exhibit 4 presents white and black renter responses to neighborhood quality. Both white and black renter responses are slightly more positive for neighborhood quality than they are for structure quality. Approximately 76 percent of white renters rate their neighborhood as excellent or good; 54 percent of black renters give their neighborhood a similar rating. The *neighborhoods* of white and black *renters* are slightly less apt to be given a poor rating than are the *structures* they occupy but are roughly three times more prone to "poor" designation than is the case for neighborhoods of white and black *owners.* The mean numeric for whites is 2.03; the equivalent for blacks is 2.44. Again both average renter opinions fall below the "good" range. The difference of .41 is 10 percent less than the difference noted for white and black owner evaluations of neighborhood but still is statistically significant at the .001 level. (See Appendix III for results by "cash rent" and "no cash rent.")

EXHIBIT 4

SPECIFICATION OF NEIGHBORHOOD QUALITY (STREET OPINION) FOR RENTERS BY RACE

	Structure Quality				
	(1)	*(2)*	*(3)*	*(4)*	
Race	*Excellent*	*Good*	*Fair*	*Poor*	*Total*
White	4,534	9,032	3,617	710	17,893
	(25.3)	(50.5)	(20.2)	(4.0)	(100.0)
Black	445	1,629	1,474	332	3,880
	(11.5)	(42.0)	(38.0)	(8.6)	(100.0)
Total	4,979	10,661	5,091	1,042	21,773

Mean for whites = 2.028; mean for blacks = 2.436 – white/black differences significant at .001 level.

Notes: 1. Data is weighted and in thousands.
2. In parentheses are the row or *race* percentages.
3. Numbers on top of columns indicate numeric assignments.

Source: U.S. Department of Commerce, U.S. Department of Housing and Urban Development, *Annual Housing Survey,* 1976.

SUMMARY

Both white versus black owners and white versus black renters have statistically significant differences of opinion on both structure and neighborhood quality. In the case of owners' opinions, the racial difference is larger on opinion of neighborhood quality than opinion of structure quality; in the case of renters the racial differences are similar for the two opinions.

Developing a Model to Isolate the True Race Effect—
Choosing the Variables

THE DATA BASE AND GROSS VARIABLE SET

Prior to developing equations to test the true race effect, a variable selection process must be undertaken. An effort will be made to concentrate on relevant objective variables first and only if R^2 remains small, to subsequently introduce additional subjective variables.

Again, specified white/black owners who have lived in their residence for more than three months serve as the primary data base. Stepwise multiple regression is undertaken for the full sample of 30,471, "90-day"—28,280 whites and 2,191 blacks—and 16,999 "90-day" renters—13,981 whites and 2,728 blacks. The choice of variables takes place according to both judgmental and mathematical criteria. Variables are included if they meet a variance explanation, i.e. addition to R^2 lower limit (which ranges from .002 to .005 depending on race and opinion). Thus the procedure is stopped when there do not exist any variables (not already in the equation) which, if added, would add sufficiently to the R^2 of the equation. This method is conservative in terms of R^2 but not so in terms of significance level. However, if significance levels were relied upon exclusively, often the case forstepwise regression, given this sample size almost any amount of variance explanation would be significant. This would lead to the inclusion of a multitude of variables in the resulting equations, making the analysis unmanageable.

For both opinion of structure and neighborhood, stepwise regression is performed on each race separately so as not to lose a variable which might be important to blacks. For instance, the presence of rats, affecting statements on either structure or neighborhood quality, if unimportant to whites and important to blacks, could be lost as important in a pooled (both races) regression due to the predominant presence of whites versus blacks in the sample.

The first group of variables to be included are those for which data is available in all cases. This primary variable set is listed below.

Primary Variable Set* (Full-information)

Geographic:	region, central city-SMSA
Socio-Economic Status (SES):	sex, marital status, age, income, education, pre-school or school-age children
Housing Age:	when built, when moved in
Housing Physical Features:	plumbing, kitchen, heating, air conditioning, phone, basement, sewer
Housing Economics:	value (owners), mortgage (owners), cash rent (renters), subsidy (renters)

This variable set is optimal for prediction and analysis purposes. Each household has complete information for this set. Thus the regression equations and the individual predicted values can be computed without any adjustments for missing data. However, if R^2 appears insufficient (say less than .20) additional variables which do not have complete information will be introduced.

Initial Variable Selection—R^2. The retained "full information" variables for white and black *owners* on *structure* quality are listed below. (Variable lists for white/black owners on neighborhood

White Owners Structure Quality	Black Owners Structure Quality
Value	Value
Plumbing	Heating
Air	Built
Built	Pre-School Children
Phone	Education
Heating	Plumbing
$R^2 = 0.164$	$R^2 = 0.113$

*See definition in Appendix I.

quality, renters on structure quality and renters on neighborhood quality appear in Appendix II.)

It is noteworhty that four variables—*value, plumbing, heating and when built*—appear as important in both white and black owner specification of structure quality. Thus, the price of a house, the exclusive use and full presence of plumbing, the quality of available heating and the house's age affect both white and black owner's specification of structure quality.

The above equation for both whites and blacks lists the four common variables as well as four additional variables *(air, phone, pre-school children and education)*. To these eight variables are added six additional variables for substantive reasons: *Income, age, when moved in, sex, marital status and the presence of school-age children*. These latter variables, which classically have been believed to affect specification of structure or neighborhood quality, are given a final chance to enter the regression equation.

Secondary Variable Set (Limited Information)—R^2. Since the first set of variables explained less than the desired "first cut" R^2 — 0.20. a selected number of these original "full information" variables are retained and combined with other variables for which full data is not available. These latter variables are those for which "no answer" is a reported response. These additional variables are far from ideal from a data manipulation perspective. They pose the statistical problem of causing the data user to either: (1) use a different number of cases in estimating individual correlations, (2) lose all cases where any information is absent, or (3) fill in missing values by some technique. The limited information variable set is:

Breakdown Variables:	toilets, rats, fuse blown, leaks, holes, electricity, exterminator, water
Repairs:	alterations done, repairs planned
Insurance:	theft insurance, refused insurance
Housing Economics II:	housing costs (owners), gross rent (renters), costs/income (owners), rent/income (renters)
Housing Physical Features II:	garage (owners, privacy, parking available (renters), crowding, live alone, trash disposal

| *Employment:* | Employed, time to work, distance to work |
| *Neighborhood:* | Nbd |

Again a stepwise regression is run for both races and both tenurial categories on structure and neighborhood opinion. (White and black owner opinions of structure quality are shown here.) This yields twelve variables for whites and seven for blacks. Since the seven black variables are subsumed within the twelve white variables, a total of twelve variables are retained for owners on opinion of structure quality. Listed below are the variables selected.

White Owners Structure Quality	*Black Owners* Structure Quality
Value	Value
Holes	Holes
Leak	Theft Insurance
Theft Insurance	Built
Garage	Rats
Built	Age
Rats	Air
Age	
Education	
Neighborhood	
Air	
Fuse Blown	
$R^2 = 0.195$	$R^2 = 0.151$

It is obvious from above that the dominant variables explaining white owner variation are quite similar to those variables which most explain black variation. This is not only true for white/black *owner* specification of *structure* quality but also holds true for white/black *renter* specification of *structure* quality. On the whole, the commonality of variables triggering white/black opinions is much more dominant in their specification of *structure* than *neighborhood*. Appendix IV lists the variables selected for (1) white/black owner specification of neighborhood quality (nine variables*,

*CC-SMSA and Region are counted as one variable each although both actually consist of three dummy variables.

four in common); (2) white/black renter specification of structure quality (nine variables, six in common) and (3) white/black renter specification of neighborhood quality (eleven variables*, three in common).

SUMMARY

Variable sets were formed for utilization in prediction equations for white/black owner/renter opinions of housing and neighborhood quality. The "full information" variables were not strong enough by themselves to adquately predict the opinions. Thus "limited information" variables were added. After including this latter set of variables, the R^2s were still relatively low.

A Model to Isolate Racial Differences in Specification of Structure and Neighborhood Quality

To analyze the "race effect"* separate regression equations are constructed for whites and blacks. The data for one group is substituted into the equation for the other to see if observed results differ significantly from predicted results. Thus for a given opinion (structure or neighborhood) and tenure an individual black's appropriate socioeconomic status and housing feature variables are entered into the white equation—yielding a predicted value for that black if he/she were to change race but keep the appropriate variables constant. This is repeated for each black and the average of these resulting numbers is the mean predicted value for blacks. This mean predicted value is then compared to the actual (i.e. observed) black mean. If the two means are identical, the race effect does not exist. If the "race effect" diminishes but still exists, then the mean of the predicted values will be somewhere between the actual black mean and the actual white mean. This procedure is then reversed for whites in the black equation.

THE UNREFINED RACE EFFECT

Exhibit 5 presents initial specification of structure and neighborhood opinion by race of respondent, unrefined by comparability

*The believed notion that whites are more positive about the housing that they occupy than blacks.

EXHIBIT 5

SPECIFICATION OF STRUCTURE AND NEIGHBORHOOD QUALITY (OWNERS AND RENTERS) BY RACE*

Opinion of Structure/ Neighborhood Quality	RACE		Black Mean Minus White Mean (Raw Race Effect)
	Black Mean	White Mean	
Structure Quality— Owners	2.000	1.646	.354
Structure Quality— Renters	2.532	2.131	.401
Neighborhood Quality— Owners	2.131	1.672	.458
Neighborhood Quality— Renters	2.450	2.039	.411

White/Black differences significant at .001 level.

*These means are based just on the people who responded to both structure and neighborhood quality questions. Thus, they are slightly different than those in Exhibit 1-4.

of socioeconomic status or housing features. What is apparent from this exhibit is that owners for both opinions and both races give higher ratings than renters and that whites rate both their housing and their neighborhood higher than blacks. On the four point scale, the average ratings for both structure and neighborhood run from 1.6 to 2.5. There is a consistent 20 to 25 percent higher average rating of structure and neighborhood by whites versus blacks. This holds true for both owners and renters. This difference is termed the "raw" race effect and appears in the last column of Exhibit 5.

THE TRUE RACE EFFECT–OBJECTIVE VARIABLE SET

Exhibit 6 shows the race effect when whites are put into the black equation and Exhibit 7 when blacks are put into the white equation. Column 1 of these exhibits shows the mean predicted value when one race is put into the other's equation; Column 2 shows the estimated race effect (±** the actual mean minus the mean of the predicted values); Column 3 the standard error of that effect; Column 4 the percentage of the raw effect than the estimated effect represents.

**The sign of the effect is adjusted so that a positive race effect always refers to whites having a more positive opinion; a negative sign means blacks have a more positive opinion.

Exhibit 6 demonstrates that when whites are put into the black equation the race effect is reduced to approximately 40 percent of its original value, i.e., the residual race effects are about 40 percent of the corresponding raw race effects. Thus the difference between black and white responses to structure and neighborhood quality has been reduced to less than half of its initial size by standardizing for socioeconomic status and housing features. Exhibit 7 shows that a similar phenomenon takes place when blacks are placed into the white equation. The raw race effect of black-white specification of structure and neighborhood quality is reduced to less than one-half of its original value by standardizing for equivalent socioeconomic status and housing features of the two groups.

In terms of absolute size, the race effect has been reduced to approximately .10 to .20 which is 3 to 7 percent of the absolute range of the evaluation scale or equivalently, 5 to 10 percent of the average responses of whites.

EXHIBIT 6

RESULTS OF RECIPROCAL REGRESSION EQUATION (WHITES IN BLACK EQUATION)

MEAN, STANDARD ERROR, % OF RACE EFFECT

Opinion of Structure/Neighborhood Quality	(1) Mean Predicted Value	(2) Estimated Race Effect	(3) Standard Error of Effect	(4) Percentage of Raw Race Effect
Structure Quality— Owners	1.752	.106	.0035	30.0
Structure Quality— Renters	2.337	.206	.0064	51.3
Neighborhood Quality— Owners	1.912	.240	.0039	52.4
Neighborhood Quality— Renters	2.188	.149	.0065	36.2

It is significant to note that while the race effect overall is relatively low, it has been reduced least by equivalency in socioeconomic status and housing features for *owners' opinion of neighborhood and renters' opinion of structure.* Equivalent white and black owners have more divergence in opinion on neighborhood quality than they do on structure quality; equivalent white and black renters have greater differences in opinion on structure quality than they do on

EXHIBIT 7

RESULTS OF RECIPROCAL REGRESSION EQUATION
(BLACKS IN WHITE EQUATION)

MEAN, STANDARD ERROR, % OF RACE EFFECT

Opinion of Structure/Neighborhood Quality	(1) Mean Predicted Value	(2) Estimated Race Effect	(3) Standard Error of Effect	(4) Percentage of Raw Race Effect
Structure Quality— Owners	1.924	.076	.0148	21.5
Structure Quality— Renters	2.372	.160	.0148	39.9
Neighborhood Quality— Owners	1.907	.223	.0161	48.7
Neighborhood Quality— Renters	2.315	.135	.0146	32.8

Source: U.S. Department of Commerce, U.S. Department of Housing and Urban Development, *Annual Housing Survey*, 1976.

neighborhood quality. Thus, based on the controls instituted at this stage, black owners are less sanguine (relative to whites) about their neighborhoods than their structures. black renters exhibit less enthusiasm (relative to whites) about their housing than their immediate geographic area.

The "raw" race effect initially observed at approximately 14 percent of the range of the scale has been reduced to less than one-half of this value by standardizing for housing features and socioeconomic status of the reporting race.

The race effect, while reduced significantly, still persists at a low level. At this point, suffice it to say than in terms of potential public meliorative actions, the effect may be viewed as zero. Yet, while for substantive reasons it is sufficiently low to be ignored, black-white differences in the specification of their housing and neighborhood continue to be identifiable.

Attempting to Determine the True Race Effect—Adding Subjective Variables, Narrowing the Geographic Focus

There are three potential statistical refinements that may be used to further investigate whether white-black reporting differences in evaluations of structure or neighborhood are attributable to race alone. First, subjective variables may be added to the data set. This assumes that the predictive equations containing just objective variables are insufficient to correctly specify substantive linkages—thus the results concernign the estimated race effect may be spurious.* Adding the subjective variables may significantly change the prediction equations (including a substantial increase in R^2) and explain the lingering race effect.**

A second procedure is to apply the analysis to a smaller portion or subgroup of the national population—i.e., regions, portions of regions etc. The rationale for this is that, since characteristics of blacks and whites differ significantly according the the region that they occupy and to their central-city/non-central-city locations, and the geographical distribution of the two races differ, an analysis that does not take these geographic variations into account may not adequately describe the data.

A third procedure is to allow one opinion to help explain another opinion—i.e., opinion of neighborhood to partially interpret opinion of structure. This assumes some level of consistency between satisfaction with structure and neighborhood such that failure to include neighborhood ignores a major reason why housing buyers act the way they do in the selection and purchase of a house. It has been shown that satisfaction with neighborhood inflates opinions of house.

THE TRUE RACE EFFECT—THE INTRODUCTION OF SUBJECTIVE VARIABLES

The first probe of the remnant white-black reporting differences consists of adding additional subjective variables to the variable set. Variable additions will be viewed both in terms of affect on R^2 and their reduction of the raw race effect.

Desire-to-move variables (occupants'expressed preference to move because of neighborhood conditions, structural deficiencies or

---

*The subjective variables incorporate some error. This leads to some bias in the regression equations and predicted results. However, since the R^2s with objective variables were low, some bias will be risked by including subjective variables.

**Of course, the estimate race effect may also increase with added variables.

neighborhood services) are entered into the regression equation after the objective variables have been included. For renters, all three of the variables are included in the regression equations for structure and neighborhood quality; for owners' opinions of *neighborhood* quality, due to an insignificant R^2 addition, the variable structural deficiencies was not retained. for owners' opinions of *structure* quality, again due to insignificant R^2, neither the variable structural deficiencies nor neighborhood services were retained.

Exhibit 8 presents the effect of the inclusion of these variables on the explanatory power (R^2) of the regression equations for both whites and blacks. The R^2 relating to opinions of *structure* quality (both owner and renter) has been increased for both races via inclusion of the subjective variables by 5 to 30 percent; for *neighborhood* quality by more than 80 percent. The subjective variables obviously increase significantly the explanatory power of equations relating to specification of *neighborhood* quality. Thus, the "desire-to-move" variables contain significant information about expressed *neighborhood* quality not contained in the objective variables.

EXHIBIT 8

EXPLANATORY POWER OF THE BASIC WHITE/BLACK REGRESSION EQUATIONS WITH AND WITHOUT THE "DESIRE-TO-MOVE" VARIABLES

RACE

Opinion of Structure/ Neighborhood Quality	BLACKS		WHITES	
	R^2 *Without*	R^2 *With*	R^2 *Without*	R^2 *With*
Structure Quality— Owners	.151	.176	.195	.206
Structure Quality— Renters	.214	.275	.171	.225
Neighborhood Quality— Owners	.116	.234	.126	.239
Neighborhood Quality— Renters	.153	.283	.106	.254

Following the format of Exhibits 6 and 7, Exhibits 9 and 10 present the results of one race placed in the regression equation of the other. As before, the regression equations are produced for both owners and renters on structure and neighborhood quality and include the subjective "desire-to-move" variables.

EXHIBIT 9

RESULTS OF RECIPROCAL REGRESSION EQUATIONS (INCLUDING THE "DESIRE-TO-MOVE" VARIABLES) (WHITES IN BLACK EQUATIONS)

| | MEANS, STANDARD ERROR, % OF RACE EFFECT | | | |
| | *(1)* | *(2)* | *(3)* | *(4)* |
Opinion of Structure/Neighborhood Quality	*Mean Predicted Value*	*Estimated Race Effect*	*Standard Error of Race Effect*	*Percentage of Raw Race Effect*
Structure Quality– Owners	1.743	.097	.0035	27.4
Structure Quality– Renters	2.329	.198	.0062	49.4
Neighborhood Quality– Owners	1.885	.213	.0036	46.5
Neighborhood Quality– Renters	2.203	.164	.0060	39.9

EXHIBIT 10

RESULTS OF RECIPROCAL REGRESSION EQUATION (INCLUDING THE "DESIRE-TO-MOVE" VARIABLES) (BLACKS IN WHITE EQUATIONS)

| | MEANS, STANDARD ERROR, % OF RACE EFFECT | | | |
| | *(1)* | *(2)* | *(3)* | *(4)* |
Opinion of Structure/Neighborhood Quality	*Mean Predicted Value*	*Estimated Race Effect*	*Standard Error of Race Effect*	*Percentage of Raw Race Effect*
Structure Quality– Owners	1.933	.067	.0146	18.9
Structure Quality– Renters	2.392	.140	.0143	34.9
Neighborhood Quality– Owners	1.942	.189	.0149	41.2
Neighborhood Quality– Renters	2.310	.140	.0135	34.1

Source: U.S. Department of Commerce, U.S. Department of Housing and Urban Development, *Annual Housing Survey*, 1976.

Using these Exhibits and comparing them with previous Exhibits 6 and 7, in 3 out of 4 cases the "desire-to-move" variables reduce the race effect by approximatetly 10 percent from the results reported in Exhibits 6 and 7. Opinion of *neighborhood* quality for *renters* is the only case where inclusion of the "desire-to-move" variables does not diminish the race effect.

Overall, inclusion of the subjective "desire-to-move" variables has increased significantly the R^2 of the regression equations (both white and black) for opinions of neighborhood quality and increased moderately the R^2 in the equations for opinions of structure quality. The race effect in most cases has been reduced by an additional 10 percent via the inclusion of these variables.

Thus, desire to move from a neighborhood impacts on both opinions of housing and surroundings within a neighborhood for both whites and blacks.* It contributes slightly to the demonstration of minimal importance of the race effect in black/white specification of structure and neighborhood.

THE TRUE EFFECT–NARROWING THE GEOGRAPHIC FOCUS

Another means of probing the race effect is to consider geographic subsets of the national sample. The previously used equations, reflecting a national distribution of a particular race, may be drawing upon too broad a base. Subleties in the race effect on opinions, not apparent using the entire group, may appear when specific subsets are scrutinized.

The first geographic subset comprises central city and suburban areas* within SMSAs. The second partitions this first subset into four Census-defined regions of the United States.**

*It is interesting to note that although R^2s were increased significantly for the opinion of neighborhood quality, the estimated race effect was only changed minimally. Thus the earlier rationale of the lingering race effect as partially due to low R^2s is not borne out, at least on opinions of neighborhood quality.

*"Suburbs" are defined as those areas within an SMSA not in the central city.

**Northeast, North Central, South, West. Technically, the variable selection procedure should be repeated when a subgroup is considered. For practical reasons and the fact that the twelve variables form a broad substantive group, variable selection will not be repeated here. However, the regression equations are recalculated for each

The analysis will be restricted to *owners'* (both white and black) opinions of *structure* quality. The original twelve objective variables plus a dummy variable for central city versus suburb will be used.

Exhibit 11 presents means and R^2s for the subsets as well as the total group. As before, the black minus white mean is the "raw race effect". Evident in the Exhibit is that the raw effect is higher in central cities and suburbs than it is for non-SMSA areas. When the suburbs and central cities are taken as a group and partitioned by region, the raw effect is higher in the Northeast and North Central regions and lower in the South and West.

EXHIBIT 11

SPECIFICATION OF STRUCTURE QUALITY (OWNERS) BY RACE (PARTITIONED BY GEOGRAPHIC REGION)

MEAN, RAW RACE EFFECT, R^3

Geographic Subset	Black Mean	White Mean	Black Minus White Mean (Raw Race Effect)	Black R^2	White R^2
Total–All Areas	2.000	1.646	.354	.151	.195
All Central Cities and Suburbs	2.000	1.605	.395	.145	.176
Central Cities/Suburbs in Northeast	2.013	1.586	.427	.277	.142
Central Cities/Suburbs in North Central	2.016	1.588	.428	.204	.206
Central Cities/Suburbs in South	1.993	1.649	.344	.135	.203
Central Cities/Suburbs in West	1.975	1.603	.372	.218	.181

White/Black difference significant at .001 level.

area. The "desire-to-move" variables had little impact on the estimated race effect so their results are not reported.

Exhibit 12 shows the results of running one race in the other's predictive regression equation. Instead of individually presenting both white-on-black and black-on-white estimates of the race effect, they are combined using a weighted average.* When one partitions by central city-suburb the race effect is approximately 30 percent of the raw race effect. Within regions, standardizing for socio-economic characteristics and housing features has least effect in the South and West. In the North Central region, the race effect, as a percentage of the raw race effect, is only 7.5 percent. in the South it is 48.3 percent. Overall, the race effect is .13 which is less than 5 percent of the 1-4 evaluation range and less than 10 percent of the average white response.

Thus, at this point of the analysis, as one moves from North Central to Northeast to West and finally, South, blacks became less sanguine than whites with equivalent housing.

EXHIBIT 12

RESULTS OF RECIPROCAL REGRESSION EQUATION SHOWING RACE EFFECT
(WEIGHTED WHITE/BLACK IN BLACK/WHITE EQUATIONS)

Geographic Subset	RACE EFFECT, STANDARD ERROR, % OF RACE EFFECT		
	Estimated Race Effect	Standard Error of Race Effect	Percentage of Raw Race Effect
Total–All Areas	.104	.0034	29.4
All Central Cities and Suburbs	.127	.0030	32.2
Central Cities/Suburbs in Northeast	.082	.0102	19.2
Central Cities/Suburbs in North Central	.032	.0090	7.5
Central Cities/Suburbs in South	.166	.0105	48.3
Central Cities/Suburbs in West	.110	.0109	29.6

Source: U.S. Department of Commerce, U.S. Department of Housing and Urban Development, *Annual Housing Survey*, 1976.

*The weight for the white-on-black estimate is the number of whites and for the black-on-white estimate the number of blacks.

The analysis of geographic subsets is carried to its final step** when the heavily populated area within regions (central cities-suburbs) are viewed individually within the same region. Again only *owner* opinions of *structure* quality are considered. Similar research questions are now asked of residents within suburbs and central cities separately—1) What is the "raw" race effect? 2) How is the effect diminished when one standardizes for socioeconomic characteristics and housing features of the respondents?

Exhibit 13 presents white and black means, R^2s and the raw race effect for owners' opinion of structure quality. The largest raw race effects (.40 to .45) appear in Northeastern and North Central central cities and Southern and Western suburbs. White owners consistently rate housing higher in suburbs than they do in central cities; black owners follow the same general pattern in only two of the four regions—Northeast and North Central.

EXHIBIT 13

SPECIFICATION OF STRUCTURE QUALITY (OWNERS) BY RACE (PARTITIONED BY GEOGRAPHIC REGION AND CENTRAL CITY/SUBURB)

MEAN, RACE EFFECT, R^2

Geographic/Areal Subset	Black Mean	White Mean	Black Minus White Mean (Raw Race Effect)	Black R^2	White R^2
Central City, Northeast	2.118	1.699	.419	.260	.129
Suburb, Northeast	1.837	1.552	.285	.434	.139
Central City, North Central	2.073	1.628	.445	.165	.226
Suburb, North Central	1.762	1.571	.191	.465	.200
Central City, South	1.968	1.666	.302	.084	.214
Suburb, South	2.047	1.639	.408	.311	.203
Central City, West	1.960	1.635	.325	.295	.193
Suburb, West	2.006	1.585	.421	.240	.178

**Further partitioning, within suburbs for instance is not feasible due to minimal sample size restrictions.

Exhibit 14 shows the results of placing one race in the other's equation to examine the race effect in both central city and suburb. Again, results for whites and blacks are not presented separately but combined, via weighting, according to sample representation. The "raw" race effect has been reduced significantly (less than 25 percent of original) in Northeastern and North Central suburbs and Western central cities.*** It is one-third to one-half its value in Northeastern and North Central central cities and Southern suburbs; it is 85 percent of its original value in Western suburbs.

EXHIBIT 14

RESULTS OF RECIPROCAL REGRESSION EQUATION SHOWING RACE EFFECT
(CENTRAL CITY-SUBURB)
(WEIGHTED WHITE/BLACK IN BLACK/WHITE EQUATIONS)

RACE EFFECT, STANDARD ERROR, % OF RACE EFFECT

Geographic/Areal Subset	Estimated Race Effect	Standard Error of Race Effect	Percentage of Raw Race Effect
Central City, Northeast	.142	.0215	33.9
Suburb, Northeast	.040	.0114	14.0
Central City, North Central	.211	.0169	47.4
Suburb, North Central	−.163	.0106	−
Central City, South	.117	.0173	38.8
Suburb, South	.195	.0132	47.8
Central City, West	.067	.0189	20.6
Suburb, West	.360	.0133	85.5

Source: U.S. Department of Commerce, U.S. Department of Housing and Urban Development, *Annual Housing Survey*, 1976.

Standardizing for comparable socioeconomic characteristics and housing features and partitioning by geographic area shows the race effect to virtually disappear in long standing, black-entry, Northeastern and North Central* suburbs and Western central cities and to be a small but distinct force in typically-segregated, North Central central-cities, Southern and Western suburbs.

***In fact, in North Central suburbs the race effect is reversed— black owners being more positive than whites about their structure quality.

*The "desire-to-move" subjective variables add little explanation here and thus have not been included in the reported analysis.

In summary, while the race effect generally remains small, it is above .14 in Northern (Northeast, North Central) central cities and Southern/Western suburbs. Its effect ranges from less than zero to .36 with most values around 0.10. This is only 3 percent of the range of the four point evaluation scale or 5 percent of the average white score.

The True Race Effect—Allowing Opinion of Neighborhood to Explain Opinion of Structure

A final analysis, to simultaneously upgrade the quality of the regressions through increased R^2s and also view the effect of race, is to use opinion of neighborhood quality as a gauge for predicting both owners' and renters' response to structure quality. The obvious link to the real world, as mentioned previously, is that people "purchase neighborhoods" rather than housing and housing satisfaction flows directly from satisfaction with neighborhood. If this is true one should expect significant increases in R^2s and relatively low race effects as opinions of neighborhood quality also become part of the standardization process between blacks and whites.

Viewing first white and black owner responses, Exhibit 15 presents R^2s of the regression equation for white and black owners' opinion of structure quality when the subjective measure of neighborhood quality is added to the twelve objective variables.* It is clear for both whites and blacks that R^2 is improved dramatically. Original R^2s around the .15 to .20 level have been raised to the .35 to .50 level—a doubling of the explanatory power for whites; a tripling for blacks.

The race effect using the above variable array is shown in Exhibit 16. It is clear from this Exhibit that the race effect is minimal in most areas when standardizing for socioeconomic status/housing features and opinions of neighborhood quality. In three instances (Northeastern/North Central suburbs and Western central cities) it is even reversed—black opinions of structure quality being higher than those of whites. Again Southern and Western suburbs and North Central central cities show lingering aspects of the race effect.

---

*The "desire-to-move" subjective variables add little explanation here and thus have not been included in the reported analysis.

EXHIBIT 15

SPECIFICATION OF STRUCTURE QUALITY (OWNERS) BY RACE (INCLUDING NEIGHBORHOOD QUALITY AS A PREDICTOR VARIABLE)

R^2

Geographic/Areal Subset	R^2 White	R^2 Black
Total–All Areas	.360	.303
All Central Cities and Suburbs	.338	.358
Central City, Northeast	.336	.409
Suburb, Northeast	.331	.530
Central City, North Central	.325	.312
Suburb, North Central	.399	.589
Central City, South	.394	.282
Suburb, South	.372	.425
Central City, West	.375	.617
Suburb, West	.363	.458

EXHIBIT 16

RESULTS OF RECIPROCAL REGRESSION EQUATION (INCLUDING NEIGHBORHOOD QUALITY AS A PREDICTOR VARIABLE) (WEIGHTED WHITE/BLACK IN BLACK/WHITE EQUATION)

Geographic/Areal Subset	RACE EFFECT, STANDARD ERROR, % OF RACE EFFECT		
	Estimated Race Effect	Standard Error of Race Effect*	Percentage of Raw Race Effect
Total–All Areas	.012	.0031	3.4
All Central Cities and Suburbs	.043	.0027	10.9
Central City, Northeast	.038	.0194	9.1
Suburb, Northeast	−.049	.0103	−
Central City, North Central	.104	.0152	23.3
Suburb, North Central	−.228	.0095	−
Central City, South	.000	.0156	−
Suburb, South	.157	.0119	38.4
Central City, West	−.087	.0170	−
Suburb, West	.227	.0120	53.9

*Standard error is computed only for total group. The other standard errors are estimates using the total group results and previous results from separate region analysis.

Source: U.S. Department of Commerce, U.S. Department of Housing and Urban Development, *Annual Housing Survey*, 1976.

Thus, two alternative scenarios present themselves. Either there is some latent discontent by blacks in Western and Southern suburbs and North Central cities or juridical differences in these areas is causing an unfair comparison.

The effect of opinions of *owners* on neighborhood quality is clearly very significant as an index of structure quality. This is true for both whites and blacks. The R^2s of the predictive equations are noticeably increased; the race effect, except in select locations, is virtually nonexistent.

A portion of this final analysis is repeated for *cash renters*. The opinion of neighborhood quality is added to the nine objective variables to predict structure quality opinion for the complete sample of cash renters.

Essentially, the results found for owners are also found here. The R^2 doubled (from .18 to .36) when neighborhood quality was added to the equation.* The raw race effect, .401, is reduced to .017 (4 percent of the raw effect) when the controls are applied. Thus, as with owners, essentially no race effect exists when the races are standardized for socioeconomic status, housing features and opinion of neighborhood quality.

Notes

1. See George Sternlieb, "The Sociology of Statistics: Measuring Substandard Housing," *Public Data Use*, Vol. 1-3 (July 1973).
2. U.S. Department of Commerce, Bureau of Census, *Measuring Housing Quality* (Washington, D.C.: Government Printing Office). pp. 1-6.
3. U.S. Department of Commerce, *U.S. Census of Housing*, 1950. Bulletin H-B14, "Non-Form Housing Characteristics" (Washington, D.C.: Government Printing Office, 1950), pp. vi-vii.
4. U.S. Department of Commerce, Bureau of Census, *U.S. Census of Housing-1960*, Series HC (2)-1, "Metropolitan Housing" (Washington,D.C.: Government Printing Office, 1960), pp. x-xi.
5. U.S. Department of Commerce, Bureau of Census, *U.S. Census of Housing*, *1970*, Series HC-6 "Plumbing Facilities and Estimates of Dilapidated Housing" (Washington, D.C.: Governement Printing Office, 1970), pp. viii-ix.

*As with owners, the "desire-to-move" variables added insignificantly to R^2 at this point.

6. U.S. Department of Commerce, Bureau of Census, Working Paper, No.25, "Measuring the Quality of Housing: An Appraisal of Census Statistics and Methods" (1967), pp. 1-5.

7. U.S. Department of Commerce, U.S. Department of Housing and Urban Development, *Annual Housing Survey-1976*, "Documentation of the Public Use Tapes" (1978).

8. U.S. Department of Health, Education and Welfare, Office of Secretary, "Memo from Subcommittee of Housing Quality" (February 1977).

9. Telephone conversation with Census Bureau personnel-1980 Decennial Census-Housing.

10. See George Sternlieb and Robert W. Burchell, *Residential Abandonment: The Tenement Landlord Revisited* (New Brunswick, N.J.: Center for Urban Policy Research, 1972).

    11. Frank M. Andrews and Stephen B. Withey, *Social Indicators of Well Being* (New York, Plenum Press, 1976).

    12. Angus Campbell, Philip E. Converse and Willard L. Rodgers, *The Quality of American Life* (New York, Russell Sage Foundation, 1976).

    13. Raymond J. Burby III and Shirley F. Weiss, *New Communities, U.S.A.* (Lexington, Massachusetts, Lexington Books, 1976).

    14. Constance A. Nathanson, Jeanne S. Newman, Elizabeth Moer and Helen Hiltabiddle, "Moving Plans Among Residents of New Towns," *A.I.P. Journal* (42), June, 1976, pp. 295-302.

    15. Roger Durand, "Some Dynamics of Urban Service Evaluations Among Blacks and Whites," *Social Science Quarterly* (56) March 1976, pp. 698-706.

    16. Nicholas P. Lovrich, Jr., "Differing Priorities in an Urban Electorate: Service Preferences Among Anglo Black and Mexican American Voters," *Social Science Quarterly* (55) December 1974, p. 704-717.

    17. Robert J. Diaiso, David M. Friedman, Lester C. Mitchell, and Eric A. Schweitzer, *Perception of the Housing Environment: A Comparison of Racial and Density Preferences* (Pittsburgh, Pa., University of Pittsburgh Graduate School of Public and International Affairs, 1971).

Other References

Robert Crosby, "An Item Analysis of the Annual Housing Survey" (Washington, D.C.: U.S. Department of Health, Education, and Welfare, January 13, 1977), unpublished, 35 pp.

Jeanne E. Goedert and John L. Goodman, Jr., "Indicators of Housing Quality:An Exploration of the Annual Housing Survey" (Washington, D.C.: The Urban Institute, November 1976), unpublished, 44 pp.

Kenneth F. Wieand, "Analysis of Multiple-Defect Indicators of Housing Quality with Data from the 1976 Annual Housing Survey" (Washington, D.C.: U.S. Department of Housing and Urban Development, June 1978), unpublished, 63pp.

William T. Bielby, "Measuring Neighborhood Quality in the Annual Housing Survey" (Santa Barbara, Calif.: University of California, November 1978), unpublished, 33pp.

Appendix I
List of Variables, Variable Definitions and Coding

Variable Codes

Full Information Variables

I GEOGRAPHIC REGION
1) *Region:* 3 dummy variables for the four regions: Northeast, North Central, West and South
2) *Central City-SMSA:* 3 dummy variables for four areas: Central City, SMSA but not Central City ("suburb"), SMSA with Central City code not specified, and outside SMSA.

II SOCIOECONOMIC STATUS
1) *Sex:* 1 = male, 0 = female
2) *Marital Status:* 1 = married, 0 = not married
3) *Age:* 14 - 19 = 1, 20 - 39 = 2, 40 - 64 = 3, 65 + = 4
4) *Income:* < $10,000 = 1, $10,000 - $19,999 = 2, $20,000 - $34,000 = 3, $35,000 + = 4
5) *Education:* < grade 9 = 1, grade 9 - 11 = 2, grade 12 = 3, 1 - 3 years college = 4, 4 years college = 5, 5 + years college = 6
6) *Pre-School or School Age Children:* 2 dummy variables for: (1) children under 6, (2) children 6 - 17 or both 6 - 17 and under 6 and (3) no children up to 17.

III HOUSING AGE
1) *(When) Built:* 1975 or 1976 = 1, 4/1970 - 1974 = 2, pre 4/1970 = 3
2) *(When) Moved-in:* 1975 or 1976 = 1, 4/1970 - 1974 = 2, 1965 - 3/1970 = 3, pre 1965 = 4

IV HOUSING PHYSICAL FEATURES
1) *Plumbing:* exclusive use = 1, else = 0
2) *Kitchen:* exclusive use = 1, else = 0
3) *Heating:* room heaters with flue or vent burning gas, oil or kerosene = 1, other means without flue = 2, none = 3
4) *Air:* have air conditioning = 1, else = 0

5) *Phone:* have one = 1, else = 0

6) *Basement:* have one = 1, else = 0

7) *Sewer:* public sewer or septic tank or cesspool = 1, else = 0

V HOUSING ECONOMICS I

1) *Value (owners):* < $20,000 = 1, $20,000 - $34,999 = 2, $35,000 - $49,999 = 3, $50,000 - $74,000 = 4, $75,000 + = 5

2) *Mortgage (owners):* have one = 1, else = 0

3) *Cash Rent (renter):* yes = 1, no = 0

4) *Subsidy (renters):* living in public housing project or receiving government rent subsidy = 1, else = 0

Limited Information Variables

VI HOUSING ECONOMICS II*

1) *Housing Costs (owners)*

2) *Gross Rent (renters)*

3) *Costs/Income (owners)*

4) *Rent/Income (renters)*

VII HOUSING PHYSICAL FEATURES II

1) *Garage (owners):* have one = 1, else = 0

2) *Privacy:* must go through bedroom to reach bath or another bedroom = 1, don't have to = 2, no bedrooms = blank

3) *Parking Available (renters):* Available = 1, else = 0

4) *Crowding:* 1 if No. of persons/room > 1, 0 else

5) *Trash Disposal:* garbage collection services not available = 1, else = 0

6) *Live alone:* yes = 1, no = 0

VIII BREAKDOWN VARIABLES

1) *Toilet:*** had breakdown = 1, else = 0

2) *Rats:*** sign of rats = 1, else = 0

3) *Leaks:* sign of basement and/or roof leak = 1, else = 0

4) *Fuse Blown:*** blown fuses or breakers = 1, else = 0

5) *Holes:* No. times answered yes to (1) cracks or holes in walls, (2) holes in floor, (3) peeling paint and (4) broken plaster

6) *Electricity:* electric wall outlets not working or wiring not concealed = 1, else = 0

7) *Exterminator:* used one = 1, else = 0

8) *Water:*** water source breakdown = 1, else = 0

IX INSURANCE

1) *Theft Insurance:* have it = 1, else = 0

2) *Refused Insurance:* yes = 1, no = 0

X EMPLOYMENT

1) *Employed:* yes = 1, no = 0

2) *Time to Work:* Codes 1 † 7 as is from H399*** (these range from under fifteen minutes = 1 to over 1 hour, 30 minutes = 7); rest = blank

3) *Distance to work:* Codes 1 † 8 on H400*** as is (these range from under one mile = 1 to over 50 miles = 8); rest = blank

XI NEIGHBORHOOD

1) *Neighborhood:* abandoned or boarded buildings noted by enumerator or (renters only) hazardous steps or stair railings on common stairways = 1, else = 0

XII REPAIRS

1) *Alterations done:* none = 1, less than $100 = 2, greater than $100 = 3

2) *Repairs Planned:* yes, in next 12 months = 1, else = 0

XIII DESIRE TO MOVE

1) *Neighborhood Conditions:* none = 0, 1 condition = 1, 2 - 4 conditions = 2, 5 + conditions = 3

2) *Structural Deficiencies:* none = 0, 1 deficiency = 1, 2 deficiencies = 2, 3 + deficiencies = 3

3) *Neighborhood Services:* not wish to move = 0, wish to move = 1

*For all four of the variables several recodes were tried. None changed the correlations with the opinion questions appreciably, so, in the end, no recodes are used.

**Applies to the last 90 days.

***See the *Data Base Dictionary* for 1976 National Annual Housing Survey, published by Data Users Services Division, Bureau of the Census.

Appendix II
Objective Variables Included in Basic White and Black Regression Equations—Not Reported in Text

EXHIBIT A-II-1

Objective Variables Included in Basic Regression Equations
For Owner's Opinions of Neighborhood Quality

WHITES	BLACKS
Value	Value
Neighborhood (NBD)	Neighborhood (NBD)
Education	Region
Age	Employed
Region	Alterations
Central City–SMSA	Income
	Central City–SMSA

EXHIBIT A-II-2

Objective Variables Included in Basic Regression Equations
For Renter's Opinions of Structure Quality

WHITES	BLACKS
Holes	Holes
Rats	Neighborhood (NBD)
Built	Rats
Leak	Leak
Theft Insurance	Age
Electric	Built
Age	
Neighborhood (NBD)	
Rent	

EXHIBIT A-II-3

Objective Variables Included in Basic Regression Equations
For Renter's Opinions of Neighborhood Quality

WHITES	BLACKS
Holes	Neighborhood (NBD)
Neighborhood (NBD)	Holes
Parking	Subsidy
Central City–SMSA	Age
Theft Insurance	Central City–SMSA
Live alone	Built
Rent	Rats

Source: U.S. Department of Commerce, U.S. Department of Housing and Urban Development, *Annual Housing Survey*, 1976.

Appendix III

Distribution and Means of Cash/No Cash Renters on Structure and Neighborhood Quality by Race

EXHIBIT A-III-1

Race by Specification of Structure Quality (House Opinion)
For Renters (For Subsets of Rental Tenure)

A. TENURE = CASH RENT

STRUCTURE QUALITY

Race	(1) Excellent	(2) Good	(3) Fair	(4) Poor	Total
White	3,558 (21.2)	8,351 (49.7)	4,044 (24.0)	862 (5.1)	16,814 (100.0)
Black	374 (10.1)	1,485 (39.9)	1,371 (36.8)	492 (13.2)	3,772 (100.0)
Total	3,933	9,836	5,414	1,354	

Mean for whites = 2.131; mean for blacks = 2.532.

B. TENURE = NO CASH RENT

STRUCTURE QUALITY

Race	(1) Excellent	(2) Good	(3) Fair	(4) Poor	Total
White	330 (30.5)	524 (48.5)	199 (18.4)	27 (2.5)	1,081 (100.0)
Black	34 (21.6)	64 (41.0)	41 (26.5)	17 (10.9)	156 (100.0)
Total	364	588	240	44	

Mean for whites = 1.927; mean for blacks = 2.263.

EXHIBIT A-III-2

Race by Specification of Neighborhood Quality (Street Opinion)
For Renters (For Subsets of Rental Tenure)

A. TENURE = CASH RENT

NEIGHBORHOOD QUALITY

Race	(1) Excellent	(2) Good	(3) Fair	(4) Poor	Total
White	4,154 (24.7)	8,524 (50.7)	3,463 (20.6)	676 (4.0)	16,817 (100.0)
Black	410 (1.0)	1,554 (41.7)	1,433 (38.5)	326 (8.8)	3,724 (18.1)
Total	4,564	10,078	4,896	1,002	20,541

Mean for whites = 2.039; mean for blacks = 2.450.

B. TENURE = NO CASH RENT

NEIGHBORHOOD QUALITY

Race	(1) Excellent	(2) Good	(3) Fair	(4) Poor	Total
White	381 (35.3)	509 (47.2)	154 (14.3)	34 (3.2)	1,078 (100.0)
Black	35 (22.3)	75 (47.6)	41 (26.1)	6 (4.0)	157 (100.0)
Total	416	584	195	41	1,235

Mean for whites = 1.852; mean for blacks = 2.115.

Appendix IV

Basic Regression Equations
for Owners/Renters on Structure
and Neighborhood Quality by Race

EXHIBIT A-IV-1

VARIABLES SELECTED BY STEPWISE REGRESSION FOR STRUCTURE AND NEIGHBORHOOD QUALITY BY RACE

OWNERS

STRUCTURE QUALITY		NEIGHBORHOOD QUALITY	
Whites	*Blacks*	*Whites*	*Blacks*
Whites	Value	Value	Value
Holes	Holes	Neighborhood	Neighborhood
Leaks	Theft Ins.	Education	Region
Theft Ins.	When Built	Age	Employed
Garage	Rats	Region	Alterations Done
When Built	Age	CCSMSA	Income
Rats	Air		CCSMSA
Age			
Education			
Neighborhood			
Air			
Fuse Blown			

CASH RENTERS

STRUCTURE QUALITY		NEIGHBORHOOD QUALITY	
Whites	*Blacks*	*Whites*	*Blacks*
Holes	Holes	Holes	Neighborhood
Rats	Neighborhood	Neighborhood	Holes
When Built	Rats	Parking Available	Subsidy
Leaks	Leaks	CCSMSA	Age
Theft Ins.	Age	Theft Ins.	CCSMSA
Electricity	When Built	Live Alone	Built
Age		Gross Rent	Rats
Neighborhood			
Gross Rent			

Source: U.S. Department of Commerce, U.S. Department of Housing and Urban Development, *Annual Housing Survey*, 1976.

EXHIBIT A-IV-2

BASIC REGRESSION EQUATIONS FOR STRUCTURE AND NEIGHBORHOOD QUALITY (OWNERS AND RENTERS WITH NEIGHBORHOOD (NBD) VARIABLE BY RACE)

OWNERS

Variables	STRUCTURE QUALITY White	STRUCTURE QUALITY Black		Variables	NEIGHBORHOOD QUALITY White	NEIGHBORHOOD QUALITY Black
Value	-.168	-.181		Value	-.158	-.213
Holes	.217	.166		Age	-.081	-.032
Leak	.119	.151		Education	-.052	.013
Built	.093	.134		Neighborhood (NBD)	.341	.254
Rats	.103	.140		Employed	-.005	.129
Garage	-.097	-.013		Income	-.025	-.103
Theft Insurance	-.149	-.097		Region 1	-.027	-.013
Age	-.059	-.029		Region 2	.092	-.094
Air Conditioning	-.038	-.101		Region 3	.034	.200
Fuse Blown	.042	.064		CCSMSA 1	-.174	-.201
Education	-.023	.005		CCSMSA 2	-.030	-.062
Neighborhood (NBD)	.111	.117		CCSMSA 3	.136	.250
				Alterations Done	.007	.047
Constant	2.225	1.994		Constant	2.504	2.505
R^2	.195	.151		R^2	.126	.116
Syx	.583	.695		Syx	.639	.740

CASH RENTERS

Variables	STRUCTURE QUALITY White	STRUCTURE QUALITY Black		Variables	NEIGHBORHOOD QUALITY White	NEIGHBORHOOD QUALITY Black
Holes	.265	.252		Holes	.157	.123
Built	.152	.195		Built	.044	.164
Leak	.236	.183		Theft Insurance	-.086	-.076
Theft Insurance	-.136	-.103		Age	-.048	-.122
Electric	.337	.112		Neighborhood (NBD)	.273	.034
Age	-.092	-.095		Rats	.114	.124
Neighborhood (NBD)	.168	.238		Gross Rent	-.001	-.001
Rats	.252	.195		CCSMSA 1	-.282	-.296
Gross Rent	.001	.002		CCSMSA 2	.025	.129
				CCSMSA 3	.170	.199
				Subsidy	.110	.240
				Parking	.152	.070
				Live Alone	-.139	-.029
Constant	1.949	1.928		Constant	2.197	1.997
R^2	.171	.214		R^2	.106	.153
Syx	.728	.751		Syx	.740	.740

Source: U.S. Department of Commerce, U.S. Department of Housing and Urban Development, *Annual Housing Survey*, 1976.

Appendix V
Analysis of the Effect of the Variable "Value" on Explaining the Race Effect

Introduction

The purpose of this Appendix is to analyze white-black differences in opinion of structure quality when a specific variable, *value*, is controlled.

For this analysis, value for owners of single-family homes is expressed in dollar ranges of the following categories:

1) less than 20,000
2) 20,000 - 34,999
3) 35,000 - 49,999
4) 50,000 - 74,999
5) 75,000 and over

The relationship of race and value is clear from the following Exhibit. On the average whites occupy much more expensive h uses than blacks do.

EXHIBIT A-V-1

Structure Value by Race
(Weighted Sample Sizes in 000's)

		VALUE						
		1	*2*	*3*	*4*	*5*	
Race	White	7,225	12,232	9,211	5,408	2,202	36,278
		(20.0%)	(33.7%)	(25.4%)	(14.9%)	(6.0%)	100%
	Black	1,424	945	349	107	25	2,850
		(50.0%)	(33.2%)	(12.2%)	(3.8%)	(0.8%)	100%

Source: U.S. Department of Commerce, U.S. Department of Housing and Urban Development, *Annual Housing Survey*, 1976.

Twenty percent of whites live in the two highest value categories of homes; the same is true for less than 5 percent of blacks. At the other extreme, one-half of all black homeowners fall into the lowest category; the figure for whites is just one-fifth.

It is important to view the strengths that *value* exhibits:

(1)   the highest simple correlation with both resident opinion of structure and neighborhood quality (-.387 and -.324, respectively).

(2) the highest partial correlations, equivalently F statistics, in the basis regression runs, and

(3) a strong relationship with race, as noted above.

Results

Exhibits A-V-2 and A-V-3 show the average structure and neighborhood quality responses by race and value of residence. These tables exhibit monotonicity in two ways. First, the average opinion in both tables and for both races becomes more positive as *value* increases and secondly, within each level of *value*, whites' average opinion is more positive than blacks'.

As indicated in Exhibit A-V-4, *value* is indeed a very strong control variable. For owner opinions of structure quality more than half of the black-white reporting difference can be explained by differences in value: for opinions of neighborhood quality, an essentially comparable figure of 40 percent is evident.*

In the aggregate and across all classifications, by itself, *value* reduces the "raw" race effect significantly. It is expecially stable across categories on opinions of structure qualtiy. Thus, this variable is quite important in attempting to explain the perceived racial differences in expressed opinions of structure and neighborhood.

Furthermore, after comparing the results in the Appendix with those in the text, it is seen that *value* alone explains a considerable amount of the race effect due to all the control variables.

---

*A tabular approach (as in this Appendix) allows a finer control for *value* than that achieved by the regression method used in the main text. However, when the regression method is used to control (for *value* alone), the results are similar to those presented in this Appendix.

EXHIBIT A-V-2

Owner's Mean Response on Structure Quality By Race and Value

		1	2	3	4,5	Weighted Average
Race	White	2.048	1.719	1.510	1.311	1.646
	Black	2.194	1.891	1.702	1.439	2.000

EXHIBIT A-V-3

Owner's Mean Response on Neighborhood Quality By Race and Value

		1	2	3	4,5	Weighted Average
Race	White	1.976	1.766	1.560	1.368	1.672
	Black	2.257	2.132	1.854	1.481	2.131

EXHIBIT A-V-4

Owner's Black-White Differences of Means on Structure And Neighborhood Quality by Value

	Black Minus White Mean	% of Differences of Means in Total Group
Structure Quality		
Total Group	.354	–
Value = 1	.146	41.2%
Value = 2	.172	48.6%
Value = 3	.192	54.2%
Value = 4,5	.128	36.2%
Neighborhood Quality		
Total Group	.459	–
Value = 1	.281	61.2%
Value = 2	.366	79.7%
Value = 3	.294	64.1%
Value = 4,5	.113	24.6%

Weighted black-white differences:

Structure Quality	.163	=	45.5% of	.354
Neighborhood Quality	.280	=	61.1% of	.459

Source: U.S. Department of Commerce, U.S. Department of Housing and Urban Development, *Annual Housing Survey*, 1976.

Appendix VI

Analysis of the Effect of the Neighborhood Variable on Explaining the Race Effect

Introduction

The purpose of this Appendix is to analyze white-black differences in opinions of structure/neighborhood quality when one aspect of neighborhood condition is controlled. This is accomplished by using the variable *neighborhood*. For owners, this variable is enumerator observation of abandoned or boarded buildings in the neighborhood; for renters, it is the same observation or observation of either hazardous steps or stair railings not firmly attached on common stairways. Hereafter, neighborhoods are classified into "good" and "bad" categories according to this variable.

In terms of gereral distribution, 4.8 percent of owned housing was evaluated as being in bad neighborhood—19.2 percent for blacks, 3.6 percent for whites. Fourteen percent of rental housing was classified as in bad neighborhoods; 28.4 percent for blacks, 10.6 percent for whites.

The neighborhood variable is the only enumerator evaluation relating to either housing or neighborhood conditions in the *Annual Housing Survey*. It thus represents the only objective measure (i.e. non-opinion of interviewee) of neighborhood quality available from this data source. Further, this variable is highly correlated with race* and thus of potentially significant value in explaining away any observed race effect.

Shortcomings in using the variable include: (1) coarseness (i.e., only a good or bad rating available for each neighborhood) (2) limited applicability (95 percent owner housing classified in good neighborhood; 85 percent of rented housing similarly classified) and (3) incompleteness (5.3 percent blank for owners; 3.7 percent blank for renters).**

Results

Overall, for both owners and renters, those residing in bad neighborhoods have lower opinions of both structure and neighborhood quality than comparable populations in good neighborhoods (see Exhibits A-VI-1, 2 and A-VI-4, 5).

*There are five times as many black owners in "bad neighborhoods" as white owners; for renters, almost three times as many.

**For the purposes of this analysis, blanks are lumped with good neighborhoods.

When the neighborhood variable is controlled in the case of owners, the white-black difference in scores (raw race effect) is reduced by one-third for those in bad neighborhood and one-tenth for those residing in good neighborhoods. Thus for owners, differences in neighborhood conditions, as measured by enumerator indication of the presence of abandoned buildings broken stairs/ railing, etc., does explain a small portion of black-white differences in opinion of structure and neighborhood quality. A great deal of these differences remains unexplained, however.

For renters, reductions in black-white opinion differences are somewhat weaker than those of owners. Also, contrary to the owner's case, *neighborhood* is a stronger control variable within good neighborhoods than within bad neighborhoods. Differences shrink about one-tenth for people in bad neighborhoods and approximately one-fifth for renters in better neighborhoods.

Thus, the results are not strong in light of the great potential that the neighborhood variable would seem to offer. This may be due to the coarseness or limited range of the variable or to the historic inconsistencies of enumerator ratings when dealing with conditions of structure or neighborhood.

EXHIBIT A-VI-1

Owner's Mean Response on Structure Quality By Race and NBD

| | | RACE | |
		WHITE	BLACK
Neighborhood (NBD)	Bad	1.965	2.194
	Good	1.634	1.954
	Weighted Average	1.646	2.000

EXHIBIT A-VI-2

Owner's Mean Response on Neighborhood Quality By Race and NBD

| | | RACE | |
		WHITE	BLACK
Neighborhood (NBD)	Bad	2.143	2.418
	Good	1.655	2.062
	Weighted Average	1.672	2.131

EXHIBIT A-VI-3

Owner's Black-White Differences of Means on Structure
And Neighborhood Quality By NBD

	Black Mean- White Mean	% of Differences of Means in Total Group
Structure Quality All People (Total Group)	.354	—
People in Bad NBD	.229	65%
People in Good NBD	.320	90%
Neighborhood Quality All People (Total Group)	.459	—
People in Bad NBD	.275	60%
People in Good NBD	.407	89%

Source: U.S. Department of Commerce, U.S. Department of Housing and Urban
Development, *Annual Housing Survey*, 1976.

EXHIBIT A-VI-4

Renter's Mean Response on Structure Quality By Race and NBD

		RACE	
		WHITE	BLACK
Neighborhood (NBD)	Bad	2.440	2.813
	Not Bad	2.081	2.405
	Weighted Average	2.119	2.521

EXHIBIT A-VI-5

Renter's Mean Respons on Neighborhood Quality By Race and NBD

		RACE	
		WHITE	BLACK
Neighborhood (NBD)	Bad	2.407	2.771
	Not Bad	1.983	2.305
	Weighted Average	2.028	2.437

EXHIBIT A-VI-6

Renter's Black-White Differences of Means on Structure
And Neighborhood Quality By NBD

	Black Mean Minus White Mean	*% of Differences of Means in Total Group*
Structure Quality		
All People (Total Group)	.402	—
People in Bad NBD	.373	93%
People in Not Bad NBD	.324	81%
Neighborhood Quality		
All People	.409	—
People in Bad NBD	.364	89%
People in Good NBD	.322	79%

Source: U.S. Department of Commerce, U.S. Department of Housing and Urban Development, *Annual Housing Survey*, 1976.

Appendix VII
Plumbing as a Control Variable Within the Basic Regression Equations

Introduction

The use of complete plumbing facilities or the lack thereof has been utilized as one component of housing quality analyses since the 1950 Census. The same information regarding plumbing is contained in the *Annual Housing Survey*. It is thus interesting to analyze the effect, if any, that the plumbing variable has on expressed opinions of structure quality. One component of this effect is investigated in this Appendix.

Results

This analysis will be restricted to the owners' opinion of structure quality. *Plumbing* (which is a dummy variable: complete use of plumbing versus non-complete use) was not one of the twelve control variables chosen for this group. Thus, for the country as a whole, *plumbing* has little predictive power for opinion of structure quality when the specified twelve variables have been controlled. However, *plumbing* may be important in some areas—while not in others—and thus might not enter the regression equation based on the full country.

Plumbing was thus considered separately within each of the four regions for central cities, suburbs and non-SMSA areas of standard Metropolitan Statistical Areas. In each of these (12) areas the weighted percentage of houses with full plumbing is computed along with the amount *plumbing* would add to R^2 if it were to be included as a thirteenth control variable.

Interestingly, all sampled black-owned houses have full plumbing in the North Central and West regions while essentially all have full plumbing in the Northeast. In the South, suburbs and non-SMSA areas show substantial lack of plumbing but its effect on R^2 is still trivial.

For whites, in all regions, the structures within central cities have 99 percent or more full plumbing. All the suburbs are also above 99 percent level, except for the South (98.5 percent). In non-SMSA areas lack of plumbing is more prevalent (up to 5 percent in the South) but *plumbing's* effect on R^2 is still relatively small.

Thus, as far as R^2 is concerned, *plumbing's* effect on opinion of structure quality is minimal. In most areas, this is because essentially all atructures have full plumbing. In the other areas *plumbing's* effect, if any, is accounted for by other control variables considered—probably *value, holes, leaks, and rats.*

EXHIBIT A-VII-1
Plumbing Means and Additions to R^2—Owner's Opinions of Structure Quality

| | | RACE | | |
| | WHITES | | BLACKS | |
Geographic Subset	Mean	Addition to R^2	Mean	Addition to R^2
NORTHEAST				
Central City	.990	.002	1.000	—
Suburb	.992	.000	.971	.000
Non-SMSA	.966	.002	1.000	—
NORTH CENTRAL				
Central City	.998	.000	1.000	—
Suburb	.992	.001	1.000	—
Non-SMSA	.964	.001	1.000	—
SOUTH				
Central City	.993	.002	.979	.000
Suburb	.985	.002	.878	.001
Non-SMSA	.953	.001	.674	.004
WEST				
Central City	1.000	—	1.000	—
Suburb	.998	.001	1.000	—
Non-SMSA	.984	.000	1.000	—

Source: U.S. Department of Commerce, U.S. Department of Housing and Urban Development, *Annual Housing Survey*, 1976.

Epilogue: A Note on Federal Housing Policy

George Sternlieb

Good consulting takes a good client—and clearcut, mutually consistent objectives. None of these conditions prevail in the development of government housing policy. The confusion is epitomized by the linkages between housing and financial market considerations which have been frequently detailed. But there are other barriers as well.

I. The Federal Role in Housing Quality Provision is Inconsistent and Contradictory not Because of Maladministration or the Specific Personalities at Work, But Rather as a Result of the Mixed Priorities and Objectives Grouped Under Housing.

The vicissitudes and changing definitions of the term "housing" could provide, in talented hands, an insight into the history of post-World War II America. In the 1940s and 1950s, it had two basic definitions, each of which had clearcut constituencies of

543

sufficient breadth to serve both as expounders and proponents. The two were viewed as relatively independent and, except by a select few, as relatively noncontradictory. The first definition, and by far the most important, dealt with the provision of housing for the newly developed middle-class. America had entered World War II with a majority of its households as renters, after a Depression-base period in which annual housing starts had drifted down the 100,000 unit mark. With war-time controls and induced savings, there was an enormous level of latent housing demand and the werewithal of creative financing to bring it to realization.

Spearheading this drive was one of the classic elements of housing through the ages—the appropriate reward for the returning hero. And, clearly, there is a well-defined line of descent from Blenheim Castle to the Levittowns of America; they both served as rewards for the warriors' return.

The agencies which served this aspect of housing tended to combine substantial patronage with political clout. While, as always, there were a few hecklers on the sidelines, the vast bulk of Americans were committed to this housing goal. Though an occasional windfall of scandal came to life, the proof of the pudding is the public's acceptance of the providers of housing—middle-class housing— as heroes of the American way.

The second definition and by far the less significant, dealt with the provision of housing amenities for the poor, most particularly the newly visible urban poor. Essentially, this was an extension of housing/planning theory that was nearly a century old. Its basic thesis was that the problems of the poor—whether disease, illiteracy, unemployment, delinquency or generalized unpleasantness—stemmed from faulty physical surroundings. In an example of commutative linkage which would have many exemplars in later legislative thinking, the implicit assumption was made that the provision of good plumbing (interpreting the term broadly) would, by definition, reverse all trauma. Even before the age of the computer and computerized regression analysis, correlation was mistaken for causality (i.e., people who live in good housing did not have many of the trauma associated with the poor—or at least it was assumed that they did not). Therefore provide good housing and traumatic problems would be removed.

Given the broadly based, much desired, politically potent first definition of housing —coupled with the much more narrowly patronized second definition—a reasonably operative constituency was developed. It was broadened and given penetration by the levels of patronage that quickly developed around the subsidized sphere. While the banking fraternity was, in general, somewhat reluctantly involved in this area, some of the more aggressive elements among the homebuilders and trade groups strongly expounded it, and a few stayed until the bitter end. (Note that when the housing moratorium was announced by President Nixon in 1973, the two principal groups which protested this action (to limited avail) included the National Council of Negro Women on the one hand—and the National Association of Homebuilders on the other.)

The coalition was an unstable one. The forms of financing, levels of subsidies, and definitions of success differed much too radically to support the marriage comfortable over a long period of time. Most importantly, there was so much success achieved in delivering the goals of the middle-class and middle-class aspirants as to minimize their future interest.

In this context, it is interesting to note an insightful comment made by William Wheaton some 25 years ago. Professor Wheaton, who at that time was advocating the development of a Cabinet-level office to be concerned with housing and urban development, suggested coupling other elements to housing, pointing to the fact that the latter by itself would be too weak without the support of a strong, more nationally acceptable goal and patronage element. He proposed that public works activity be joined either with urban development (in which he included housing for poor people) or with housing generally. In either case, he saw both alternatives as equally potent dray horses with which to pull the cause of the less fortunate along. Ultimately, Dr. Wheaton preferred the grouping of housing and urban development. He pointed to the former as having most significant strength and indeed stated "only in the event of a sustained prosperity could the housing agency lose importance in the popular mind."[1] But that is just what has happened. Will it continue? A number of other facets in the provision of housing must be touched on before a return to the question.

II. The Dilemma of Housing Quality: The Consumer, The Audience, The Professionals

The generation which heard President Franklin Delano Roosevelt give his famous speech on "one-third of a nation ill-housed—" is beginning to withdraw from the scene, most of them content with the stored capital value derived through homeownership, and with their need for adequate shelter long requited. The old era of absolute housing want has largely come to an end. This is not to suggest that there are not significant groups of Americans ill housed. The sad condition of much of rural housing as well as of hard core center city locations desperately need rectification. But this is the concern of the relatively few. *The vast bulk of the Americans, both rural and urban, are substantially satisfied with their housing.*

There were indications of this satisfaction as early as the aftermath of the 1960 Census. Shortly after its conclusion, the Census Bureau tested the results of the housing surveys which were conducted at that time. The results exemplified in *Working Paper No. 25* were the apothesis of the statistician's nightmare—the non-replicability of field results. They indicated that there was little problem in rating good housing, that there were relatively small problems with very bad housing, but that the standards for the in-between category, of less-than-sound units, simply were not adequate to bear replicability. When tested by alternate field crews, the results were completely random. A basic crisis in field work had arisen. The state of the art permitted consistent counting of plumbing facilities but it was no longer adequate for very much more than that. While this was a cause of despair with those concerned with housing enumeration in the Census Bureau, it should have been a moment of elation for the rest of us. It indicated that the vast bulk of housing want had largely been obviated.

Statistical procedures and their bureaucratic patrons however, abhor vacuums and so the *Annual Housing Survey* was developed. This is an approximately 70,000-household probability sampling conducted annually on a national base. It is further fortified with a series of more intensive analyses of some 60 metropolitan areas, with 15 of them done every year. Thus the series is replicated every fifth year. (Note that this latter procedure has varied somewhat over time as has the precise number of households involved in the national sample.)

Instead of the simple physical counts of earlier census work, now made obsolete by the fact that all but a very few Americans had appropriate plumbing facilities, an effort was made to utilize functional questions. Not merely whether the unit has running water, if it does, how frequently are there interruptions, etc.

There has been, as yet, relatively little intensive analysis of the findings of this effort, though the first field work was conducted in 1973. A part of the problem is the "counter intuitive" nature of the findings. Instead of finding a rich band of trauma and specific physical and/or operational disability which could be linked into overall housing and/or neighborhood satisfaction (thus serving as an inspiration for future housing legislation), the complaints have been relatively random. For example, with some deviance at the very top and the very bottom of the rental scale, the level of complaint is relatively consistent, i.e., high-rent payers and low-rent payers have the same complaints. High-cost housing occupants and low-cost housing occupants indicate similar levels of toilet stoppage, of rodent infestation and the like.

Suffice it to say, the vast bulk of Americans—approximately 90 percent—are satisfied with their housing. This generalization holds true both of owners and of renters, though the latter are slightly more negative. It seems to hold true again with the same caveat of both whites and blacks and, surprisingly, among those with modest incomes as well as the rich.

If we were to take social science research seriously, we would have to say that what we are dealing with is a race between the realities and aspiration/expectation levels and further, that their relationship seem to be a constant. Since the inspiration of this study is more action-oriented than fact-finding *per se*, the results of the survey—rather than being viewed as a positive indication of the resolution of the broad housing problem of yesteryear—have largely been permitted to languish. How can a bureaucracy hope to perpetuate itself if its target (now largely confined to the insufficiently housed) seems to have diminished so very substantially. Housing by this bureacratic definition *must* be a problem. If its consumers do not envision the housing problem as being significant, then the issue is their low aspirations which must be raised!

And so we have a new definition of the housing target goal. It is no longer the absolute issues of shelter, but it is rather the relative issues of housing costs. In the much cited studies of housing need, yielding the 26-million, 10-year unit target figure, the largest single element added into the equation, is the housing units for which people are paying more than some arbitrary proportion of their incomes. The housing issue of yesteryear then, of absolute shelter deprivation, has been unobtrusively replaced. Its new surrogate must be viewed as income redistribution rather than provision of housing shelter *per se.*

There are two codicils to this logic.

1. There is little evidence of housing shelter improvement as having high priority among poor consumers. Reform is a juggernaut which, when set in motion, tends to demolish research and thoughtful analysis. Patrons view research results with a selective eye, skimming over the unacceptable, reciting only these findings most consonant with their *a priori* prejudices. While there has been a number of efforts to prove the linkage between improvement in housing quality and a variety of equivalent alleviations of other social trauma, in general these efforts have yielded null findings. While by no means belittling the problems of research in this arena, what little we have in the way of results certainly does not support the curative nature of physical improvement in housing.

2. Housing for the poor has become a form of symbolic action. Its major justification is viewed not in terms of a shelter utility function, but rather to indicate concern. The triumph of this art form is the efforts to breathe new housing life into the South Bronx, an area whose basic isolation and social trauma defy adequate description. As an investment for its ulterior purpose, i.e., to improve the environment, it can have but little hope of success. As a form of public ritual and communication to the broad audience of the poor generally and black leadership specifically, it conveys a message of care and solicitude. By the time this is a physical reality—if ever—and it fails—well then, there will be other avenues for symbolism. Could there be more functional approaches? Are there efforts which would yield greater results for the client? We will have to leave these issues to the future.

However, for the monent, at least, we have some very significant indications of consumer attitude as a result of one of the largest controlled, social science field experiments in our history; that of the housing assistance supply experiment. In this effort which is being conducted in Brown County (Wisconsin) and St. Joseph County(Indiana), owners and tenants of low income qualify for generous housing allowances (averaging currently $900 a year) when they meet the program's housing standards. As pointed out by the Rand Corporation who is the chief contractor,

"although the option of moving may bolster renters in their dealings with landlords, it is only occasionally exercised as a means of securing certifiable housing. Those in substandard housing who qualify for payments usually do so by repairing (or pursuading their landlords to repair) their homes".

Rand, *4th Annual Report of the Housing Assistance Supply Experiment,* March, 1978, Santa Monica, California, page 7.

What are these defects and how consequential are they? Typically they are remedied by amateur labor with professional contractors doing barely one-in-eight of all initial repairs. The others are done by homeowners, landlords, tenants, or their friends. The median cash outlay, as pointed out by the Rand Corporation, for repaired dwellings is only $10 with three-out-of-four substandard dwellings being repaired for under $30.

Thus we have a situation in which, prior to federal intervention, at least half of the enrollees are housed in what middle-class standards bearers, i.e., federal contractors employed in the study, find to be substandard facilities. The level of investment required to repair these rental facilities is trivial. The renters do not make them because they are unimportant to them. The cash outlay required is trivial even to the poor. *What is required then is a substantial federal bonus in order to secure housing improvement which could be done by the tenants within their own resources, if (and let me stress the "if") these improvements had any measure of significant priority. The Rand Corporation summarizes this generalization quite adequately.*

"Understandably most clients are more interested in budgetary relief than housing improvement. Only a minority respond immediately to the receipt of an allowance by moving or by markedly increasing their housing outlays. most do what is required to meet the program's housing standards and treat the allowance as a budgetary supplement. Consequently the program's housing requirements are needed to achieve its housing objectives. If allowance were unrestricted cash transfers, we are reasonably sure that few recipients would voluntarily repair their home to HAO standards or increase their housing expenditures much beyond what was needed to counter inflation." Rand, *op. cit.,* 8-9.

Clearly, what is evident in the experiment is an income transfer thinly masquarading as a housing device. While reports on experience under Section 8 are still tentative, they seem to indicate somewhat similar generalizations to be appropriate.

Why then do we go through the motions? One can only think of the mountaineer's explanation for risking his neck—"It's there!"

The problem with appropriate formations of social policies and inputs are not that we lack adequate research on the pressure points, but rather that the forms of ritual, custom and developed bureaucracy impede the acceptance of what research tells us.

Again, those involved in the field are far from unique in sponsoring research and avoiding its results, but perhaps occasionally it is worth highlighting the cleavage. There is substantial evidence that in urban areas, particularly, the issue of neighborhood quality is much more significant as a felt detriment to the housing environment than physical structure, *per se.* This is not to indicate that the absolute levels, certainly in proportion of total, are very impressive. In Exhibits 1, 2 and 3 are shown central city/suburban comparisons of black occupant responses to their neighborhoods, to their housing, and in terms of wish to move. From the perspectives of this group clearly the central city is seen in a much less sanguine view by its residents than is the case for suburban-located individuals. The most negative of all are the respondents inside the central cities of the Northeast, both in terms of neighborhood and of housing. but even in this most accentuated of cases as shown in Table 3, the wish to move is limited to approximately a third of the respondents. (In analysis currently underway by a variety of groups, cross tabulations of the motivation for wish to move and its correlation with housing satisfaction proved to be less than determinative. The variable is a most noisy one with job location and relocation, for example, playing a major role as against the factors of environment *per se.*)

Thus, major problems of housing policy for the poor (at least from their perspective) would seem to revolve largely around 1) cost, 2) the improvement of the neighborhood, 3) in targeting absolute housing improvements for those in need. We know how to do the first and third of these elements, the second is still wrapped in mystery even though there are many energetic efforts under way, in a variety of communities, to provide both the physical elements and the mystique involved in the neighborhood upgrading.

Just as the scale of the problem of housing quality seems to have been brought down to manageable proportions, however, the provision of funding for that purpose would seem to have been seriously impacted. The vast upgrading of housing supported by the middle class, which provided as a spill-over effect, relatively uncrowded and physically competent dwelling units for the less well-endowed, has given way to new phenomena, perhaps with less happy secondary impacts upon the poor.

The new problem of America's housing provision will be to cushion the shock of reduced housing quality to the middle class. The long line of housing improvement stretching the two generations from World War II to the present has aborted. We face a future bereft of the old guidelines. The decline in America's housing buying power is not an acute attack similar to those experienced in earlier, soon over recessions—it is rather the new reality.

Notes

1. Wm. Wheaton, *The Evolution of Federal Housing Programs*, 519 (Chicago, 1953).

EXHIBIT 1

CENTRAL CITY-SUBURB BLACK COMPARISONS NEIGHBORHOOD RATING, BY SMSA LOCATION U.S. AND REGIONS, 1975

(Percents)

Neighborhood Rating	United States		Northeast		North Central		South		West	
	Inside Central City	Outside Central City	Inside Central City	Outside Central City	Inside Central City	Outside Central City	Inside Central City	Outside Central City	Inside Central City	Outside Central City
Excellent	11.3	19.9	7.0	20.2	9.9	20.1	14.4	22.8	16.3	12.7
Good	41.4	52.6	35.6	53.0	40.1	49.3	45.5	51.1	45.8	58.4
Fair	38.4	23.8	45.9	22.0	39.3	26.3	33.9	22.1	31.7	27.4
Poor	8.9	3.8	11.5	4.8	10.7	4.2	6.2	4.0	6.4	1.5
Total	100.0	100.0	100.0	100.0	100.0	100.0	100.0	100.0	100.0	100.0
	(3776)	(990)	(1032)	(243)	(1049)	(172)	(1241)	(398)	(454)	(177)

Note:　Marginal totals in thousands of units.

Source:　Annual Housing Survey, 1975.

EXHIBIT 2

CENTRAL CITY-SUBURB BLACK COMPARISONS HOUSING RATING, BY SMSA LOCATION U.S. AND REGIONS, 1975

(Percents)

Neighborhood Rating	United States Inside Central City	United States Outside Central City	Northeast Inside Central City	Northeast Outside Central City	North Central Inside Central City	North Central Outside Central City	South Inside Central City	South Outside Central City	West Inside Central City	West Outside Central City
Excellent	14.9	23.2	11.8	25.5	14.7	29.9	16.6	20.9	17.6	18.6
Good	43.2	48.5	38.3	43.1	46.2	44.5	43.4	51.3	46.8	53.3
Fair	32.6	23.0	35.9	26.0	31.7	20.0	31.8	22.6	29.7	22.5
Poor	9.3	5.3	14.0	5.3	7.4	5.5	8.2	5.1	5.9	5.6
Total	100.0 (3771)	100.0 (988)	100.0 (1029)	100.0 (243)	100.0 (1045)	100.0 (172)	100.0 (1241)	100.0 (397)	100.0 (455)	100.0 (177)

Note: Marginal totals in thousands of units.

Source: Annual Housing Survey, 1975.

EXHIBIT 3

CENTRAL CITY-SUBURB BLACK COMPARISONS WISH TO MOVE, BY SMSA LOCATION U.S. AND REGIONS, 1975

(Percents)

Wish to Move	United States		Northeast		North Central		South		West	
	Inside Central City	Outside Central City	Inside Central City	Outside Central City	Inside Central City	Outside Central City	Inside Central City	Outside Central City	Inside Central City	Outside Central City
YES	29.5	17.5	34.6	19.9	28.5	12.5	28.0	18.2	16.7	16.7
NO	70.5	82.5	65.4	80.1	71.5	87.5	72.0	81.8	83.3	83.3
TOTAL	100.0 (1076)	100.0 (265)	100.0 (339)	100.0 (86)	100.0 (341)	100.0 (54)	100.0 (325)	100.0 (109)	100.0 (72)	100.0 (16)

Note:　Marginal totals in thousands of units.
Source:　Annual Housing Survey, 1975.

Index